THE CITY IN HISTORY

P9-CJM-058

Books by Lewis Mumford

THE STORY OF UTOPIAS 1922

STICKS AND STONES 1924

THE GOLDEN DAY 1926

HERMAN MELVILLE 1929

THE BROWN DECADES 1931

TECHNICS AND CIVILIZATION 1934

THE CULTURE OF CITIES 1938

MEN MUST ACT 1939

FAITH FOR LIVING 1940

THE SOUTH IN ARCHITECTURE 1941

THE CONDITION OF MAN 1944

CITY DEVELOPMENT 1945

VALUES FOR SURVIVAL 1946

GREEN MEMORIES 1947

THE CONDUCT OF LIFE 1951

ART AND TECHNICS 1952

IN THE NAME OF SANITY 1954

FROM THE GROUND UP 1956

THE TRANSFORMATIONS OF MAN 1956

THE HIGHWAY AND THE CITY 1963

THE MYTH OF THE MACHINE 1967

THE URBAN PROSPECT 1968

THE CITY IN

HISTORY Its Origins,

Its Transformations, and Its Prospects

by LEWIS MUMFORD

HARCOURT, BRACE & WORLD, INC.

A HARBINGER BOOK · NEW YORK

ISBN 0-15-618035-9

C.6.70

CONTENTS

ILLUSTRATIONS

GRAPHIC SECTION IV
Between pages 432 and 433

This book opens with a city that was, symbolically, a world: it closes with a world that has become, in many practical aspects, a city. In following through this development I have attempted to deal with the forms and functions of the city, and with the purposes that have emerged from it; and I have demonstrated, I trust, that the city will have an even more significant part to play in the future than it has played in the past, if once the original disabilities that have accompanied it through history are sloughed off.

As in all my other studies of the city, I have confined myself as far as possible to cities and regions I am acquainted with at first hand, and to data in which I have long been immersed. This has limited me to Western civilization, and even there I have been forced to leave out large significant tracts: namely, Spain and Latin America, Palestine, Eastern Europe, Soviet Russia. I regret these omissions; but since my method demands personal experience and observation, something unreplaceable by books, it would take another lifetime to make them good.

'The City in History,' incidentally, replaces the limited historical sections of 'The Culture of Cities': parts of those four original chapters now lie embedded in the eighteen chapters of the present work, which is more than twice as long. If the reader occasionally stumbles upon a ruined portion of that earlier edifice, preserved under a quite different building, like a fragment of the Servian wall in Rome, let him not tax me with undue piety. I have kept only so much as I was not skillful enough to improve or resourceful enough to expand. The material thus retained should give the book an organic continuity and solidity that would have been lacking, perhaps, had I ignored the earlier structure and, like a speculative builder with a bulldozer, levelled the whole tract. In this it reflects with symbolic aptness the historic growth of the city itself.

— L. M.

Amenia, New York

THE CITY IN HISTORY

CHAPTER ONE

Sanctuary, Village, and Stronghold

1: THE CITY IN HISTORY

What is the city? How did it come into existence? What processes does it further: what functions does it perform: what purposes does it fulfill? No single definition will apply to all its manifestations and no single description will cover all its transformations, from the embryonic social nucleus to the complex forms of its maturity and the corporeal disintegration of its old age. The origins of the city are obscure, a large part of its past buried or effaced beyond recovery, and its further prospects are difficult to weigh.

Will the city disappear or will the whole planet turn into a vast urban hive?—which would be another mode of disappearance. Can the needs and desires that have impelled men to live in cities recover, at a still higher level, all that Jerusalem, Athens, or Florence once seemed to promise? Is there still a living choice between Necropolis and Utopia: the possibility of building a new kind of city that will, freed of inner contradictions, positively enrich and further human development?

If we would lay a new foundation for urban life, we must understand the historic nature of the city, and distinguish between its original functions, those that have emerged from it, and those that may still be called forth. Without a long running start in history, we shall not have the momentum needed, in our own consciousness, to take a sufficiently bold leap into the future; for a large part of our present plans, not least many that pride themselves on being 'advanced' or 'progressive,' are dreary mechanical caricatures of the urban and regional forms that are now potentially within our grasp.

Since it has taken more than five thousand years to arrive at even a partial understanding of the city's nature and drama, it may require

3

an even longer period to exhaust the city's still unrealized potentialities. At the dawn of history, the city is already a mature form. In our attempt to achieve a better insight into the present state of the city, we must peer over the edge of the historic horizon, to detect the dim traces of still earlier structures and more primitive functions. That is our first task. But we shall not leave this trail till we have followed it forward, with all its meanderings and back tracks, through five thousand years of recorded history, into the emerging future.

When we finally reach our own age, we shall find that urban society has come to a parting of the ways. Here, with a heightened consciousness of our past and a clearer insight into decisions made long ago, which often still control us, we shall be able to face the immediate decision that now confronts man and will, one way or another, ultimately transform him: namely, whether he shall devote himself to the development of his own deepest humanity, or whether he shall surrender himself to the now almost automatic forces he himself has set in motion and yield place to his dehumanized alter ego, 'Post-historic Man.' That second choice will bring with it a progressive loss of feeling, emotion, creative audacity, and finally consciousness.

Many cities, many existing educational institutions and political organizations have already made their commitment to Post-historic Man. This obedient creature will have no need for the city: what was once a city will shrink to the dimensions of an underground control center, for in the interests of control and automatism all other attributes of life will be forfeited. Before the majority of mankind drifts into accepting this prospect, lured by little promises of 'pneumatic bliss' that obscure the total threat, it will be well to take a fresh look at man's historic development as shaped and molded by the city. To get a sufficient perspective upon the immediate tasks of the moment, I purpose to go back to the beginnings of the city. We need a new image of order, which shall include the organic and personal, and eventually embrace all the offices and functions of man. Only if we can project that image shall we be able to find a new form for the city.

2: ANIMAL PROMPTINGS AND FORESHADOWINGS

In seeking the origins of the city, one may too easily be tempted to look only for its physical remains. But as with the picture of early man, when we center on his bones and shards, his tools and weapons, we do less than justice to inventions like language and ritual that have left few, if any, material traces. Some of the functions of the city may have been performed, some of its purposes fulfilled, some of the sites later used may already have been temporarily occupied, before anything that we should now recognize as a city had come into existence.

We beg the whole question of the nature of the city if we look only for permanent structures huddled together behind a wall. To come close to the origins of the city we must, I submit, supplement the work of the archaeologist who seeks to find the deepest layer in which he can recognize a shadowy ground plan that indicates urban order. If we are to identify the city, we must follow the trail backward, from the fullest known urban structures and functions to their original components, however remote in time and space and culture from the first 'tells' that have been opened up. Before the city there was the hamlet and the shrine and the village: before the village, the camp, the cache, the cave, the cairn; and before all these there was a disposition to social life that man plainly shares with many other animal species.

Human life swings between two poles: movement and settlement. The contrast between these modes may be traced back to the original break between the mainly free-moving protozoa that formed the animal kingdom and the relatively sessile organisms that belong to the vegetable kingdom. The first, like the oyster, sometimes become overadapted to a fixed position and lose the power of movement; while many plants free themselves in some degree by underground rootings and above all, by the detachment and migration of the seed. At every level of life one trades mobility for security, or in reverse, immobility for adventure. Certainly, some tendency to settle and rest, to go back to a favored spot that offers shelter or good feeding exists in many animal species; and, as Carl O. Sauer has suggested, a propensity to store and settle down may itself be an original human trait.

But even more significant contributions to stability and continuity come forward from our animal past. Many creatures, even fish, come together in herds and schools for mating and for rearing their young. With birds, there is sometimes attachment to the same nest from season to season, and among the flocking species there is a habit of communal settlement at breeding time in protected areas like islands and marshes. Larger mating groups, drawing on diverse strains, introduce possibilities of genetic variation that small inbred human groups lack. These breeding and feeding grounds are plainly prototypes of the most primitive kind of permanent human settlement, the hamlet or village. One aspect of the early town, its sense of defensive isolation—along with its birdlike claim of 'territoriality'—has this long foreground in animal evolution.

Even the technological complexity of the human town does not lack animal precedent. With certain species, notably the beavers, colonization brings a deliberate remolding of the environment: tree-felling, dam-raising, lodge-building. These engineering operations transform a close family congregation into a somewhat looser association of numerous families, cooperating on common tasks and improving the common habitat. If the beaver colony lacks many of the attributes of a town, it is already close to those early villages which also performed feats of hydraulic engineering.

For all that, the nearest approach to a collective dwelling place among other animals was a long way from the most rudimentary urban community. Rather, it is along a quite different evolutionary line, represented by the social insects, that one finds the closest approach to both 'civilized life' and the city. The social functions of the beehive, the termitary, and the ant-hill—structures often imposing in size, skillfully wrought—have indeed so many resemblances to those of the city that I shall put off further observations till the city comes into view. Even the division of labor, the differentiation of castes, the practice of war, the institution of royalty, the domestication of other species, and the employment of slavery, existed in certain 'ant empires' millions of years before they coalesced in the ancient city. But note: there is no question here of biological continuity. Rather, this is an example of parallelism and convergence.

3: CEMETERIES AND SHRINES

In the development of permanent human settlements, we find an expression of animal needs similar to those in other social species; but even the most primitive urban beginnings reveal more than this. Soon after one picks up man's trail in the earliest campfire or chipped-stone tool one finds evidence of interests and anxieties that have no animal counterpart; in particular, a ceremonious concern for the dead, manifested in their deliberate burial—with growing evidences of pious apprehension and dread.

Early man's respect for the dead, itself an expression of fascination with his powerful images of daylight fantasy and nightly dream, perhaps had an even greater role than more practical needs in causing him to seek a fixed meeting place and eventually a continuous settlement. Mid the uneasy wanderings of paleolithic man, the dead were the first to have a permanent dwelling: a cavern, a mound marked by a cairn, a collective barrow. These were landmarks to which the living probably returned at intervals, to commune with or placate the ancestral spirits. Though food-gathering and hunting do not encourage the permanent occupation of a single site, the dead at least claim that privilege. Long ago the Jews claimed as their patrimony the land where the graves of their forefathers were situated; and that well-attested claim seems a primordial one. The city of the dead antedates the city of the living. In one sense, indeed, the city of the dead is the forerunner, almost the core, of every living city. Urban life spans the historic space between the earliest burial ground for dawn man and the final cemetery, the Necropolis, in which one civilization after another has met its end.

In all this, there are ironic overtones. The first greeting of a traveller, as he approached a Greek or a Roman city, was the row of graves and tombstones that lined the roads to the city. As for Egypt, most of what is left of that great civilization, with its joyous saturation in every expression of organic life, are its temples and its tombs. Even in the crowded modern city, the first general exodus to a more desirable dwelling place in the country was the migration of the dead to the romantic Elysium of a suburban cemetery.

But there is still another part of the environment that paleolithic man not merely used but periodically came back to: the cave. There is plenty of evidence, all over the world, of the aboriginal occupation or visitation of caves. In the limestone caves of the Dordogne in France, for instance, early man's successive occupations can be traced in layers, as the erosion of the rock lowered the river bed, raising old shelters and exposing new platforms lower down. But more important than its use for domestic purposes was the part that the cave played in art and ritual. Though caves like those at Lascaux and Altamira were not inhabited, they seem to have been ceremonial centers of some kind, as much as Nippur or Abydos. As late as the fourth century B.C. one finds the carved representation of a cave dedicated to the Nymphs, showing Hermes and Pan—the carving itself being found in the Cave of the Nymphs on Mount Pentelicon.

In the inner recesses of such special ritual centers, usually reached by low passages, demanding a tortuous and frequently dangerous crawl, one finds great natural chambers, covered with paintings of astonishing vividness of form and facility of design, chiefly of exquisitely realistic animals, occasionally of highly formalized and stylized men and women. In some places this art exhibited an esthetic mastery not touched again till we reach the temples and palaces of a period more than fifteen thousand years later.

If the esthetic design was, as some hold, only an incidental by-product of magic, did it not nevertheless exert a special magic of its own, which drew men back to the scene of this first triumphant expression?

Even in their most primitive form, these practices survived their period and made their way into the later city. A paleolithic drawing in the Caverne des Trois Frères at Ariège depicts a man dressed in a stag's skin, wearing antlers on his head, presumably a wizard, while a bone engraving of the same period in an English cave depicts a man whose face is masked by a horse's head. Now as late as the seventh century A.D. in England, according to Christina Hole, the calends of January were observed by men dressed in the skins and heads of animals, who ran leaping and prancing through the streets: the practice was in fact forbidden by the Archbishop of Canterbury because it was, he said, "devilish." If there is reason for suspecting some dim ancestral continuity in this custom, there is even better reason for finding in the rites of the cave the social and religious impulses that conspired to draw men finally into cities, where all the original feelings of awe, reverence, pride, and joy would be further magnified by art, and multiplied by the number of responsive participants.

In these ancient paleolithic sanctuaries, as in the first grave mounds and tombs, we have, if anywhere, the first hints of civic life, probably well before any permanent village settlement can even be suspected. This was no mere coming together during the mating season, no famished return to a sure source of water or food, no occasional interchange, in some convenient tabooed spot, of amber, salt, jade, or even perhaps shaped tools. Here, in the ceremonial center, was an association dedicated to a life more abundant: not merely an increase of food, but an increase of social enjoyment through the fuller use of symbolized fantasy and art, with a shared vision of a better life, more meaningful as well as esthetically enchanting, such a good life in embryo as Aristotle would one day describe in the 'Politics': the first glimpse of Eutopia. For who can doubt that in the very effort to ensure a more abundant supply of animal food—if that was in fact the magical purpose of painting and rite—the performance of art itself added something just as essential to primitive man's life as the carnal rewards of the hunt. All this has a bearing on the nature of the historic city.

The paleolithic cave brings to mind many other venerable shrines that likewise embodied sacred properties and powers, and drew men from afar into their precincts: great stones, sacred groves, monumental trees, holy wells, like the Chalice Well at Glastonbury where Joseph of Arimathea supposedly dropped the Holy Grail. These fixed landmarks and holy meeting places called together, periodically or permanently, those who shared the same magical practices or religious beliefs. Mecca, Rome, Jerusalem, Benares, Peiping, Kyoto, Lourdes still recall and carry on these original purposes.

While these elemental properties, closely tied to natural features, are not in themselves sufficient to found or support a city, they constitute the larger part of the central nucleus that originally dominated the historic city. Not least, perhaps, the cave gave early man his first conception of architectural space, his first glimpse of the power of a walled enclosure to intensify spiritual receptivity and emotional exaltation. The painted chamber within a mountain prefigures the tomb of the Egyptian pyramid, itself a man-made mountain, deliberately imitative. The variations on this theme are endless; yet despite their differences, the pyramid, the ziggurat, the Mithraic grotto, the Christian crypt all have their prototypes in the mountain cave. Both the form and the purpose played a part in the ultimate development of the city.

In going back so far for the origins of the city, one must not of course overlook the practical needs that drew family groups and tribes together seasonally in a common habitat, a series of camp sites, even in a collecting or a hunting economy. These played their parts, too; and long before agricultural villages and towns became a feature of the neolithic culture, the favorable sites for them had probably been prospected: the pure spring with its year-round supply of water, the solid hummock of land, accessible, yet protected by river or swamp, the nearby estuary heavily stocked with fish and shellfish—all these served already in many regions for the intermediary mesolithic economy, on sites whose permanence is witnessed by huge mounds of opened shells.

But settlement may even have antedated these hamlets: the remains of paleolithic buildings, seemingly part of a hamlet, in southern Russia warn one against fixing too late a date for the appearance of the permanent village. Eventually we shall find the hunter's camp sinking into a permanent roosting spot: a dominant paleolithic enclave walled off from the neolithic villages at its base.

But note that two of the three original aspects of temporary settlement have to do with sacred things, not just with physical survival: they relate to a more valuable and meaningful kind of life, with a consciousness that entertains past and future, apprehending the primal mystery of sexual generation and the ultimate mystery of death and what may lie beyond death. As the city takes form, much more will be added: but these central concerns abide as the very reason for the city's existence, inseparable from the economic substance that makes it possible. In the earliest gathering about a grave or a painted symbol, a great stone or a sacred grove, one has the beginning of a succession of civic institutions that range from the temple to the astronomical observatory, from the theater to the university.

Thus even before the city is a place of fixed residence, it begins as a meeting place to which people periodically return: the magnet comes before the container, and this ability to attract non-residents to it for intercourse and spiritual stimulus no less than trade remains one of the essential criteria of the city, a witness to its inherent dynamism, as opposed to the more fixed and indrawn form of the village, hostile to the outsider.

The first germ of the city, then, is in the ceremonial meeting place that serves as the goal for pilgrimage: a site to which family or clan groups are drawn back, at seasonable intervals, because it concentrates, in addition to any natural advantages it may have, certain 'spiritual' or supernatural powers, powers of higher potency and greater duration, of wider cosmic significance, than the ordinary processes of life. And though the human performances may be occasional and temporary, the structure that supports it, whether a paleolithic grotto or a Mayan ceremonial center with its lofty pyramid, will be endowed with a more lasting cosmic image.

Once detached from its immediate animal needs, the mind begins to play freely over the whole canvas of existence, and to leave its imprint on both natural structures, like caves and trees and springs, and man-made artifacts, elaborated in their image. Some of the functions and purposes of the city, accordingly, existed in such simple structures long before the complex association of the city had come into existence and re-fashioned the whole environment to give them sustenance and support. But this is only part of the story: so let us look further.

4: DOMESTICATION AND THE VILLAGE

Though some of the seeds of later urban life were already present in paleolithic culture, the soil to nourish them was lacking. Hunting and food-gathering sustain less than ten people per square mile: to be sure of a living, paleolithic man needed a wide range and great freedom of movement. Chance and luck compete with cunning and skill in early man's economy: now he feasts, now he starves: and until he learns to smoke and salt his meat, he must live from day to day, keeping to small, mobile groups, not heavily impeded by possessions, not tied to a fixed habitation.

The first condition for an ample, reliable food supply arose in the mesolithic period, perhaps fifteen thousand years ago. At this point the archaeologist begins to find definite traces of permanent settlements, from India to the Baltic area: a culture based on the use of shellfish and fish, possibly seaweed, and planted tubers, doubtless supplemented by other less certain supplies of food. With these mesolithic hamlets come the first clearings for agricultural purposes: likewise the earliest domestic animals, the household pets and guardians: pig, fowl, duck, goose, and above all, the dog, man's oldest animal companion. The practice of reproducing food plants by cuttings—as with the date palm, the olive, the fig, the apple, and the grape—probably derives from this mesolithic culture. The time required for the growth of fruit-bearing trees itself denotes a continuous occupation and persistent care.

The richness of this greatly augmented food supply, once the last Ice Age had receded, may have had a stirring effect upon both the mind and the sexual organs. The easy picking, the extra security, afforded leisure; while the relief from forced fasting, that long-proved diminisher of sexual appetite, may have given to sexuality in every form an early maturation, a persistence, indeed a potency, it perhaps lacked in the anxious, often half-starved life of hunting and collecting peoples. Both the diet and the erotic customs of the Polynesians, as they existed when Western man discovered them, suggest this mesolithic picture.

This process of settlement, domestication, dietary regularity, entered a second stage, possibly ten or twelve thousand years ago. With this came the systematic gathering and planting of the seeds from certain grasses, the taming of other seed plants, like the squashes and the beans, and the utilization of herd animals, the ox, the sheep, finally the ass and the horse. By one or another of these creatures, food, pulling power, and collective mobility were increased. Neither phase of this great agricultural revolution could have come about, in all probability, among chronic nomads: it needed something like the permanent occupation of an area, prolonged enough to follow the whole cycle of growth, to prompt primitive folk to have an insight into natural processes and to duplicate them more systematically. Perhaps the central event in this whole development was the domestication of man himself, itself an evidence of a growing interest in sexuality and reproduction.

Here one cannot dismiss the suggestion of A. M. Hocart that both domestication and the use of manures may have had their origin in fertility rites and magic sacrifices, just as the ceremonial use of body decoration and purely symbolic costume almost certainly preceded the fabrication of clothes as a protection against the weather. In any event, general domestication was the final product of a growing interest in sexuality and reproduction; and it was accompanied by an enlarged role for woman in every department. Predation yielded to symbiosis. Fortunately for human development, woman's sexuality never became segregated and exaggerated in the mammoth form of, say, the termite queen, who took over the egg-laying function for the whole termitary.

What is called the agricultural revolution was preceded, very possibly, by a sexual revolution: a change that gave predominance, not to the hunting male, agile, swift of foot, ready to kill, ruthless by vocational necessity, but to the more passive female, attached to her children, slowed down in movement to a child's pace, guarding and nurturing the young of all sorts, even suckling little animals on occasion, if the mother had died, planting seeds and watching over the seedlings, perhaps first in a fertility rite, before the growth and multiplication of seeds suggested a further possibility of enlarging the food crop.

Let me emphasize neolithic man's concentration on organic life and growth: not merely a sampling and testing of what nature had provided, but a discriminating selection and propagation, to such good purpose that historic man has not added a plant or animal of major importance to those domesticated or cultivated by neolithic communities. Domestication in all its aspects implies two large changes: permanence and continuity in residence, and the exercise of control and foresight over processes once subject to the caprices of nature. With this go habits of gentling and nurturing and breeding. Here woman's needs, woman's solicitudes, woman's intimacy with the processes of growth, woman's capacity for tenderness and love, must have played a dominating part. With the great enlargement of the food supply that resulted from the cumulative domestication of plants and animals, woman's central place in the new economy was established.

Certainly 'home and mother' are written over every phase of neolithic agriculture, and not least over the new village centers, at last identifiable in the foundations of houses and in graves. It was woman who wielded the digging stick or the hoe: she who tended the garden crops and accomplished those masterpieces of selection and cross-fertilization which turned raw wild species into the prolific and richly nutritious domestic varieties: it was woman who made the first containers, weaving baskets and coiling the first clay pots. In form, the village, too, is her creation: for whatever else the village might be, it was a collective nest for the care and nurture of the young. Here she lengthened the period of child-care and playful irresponsibility, on which so much of man's higher development depends. Stable village life had an advantage over looser itinerant forms of association in smaller groups in that it provided the maximum facilities for fecundity, nutrition, and protection. By communal sharing of the care of the young, larger numbers could prosper. Without this long period of agricultural and domestic development, the surplus of food and manpower that made urban life possible would not have been forthcoming. And without the forethought and conscious moral discipline that neolithic culture introduced in every department, it is doubtful if the more complex social co-operation brought in with the city could have emerged.

Woman's presence made itself felt in every part of the village: not least in its physical structures, with their protective enclosures, whose further symbolic meanings psychoanalysis has now tardily brought to light. Security, receptivity, enclosure, nurture—these functions belong to woman; and they take structural expression in every part of the village, in the house and the oven, the byre and the bin, the cistern, the storage pit, the granary, and from there pass on to the city, in the wall and the moat, and all inner spaces, from the atrium to the cloister. House and village, eventually the town itself, are woman writ large. If this seems a wild psychoanalytic conjecture, the ancient Egyptians stand ready to vouch for the identification. In Egyptian hieroglyphics, 'house' or 'town' may stand as symbols for 'mother,' as if to confirm the similarity of the individual and the collective nurturing function. In line with this, the more primitive structures—houses, rooms, tombs—are usually round ones: like the original bowl described in Greek myth, which was modelled on Aphrodite's breast.

The village, in the midst of its garden plots and fields, formed a new kind of settlement: a permanent association of families and neighbors, of birds and animals, of houses and storage pits and barns, all rooted in the ancestral soil, in which each generation formed the compost for the next. The daily round was centered in food and sex: the sustenance and the reproduction of life. Right into historic times, the phallus and the vulva loom large in village ritual. In monumental form they make their way later into the city, not merely disguised as obelisks, columns, towers, domed enclosures, but in such naked forms as the huge penis, broken off but erect, still on view at Delos.

In primitive form, many urban structures and symbols were present in the agricultural village: even the wall may have existed in the form of a stockade or mound, if one can judge from much later evidence, as a protection against marauding animals. Within such an enclosure children might safely play, otherwise unguarded; and at night the cattle could rest unmolested by wolf or tiger. Yet many early hamlets, according to V. Gordon Childe, were open: so the very existence of such safeguards perhaps indicates a later period of pressure or danger, in which the static encirclement of the wall served instead of vigilant weapons to keep the marauder at bay.

Into this life with its erotic exuberance a new order, a new regularity, a new security had entered; for the food supply was more abundant than it had ever been before: almost certainly more children were born and more survived in these neolithic communities than any earlier culture could sustain, except under unusually happy circumstances. The ground and polished tools that were once treated as the main criteria of neolithic culture bear witness to patience and systematic effort, far different from that needed for flint-knapping or hunting. All these new habits and functions made their contribution to the city, when it finally emerged; and without this village component, the larger urban community would have lacked an essential base for physical permanence and social continuity.

Even without any conscious push in that direction, this new symbiotic association of man and animals and plants was favorable to the later development of the city. Originally the dog was less a hunting animal than a watchman and a scavenger: without the dog and the pig it is doubtful if the close-packed community could have survived its sanitary misdemeanors: indeed, the pig served as an auxiliary department of sanitation right down to the nineteenth century, in supposedly progressive towns like New York and Manchester. Then, too, when grains became plentiful, the cat— and in Egypt the domesticated snake—served to keep down the rodents that carried disease and sapped the food supply. But one must add, in fairness, a word about the negative side: the mouse, the rat, and the cockroach also took advantage of the new settlements, and formed an all-too-permanent attachment.

This new partnership with animals antedated their use for food: as with costume and body decoration, they were decorative before they were useful. But the close quartering of men and animals must have had a further stabilizing effect on agriculture: it turned the village environs, willy-nilly, into a compost heap. The term fertilization today has a double sense in English; and that connection may have been an old one, for these early cultivators were nothing if not observant. If they understood the obscure process of cross-fertilization as in the date palm, they probably had also observed that both forms of 'fertilization' furthered vegetable growth. Primitive man, like the little child, regards with interest, even with awe, all the excretions of the body: only the uncontrolled periodic discharge of the menses arouses his fear and prompts precautionary measures. He values these self-made products as evidences of a kind of spontaneous creativity, common to both man and his animal partners. In the village, mere numbers made manure abundant, for it was even mixed with mud to plaster the reed-mat walls of Mesopotamian huts.

Thus the very act of settlement in villages helped to make agriculture self-sustaining, except in the New World tropics where later, with more primitive methods of cultivation, using fire to clear the jungle, the village lacked stability, and the ceremonial centers often had no permanent population. But where human as well as animal dung was fully used, as in China, even the growing city offset its own blotting out of valuable agricultural land by enriching the surrounding fields. If we knew where and when this practice began we would have a deeper insight into the natural history of early cities. Water closets, sewer mains, and river pollution give a closing date to the process: a backward step ecologically, and so far a somewhat superficial technical advance.

Village life is embedded in the primary association of birth and place, blood and soil. Each member of it is a whole human being, performing all the functions appropriate to each phase of life, from birth to death, in alliance with natural forces that he venerates and submits to, even though he may be tempted to invoke magical powers to control them in his group's interest. Before the city came into existence, the village had brought forth the neighbor: he who lives near at hand, within calling distance, sharing the crises of life, watching over the dying, weeping sympathetically for the dead, rejoicing at a marriage feast or a childbirth. Neighbors hurry to your aid, as Hesiod reminds us, while even kinsmen "dawdle over their gear."

The order and stability of the village, along with its maternal enclosure and intimacy and its oneness with the forces of nature, were carried over into the city: if lost in the city at large, through its overexpansion, it nevertheless remains in the quarter or the neighborhood. Without this communal identification and mothering, the young become demoralized: indeed, their very power to become fully human may vanish, along with neolithic man's first obligation—the cherishing and nurturing of life. What we call morality began in the mores, the life-conserving customs, of the village. When these primary bonds dissolve, when the intimate visible community ceases to be a watchful, identifiable, deeply concerned group, then the 'We' becomes a buzzing swarm of 'I's', and secondary ties and allegiances become too feeble to halt the disintegration of the urban community. Only now that village ways are rapidly disappearing throughout the world can we estimate all that the city owes to them for the vital energy and loving nurture that made possible man's further development.

5: CERAMICS, HYDRAULICS, AND GEOTECHNICS

With the village came a new technology: the masculine weapons and tools of the hunter and miner—the spear, the bow, the hammer, the ax, the knife —were supplemented by typically neolithic forms, of feminine origin: even the very smoothness of ground tools, in contrast to chipped forms, may be considered a feminine trait. The great fact about neolithic technics is that its main innovations were not in weapons and tools but containers.

Paleolithic tools and weapons mainly were addressed to movements and muscular efforts: instruments of chipping, hacking, digging, burrowing, cleaving, dissecting, exerting force swiftly at a distance; in short, every manner of aggressive activity. The bones and muscles of the male dominate his technical contributions: even his limp penis is useless, sexually speaking, until it is as hard as a bone—as vulgar speech recognizes. But in woman the soft internal organs are the center of her life: her arms and legs serve less significantly for movement than for holding and enclosing, whether it be a lover or a child; and it is in the orifices and sacs, in mouth, vulva, vagina, breast, womb, that her sexually individualized activities take place.

Under woman's dominance, the neolithic period is pre-eminently one of containers: it is an age of stone and pottery utensils, of vases, jars, vats, cisterns, bins, barns, granaries, houses, not least great collective containers, like irrigation ditches and villages. The uniqueness and significance of this contribution has too often been overlooked by modern scholars who gauge all technical advances in terms of the machine.

The most primitive dwelling that has yet been discovered in Mesopotamia, according to Robert Braidwood, is a hole dug out of the soil, sundried to brick hardness; and what is more remarkable, this first house seems to antedate any form of earthenware pottery. Wherever a surplus must be preserved and stored, containers are important. Even though shells and skins were available, the paleolithic hunter had little use for containers: like the surviving Bushman in Africa, he made his swollen belly serve as a container. But as soon as agriculture brought a surplus of food and permanent settlement, storage utensils of all kinds were essential.

Without tight containers, the neolithic villager could not store beer, wine, oil; without sealable stone or clay jars, he could not keep out rodents or insects; without bins, cisterns, barns, he could not make his food keep from season to season. Without the permanent dwelling house, the young, the ill, and the aged could not be securely kept together nor tenderly cherished. It was in permanent containers that neolithic invention outshone all earlier cultures: so well that we are still using many of their methods, materials, and forms. The modern city itself, for all its steel and glass, is still essentially an earth-bound Stone Age structure. The early use of baked clay for written records gave a permanence to human thought that no other medium can rival, as the cuneiform inscriptions from Babylonia still witness. Though ancient cities were often destroyed, their permanent records were waterproof and fireproof. With storage came continuity as well as a surplus to draw on in lean seasons. The safe setting aside of unconsumed seeds for next year's sowing was the first step toward capital accumulation.

Mark how much the city owes technically to the village: out of it came, directly or by elaboration, the granary, the bank, the arsenal, the library, the store. Remember, too, that the irrigation ditch, the canal, the reservoir, the moat, the aqueduct, the drain, the sewer are also containers, for automatic transport or storage. The first of these was invented long before the city; and without this whole range of inventions the ancient city could not have taken the form it finally did; for it was nothing less than a container of containers.

Before the potter's wheel, the war chariot, or the plow had been invented, that is, well before 3500 B.C., all the chief forms of container had had a long career. Karl A. Wittfogel is correct in emphasizing the collective control of water as one of the distinguishing features of the totalitarian states that flourished in the stone-and-copper age. But there is evidence that the early villagers dispersed along the Nile and the Euphrates had already begun to master this art. Mud and water, as children know, are plastic and responsive. The lesson learned in modelling house and cistern, irrigation ditch and canal, was passed on to every other part of the landscape. In fact, the domestication of plants and animals, the domestication of man, and the domestication of the natural landscape all went hand in hand.

In short, the shaping of the earth was an integral part of the shaping of the city—and preceded it. That intimate biotechnic relationship is one that modern man, with his plans for replacing complex earth-forms and ecological associations with saleable artificial substitutes, disrupts at his peril.

Hundreds, perhaps thousands, of little villages, in favored parts of the world, from Egypt to India, had applied these arts, in a modest but decisive way, to every feature of their life. So woodland and grassland yielded to hand cultivation, and close to the desert or near-desert, as in the Valley of the Jordan, little oases, based on sure supplies of water, hoarded in great cisterns, became visible. Without that foundation, without that containment, without that enclosure and order, the city might never have been conceived. These neolithic functions were basic to the city's emergent purposes, which turned them to extravagantly different ends.

6: THE CONTRIBUTION OF THE VILLAGE

Let us look more closely at the early village, as one must picture it in Mesopotamia and the Valley of the Nile between, say, 9000 and 4000 B.C. A heap of mud huts, baked, or of mud-and-reed construction, cramped in size, at first little better than a beaver's lodge. Around these villages lie garden plots and patches, all the dimensions modest; not yet the broad but bounded fields, rectangular in shape, that come in with the plow. Nearby, in swamp and river, are birds to snare, fish to net, extra food to tide over a bad crop or enrich the daily diet. But even in the most primitive hamlet, such as the delta village of Merimdeh Beni-Salameh, there was a "jar sunk into the flooring to drain off the rainwater coming through the roof," as John A. Wilson observed. In addition "the village had a communal granary, consisting of woven baskets sunk into the ground."

Most of what one knows about the structure and mode of life of the neolithic hamlets and villages comes from the rough remains preserved in Polish swamps, Swiss lake bottoms, Egyptian delta mud, or from snatches of song and story recorded much later in the literate, urbanized culture of the Sumerians, the Egyptians, and the Greeks. No reference to village life among surviving tribes, supposedly primitive, can hope to give a true account of that early inchoate culture, still in the making. For what we call primitive today, even when it shows few traces of recent contact with more developed cultures, has behind it continuous linkages and changes over as great a span of history as any more complex national group or urban unit. Perhaps the best sources of early village culture remain in the surviving customs and superstitions, still kept alive in rural areas almost until our own day. This archaic culture, as André Varagnac called it, seems to be the unweathered stratum beneath all the Old World cultures, however civilized and urbanized.

Everywhere, the village is a small cluster of families, from half a dozen to threescore perhaps, each with its own hearth, its own household god, its own shrine, its own burial plot, within the house or in some common burial ground. Speaking the same tongue, meeting together under the same tree or in the shadow of the same upstanding stone, walking along the same footway trodden by their cattle, each family follows the same way of life and participates in the same labors. If there is any division of labor, it is of the most rudimentary kind, determined more by age and strength than vocational aptitude: whoever looks into his neighbor's face sees his own image. For the most part, time has dissolved the material structure of the village into the landscape: only its shards and shells claim permanence; but the social structure has remained tough and durable, for it is based on precepts, saws, family histories, heroic examples, moral injunctions, treasured and passed on without deviation from the old to the young.

As the routine of neolithic agriculture became more successful, it probably tended to become more fixed and conservative. By the end of this period, all the adventurous experiments that distinguished food plants from indigestible or poisonous ones, that had discovered the secrets of rooting and seeding and cross-fertilization and selection, that had picked out the docile and tractable animals which became man's helpers, had tapered off, if not come to an end. Conformity, repetition, patience, were the keys to this culture, once it had solidified. Doubtless it took thousands of years for the neolithic economy to establish its limits: but once it reached them, it had little inner impulse to further development. "Hold fast to what is good and seek no further" was the formula for its contentment.

Before water transport was well developed, each village was, in effect, a world in itself: cut off as much by sleepy self-absorption and narcissism, perhaps, as by mere physical barriers. Even under primitive conditions that conformity was never absolute, that sufficiency never complete, those limitations never unbreakable. One might have to go elsewhere to fetch a tool or 'capture' a bride. Yet the villagers' ideal remained that pictured much later by Lao-tse: "to delight in their food, to be proud of their clothes, to be content with their home, to rejoice in their customs." Then "they might be within sight of a neighboring village within hearing of the cocks and dogs, yet grow old and die before they visited one another." Such villages might reproduce and multiply without any impulse to change their pattern of life: as long as nutrition and reproduction, the pleasures of the belly and the genitals, were the chief ends of life, neolithic village culture met every requirement.

Doubtless this general picture needs qualification. We now perhaps are tempted to exaggerate the static qualities of the neolithic village, and read back into its more fluid characteristics the stabilities and repetitions and fixations that accumulated over thousands of years. Over the millennia there must have been some fresh accumulation and adventurous growth. In outward form, the neolithic village already had many of the character-istics of small cities, like Lagash in Mesopotamia: indeed, as purely phys-ical artifacts the remains of the large village and the small town are indistinguishable. If more physical traces were visible, we might even find as many varieties in layout as Meitzen found for a much later period in Central Europe.

For all that, the embryonic structure of the city already existed in the village. House, shrine, cistern, public way, agora—not yet a specialized market—all first took form in the village: inventions and organic differen-tiations waiting to be carried further in the more complex structure of the city. What holds for the general structure of the village also holds for its institutions. The beginnings of organized morality, government, law, and justice existed in the village Council of Elders. Thorkild Jacobsen has dem-onstrated that this representative group, the repository of tradition, the censor of morals, the judges of right and wrong, was already discernible in the fourth millennium B.C. in Mesopotamia, though its origins must pre-date any record. This rudimentary organ of government seems to char-acterize village communities at all periods. So important was this institution, that it left its mark on both religious myth and the actual functioning of the Mesopotamian city state; for thousands of years later a Babylonian Council of the Gods still followed the archaic village pattern.

Such spontaneous councils, unified by use and wont, expressed the human consensus, not so much ruling and making new decisions as giving some immediate application to accepted rules and to decisions made in an immemorial past. In an oral culture, only the aged have had enough time to assimilate all that is to be known: their influence can still be felt in village communities in Africa, Asia, South America: indeed, without cere-monial forms, they were often vestigially active in occasional American villages until today. The elders personified the hoarded wisdom of the community: all participated, all conformed, all joined in restoring a communal order each time it was momentarily upset by misunderstanding or strife. The ancient Greeks thought that their own respect for custom and common law, as against tyrannous caprice, was a unique product of their culture. But actually it was a witness to their continuity with an older village democracy we first meet in Mesopotamia: an institution that seems to precede all more sophisticated exercise of control by a dominant minority, imposing their alien traditions or their equally alien upper-class innovations upon a subjugated if acquiescent population.

So with religion itself: it remained on the familiar, human level. Though each village might have its local shrine and cult, common to all the neighbors, there was a further diffusion of religious sentiment through totem and ancestor worship: each household had its own gods as its true and inalienable property, and the head of the household performed priestly functions of sacrifice and prayer, as he still does in orthodox Jewish families at Passover. In general, the village made for a diffusion of power and responsibility: the potentialities for differentiation and specialization remained largely in abeyance, while detachment, non-conformity, innovation, and invention were reduced to the barest tolerable minimum, if not ruthlessly extirpated. In such closeness and intimacy, with daily face-to-face meeting, each member stood at eye level. Only age established precedence and authority.

Once the main neolithic inventions and institutions were established, village life might continue at that level for thousands of years, happy merely to hold its own. The last great departure came with plow culture and the substitution of metal tools for stone. There must have been a fairly long period when nothing that could be called a complete, fully differentiated city had come into existence. Yet the gradations between neolithic villages and neolithic towns are so smooth, and the points of resemblance so many, that one is tempted to take them as simply the youthful and adult forms of the same species. This applies in large measure to its physical form, but not to its social institutions. Much of the city was latent, indeed visibly present, in the village: but the latter existed as the unfertilized ovum, rather than as the developing embryo; for it needed a whole set of complementary chromosomes from a male parent to bring about the further processes of differentiation and complex cultural development.

7: THE NEW ROLE OF THE HUNTER

In seeking to interpret the succession of cultures, one runs the risk of taking their stratification too seriously. Though a due respect for strata is a necessity for archaeology, a way of defining cultural affiliations and temporal successions, only a material culture that is dead and buried ever remains stratified, without undergoing displacements and upheavals; while non-material culture is mainly fibrous in nature; though its long threads may often be broken, they go through every stratum, and even when out of sight they may play an active part.

So though on the present evidence we properly date the physical town from the later phases of neolithic culture, the actual emergence of the city came as the ultimate result of an earlier union between the paleolithic and the neolithic components. This union, if I surmise correctly, was supported, if not brought about, by the last great advance in the agricultural revolution, the domestication of grains and the introduction of plow culture and irrigation. The final result was the coalescence of the whole group of institutions and controls that characterize 'civilization.'

At that moment, the masculine contribution, curbed and tamed, if not rejected, by the earlier acts of domestication, suddenly returned with redoubled vigor, bringing with it a new dynamism, expressing itself as a desire to tame and control nature, to dominate and master strong or mettlesome animals, ass, horse, camel, elephant, above all, to exercise, partly by command of weapons, a predatory power over other human groups. Neither paleolithic nor neolithic culture was capable of doing by itself what both actually succeeded in accomplishing by a union of their complementary talents and functions.

Certainly the notion that paleolithic culture was wholly replaced by neolithic culture is an illusion. Even today, around every big city on a spring Sunday, thousands of fishermen will line riverbanks and lakesides, practicing the ancient paleolithic occupation of fishing, while later in the year, and farther afield, others will follow an even earlier practice, picking mushrooms, berries, or nuts, gathering shells and driftwood, or digging for clams on the seashore: still doing for pleasure what early man did for survival.

What, we must ask, happened to the paleolithic hunter when hoe cultivation and tree culture made village settlement possible? Doubtless he was pushed out of the agricultural areas, for if small game could be found there it would be snared or hunted by the villagers, while the big animals were driven into the swamps and highlands; or if not, would be regarded as a peril to the crops rather than as a welcome source of food. With agriculture, the hunter's opportunities shrank. If we recall Leatherstocking's attitude toward the pioneer agricultural clearings we shall be close to recognizing this primitive reaction. But in time perhaps the comforts and sociabilities of the little village hamlet aroused a measure of dissatisfaction and envy, contemptuously though the hunter might reject the repetitious routine, the unadventurous security, that successful agriculture brought with it.

Now apart from a few dubious cave paintings of men with drawn bows facing each other, there is no early evidence to suggest that hunters preyed on other hunters. For long, the victims of the chase were only animals and birds, not other men. But there is plenty of support from the animal and insect world for the belief that predators, given a choice, often prefer a soft mode of existence to a hard one, and become so addicted to the easier life that they become committed to parasitism, living off a passive, if not wholly complaisant, host. Yet up to a point, this relation may be a helpfully symbiotic one, too: in return for his share of abundance, the predator may guard the nest against other enemies.

The actual evidence for this accommodating interchange is lacking, for it precedes the historic record: even the suggestive material remains that would indicate a new relation between paleolithic and neolithic groups are scanty, and open to diverse interpretations. But before the city springs into being, there are definite indications in Palestine that the hunter's temporary camp has turned into a continuously occupied stronghold. This stronghold is held by someone that the archaeologist somewhat too vaguely describes as the "local chieftain," obviously not alone, but with a supporting band of followers. At first such hunters might not merely have been tolerated, but actively welcome. For the hunter played a useful part in the neolithic economy. With his mastery of weapons, with his hunting skills, he would protect the village against its most serious, probably its only, enemies: the lion, the tiger, the wolf, the alligator. The hunter still knew how to stalk and kill these beasts, whereas the villager probably lacked the weapons, and still more the needed audacity to do so. Over the centuries security may have made the villager passive and timid.

At this point the written record comes to our aid, though the first reciprocal arrangement between village and stronghold must long have preceded it. The archetypal chieftain in Sumerian legend is Gilgamesh: the heroic hunter, the strong protector, not least significantly, the builder of the wall around Uruk. And in the old Babylonian account of the feats of still another hunter, Enkidu, we read: He "took his weapon to chase the lions: the shepherds might rest at night, he caught the wolves: he captured the lions: the chief cattlemen could lie down. Enkidu is their watchman, the bold man, the unique hero."

This was not servile praise to a conqueror but civil gratitude to a friendly protector, whose services long continued to be needed. As late as the seventh century B.C., a stele erected by Assurbanipal recounts the ferocity of the lions and tigers after torrential rains had turned the land into a reedy jungle: he boasts of his efficiency in stamping out these beasts in their lairs. But by this time, unfortunately, the hunter's beneficent role had become soiled by the sadistic lust for power: not being able to count on a voluntary response from the community, the hunter-king filled the silence with his self-praise.

Conceivably, the villages protected by the hunter flourished better than those whose crops might be trampled by wild herds, or whose children might be mangled and devoured by marauding beasts. But the very prosperity and peaceableness of the neolithic village may have caused its protectors to exchange the watchdog's role for the wolf's, demanding 'protection money,' so to say, in an increasingly one-sided transaction. Our Victorian forebears might not have understood this so well; but in the United States of today, with one gang chieftain or another controlling prosperous business enterprises and powerful labor unions, laying huge if under-cover taxes on amusement, transportation, and building, brazenly suborning judges and enlisting policemen in partnership, we are in a position to understand the success of these earlier chieftains. The cowed villagers submitted, lest the protector show uglier teeth than animals he offered protection against. This natural evolution of the hunter into political chieftain probably paved the way for his further ascent into power. Already in the proto-literate monuments, as Henri Frankfort pointed out, "the hunter appears in the dress and with the distinctive coiffure which characterizes leaders, perhaps kings."

Yet one must not exaggerate the element of coercion, especially at the beginning: that probably came in only with the further concentration of technical, political, and religious power, which transformed the uncouth, primitive chieftain into the awe-inspiring king. From the first, there was a benign side to this relation, perhaps an actual shift in interest from the wild animal to be tracked down and killed to the tame animal to be herded and protected: from the immediate seizure of food, in response to hunger and want, to the process of fattening the eventual victim and seizing the right moment for slaughtering it.

There is a line in an early Mesopotamian poem that shows the shepherd was not unwelcome when he pastured his flocks on the farmer's meadowland, perhaps because the cultivator had already learned the value of manure. The unrestricted roamings of the herdsman and his flocks bring him closer in spirit to the hunter than they do to the peasants, tied down to the glebe. Both of them appear in fable as admirable heroic figures, while the productive peasant plays a lowly role, if not the evil one Cain enacts in Genesis. In his encounter with the shepherd Dumuzi, the farmer is conciliatory and resigned to taking second place. The shepherd may in fact be looked upon as the spiritual brother of the hunter, his better self, stressing the protective rather than the predatory function. Etana, one of the early kings, was a shepherd, so were the gods Lugubanda and Dumuzi in Mesopotamian myth, and so was David in Israel at a much later period; while Hammurabi, a great organizer and conqueror, still put himself forward as a shepherd of his peoples.

Both vocations call forth leadership and responsibility above, and demand docile compliance below. But that of the hunter elevated the will-to-power and eventually transferred his skill in slaughtering game to the more highly organized vocation of regimenting or slaughtering other men; while that of the shepherd moved toward the curbing of force and violence and the institution of some measure of justice, through which even the weakest member of the flock might be protected and nurtured. Certainly coercion and persuasion, aggression and protection, war and law, power and love, were alike solidified in the stones of the earliest urban communities, when they finally take form. When kingship appeared, the war lord and the law lord became land lord too.

If this is necessarily a mythic extrapolation from the known facts, it may nevertheless suggest how voluntary offerings would turn into tribute, and tribute itself would later be regularized as tithes, taxes, forced labor, sacrificial offerings, and even human sacrifice. At this point, I submit, war is not yet in evidence. Such neolithic villages as have been exhumed show a remarkable lack of anything that could be called weapons; and though this is negative proof, it fits well into the picture of self-contained communities, too tiny, too lacking in surplus manpower, too far apart, and too poor in easy means of movement until boats were invented, to have any need to crowd one another or encroach on each other's domains. The primal war of "each against all" is a fairy tale: Hobbes' bellicose primitive man has even less historic reality than Rousseau's noble savage. As with the birds, 'territoriality' may have amicably settled boundary claims that only later, under more 'civilized' concern for property and privilege, led to savage conflicts.

What the early castles and strongholds point to is not war and conflict between opposing communities, but the one-sided domination of a relatively large group by a small minority. Such compulsion and control as arms may have imposed were within the community, and not at first in struggles against other communities: it was by the wielding of arms that the 'nobles' at first achieved their age-old power over *their own peasantry.* Competition, conflict, violence, and outright murder may all have existed in various degrees in every group, though they have probably been exaggerated by modern scholars who gratuitously read back into primitive times the aberrations and offenses peculiar on a magnified scale to 'higher' civilizations. But Bronislaw Malinowski's judgment on this subject seems to me sound: "If we insist that war is a fight between two independent and politically organized groups, war does not occur at the primitive level."

Collective military aggression, I submit, is as much a special invention of civilization as is the collective expression of curiosity through systematic scientific investigation. The fact that human beings are naturally curious did not lead inevitably to organized science; and the fact that they are given to anger and pugnacity was not sufficient in itself to create the institution of war. The latter, like science, is an historic, culture-bound achievement—witness to a much more devious connection between complexity, crisis, frustration, and aggression. Here the ants have more to teach us than the apes—or the supposedly combative 'cave man,' whose purely imaginary traits strangely resemble those of a nineteenth-century capitalist enterpriser.

8: THE PALEOLITHIC-NEOLITHIC UNION

What actually happened before the city came into existence can only be conjectured. Perhaps residual paleolithic hunting groups and the new neolithic settlers, each still too sparse to have the upper hand, began to occupy the same territory and stayed together long enough to absorb some of each other's ways and interchange some of their kit of tools. If one dare to call this a marriage of the two cultures, they were probably at first equal partners, but the relationship became increasingly one-sided, as the weapons and coercive habits of the aggressive minority were re-enforced by the patient capacity for work that the stone-grinding neolithic peoples showed. As often happens, the rejected component of the earlier culture (hunting) became the new dominant in the agricultural community, but it was now made to do duty for the governance of a superior kind of settlement. Weapons served now not just to kill animals but to threaten and command men.

The interplay between the two cultures took place over a long period; but in the end the masculine processes over-rode by sheer dynamism the more passive life-nurturing activities that bore woman's imprint. The very elements of procreation were taken out of woman's sphere, at least in the imagination: one of the early Egyptian texts pictures Atum creating the universe out of his own body, by masturbation. The proud male could scarcely have used plainer words to indicate that, in the new scheme of life, woman no longer counted. In the early neolithic society, before the domestication of grain, woman had been supreme: sex itself was power.

This was no mere expression of fantasy, heightened by lust, for woman's interest in child nurture and plant care had changed the anxious, timorous, apprehensive existence of early man into one of competent foresight, with reasonable assurance of continuity—no longer entirely at the mercy of forces outside human control. Even in the form of physical energy, the agricultural revolution, through domestication, was the most fundamental step forward in harnessing the sun's energy: not rivalled again until the series of inventions that began with the water mill and reached its climax in nuclear power. This was like that "explosion of flowers," as Loren Eiseley has beautifully put it, which transformed the vegetable world millions of years earlier. Neolithic woman had as much reason to be proud of her contribution as Nuclear Age woman has reason to be apprehensive over the fate of her children and her world.

If one had any doubt about woman's commanding original part, one could get confirmation from the earliest religious myths; for in them her dominating femininity also manifests extremely savage attributes that suggest she had taken over far too much of the masculine role. These attributes linger today in the terrible figure of the Hindu goddess, Kali. Certainly the most ancient Mesopotamian deity was Tiamat, the primeval mother of waters, as hostile to her rebellious sons as the classic Freudian patriarch; while the cult of Kybele, the Great Mother, as lover and fierce mistress, commanding lions, lingered far into historic times in Asia Minor, though she was supplemented by more gentle, maternal images, such as Demeter, Mother of Harvests.

Possibly it was by yielding this power element to more masculine gods, that woman was able to concentrate on less primitive aspects of her sexuality, tenderness, beauty, erotic delight: Ishtar, Astarte, Aphrodite. At the same time, the male over-reacted against the feminine side of his own nature: the new hunter-hero glories in his masculine prowess, feats of strength, displays of animal courage, slaying deadly wild beasts, conquering rival men—but often turning his back on woman in order to keep more single-mindedly to his task and trial, fearing to lose his strength, like Samson or a modern prize fighter, in woman's arms. So Gilgamesh spurned the advances of Inanna.

By the same token, Enkidu was subdued by being entrapped into having intercourse with a harlot from Uruk: after which exhibition of weakness the gazelles and the wild beasts of the steppe ran away from him! Traditionally, the hunter-hero's special virtue lay in feats of daring and muscular strength: moving huge boulders, turning the course of rivers, showing contempt for danger and death. In his big and burly person occurs the first general enlargement of dimensions that comes in with the city. Likewise the first concentration on physical prowess and mechanical power as ends in themselves.

The city, then, if I interpret its origins correctly, was the chief fruit of the union between neolithic and a more archaic paleolithic culture. In the new proto-urban milieu, the male became the leading figure; woman took second place. Her digging stick and hoe were replaced by the more efficient plow, capable, with ox-drawn power, of cleaving the heavier soils of the bottom lands. Even the female goddesses yielded in some degree to Osiris and Bacchus, precisely in the realms of agriculture and invention where woman had been most active. Woman's strength had lain in her special wiles and spells, in the mysteries of menstruation and copulation and child-birth, the arts of life. Man's strength now lay in feats of aggression and force, in showing his ability to kill and his own contempt for death: in conquering obstacles and forcing his will on other men, destroying them if they resisted.

As a result of this union of the two cultures, the widest sort of cross-breeding and intermixture probably took place all along the line. This gave the city potentialities and capabilities that neither the hunter, the miner, the stockbreeder, nor the peasant would ever, if left to themselves in their regional habitat, have been able to exploit. Where hoe culture supported hamlets, plow culture could support whole cities and regions. Where local effort could build only minor embankments and ditches, the large scale co-operations of the city could turn a whole river valley into a unified organization of canals and irrigation works for food production and transport—shifting men, supplies, and raw material about, as need dictated.

This change soon left its mark over the whole landscape. Even more, it left an impress on human relations within the community. Male sym-bolisms and abstractions now become manifest: they show themselves in the insistent straight line, the rectangle, the firmly bounded geometric plan, the phallic tower and the obelisk, finally, in the beginnings of mathe-matics and astronomy, whose effective abstractions were progressively detached from the variegated matrix of myth. It is perhaps significant that while the early cities seem largely circular in form, the ruler's citadel and the sacred precinct are more usually enclosed by a rectangle.

In the city, new ways, rigorous, efficient, often harsh, even sadistic, took the place of ancient customs and comfortable easy-paced routine. Work itself was detached from other activities and canalized into the 'working day' of unceasing toil under a taskmaster: the first step in that 'managerial revolution' which has reached its climax in our day. Struggle, domination, mastery, conquest were the new themes: not the protectiveness and prudence, the holding fast or the passive endurance of the village. With this all-too-plenteous enlargement of power, the isolated village—even a thousand isolated villages—could not cope: it existed as a container for more limited functions and more strictly maternal and organic concerns.

But that part of village culture which was capable of having a share in this development was drawn into the city and systematically harnessed to its new mode of life.

For all this, the original components of the city have never entirely disappeared; indeed, each continued to flourish in its own right, even though some portion of its existence might be absorbed by the city. Thus the village multiplied and spread over the entire earth more rapidly and more effectively than the city; and though it is now on the verge of being overwhelmed by urbanization, it maintained the ancient folkways for thousands of years and survived the continued rise and destruction of its bigger, richer, and more alluring rivals. There was sound historic justification, Patrick Geddes pointed out, for the boast of the village of Musselburgh:

> "Musselburgh was a burgh
> When Edinburgh was nane,
> And Musselburgh will be a burgh
> When Edinburgh is gane."

The citadel, too, persists. Though the forms and functions of government have changed during the last four thousand years, the citadel has had a continued existence, and is still visible. From the Castel San Angelo to the concrete bunker by the Admiralty Arch in London, from the Kremlin to the Pentagon, and thence to new underground control centers, the citadel still stands for both the absolutisms and the irrationalities of its earliest exemplars. The shrine, too, has retained an independent existence. Some of the most famous shrines never became great cities in their own right, though bigger centers often play second fiddle to them. Religiously speaking, London and Baghdad are secondary to Canterbury and Mecca; while cities that have formed special objects of pilgrimage, like Santiago de Compostela and Lourdes, have not usually fostered other urban functions, except those that minister to the shrine. Each new component of the city, by the same token, has usually first appeared outside its boundaries, before the city has taken it over.

CHAPTER TWO

The Crystallization of the City

1: THE FIRST URBAN TRANSFORMATION

In view of its satisfying rituals but limited capabilities, no mere increase in numbers would, in all probability, suffice to turn a village into a city. This change needed an outer challenge to pull the community sharply away from the central concerns of nutrition and reproduction: a purpose beyond mere survival. The larger part of the world's population never in fact responded to this challenge: until the present period of urbanization, cities contained only a small fraction of mankind.

The city came as a definite emergent in the paleo-neolithic community: an emergent in the definite sense that Lloyd Morgan and William Morton Wheeler used that concept. In emergent evolution, the introduction of a new factor does not just add to the existing mass, but produces an over-all change, a new configuration, which alters its properties. Potentialities that could not be recognized in the pre-emergent stage, like the possibility of organic life developing from relatively stable and unorganized 'dead' matter, then for the first time become visible. So with the leap from village culture. On the new plane, the old components of the village were carried along and incorporated in the new urban unit; but through the action of new factors, they were recomposed in a more complex and unstable pattern than that of the village—yet in a fashion that promoted further transformations and developments. The human composition of the new unit likewise became more complex: in addition to the hunter, the peasant, and the shepherd, other primitive types entered the city and made their contribution to its existence: the miner, the woodman, the fisherman, each bringing with him the tools and skills and habits of life formed under other pressures. The engineer, the boatman, the sailor arise from this more generalized primitive background, at one point or another in the valley section: from all these original types still other occupation groups develop, the soldier, the banker, the merchant, the priest. Out of this complexity the city created a higher unity.

This new urban mixture resulted in an enormous expansion of human capabilities in every direction. The city effected a mobilization of manpower, a command over long distance transportation, an intensification of communication over long distances in space and time, an outburst of invention along with a large scale development of civil engineering, and, not least, it promoted a tremendous further rise in agricultural productivity.

That urban transformation was accompanied, perhaps preceded, by similar outpourings from the collective unconscious. At some moment, it would seem, the local familiar gods, close to the hearth fire, were overpowered and partly replaced, certainly outranked, by the distant sky gods or earth gods, identified with the sun, the moon, the waters of life, the thunderstorm, the desert. The local chieftain turned into the towering king, and became likewise the chief priestly guardian of the shrine, now endowed with divine or almost divine attributes. The village neighbors would now be kept at a distance: no longer familiars and equals, they were reduced to subjects, whose lives were supervised and directed by military and civil officers, governors, viziers, tax-gatherers, soldiers, directly accountable to the king.

Even the ancient village habits and customs might be altered in obedience to divine command. No longer was it sufficient for the village farmer to produce enough to feed his family or his village: he must now work harder and practice self-denial to support a royal and priestly officialdom with a large surplus. For the new rulers were greedy feeders, and openly measured their power not only in arms, but in loaves of bread and jugs of beer. In the new urban society, the wisdom of the aged no longer carried authority: it was the young men of Uruk who, against the advice of the Elders, supported Gilgamesh when he proposed to attack Kish instead of surrendering to the demands of the ruler of Kish. Though family connections still counted in urban society, vocational ability and youthful audacity counted even more, if it gained the support of the King.

When all this happened, the archaic village culture yielded to urban 'civilization,' that peculiar combination of creativity and control, of expression and repression, of tension and release, whose outward manifestation has been the historic city. From its origins onward, indeed, the city may be described as a structure specially equipped to store and transmit the goods of civilization, sufficiently condensed to afford the maximum amount of facilities in a minimum space, but also capable of structural enlargement to enable it to find a place for the changing needs and the more complex forms of a growing society and its cumulative social heritage. The invention of such forms as the written record, the library, the archive, the school, and the university is one of the earliest and most characteristic achievements of the city.

The transformation I now seek to describe was first called by Childe the Urban Revolution. This term does justice to the active and critically important role of the city; but it does not accurately indicate the process; for a revolution implies a turning things upside down, and a progressive movement away from outworn institutions that have been left behind. Seen from the vantage point of our own age, it seems to indicate something like the same general shift that occurred with our own industrial revolution, with the same sort of emphasis on economic activities. This obscures rather than clarifies what actually occurred. The rise of the city, so far from wiping out earlier elements in the culture, actually brought them together and increased their efficacy and scope. Even the fostering of non-agricultural occupations heightened the demand for food and probably caused villages to multiply, and still more land to be brought under cultivation. Within the city, very little of the old order was at first excluded: agriculture itself in Sumer, for example, continued to be practiced on a large scale by those who lived permanently within the new walled towns.

What happened rather with the rise of cities, was that many functions that had heretofore been scattered and unorganized were brought together within a limited area, and the components of the community were kept in a state of dynamic tension and interaction. In this union, made almost compulsory by the strict enclosure of the city wall, the already well-established parts of the proto-city—shrine, spring, village, market, stronghold—participated in the general enlargement and concentration of numbers, and underwent a structural differentiation that gave them forms recognizable in every subsequent phase of urban culture. The city proved not merely a means of expressing in concrete terms the magnification of sacred and secular power, but in a manner that went far beyond any conscious intention it also enlarged all the dimensions of life. Beginning as a representation of the cosmos, a means of bringing heaven down to earth, the city became a symbol of the possible. Utopia was an integral part of its original constitution, and precisely because it first took form as an ideal projection, it brought into existence realities that might have remained latent for an indefinite time in more soberly governed small communities, pitched to lower expectations and unwilling to make exertions that transcended both their workaday habits and their mundane hopes.

In this emergence of the city, the dynamic element came, as we have seen, from outside the village. Here one must give the new rulers their due, for their hunting practices had accustomed them to a wider horizon than village culture habitually viewed. Archaeologists have pointed out that there is even the possibility that the earliest grain-gatherers, in the uplands of the Near East, may have been hunters who gathered the seeds in their pouch, for current rations, long before they knew how to plant them. The hunter's exploratory mobility, his willingness to gamble and take risks, his need to make prompt decisions, his readiness to undergo bitter deprivation and intense fatigue in pursuit of his game, his willingness to face death in coming to grips with fierce animals—either to kill or be killed—all gave him special qualifications for confident leadership. These traits were the foundations of aristocratic dominance. Faced with the complexities of large-scale community life, individualistic audacity was more viable than the slow communal responses that the agricultural village fostered.

In a society confronting numerous social changes brought on by its own mechanical and agricultural improvements, which provoked serious crises that called for prompt action, under unified command, the hoarded folk wisdom born solely of past experience in long-familiar situations was impotent. Only the self-confident and adventurous could in some degree control these new forces and have sufficient imagination to use them for hitherto unimaginable purposes. Neolithic 'togetherness' was not enough. Many a village, baffled and beset by flooded fields or ruined crops, must have turned away from its slow-moving, overcautious council of elders to a single figure who spoke with authority and promptly gave commands as if he expected instantly to be obeyed.

Doubtless the hunter's imagination, no less than his prowess, was there from the beginning, long before either flowed into political channels: for surely there is a more commanding esthetic sense in the paleolithic hunter's cave than there is in any early neolithic pottery or sculpture. Nothing like the same superb esthetic flair as we find in the Aurignacian caves came back till the stone-and-copper age. But now heroic exertions, once confined mainly to the hunt, were applied to the entire physical environment. Nothing the mind projected seemed impossible. What one singularly self-assured man dared to dream of, under favor of the gods, a whole city obedient to his will might do. No longer would wild animals alone be subdued: rivers, mountains, swamps, masses of men, would be attacked collectively at the King's command and reduced to order. Backbreaking exertions that no little community would impose on itself, so long as nature met its customary needs, were now undertaken: the hunter-hero, from Gilgamesh to Herakles, set the example in his superhuman acts of strength. In conquering hard physical tasks every man became a bit of a hero, surpassing his own natural limits—if only to escape the overseer's lash.

The expansion of human energies, the enlargements of the human ego, perhaps for the first time detached from its immediate communal envelope the differentiation of common human activities into specialized vocations, and the expression of this expansion and differentiation at many points in the structure of the city, were all aspects of a single transformation: the rise of civilization. We cannot follow this change at the moment it occurred, for, as Teilhard de Chardin notes of other evolutionary changes, it is the unstable and fluid emerging forms that leave no record behind. But later crystallizations clearly point to the nature of the earlier evolution.

To interpret what happened in the city, one must deal equally with technics, politics, and religion, above all with the religious side of the transformation. If at the beginning all these aspects of life were inseparably mingled, it was religion that took precedence and claimed primacy, probably because unconscious imagery and subjective projections dominated every aspect of reality, allowing nature to become visible only in so far as it could be worked into the tissue of desire and dream. Surviving monuments and records show that this general magnification of power was accompanied by equally exorbitant images, issuing from the unconscious, transposed into the 'eternal' forms of art.

As we have seen, the formative stages of this process possibly took many thousands of years: even the last steps in the transition from the neolithic country town, little more than an overgrown village, to the full-blown city, the home of new institutional forms, may have taken centuries, even millennia; so long that many institutions that we have definite historic record of in other parts of the world—such as ceremonial human sacrifice —may have had time both to flourish and to be largely cut down in Egypt or Mesopotamia.

The enormous time gap between the earliest foundations in the Valley of the Jordan, if their latest datings are correct, and those of the Sumerian cities allows of many profound if unrecorded changes. But the final outbreak of inventions that attended the birth of the city probably happened within a few centuries, or even, as Frankfort suggested of kingship, within a few generations. Pretty surely it took place within a span of years no greater than the seven centuries between the invention of the mechanical clock and the unlocking of atomic power.

As far as the present record stands, grain cultivation, the plow, the potter's wheel, the sailboat, the draw loom, copper metallurgy, abstract mathematics, exact astronomical observation, the calendar, writing and other modes of intelligible discourse in permanent form, all came into existence at roughly the same time, around 3000 B.C. give or take a few centuries. The most ancient urban remains now known, except Jericho, date from this period. This constituted a singular technological expansion of human power whose only parallel is the change that has taken place in our own time. In both cases men, suddenly exalted, behaved like gods: but with little sense of their latent human limitations and infirmities, or of the neurotic and criminal natures often freely projected upon their deities.

There is nevertheless one outstanding difference between the first urban epoch and our own. Ours is an age of a multitude of socially undirected technical advances, divorced from any other ends than the advancement of science and technology. We live in fact in an exploding universe of mechanical and electronic invention, whose parts are moving at a rapid pace ever further and further away from their human center, and from any rational, autonomous human purposes. This technological explosion has produced a similar explosion of the city itself: the city has burst open and scattered its complex organs and organizations over the entire landscape. The walled urban container indeed has not merely been broken open: it has also been largely demagnetized, with the result that we are witnessing a sort of devolution of urban power into a state of randomness and unpredictability. In short, our civilization is running out of control, overwhelmed by its own resources and opportunities, as well as its superabundant fecundity. The totalitarian states that seek ruthlessly to impose control are as much the victim of their clumsy brakes as the seemingly freer economies coasting downhill are at the mercy of their runaway vehicles.

Just the opposite happened with the first great expansion of civilization: instead of an explosion of power, there was rather an *implosion*. The many diverse elements of the community hitherto scattered over a great valley system and occasionally into regions far beyond, were mobilized and packed together under pressure, behind the massive walls of the city. Even the gigantic forces of nature were brought under conscious human direction: tens of thousands of men moved into action as one machine under centralized command, building irrigation ditches, canals, urban mounds, ziggurats, temples, palaces, pyramids, on a scale hitherto inconceivable. As an immediate outcome of the new power mythology, the machine itself had been invented: long invisible to archaeologists because the substance of which it was composed—human bodies—had been dismantled and decomposed. The city was the container that brought about this implosion, and through its very form held together the new forces, intensified their internal reactions, and raised the whole level of achievement.

This implosion happened at the very moment that the area of intercourse was greatly enlarged, through raidings and tradings, through seizures and commandeerings, through migrations and enslavements, through taxgatherings and the wholesale conscription of labor. Under pressure of one master institution, that of kingship, a multitude of diverse social particles, long separate and self-centered, if not mutually antagonistic, were brought together in a concentrated urban area. As with a gas, the very pressure of the molecules within that limited space produced more social collisions and interactions within a generation than would have occurred in many centuries if still isolated in their native habitats, without boundaries. Or to put it in more organic terms, little communal village cells, undifferentiated and uncomplicated, every part performing equally every function, turned into complex structures organized on an axiate principle, with differentiated tissues and specialized organs, and with one part, the central nervous system, thinking for and directing the whole.

What made this concentration and mobilization of power possible? What gave it the special form it took in the city, with a central religious and political nucleus, the citadel, dominating the entire social structure and giving centralized direction to activities that had once been dispersed and undirected, or at least locally self governed? What I am going to suggest as the key development here had already been presaged, at a much earlier stage, by the apparent evolution of the protective hunter into the tribute-gathering chief: a figure repeatedly attested in similar developments in many later cycles of civilization. Suddenly this figure assumed superhuman proportions: all his powers and prerogatives became immensely magnified, while those of his subjects, who no longer had a will of their own or could claim any life apart from that of the ruler, were correspondingly diminished.

Now I would hardly be bold enough to advance this explanation if one of the most brilliant of modern archaeologists, the late Henri Frankfort, had not provided most of the necessary data, and unconsciously foreshadowed if not foreseen this conclusion. What I would suggest is that the most important agent in effecting the change from a decentralized village economy to a highly organized urban economy, was the king, or rather, the institution of Kingship. The industrialization and commercialization we now associate with urban growth was for centuries a subordinate phenomenon, probably even emerging later in time: the very word merchant does not appear in Mesopotamian writing till the second millennium, "when it designates the official of a temple privileged to trade abroad." Going beyond Frankfort, I suggest that one of the attributes of the ancient Egyptian god, Ptah, as revealed in a document derived from the third millennium B.C.—*that he founded cities*—is the special and all but universal function of kings. In the urban implosion, the king stands at the center: he is the polar magnet that draws to the heart of the city and brings under the control of the palace and temple all the new forces of civilization. Sometimes the king founded new cities; sometimes he transformed old country towns that had long been a-building, placing them under the authority of his governors: in either case his rule made a decisive change in their form and contents.

2: THE FIRST URBAN IMPLOSION

At the brink of recorded history this great urban transformation took place. In the final creation of the city, the 'little city,' the citadel, towered above the village and overwhelmed the humble village ways. No mere enlargement of its parts could turn the village into the new urban image; for the city was a new symbolic world, representing not only a people, but a whole cosmos and its gods.

What happened here again antedates the written record; but if the previous interpretation of the hunter-chieftain's relation to the nearby communities holds, the citadel was not in origin mainly a defensive place of refuge for the villager threatened by 'invading nomads.' Once war became an established institution there is no doubt that the stronghold more and more served in this fashion. But the fact that citadels are surrounded by walls, even when cities are not, does not necessarily give its military functions primacy in time; for the first use of the wall may have been a religious one: to define the sacred limits of the temenos, and to keep at bay evil spirits rather than inimical men.

In so far as it had a quasi-military use, the primitive citadel was rather a holding point, where the chieftain's booty, mainly grain and possibly women, would be safe against purely local depredations—safe, that is to say, against attack by the resentful villagers. He who controlled the annual agricultural surplus exercised the powers of life and death over his neighbors. That artificial creation of scarcity in the midst of increasing natural abundance was one of the first characteristic triumphs of the new economy of civilized exploitation: an economy profoundly contrary to the mores of the village.

But such a crude system of control had inherent limitations. Mere physical power, even if backed by systematic terrorism, does not produce a smoothly flowing movement of goods to a collecting point, still less a maximum communal devotion to productive enterprise. Sooner or later every totalitarian state, from Imperial Rome to Soviet Russia, finds this out. To achieve willing compliance without undue waste in constant police supervision, the governing body must create an appearance of beneficence and helpfulness, sufficient to awaken some degree of affection and trust and loyalty.

In effecting this change religion may well have played an essential role. Without the help of the rising priestly caste, the hunting chieftain could never have achieved the enlarged powers and cosmic authority that attended his elevation to kingship and widened his sphere of control. Here the natural course of development, on lines open to simple economic interpretation, was enhanced by a supernatural development that altered the contents and the very meaning of the whole process. Both sacred power and temporal power became swollen by absorbing the new inventions of civilization; and the very need for an intelligent control of every part of the environment gave additional authority to those dedicated either to intelligence or control, the priest or monarch, often united in a single office.

Thus what brute coercion could not accomplish alone, what magic and ritual could not achieve alone, the two were able to effect within the growing town by reciprocal understanding and joint action on a scale never before even conceivable. The modest foundations of the village had been laid in the earth: but the city reversed the village's values, and turned the peasant's universe upside down, by placing the foundations in the heavens. All eyes now turned skywards. Belief in the eternal and the infinite, the omniscient and the omnipotent succeeded, over the millenniums, in exalting the very possibilities of human existence. Those who made the most of the city were not chagrined by the animal limitations of human existence: they sought deliberately, by a concentrated act of will, to transcend them.

At what point all this happened no one can say: doubtless there were many partial or ephemeral unions between the stronghold and the shrine, before they became one. But it is significant that, according to Childe, "shrines occupied the central place in protoliterate villages in Mesopotamia." At some point the shrine must have moved into the citadel, or else the sacred bounds of the shrine must have been thrown around the stronghold, making it likewise a sacred and inviolable precinct.

Certainly by the time the archaeologist's spade unearths a recognizable city, he finds a walled precinct, a citadel, made of durable materials, even if the rest of the town lacks a wall or permanent structures. This holds from Uruk to Harappa. Within that precinct he usually finds three huge stone or baked-brick buildings, buildings whose very magnitude sets them aside from the other structures in the city: the palace, the granary, and the temple. The citadel itself has many marks of a sacred enclosure: the exaggerated height and thickness of these walls in the earliest cities, rivalling even eighth century Khorsabad, is significantly out of all proportion to the military means that then existed for assaulting them. It is only for their gods that men exert themselves so extravagantly. But what first was designed to ensure the god's favor, may later have paid off in practice as more effective military protection. The symbolic purpose probably antedated the military function. On that matter I agree with Mircea Eliade.

In the epoch when this alliance between the political, the economic, and the religious agencies was in the making, many later distinctions had not yet clarified. We may suppose a considerable period before kingship reached its final, inflated proportions. At the beginning chief, medicine man, magician, prophet, astronomer, elder, priest, were not separate functionaries or castes: their duties overlapped and the same person was at home in alternative roles. Even in relatively late historic times kings have readily assumed the leadership of national churches, whilst Christian bishops and popes have governed cities and led armies. But at some point a great elevation of the ruler and the priest took place: apparently after 3000 B.C., when there was a similar expansion of human powers in many other departments. With this came vocational differentiation and specialization in every field. The early city, as distinct from the village community, is a caste-managed society, organized for the satisfaction of a dominant minority: no longer a community of humble families living by mutual aid.

At that point kingly power claimed and received a supernatural sanction: the king became a mediator between heaven and earth, incarnating in his own person the whole life and being of the land and its people. Sometimes a king would be appointed by the priesthood; but even if he were a usurper, he needed some sign of divine favor, in order to rule successfully by divine right. The ancient King List of Sumer records that kingship "was lowered down from heaven." The five kings appointed by deity were given five cities "in . . . pure places": Eridu, Badtbira, Larak, Sippar, Shuruppak, all appointed as cult centers.

Does all this not indicate a fusion of secular and sacred power, and was it not this fusion process that, as in a nuclear reaction, produced the otherwise unaccountable explosion of human energy? The evidence seems to point that way. When Kish was defeated in battle, this same King List tells us, the kingship was removed to the sacred precinct of Uruk, where the new monarch, the son of the sun god, Utu, became high priest as well as king. Out of this union, I suggest, came the forces that brought together all the inchoate parts of the city and gave them a fresh form, visibly greater and more awe-inspiring than any other work of man. Once this great magnification had taken place, the masters of the citadel not merely commanded the destinies of the city: they actually set the new mold of civilization, which combined the maximum possible social and vocational differentiation consistent with the widening processes of unification and integration. Kingship enlarged the offices of the priesthood and gave the sacerdotal class a commanding place in the community, made visible in the great temples that only kings had sufficient resources to build. This priesthood measured time, bounded space, predicted seasonal events. Those who had mastered time and space could control great masses of men.

Not merely the priesthood, but a new intellectual class, thus came into existence, the scribes, the doctors, the magicians, the diviners, as well as "the palace officials who dwell in the city and have taken an oath to the gods," as Georges Contenau quotes from a letter. In return for their support, the early kings gave these representatives of the 'spiritual power' security, leisure, status, and collective habitations of great magnificence. By helping to turn a mere shrine into a vast temple, they also endowed the temple with ample economic foundations, the compulsory labor of a whole community. Not perhaps by accident do we find the earliest tablets at Erech were memoranda to assist the organization of the temple as workshop and warehouse.

Was the building of the temple with all the vast physical resources the community now commanded the critical event that brought the sacred and secular leaders together? Surely the approval of the priesthood and the gods was as necessary for the exercise of the king's power as his command of weapons and his ruthless domination of large human forces was required to enhance theirs.

The erection of a great temple, itself architecturally and symbolically imposing, sealed this union. This connection was so vital to kingship that, as E. A. Speiser has pointed out, the later Mesopotamian rulers boasted of rebuilding a temple at Assur after many centuries had passed. Assurbanipal went so far as to recapture the image of the Goddess Nan, who had been carried off from Uruk to Susa no less than 1,635 years before. Does not this suggest that the rebuilding and restoration of the ancient temple was no mere act of formal piety, but a necessary establishment of lawful continuity, indeed, a re-validation of the original 'covenant' between the shrine and the palace; for this hypothetical pact, as we have seen, transformed the local chieftain into a colossal emblem of both sacred and secular power, in a process that released social energies latent in the whole community. The very magnitude of the new temple, with its extravagant decorations and adornments, would testify to the powers of both god and king.

3: ANXIETY, SACRIFICE, AND AGGRESSION

The historic development of kingship seems to have been accompanied by a collective shift from the rites of fertility to the wider cult of physical power. This displacement was never complete, for Osiris, Bacchus, and Kybele lived on and even reclaimed their old position. But at the opening of civilization it brought about a change of outlook, accompanied by a progressive loss of understanding of the needs of life, and a gross overestimation of the role of physical prowess and organized control as determinants of communal life, not just in a crisis but in the daily routine. Backed by military force, the king's word was law. The power to command, to seize property, to kill, to destroy—all these were, and have remained, 'sovereign powers.' Thus a paranoid psychal structure was preserved and transmitted by the walled city: the collective expression of a too heavily armored personality.

As the physical means increased, this one-sided power mythology, sterile, indeed hostile to life, pushed its way into every corner of the urban scene and found, in the *new* institution of organized war, its completest expression.

To understand the nature of this regression, which left its unmistakable mark upon the structure of the city, one must go further into the origins of kingship itself. On this matter, both Hocart and Frankfort have brought together much scattered evidence that has, I believe, a bearing upon the nature of the city. Hocart, following Sir James Frazer, points out that all over the world one still finds evidence of totemic rites, with almost identic formulae, aimed at securing an abundance of food. These rites indicate a fertility cult that may be even older than the practice of agriculture. Everywhere, in both Old World and New, the birth and death of vegetation was associated with the birth and death of the corn god, the lord of the human arts of sowing and planting. With kingship, the two figures, god and king, became virtually interchangeable, for with his assumption of divine powers the ruler himself personified the pervading forces of nature at the same time that he personified his own particular community, and accepted responsibility for its biological and cultural existence.

Now, with the growth of population under neolithic agriculture, the proto-urban community became increasingly dependent upon natural forces outside its control: a flood or a plague of locusts might cause widespread suffering or death in these inchoate urban centers too big to be easily evacuated or supplied with food from afar. The more complex and interdependent the process of urban association, the greater the material well-being, but the greater the expectation of material well-being, the less reconciled would people be to its interruption, and the more widespread the anxiety over its possible withdrawal.

To mobilize these new forces and bring them under control, the king gathered to himself extraordinary sacred powers; he not only incarnated the community, but by his very assumptions held its fate in his hands. This shifted the ground for a state of collective anxiety. Thousands of years after the first urban implosion, the Egyptian Pharaoh's name could not be uttered without injecting the prayer: "Life! Prosperity! Health!" Along with this whole development went, it would seem, an intensified consciousness of the desirability of life, or at least the desirability of prolonging it and avoiding death. Urban man sought to control natural events his more primitive forerunners once accepted with dumb grace.

Did kingship pay for this exorbitant increase of magical power? There is scattered evidence, too ancient and too widespread to be wholly disregarded, that fertility rites to ensure the growth of crops were consummated by human sacrifice. In times of crisis, through dearth and starvation, the need to win over the gods would be peremptory. Very possibly the original subject of the sacrifice was the most precious member of the community, the god-king himself. By voluntarily inflicting death, primitive magic sought to avert divine wrath and resume control over the forces of life.

Unfortunately, urban cultures were too far advanced in their development by the time writing was invented to record any of the early stages of royal human sacrifice, though the religious slaughter of children, captives, and animals significantly went on through the greater part of ancient history. Only the Babylonian Berossus (third century B.C.) left an account of the New Year's Festivals, which indicates that the custom of choosing a substitute for the king, who might otherwise have been sacrificed with the dying year to ensure the birth of the new vegetation in the coming one, was long maintained.

Frazer sardonically points out that the practice of sacrificing the king to ensure the community's prosperity somewhat lessened the attraction of that noble office. As soon as the organizational skill and intelligence of the leader became as important as his imputed magical functions, a more rational method would suggest itself: the selection of a 'stand-in,' who would first be identified with the king by being temporarily treated with all the honors and privileges of kingship, in order finally to be ceremoniously slaughtered in his place on the altar.

If such customs once prevailed in Egypt or Mesopotamia, they came at a far too early date to leave any direct traces. That is, one must admit, a serious hiatus: for it is only in spots that one can directly connect war and ceremonial human sacrifice. Still, the spots themselves are significant, for in the unmistakable evidence we derive from the Aztecs, we also have the witness of a community at about the same general level of development as we find in the earliest urban centers. Among the Aztecs, the need for sacrificial victims—as many as twenty thousand in a single year—was the main reason for the ferocious wars these people waged.

As with many other institutions, both war and human sacrifice may have had more than one point of origin; and perhaps only in a limited number of places was the connection between them a causal one. Invasions in force to round up captives for slavery, rather than sacrifice, may well have been an independent source of war. The Sumerian raids for wood and ore upon the mountains to the north probably also brought back useful captives: suggestively, the Sumerian sign for slave is "mountain woman." These raids and foraging parties were at first too one-sided to be called either war or trade, for it takes two to make a fight, and until the mountain people had increased in numbers and had improved their arms, they were no match for either the Egyptian or the Mesopotamian 'armies.' But in the end reprisals and two-sided hostilities, bitter and merciless, became all but inevitable; and the province of war steadily widened. During the nineteenth century the raiding Arab slave-traders in the heart of Africa brought on a similar cycle of violence.

If the city had not served as a focal center for organized aggression, the search for sacrificial victims need never have gone beyond the relatively innocent limits that were still visible in many primitive tribal communities down to the nineteenth century—a perverse but selective effort to obtain a few symbolic captives from another community. This practice was misinterpreted by missionaries and even by anthropologists; and urban historians like Henri Pirenne, who took for granted that "war is as old as humanity," never bothered to look carefully at the actual evidence, or to examine the basis of their own gratuitous convictions. But the object of primitive interchanges of blows between armed men was not the killing of a mass of people in battle or the robbing and razing of their village—but rather the singling out of a few live captives for ceremonial slaughter, and eventual serving up in a cannibal feast, itself a magico-religious rite.

Once the city came into existence, with its collective increase in power in every department, this whole situation underwent a change. Instead of raids and sallies for single victims, mass extermination and mass destruction came to prevail. What had once been a magic sacrifice to ensure fertility and abundant crops, an irrational act to promote a rational purpose, was turned into the exhibition of the power of one community, under its wrathful god and priest-king, to control, subdue, or totally wipe out another community. Much of this aggression was unprovoked, and morally unjustified by the aggressor; though by the time the historic record becomes clear, some economic color would be given to war by reason of political tensions arising over disputed boundaries or water rights. But the resulting human and economic losses, in earliest times no less than today, were out of all proportion to the tangible stakes for which they were fought. The urban institution of war thus was rooted to the magic of a more primitive society: a childish dream that, with the further growth of mechanical power, became an adult nightmare. This infantile trauma has remained in existence to warp the development of all subsequent societies: not least our own.

If anything were needed to make the magical origins of war plausible, it is the fact that war, even when it is disguised by seemingly hardheaded economic demands, uniformly turns into a religious performance; nothing less than a wholesale ritual sacrifice. As the central agent in this sacrifice, the king had from the very beginnings an office to perform. To accumulate power, to hold power, to express power by deliberate acts of murderous destruction—this became the constant obsession of kingship. In displaying such power the king could do no wrong. By the very act of war the victorious king demonstrated the maximum possibilities of royal control and invoked further divine support by the wholesale infliction of death. That, as Isaiah reminds us, is the burden of Egypt and Babylon and Tyre.

Thus by a curious act of transvestiture a ceremony that began by the invocation of more abundant life, turned into its very opposite: it invited a centralized military control, systematic robbery, and economic parasitism —all institutions that worked against the life-promoting aspects of urban civilization, and finally brought one city after another to its ruin. That was a final ambivalence and contradiction: for the many gains made through the wider associations and laborious co-operations of the city were duly offset by the negative economic activity of war. That cyclic disorder was embedded in the very constitution of the ancient city.

But this much must be conceded. As soon as war had become one of the reasons for the city's existence, the city's own wealth and power made it a natural target. The presence of thriving cities gave collective aggression a visible object that had never beckoned before: the city itself, with its growing accumulation of tools and mechanical equipment, its hoards of gold, silver, and jewels, heaped in palace and temple, its well filled granaries and storehouses: not least, perhaps, its surplus women. If war had originated in one-way raiding parties, sent out by the city, the existence of a new professional caste, armed warriors, may have turned those raids more and more away from the source of raw materials to the places that held the largest store of finished products. Cities that had first drawn tribute from primitive folk now learned to prey on each other.

Meanwhile, once war became fully established and institutionalized, it would naturally spread beyond its original urban centers. Primitive peoples, once peacefully disposed, or at worst content to express their anxiety and aggression by token human sacrifices, would imitate the new technics and make bolder use of the new weapons: all the more readily if invasion and robbery and enslavement by urban expeditions moved the more primitive group to revenge. As with kingship and the city itself war gained a worldwide diffusion, and was practiced by peoples who "knew not kingship," like the invaders of Akkad, a century after Sargon. Under the aegis of the city, violence thus became normalized, and spread far beyond the centers where the great collective manhunts and sacrificial orgies were first instituted. Throughout the greater part of history, enslavement, forced labor, and destruction have accompanied—and penalized—the growth of urban civilization.

Though anything like satisfactory proof of the early connection between kingship, sacrifice, war and urban development will always be lacking, I have put together enough of the surviving fragments to cast serious doubts on the assumptions of either a biologically inherited belligerence or an 'original sin' as the sufficient operative cause in producing the complex historic institution of war. But here, if anywhere, the doctrine of natural selection worked with classic exactitude, for in the course of five or six thousand years many of the milder, gentler, more co-operative stocks were killed off or discouraged from breeding, while the more aggressive, bellicose types survived and flourished at the centers of civilization. The peripheral successes of urban culture bolstered up its central failure—its commitment to war as the elixir of sovereign power and the most effective purgative for popular discontent with that power.

Too easily have historians imputed war chiefly to man's savage past, and have looked upon war as an incursion of so-called primitive nomads, the 'have-nots,' against normally 'peaceful' centers of industry and trade. Nothing could be farther from the historic truth. War and domination, rather than peace and co-operation, were ingrained in the original structure of the ancient city. No doubt the urban surplus tempted poorer folk, for each city must have seemed a sitting duck to swift-moving raiders from the highlands or steppes: but the very facilities that enabled them to move swiftly, with horses and boats, came only after the city itself had been founded. The earliest settlements in Sumer are so near together that they, too, may easily have antedated organized warfare. In later times, nomads might indeed, like the Hyksos shepherd kings, take over a whole country. But once war was established, the chief enemy of the city was another city under another god that claimed equal powers.

We must not forget that in the general expansion of power, the capacity to kill increased, too; and the exhibition of armed might became one of the most important attributes of kingship. The city, with its buttressed walls, its ramparts and moats, stood as an outstanding display of ever-threatening aggression, which achieved lethal concentrations of suspicion and vengeful hatred and non-cooperation in the proclamations of kings. Egyptian monarchs no less than their Mesopotamian counterparts boasted on their monuments and tablets of their personal feats in mutilating, torturing, and killing with their own hands their chief captives. They did in person what sicklier paranoids like Hitler performed through their agents. Under this leadership the local urban deity matched his magic potencies against each threatening foreign deity: the temple became both the starting point and the object of aggressive action. Thus, incited by exorbitant religious fantasies, ever greater numbers with ever more effective weapons for siege and assault were drawn into the insensate rituals of war.

In this development the city operated in a new capacity: with the king's command of its entire manpower, the city became, so to say, a permanently mobilized standing army, held in reserve. This power of massed numbers in itself gave the city a superiority over the thinly populated widely scattered villages, and served as an incentive to further growth in both internal area and numbers. To meet this challenge, the aboriginal villages may themselves have often combined into larger urban units, as later the Phoceans gathered their populations into a single city, Megalopolis, in order to resist the threat of conquest by the Lacedemonians.

With concentration on war as the supreme 'sport of kings,' an ever larger portion of the city's new resources in industrial production went into the manufacture of new weapons, like the Bronze Age chariot and the battering ram. The very existence of a reserve of military manpower, no longer needed for agriculture, fomented fantasies of unqualified violence among the ruling classes, such as we have seen erupt once more in our own age, even among supposedly rational minds trained in exact science. Every city became a pocket of insolent power, indifferent to those humane means of conciliation and intercourse which the city, in another mood, had promoted.

Thus both the physical form and the institutional life of the city, from the very beginning of the urban implosion, were shaped in no small measure by the irrational and magical purposes of war. From this source sprang the elaborate system of fortifications, with walls, ramparts, towers, canals, ditches, that continued to characterize the chief historic cities, apart from certain special cases—as during the Pax Romana—down to the eighteenth century. The physical structure of the city, in turn, perpetuated the animus, the isolation and self-assertion, that favored the new institution.

But, even more, war fostered practices of regimentation, militarization, compulsive conformity. War brought concentration of social leadership and political power in the hands of a weapons-bearing minority, abetted by a priesthood exercising sacred powers and possessing secret but valuable scientific and magical knowledge. If civilized society has not yet outgrown war, as it outgrew less respectable manifestations of primitive magic, like child sacrifice and cannibalism, it is partly because the city itself in its structure and institutions continued to give war both a durable concrete form and a magical pretext for existence. Beneath all war's technical improvements lay an irrational belief, still deeply imbedded in the collective unconscious: only by wholesale human sacrifice can the community be saved.

If war has no sufficient basis in any wild ancestral pugnacity, we must look for its origins in quite another direction. To find a parallel for war we must look into the animal world—namely into the perversions and fixations of a far earlier kind of society, the termitary or the ant-hill. Plainly there is both combativeness and assault with intent to kill in the animal world: but the first is almost exclusively sexual, between old and young males, and the latter is entirely a matter of one species preying on another or killing its members for food. Apart from human communities, war exists only among the social insects, which anticipated urban man in achieving a complex community of highly specialized parts.

As far as external observations can show, one certainly does not find religion or ritual sacrifice in these insect communities. But the other institutions that accompanied the rise of the city are all present: the strict division of labor, the creation of a specialized military caste, the technique of collective destruction, accompanied by mutilation and murder, the institution of slavery, and even, in certain species, the domestication of plants and animals. Most significant of all, the insect communities that exhibit these traits boast the institution I have taken to be central in this whole development: the institution of kingship. Kingship, or rather, its feminine equivalent, queenship, has been incorporated as a supreme biological fact in these insect societies; so that what is only a magic belief in early cities, that the life of the whole community depends on the life of the monarch, is an actual condition in Insectopolis. On the queen's health, safety, and reproductive capacity the continued existence of the hive does in fact depend. Here, and only here, does one find such organized collective aggression by a specialized military force as one finds first in the ancient cities.

In following these clues to the emergence of the city, we have I think laid bare the sorriest events in urban history, whose shame is still with us. No matter how many valuable functions the city has furthered, it has also served, throughout most of its history, as a container of organized violence and a transmitter of war. The few cultures that for a time avoided this are those that retained their village basis and yielded without force to a seemingly benign central command.

One may even carry the point further. Not merely did the walled city give a permanent collective structure to the paranoid claims and delusions of kingship, augmenting suspicion, hostility, non-cooperation, but the division of labor and castes, pushed to the extreme, normalized schizophrenia; while the compulsive repetitious labor imposed on a large part of the urban population under slavery, reproduced the structure of a compulsion neurosis. Thus the ancient city, in its very constitution, tended to transmit a collective personality structure whose more extreme manifestations are now recognized in individuals as pathological. That structure is still visible in our own day, though the outer walls have given way to iron curtains.

4: LAW AND URBAN ORDER

From the beginning, then, the city exhibited an ambivalent character it has never wholly lost: it combined the maximum amount of protection with the greatest incentives to aggression: it offered the widest possible freedom and diversity, yet imposed a drastic system of compulsion and regimentation which, along with its military aggression and destruction, has become 'second nature' to civilized man and is often erroneously identified with his original biological proclivities. Thus the city had both a despotic and a divine aspect. Partly it was a *Zwingburg*, a royal control center: partly a replica of heaven, a transformer of remote cosmic power into immediate operating institutions. Its center of gravity shifted from castle to temple, from citadel to marketplace and neighborhood, and back again. Long before the biblical Noah, "the earth was filled with violence." That some measure of law and order nevertheless emerged is a testimonial to the socializing power of the city.

To understand the city's processes and functions, above all its purposes, in more concrete terms one must pierce the foggy territory of the proto-literate period, when the new institution of kingship was taking shape. Perhaps the best way to substantiate the role of the king as city builder would be to work back from the late historic evidence to a period when only a handful of artifacts and bones in royal tombs provides material for deduction and speculation.

Herodotus' account of the rise of Deioces to absolute power over the Medes deals with a very late period, largely free from the flood of magic and religious ideas that overflowed the late Stone and early Bronze Ages; so it gives a highly rationalized account of the passage from village culture to urban culture. The Medes were then distributed, the ancient Greek historian tells us, into villages. And in this case, so prevalent were disorder and violence that Deioces obtained a high reputation among them, as a councillor, in exercising even-handed, fearless justice. This reputation caused people from other villages to come before him for judgment, when in conflict; and so constant was the need for his offices that they decided to make him into their supreme ruler.

Deioces' first act was to build a palace suitable for a king, and to ask for "guards for the security of his person." One may justifiably assume that in older days the guards themselves preceded or accompanied the erection of the citadel and the palace, and that the palace itself existed, as a visible seat of power and the repository of tribute, before the function of justice was exercised by the king. "Being thus possessed of power," Deioces "compelled the Medes to build one city, and having carefully adorned that to pay less attention to others." I would emphasize the last phrase: the deliberate establishment of a monopoly, economic and political, has been one of the pre-requisites for the rapid growth of the city. And as the Medes obeyed Deioces in this, also, he built "lofty and strong walls, one placed in a circle within the other. . . . Deioces then built fortifications for himself, around his own palace; and he commanded the rest of the people to fix their habitations round the fortification." Perhaps the best definition for the inhabitants of an early city is that they are a permanently captive farm population.

Note that in lessening the physical distance by concentrating population in the city, Deioces took care to increase the psychological distance by isolating himself and by making access to his person formidable. This combination of concentration and mixture, with isolation and differentiation, is one of the characteristic marks of the new urban culture. On the positive side there was friendly cohabitation, spiritual communion, wide communication, and a complex system of vocational co-operation. But on the negative side, the citadel introduced class segregation, unfeelingness and irresponsiveness, secrecy, authoritarian control, and ultimate violence.

Herodotus' account condenses into a single lifetime changes that probably took place in many different places, under varying conditions, over thousands of years; for even the rise of the chieftain to purely local leadership based on command of weapons, may have been a slow process. Frankfort noted that there are no pre-dynastic graves in Egypt that indicate, as later tombs do, the eminence of any single figure or family. But the critical change that brought both kingship and the city into existence, the first as the incarnation, the second as the embodiment of 'civilization,' probably took place within a short period: part of the general release of energy and implosion of power that followed some time after the middle of the fourth millennium.

No less important to the citadel than its enclosure was its centrality: both enclosure and centrality were attributes of the sanctuary, before they were passed on to the bigger urban community. Once the urban transformation had been effected, the city as a whole became a sacred precinct under the protection of its god: the very axis of the universe went, as Mircea Eliade has made clear, through the temple; while the wall, under pressure of the new institution of war, was both a physical rampart for defense and a spiritual boundary of even greater significance, for it preserved those within from the chaos and formless evil that encompassed them. The 'innerness' needed for further human development found in the city— above all in the sacred precinct—the collective form that would help call it forth.

Behind the walls of the city life rested on a common foundation, set as deep as the universe itself: the city was nothing less than the home of a powerful god. The architectural and sculptural symbols that made this fact visible lifted the city far above the village or country town. Without the sacred powers that were contained within the palace and the temple precinct, the ancient city would have been purposeless and meaningless. Once those powers were established by the king, widening the area of communication and unifying behavior through law, life prospered here as it could not hope to prosper anywhere else. What began as control ended as communion and rational understanding.

Significantly enough, the Egyptian text that takes us close to the early period of city founding, in describing the powers of the dominant deity Ptah, states not only that he "founded nomes"—but that *he put the gods in their shrines.* Scribes who were still relatively near to these acts saw both functions correctly, I believe, as essential to the exercise of those enlarged powers that came in with civilization.

Without the religious potencies of the city, the wall alone could not have succeeded in molding the character as well as controlling the activities of the city's inhabitants. But for religion, and all the social rites and economic advantages that accompanied it, the wall would have turned the city into a prison, whose inmates would have had only one ambition: to destroy their keepers and break out. This brings to light another urban ambivalence. In a townless culture, like that of the Spartans, living in open villages and declining to take refuge behind walls, the ruling classes had to remain savagely alert and threatening, under arms at all times, lest they be overthrown by the enslaved helots. Whereas such rulers had to back their naked power by overt terrorism, in walled cities the wall itself was worth a whole army in controlling the unruly, keeping rivals under surveillance, and blocking the desperate from escaping. The early cities thus developed something of the same concentration of command one finds in a ship: its inhabitants were 'all in the same boat,' and learned to trust the captain and to execute orders promptly.

From the beginning, however, law and order supplemented brute force. The city, as it took form around the royal citadel, was a man-made replica of the universe. This opened an attractive vista: indeed a glimpse of heaven itself. To be a resident of the city was to have a place in man's true home, the great cosmos itself, and this very choice was itself a witness of the general enlargement of powers and potentialities that took place in every direction. At the same time, living in the city, within sight of the gods and their king, was to fulfill the utmost potentialities of life. Spiritual identification and vicarious participation made it easy to submit to the divine commands that governed the community, inscrutable and difficult to interpret or inwardly submit to as they might be.

Though power in all its manifestations, cosmic and human, was the mainstay of the new city, it became increasingly shaped and directed by new institutions of law and order and social comity. This comes out plainly again in the story of Deioces, which skips over the earlier religious origins of king and city. At some point, power and control brightened into justice. With the coming together of people of many different languages and customs in the new center, the slow process of reconciliation and accommodation was hastened by royal intervention: obedience to stern external command doubtless was preferable to wrangling non-conformity and endless dissension. Even beneficial customs tend to carry with them accidental and irrational residues which become as sacred as the more central human purposes that custom embodies. That was the weakness of the village. Written law, like written language, tended to filter out these residues, and produced a canon of equity and justice that appealed to a higher principle:

the king's will, which was another name for divine command. The essence of law, as the scientist Wilhelm Ostwald put it half a century ago, is "predictable behavior," made possible in society by uniform rules, uniform criteria of judgment, uniform penalties for disobedience. These wider uniformities came in with the city, transcending a thousand meaningless local differences.

The growth of self-consciousness in the city, through the clash of village customs and regional differences, produced the beginnings of reflective morality; for the Egyptian ruler himself had, at a quite early date, to account for his own conduct before the gods, and to prove that he avoided evil and furthered goodness. As society itself became more secularized, through the increasing pressure of trade and industry, the part played by the city as a seat of law and justice, reason and equity, supplemented that it played as a religious representation of the cosmos. To appeal from irrational custom or lawless violence, one must seek the protection of the court of law in the city.

By putting power in some measure at the service of justice, the city, departing from the tedious archaic reign of the village, brought order more swiftly into its internal affairs: but it left an unguarded lawless wasteland in the area between cities, where no local god could exercise power or establish moral jurisdiction without colliding with another god. And as internal frustrations increased, external aggressions tended to multiply: the animus against the local oppressor would be profitably turned against the external enemy.

5: FROM 'PROTECTION' TO

DESTRUCTION

Being partly an expression of intensified anxiety and aggression, the walled city replaced an older image of rural tranquillity and peace. The early Sumerian bards looked back to a pre-urban golden age, where "there was no snake, no scorpion, no hyena, no lion, no wild dog, no wolf": when "there was no fear, nor terror; man had no rival." That mythical age of course never existed, and doubtless the Sumerians themselves were dimly aware of this fact. But the poisonous and dangerous animals whose presence awakened their dread had, with the development of human sacrifice and unrestrained war, taken on a new form: they symbolized the realities of human antagonism and enmity. In the act of expanding all his powers, civilized man had given these savage creatures a gigantic place in his own make-up.

Unarmed, exposed, naked, primitive man had been cunning enough to dominate all his natural rivals. But now at last he had created a being whose presence would repeatedly strike terror to his soul: the Human Enemy, his other self and counterpart, possessed by another god, congregated in another city, capable of attacking him as Ur was attacked, without provocation.

The very implosion that had magnified the powers of god, king, and city and held the complex forces of the community in a state of tension, also deepened collective anxieties and extended the powers of destruction. Were not civilized man's increased collective powers themselves something of an affront to the gods, who would be appeased only by destroying utterly the claims and presumptions of rival gods? Who was the enemy? Anyone who worshipped another god: who rivalled the king's powers or resisted the king's will. Thus the increasingly complex symbiosis within the city and its nearby agricultural domain was counterbalanced by a destructive and predatory relation with all possible rivals: indeed, as the activities of the city became more rational and benign within, they became in almost the same degree more irrational and malign in their external relations. That holds even today of the larger aggregations that have succeeded the city.

Royal power itself measured its strength and divine favor by its capacities, not merely for creation but even more for pillage, destruction, and extermination. "In reality," as Plato declared in 'The Laws,' "every city is in a natural state of war with every other." This was a simple fact of observation. Thus the original perversions of power that accompanied the great technical and cultural advances of civilization, have undermined and often nullified the great achievements of the city down to our own age. Is it merely by chance that the earliest surviving images of the city, those on the pre-dynastic Egyptian palettes, picture its destruction?

In the very act of transforming loose groups of villages into powerful urban communities, capable of maintaining wider intercourse and building greater structures, every part of life became a struggle, an agony, a gladiatorial contest fought to a corporeal or symbolic death. While the sacral copulation of Babylonian king and priestess in the divine bedchamber that crowned the ziggurat recalled an earlier fertility cult, dedicated to life, the new myths were mainly expressions of relentless opposition, struggle, aggression, unqualified power: the powers of darkness against the powers of light, Seth against his enemy Osiris, Marduk against Tiamat. Among the Aztecs even the stars were grouped into hostile armies of the East and West.

Though the more co-operative village practices retained their hold in the workshop and the field, it is precisely in the new functions of the city that the truncheon and the whip—called politely the scepter—made themselves felt. Given time, the village cultivator would learn many wiles and dodges for resisting the coercions and demands of the governmental agents: even his seeming stupidity would often be a method of 'not hearing' orders he did not propose to obey. But those caught within the city had little choice but to obey, whether they were openly enslaved or more subtly enthralled. To preserve his self-respect, mid all the new impositions of the ruling classes, the urban subject, not yet a full-fledged citizen, would identify his own interests with those of his masters. The next best thing to successfully opposing a conqueror is to join his side, and have a chance at some of the prospective booty.

The city, almost from its earliest emergence, despite its appearance of protection and security, brought with it the expectation not only of outward assault but likewise of intensified struggle within: a thousand little wars were fought in the marketplace, in the law courts, in the ball game or the arena. Herodotus was eyewitness of a bloody ritual fight with clubs between the forces of Light and Darkness, held within an Egyptian temple precinct. To exert power in every form was the essence of civilization: the city found a score of ways of expressing struggle, aggression, domination, conquest —and servitude. Is it any wonder that early man looked back to the period *before* the city as the Golden Age, or that, like Hesiod, he regarded each improvement of metallurgy and weapons as a worsening of life's prospects, so that the lowest human state was that of the Iron Age. (He could not anticipate how much lower the precise scientific technics of total extermination by nuclear or bacterial agents would degrade man.)

Now all organic phenomena have limits of growth and extension, which are set by their very need to remain self-sustaining and self-directing: they can grow at the expense of their neighbors only by losing the very facilities that their neighbors' activities contribute to their own life. Small primitive communities accepted these limitations and this dynamic balance, just as natural ecologic communities register them.

Urban communities, engrossed in the new expansion of power, forfeited this sense of limits: the cult of power exulted in its own boundless display: it offered the delights of a game played for its own sake, as well as the rewards of labor without the need for daily drudgery, by forcible collective seizure and wholesale enslavement. The sky was the limit. We have the evidence of this sudden sense of exaltation in the increasing dimensions of the great pyramids; as we have the mythological representation of it in the story of the ambitious Tower of Babel, though that was curbed by a failure of communication, which an over-extension of linguistic territory and culture may in turn have repeatedly brought about.

That cycle of indefinite expansion from city to empire is easy to follow.

As a city's population grew, it was necessary either to extend the area of immediate food production or to extend the supply lines, and draw by co-operation, barter, and trade, or by forced tribute, expropriation, and extermination, upon another community. Predation or symbiosis? Conquest or co-operation? A power myth knows only one answer. Thus the very success of urban civilization gave sanction to bellicose habits and demands that continually undermined it and nullified its benefits. What began as a self-contained urban droplet would be forcibly blown into an iridescent soap bubble of empire, imposing in its dimensions, but fragile in proportion to its size. Lacking an inner cohesion, the more warlike capitals were under pressure to continue the technique of expansion, lest power flow back again to the autonomous village and urban centers where it had first flourished. Such a recession did in fact happen during the Egyptian feudal inter-regnum.

If I interpret the evidence correctly, the co-operative forms of urban polity were undermined and vitiated from the outset by the destructive, death-oriented myths which attended, and perhaps partly prompted, the exorbitant expansion of physical power and technological adroitness. The positive urban symbiosis was repeatedly displaced by an equally complex negative symbiosis. So conscious were Bronze Age rulers of these disastrous negative results, that they sometimes counterbalanced their many boasts of conquest and extermination by pointing to their activities on behalf of peace and justice. Hammurabi, for example, proudly proclaimed: "I made an end of war; I promoted the welfare of the land; I made the peoples rest in friendly habitations; I did not let them have anyone terrorize them." But hardly were the words out of his mouth when the cycle of expansion, exploitation, and destruction began again. On the favored terms desired by gods and kings, no city could secure its own expansion except by ruining and destroying other cities.

Thus the most precious collective invention of civilization, the city, second only to language itself in the transmission of culture, became from the outset the container of disruptive internal forces, directed toward cease-less destruction and extermination. As a result of that deep-rutted heritage, the very survival of civilization, or indeed of any large and unmutilated portion of the human race, is now in doubt—and may long remain in doubt whatever temporary accommodations may be made. Each historic civiliza-tion, as Patrick Geddes long ago pointed out, begins with a living urban core, the polis, and ends in a common graveyard of dust and bones, a Necropolis, or city of the dead: fire-scorched ruins, shattered buildings, empty workshops, heaps of meaningless refuse, the population massacred or driven into slavery.

"And he took the city," we read in Judges; "and slew the people therein; and he beat down the city and served it with salt." The terror of this final episode, with its cold misery and blank despair, is the human climax toward which the 'Iliad' moves; but long before that, as Heinrich Schliemann proved, six other cities were destroyed; and long before the 'Iliad' one finds a lamentation, equally bitter and heartfelt, for that marvel among ancient cities, Ur itself, a wail uttered by the goddess of the city:

"Verily all my birds and winged creatures have flown away—
'Alas! for my city,' I will say.
'My daughters and my sons have been carried off—
'Alas! for my men,' I will say.
'O my city which exists no longer, my [city] attacked without cause,
'O my [city] attacked and destroyed!' "*

Finally, consider Sennacherib's inscription on the total annihilation of Babylon: "The city and [its] houses, from its foundation to its top, I destroyed, I devastated, I burned with fire. The wall and the outer wall, temples and gods, temple towers of brick and earth, as many as they were, I razed and dumped them into the Arakhtu Canal. Through the midst of that city I dug canals, I flooded its site with water, and the very foundations thereof I destroyed. I made its destruction more complete than that by a flood." Both the act and the morals anticipated the ferocious extravagances of our own Nuclear Age; Sennacherib lacked only our swift scientific dexterity and our massive hypocrisy in disguising our intentions even from ourselves.

Yet again and again the positive forces of co-operation and sentimental communion have brought people back to the devastated urban sites, "to repair the wasted cities, the desolation of many generations." Ironically— yet consolingly—cities have repeatedly outlived the military empires that seemingly destroyed them forever. Damascus, Baghdad, Jerusalem, Athens still stand on the sites they originally occupied, alive though little more than fragments of their ancient foundations remain in view.

The chronic miscarriages of life in the city might well have caused their abandonment, might even have led to a wholesale renunciation of city life and all its ambivalent gifts, but for one fact: the constant recruitment of new life, fresh and unsophisticated, from rural regions, full of crude muscular strength, sexual vitality, procreative zeal, animal faith. These rural folk replenished the city with their blood, and still more with their hopes. Even today, according to the French geographer Max Sorre, four-fifths of the population of the world lives in villages, functionally closer to their neolithic prototype than to the highly organized metropolises that have begun to suck the village into their orbits and, ever more swiftly, to undermine their ancient mode of life. But once we allow the village to disappear, this ancient factor of safety will vanish. That danger mankind has still to reckon with and forfend.

*Unless otherwise noted, this and other quotations from Mesopotamian or Egyptian texts are taken from 'Ancient Near Eastern Texts,' edited by James E. Pritchard (Princeton University Press).

CHAPTER THREE

Ancestral Forms and Patterns

1: CITIES OF THE PLAIN

This inquiry into the origins of the city would read more clearly were it not for the fact that perhaps most of the critical changes took place before the historic record opens. By the time the city comes plainly into view it is already old: the new institutions of civilization have firmly shaped it. But there are other difficulties no less formidable; for no ancient town has yet been completely excavated and some of the most ancient cities which might reveal much, still continue in existence as dwelling places, smugly immune to the excavator's spade.

The gaps in the evidence then, are baffling: five thousand years of urban history and perhaps as many of proto-urban history are spread over a few score of only partly explored sites. The great urban landmarks, Ur, Nippur, Uruk, Thebes, Heliopolis, Assur, Nineveh, Babylon, cover a span of three thousand years whose vast emptiness we cannot hope to fill with a handful of monuments and a few hundred pages of written records. On such swampy ground even the most solid hummock of fact may prove treacherous, and too often one must choose between not advancing at all and being dragged down into a bottomless bog of speculation. Let the reader be warned: he proceeds at his own risk!

In addition to the imperfection of the visible remains, the two great civilizations in which the city first probably took shape, Egypt and Mesopotamia, present disconcerting contrasts, which only become sharper if one includes Palestine, Iran, and the Indus Valley. While all these differences bring out significant alternatives in urban evolution, they make it difficult to give anything like a generalized picture of the origin of the city.

The narrow geographic provenance of the aboriginal cities must first be noted. As a special organ of civilization, the city seems to have sprung up in a few great river valleys: the Nile, the Tigris-Euphrates, the Indus, the Hwang Ho. Villages might exist wherever there were possibilities of rudimentary farming and cattle-raising. Even bigger settlements could take root in regions like the Negev in Palestine, as soon as there was sufficient manpower to build cisterns and reservoirs to tide over the dry season. Not merely villages but much larger country towns, contemporary with what has come to light in Jericho, may still be buried beyond recall in the muddy deltas of the Nile and the Euphrates. In all probability most of the physical organs of a close urban settlement had taken form before the new cultural complex that the city embodied and transmitted had matured.

But the mark of the city is that it escapes these rural limitations and this nearby horizon: it is the product of an enormous mobilization of vitality, power, and wealth, which was at first necessarily confined to a few great rivers in exceptionally favored regions. Once swamps were drained and the water level regulated, the land of these valleys proved extremely fertile. Even without animal manure, the rich silt deposited at floodtime guaranteed crops almost a hundred times greater than the original seed: sometimes two or three crops a year.

In Palestine, the middle of the Fertile Crescent whose tips are the Upper Nile and the Lower Euphrates, emmer, the wild ancestor of wheat, was found and gathered before neolithic man learned to plant crops systematically. Two brother gods, according to a tablet now in Jena, brought barley from the mountains down to Sumer, "which knew no barley." Possibly they brought the image of the sacred mountain and the wall-hemmed citadel along with this tangible gift. With the improvement of these first grains, wheat, barley, sesame, it needed only the invention of the plow and the domestication of draft animals to make the heavy soils immensely productive. By commanding a store of hard-grains, rich in proteins, resisting spoilage if kept dry, large urban populations could, for the first time, be fed. Thanks to the cultivation of the date palm, the Mesopotamian culture had an even more diversified agricultural resource: for from this tree it obtained food, wine, matting, basketry, roofing, stems for columns, and fiber for rope.

The rivers themselves were the first highroads, once boats were invented: moving belts of water, six hundred miles long in Egypt and Mesopotamia, a thousand miles in the Indus Valley. They formed a spinal transportation system which served as model for the irrigation ditch and the canal; while their sudden floods or periodic inundations made it necessary for the village cultivators to band together to repair the storm damage, to guide the water around their fields to fend off drought, to create finally a whole network of embankments and canals and irrigation works. The construction of these utilities demanded a degree of social intercourse, co-operation, and long-range planning that the old self-contained village culture, complacently accepting its limitations, did not need or encourage. The very conditions that made large urban settlements a physical possibility also made them a social necessity.

Though village culture had achieved an inner stability and harmony that urban culture was rarely to know, the little individual settlement was at the mercy of the elements: it might be swept away in a storm or starved to death in a drought, without being able to draw help from its nearest neighbor a few miles away. This condition changed when the city could mobilize manpower and exercise centralized control. In the transfer of authority to the city, the villager doubtless lost in no little degree his powers of self-government, and his feeling of being entirely at home in an environment in which every human being, almost every animal, every patch of land or flow of water, was thoroughly known to him. Yet to the extent that the villager submitted to the new forces at work in the city and even identified his own life with them, he was rewarded with a prosperity and a security that he had never before enjoyed.

Thus the transformation of village into city was no mere change of size and scale, though both these factors entered into it: rather, it was a change of direction and purpose, manifested in a new type of organization.

Perhaps the greatest bond between Egypt and Mesopotamia is that they had common pre-conditions of geographic existence; for the desiccation of the climate, from 7000 B.C. on, which turned grassland into steppe and desert, made the marshy valley of the great rivers open to agricultural occupation. Here and there little settlements would appear in the boundless plain, attracted by the abundance of wild fowl, small game, and fish, the last the commonest source of animal protein. The inhabitants used bundles of rushes to construct the most primitive form of boat, for making their way about this watery waste, boats that James Henry Breasted was delighted to find still in use half a century ago. A primitive life: but not too different from that lived till yesterday by the trappers and hunters in the marshes of the lower Rhone.

This slow drying up of the plains was accompanied by a progressive contraction of the population into the emerging clumps of solid land; and as it went on, the area of these clumps multiplied and the new methods of cultivation brought about an enlargement and definition of meadow and field, while in time, the coming of dry spells that threatened to wither crops under the intense tropical heat would be offset by the digging of water channels, and finally by the invention of a machine (the noria) for lifting water from the low river to the banks above.

Even while the peoples in these spinal river valleys lived under primitive conditions in crude hamlets, foreign materials found in pre-dynastic graves show that trade of some kind ranged as far abroad as Iran, perhaps moving in slow stages by a chain of short hauls and barters. Necessarily, it was along the riverbanks that population thickened. In Egypt, Flinders Petrie noted, the peasants cultivated the rich lands by river and canal, the temple serfs the poorer inner area, while the soldiers worked the even poorer inundated land, a mixture of swamp and waste, toward the desert.

Neither mountains nor impenetrable jungles crowded close to these fertile plains; and though agriculture could not develop in a large way until the swamps were drained and the wild waters of Mesopotamia placed under control, with co-operative effort and patience the water could be canalized with the same plastic facility that a child shows in sluicing water and building dams on a beach. If the inhabitants, indeed, did not mold the land in an orderly way, nature would do so in her own cruder manner, by yearly inundation with silt, in the Valley of the Nile, or by upheaval and raging flood, by clogging up passages and changing river courses, in the valley of the sluggish Euphrates and the turbulent Tigris.

To avoid the extremes of desert and fen, the inhabitants of Mesopotamia, beginning probably in isolated villages, began to build local networks of irrigation ditches and canals and embanked dwelling places, making use of timber and bitumen from the upper valley to the north for shoring and waterproofing. This management of water was the price of communal survival; for there was a natural threat of water shortage at the beginning of the growing season and a likelihood of storms and floods at harvest time. Agricultural productivity here rested on unceasing vigilance and collective effort.

In accepting this hard challenge, the villages at an early stage learned the advantage of mutual aid, long-term planning, patient application to a common task, all repeated season after season. The long-surviving authority of the Council of Elders points to an early communal mobilization of manpower under competent but local leadership. This measure of communal co-operation may in turn have given Mesopotamian kingship just those human limitations that contrast with its Egyptian counterpart: yet they paved the way for a more centralized authority that could handle a larger area.

But in Mesopotamia, once the Storm God was appeased—and circumvented—the potential surplus in food and human vitality was enormous. Even the fleece of the sheep in these valleys was thicker and finer than the product of drier pastures: Babylon's woolen textiles became as famous as Egypt's cottons. The risks were great, and the efforts to overcome them heartbreaking; but the rewards were immense.

So it is natural that out of this first great surplus Sumer almost surely, as most Mesopotamian archaeologists stoutly hold, took the lead: beginning in the nest of cities in the torrid delta lands near the Persian Gulf. Not merely did these cities inspire the earliest monumental brick architecture in Egypt; but in astronomy, writing, military organization, canal-building, irrigation, and not least in commerce and manufacture, they pushed forward steadily, and through trade and perhaps even more intimate intercourse left their impress upon the distant cities of the Indus Valley.

Egypt presents a whole series of contrasts with Mesopotamia that cleaves through every aspect of their life and thought: even the principal rivers differ in character and flow in opposite directions. Under the blander conditions of Egypt, with cloudless skies, and a smooth-spreading predictable annual flood, a tempered regularity contrasts with the storm and strife, the lightning flashes, the catastrophic torrents and inundations of the more eastern region, where violences of nature were mirrored in the violences of men. Once the new grains and plow-culture were introduced into Egypt, there was a similar surplus of food, and out of that, no doubt, a surplus of babies. But all of Egypt's feats of domestication were accomplished under a halcyon sky, unclouded by storms, untouched by dark uncertainties, unembittered and undismayed by repeated defeats. Life was good: eternal life was the highest imaginable good. Even in the midst of the violence that marked the breakdown of the Old Kingdom, Ipu-wer would say: "It is still good when the hands of men construct pyramids, when canals are dug, and when groves of trees are made for the Gods."

One of Mesopotamia's earliest myths, in contrast, reveals how the herb that would have given Gilgamesh immortality, was devoured by a serpent when he slept. The 'black-headed people' put little faith in immortality as a sufficient offset to all their perpetual disappointments. If an after-life existed, it did not so much promise bliss as something more to dread. But the Egyptians loved life so much they even embraced death: they utilized every material and magical resource to keep the dead alive in bodily form, and to assure them of all the familiar comforts and joys of earthly existence. If the Pharaoh was immortal, so in the end, by identification, was the whole community. These differences in part account for the contrasts in their urban heritages. In Egypt the dead everywhere tower benignly above the living: even house cats were mummified to ensure their future existence.

Despite this the Valley of the Nile made the same leap from a tribal, self-contained village culture to a centralized urban culture, dominated by the temple and the palace—though the city in Egypt took a different form. In both lands the same implosion of forces took place, and in both the same magnification of centralized power and release of communal energies. In both a new will-to-power, hitherto exercised only in the rituals of magic, expressed itself in exorbitant fantasies and audacious practical achievement. Whatever a god might do in mythical deeds in one generation, a hero or a king would undertake in the next.

Under these conditions the unconscious itself now released explosive powers. If the tricky goddesses and ferocious gods seem often as ruthless as civilized man, it will be equally true that men in cities could become as exalted as gods, released from inhibiting conformities and a paralyzing sense of their own pettiness. Re-enforced by the visible presence of great numbers of their own kind—numbers never seen in any more primitive gatherings of men—the kings and governors and their subjects joined in a relentless collective assault on every part of the environment: now form-giving, now expressionist and exhibitionistic, now purely destructive.

This expansion of human powers paved the way for the city; but it was already visible in Egypt during the Pyramid Age before any cities that can now be identified were built. Whether the legendary Menes, when he first unified the 'Two Lands,' Upper and Lower Egypt, built the city of Thebes, is still somewhat in doubt; but that he altered the course of the Nile at this point seems less open to question. In technical improvements the Neolithic Age of containers joined its facilities with the Bronze Age of machines. The new machines themselves have long awaited recognition, or rather, proper identification. For the earliest complex power machines were composed, not of wood or metal, but of perishable human parts, each having a specialized function in a larger mechanism under centralized human control. The vast army of priests, scientists, engineers, architects, foremen, and day laborers, some hundred thousand strong, who built the Great Pyramid, formed the first complex machine, invented when technology itself had produced only a few simple 'machines' like the inclined plane and the sled, and had not yet invented wheeled vehicles.

No works of civil engineering modern man can now conceive, with all his locomotive and hoisting machinery, were beyond the capacity of these first great human machines. Even speed was not lacking in this homo-mechanized economy. While the cathedrals of the Middle Ages often required centuries for completion, many an Egyptian tomb was finished within the lifetime of the Pharaoh whose mummy was destined to be placed in it, sometimes within a single generation. No wonder the central authority that set such machines in motion seemed authentically godlike.

It was in these contrasting natural and social environments that the city's foundations were now superimposed on the modest dimensions of village and country town. The feat of city building itself was made possible by the fertility and productivity of the great valleys, by the reproductive capacities of the small village, well nourished and oriented wholly to life, by the traffic of water systems, and by the availability of ample material means and energy for supporting whole classes exempt from both the ancient village tutelage and harassing manual toil. The urban surplus was a many-sided one, and the lengthening of transportation systems and trade routes began long before the historic record could follow them. In earliest Jarmo one finds evidence of an obsidian industry, though this stone was imported from a great distance. Along with this far flung traffic went a steady amalgamation of peoples and cultures, as in the fusion of 'Ubaid, Uruk, and Jamdat Nasr culture in the city of Ur.

2: THE ENIGMA OF THE URBAN RUINS

Though the existing ruins of cities give an occasional clue to the institutions and the institutional life that accompanied them, nothing like a consecutive record of the first four thousand years of the city's existence is available; and even with a civilization as heavily monumented and documented as that of Rome, there are many large patches that remain blank. Yet the dispersed and dismembered fragments are worth looking at separately before we try to put them together and fathom their value and significance.

The first thing we note, to mark the passage from village to city, is an increase in the built-up area and population. Yet this difference is far from being decisive, since in the late neolithic culture the more developed villages at some natural meeting point between regions may have gained in population and arable land without any other important developments. It is not the numbers of people in a limited area alone, but the number that can be brought under unified control to form a highly differentiated community, serving purposes that transcend nurture and survival, that have decisive urban significance.

Among the bigger early remains, Megiddo in Palestine, covered three and a half acres; Gurnia, in Crete, containing sixty houses, measured superficially only six and a half acres—both plainly villages. Though early villages might occupy as little as an acre or two, and harbor less than a dozen families. Much later the walled area at Mycenae, the richest town of Greece in its period, contained not more than twelve acres; closer to a citadel than to a full-grown city: for about the same time Karkemish, on the Euphrates in Syria, covered two hundred and forty acres, while even earlier, in the third millennium, Mohenjo-Daro, one of the great capitals of the Indus civilization, covered six hundred acres.

Nevertheless, the city represented a new degree of human concentration, a new magnitude in settlement. The ancient city of Ur, the early home of Abraham, with its canals, harbors, and temples, occupied two hundred and twenty acres, while the walls of Uruk encompassed an area of just over two square miles. In part, this points to an extension of the area of food-growing, in part to an increase of transport facilities and other technological equipment; for in the Iron Age, with more efficient equipment and cutting tools, and with the use of metal for agricultural implements, with a more widespread system of canals, the area covered by the city widened farther. Khorsabad, in Assyria, about 700 B.C., enclosed some 740 acres; Nineveh, a century later, perhaps 1,800 acres; while later still, Babylon, before its destruction by the Persians, was surrounded by at least eleven miles of walls. If one skips about in supplying these statistics, it is because the evidence itself is so poor and spotty.

What is harder to estimate is the population of these ancient towns. They were at first limited by the same difficulties in transport as early medieval Western towns, and seem to have had populations of the same order, that is, from about two thousand to twenty thousand people. Probably the normal size of an early city was close to what we would now call a neighborhood unit: five thousand souls or less. So at the beginning of differentiated urban association, the city still retained the intimacies and solidarities of the primary community.

Frankfort, digging in Ur, Eshnunna, and Khafaje, which flourished about 2000 B.C., found that the houses numbered about twenty to the acre, which gave a density, he calculated, of from 120 to 200 people per acre, a density certainly in excess of what was hygienically desirable, but no worse than that of the more crowded workmen's quarters in Amsterdam in the seventeenth century: in both cases perhaps offset a little by the presence of canals. Even when Ur was an imperial capital, Frankfort does not put the population above 24,000, while Khafaje held only half as many. Leonard Woolley's estimate for the walled 'Old Town' of Ur —34,000—does not seriously differ; though he points out that this was but one-sixth of greater Ur, the later manufacturing center with its far-flung trade. That metropolis, he estimates, may have held a quarter of a million people.

The evidence for the size and density of dwelling houses is equally random; and even further digging may not make it possible to present figures in which one can have much confidence, since much depends upon the density per room if one would distinguish a decent family dwelling from a slum. On such matters no data seem likely to come forth. But it is interesting to note that the small houses found in Mohenjo-Daro, from about the middle of the third millennium B.C., were two stories high and about thirty by twenty-seven feet: about the same size as a modest house in Greek Priene about 200 B.C., which measured twenty-six feet by twenty. Neither would have seemed out of place in the East End of London in the eighteenth century, and the oldest house cited is actually a little bigger than the five-room house I once occupied in Sunnyside Gardens, Long Island, in what was designed to be a model housing estate.

What is most significant in these figures is their remarkable constancy over a period of some five thousand years. As for the more commodious dwellings of the wealthier classes, they originally expressed the same differences we observe today: for the latter range from houses of ten rooms, from 85 by 56 feet to 97 by 72 feet, in Eshnunna, Babylon, Assur, and Olynthos, to many-roomed palaces. These figures cover a period that spans about two thousand years and includes four well-differentiated cultures. But with a few exceptions like Mohenjo-Daro, the detached house did not apparently exist within early towns, any more than in the Polish Iron Age village of Biskupin, whose wooden ramparts and row houses have been excavated in our own day. Detachment and openness were originally attributes of the palace, reserved, with many other habits and properties, for the small group of nobles and officials who served the rulers of the early cities. The free-standing suburban villa set in a garden shows up quite early in Egyptian paintings and tomb models.

The next mark of the city is the walled citadel, ringed by one or more settlements. Probably the discovery of the value of the wall as a means of protection for the ruling group led to its being used to encircle and keep in order the tributary villages. That the wall is essential to a definition of the city, as Max Weber held, is a parochial misconception. But it is true that the wall continued to be one of the most prominent features of the city, in most countries, right down to the eighteenth century—the chief exceptions being early Egypt, Japan, and England, where natural barriers gave their towns and villages at certain periods a collective immunity; or where, as in imperial Rome and imperial China, a vast army or a colossal cross-country deployment of masonry barricades dispensed with local walls.

But there is one conditioning factor in the size of cities that is too often overlooked: not just the availability of water or food, but the range of collective communication systems. Plato limited the size of his ideal city to the number of citizens who might be addressed by a single voice: even so, there was a more common limitation on the number who might come together within the sacred precincts to take part in the great seasonal ceremonies. If cities soon grew beyond a point where all their citizens were within hailing distance of each other, they nevertheless were probably long limited to the number that could respond promptly to a summons from headquarters. Mesopotamian cities had an assembly drum, just as medieval cities used a bell in a church tower to call their citizens together: only a short while ago, faced with invasion and the possibly total disruption of communication by telegraph and radio, England fell back on the universal ringing of church bells as the proposed signal for the beginning of a German landing.

Early cities did not grow beyond walking distance or hearing distance. In the Middle Ages to be within sound of Bow Bells defined the limits of the City of London; and until other systems of mass communication were invented in the nineteenth century, these were among the effective limits to urban growth. For the city, as it develops, becomes the center of a network of communications: the gossip of the well or the town pump, the talk at the pub or the washboard, the proclamations of messenger and heralds, the confidences of friends, the rumors of the exchange and the market, the guarded intercourse of scholars, the interchange of letters and reports, bills and accounts, the multiplication of books—all these are central activities of the city. In this respect the permissive size of the city partly varies with the velocity and the effective range of communication.

The restricted size of the early city tells us something about an early restriction on urban life, or at least on intelligent voluntary co-operation: it was only in the palace and the temple that the means of communication multiplied—all the more because they were effectively segregated from the population as a whole. The great secret of centralized power was secrecy itself. That holds of all totalitarian states down to our own day.

3: URBANISM AND MONUMENTALITY

Probably because it is a relatively compact mass, and almost certainly the repository of the richest relics in art and technics, the citadel of the ancient city is its most thoroughly explored quarter. The proto-city had, as I pointed out, the beginnings of its institutional life in the fortified camp and the shrine, not necessarily occupying a common site. The mark of the city, let me repeat, is the coming together of these two institutions in a special precinct, set apart from the profane world. Thus Enkidu sought out mighty Gilgamesh in Uruk's "holy temple, the abode of Anu and Ishtar." Though subordinate temples are found in other parts of the city, and in the case of Khorsabad, a subordinate palace as well, the great palace of the king and the great temple stand close together within the citadel: part of the dual system of government that so long prevailed.

The stone core of the citadel can be traced in more than one city, indeed the ziggurat may still tower above the sandy mound and its buried debris, called *tillu* (ruin heap) in ancient Babylonian, and still called 'Tell': sometimes a hundred feet high. But the shape of the city that surrounded it is known only from late examples, and the glyphs that are left, which should reveal an even earlier form, are bafflingly obscure. Strangely, the characters for 'temple,' for 'tower,' for 'water,' for 'garden,' for 'woods,' for 'high-road,' for 'market' are graphically clear in Ur and Kish, either as picture or symbol: but not the city. Cultivated land is represented as an oblong of fifteen squares or the rectangular marks of a plow in an oblong field, open at one side; but the city is either an oblong with two inner vertical lines, or an L-shaped block with a short riser; and it is hard to understand what either figure signified, unless the latter be the outline of an actual house minus the door and the smaller structure stands for the bigger.

With the very foundation of the city one should expect definitions and boundaries, limits of sacred authority, royal jurisdiction, and property. Were there, for example, such boundaries to define the neighborhoods that served the sub-temples; or did they merely melt into each other invisibly, without canal or other open space to separate them? We do not know. Even the most superficial inquirer can ask more pertinent questions than the most learned archaeologist can yet answer.

In the citadel the new mark of the city is obvious: a change of scale, deliberately meant to awe and overpower the beholder. Though the mass of inhabitants might be poorly fed and overworked, no expense was spared to create temples and palaces whose sheer bulk and upward thrust would dominate the rest of the city. The heavy walls of hard-baked clay or solid stone would give to the ephemeral offices of state the assurance of stability and security, of unrelenting power and unshakable authority. What we now call 'monumental architecture' is first of all the expression of power, and that power exhibits itself in the assemblage of costly building materials and of all the resources of art, as well as in a command of all manner of sacred adjuncts, great lions and bulls and eagles, with whose mighty virtues the head of the state identifies his own frailer abilities. The purpose of this art was to produce respectful terror, as in the contemporary confession quoted by Contenau: "I am as a dead man, I am faint after the sight of the King my master."

Both the citadel and its walled ramparts may have begun in a more humble way, with prudent practical considerations in view. W. F. Albright notes that as late as 1750 B.C. in Palestine the tribal chieftains occupied fortresses, while most of their subjects lived in surrounding hamlets, and moved into the fortified enclosure only in times of peril, or when the winter weather forced them out of the improvised shelters of stones and boughs where they lived in the summer, especially during the grape harvest. This probably continued the earliest pattern; and Fustel de Coulanges long ago correctly characterized it as the primordial form of the city.

Either a steep natural pile of rock or a man-made wall uniformly protected the citadel; but this was not necessarily true of the early village or even town. Gertrude Levy notes that Arpachiyeh, an old painted-pottery center, had no defenses, and shows in its remains no weapons: so that a specialized small town, little more than an overgrown village, under the protection of a powerful metropolis like Nineveh, could perhaps forgo the building of a wall even in a period when war was constant and ever threatening. But with the invention of the arts of organized collective extermination and destruction, the wall plainly became a practical necessity, not just a symbol, and it imposed a definite form upon the city. This happened, it would seem, in the early communities near the Euphrates, and it played a part in setting the physical limits to facile urban expansion. At the same time it magnified the selfish absorptions and the anxious preoccupations of the city's king or governor, bent on bringing within the walls all that lay outside them.

The wall, then, served as both a military device and an agent of effective command over the urban population. Esthetically it made a clean break between city and countryside; while socially it emphasized the difference between the insider and outsider, between the open field, subject to the depredations of wild animals, nomadic robbers, invading armies, and the fully enclosed city, where one could work and sleep with a sense of utter security, even in times of military peril. With a sufficient supply of water within, and a sufficient amount of stored grain in bins and granaries, that security would seem absolute.

The openings in the city wall were as carefully controlled as the sluice gates in an irrigation system; and one must remember that, except for the daily passage to and from the surrounding fields, only a trickle of people would come by boat or caravan into the city. Not indeed till the city at length reached the dimensions of a metropolis was there any problem of congestion around the city's gates, causing the trading population to back up there, with inns, stables, and warehouses of their own, to form a merchant's quarter and entrepôt, or 'port.' We shall find the same formations again in the Middle Ages.

The gates that guarded these ancestral cities would be symbolically re-enforced, like the palace itself, by threatening bulls or lions, huge magic images of deified power. Such bronze portals served to discourage the attacking army and to inculcate respect in the most peaceable visiting stranger. Very early, the ramparts had the general form that they retained down to the sixteenth century A.D.: with towers and bastions jutting from a solid girdle of masonry, often broad enough for three chariots to drive abreast at the top, to permit the easy use of counter-weapons.

With the growth of military skill and political suspicion, the wall might turn into a complicated system, with enclosures within enclosures: so that stratagem and treason served better than engines of assault in Babylon as in Troy, for gaining entrance into the city. Certainly the presence of encircling moats and canals, as well as walls, did not make the attacker's task any easier. Without this great advantage for defense, small cities would not have resisted capture and demolition as well as they sometimes did; while but for human weaknesses—envy, inner contention and treason—great cities might have remained invulnerable.

If the inhabitant of the city exulted in his powerful gods, he was no less proudly conscious of the encircling and all-containing wall: to contemporaries it seemed the great gods had fashioned the city and its temple—"the house descending from heaven"—and above all "its great wall touching the clouds." On both these matters one happily has sure contemporary evidence, in various versions of the Gilgamesh epic, which characteristically exhibit this early hero and king as a builder of Uruk's wall and its great temple: the two great acts that gave form to the 'urban implosion.' In this instance, a few words are worth large heaps of ruined masonry:

> Of ramparted Uruk the wall he built,
> Of hallowed Eanna [the temple of Anu and Ishtar]
>   the pure sanctuary.
> Behold its outer wall, whose cornice is like copper,
> Peer at the inner wall, which none can equal!
> Seize upon the threshold, which is of old.
> ... Go up and walk on the walls of Uruk,
> Inspect the base terrace, examine the brickwork:
> Is not its brickwork of burnt brick?
> Did not the Seven [Sages] lay its foundations?

But besides the functions of military defense and control, of religious unification and protection, the wall had still another part to play: it established a clean, formal contrast between town and country. Trees, gardens, fields, cattle byres might exist within the city; but the wall, by engirdling the built-up area, ensured a permanent margin of agricultural land about it. This sharp division must have produced an equally bold esthetic effect.

In these wide valleys, both in Mesopotamia and Egypt, the cities were often erected, alike for safety and defense, on platforms; so that Herodotus, speaking of the landscape in Egypt at floodtime, described its cities as looking "very like the islands of the Aegean sea." The mud platform itself, sometimes only of the base of the citadel, sometimes of the whole city, might rise to a height of forty feet: in the temple of Anu such a base, according to Frankfort, covered 420,000 square feet. Above that mound, the ramparts might lift another hundred feet, probably concealing all the other buildings from the distance, except the main temple. By its very form the city was an assertion of the collective will to dominate the land: to the outward eye a sort of brown table mountain on a verdant carpet, its close-built sun-baked clay structures, its profile of battlement, tower, and ziggurat, surrounded and crisscrossed by canals and irrigation ditches, the whole plumed by occasional palm trees, by feathery acacias and flowering tamarisks. If the wall towered and the gates grimly lowered, the landscape beyond smiled; while once inside the wall the hum of the busy hive, the color and glow of its dense-packed life, contrasted with the thinned-out, spotty, almost invisible activities of the village.

The visible external order of the citadel and its city would be matched by the inward order of the palace and the temple, sometimes at one side of the circuit of the walls, sometimes in the very center. Power radiated outward from these two sacred sources; and in turn, human tribute in every form, gold, silver, copper, tin, lapis lazuli, food, daily labor, life itself, streamed back to these same centers. If the houses were crowded and sometimes airless, the sacred precinct was spacious, with rectangular inner courts that could hold a multitude. Here art came in to establish and reenforce, with an effect beyond that of mere words, all that the new order had brought in to alter the dimensions of the older, purely agricultural regime: above all, the power of the disciplined imagination itself to translate the possible into the actual, and to enlarge the humble habits of everyday life into structures of magnificence.

While villages can be identified by house foundations and shards of pottery, the ancient city can be most reliably identified by its wealth of monumental images. The forms of urban art better indicate the total transformation than any census of houses or any measurement of area. In his classic 'Principles of Psychology,' William James well described the way in which a man's house and possessions become as much a part of his complete personality as his knowledge and sentiments, his opinions and acts. If that is true of the individual, it is even more massively true of the community: for it was by means of new esthetic structures that the city defined the new collective personality that had emerged, and looked with a fresh pride at its own face. If the king or the governor were too high and mighty to be approached except in extremity, the meanest inhabitant could nevertheless identify himself with the personality of the city, in all its power and radiance.

The round of agriculture had tied men to their daily task: they were addicted to the commonplace and accustomed to their own littleness and their short tether. In the city, even the humblest could vicariously participate in greatness and claim it for his own: there was ceremonious leisure and playful detachment, open to all, through the new agencies the municipality commanded. Again I turn to the ancient Akkadian text for confirmation:

> Come then, O Enkidu, to ramparted Uruk
> Where people are resplendent in festal attire,
> Where each day is made a holiday.

This perhaps was an exaggeration akin to that one might find today in a travel folder; but at bottom, it revealed a sense of the splendor and joy expressed in music, song, and costume, as well as architecture, that men began to associate with cities. Without these goods their many sordid and oppressive actualities could hardly have been endured.

Note the magical attraction of the city. People came to that sacred place to be under the care of a mighty god and almost equally mighty king, who exhibited in his own person new attributes—a power of command and understanding, a power of decision and free will—which might run counter to the venerable ways of the tribe. Until this moment the human character had been molded by the local group and had no other identity or individuality. But in the city, under the institution of kingship, personality itself first emerged: self-directed, self-governing, self-centered, claiming for the single magnified 'I,' as divine representative of the larger collectivity, all that had once belonged to the now-diminished 'Us.'

To understand the importance of this change, one may happily fall back on the Chinese philosopher, Mencius. "When men are subdued by force," he observed, "they do not submit in their minds, but only because their strength is inadequate. When men are subdued by power in personality they are pleased to their very heart's core and do really submit." "Power in personality" was what the city and its gods provided: that was the chief source of the great accomplishments that kingship itself made possible. Thousands of years elapsed before the city passed on this personal power to the rest of its inhabitants.

Deprived of such sacred powers, the ancient city could have been only a heap of baked mud or stones, formless, purposeless, meaningless; since without such cosmic magnifications, the common man could live an equally good or even far better life in the village. But once life was conceived sacrally, as an imitation of the gods, the ancient city itself became, and remained right into Roman times, a simulacrum of heaven: even its seeming durability, the freedom of its sacred buildings from the decay and dilapidation of the cramped peasant's hut, only made it come closer to the eternal pattern that man's growing consciousness of the cosmos itself made so attractive. So Thebes, the center of the Sun God cult, became in sacred legend the original site of creation itself.

In the early cities, human life and energy were translated into the form of art on a scale that had been unattainable before. Each generation could now leave its deposit of ideal forms and images: shrines, temples, palaces, statues, portraits, inscriptions, carved and painted records on walls and columns, that satisfied man's earliest wish for immortality through being present in the minds of later generations. Even when threatened with extinction, pride and ambition clung to the stones of the city; for art preceded the written word in fixing into 'eternal' symbolic forms that which would otherwise pass away. In the Babylonian version of the Gilgamesh epic, the hero, though acknowledging the limitations that dog man's days and his achievements, knowing that no mere human "can scale heaven," nevertheless cherishes the consoling thought of the new urban man: "Should I fall, I shall have made me a name. 'Gilgamesh,' they will say, '. . . has fallen. [Long] after my offspring has been born in my house.'" 'Fame' spurs the city dweller to acts destined in graven memory to outlast his lifetime.

In the city, the great archetypes of the unconscious, godlike kings, winged bulls, hawk-headed men, lionlike women, hugely magnified, erupted in clay, stone, brass, and gold. It is not merely in the theater that the spectator feels that the actors are bigger than their actual life size. This a characteristic illusion produced by the city, because the urban center is in fact a theater. From what Adelbert Ames experimentally demonstrated about the part played by subjective values and purposes in altering apparently neutral sensations, one can hardly doubt that, in the midst of the general magnification of human activity that took place in the fourth millennium B.C., the godlike king or the chief priest actually looked as large in 'real life' as he was represented in painted or sculptured image—at least when he was performing those sacred rituals which enhanced all his powers. The detachment that Deioces was so careful to provide for himself on being elevated from village councillor to king, helps to bring about this enlargement: for psychal distance, prolonged by awe and reverence and fear, enlarges the single object focussed upon, and shrinks and blurs the mass of urban denizens, who are 'out of focus,' like objects outside the field of a magnifying glass.

Yet the actor needs an audience to re-enforce his own ego and lend importance to his role. What actor can perform at his best in an empty house? If the kings were in fact to exercise the powers they claimed, they needed the constant attention and applause of a many-headed urban audience. Thus the old active participants in the village ritual soon became the passive chorus, the spectators and commentators in the new urban drama. Once upon a time in the old village these lookers-on had a full share in what went on, and could perform successfully all the roles, by turns actor and spectator. Now, in the city, they were diminished into supernumeraries. Perhaps not the least mission of urban monumental art was the reduction of the common man to this abject position, making him easier to govern, while the illusion lasted.

4: RIVER, HIGHWAY, AND MARKET

But potent though all the citadel's functions were in focussing and expanding both religious and political power, it probably played an equal part in the economic life of the city. If at first one can find no open space that can be called a market, it is perhaps because this space was a part of the temple precinct, and only at a later date found an opening for itself in the plebeian quarters of the city. In this, the market resembles those governmental offices which may have had an assigned place in the old palace as soon as they began to be differentiated; for surely what we now call the palace was also a barracks, a prison, a court, an administrative compound.

I have left to the last the dynamic component of the city, without which it could not have continued to increase in size and scope and productivity: this is the first efficient means of mass transport, the waterway. That the first growth of cities should have taken place in river valleys is no accident; and the rise of the city is contemporaneous with improvements in navigation, from the floating bundle of rushes or logs to the boat powered by oars and sails. After this, the ass, the horse, the camel, the wheeled vehicle, and finally the paved road widened the province of transportation, and gave the city command over men and resources in distant areas. Transport made it possible to equalize surpluses and to get access to distant specialities: these were the functions of a new urban institution, the market, itself largely a product of the securities and regularities of urban life. In the cities where we have the earliest records, we find that the functions of the market—procurement, storage, distribution—were undertaken by the temple, though possibly, as in Soviet Russia today, a portion of the peasant's product might be privately consumed or exchanged, once the collective demand was satisfied.

Like the other original components of the city, the market may exist as a separate entity, without bringing into existence more than temporary shelters: some of this evanescent quality still remains in weekly markets in European towns, even big ones, with their motor caravans of sellers and their temporary booths. What gives the market a permanent place in the city is a population big enough to offer a handsome living to merchants with distant connections and costly commodities, and sufficient local productivity to enable the surplus of urban workshops to be offered for general sale. But these conditions are a result, not an original cause, of the growth of population.

More important, in the long run, than the wider distribution of the goods in the market was the wider communication system that grew up along with it: the permanent record seems to be at first a by-product of market transactions, and the greatest invention after linguistic and numerical notations themselves was the invention of the alphabet, the work of Phoenician traders. With trade came human intercourse on a wider scale than ever before. Sumer was characterized as the "many-tongued," and the diffusion and standardization of local languages gave the city its special status as a communication center, the seat of a common literature in which other centers would eventually share.

If transportation was the most dynamic element in the city, apart from war, the lack of transport, or the ease with which it could be disrupted along a river route by a community that denied passage to boats, was a threat to its growth, indeed to its very existence. This doubtless accounts for the tendency of powerful cities to extend their frontiers and to destroy cities that might block their trade routes: it was important to safeguard the 'life lines.' This would partly explain the political route from urban center to empire.

In one of S. N. Kramer's translations, one finds a reference to the "market street of Ur," and Enkidu's struggle with Gilgamesh took place in the "Market of the Land." The Sumerian ideogram for market, a Y, would indicate perhaps that the idea of the market as a juncture of traffic routes was already recognized. There is no need to doubt the early coming in of the market to handle local barter long before any 'market economy,' based on transactions aimed at monetary gain and private capital accumulation, came into existence. If these allusions to the market can be safely taken as indicating more general usage, the two classic forms of the market, the open place or covered bazaar, and the booth or shop-lined street, had possibly found their urban form by 2000 B.C. at latest. But it may be they were both preceded by the even more ancient form of the supermarket—within the temple precinct. In this case, the market was a monopoly of the god and his priesthood, not a money-making corporation, where possibly every form of goods, agricultural and industrial, would be brought for direct taxation before redistribution.

In the early stages of ancient city development, we seem indeed to be dealing with a controlled totalitarian economy, centered in the temple. It is not alone that the god owns the neighboring land and exacts service from everyone: a portion of the year must be devoted to forced labor for the benefit of the community. But in addition, the temple precinct itself was not purely a religious area: it served also as a 'trading estate,' where goods were manufactured, and as a 'shopping center,' where they were stored and distributed. The storehouses, Frankfort points out, contained "an immense variety of articles: grain, sesame seed as the raw material for oil, vegetables, beer, dates, wine, fish (dried or salted), fat, wool, skins, huge quantities of reeds and rushes, mats, asphalt, stones." Wool-plucking, grain-milling, tanning, spinning, and weaving were all done within the temple precinct. Only with the growth of the urban population and the increasing complexity of economic operations was a portion of this economy released to more purely secular enterprise, in other quarters of the town.

Even in the crudest economy, some mode of distributing the surplus and exchanging special products in limited demand must be found, whether by barter, by gift, or by feast. Early urban consumers depended not merely upon the peasant's products, but upon the activities of the fisherman, the fowler, the potter, the weaver, the smith, and indeed, this full-time concentration upon a single activity was one of the distinguishing marks of the new urban economy—even though an older order might be kept alive in remoter villages and on country estates.

Petrie pointed out that the early nome capitals of the Delta, and the early cities of Mesopotamia were on the average some twenty miles apart, sometimes less; and he reasonably suggested that this uniformity could be interpreted as due to the need for an easily accessible central storage for grain. So long as payments between traders were made in grain, both storage and credit must have multiplied the market centers under the protection of some august local god. The very closeness of these early towns may well indicate, at the time of their foundation, a state of security and peace not attested by later records of strife and war.

5: TECHNICAL INNOVATIONS AND

DEFICIENCIES

Though the size of the typical early city was modest and its scope largely confined to its neighboring region, the scale of the citadel and its chief buildings might verge on the colossal: no sacrifice was too great to enchance its prestige and its power, or to ensure its permanence. Strangely enough, though, some of the earliest cities show physical features in the residential quarters that were lost in the later development of the city, though the rulers might still retain them. The regular street plan, the row houses, the bathrooms and the inside latrines, the pottery pipes, the bricklined drainage channels in the streets, the culverts to carry off the rain water—all these the digger finds in the ruins of Mohenjo-Daro and finds again, with minor variations, in spreading Ur or little Lagash.

The broad street had come in before the invention of wheeled vehicles, for it was probably first laid out for sacred processions and for marching soldiers. The frequent orientation of the main avenues to the points of the compass perhaps indicates the growing dominance of the sky gods; this layout sometimes flouted more practical considerations, such as tempering the heat or catching the prevailing winds. Yet many of these improvements dropped out of sight in the later development of cities, and still were absent till recently from many big 'progressive' cities in the Western world —I refer particularly to bathrooms, inside latrines, and pottery pipes—at the beginning of the nineteenth century. So much for the doctrine of continuous material progress.

In the earliest cities, as the excavations at Ur show, the street as an open, articulated means of circulation was exceptional: the narrow tortuous alley, well-shaded from the torrid sun, was the usual channel of traffic, better adapted to the climate than a wide thoroughfare. What Sumerian scholars sometimes translate as "boulevard" must not be confused with the later seventeenth-century boulevard carved out of a destroyed 'bulwark' (earthwork): it was rather a Broad Way, wide enough for crowds, where one might go for a stroll in the evening, to watch the dancing, listen to the music, or meet for gossip, as an old document reveals: in short, it served as the classic 'Main Street.'

Lack of adequate artificial light remained one of the greatest technical imperfections of the city till the nineteenth century. But by 2000 B.C., at all events, most of the major physical organs of the city had been created. The nineteenth-century observer would hardly have felt at home in the confused mythological conceptions, the bold sexual obscenities, or the bloody sacrificial rituals of the dominant urban religions; but scarcely any part of the physical city would have been unfamiliar to him. Those of us who are sufficiently conscious of the collective irrationality and decadence of the present age would feel equally at ease—or, better, equally ill at ease—in both territories.

The general appearance of these ancient Mesopotamian cities must have been—as Leonard Woolley pointed out—very much like that of a walled North African city today: the same network of narrow streets or rather, alleys, perhaps no more than eight feet wide, with the same one, two, and three story houses, the same usable roof tops, the same inner courts, and finally, the steep pyramid of the ziggurat dominating it all, as the towers of the Mosque now dominate the Moslem city. Beyond the walled but spacious temple precinct, spread a series of more or less coherent neighborhoods in which smaller shrines and temples serve for the householder. Every citizen in ancient Mesopotamia, it would seem, belonged to a particular temple and its god, and did work for him: the basis of 'citizenship' was in this particular religious affiliation. Frankfort points out that a temple community—in visible form a 'neighborhood unit'—comprised priests, officials, gardeners, craftsmen, stonecutters, merchants, and even slaves—all the people of the god. For a long time, the inhabitants were subjects or serfs bound to their religious lord, not citizens: they took orders but probably did not dare to give them even in the fashion that a village council might give them to its own members. The 'City Description of Assur,' dating from around 700 B.C., when Assur was no longer a royal town, records thirty-four temples and chapels. Every feature of the early city revealed the belief that man was created for no other purpose than to magnify and serve his gods. That was the city's ultimate reason for existence.

Though Woolley's comparison of ancient and modern towns of the Near East is probably fair, it takes the early city at a late stage, when, as with our own late medieval cities, overcrowding, overbuilding, and a reckless accumulation of debris had wiped out the open spaces with which it had begun. Even at an advanced point in its growth, however, we know that there were open fields within the walls of Babylon; and a large part of the inhabitants of ancient cities worked in the fields and gardens outside, as they still do in many Greek and Italian country towns. Such agricultural 'allotment gardens' may have been preserved within the walls for a long time, since gardens and cattle were an insurance against starvation under a long siege.

But at an early date the slack rural ways of disposing of rubbish and excrement became a menace in crowded urban quarters, without apparently spurring sufficient efforts for the improvement of urban sanitation and hygiene. Then, as now in Africa, Woolley remarks, "the sweepings of the house floors and the contents of the rubbish bins were simply flung on the streets," so steadily that in these old cities the street levels were gradually raised and new houses would be built above the risen level of the street, while the thresholds of the old houses would sink below.

For thousands of years city dwellers put up with defective, often quite vile, sanitary arrangements, wallowing in rubbish and filth they certainly had the power to remove, for the occasional task of removal could hardly have been more loathsome than walking and breathing in the constant presence of such ordure. If one had any sufficient explanation of this indifference to dirt and odor that are repulsive to many animals, even pigs, who take pains to keep themselves and their lairs clean, one might also have a clue to the slow and fitful nature of technological improvement itself, in the five millennia that followed the birth of the city.

Yet there is another side to this picture, which one discovers in the biblical description of the new cities for the Levites in Palestine, and one finds in an even earlier passage in a poem from which I have already quoted. There was more openness and natural beauty in the urban *ambiance* than the dusty remains encourage us to suspect. Whatever unit the word 'sar' represented, in Uruk, according to Gilgamesh, "one 'sar' was city, one 'sar' was orchards, one 'sar' was 'margin lands'; [further there was] the precinct of the temple of Ishtar." Three 'sar' and the sacred precinct comprised Uruk: thus half the city was dedicated to open spaces. What the translator calls margin land may in fact be a suburb, with detached houses and gardens or possibly a greenbelt of market gardens. Certainly the large amount of land under cultivation suggests easy access to fresh air, the sanifying sunlight, and the sight of growing things. As long as the city remained under thirty thousand in population, its outer green belt was more accessible from the center by foot than it is today even in an English New Town—and, except for the outward expansion of the town, it was even less liable to non-agricultural encroachments.

6: CONTEMPORARY GLIMPSES OF THE CITY

Even the partial excavations of the ruins give the archaeologist many clues to the life, as well as the form, of the ancient cities: yet when he attempts to bring the dry bones together and breathe life into them, the graphic model is not only too patently 'synthetic,' but worse, is dead. It is to ancient art, that is, to legend and graphic representation, that one must turn to fill out the eroded forms disclosed by the excavator's spade. Even then, one is left with a static picture, a cross section, not with life in its flow and multitudinous movement; but it has the touch of the living hand and the eye that originally bore witness.

I shall confine myself to three contemporary sources: the monuments Layard unearthed at Nineveh, the map of Nippur, dating from 1500 B.C. that Professor Kramer discovered in the Hilprecht collection at Jena, and the classic account that Herodotus left of Babylon. The first not only show us buildings, trees, gardens, but also men in action: soldiers assaulting a city from movable towers, swimming rivers in full armor with the aid of bladders, slaying captives, scaling walls. If this is not the everyday life of the city, it is that part of it which left the deepest scar on all its organs. The pictures lack any sense of crowds, as one might find them in the market or the temple precinct; but the outlines are there. The stone carvings, the glazed colored tiles, the written descriptions, confirm each other.

The map of Nippur is closer to the outlines traced by the archaeologists, for that is the nature of town plans: but its very irregularity discloses a high order of technical skill and the ability to transpose irregular figures to a plane surface without reducing them to a conventional symbol. Here, in "the oldest map known to history," are the outlines of a real Mesopotamian city, with its walls and gates, and its canals, its temples (the god Enlil himself elsewhere is addressed as a mountain, symbol of protection), its 'Lofty Shrine,' its 'Central Park,' so called though not actually centered.

The citadel unfortunately cannot itself be identified; but the salient position of the Central Park might suggest that the palace and the stronghold, otherwise unidentified by the scribe who composed the map, were here, though the park might surround the palace as it does the Pitti Palace in Florence. The mid-city canal, eighty feet wide, divides the city roughly into two equal parts, that to the southeast indicating the temenos of the Mountain House, the principal temple. This city plan indicates not only the disposition of the main elements of the city—the canals, the parks, the civic precincts—it also indicates the presence of the kind of learning and vocational skill capable of thinking in abstractions, and representing them; so that even if we knew nothing about Babylonian mathematics we would have to assume its existence. If we want to fill up these early pictures, we shall have to supplement them by a literary description, this time not an archaeologist's, but that of an eyewitness who saw only the remains, perhaps partly rebuilt for a third time, of the fallen city of Babylon.

Herodotus' observations are all the more significant because in his century power and influence were leaving the mother cities of Mesopotamia, going eastward to Iran, northward to Macedonia, and westward, as well as northward, to Rome. The last of the great cities in this area, and perhaps the greatest of them, which united the older elements in its civilization, was Babylon. "The following," says Herodotus, "is a description of the place:

"The city stands on a broad plain and is an exact square, a hundred and twenty furlongs each way, so that the entire city is four hundred and eighty furlongs [in circumference]. While such is its size, there is no other city that approaches it. It is surrounded in the first place by a broad and deep moat, full of water, behind which rises a wall fifty royal cubits in width and two hundred feet in height. And here I may not omit to tell the use to which the mud dug out of the great moat was turned, nor the manner in which the wall was wrought. As fast as they dug the moat, the soil which they got from the cutting was made into bricks; and when a sufficient number were completed, they baked the brick in kilns. Then they set to the building and began bricking the borders of the moat, after which they proceeded to construct the wall itself, using for their cement hot bitumen, and interposing a layer of wattled reeds at every course of bricks. On the top, along the edges of the wall, they constructed buildings of a single chamber, leaving between them room for a four horse chariot to turn. In the circuit of the wall are a hundred gates, all of brass, with brazen lintels and side posts. . . . The city is divided into two portions by the river which runs through the middle of it. This river is the Euphrates, a broad, deep, swift stream, which rises in Armenia and falls into the Red Sea.

"The wall on either bank has an elbow carried down to the river; thence, from the corners of the wall, is carried along each bank of the river a wall of burnt bricks. The houses are mostly three and four stories high; the streets all run in straight lines, not only those parallel to the river, but also the cross streets which lead down to the waterside. At the river end of these cross streets are low gates in the wall that skirts the stream.

"The outer wall is the main defence of the city. There is, however, an inner wall, of less thickness than the first, but very little inferior in strength. The center of each division of the town is occupied by a fortress. . . . In the one stood the palace of the kings, surrounded by a wall of great strength and size; in the other was the sacred precinct of Jupiter Belus, a square enclosure two furlongs each way, with gates of solid brass; which was also remaining in my time. In the middle of the precinct there was a tower of solid masonry, a furlong in length and breadth, upon which was raised a second tower, and on that a third, and so on up to eight"—in short, a ziggurat, a form that had been passed on without substantial change for tens of centuries. "The ascent to the top is on the outside, by a path which winds round all the towers. When one is about half way up one finds a resting place and seats. . . . On the topmost tower there is a spacious temple where, just as the Egyptians reported at Thebes, there was once a large couch where the god was supposed to have intercourse with a priestess, and by the side of this couch was a table of gold." The ancient fertility ceremony whereby the divine king magically assured the continuance of the procreative functions throughout nature was still enacted under sacred auspices, or at least the tradition had stayed alive in memory.

Though Herodotus could have seen only the shattered remains of this great city, he was close enough to it to convey a last exhalation of life, something that the richest archaeological remains hardly any longer contain. His account would be precious, even if it only told us how chunks of bitumen, so useful in waterproofing, were carried by a tributary stream into the Euphrates, and thus floated down to Babylon, or how the traders bringing casks of palm wine had used the traditional round raft, of bound reeds, with ribs of willow, covered with skins, to bring goods to the city; after which they would sell the ribs—wood was valuable on the treeless plain—pack the hides on a donkey they had carried aboard with them, and go back overland to the hills whence they came, since the swift current of the Euphrates did not permit them to pole back upstream.

In both Herodotus' account and in those of the archaelogists only one group in the city's life seems hard to spot. Where are the children? Part of the day, we know, they were at school: the records of Ur not merely show us a school, but likewise recall a little friendly bribery of the schoolmaster, by dining him at home. From a Sumerian letter, dating back 3,700 years, we have a better picture of the adolescent, excused by his too-indulgent father from working in the fields, carrying rushes, digging and plowing. Not having anything serious to do when school is over, the idle youth wanders about the street, according to his father, and loiters in the public square. He seeks pleasure, is somewhat insolent, and is indifferent to his inherited vocation's opportunities, it would seem, with no disposition to follow the scribal calling of his father. This little touch of actual life, which the author of 'History Begins at Sumer' has brought before us, suddenly closes the gap of millennia between ourselves and these early city dwellers. The human drama of the outraged but loving father and the bored, rebellious son seems all too close to our own age.

The city, as we first discover it, seems to belong exclusively to the adult population. Probably the larger portion of the child population worked, as the above passage would indicate, in the fields: saved from both school and delinquency by their agricultural labor. But where in these crowded streets, these narrow ways, these constricted housing quarters, do the common children play? Thousands of years will pass before, in the heart of the city, in the grounds around the school and in the nearby playing fields—first in the medieval towns, but most notably now in the British New Towns—the playtime activities of the children will claim large swathes of open space.

7: EGYPT AND THE OPEN CITY

The story of the city as it unfolds in Mesopotamia cannot be told over again for Egypt without numerous qualifications, contrasts, and particularizations. This fact emphasizes a more general truth about cities: their marked individuality, so strong, so full of 'character' from the beginning that they have many of the attributes of human personalities.

The dawning civilization of the fourth millennium B.C. shows many of the same forceful features in Egypt that it does in Sumer; indeed, in its centralized absolutisms, in the overwhelming devotion to religious cult, in the deification of the Pharaoh, who for long alone shared with the gods the gift of immortality, this implosion and concentration of powers and agents seems to go farther in Egypt than in Mesopotamia.

In Egypt, there was much turbulence and change on the cultural surface, a plentitude of great and little gods, a variety of tribal totems, a mixture of the eternal and the ephemeral, the animal and the human, as if every manifestation of life were precious and no part of it that once showed life might be denied or lost. But these are scratchings and daubings on a vast granite monolith set deep in the Nile mud, which showed little weathering in its main forms after thousands of years. For the Egyptians there was nothing so valuable as the second life, after death; and the early folk must at least have dreamed of having a share of immortality before the priesthood, in response to a devastating popular revolution, granted all of them the possibility of a passage to heaven, guaranteed by mummification and magic spells. After that, everything returned more or less to its original position.

But one looks in vain for the visible remains of the city in Egypt comparable to those one finds as early as 2500 B.C. in Sumer, though the pyramids are early and more unshakably permanent. One contemporary scholar has even said, with his tongue in his cheek perhaps, that the Egyptian city did not exist till 1500 B.C. That statement is not so much a challenge to further digging, as a call for a more adequate definition of a city than that which urbanists and sociologists have so far been content with.

True, one does not at first find in the Nile Valley the archetypal city of history, the walled town, solidly bounded and ramparted, built for permanence. Everything else in Egypt seems to have found a durable form except the city. The temples at Luxor and Karnak have shown their mighty outlines throughout historic times: the great and little pyramids are still visible, though the fashion for pyramids flourished and died down almost as swiftly as the fashion for elaborate starlike fortifications in the late Renascence. Of independent structures that testify to the universal magnification of power at the onset of civilization there is no lack: obelisks, majestic processional ways, colonnades, granite and diorite sculptures on the grandest scale, all these testify to the kind of life we expect to find in the city. But the city is transitory. Each Pharaoh builds his own capital, with no desire to continue the work of his predecessors or aggrandize his city. His urban home is as exclusive as his tomb—perhaps for the same egoistic reason. Even where the same general site is respected, as in Thebes, the growth is by a sort of loose suburban accretion.

Yet certainly if I am right in thinking that monumental art is one of the surest marks of the classic city's existence, the city is inescapably 'there.' We can inspect likewise all the accessory specialized institutions of the city in the little wooden models taken out of the tombs: the butcher's shop, the barge, the embalmer's establishment, the bakehouse; and of course there are temples and palaces on the greatest scale, long before 1500 B.C. There must have been visible centers of control, too: for the office of the Grand Vizier came into existence as early as the Fourth Dynasty, he who served as chief justice, head of the archives and the exchequer, mayor of the palace, that is, military governor of the citadel. All these are focal civic functions.

Now, if the city in the same architectural form we find in Mesopotamia, cannot be uncovered before the relatively late period of Tell-el-Amarna (early fourteenth century B.C.), this may be because the walled city in Egypt was an *early* form, whose military features disappeared once the great Pharaohs had established a universal order and a unified command, resting mainly on religious belief and voluntary support, rather than on physical coercion. This ideology prevailed through the whole Nile Valley. It is certain, H. W. Fairman points out, that during the Negada II period, towns with enclosing brick walls were in existence. On the stone palettes of the late pre-dynastic and early dynastic times, towns are shown as circles or ovals, surrounded by stout walls and often provided with buttresses.

This perhaps explains the otherwise inexplicable hieroglyph for city, an oval or circular enclosure, whose crossroads (if they are crossroads) divide the city into four quarters. If this is in fact a symbolic plan, it would be the best possible symbol for the classic city. The fact that this sign was used from the very beginning of writing points to an even more ancient origin; indeed the circular form in itself would make an early dating probable, though it was repeated, apparently, in later Hittite towns, and though one finds a similar pattern on early pre-dynastic bowls. The city of El Kab, in Upper Egypt, between Latopolis and Hierakonopolis, lies in an area rich in tombs from the Fifth and Sixth Dynasties. The bigger city, enclosed in a wall about 1,600 feet square, probably flourished around 1788-1580 B.C. But this wall intersects that of a more primitive town in the form of an oval or a circle, protected by a double wall. Both the form and the date are significant.

In Mesopotamia each city was a separate world. In Pharaonic Egypt the cities did not, probably, hold so large a part of the population: the functions of the city—enclosure, assembly, intermixture—were performed by the land itself. Desert and mountain constituted the 'wall,' the nomes and totem groups formed the 'neighborhoods,' and the Pharaohs' tombs and temples served as otherworldly 'citadels.' It was the Pharaoh himself, not the city's familiar deity, who incarnated the community: his divine powers pervaded the entire realm. But in the pre-dynastic period, and in the two great relapses into feudal localism and dispersal, if one follows Jacques Pirenne's account, cities were detached, self-governing entities, whose citizens were free from the restrictions of serfdom, able to travel at will, capable of conducting private business—at least in Lower Egypt. Curiously, this 'relapse' into autonomy closely parallels a similar escape from central control and a similar expression of municipal independence in the European Middle Ages after the collapse of the Western Roman Empire.

Is it not possible, then, that the very success of the Pharaonic religio-political system, after Menes, removed the need for the walled control center? The success of the first dynasties in evolving a religious form of government, centering in a king who was popularly accepted as a living god, changed the problem of city building in two ways. It eliminated need for enclosure as a means of coercion and control; and it created a unique type of city, fully developed only in Egypt: the city of the dead. Around the central pyramids of Gizeh we find a veritable urban settlement of corpses with the tombs placed in orderly rows, in streets and cross streets; the mastabas of the nobles even have the appearance of houses. With such a heavy investment in permanence in these monumental structures, there is little wonder that the city of the living lacked the means, as well perhaps as the will, to take more durable form.

In this inverted theology, the dead took precedence over the living; and what followed from this was that the peasant was permitted to remain in his village and little market town, and for the ordinary needs of life, village culture sufficed. Even though this civilization produced written records and monuments in abundance, their provenance was restricted to the ruling classes. Except on the occasions of the great festivals, which drew large masses of people to the great temple communities, like Abydos, there was no need to herd this docile and contented village population into mighty urban centers. Happy with their minor gods and minor duties, in field, household, and hamlet, they cheerfully followed the beneficent rule of the Pharaoh. If his officers collected a portion of the crop, they also kept the irrigation system in order and re-defined the field boundaries between village and village after the annual flood. That law and order, in the long run, ensured a greater prosperity for the growing population.

Until feudal lords in their local strongholds and later foreign invaders challenged the central monarchy, political power transcended the limitations of the city and had no military need for it. The royal capitals themselves continued to have a temporary and improvised air: only the tomb and the city of the dead were built as if for permanent occupancy. Even as late as 1369-1354 B.C. the new capital city of Akhetaton was inhabited for only sixteen years. But temple cities, like Memphis, remained a sacred community for fifteen hundred years.

If between the pre-dynastic or early dynastic towns and those of the Empire there were no walls, did some other mode of organization bring about the mixtures and interchanges of the stone-encased city? Under what form, if at all, did these urban functions exist after Upper and Lower Egypt were unified? Can one speak, in such a situation, of an urban implosion, any more than of an urban structure?

So far, in analyzing the components of the city, I have emphasized the essential function of the closed container, which concentrated the social agents and gave them a closed field that promoted the maximum interaction. But the city is not merely a container: before it has anything to hold, it must attract the people and the institutions that carry on its life. To this aspect of city life, Ebenezer Howard properly applied the term magnet; and that term is all the more useful in description because with the magnet we associate the existence of a 'field' and the possibility of action at a distance, visible in the 'lines of social force,' which draw to the center particles of a different nature. Organized religion played such a role in the early city, for religion constituted the better part of life; indeed, it was through religion that men enhanced their own vitality and that of their crops and animals; and it was through the immortality imputed to the gods that man was encouraged to take measures to ensure his own immortality, first the Pharaoh, because he was also a god, but eventually all men who had followed the laws, attended to the ceremonials, and dealt with one another, in the spirit of Ma'at, with order and justice.

Here we note a significant difference between early Egypt and Mesopotamia. In Mesopotamia, the king was not a god, and the gods themselves were with a few exceptions neither loving nor reasonable nor admirers of civic virtue: indeed, more than one record refers to the impossibility of pleasing them, or of hoping, by good conduct, to win their favor. 'Insecurity' and 'intimidation' were written all over the Mesopotamian record: even the school maintained a functionary with a lash to keep order. These practices left their impression on every part of life, in repeated acts of cruelty and violence, which reached a certain climax of wanton ferocity in the Assyrian monarch, Assurbanipal. The cosmic powers themselves so far from endowing rulers with the more humane virtues sanctioned a policy of terrorization, so much so, that as late as the time of Hammurabi, the very code of law for which he is famous contained an endless list of offenses, many of them trivial, punishable by death or mutilation, on the strict principle of an eye for an eye or a tooth for a tooth, with sometimes a few other organs added as makeweight. Even without the incessant outbreak of war, there was an undercurrent of terrorism and sadistic punishment in such a regime, similar to that which has been resurrected in the totalitarian states of our own day, which bear so many resemblances to these archaic absolutisms. Under such conditions, the necessary co-operations of urban living require the constant application of the police power, and the city becomes a kind of prison whose inhabitants are under constant surveillance: a state not merely symbolized but effectively perpetuated by the town wall and its barred gates.

Two sets of deities towered above the rest of the Egyptian pantheon: Re and Osiris, Ptah and Hathor. The benign sun and the forces of fertility and every kind of creativeness. In Egypt, as a result, the magnet, the center of attraction and aspiration, seems to have prevailed from the earliest moments over the more compulsive container; and this perhaps accounts for the different form that the city took there. There was both an external and an internal unity to Egyptian life. Despite differences between the Upper and the Lower Nile, the whole valley was a single unit, with an almost uniform belt of vegetation, serene skies, a predictable climatic cycle, a benign atmosphere. One had only to float with the river's current to reach the mouth, or to hoist sail, once sails were invented, to go up the river with a wind usually behind one. In Mesopotamia, one had to defy nature, meeting blow with counterblow: in Egypt to submit was sufficient to guarantee that one year would be happily like the other. This static harmony, this deep inward equilibrium, simplified the problem of wielding the new technical powers that civilization had brought into existence: an outer uniformity was accompanied by an inner unity, indeed a docile and affable unanimity.

As god, the Pharaoh incarnated the friendly attributes of the sun and the living vegetation and animal fertility; and as early as 3000 B.C., Breasted notes, both 'command' and 'understanding' had become attributes of Re, the sun god, who in one form or another became the presiding member of a vast pantheon that held some four hundred deities. For such a ruler the temple played a more important part than the castle and the armed guard. What need for terrorism when obedience was so easily forthcoming—when the presence of a living god in one's midst guaranteed abundance and security, order and regularity, justice in this world and at least a vicarious immortality in the next?

8: FROM CEREMONIAL CENTER TO CONTROL CENTER

After the Sixth Dynasty, when a breakdown of centralized power and a period of feudal separatism began, there was a remarkable absence of tension, if one considers the formidable bureaucratic and para-military organization that was required to collect taxes, mobilize labor, and build the great tombs and temples: in short, to govern a country of perhaps three million people. If 'war' existed, between the ascendancy of Menes and the Hyksos invasion, it played a minor role: so much so that an absence of walls around the little country towns and villages would not, I repeat, be a surprise. What passed for war were gigantic, one-sided raiding expeditions, which brought back malachite, copper, wood, and gold.

The unity that the Mesopotamian peoples achieved only through the active enforcement of the city, the Egyptian achieved as a gift of nature in the Nile Valley. As noted before the region itself had the features of a walled city, for mountain, desert, and sea over a long period served as ramparts and kept the Egyptians virtually free from invasion. This very uniformity and harmony perhaps accounts for the other durable qualities

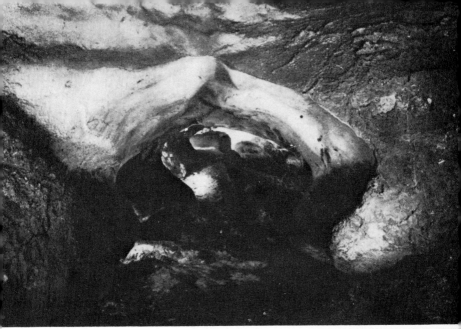

1: CEREMONIES AND MEMORIALS

2: URBAN NUCLEUS

3: MONUMENTAL SCALE

4: TOMB-ORIENTED CITIES

5: ROYAL MAKERS AND BREAKERS

6: THE TRAUMA OF CIVILIZATION

7: CITY AND WORKING QUARTER

8: SACRED MOUNTAIN: DELPHI

9: ATHENIAN POWER AND FORM

10: ANCIENT WAYS, MODERN DAYS

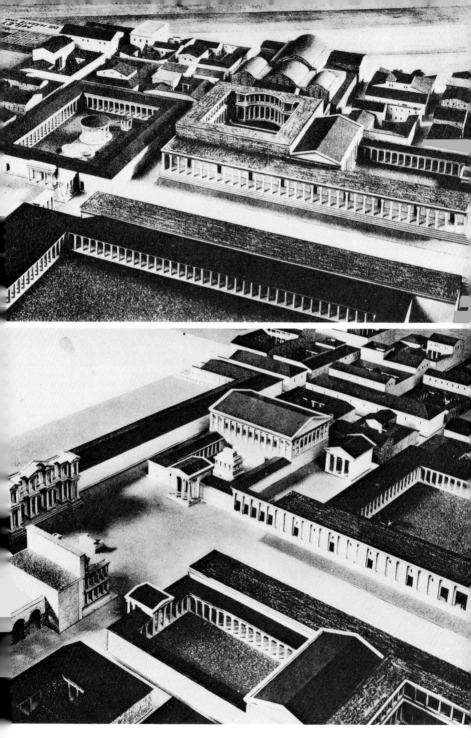

11: MILESIAN ORDER

12: CLASSIC CORE: POMPEII

13: POMPEIIAN DAILY LIFE

14: POMPEII AND PAVIA

15: TEMPLE AND SUPERMARKET

16: CROWD CONTAINERS

1 : CEREMONIES AND MEMORIALS

The ceremonious burial of the dead in graves marked by a cairn, a tree, or a tall rock, formed perhaps the first permanent meeting place for the living: the home of the ancestral spirits, the shrine of a god, the embryo of a city. Like the grave, the cave is a womb to which primitive man returns for security and secrecy: here [upper] in the caves of Lascaux magic rites were possibly performed and paintings were limned by the artists of the Aurignacian culture: prototype of later monumental art, whose superb quality of stylized representation here and in Altamira contrasts with the crudeness of the wall surface and primitive tools and utensils. The symbolic aspects of the early ceremonial mountain caves were retained in the great Egyptian monuments, even the cramped tortuous entrance to the interior. The mountain, rising from the flood, was for the Egyptians an expression of divine creativity as well as a symbol of the eternal: a sacred form translated into a man-made pyramid to attest the Pharaoh's power. Pyramid, ziggurat, tower, dome, spire, all of them charged with religious meaning, formed the sacred core of the city for the greater part of history. Grave, shrine, ceremonial center, anticipated market, workshop, and fort: their purpose, to enhance the meaning and values of life, ensured collective participation, willing sacrifice, and pious continuity.

[Upper] Entrance to the caves at Lascaux. [Lower] Pyramid and Sphinx at Gizeh, whose size and technical perfection reflect the general magnification of power at the first stage of the urban implosion. Photograph by G. E. Kidder Smith.

2 : URBAN NUCLEUS

The earliest ruins recognizable as cities usually disclose only the original dominants, the temple and the palace, sometimes the granary, within the walled citadel or sacred precinct. This was the activating nucleus in the urban implosion. The only complete early 'cities' of permanent materials are the 'cities of the dead,' such as that at Saqqarah built around the step pyramid tomb of Zoser [upper], c. 2700-2650. Since the Egyptians took pains in their tombs to reproduce in miniature all the necessary facilities for daily life, there is good reason, many Egyptian scholars believe, to suppose that this mortuary 'city' reproduced with equal faithfulness the layout and buildings of its secular counterpart. This likelihood is further backed by the reproduction in stone of the royal palace, which was probably built in less permanent sun-baked bricks, together with a sacred temple, government buildings, chapels of national divinities, and a storehouse. In Pharaonic times orthogonal planning governed equally the walled sacred precinct, the workmen's village, or the priests' quarter. The same kind-of order, with the same institutional nucleus, prevailed in New World centers such as Chichen-Itza, along with the pyramid temple. In the religious center at Xochicalco, A.D. ninth to tenth century, [lower] we find the classic components of the historic city: a sacred precinct on a steep hill, also fortified, linked to the religious nucleus by a paved way, lined with walls: probably surrounded by a group of villages and feudal estates that, here as in Egypt, have left no traces. The political, scientific, and religious components of the city, its civilizing inheritance, were transmitted by this cultural nucleus. This general pattern prevailed with minor variations at every place and period. Permanence, continuity, accumulation here take architectural form.

[Upper] Pyramid of King Neterkhet-Zoser, c. 2700 B.C. from 'Fouilles à Saqqarah' Tome II, by Jean Philippe Laver. [Lower] Xochicalco, Mexico. Photograph: Campañia Mexicana Aerofoto, S. A.

3 : MONUMENTAL SCALE

From the fourth millennium onward, magnification of power and personality went hand in hand, creating a wider horizon of effort in technics, and a new scale of expression in art. Monumentalism springs out of the same concentration of social and economic and religious effort that created the city, as the container for a complex civilization, distinguished from the homely country town, its simpler prototype, derived mainly from rural needs. Probably cosmic images of a heightened divine power preceded the institution of absolute rulership: a god, for example, had the title of 'Ruler of the Four Quarters' before an Akkadian king, Naram-Sin, adopted it. The magnification of Amenophis III in the mortuary temple at Luxor —note the human figure in the middle—has its parallel in our time in the more ephemeral posters that puffed up the photographic image of a Hitler or a Stalin: attempts to suggest divine proportions sufficient to conceal merely human frailty, fallibility, or mortality. (Contrast these inflated monuments and inscriptions with those on fifth century Greek tombstones, cut to the human measure.) Ramses II defaced these figures and substituted his own name, setting a precedent in the re-writing of history still faithfully followed by the totalitarian regimes of our own day.

Identification: Statues at Luxor. Photograph: Ewing Galloway, New York.

4 : TOMB-ORIENTED CITIES

"Each pharaoh took up residence near the site chosen for his tomb, where, during the best part of his lifetime, the work on the pyramid and its temple continued, while government functioned in the neighboring city.

But after his death the place was abandoned to the priests and officials who maintained his cult and managed his mortuary estate, unless the new king decided to continue in residence because the adjoining desert offered a suitable site for his own tomb. Until the middle of the second millennium B.C. *(when Thebes assumed a metropolitan character) there was no truly permanent capital in Egypt." Thus Henri Frankfort. These royal tomb cities were thus the earliest form of permanent 'Residenzstadt,' like Versailles or Karlsruhe; but this does not mean that they were without neighboring workshops, markets, or shipping facilities: the numerous priesthood alone guaranteed a large body of consumers, who required goods and services near at hand. Religious cult centers like Memphis and Abydos, the royal burial centers like many-tombed Thebes had a continued existence. The more secular part of the town probably showed a similar kind of spatial order, expressed in buildings of more modest scale. The white limestone temple of Queen Hatshepsut at Thebes (1520-1480* B.C.*), a kind of inverted acropolis beneath the cliff, was built when Pyramids were long out of fashion. The royal architect, Senmout, gave this temple an almost Hellenic serenity and austerity in both form and layout. Built on a series of retreating terraces, invisible on the photograph, the buildings form open quadrangles that mark a departure from the enclosed and heavily occupied space of the orthodox temples: an early mutation that apparently was not copied. Note the great temple and mortuary chapel at Thebes [upper]: a religious precinct dedicated to the main business of life: preparation for death and insurance of immortality by every device of mimicry and magic. The obelisk, over 97 feet high, was one of two cut as single stones in seven months, transported by water, and erected after the surrounding building was built. The functions and powers of the Egyptian city intersected not at the marketplace but at the tomb and the temple.*

[Upper] Temple and mortuary chapel at Karnak. [Lower] Queen Hatshepsut's temple at Der-el-Bahri. For fuller description see J. H. Breasted's 'History of Egypt.' Photographs by G. E. Kidder Smith.

5 : ROYAL MAKERS AND BREAKERS

The Narmer palette celebrates the First Dynasty's success in unifying the 'Two Lands,' Upper and Lower Egypt, though country towns probably existed and Kingship had been established for hundreds, possibly thousands of years—elsewhere if not in the Nile Valley. On earlier carvings, the Hunters' palette and the ivory knife handle from Gebel el Arak show groups of hunters and warriors, Frankfort points out, engaged in a common task. But on the Narmer palette, as on the 'Scorpion' mace-

head, the king has displaced the co-operative group. He alone opens a canal or conquers a city. On the reverse of the Narmer palette, shown here [left] the king wields a mace and subdues his enemy: on the obverse side his beheaded victims, perhaps the kings of the conquered regions, attest his prowess. The tiny rectangular figure [bottom left] seems to represent either a citadel or a city, for it is of the same order as the cities on the Cairo palette (early dynastic) exhibited next to the copy of the Narmer palette in the Metropolitan Museum of Art. If kings were not the sole builders of cities, the bottom of the obverse side leaves no doubt that they were the appointed destroyers of cities. Here the king, in the form of a bull, tramples open a walled city. Though Egyptologists usually call such walled structures forts, attributing to them the functions of the specialized military strongholds in the Middle Kingdom, there is good reason for supposing they were cities, all the more because they correspond in shape to the original round hieroglyph for city. The circular enclosure was possibly an early (maternal) neolithic form, antedating the rectangular (male-oriented) divisions of plowed fields. The wall on the Narmer palette is the same type one finds some three thousand years later in the painting of the Flight of Icarus in Pompeii. Here is succinct, if over-condensed, testimony to the relation of kingship to war and urban control.

Narmer Palette. [Left] Reverse. [Right] Obverse. From 'Birth of Civilization in the Near East,' by Henri Frankfort. Courtesy of the Indiana University Press.

6: THE TRAUMA OF CIVILIZATION

With the rise of kingship, organized violence became the supreme art of cities: all the more because the many internal frustrations and anxieties arising in a complex community stimulated aggressions that could be turned against the 'Enemy,' that is the Outsider. When the city becomes visible in Mesopotamian art it is already fully formed, both as 'Kulturstadt' and 'Polizeistadt,' largely dedicated to internal control and external domination. The relief presented here, one of a series of similar Assyrian monuments published by the Victorian archaeologist, Austen Henry Layard, reveals the aftermath of urban conquest: the triumphal procession, the unmanned chariots, the dead bodies floating in the river: one of a long series of carved slabs and columns depicting assaults on cities and the slaughter of their inhabitants. But the plan of the walled town is instructive: consider the protective river and canal, the rectangular layout, the heavy wall, the varied house types, the regular and irregular placement of buildings within: also the seemingly more important free-standing buildings outside the walls, surrounded by palm trees and doubtless gar-

dens: perhaps an upper class villa quarter or suburb, as in Egypt. The building on the raised mound outside the wall next to the gate has been interpreted as the storehouse, if not the market hall, of the port.

From A. H. Layard's 'The Monuments of Nineveh.'

7: CITY AND WORKING QUARTER

If the Narmer palette gives the first image of the city, the remarkable little Nippur tablet (c. 1500 B.C.) presents the first cartographic city plan so far unearthed. Here is Nippur, with its canals and the Euphrates itself, its walls and gates, its temple (Mountain House) and, on the outskirts, its lofty shrine—all apparently drawn to scale. The other side of urban work, the activities of regimented gangs of forced labor, digging canals and moats, and raising the mounds on which cities and temples were built, could be heavily illustrated from both Mesopotamian and Egyptian monuments. These outlines of the principal components of the town, as interpreted by Dr. S. N. Kramer, leave out only one essential feature, the citadel: perhaps to be explained by Nippur's eminence as a sacred cult center, or possibly by its destruction. Was the area that Kramer interprets as 'Central Park' originally a citadel which, by disuse, had been turned into a public pleasance, much like the Palatine Hill in Rome? The main picture, with the king seated on a throne within a conquered city's walls comes from Nineveh. Note the circular walls and buttresses. The big building is perhaps the palace, to which the captives with bound arms are brought. What is even more significant seems to be the representation of a workers' quarter with their equipment and varied occupations. Though Layard interpreted these workshops as tents, their method of construction may indicate that they were huts, covered with reeds, such as the traveller still finds in Basra. Whether tent or hut, camp or city, the space devoted to the crafts on such a memorial would indicate their importance in the urban economy.

[Inset] Map of Nippur from the Hilprecht Collection, at the Friedrich Schiller University, Jena. Interpretation by S. N. Kramer in 'History Begins at Sumer,' Appendix A. [Main view] Sennacherib within the walls of a conquered city, showing three houses and six huts or tents. Layard's 'The Monuments of Nineveh.' Plate 77. First series.

8: SACRED MOUNTAIN: DELPHI

Delphi was not only the navel of the Hellenic world but the activating civic nucleus that gave measure and order to its cities. Enthroned on a sacred mountain, Parnassus, Delphi is no miniature man-made reproduction. The primeval earth-cult, with its snakes and heady vapors and orac-

ular Pythoness have disappeared, but the earthquakes that once and again destroyed the temples are still a possibility. These dark forces of the earth and the human unconscious only accentuate the sanctity and peace that pervade the landscape, where the olive groves of Amphissa spread like a green lake running down to the sea. The three parts of the ancient community stand on three narrow shelves. In the middle, Apollo's temple and the theater of his fellow-god Dionysus: a sacred precinct surrounded by a rectangular wall. High above, the narrow stadium cut into the hillside, where the Pythian Games were held and where the boys of the village still play football. Below, the Castalian spring in the rocks, and the sacred way leading past the little 'Treasury' buildings, to the gymnasium, and terminating in the circular tholos. Here was the cultural core of the Greek city. Without the means to sustain a permanent population Delphi remained a ceremonial center, an object of pilgrimage, a place apart, which like Olympia, never became a full-fledged city.

[Upper Left] Theater of Dionysus, with remains of Apollo's temple at its foot. [Upper Right] The way down to the lowest level, with the Athenian 'Treasury.' [Lower] Lowest level, the tholos, shown not so much for the ruins as for the glimpse of the exalting scenery in which Delphi was set. Courtesy of the Museum at Delphi.

9 : ATHENIAN POWER AND FORM

With its Acropolis dominating the whole plain, yet safely distant from the sea, Athens is the archetypal Greek city. The Acropolis itself is a fortress rock, a true citadel, but also a 'temenos,' a precinct sacred to the gods, with its ancient burial pits and caves in the side of the hill, and many sacred shrines and memorials, now obliterated, whose existence accounts partly for the irregular placement of the buildings. The religious processions, winding up these heights, had the experience of earth and sky, the distant sea and the nearby city, as an accompaniment to their civic ritual. Their gods, if as capricious and inscrutable as their Mesopotamian predecessors, were more friendly: their easy relaxed postures in the panathenaic frieze tell as much. The beauty of the Parthenon, and more especially of that delicate frieze, has obscured the architectonic quality of the Acropolis as a whole. The esthetic effect of the topmost structures is heightened by the roughness of their rocky base, of powder-blue and rust-pink stone, and the sheer fortification walls. The whole is an eruption out of profound depths which finally cooled off into a few immense and perfect, highly colored crystals. The sharp ascent to the Propylaea [lower] emphasizes the monumentality of the buildings, by inducing a proper deliberation and humility in the ascending worshipper: a note well copied in the Lincoln Memorial in Washington. But the human *scale was preserved in fountains and stelae and gravestones, as delicately incisive in their carving as in their inscriptions.*

[Upper] The Acropolis, with Propylaea (left), the Parthenon (middle), and Mt. Lycabettus (right) in distance. [Lower] Entrance to Propylaea. Both photographs: Ewing Galloway.

10: ANCIENT WAYS, MODERN DAYS

Though one is not astounded to see the stone seats of the theater of Dionysus, on the southern slope of the Acropolis [top left] one feels almost closer to the fifth century city when one leans over the eastern parapet of the Acropolis [top right] and discovers such a huddle of one-story houses as one might have found there in the time of Solon or even Pericles. The view from the southeast side [middle right] showing the Acropolis in its role of a mighty citadel likewise takes one back in time —more so than the Choragic Monument, which one will find, displaced from its original setting on the Acropolis, in a little neighborhood park to the east below. As for the open pavilion [middle left] with its garden and its nearby stone church, on the road that leads up the Pnyx, it has a sixth century B.C. touch, simple and 'primitive' but finely proportioned, that reveals a contemporary mind deeply steeped in the ancient culture, but free from any temptation to imitate the inimitable. This group mingles the sacred and the secular, as in the ancient Agora. The cave [bottom left] recalls an older prototype of the chapel; while the open shop [bottom right], not far from the original Agora on the northwest side of the Acropolis, is the modern equivalent of those one encounters on Greek vases, though the new metal workers may be fashioning an aluminum pot. Such snatches of contemporary life reveal the continuity of the urban container better than the painstaking reconstruction of the Stoa of Attalos in the Agora; though that American contribution serves admirably as a museum, full of objects that bring the daily life near, from a clay sausage-griddle to a ceramic potty-seat with holes for the child's legs, and an Attic representation of a mother anxiously encouraging the seated infant. At the beginning of the nineteenth century this whole area was depopulated, but the original functions were often picked up again near the same spot, giving Athens almost as much continuity as Erbil or Damascus.

[Middle left] The buildings and the remarkable landscaping in this area are by Demetrius Pikionis. Here and in his design for a small recreation areas at Phylothei he sets a new standard of beauty for playgrounds, rivalled only by the work of Harry Sims Bent in Honolulu.

11: MILESIAN ORDER

For once one resorts to a model to illustrate the all-too-broken remains of the Greek city. Happily this type of plan loses little by such a presentation, though it would gain by the presence of human figures. Here is the wide avenue, the colonnaded street, the enclosed quadrangle, the open meeting place, and the buildings that appertained to them: the temple (Delphinion), and the gymnasium. This is the living prototype of the pallid, orderly Greece once beloved by the academic imagination. The public buildings of the city were no longer considered as independent entities bound up with historic or sacred sites; they became parts of unified architectural groups, forming esthetic wholes whose approach was controlled by equally regular streets: in a sense the frame superseded the picture. Such order, open and understandable almost at a glance, was doubtless helpful to the visitor and trader, who made up no small part of the daily population of such busy metropolises as Miletus.

[Upper] Delphinion and gymnasium. [Lower] Place before the Bouleuterion (Town Hall). From 'L'Urbanisme dans la Grèce Antique,' by Roland Martin. By courtesy of Editions A. & J. Picard & Cie.

12: CLASSIC CORE: POMPEII

Through its two great misfortunes, the second fatal—complete burial under volcanic ashes in A.D. 79—Pompeii has the distinction of being the only city in the ancient world preserved intact, with all its houses, streets, buildings, untouched by time, except where the careless curiosity of eighteenth century investigators opened them up indiscreetly and carried off fragments that might have better been preserved on the spot. About a third of the area, which totals 161 acres, still remains to be excavated. Pompeii, because it has been a relatively easy nut to crack, has been disparaged as a commonplace 'uninteresting' town. This is archaeological snobbism: actually Pompeii remains a living witness to the charm and glory of Greco-Roman town life in the first century A.D., all the better because of its varied origin (Oscans, Samnites, Greeks) and its many-sided life. What modern town of from twenty to thirty thousand people, can point to as well-ordered a group of public buildings around such a comely forum; as many handsome examples of bath, theater, odeon, arena, gymnasium, or generally, as rich an investment in the common life? Ostia, the seaport of Rome, now at last reveals many of the same advantages: so one must regard Pompeii's admirable features as quite typical of the smaller municipalities, though Ostia's 'Garden Apartments,' like Hercu-

laneum's more cramped workers' quarters, show that Pompeii's spaciousness was perhaps due to its high general level of prosperity as a regional
center. As in other Latin cities, the central nucleus was the Forum, whose
dimensions in Pompeii were 466 by 124 feet. Barred to wheeled traffic,
as the bollards show, entered through archways, the Forum formed a pedestrian mall around which the law courts, the temples, and the public
market were concentrated. Within this area was the maximum provision
for civic meeting and association. From the Avenue of Tombs, which
marks one approach, to the Tower of Mercurio set in the wall, from the
suburban villas on the outskirts—such as the House of Mysteries—to the
varied biuldings and open spaces within, one gets a clear impression of
Roman city design at its best and fullest.

[Upper and Lower] Views of Forum from above showing Temple of Jupiter at near
end. From 'Pompeii,' by Amedeo Maiuri. By courtesy of the Istituto Geografico de
Agostinie, Novara.

13: POMPEIIAN DAILY LIFE

Pompeii's ruins preserve many of the intimacies of its workaday life: not
least the signs and advertisements and adolescent scrawls on its smooth
inviting walls [upper left] particularly in the business street known as
the Street of Abundance. Here we find election advertisements of candi-
dates for public office, messages between sweethearts, bits of local gossip, quotations from Virgil and Propertius: some 15,000 items in all; and
these are supplemented by shop signs which picture the actual work of
the craftsmen. Helen Tanzer's 'Common People of Pompeii' draws heavily
on these grafitti for evidence. For the first time one has a full picture of
the workaday occupations and the quarters in which they were carried
on—sometimes in old residences made over, when the population grew,
into a fulling mill, a bakery, [upper right] or a cookshop, with the owner
living at the rear or on the upper floor. Note one of the narrow streets
[lower left] meant for human and animal burden-bearers, with its raised
sidewalks and its stepping stones for pedestrians, its fountain, its heavy
stone paving—which on the wider wagon ways was grooved for, or by,
vehicles. While Pompeii exhibits many classic town houses, each with its
spacious inner court (the atrium), its fountains, statues, and wall paintings, not the least interesting house is this modest brothel [lower right]
with overhanging second story, often represented, with a sniggering whis-
per, as filled with obscene pictures 'For Men Only.' Actually, the only
decorations for the little cubicles with their stony beds are small plaques
above the doorways chastely illustrating the classic positions for sexual
intercourse: somewhat superfluous, but charming. Like Pompeiian wall

paintings generally, these plaques testify to a certain delicacy and refinement of taste that mark the period and the province.

[Upper Right] Photograph: Ewing Galloway.

14: POMPEII AND PAVIA

Pompeii was in existence in the seventh century—indeed some recently unearthed prehistoric burial vaults in the hillside point to much earlier settlement—when the Greeks began to colonize southern Italy. At some point in Pompeii's growth its more orderly layout in rectangular blocks must have been ordained, possibly after the Roman victory over the Samnites. Deviations in the street plan, in width, in direction, or in both, as in the via dell'Abondanza, suggest a slow organic growth. The oblong blocks are 310 or 380 feet long by 110 feet wide, the square blocks are 200 feet each way. Note that the public places and buildings (the forum and theater) are correctly placed at one side of the arteries. When the Romans began to build colonial towns, they extended their rectangular order to the surrounding countryside, by introducing the system of 'centuriation,' similar to the nineteenth century American system of sections and quarter-sections. The basic unit was the heredium, 1.25 acres; and a hundred heredia made a centuria. This produced a typical geometric pattern in the landscape, still visible from the air today. True colonial towns, which were planned as complete units, show a stricter order, as the ruins of Timgad witness. Substantially, all the elements of the Roman plan, with small square blocks, are still visible in Pavia: note the characteristic crossing of cardo and decumannus. The main bridge across the Ticino, shown here, is on the site of the original Roman bridge, leading to the main artery: and the present population of the town, c. 50,000, touches the upper limit of the old colonization towns. The fact that this is still essentially the same town shown in a print of 1599—but for the partial building over of the big piazza on the site of the old Forum—enabled Pavia, like many other small European cities, to keep the railroad station and yards at a distance from its built up area. The marvellous vigor and continuity of this little town contrasts favorably with overgrown and disintegrated Rome. Pavia marks a signal victory for Howard's principle of planned dispersal in small urban centers.

[Upper] Pompeii from the air in the 1930's. Official Photograph by courtesy of Italian Air Ministry. [Lower] Pavia. British Crown Copyright Reserved.

15: TEMPLE AND SUPERMARKET

The Pantheon [upper] the finest single monument Rome has left, symbolizes the power and aspiration of Rome at its best. The interior, with its dome open to the sky, conjures a depth of religious feeling that turns St. Peter's into a monument of spectacular vulgarity, unredeemed by the Sistine Chapel. Here the gods from the countries and cities Rome conquered were placed on view: in its day, a sort of living museum of comparative religions, some of which, like the cult of Isis and Serapis, or the Mithraic religion of salvation, proved more attractive than Rome's gods, before Christianity swept them away. The Market of Trajan [lower], with its concentration of shops on three levels, vies with any American supermarket today, though the layout of the shops on the top terrace [right] would indicate more diversified individual proprietorship. Since Roman customers were seemingly as undaunted by stairs as Italians still are, Trajan's market is a miracle of compact planning. Both the Pantheon and the market bridged the gap between ancient and medieval Rome, the first becoming a Christian Church, as it still is, the second being occupied for residence, as the houses above the market testify. This 'making do' by using the old structures almost unaltered for new needs and purposes eased the poverty and sordor of the transitional period between the fifth and the tenth, or in Rome's case, the fifteenth century. Meanwhile, the Rome of the Republic and the Rome of the Caesars left behind ghosts that not merely stalked through the ruins but rattled their chains in many distant cities where Roman power had once been felt. Wherever centralized power and order coalesced in the West, some image of the imperial Roman style has usually accompanied them, even in areas as remote as New Delhi.

[Upper] The Pantheon. Photograph by G. E. Kidder Smith. [Lower] Market of Trajan, across from the Forum Romanum, as seen from below and above. The form of the open shops still visible along the via Biberatica was carried into the Middle Ages.

16 : CROWD CONTAINERS

By bringing together a view of the Roman Colosseum [lower] and one of the theater and amphitheater area at Arles [upper], one has with half-closed eyes a synthetic image equivalent to what an eagle might have commanded over third century Rome. The amphitheaters were sufficiently big and sufficiently numerous to hold, along with arenas and stage theaters and baths, the greater part of the population of the city: more than can be said of even the most extravagant supply of such buildings today. Those who occupied the upper tiers of the circus had not merely a breathtaking climb but a dizzy sense of distance when they reached the top. Rome after Julius Caesar was not encumbered by wheeled vehicles in the daytime, but the residential areas within the Aurelian Wall were within walking distance. The assemblage and dispersal of the attendant crowds,

*though doubtless slow, was not as tedious as the exit from such struc-
tures is today, by way of the parking lot and the fictitiously rapid motorway whose speed decreases directly with density of land use and the immediate load. The coming back of these amphitheaters and stadiums into
the modern city signifies not merely the revival of athletics, but of more
brutalized forms of sport, in partial compensation for the emasculated,
over-regimented existence of the metropolitan economy.*

in Egyptian civilization: even after it encountered periods of social disruption, it did so only to return to the same institutions under the same
religious and political leadership it had known in its formative period.
Under such conditions, the city itself naturally took a different form, more
open, more widely diffused: essentially it was a ceremonial center, a
complex of palace, temple, shrine, probably unwalled in a military sense,
though perhaps symbolically enclosed, and surrounded by a group of
villages. This would not be very different from the ancient Maya ceremonial and governmental centers. And only if one treated the dense occupation of a limited walled area as the critical mark of the early city, could
one withhold from this open urban formation the title of city.

Now it is precisely the overparticularized definition of the city that one
must sharply call in question: congestion, large numbers, an encircling
wall are accidental characters of the city, not essential ones, though the
growth of warfare did in fact turn them into dominant and persistent
urban features almost down to the present age. The city is not so much a
mass of structures as a complex of inter-related and constantly interacting
functions—not alone a concentration of power, but polarization of culture.

As Morley remarks of Landa's account of a new empire settlement
among the Maya, it is clear that "he is describing a town, even in the
modern sense of the word. Two important differences, however, must be
admitted: first, Maya centers of population were not so concentrated, not
so densely packed into congested blocks as our modern cities and towns.
On the contrary, they were scattered over extensive, more lightly inhabited
suburbs, fringing out into continuous small forms—a suburban, as contrasted to a closely concentrated urban type of occupation. Second, the
assemblages of public buildings, temples, sanctuaries, palaces, pyramids,
monasteries, ball courts, observatories, dance platforms were not usually
disposed along streets and avenues. . . . Instead the buildings were erected
around the sides of courts and plazas which were religious precincts, governmental and trading sections of the city." With this broader interpretation
of the city I am in full agreement; the social core is more significant than
any particular physical manifestation, for here ideal human purposes prevail over the preparatory agents and means.

Yet at a later period in their development, the kind of enclosure that
took place in the Mesopotamian city seems to have taken place among both
the Egyptians and the Maya, for the same reason. Pedro Armillas has
pointed out that the crisis that seems to have developed in Meso-American
society around A.D. 900 resulted in a change from a theocratic pattern to
a secular-militaristic one, "in which religion was still a powerful force of
social control, but the priesthood was in a subordinate position of temporal power, and there was a correlative change in the settlement pattern."
Before this crisis almost all known sites were on open ground, with no

natural and seemingly no artificial means of defense. This would account for the existence of a functional 'city' on a more porous open pattern, with a larger place for the village, and with a more pacific and presumably co-operative way of life.

A good four thousand years and an equivalent stretch of miles separate the Mayan cities from the early dynastic Egyptian. Only one vital connection between their forms can as yet be established. Both first flourished under a secure political order in which war was absent, or almost absent, where force was minimized, and the monopoly of sacred power and sacred knowledge by the ruling classes, the many-privileged nobles and priests, was accepted without serious contention over a long period. Under these circumstances the citadel minority had no need for protection against the neighboring villages: populous, potentially stronger, but submissive. Had these conditions been universal, the open city might always have been the dominant type: open, but still, in its cohesions and interactions, in its emergent potencies and creativities, a true city.

So much for the genesis of the Egyptian city. All the essential elements brought into operation by civilization were present from the beginning: but they were at first held together, perhaps, not by separately established urban walls, but by the common natural walls about the whole country, as they were polarized, not only by the many local deities and shrines, but by the single presence of the Divine Pharaoh, in a kind of political monotheism that preceded any theological creed of the same nature. In short, the magnet was more important than the container, because the religious assumption was more persuasive, in contrast to the secular pressures and coercions of Sumer and Akkad. This might be accompanied not only by a freedom from neurotic anxiety, but by a letdown in psychological tension. In that sense of general relaxation, in that diminution of ambitious drive, the early Egyptian city might even be called suburban; or it might be more correct, as well as more charitable, to say that it preserved, despite its immense physical magnifications, the pious conformities and warm life-sense of the village.

In time the more typical forms of the city made their appearance in Egypt, and probably Pierre Lavedan is correct in thinking that the same regularity of plan and the same orientation to the points of the compass of its main streets characterized the secular city as in the austere cities of the dead, like those at Gizeh and Saqqarah. The gridiron plan such as we find in Tell-el-Amarna and Kahun is, if anything, a negative adaptation to the climate: with the wide streets of Tell-el-Amarna—the Street of the Grand Priest, probably a major processional way, was 180 feet wide —there was maximum exposure to the torrid sun.

But if religion was one of the motives for this inflexible kind of order, there was still another more practical reason that would be repeated again in the Greek and Roman colonization towns, in the medieval bastides, and in the American pioneer towns: speed and mechanization. Alexandre Moret has even discovered a 'New Towns' policy with charters of privilege in the Ancient Empire. City building under the Pharaohs was a swift, one-stage operation: a simple geometric plan was a condition for rapid building, all the more because the main settlements, if not the citadels, were on level land. More organic plans, representing the slowly developing needs and decisions of many generations, require time to achieve their more subtle and complex richness of form.

There may have been a different order of planning in the old country towns that still dotted the administrative area called the nome, the equivalent of the English county, with its villages, its small towns, its governmental capital, where the tax collector and the local governor and judge held forth. Possibly such government capitals were relics of the feudal strongholds whose growth accompanied the dispersal of centralized authority around 2625 B.C., after the reign of Unis: but in some cases they may have been new centers specially built for administration. Childe's suggestion that the nome largely takes the place of the city in Egypt cannot be dismissed: this open township pattern, familiar in New England, is perhaps the symbiotic version of the city: a viable alternative to the predatory type that came in with war and walled enclosures. There may thus have been different degrees of order and regularity in Egyptian cities, even as there were surely different degrees of monumental magnificence. But whatever disagreement remains between Egyptologists as to the origin and nature of the Egyptian city, it seems to me plain that all the elements for the urban implosion were present and that the city, in one form or another, performed its special function—that of a complex receptacle for maximizing the possibilities of human intercourse and passing on the contents of civilization.

By the Nineteenth Dynasty (1350-1200 B.C.) the lack of archaeological material need not bother us; for there is no doubt about the existence of the city. Even as late as this, however, it still exhales an earthy fragrance that bears witness to its flourishing rural background. Consider the eulogy of the city of Ramses:

"I have reached Per-Ramses and have found it in very good condition, a beautiful district, without its like, after the pattern of Thebes. It was [Re] himself [who founded it].

"The residence is pleasant in life; its field is full of everything good; it is [full] of supplies and food every day, its ponds with fish, its lakes with birds. Its meadows are verdant with grass; its banks bear dates; its melons are abundant on the sands. . . . Its granaries are [so] full of barley and emmer [that] they come near to the sky. Onions and leeks are *for food*, and lettuce of the garden, pomegranates, apples, and olives, figs of the orchard, sweet wine of *Ka*—of Egypt, surpassing honey, red *wedj*-fish of the canal of the Residence City, which live on Lotus flowers, bedin-fish of the Hari waters. . . . One rejoices to dwell within it, and there is none who says: 'Would that!' to it. The small in it are like the great."

This says nothing about the form of the city and very little about the social contents, except that they point to at least the possibility of a high level of well-being and contentment, not unrelated to the very religious homogeneity that perhaps explains both the incomparable success of the Egyptian state and the peculiar form of the Egyptian city. All this re-enforces Frankfort, in his emphasis that "all were commoners before the throne." So even in the city, the existence of a hierarchical division of classes and functions, from which many of the structural differentiations of the city derived, did not keep the small from at least feeling like the great, and perhaps even registering their personal approbation of that very greatness.

To sum up: Probably, the walled town made its appearance in Egypt before the dynastic centralization of power; but there may well have been a long period, a Pax Egyptiana, that relaxed both the internal tensions and the need for external protection. When the walled city came back again, it was more of an agent of common defense against foreign invaders than a means of making local coercion effective. But from the Hyksos inter-regnum onward, much of what we have learned about Mesopotamian cities would apply, with modifications, to Egypt, even as it applied to other towns from Palestine to the Iranian highlands and beyond. The picture presented by the cities of the Indus Valley shows the inflexible order and regimentation that was one of the indices of the urban implosion, with its overemphasis of control. If we knew more of the details, we should perhaps be aware of many enlivening inner and outer differences, such as the archaeologist detects in the towns built on irregular sites—notably Assur, the old capital of Assyria, or the Hittite capital of Boghaz-Keui, where the planners, instead of blindly keeping to an abstract scheme, boldly utilized the terrain to create a silhouette that was probably not less striking than that of medieval Durham in England.

When we have allowed for many variations and departures, one larger fact nevertheless begins to emerge: two contrasting archetypal patterns of urban life seem to have been formed in the great river valleys of the Near East. One expressed calmness and confidence, the other tempestuous uncertainty; one, beset with danger and anxiety, piled up the symbols of power and fortified itself with heavy walls to keep off those who "were planning evil": the other, trusting in the beneficence of the sun and Father Nile, knowing that one year would be like the next, imposed order in the name of justice and enthroned death in the gay garments of life. In one, the citadel formed the hard kernel of power that, by its very explosion, destroyed itself as well as its object: in the other, the organic rituals of the village tempered and humanized all the new forces that were at the disposal of civilization: in that city, the Eloquent Peasant would still be heard. These polar contrasts, under new masks, are still in existence.

Thus at the very beginning the urban heritage bifurcated; and the differences between the two great valley systems remain visible, though often disguised, throughout urban history. Two ways were in fact open for the development of human culture, once it had passed beyond the stage reached in the neolithic community—the way of the village or the way of the citadel: or, to speak in biological terms, the symbiotic and the predatory. They were not absolute choices, but they pointed in different directions. The first was the path of voluntary co-operation, mutual accommodation, wider communication and understanding: its outcome would be an organic association, of a more complex nature, on a higher level than that offered by the village community and its nearby lands. The other was that of predatory domination, leading to heartless exploitation and eventually to parasitic enfeeblement: the way of expansion, with its violence, its conflicts, its anxieties, turning the city itself into an instrument, as Childe properly observes, for the "extraction and concentration of the surplus." This second form has largely dominated urban history till our own age, and it accounts in no small degree for the enclosure and collapse of one civilization after another.

Now, there were large elements of coercion even in the most gentle moments of the Egyptian rule, and there were many joyful expressions of human co-operation and intellectual and emotional enrichment even under the most ruthless of totalitarian monarchs in Mesopotamia. In both cases, many of the higher functions of the city were promoted and enlarged. Neither Egyptian nor Mesopotamian form, then, was pure; for the more co-operative kind of local grouping had features that raised disturbing parallels with insect societies in their tendency to fixation and self-stultification; while in the communities most lamed by neurotic anxieties and irrational aggressive compulsions, there was nevertheless a sufficient cultivation of the more positive aspects of life to create a system of law and order, with reciprocal obligations, and to develop some degree of morality for insiders, even though a growing number of these insiders were slaves, captured in war, or remained the cowed inhabitants of villages compelled under threat of starvation to labor like slaves. So much for the forces that in the early stages of civilization brought the city into existence. We shall soon make a provisional appraisal of the cultural results.

9: ARCHETYPES OR GENES?

By 2500 B.C. all the essential features of the city had taken form, and had found a place for themselves in the citadel, if not in the whole urban community. The walled enclosure, the street, the house-block, the market, the temple precinct with its inner courts, the administrative precinct, the workshop precinct—all these existed in at least rudimentary form; and the city itself, as a complex and powerful esthetic symbol, magnifying and enriching human potentiality, was visible. The durability of these institutions and forms is almost as striking as the wide range of variations to which they have lent themselves.

Even on the other side of the world, among the Mayas, the Peruvians, and the Aztecs, we find, in pre-Columbian times, similar institutions and habits of life, embodied in similar structures, associated with similar myths, ideologies, scientific observations, ceremonies, customs, even similar psychological stresses and torments. Since it was long held that the immigration into the New World ceased some ten or twelve thousand years ago, this similarity raises an important question. Is the city a natural habitation, like a snail's shell, or a deliberate human artifact, a specific invention that came into existence at one or more places under the influence of urban ideological convictions and economic pressures? An aboriginal predisposition toward social life, even toward group settlement, may well characterize the human species; but could such a general tendency make man everywhere produce the city as inevitably as a spider produces her web? Could the same dispositions that gave the camp or the hamlet a planetary distribution likewise account for such a many-faceted cultural complex as the city?

If one hold to the isolationist premises of the older generation of American anthropologists and archaeologists, one must treat the forms of Mayan, Aztec, and Peruvian cultures as a completely independent invention of the New World. This is possible, but there are many facts that keep it from being wholly plausible. If cultures were in fact as different as biological species, these resemblances might be as unrelated as the no less striking resemblances between the termitary and the anthill. But what one finds in the New World is not just a collection of houses and buildings, which might have had the same common ancestor in the mesolithic hamlet. One discovers, rather, a parallel collection of cultural traits: highly developed fertility ceremonies, a pantheon of cosmic deities, a magnified ruler and central authority who personifies the whole community, great temples whose forms recall such functionally different structures as the pyramid and the ziggurat, along with the same domination of a peasantry by an original hunter-warrior group, or (among the early Mayas) an even more ancient priesthood. Likewise the same division of castes and specialization of vocational groups, and the beginnings of writing, time-measuring, and the calendar—including an immense extension of time perspectives among the Mayas, which surpasses in complexity and accuracy even what we know of the cosmic periods of the Babylonians and the Egyptians. These traits seem too specific to have been spontaneously repeated in a whole constellation.

Admittedly, there are many contrasts between the cities of Sumer and Egypt and those of the Mayas a millennium or two later, as there are, for that matter, between those of Peru and Mexico. But these differences are precisely what one would expect in cultures remote in space and time, connected only through a passage of ideas borne by traders, explorers, even religious missionaries, rather than by any wholesale immigration or invasion in force. The vehicles of this passage, boats and even islands, may well have sunk out of sight long before the ideas themselves reached the New World. If the cultural dispersion began very early, it might well have included the archetypal form of the pyramid or ziggurat, but not the plow or the wheel: it might bring the memory of the city without transporting the ox or the ass. If Mesopotamian writing prompted the Egyptians to develop writing, as many archaeologists believe, the form of the Egyptian hieroglyphs is no farther removed from its immediate exemplar than Mayan signs are from either. Thus one may account for the many differences between Egyptian, Sumerian, Indian, Chinese, Cambodian, Mayan, Peruvian, and Aztec urban centers, without denying their underlying similarities, and without setting any arbitrary barrier, not even the Pacific Ocean, against the possibility of their slow diffusion from a few points. That the pyramid form would be used as a tomb and would represent the mountain of creation among the Egyptians, and would be transformed into a temple for collective religious ceremonies among the Mayas and the Aztecs, is no more implausible than the transformation of the gridiron street system from an original Etruscan symbol of cosmic order to a convenient pattern for creating American pioneer towns—or speculating in real estate.

Was this New World urban complex due to an original predisposition toward urban life carried in the genes? Or is it an instance of a Jungian collective archetype, transmitted even more mysteriously? Or is the New World urban complex the result of an astonishing conspiracy of accidents whose ultimate convergence with those of the Old World would be nothing short of a miracle? Would it not be more sensible, now that the mobility of early peoples, even on the sea, is becoming apparent, to admit that the idea of the city may have reached the New World from afar, though the route cannot be traced and more positive evidence will possibly always be lacking. Unfortunately, the old diffusionists, like G. Elliott Smith, who jumped too quickly at an answer, cast discredit on the question. But the problem remains; for both isolation and diffusion are anthropological facts:

likewise some inventions are unique, and some are widespread and independently repetitive.

If the city were in fact bound to come into existence when certain natural and economic conditions favored close human settlement, the existence of the city in the New World raises, as V. Gordon Childe was frank enough to admit, a serious problem. For the fact is that most of these favoring external conditions seem conspicuously absent. The New World cities arose, not in the great river valleys of the Amazon, the Plata, or the Mississippi, but in relatively unfavorable spots, poor in natural means of communication and transport, and they required a maximum human effort, in jungle clearing or in soil building, to provide their own food—in contrast to the relatively easy life of the grain growers and the palm cultivators in the Old World. The great roads between the Mayan and the Peruvian cities could not exist until a central authority had established the collective organization capable of building them. Even in their most flourishing periods, the Meso-American cities rested on an unstable system of tropical agriculture, largely dependent upon a single grain, maize: this system relied on shifting the cultivation patches and burning the quick undergrowth on the exhausted land for soil replenishment. There was no pressure toward centralized organization from the need to control floods or plan irrigation systems. Without metal tools, draught animals, the wheel, or the plow, this culture lacked most of the technological facilities for the first urban implosion. As far as natural conditions favored anything, they favored the isolated village, small, primitive, and shiftable.

But if the economic foundations of the New World city were inadequate, and the geographic pressures were absent, its formative ideal nucleus was present: purpose over-rode function. Right into recent historic times, one finds evidence of the fusion of temporal and sacred powers that accompanied the emergence of the city in the Old World. The very lack of a favorable environment and of technological improvements only makes the ideal pattern itself more striking—and more difficult to account for as a 'natural' growth under circumstances closely similar to those we find in the Near East. Significantly the necessary cultural conditions were present: a skyward orientation of religion, the recognition of the prevailing power of the sun, and the concentration of that power in the person of a king, toward whom the life of the whole community was focussed. The political and intellectual achievements, including the rigorous mathematical calculations and time-sense of the Mayas, sufficed to bring a new order, based on cosmic perspectives, into existence; and out of that concentrated energy of mind the city itself took form, from Tenochtitlan to Chichen-Itza. Was this mobilization and magnification of power original or derivative? On the basis of the existing evidence, one cannot answer; but one should, I believe, keep an open mind.

Plainly, these are only hints and speculations: the data do not even faintly indicate the actual process whereby the image of the city and the purpose of its institutions were carried to the New World—or if in fact this occurred. But the circumstantial evidence casts at least a shadow of doubt over the likelihood of an entirely independent invention of this highly complex organism at a date much later than that when the cities of Mesopotamia and the Indus Valley took form. After the city was successfully established as both a permanent container and an institutional structure, capable of storing and handing on the contents of civilization, it might (as an image) travel far, and detached fragments of its culture, transmitted mainly by living people, might take root in soil too arid to have brought to maturity the first urban mutants. Eventually cities would be established in geographic areas as unfavorable as Tibet, Iceland, and the High Andes.

Once established, the physical structures, even the general pattern of the city, might be copied by groups that resisted this or that feature of its institutional structure. Thus granules of urban life, amorphous collections of buildings and streets, reproducing only the barest externals of a city, its huddled shelters and its market, would spread everywhere, often lacking in their random assemblage the social facilities of even a village. These urban granules have been multiplying and coalescing with great rapidity in our time; but however big the ultimate mass, it is only by a stretch of meaning that one may call them cities: they are rather urbanized conglomerations. To define the city one must look for its organizing nucleus, trace its boundaries, follow its social lines of force, establish its subsidiary centers for association and communication, and analyze the differentiation and integration of its groups and institutions. While the city brought together and welded into a visible unity village, shrine, stronghold, workplace and market, its character altered from region to region, from age to age, as one or another component dominated and colored the rest. But always, as in a living cell, the organizing nucleus was essential to direct the growth and the organic differentiation of the whole.

At every stage, then, one must distinguish the close grouping of urban structures, with a mere thickening of population, from the complex dynamic organization of the city, in which old structures and functions served new purposes. In many ways the simpler kind of town or suburb has, like the village, many of the potentialities of the city. Yet one must remember Rousseau's definition: "Houses make a town, but citizens make a city." The ability to transmit in symbolic forms and human patterns a representative portion of a culture is the great mark of the city: this is the condition for encouraging the fullest expression of human capacities and potentialities, even in the rural and primitive areas beyond. In making this possible, the early builders of the city indeed builded better than they knew.

CHAPTER FOUR

The Nature of the Ancient City

1: DEVELOPMENT OF URBAN FUNCTIONS

We may no longer imagine that the physical structure of the city was—any more than its ancient cultural fibers—the product of an altogether sudden growth. This supposition, natural when only the ruins of Babylonia were in view, has been upset by the discovery of a walled town, with a sanctuary, and a singularly subtle type of portrait art, in one of the lowest strata in Jericho: many millennia before any known remains elsewhere. The diggings disclose the presence of great cisterns to ensure a continuous water supply, still giving one thousand gallons a minute. The earliest houses uncovered have rooms whose round shapes point to the early 'matriarchal' accompaniments of domestication.

There seems a strong possibility that a great part of the physical shell antedated the institution of kingship: it is significant that the word 'Lugal' (Big Man, King) has not been found in the proto-literate texts. Yet the shift of emphasis, from chieftain to king, like the shift from hoe to plow culture, may have gone on for a long while before the fully dimensioned city finally leaped forth. This final act of formal organization might have occurred within as narrow a span of time as brought about the evolution of the Egyptian pyramid tomb. But once the institutional structures of the city had crystallized, the ideal or archetypal form of the city underwent surprisingly few alterations. Beginning as a concentration of manpower under a firm, unified, self-reliant leadership, the ancestral city was primarily an instrument for regimenting men and mastering nature, directing the community itself to the service of the gods.

That divine object sanctified every sacrifice, counteracted every abnegation. All the higher institutions that the city fostered rested on this original base; and the same principles of leadership were applied in turn to other institutions. Witness the objurgation of the Eloquent Peasant, faced with injustice: "Behold thou art a town which has no mayor, like a company which has no chief, like a ship in which there is no pilot, a confederacy which has no leader." Concentrated personal responsibility, with an accompanying freedom of action, was one of the necessary devices of government in complex communities that kingship passed on to the city. Yet beneath this organization there fortunately persisted, even within the most centralized city government, an older body of custom, based on ancestral pieties, democratic participation, mutual aid, all carried over from the more ancient village.

In making a tally of the city's activities, one must distinguish between two aspects: the common human functions, performed everywhere, but sometimes greatly aided and enriched by the constitution of the city, and the special urban functions, the product of its historic affiliations and its unique complex structure, performed only within the city. For the sake of keeping this second set of activities more clearly in mind, I would group them, mnemonically, as mobilization, mixture, and magnification. But out of these functions and processes arises a higher capacity for co-operation, and a widening of the area of communication and emotional communion; and from these emerge new purposes, no longer attached to the original needs that brought the city into existence.

Starting as a sacred spot, to which scattered groups returned periodically for ceremonials and rituals, the ancient city was first of all a permanent meeting place. The attractive, life-bestowing qualities of the city may have been immensely increased by the ability of the cities of Mesopotamia, set on their great mounds, to survive the floods that periodically obliterated the entire plain and with that the population of its villages: not Utnapishtim's ark, but the earliest cities, may have been, as Woolley suggests, the chief agents that ensured survival in one almost overwhelming catastrophe.

But fresh human opportunities as well as natural dangers drew people from farther regions toward the new urban settlements. Different racial stocks, different cultures, different technological traditions, different languages, came together and intermingled. At a very early period Delta men occupied places of authority in the White City of the Upper Nile. Everywhere the rise of the city seems accompanied by a deliberate effort to break down the isolation and self-sufficiency of the village. We have historic record in Greece of Cleisthenes' mixing of the men of the hills, the men of the plain, and the men of the coast. This mobilization and mixture may even have had special biological advantages, for in the city the dangers of breeding too long from a limited stock disappeared, and wide biological hybridization probably took place.

Though we can know too little about this extremely complex process to make even a limited assessment of its contribution, the analogies of plant and animal breeding suggest that the urban intermixture may have had a similar effect in producing happy variations: so that Flinders Petrie may have been right, in 'The Revolution of Civilizations,' in attributing partly to hybrid biological vigor some of the dynamic phenomena of civilization. Such conjectures are not open to proof.

But about the benefits of the cultural intermixture there can be less doubt: the city broke down the parsimonious self-sufficiency and dreamy narcissism of village culture. In bringing people from the most distant parts of the valley into the same milieu, the city gave continuity of meeting place to those who had lived a nomadic life, and it gave the challenge of 'outside' experiences to those who lived at home. The surplus population produced by these riverine communities in itself led to wider movements, nomadizing or colonizing, exploring or migrating—not seldom to mass population shifts by enslavement or conquest.

Thus what began mainly, it would seem, as a system of glorified servitude, imposed on domesticated agricultural groups that could not escape such control, became in time, at least partly, a responsive act of choice. Increasingly people sought out the city and became part of it by willing adoption and participation. Whereas one gains membership in a primary group like the village or clan solely by the accident of birth or marriage, the city, probably from the first, offered an opening to strangers and outsiders. But so strong was the impress of the village that the Greeks maintained for long the fiction that all the citizens of the city were in fact descendants of a common ancestor.

Arnold J. Toynbee's 'A Study of History' has given our generation a fresh insight into the role that 'encounters' and 'challenges' play in the development of a civilization no less than in that of an individual. But what is curiously lacking in his otherwise almost too-exhaustive essay is a realization of the fact that it is in the city—and only there, on an effective scale, with sufficient continuity—that these interactions and transactions, these proposals and responses, take place.

If early man had deliberately sought to break through the isolations and encystments of a too-stabilized community, set in its ways and reluctant to break into its happy routines, he could hardly have devised a better answer to that problem than the city. The very growth of the city depended on bringing in food, raw materials, skills, and men from other communities either by conquest or trade. In doing this the city multiplied the opportunities for psychological shock and stimulus.

For this reason the stranger, the outsider, the traveller, the trader, the refugee, the slave, yes, even the invading enemy, have had a special part in urban development at every stage. In the 'Odyssey,' Homer enumerates the strangers that even a simple community would "call from abroad"—

the "master of some craft, a prophet, a healer of disease, a builder or else a wondrous bard." In contrast to the original peasants and chiefs these are the new inhabitants of the city. Where they were lacking, the country town remained sunk in a somnolent provincialism.

For a great part of urban history, the functions of the container remained more important than those of the magnet; for the city was primarily a storehouse, a conservator and accumulator. It was by its command of these functions that the city served its ultimate function, that of transformer. Through its municipal utilities the kinetic energies of the community were channelled into storable symbolic forms. Society, as a succession of observers have noted, from Auguste Comte to W. M. Wheeler, is an 'accumulative activity': and the city became the essential organ of that process.

It is no accident that the emergence of the city as a self-contained unit, with all its historic organs fully differentiated and active, coincided with the development of the permanent record: with glyphs, ideograms, and script, with the first abstractions of number and verbal signs. By the time this happened, the amount of culture to be transmitted orally was beyond the capacity of a small group to achieve even in a long lifetime. It was no longer sufficient that the funded experience of the community should repose in the minds of the most aged members.

In daily transactions, the same need for permanent notations and signs was even more obvious: to act at a distance through agents and factors, to give commands and make contracts, some extra-personal device was needed. The earliest tablets from Ur are mere lists and tallies: they record amounts of flour, bread, beer, livestock, men's names, the gods and their temples—bare factual notations for enabling the community to keep track of quantities that might otherwise be uncertain or escape notice.

Fortunately, the control of such activities was at first largely in the hands of a priestly class, freed from the constant necessity of manual labor, and increasingly conscious of the mediating functions of mind. By progressive degrees of abstraction and symbolization, they were able to turn the written record into a device for preserving and transmitting ideas and feelings and emotions that had never taken any visible or material form.

By means of such records, the rulers of the city lived a multiple life: once in action, again in monuments and inscriptions, and still another time in the effect of the recorded events upon the minds of later people, furnishing them with models for imitation, warnings of danger, incentives to achievement. Living *by* the record and *for* the record became one of the great stigmata of urban existence: indeed life as recorded—with all its temptations to overdramatization, illusory inflation, and deliberate falsification—tended often to become more important than life as lived. Hence the perversions of monumentalism, ironically climaxed by the boasts of

Ozymandias. This tendency has been heightened in our own day in motion pictures, wherewith fictitious performances are staged, before or after the real event, in order to leave an 'accurate' record for posterity.

The development of symbolic methods of storage immensely increased the capacity of the city as a container: it not merely held together a larger body of people and institutions than any other kind of community, but it maintained and transmitted a larger portion of their lives than individual human memories could transmit by word of mouth. This condensation and storage, for the purpose of enlarging the boundaries of the community in time and space, is one of the singular functions performed by the city; and the degree to which it is performed partly establishes the rank and value of the city; for other municipal functions, however essential, are mainly accessory and preparatory. The city, as Emerson well observed, "lives by remembering."

Through its durable buildings and institutional structures and even more durable symbolic forms of literature and art, the city unites times past, times present, and times to come. Within the historic precincts of the city time clashes with time: time challenges time. Because the structures of the city outlast the functions and purposes that originally molded them, the city sometimes preserves for the future ideas that have been wantonly discarded or rejected by an earlier generation; but, on the debit side, it transmits to later generations maladaptations that might have been cast off, if they had not materialized in the city and left their imprint there— just as the body itself transmits as a scar or a recurrent rash some painful long-past injury or disorder. Our generation has a special obligation to re-examine that urban outcome in the worst of chronic injuries—war.

Doubtless it is in the nature of good containers not to be changed in composition by the reaction that goes on within them; for if containers altered as rapidly as their contents, both would disappear. Yet if the urban container were too rigorously selective it would lose one of its most important attributes, its social capaciousness, its facility for fulfilling life in many ways, lest, as the Victorian poet put it, "one good custom should corrupt the world."

Thus the urban jar that, figuratively speaking, first held Mesopotamian barley would also hold Athenian olives, Egyptian beer, or Roman sausages. Sometimes the urban form would crack and leak; repeatedly it would be dashed to the ground and broken, with its contents spilled, and irretrievably damaged. This repeated damage probably accounts for the relative poverty of mechanical invention, except in war, once the Bronze Age had dawned. But, at least up to the seventeenth century, the city endured, without any radical change of form: the mold in which the activities of 'civilized man' had cooled and congealed.

2 : MONOPOLY OF CREATIVITY

In terms of current psycho-social jargon, the city is a special receptacle for storing and transmitting messages. At the beginning all its creative offices were tied to religion, and the most significant messages were sacred ones. These sacred messages, written in the stars or the entrails of beasts, in dreams, hallucinations, prophecies, came within the special province of priesthood. For long they monopolized the creative powers, and the forms of the city expressed that monopoly.

Creativity is, by its nature, fitful and inconstant, easily upset by constraint, foreboding, insecurity, external pressure. Any great preoccupation with the problems of ensuring animal survival exhausts the energies and disturbs the receptivity of the sensitive mind. Such creativity as was first achieved in the city came about largely through an arrogation of the economic means of production and distribution by a small minority, attached to the temple and the palace. In the epic of creation Marduk remarks of man: "Let him be burdened with the toil of the gods that they may freely breathe." Shall we err greatly if we translate this as: "Let our subjects be burdened with daily toil that the king and the priesthood may freely breathe"?

Vast resources were pre-empted by this small group alone, for they considered themselves under no obligation to lift to their own level the life of the majority of peasants and craftsmen. First by assuming control over the sacred powers in the building of shrines and the elaboration of ritual, then by secreting the permanent record, or rather, the magic incantations, the mathematical notations, the scientific observations preserved by the record, the priesthood re-enforced royal authority backed otherwise merely by bureaucratic and military organization.

Many of the messages coded in the temple never got beyond the slot into which they were dropped: some of this knowledge, which included the properties of sedatives and anesthetics, was probably lost more than once because of the very secrecy employed in transmitting it; while the repeated destruction of temples in warfare did far worse damage than merely defacing or obliterating great works of art. As a result of this combination of secrecy in peace and destructiveness in war, a large part of the achievements of the new urban community were wantonly squandered, and an even greater part of its potential was never developed.

If anything proves that the city was primarily a control center, long before it became a center of communication, the persistent restrictions exercised over the extension and communication of knowledge would support this interpretation. As in the United States and Soviet Russia today, the great business of the citadel was to 'keep the official secrets.' These secrets created a gap between the rulers and the ruled that almost turned them into different biological species; and it was not until the achievements of civilization themselves were called into question, by popular revolt, that any part of these secrets was shared.

There is a bitter lament from Egypt's first great popular uprising that reveals the indignation of the upper classes, because the lower orders had broken into their precincts, and not merely turned their wives into prostitutes, but, what seemed equally bad, captured knowledge that had been withheld from them. "The writings of the august enclosure [the temple] are read. . . . The place of secrets . . . is [now] laid bare. . . . Magic is exposed." (Admonitions of Ipu-wer: 2300-2050 B.C.?)

Yet the ruling classes, in their very monopoly of the creative processes, had discovered a principle of general importance to human development. This principle remains only fitfully understood and intermittently applied even today. I mean the use of deliberate withdrawal and detachment to break into the purely repetitive cycle of birth, nutrition, and reproduction, or of production, exchange, and consumption. Though a large part of the surplus produced in urban society was wasted on extravagant consumption and even more extravagant acts of military destruction, a considerable part went into leisure, uncommitted time, released from the daily routine, devoted to the contemplation of nature and discipline of the human mind.

As the outer shell of the city grew, so to say, its interior likewise expanded: not merely its inner spaces, within the sacred precinct, but its inner life. Dreams welled up out of that interior and took form; fantasies turned into drama, and sexual desire flowered into poetry and dance and music. The city itself thus became a collective expression of love, detached from the urgencies of sexual reproduction. Activities that sprang to life only on festal occasions in ruder communities became part of the daily existence of the city. And what began as a wholesale transformation of the environment became a transformation of man.

This release of creativity was not, I need hardly emphasize, one of the original purposes of human settlement, nor yet of the urban implosion itself; and it is only partially and fitfully that it has characterized the development of cities. Even today, only a small part of the total energies of the community go into education and expression: we sacrifice far more to the arts of destruction and extermination than to the arts of creation. But it is through the performance of creative acts, in art, in thought, in personal relationships, that the city can be identified as something more than a purely functional organization of factories and warehouses, barracks, courts, prisons, and control centers. The towers and domes of the historic city are reminders of that still unfulfilled promise.

3 : CULTURAL SEEPAGE

So far I have dwelt on one phase of the monopoly of knowledge and power originally exercised by the rulers of the citadel. But as a matter of fact, this monopoly covered most of the functions which were later taken over and collectively distributed by the municipality only after many thousands of years. One might call this the law of cultural seepage.

In the citadel's bodyguard, we find the first army and the first police officers; and though we cannot identify the separate buildings until a late date, the first housing for such military functionaries, the barracks. Here, too, we find the first foreign office, the first bureaucracy, the first court of law (at the gate of the palace), likewise, from the temple quarter, the first astronomical observatory, the first library, the first school and college: not least, the first 'theater.' All these flourished in the citadel before there were any independent municipal equivalents with a larger domain to work in, or any question of democratic participation.

This royal monopoly held for many technical innovations, which made their appearance in the citadel long before they spread to the rest of the city. It was in the citadel that fireproof buildings, in permanent materials, first appeared: likewise paving. It was here, in one region or another, that before 2000 B.C. drains, running water, bathtubs, water closets, private sleeping apartments, were constructed; and it was in the palace precinct, at a time when the rest of the city had become a compact mass of houses, densely occupied, that the king and his court enjoyed what is still the greatest and most aristocratic of urban luxuries—an amplitude of open space, stretching beyond the dwelling itself into gardens and pleasances, sometimes forming a whole villa quarter for nobles and high officials.

Even the urban industrial crafts owed their existence in no small measure to the king's patronage: an ancient fact still symbolized in England by the legend 'By appointment to Her Majesty the Queen.' Royal foraging expeditions first provided the fruits of trade by a one-way process of gathering raw materials: under royal command, armor was made, weapons forged, chariots built. For the king's wives and concubines, and for his fellow nobles, the goldsmiths and the jewelers first practiced their arts. When thousands of years later fine porcelain china was introduced into Europe, it was not by accident that the new product was made in royal porcelain works, Sèvres, Dresden, Meissen, Copenhagen. Industrial production got its start in luxury wares for the court; and even mass production began, not in necessities, but in cheap imitations of upper-class luxury products, like eighteenth-century Birmingham jewelry or twentieth-century motorcars.

These facts about the origins of the city proper within the citadel or 'little city' seem essential to an inclusive picture of its functions and purposes. In current economic parlance, the citadel served as the original pilot project for the city; and this accounts for the fact that so many of the characteristics of both city and state today bear the imprint of ancient myths and magical aberrations, of obsolete privileges and prerogatives originally based on royal claims: witness the myth of absolute sovereignty. Fortunately, in uniting village and citadel, shrine and market, the city still rested on the moral underpinning of the village: the habits of regular labor and daily collaboration in a common task, the nurture, reproduction, and consecration of life. Even the village shrine was never completely absorbed by the central ceremonial center; for subordinate cults and shrines formed the nucleus of temple parishes in Mesopotamia. In Khafaje, archaeologists found such a neighborhood unit with its footways converging toward the temple.

4: URBAN DIVISION OF LABOR

Though we apply terms like hunter, miner, herdsman, peasant to Stone Age groups, we are thus actually transferring a later urban usage to an early phase of human development. If we could recapture the mentality of early peoples, we should probably find that they were, to themselves, simply men who fished or chipped flint or dug as the moment or the place might demand. That they should hunt every day or dig every day, confined to a single spot, performing a single job or a single part of a job, could hardly have occurred to them as an imaginable or tolerable mode of life. Even in our times primitive peoples so despise this form of work that their European exploiters have been forced to use every kind of legal chicane to secure their services.

The very notion of a settled division of labor, of fixation of many natural activities into a single life occupation, of confinement to a single craft, probably dates, as Childe indicates, from the founding of cities. Urban man paid for his vast collective expansion of power and environmental control by a contraction of personal life. The old Stone Age community, entering the city, was dismembered into a score of parts: castes, classes, professions, trades, crafts.

Admittedly, the first evidence of specialization and division of labor may go back to paleolithic times, in the special powers exercised by the magician or leader of the ritual; and this may have come at a time when there was also, perhaps, some occupational specialization among those adept at mining or chipping flint. Hocart has suggested that the division of labor was originally a hereditary division of the offices in ritual; and since primitive people regard ritual as no less important than work, indeed as the most efficacious form of work, there is no need to assume that the two forms of specialization were exclusive: rather, we should expect them to be mingled and confounded, as the magical rites of fertilization mingled with the practical seeding and watering of crops.

Even before the city took form, there may have been some fixation in special castes and occupations, through the handing down, within a particular family, of secret knowledge of processes or ancestral skills. But the first true urban specialists were probably the members of armed hunting bands who disdained repetitive daily labor with their hands, and the guardians of the shrine who were probably exempt from manual drudgeries.

In early communities, labor itself is a part-time activity, impossible to segregate completely from other functions of life, like religion, play, communal intercourse, even sexuality. In the city specialized work became for the first time an all-day, year-round occupation. As a result, the specialized worker, a magnified hand, or arm, or eye, achieved excellence and efficiency in the part, to a degree impossible to reach except by such specialization; but he lost his grip on life as a whole. This sacrifice was one of the chronic miscarriages of civilization: so universal that it has become 'second nature' to urban man. The blessing of a varied, fully humanized life, released from occupational constraints, was monopolized by the ruling classes. The nobles recognized this; and in more than one culture reserved the title 'true men' for themselves.

Since Adam Smith, everyone is well aware of the gains in productivity that specialized labor ensured, long before the invention of complex machines. The fact that urban culture developed such specialization was not the least reason for the accumulation of capital and the rise in income that accompanied the rise of the city before there were any comparable advances in mechanical invention. While many of the inhabitants of early cities worked in the temple fields or had outlying farms, a growing proportion of the population practiced other trades and callings, first as servants of the temple, then as part or whole time craftsmen, working directly to order or for the market.

In the so-called 'Satire on the Trades,' which may date back to the second millennium B.C. in Egypt, the writer mentions some eighteen different trades, besides his own, that of the scribe—but he omitted the higher professions, the priest, the soldier, the physician, the architect, which he must have piously regarded as quite above criticism or denigration; for indeed it was partly for the privilege of meeting with such august figures that he valued the profession he himself followed. The trades the scribe mentions range from the barber to the embalmer, from the carpenter to the cobbler and the currier; and in each case he stresses their hardships, their occupational disabilities and deformities as compared with the opportunities offered the scribe, who lived at ease and mingled with the great.

In the city it was possible for the first time to spend an entire life in a fractional occupation: the worker was a uniform replaceable part in a complex social machine, fixed in the same position, repeating the same operations, confined within the same quarter, throughout his life. Petrie notes that even outside the city, in the realm of mining, "we know from the mummy records how minutely work was subdivided. Every detail was allotted to the responsibility of an individual; one man prospected, another tested the rock, a third took charge of the products. There are over fifty different qualities and grades of officials and laborers named in the mining expeditions."

These divisions were embedded in the very nature of the city, for it was only by its capacity to mobilize and apportion manpower that these interlocking operations could be performed in every part of the economy. By the time Herodotus visited Egypt in the fifth century B.C., the over-all division of labor and the minute subdivision into specialisms had reached a point comparable to that which it has come to again in our own time; for he records that "some physicians are for the eyes, others for the head, others for the teeth, others for the belly, and others for internal disorders."

Thus while the new urban form brought together and united a larger group of co-operating and interacting people than had ever existed in one place before, it also divided them into tightly separated strands, each deeply dyed in its occupational colors. The whole system of specialized labor was pushed to the point of caricature in India, where the castes, even minute divisions within the castes, became hereditary; but by the time of Plato, this division had become so ingrained in thought that, like slavery itself, it was taken almost as a fact of nature. Toynbee characterizes caste and vocational specialization as outstanding features of 'arrested civilization'; but in various degrees this arrest characterizes all urban communities. Even today many people are still unable to imagine any further human development beyond this. Released from physical labor by automatic machines, they would still apply the same vocational fixations and limitations to sport, play, scholarship, science.

Occupational and caste stratification produced in the ancient city an urban pyramid, which rose to a peak in the absolute ruler: king, priest, warrior, scribe formed the apex of the pyramid; but the king alone, at the highest point, caught the full rays of the sun. Below him, the layers widened out into merchants, craftsmen, peasants, sailors, house servants, freed men, slaves, the lowest layer deep in perpetual shadow. These divisions were distinguished and sharpened by the ownership, or lack, of property in various degrees; and they were further expressed in costume, in habit of life, in food, and in dwelling place.

Segregated economic functions and segregated social roles in turn created equivalent precincts within the city: not least—if not first—the marketplace. If the local temple was the magnet for residents of a whole neighborhood, there would also be a partly visible occupational wall, identifiable by house types, to serve as class envelope. That practice lingers today in the spontaneous grouping of certain occupations, even without the pressure of any municipal zoning ordinance. Thus in Philadelphia, the city where I am now writing these words, the physicians congregate in a small area whose axis is Spruce Street, while the insurance agents fill a whole quarter between Independence Hall and the wholesale provision district. 'Harley Street,' 'Madison Avenue,' 'State Street,' are shorthand expressions not just for occupations, but for a whole way of life that they embody. Rome and Antioch, yes, probably Nineveh and Ur, had their equivalents.

The division of labor and the segregation of functions antedated the money economy: in one sense it was an extension of the practice of sacrifice, in the abandonment or postponement of a variety of functions and freely shifting roles in order to concentrate on a single activity for the benefit of king, god, and city. Whether or not prostitution is the oldest profession in the world, it is remarkable that specialists in sex-play should make their appearance so early in the texts that bear on urban life. We read that while "Gilgamesh called the craftsmen, the armorers," Ishtar assembled "the pleasure girls and the temple harlots."

This early sexual specialization suggests that in the ancient cities there may have been a disproportionate number of unmarried males; but it also shows a more general process, whereby functions that once were united in the village household—sleeping, drinking, eating, talking, mating, educating—in time were sorted out, magnified, and segregated in definite buildings and quarters in the city. The inn, the tavern, the marketplace, the temple, the school, the harlot's house would all be under the auspices of full-time professionals. In that sense, the city became a magnified collective household. With this differentiation went a certain detachment: all the necessary functions, even the bodily ones, took a playful form, pursued and prolonged more for their sociable occasions than for their practical ends.

This abstraction of specialized and differentiated functions from the matrix of the common life was furthered by the introduction of writing and money; for with the development of long-distance trade all the varied human values that had been expressed only in terms of immediate living were translated into a neutral medium, which could be bargained for, stored, and used as a source of power to command the labor of other men.

Originally, the main forms of urban specialization may have begun in the temple, with the first growth of rationalization and regimentation in those sacred quarters. Prostitution itself possibly derives from the employment of priestesses in the fertility rites; for the custom of temple prostitution has not merely been preserved down to our own day in countries like India, but the temples of the goddesses of love, of Ishtar, Aphrodite, Venus, Isis, were traditionally the favored places of assignation for lovers. Temple prostitution scandalized Herodotus, for in Babylon it seems to have demanded the conscription of all women, even the married, for at least one day a year; and the uglier conscripts had to remain within the temple indefinitely until someone took pity on them and lay with them.

All this emphasizes a more general characteristic of the city: the way in which it gave a specialized, abstract, professional, collective form to human needs that no one had hitherto ever thought of dedicating a whole lifetime to fulfilling.

Now here we must note again the contradictory and ambivalent part played by the city. Biologically, man had developed farther than other species because he had remained unspecialized—omnivorous, free-moving, 'handy,' omni-competent, yet always somewhat unformed and incomplete, never fully adapting himself to any one situation, even though it might continue as long as the last Ice Age. Instead of cramping his activities by producing specialized organs to ensure effective adaptation, man put all his organic capital, so to say, into one feature of animal development that could invent substitutes for such specialized organs—the central nervous system. Thanks to the enlarged growth of the brain, far beyond any immediate functional needs, man was capable of extrapolating new organs outside the body without being bound, as in other organic adaptations, to their indefinite perpetuation. By remaining non-specialized, man opened up a thousand fresh paths for his own further development.

Civilization, as it developed in the city, partly reversed this process. The more successful urban types were those committed to specialization; and their partial lives depended upon the successful interlocking of a whole organization, in which each group accepted the limitations of its allotted role. The early Egyptian craftsman was forbidden to change his hereditary calling; and early apprenticeship and habituation made this legal injunction almost unnecessary. Everywhere the worker was always a worker, the slave always a slave, the noble always a noble—at least until the slave revolted or bought his freedom, or the noble was taken in battle and lost his.

The city thus at an early date recaptured the polymorphism of the insect hive: by social means it achieved the equivalent of the physiological differentiations that accompany the integration of insect societies. True, this division of labor allowed for far greater internal mobility than insect communities know. Even prostitution, though it condemned a whole class to the drudgeries of sexual intercourse, never reached the point of creating a single class of sexual breeders, segregated for childbearing. (That horror possibly awaits the triumph of Post-historic Man.) Nevertheless, the parallel between human and insect societies applies even to the working life; for within a single lifetime the differences between vocations still cause characteristic diseases and disabilities, even changes in bodily structure. These differences still affect the death rate and the span of life of each major occupation.

5: PROPERTY AND PERSONALITY

With the growth of numbers and the increase of wealth in the city rose another kind of division: that between the rich and the poor, which came in with the next great innovation of urban life, the institution of property. Property, in the civilized sense of the word, did not exist in primitive communities: if anything, people belonged to their land, more than the land belonged to them; and they shared its products, in feast or famine. It remained for civilization to create artificial famines to keep the worker chained to his task, so that the surplus might ensure the rich man's feast.

In the change-over from the village to the city, there is some further confirmation of this reading of communal ways: for the land and all it brought forth became the property of the temple and the god; even the peasants who worked it belonged to the temple, and all the other members of the community belonged to the land, too, and were obliged to give part of their labor to the common tasks of digging and embanking and building. These possessions, with the extension of the secular powers of kingship, would become the royal estate; and identification of the common domain with the sovereign power sank so deep that even in modern states most sharply conscious of the rights of private property, the state itself is the ultimate owner and residuary legatee, with that power to commandeer and to tax which is ultimately the power to possess or destroy.

Private property begins, not as Proudhon thought with robbery, but with the treatment of all common property as the private possession of the king, whose life and welfare were identified with that of the community. Property was an extension and enlargement of his own personality, as the unique representative of the collective whole. But once this claim was accepted, property could for the first time be alienated, that is, removed from the community by the individual gift of the king.

This conception of the royal possessions remained in its original form well past the time of Louis XIV. That Sun King, a little uneasy over the heavy taxes he desired to impose, called together the learned Doctors of Paris to decide if his exactions were morally justifiable. Their theology was equal to the occasion. They explained that the entire realm was his by divine right: hence in laying on these new taxes he was only taxing himself. This prerogative was passed on, undefiled, to the 'sovereign state,' which in emergencies falls back, without scruple, on ancient magic and myth.

The separation and division of property began with the bestowal of gifts by the absolute rulers upon their fellow nobles, their adherents, their servants, in reward for services done. When it had escaped from the common domain, it could be passed on, subdivided, or augmented. By a fairly early date, around 1700 B.C., when the Code of Hammurabi was promulgated, detailed laws dealing with private property, its transfer, its loan, its bequest, reveal the rise of this new legal entity.

Within the city, property rights acquire a special sanctity; and as class differentiations increased they became correspondingly more important—indeed often more sacred than human life itself. In the protection of these rights, the early rulers did not hesitate to maim or mutilate the body of the offender. But the general gap between the rich and the poor made itself felt even here: there were different degrees of punishment for each class.

These forms of legalized violence were not holdovers from an even more vicious primitive regime, as the old apostles of progress liked to believe: they were rather, like war itself, a new kind of ferocity peculiar to urban culture: what Giambattista Vico properly characterized as the "barbarism of civilization."

Specialization, division, compulsion, and depersonalization produced an inner tension within the city. This resulted throughout history in an undercurrent of covert resentment and outright rebellion that was perhaps never fully recorded, since it would come plainly into view only momentarily when a slaves' rebellion, like that under the Gracchi, was put down with a bloody massacre of the rebels.

But the fact that the city has from the beginning been based on forced labor, and that forced labor was produced, not only by enslavement, but by monopoly of the food supply, seems to be indisputably incised on the walls of the ancient city. Planned scarcity and the recurrent threat of starvation played a part from the beginning in the effective regimentation of the urban labor force. No wonder Sir Mortimer Wheeler exulted when he at last identified the great granary in the citadel of Mohenjo-Daro: for the guardians of the granary, with the support of an armed soldiery, held powers of life and death over the whole community. It was not for nothing that this great storehouse was *within* the heavy walls of the citadel, protected *against the inhabitants of the city.*

What made the division of labor, for all its life-limiting qualities, tolerated if not wholly tolerable, through so many centuries and millennia? There are various ways of accounting for its acceptance; and to begin with it helped to create the first economy of abundance, whose advantages were at first more easily recognized than its ultimate disabilities and weaknesses. This is one of a number of facts that unites the late neolithic magnification of human power to the similar changes that have taken place in our own age. Despite the royal and priestly monopolies, some portion of the vast quantity of goods produced did in fact filter down to lower levels of the social pyramid; and the city dweller, however poor, got a larger portion than the village laborer, if only because he was nearer to the source of supply. The city dweller could not, indeed, drink at the royal fountain; but in contrast to the villager, he was near at hand and caught some of the overflow.

Happily, the social constitution of the city helped to overcome its human constrictions and compulsions. If it dismembered the whole man and forced him to spend a long lifetime at a single task, it re-assembled him in a new collective entity; so that while his individual life might be narrow and constrained, the urban pattern so woven was all the richer in texture because of the variegated threads that formed it. Not merely did each special group find more of its own kind in the city: each could discover in the give-and-take of daily intercourse a wealth of human potentialities that remained invisible at a humbler level.

If there is likely to be one person of exceptional ability in every generation in, say, ten thousand people, a group of only one thousand may have to wait many generations before it has the advantage of a superior mind; and that mind, by its very isolation, may lack the stimulus from other minds that will help it to find itself. But a hundred thousand people, in Sumer or Babylon, in Jerusalem or Athens, in Baghdad or Benares, might produce at least fifty exceptional minds in a single lifetime; and these minds, by the very closeness of urban communication, would be open to a far greater variety of challenges and suggestions than if they appeared in a smaller community.

Finally, if the subdivided urban man, or *Teilmensch,* forfeited the unconscious wholeness of the simpler village type, he achieved, at least vicariously, a new sense of the individual personality, emerging from the chrysalis of tribe, clan, family, and village. For at the opposite pole to the vocational specialist, an individual person now stood forth in the role of the monarch himself: the Pharaoh of Egypt or the Lugal of Sumer. At the bottom there might be slavery and compulsion; but at the top—for long only at the top—there were freedom, autonomy, choice, all of them emerging attributes of personality, hardly possible in a regime based on family togetherness and tribal unanimity.

The royal fiat, as Frankfort pointed out, gave to the actions of a whole community the attributes of an integrated person: the willingness to assume risks, to make choices, to pursue distant and difficult goals. Whatever the deprivations and hardships imposed by large-scale urban organization, the meanest member of the community participated vicariously in the enlargement of the king's functions and in the contemplation of even more divine attributes in which, as the citizen of no mean city, he also shared. In that sense the whole city belonged to the meanest inhabitant.

In the king, I repeat, the person first emerged, in a position of responsibility superior to the group, detached from his communal matrix. With the rise of the city the king incarnated a new idea of human development, and the city became nothing less than the corporate embodiment of this evolving idea. One by one, the privileges and prerogatives of kingship were transferred to the city, and its citizens. Thousands of years were needed to effect this change; and by the time it was consummated men had forgotten where and how it had begun.

Thus the city became a special environment, not just for supporting kings but for making persons: beings who were more fully open to the realities of the cosmos, more ready to transcend the claims of tribal society and custom, more capable of assimilating old values and creating new ones, of making decisions and taking new directions, than their fellows in more limited situations. The first royal prerogative that was, somewhat grudgingly, passed on to the other members of the community was immortality, as conceived by the Egyptians, but in time other attributes followed.

In the end, the city itself became the chief agent of man's transformation, the organ for the fullest expression of personality. Into the city go a long procession of gods: out of it there come, at long intervals, men and women, at home in their world, able to transcend the limitations of their gods. But it was with no thought of this final possibility that men originally shaped the city. Power and property had unwittingly prepared a nest for personality. And eventually personality would undermine their inflated pretensions and claims.

6 : RHYTHM OF DEVELOPMENT

Groups of organisms may occupy a common environment and make use of each other's activities without any one organism reaching its fullest growth, or achieving its maximum potentialities for development. As a matter of fact, they may live together for a long time while undergoing a steady deterioration, marked by physical malformations, lowered resistance to disease, and a shortened span of life. Survival by itself indicates nothing about the development or rank of the organism that survives.

In the original formation of the city, the positive symbiosis of the neolithic village community was largely replaced, or at least undermined, by a negative symbiosis resting on war, exploitation, enslavement, parasitism. The first had achieved stability in an equilibrium too firmly guarded to permit growth. With the introduction of predatory-parasitic elements into the forming urban community, a fresh stimulus to growth came into existence, which accounts for the over-enlargement of all the functions of the citadel. But the very means of achieving this growth oriented the community to sacrifice, constriction of life, and premature destruction and death.

The fact is that the parasitism practiced by the rulers of the citadel increased, growing ever more exorbitant with their demand for visible wealth and power; instead of submitting these claims to the ordeal of reality and sharing more of the goods they monopolized with their fellow-citizens they inflated their demands beyond the possibility of their being locally executed.

These impositions could be met only by extending the area of exploitation: so that the growth of the great capital cities, like Nineveh, Babylon, and Rome, was effected only by enlarging the dimensions of the tributary hinterland and by bringing about a negative symbiosis based on terrified expectation of destruction and extermination.

"It is perfectly clear," Contenau remarks, "that the immense wealth of the Assyrian and Babylonian Empire, to name no more, was largely dependent upon the institution of slavery." Likewise it should be equally clear that this wealth would have been far greater and the power displayed far more durable, if the rulers of these empires had not given such full scope to their insensate sadism. Yet this widened area of exploitation was also an area of potential association and constructive interchange. All the energies of the growing city might—if not absorbed by the infliction and reparation of injuries—have gone into the fabrication of a wider kind of co-partnership.

Despite its negations, the city produced a purposeful life that at many points magnificently over-rode the original aims that had brought it into existence. Aristotle put into words the nature of this transition from the preparatory urban processes and functions to emergent human purposes, in terms it would be hard to improve: "Men come together in the city to live; they remain there in order to live the good life." To define the nature of the city in any particular cultural setting would be in part to define both the local and the more universal qualities of the good life.

But even for the classes that were the special beneficiaries of this effort, the life of civilized man as carried on in the great cities turned out repeatedly to be empty and hateful. Is it an accident that both Egyptian and Mesopotamian cultures have left us two classic dialogues on suicide, occasioned by despair over the emptiness of civilized life? These dialogues reveal that urban man, in surmounting the limitations of the village community had nevertheless not been able to overcome the weakening of his own animal faith, promoted by his removal from the sources of life and his exclusive concentration on power and wealth. Even the early civilizations of the East, perhaps *especially* these, suffered from the vice that now threatens to overwhelm our own civilization in the very midst of its technological advancement: purposeless materialism. Urban life was arrested, at an early date, by the error of treating materialization as an end in itself.

Toynbee has demonstrated that there is no uniformly favorable relation between man's increasing domination over his physical environment, with a growing complexity of technical apparatus, and the quality of human culture. If anything, there is an inverse relation: for cultures that remain static and uncreative in the human sphere often promote ingenious technical adaptations and inventions, whereas more creative cultures transmute their energies into higher and more refined forms: so that even their technical apparatus becomes progressively de-materialized, lessened in bulk or weight, simplified in design or operation. Toynbee calls this process 'etherialization.'

Compare the vast clanking mechanism of the medieval clock in the Marienkirche in Lübeck with a fine modern Geneva watch, an infinitesimal fraction of its weight and size, but almost infinitely superior in accuracy. This transformation takes place, in various degrees, all along the line. In the case of urban structures, it means a thinning of the container and a strengthening of the magnet.

When etherialization goes on, an ever larger part of the environment, in space and time, becomes available for further human development, precisely because it has been concentrated in symbolic form. Whereas other organisms need only so much of the past as they carry in their genes, so much of their environment as is concretely present, man's own capability depends upon his having access to remoter events, remembered or projected, and to remote or inaccessible parts of the environment. When the process of etherialization is arrested, nothing like an equivalent amount of experience can be achieved by direct effort, within a single lifetime.

Toynbee does not draw this conclusion, but it seems plain that etherialization is one of the main justifications for the city—though an emergent one, not envisaged by its original creators—or even fully appreciated today. Art and science, in all their manifold expressions, are the easily recognized symbols of this release. In a positive symbiosis these functions re-enforce each other and flow forth in a great variety of activities; for life is in the living, and even the highest by-products of life are only incentives for more intense modes of living, not substitutes for it. Accordingly, all the sacrifices that have helped bring the city into existence come to nothing if the life that the city makes possible is not its own reward. Neither augmented power nor unlimited material wealth can atone for a day that lacks a glimpse of beauty, a flash of joy, a quickening and sharing of fellowship.

But in addition, the city performs an equally important function that I have described elsewhere: the function of materialization. Though Toynbee completely overlooks this aspect of the social process, it stares one in the face as one walks around the city; for the buildings speak and act, no less than the people who inhabit them; and through the physical structures of the city past events, decisions made long ago, values formulated and achieved, remain alive and exert an influence.

The rhythm of life in cities seems to be an alternation between materialization and etherialization: the concrete structure, detaching itself through a human response, takes on a symbolic meaning, uniting the knower and the known; while subjective images, ideas, intuitions, only partly formed in their original expression, likewise take on material attributes, in visible structures, whose very size, position, complexity, organization, and esthetic form extend the area of meaning and value, otherwise inexpressible. City design is thus the culminating point of a socially adequate process of materialization.

Even when an idea is incarnated in a human personality, the influence of that personality does not depend merely on direct intercourse and imitation. To complete his own integration, to last beyond his own lifetime and his limited circle, the person needs the further collective backing of institutions and buildings. The translation of ideas into common habits and customs, of personal choices and designs into urban structures, is one of the prime functions of the city.

On this interpretation, both etherialization and materialization are indispensable to progressive human development. When life prospers, one process alternates with another as naturally as the intake and expulsion of breath. Growth is not, as Toynbee would have it, a single process of progressive de-materialization, a transposition of earthly life into a heavenly simulacrum. It is not for nothing that the building stones of the universe are the durable elements, while the most 'etherial' elements, those that have a life of a few seconds, would make continuity of any kind impossible if they preponderated. Both stability and constant creativity are needed, and that combination was the supreme gift of the city.

Heaven and Utopia both had a place in the structure of ancient cities; yet to the extent that the best human plans may miscarry and the most successful human dreams may, through their very success, succumb to internal perversities, Hell became part of the formative structure, too. The resulting material form often outlasted the ideal that originally quickened it: as is the fashion of containers, old buildings and public ways may serve, with minor changes, to hold a new dream. But that is a late development. So important was the symbol itself for early urban rulers, that more than one city was razed to the ground, to be rebuilt again by the destroyer on the same site. No rule of common sense or economics can explain that.

7: THE URBAN DRAMA

The characteristic activities of the ancient city have, finally, a special quality: they exist in a state of tension and interplay that moves periodically toward a crisis or a climax. This is characterized at an early state in the city's development by a new art, the art of the drama. There are at least two sources of the drama which prepare for its appearance in the city. One of them was admirably explored by Jane Harrison in her 'Ancient Art and Ritual.' There she shows how drama, the 'thing done,' originated in the ancient seasonal rituals of the village, in which all the villagers had a part to play. The very notion of playing a part, of performing a role, may in fact have had its beginning in magical and religious ceremonial, before it took on any other form.

These rites reflected the static qualities of the village community. In the translation of such rites to the city, the roles became magnified; and though the themes would remain close to the original myths and legends, a growing self-consciousness in playwright and actor would stimulate improvisations and departures. That passage from ritual to drama, from the stable and the repetitive to the dynamic, the adventurous, the rationally critical, the self-conscious and reflective, and in some degree non-conformist, was one of the marked achievements of the city.

In entering the city, the drama got re-enforcement from another tribal ceremony, the contest or agon: sometimes a battle of wits, sometimes a competitive exhibition of bodily strength and skill. Originally these competitions may have accompanied religious ceremonies, like the funerary games. Certainly when the gods make their appearance in history, the cosmic events they symbolize stand forth very largely as contests, like that between Light and Darkness, Water and Land, Field and Desert, Good and Evil. These machinations and struggles appeared first perhaps as unconscious drives and wishes, before they found in the city a theater of action.

The playful aspect of this struggle was never completely absorbed by the economic and political apparatus of the city: so that athletic and gladiatorial contests existed side by side with more aggressive struggles for power: not so much a sublimation of the aggressive impulses as a more innocent preparatory schooling in the art, as in a little girl's play with dolls. To form a circle of spectators around the actors in a contest was the first office, probably, of the agora or forum; and the practice of holding such contests passed on to later cities. In fifth-century Athens the ecclesia, W. S. Ferguson points out, was a great 'agon' or contest of statesmen: and there were contests of potters, we learn from a boastful gravestone, as well as contests of horse-breeders, singers, military companies, composers, and dramatists. The practice of choosing leaders and 'taking sides' was one of the earliest forms of social differentiation. The city magnified this process and multiplied its occasions.

Apart from the text of the mystery play performed at Abydos, among the earliest urban literary texts we find are those of the Sumerians, simple disputations between opposite characters, the elementary black and white of both primitive drama and dialectic: disputations between Summer and Winter, between the Plow and the Pick-Ax, between the Shepherd and the Farmer. With urban self-consciousness, there comes also an acuter sense of differences, first expressed in gross contrasts, but eventually in all the fine shadings and incisive lines that make up 'character,' partly formed by the role, partly by endless individual variations upon the common type.

With this perhaps goes a heightened enjoyment of the encounter itself, that is the confrontation and struggle of man with man, as the very essence of urban existence; and along with this greater tension went a fiercer aggressiveness, so that the contestants hurl insults at each other and swear oaths that would be treated as mortal offenses but for the saving sense of drama itself—that all this goes with the role, that life *as acted* is a sort of make-believe. So long as the city performs its essential functions, it keeps struggle and tension within bounds, and heightens their significance.

The ancient city, then, is above all things a theater, in which common life itself takes on the features of a drama, heightened by every device of costume and scenery, for the setting itself magnifies the voice and increases the apparent stature of the actors. This urban life, however heavily committed to ritual, is still full of new situations, for which the proverbial wisdom and the time-honored responses are no longer adequate. If we trace the components of this drama back far enough, we shall find that each of them, not the theater alone, derives from religion; and just as the first recorded contests were those of the gods and the heroes, so the first well-defined dramas themselves were performed in the temple.

Situation, plot, conflict, crisis, resolution—in these terms the acted drama translates into the new life lived in the city, and in reflection of the symbol, the tensions and excitements of that life in turn take on a greater significance. As the cast of characters lengthened, the plot thickened and the outcome became less and less predictable.

The "remaking of man was the work of the city." This observation of Robert Redfield, a wise student of more primitive folk cultures, goes deeper than most sociologists and psychologists, with the exception of J. L. Moreno, have usually allowed. Primitive communities certainly remade man; but once they had found their special mold, common to the whole, they sought to forfend or circumscribe further changes. In the city, on the contrary, the making and remaking of selves is one of its principal functions. In any generation, each urban period provides a multitude of new roles and an equal diversity of new potentialities. These bring about corresponding changes in laws, manners, moral evaluations, costume, and architecture, and finally they transform the city as a living whole.

Such individuation of character, with its suppression of the tribal or communal mask, goes along with the development of other higher functions; for it is not merely the intelligence that is quickened by systematic observation and record, but the feelings are tempered and the emotions are refined and disciplined by their constant interplay with those of other men, against a setting of art. Here, by action and participation, and again by detachment and reflection, urban man may give to a larger portion of life the benefit of a continued play of the collective mind and spirit. What began as an outer struggle against hostile natural forces culminates in an inner drama whose resolution is not any physical victory but a more intimate self-understanding, and a richer inner development.

The daily routines of the city, the work of household, craft, profession, can be performed almost anywhere: even when they take a highly specialized form, they may function in an independent enclave outside the city—as so many big, quasi-feudal organizations have begun to again in our own day. But only in a city can a full cast of characters for the human drama be assembled: hence only in the city is there sufficient diversity and competition to enliven the plot and bring the performers up to the highest pitch of skilled, intensely conscious participation.

Take away the dramatic occasions of urban life, those of the arena, the law court, the trial, the parliament, the sport field, the council meeting, the debate, and half the essential activities of the city would vanish and more than half of its meanings and values would be diminished, if not nullified. Out of ritual and dramatic action, in all their forms, something even more important emerged: nothing less than the human dialogue. Perhaps the best definition of the city in its higher aspects is to say that it is a place designed to offer the widest facilities for significant conversation.

The dialogue is one of the ultimate expressions of life in the city: the delicate flower of its long vegetative growth. Certainly, the dialogue developed with difficulty, if it developed at all, in the early city; for the first urban communities were based rather on the monologue of power; and once the priestly behest or the royal command had gone forth, it was not wise to answer back.

Dialogue was, in fact, the first step out of that tribal conformity which is an obstacle both to self-consciousness and to development. Gaining confidence through numbers, the dialogue challenged the deadly unanimity promoted by a centralized absolutism. The Egyptian 'Complaint of the Eloquent Peasant' may not have been repeated often: but this first answering back brought such a breath-taking change of atmosphere that the story was copied and told for thousands of years, if only because it anticipated the coming of a genuine and more universal dialogue.

Like so many other emergent attributes of the city, the dialogue was no part of its original plan or function; but it was made possible by the inclusion of human diversities within the enclosed urban amphitheater. This turned dialogue into drama. By its very growth of differentiated occupations and characters, the city ceased to be a wholly like-minded community, wholly obedient to a central control. "A city that is of one man only is no city," says Haemon in Sophocles' 'Antigone.' Only where differences are valued and opposition tolerated can struggle be transmuted into dialectic: so in its internal economy the city is a place—to twist Blake's dictum—that depresses corporeal and promotes mental war.

This special function of the city was put with classic succinctness by that able observer of cities, the Elizabethan, John Stow: "Men by this nearness of conversation are withdrawn from barbarous feritie and force, to certain mildness of manners, and to humanity and justice, whereby they are contented to give and take right, to and from their equals and inferiors, and to hear and obey their heads and superiors."

And if provision for dialogue and drama, in all their ramifications, is one of the essential offices of the city, then one key to urban development should be plain—it lies in the widening of the circle of those capable of participating in it, till in the end all men will take part in the conversation. In this process the original roles cut out for men in cities, with a lifetime devoted to a single office, must be recognized for what they always were: limitations upon the whole scope and significance of the human drama, institutional blockages of the free and full development of the personality. In submitting too tamely to this limitation, Old World man left an unfinished task to his latterday successors.

Not by accident, then, has more than one historic city reached its climax in a dialogue that sums up its total experience of life. In the Book of Job, one beholds Jerusalem; in Plato, Sophocles, and Euripides, Athens; in Shakespeare and Marlowe, Dekker and Webster, Elizabethan London. In a sense the dramatic dialogue is both the fullest symbol and the final justification of the city's life. For the same reason, the most revealing symbol of the city's failure, of its very non-existence as a social personality, is the absence of dialogue—not necessarily a silence, but equally the loud sound of a chorus uttering the same words in cowed if complacent conformity. The silence of a dead city has more dignity than the vocalisms of a community that knows neither detachment nor dialectic opposition, neither ironic comment nor stimulating disparity, neither an intelligent conflict nor an active moral resolution. Such a drama is bound to have a fatal last act.

CHAPTER FIVE

Emergence of the Polis

1: STRONGHOLDS OF MINOS

When we turn from the river valleys, where cities first multiplied, to the rocky islands of the Aegean and the mountain masses and wide plains of the Balkan peninsula, we at first find the change in the milieu more striking than any change in the essential urban institutions. But both geographic conditions and human purposes brought about many modifications in the outward form of the city. Here, as everywhere, the soil, the climate, the geological formation, the vegetation, the whole regional matrix, left their mark, even on the health of the inhabitants, as well as upon their economic activities and their general view of life.

If the ancient cities of Mesopotamia were mobilizing centers for river control and for coping with storm damage, there was nothing in the Aegean towns to promote that sort of large scale co-operation and unification: the terrain itself did not admit of much human remodelling. How far could a quarry make an impression on the Isle of Paros when the whole mountain was a mass of marble? But if, apart from differences between north and south, fairly uniform conditions prevailed among the Cities of the Plain, just the opposite held in these Aegean communities. Within a narrow span of perhaps twenty miles, from sea to mountaintop, nature provided a great variety of climates and types of vegetation. If grain crops were plentiful on the heavy soils of the lower valleys, fruit and nut-bearing trees, especially the olive and the chestnut, partly released the thrifty occupants from the slavery of unremitting toil. Even peasants in the Aegean might know leisure and enjoy its fruits.

In Crete and Greece we pass from a barley and beer culture to a wine and olive culture: from fat sheep, maintaining the fertility of an already rich soil, to wiry goats, ravenously devouring the hillside seedlings and eventually opening to erosion the thin soil that covers them. At the same time, the deep clefts of the mountains, with their spasmodic rivers, enforced communal isolation. If the Nile and the Euphrates were helpful highways to early man, the sea was almost as much of an obstacle to these Aegean communities as the mountain passes themselves: even after the invention of boats and ships, sailing was a fair-weather occupation, abandoned in winter, for the sailors worked their way across the isle-studded sea, from headland to headland, never far from a landing place. Instead of drifting with the river's current to their only possible destination, the sea demanded daring effort, vigilant choice.

The submerged mountains that formed these island pinnacles and the continuous mountain system of the Balkan peninsula were formidably rugged in topography. Though their limestone masses furnished admirable building materials, stone neither too hard to be worked easily nor too soft to endure, the surface of the land could not be shaped and defined, as the alluvium of the Nile or the Euphrates could be defined by embankments and canals: at most, with backbreaking effort, the steep hillsides could be terraced for cultivation. No one dared to think of any larger shaping till the time of Alexander, when his architect, Deinocrates, proposed to carve his image in super-heroic sculpture out of Mount Athos. Not merely did the islands of the Aegean present so many isolated stepping stones, but each valley in the larger islands and on the mainland was a kind of inverted pinnacle, as insular as any natural island and even more unapproachable. Few of the conditions that favored the growth of the aboriginal city were present: not even adequate building sites. One scraped an urban site out of a ledge of almost bare rock, as at Delphi. Even on the plains, the cultivator forfeited arable land to urban building with justifiable reluctance.

City development in this part of the world began in Crete. The fertile lowlands of Crete supported neolithic agriculture; and on the hillsides, the chestnut, the fig, the olive, and the grape rounded out a diet of lowland grain and salt-water fish. These early villages, according to Childe, formed distinct communities, not subject to any common system of control, "not yet fused to form a single people with an homogeneous culture. But they seem to have lived together peaceably, as no fortifications have been found, and as members of a single economic system, in view of the uniformities in types of metal tools, stone vases, etc." The ruins of one of these neolithic villages, forming a tell more than eighteen feet high—an evidence of long occupation—have been found beneath the oldest Minoan level at Knossos, in central Crete.

Once again, in Knossos, we can identify the core of the early city, the citadel, with the temple itself apparently embedded in the palace. What indeed was this mountainous island itself, girt with the sea as its moat, but a vast citadel? Crete's immunity to invasion under primitive conditions gave it the same kind of peaceful isolation that Egypt once had and that Iceland and England were later to have. Thus Crete enjoyed a certain freedom from fear, an absence of disruptive tensions, that permitted life to flower during the early phases of Minoan culture. The whole island of Crete, now given over to shepherds and peasants, was once dotted with villages, cities, granaries, and monumental cemeteries. From this fact alone one might deduce, without further evidence, that the lords of the citadel, the Sea Kings, in the Middle Minoan Age, commanded great fleets, both armed and mercantile, capable of keeping down pirates and bringing back food and raw materials as well as finished products to these well-protected towns: strongholds within a stronghold. The stone walls and tiled conduits at Knossos tell us of a concentration of labor and engineering skill comparable to that which built Sumer; and the interior fittings of the palace corroborate that tale.

Though Cretan ruins like those of Gurnia give little information about the nature of the city not already disclosed in Mesopotamia, there is one stunning fragment—a series of faience plaques found in the Palace of Minos—that establishes more about the character and appearance of the Minoan city than can be put together from the palaces that have so far been unearthed.

These plaques were found by Sir Arthur Evans; and one cannot describe them better than in his own words. "The central features," he notes, "consisted of the towers and houses and a fortified town. There were, however, abundant remains of inlays of another class, trees and water, goats and oxen, marching warriors, spearmen and archers, arms and equipment, the prow apparently of a ship, and curious negroid figures. . . . The appearance of these house façades, with their two and three story roof attics and their windows of four and even six panes is perhaps the most astonishing. That windows of four and even six panes, containing some substitute for window glass, should already have existed at this time is only another proof of the extraordinary anticipation of modern civilized usage achieved in the great days of Minoan history—an anticipation not less marked in their hydraulic and sanitary appliances." Evans dated these plaques "not later probably than the last half of the eighteenth century" [B.C.].

Some of the mystery of this discovery has been lifted during the last half century since it was made. As archaeologists have overcome their natural if professionally nearsighted preoccupation with the immediate find, they have begun to see the particulars of this or that culture in the wider context of transportation routes, invasions, migrations, conquests, interchanges, which turn out to be much earlier and much wider in their provenance than nineteenth-century scholars suspected. The "curious negroid figures" do not now seem so strange: if they were too negroid to be the black-headed folk of Sumer, or their descendants, they may have been Numidians from Africa. The advanced designs of the dwelling house, or the equally resourceful technics of sanitation found in the palaces, distinctly recall Sumer. The sophisticated façades of the houses suggest that they, like the palaces, may have had equally elaborate interior fittings, and may have been served with internal conduits and drains, perhaps even water closets, similar to those for which there is evidence in Indus cities like Harappa and Mohenjo-Daro, according to Wheeler, before 1500 B.C.

But the great novelty in Crete is the window, for here Knossos leaves behind the dark windowless dwellings of Sumer, lighted only from a narrow courtyard or clerestory, if at all. This is all the more significant—and all the more mysterious from the standpoint of technological history—since they must have been covered in a transparent material, still unknown, producible in relatively large quantities. The palace at Phaestos, moreover, had a sewer and drinking-water pipes of terra cotta; and these pipes imply a mountain source, perhaps stone aqueducts and reservoirs as well.

Only yesterday, so to speak, Lewis Farnell made a bold inquiry into the religions of Babylon, Anatolia, and Greece, to test, in the light of evidence available in 1911, the suggestion of Morris Jastrow and other Mesopotamian scholars that early Greek religion derived from the Babylonian, as much as Greek astrology later did. Farnell in the end dismissed the resemblances between the two; but the very fact that he opened up the question redounds to his credit. Today Herodotus' emphasis on the debt of Greece to Egypt does not seem as absurd, indeed as outrageous, as it used to seem to Greek scholars in the nineteenth century, who mistakenly looked upon Greek culture as a unique, or rather, an underived phenomenon. If later scholars, like F. M. Cornford, following Farnell's lead, have shifted the religious part of the debt from Egypt to Babylon, matching god for god, myth for myth, in the two theologies, this only leads us to look for further resemblances between the Mesopotamian and the Aegean cultures, though one arose from the river, like a hippopotamus, and the other, like Aphrodite from the sea.

The evidence from Crete is rich but fragmentary, and therefore tantalizing: especially as concerns the city. If Cretans went to the tops of mountains to worship their god, one of the chief components of the city perhaps never descended to the center. Apart from the Cretan town pictures, obviously the crown of a long technical and urban development, some fifteen hundred or two thousand years of urban history remains unknown to us except in dim, broken outlines. Even if all the Minoan scripts are finally deciphered, it is not likely that they will tell us much more than we already know about the city, for the literary debris of these early cultures was never the work of urban sociologists or of gifted generalists like Aristotle; even the chance of translating an early Cretan Herodotus is slim. Merchants' letters and accounts; rulers' laws and boastings; magical prescriptions and religious rituals may come to light here as elsewhere; but though they may tell us something about the contents of urban life, they are likely to tell little about the shell.

Crete, figuratively speaking, is another Atlantis: it suddenly "disappears into the sea." Or what is almost the same thing, its refined habits of life, its seemingly unchallengeable security, may eventually have bred a decadent ruling class; and some centuries after a devastating earthquake, all its creations were swept away by the Mycenaean war bands, probably operating from strongholds of their own, notably Mycenae and Tiryns. One can guess that the new conquerors were similar to the hardy, swaggering males one finds later in the 'Iliad': quick to pick a quarrel, zealous in hunting, skilled in violence and theft, audacious at piracy, even making raids on the Egyptian seaboard; but they retained the old contempt of the blooded aristocrat for honest work, and no less for honest trade. Their continued occupation of Crete turned that island into a kind of political fossil of the military state, dear to Plato.

With the wholesale destruction of Cretan towns and palaces, urban activities shrank to the meager occupations of the citadel, the *Zwingburg,* with the armed conquerors keeping a watchful eye over the helot population that worked the soil. Down to Plato's day, Crete remained a counterpart of Sparta: hence he regarded them as equally admirable. Did he not, in lieu of a then odious Spartan, introduce a Cretan as one of the principal participants in his final utopian dialogue? Surely it was not an accident that war and athletic exercises in preparation for war were the main elements in training the elite in both countries. The common table that both Cretans and Spartans boasted may have had one leg in the temple, but the other was in the barracks.

Some of the habits fostered by this Mycenaean aristocracy and their like-minded Achaean and Dorian successors must have entered the Greek city, as it took form around the seventh century B.C. Though their strongholds became urban backwaters, their very existence and power may have given the legendary Theseus insight into the part that the city could play as a rallying point, indeed as a permanent winter residence, too, for the peasants and fishermen in their otherwise defenseless condition.

For that reason, one takes special note of the prelude in Minoan Crete, though so little apparently was passed on. As for the Mycenaean settlements, they lapsed into a more primitive urban form, though possibly with large aggregations of houses, dense habitations, in towns closer to the lowest layers of Jericho than to the upper-crust sophistications of Knossos. But the Mycenaean ascendancy seems never to have developed the permanent urban forces essential to further growth: the code of written law, the bureaucratic controls, the system of taxation, that would have ensured its continuity for even a millennium. Power, dependent chiefly on personal force, soon crumbled.

Between the eighth and the sixth century B.C., a new urban fabric began to knit together over the Aegean. This was a period stamped by the introduction of the alphabet and, around 650 B.C., by the invention of coined money; and it was marked by a devolution of power from the citadel to the democratic village-based community, and by the rise of the village itself to a new degree of self-consciousness and cosmic insight, to which the 'Works and Days' and the 'Theogony' of Hesiod both bear testimony. Hesiod's mixture of homely practical insight and religious myth and speculation established the temper and tone for the new urban order: both aspects of life came to a fuller consciousness in the Greek polis. The powers of the fabled kings and bellicose warriors who occupied the Acropolis were passed on to the city. Then, beginning on mainland Ionia, on the Black Sea, the cities rose, multiplied, flourished, colonized. As early as 734 B.C. Corinth founded Syracuse and Corcyra; and for over a century, roughly from 734 to 585 B.C., a strenuous program of colonization by representative groups, bearing all the essential institutions and equipment of the mother city, spread the Greek polis and Greek culture far and wide, from Naucratis in Egypt to Marseille in Gaul, from Sicily to the farther shores of the Black Sea. This movement at first was due to agricultural pressure rather than commercial ambition; and it spread the Hellenic way of life far beyond the Aegean.

Greek city development made many promising institutional departures from the original pattern of the city, as it had developed both in Mesopotamia and in the Egypt of the Empire. The Greeks, it seemed, had in some degree freed themselves from the outrageous fantasies of unqualified power that Bronze Age religion and Iron Age technology had fostered: their cities were cut closer to the human measure, and were delivered from the paranoid claims of quasi-divine monarchs, with all the attending compulsions and regimentations of militarism and bureaucracy. The Greeks broke down, indeed they had hardly yet developed, the hard caste and occupational divisions that had come in with civilization itself: at this early moment, they had the flexibility and inventiveness of the amateur, not willing to sacrifice too much of his life to specialized competence.

As the city developed, the democratic habits of the village would be often carried into its heretofore specialized activities, with a constant rotation of human functions and civic duties, and with a full participation by each citizen in every aspect of the common life. This sparse material culture, in many places little better than a subsistence regimen, gave rise to a new kind of economy of abundance, for it opened up virgin territories of mind and spirit that had hardly been explored, let alone cultivated. The result was not merely a torrential outpouring of ideas and images in drama, poetry, sculpture, painting, logic, mathematics, and philosophy; but a collective life more highly energized, more heightened in its capacity for esthetic expression and rational evaluation, than had ever been achieved before. Within a couple of centuries the Greeks discovered more about the nature and potentialities of man than the Egyptians or the Sumerians seem to have discovered in as many millennia. All these achievements were concentrated in the Greek polis, and in particular, in the greatest of these cities, Athens.

Supreme in every department except colonization, Athens was the embodiment of all these fresh promises. But while Athens created a cultural legacy to which every succeeding age has been indebted, it sought to pre-empt for its own vainglory the goods that every other city had contributed to, and had a right equally to share in. Though conserving, indeed cultivating, the benefits of internal democracy, Athens chose to act the king among lesser cities, demanding homage and tribute, in tyrannous fashion, in return for protection. The excrement of early civilization —war, exploitation, enslavement, mass extermination—backed up on Athens, as from an ancient sewer. In the end these forces overcame a movement toward a wider fellowship, with more humane goals, that was already visible in the seventh century. Had Greece's intellectual leaders fully grasped the implications of this universalism, they might have liberated urban culture from its chronic involvement in the practice of human sacrifice for perverse and irrational ends.

At a decisive moment, it was Athens' refusal to give freedom to its tributary cities, not Sparta's truculent challenge, that brought on the fatal Peloponnesian War. In bringing to light both the potentialities that never fully flowered, and the frustrations and defeats that were the outcome of the challenge not taken, the life unlived, Athens may well serve as an exemplar of all other great cities, equally varied and highly individuated. This opportunity is in fact also a necessity, for apart from archaeological findings, themselves still scattered and incomplete, most of the documents on Greek urban development come from Athens. Yet what was true of Athens probably holds, with sundry degrees of qualification, for most other Greek cities, at similar moments of their development. Their chief difference would be a quantitative one, for many sister Greek cities, distinguished in history, never held more than three or four thousand inhabitants. Contrary to the convictions of census statisticians, it is art, culture, and political purpose, not numbers, that define a city.

2: THE VOICE OF THE VILLAGE

If one finds fleeting pictures of the Mycenaean or post-Mycenaean palaces
and towns in Homer, one discovers the background of village culture
out of which the Aegean city and its colonies grew, in Hesiod's 'Works
and Days.' The scene shifts from Crete to the western Aegean, though the
fullest development of the city, before the fifth century, actually took
place in Ionia, in the ports that served as outlets for Asia Minor and
for the distant provinces beyond.

As we have noted, these mountain-locked valleys provided no easy
means of subsistence, and could support only a meager village population. When numbers increased, the plains of Thessaly and Boeotia would
at first supply the grain. But in urban terms they counted as backward
parts of Greece. Though poor in barley and wheat, the villages near the
sea got from it an extra store of food: the fisherman became a sailor and
the sailor a merchant—albeit malice or misfortune might turn all three,
on occasion, into pirates, and piracy, with its goods-looting and body-
snatching, might lead to war. Villages that were a few miles inland, under
the shadow of a steep hill, had a double protection against piratical raids;
and in contrast to landbound Mycenae or Sparta, it was the towns with
access to the sea, yet with a strip of land between, like Athens and
Corinth, that turned into great metropolises.

The pattern of a natural stronghold, with abrupt rugged slopes easy
to defend without extra fortification, surrounded by a group of villages—
this is a common feature of both Greece and Italy, from Asia Minor in
fact to Sicily and to Etruria. The remains of such settlements, often
lapsing back into their earliest state, are visible today. These natural
defensive sites usually had a feature that made them more desirable—
a spring—and the spring itself might put the spot under the protection
of a god and the permanent guardianship of a single family. If in times
of danger the clustered villagers withstood the attack well, the common
shrine would only become more venerable.

Villages, once isolated, would keep up their religious association when
the military necessity was gone: if not the presence of danger, then the
desire to forfend it by pious observances, would draw them back to the
natural acropolis. Here the sacred fire would be lighted, and kept lighted,
supplementing that of the household hearth—both pieties symbolizing
the common bond—while the shrine itself would draw to its neighborhood
other household or village shrines and even absorb them in the larger
cult. It is significant that no man who neglected the plot where his dead
lay might hold the chief magistracies in Athens. The Hellenic city is,

typically, such a union of villages, or synoecism: sometimes brought about by voluntary democratic action, sometimes, as in the case of Athens itself, by kingly compulsion. But the adhesion was never complete and the rule of the city never absolute.

Among the Hellenes, the original ingredients for kingship and city building were much the same as we have found in Mesopotamia; but with a difference. For in Greece, the abundance of naturally defensible sites lessened dependence upon engineering skill: a handful of brave men could successfully hold a mountain pass against seemingly overwhelming numbers, and they had a similar advantage on the rocky slopes of their natural citadel. A sparse population, moreover, cannot be regimented in masses or kept in order at a formidable distance from their rulers. Made independent by his isolation, inured to his poverty, the underdog will not take a beating from his superiors without snapping back: even Thersites in the 'Iliad,' though unfriended and at a disadvantage, indeed an object of contempt, did not hesitate to tell the chiefs off.

Poor peasants and shepherds, if they were willing to live leanly, could keep going without submission to a vast collective organization; and since the tempting surplus was lacking, they could not so easily be bribed by bread and shows. If there was thus less opportunity for one-sided exploitation, there was less need for a strict, over-all control. Hence, perhaps, a somewhat looser form of organization grew up, less formalized, less stiffly ranged in hierarchic rank. With this came personal independence: alike in judgment and in action. Independence and self-reliance were as engrained in pre-imperialist Greece as in Emersonian New England: there was pride in the old saying: "Greece and poverty are twins." The Greek poleis in their best days had no great surplus of goods: what they had was a surplus of time, that is, leisure, free and untrammeled, not committed —as in America today—to excessive materialistic consumption, but available for conversation, sexual passion, intellectual reflection, and esthetic delight.

Is it an accident that in the short Ephebic Oath the vow to do one's duty *"single-handed* or with the support of all" is uttered twice? The boast of pliability and of freedom from the constraints of specialization which Thucydides put into Pericles' mouth as a special attribute of the Athenians, had its roots in the village. Athens had no patent on these virtues: those who live in villages and value their intimacies do not confuse size with significance. Lonely courage played a part that mass obedience to the leader's command could never rival. Such courage produced heroes of the mind as well as of the battlefield, often in the same person.

In their formative period the Greek cities never lost their connections with their countryside or their villages: there was a tidal drifting in and out of the city with the seasons. As late as 400 B.C., according to Elizabeth Visser, three-quarters of the Athenian burghers owned some land in Attica. In many places, the archaic village component seems much stronger than that of the citadel. Aristotle, with some historic justification, associated fortified hill sites with monarchy and oligarchy, while he equated the lowland cities with democracy; but in actual operation, the two were not so far apart and the dividing line not too rigid. The writer of 'The Government of Athens' wryly noted that the Athenians "everywhere give more weight to the less higher class," and what could be more characteristic of village democracy?

The village measure prevailed in the development of Greek cities, down to the fourth century: the modest dimensions of stele and gravestone, delicately pithy inscriptions, the touches of humor—all far from the grandiose, the monumental, the inflated. In these communities, poverty was not an embarrassment: if anything, riches were suspect. Nor was smallness a sign of inferiority. The democratic practices of the village, without strong class or vocational cleavages, fostered a habit of taking counsel together. The best excuse for the city as a larger village was that it widened the circle of possible talkers. If the Spartans were an exception, their laconic habits of speech were perhaps bred of the need to keep their intentions secret from the people they so brutally held in slavery: thus they had no use for the city.

These village ways made the post-Homeric Greeks distrustful of kingly power and centralized rule: even at Troy that was plain. The mystique of kingship did not fit in well with either their village parochialism or their inbred self-respect: they valued the intellectual cunning of an Odysseus no less than the schoolboy valor of an Achilles, and though they worshipped the gods, they never encouraged, any more than their Persian rivals, the notion that the ruler himself might be a god. Agamemnon reproached Clytemnestra for her servile effusiveness of speech: "As a man, not as a god, let me be honored." The delusion of divinity in a ruler was a product of their civic decadence.

Even the growth of imperialism in the fifth century, though it turned Athens itself into a ruthless exploiter of smaller Greek cities, did not bring about the restoration of kingship or enlarge the dominion of the Olympian gods. Quite the contrary: not merely did the Greeks discard the more superstitious claims of royalty, making their leaders dependent upon popular support, cutting them down to human dimensions, but their gods are represented either as of the same build as other human figures, as in the Parthenon frieze, or as slightly larger creatures of the same mold. By the fifth century they even made the gods themselves a little ridiculous, if not contemptible, by playing up their amorous foibles and jealous rivalries.

Not till the barbarous Macedonian, Alexander, set out on his conquests were the aboriginal claims of the divine king revived: perhaps a sign that this ancient cult had taken refuge in the mountains, as Manichaeism was later to do. When tyrants assumed power in Greek cities, they did so, more often than not, by espousing the popular cause and challenging the old feudal oligarchy of the 'best families'—the landed proprietors who not merely claimed a larger share of wealth, but who alone inherited the priestly offices and could alone perform some of the higher municipal functions.

This maintenance of the old connections with farm and village, this keeping up of tribal and family associations, was a source of strength to the Greek city in a time of troubles. But it also tended to restrict its advantages. When the population of the city increased through trade and immigration, it reduced an ever larger part of its inhabitants to the status of irresponsible, second-class citizens, who were in fact excluded from public office and even from some of the important civic festivals.

True: it was not until the fourth century that any large part of the population in a Greek city might be foreigners, with no right to possess property in land; and by this time war had sent many native citizens into perpetual exile or slavery. Yet the roots of village life were so deep that even the displaced victims of a savage conquest could sometimes survive the destruction of the city. When the Spartans, for example, compelled the inhabitants of Mantinea to destroy their own city—a refinement of cruelty comparable to the Nazis' compelling their victims to dig their own graves—these miserable people retired to their rural *demes,* from which they had never been completely severed.

As long indeed as the Greek cities remained small, the countryside was within easy walking distance: the sea of houses that today stretches between Athens and the Piraeus was under cultivation, like the country-side along the sacred road to Eleusis, now given over to cement plants. Even in growing Athens, it was natural for Socrates and Phaedrus, on a hot summer's day, to stroll beyond the city, paddling in the shallow Ilyssus, in the shade of the plane trees, to find rural peace and solitude. The landed families would send their oil, their wine, their honey, their figs, and their wool from the country to their own urban household, thus keeping partly independent of the market and the need for money exchanges. That must have re-enforced their contempt for outsiders who had to devote themselves to money-making in order to buy such products. As Emil Kuhn remarked long ago, in his noteworthy 'Staedte der Alten,' city and country formed a unity among the Greeks, not two antagonistic modes of life.

This closeness to rural ways no doubt partly accounts for the primitive housing accommodations and sanitary facilities that characterized the Greek cities right into the fourth century and even later. The houses were lightly built of wood and sun-dried clay: so flimsy were the walls that the quickest way for a burglar to enter a house was by digging through the wall. Residentially speaking, the biggest cities were little better at first than overgrown villages; indeed, precisely because of their overgrowth and density of site occupation, they were certainly much worse, because they lacked the open spaces of the farmyard and neighboring field.

Thus the highest culture of the ancient world, that of Athens, reached its apex in what was, from the standpoint of town planning and hygiene, a deplorably backward municipality. The varied sanitary facilities that Ur and Harappa had boasted two thousand years before hardly existed even in vestigial form in fifth-century Athens. The streets of any Greek city, down to Hellenistic times, were little more than alleys, and many of these alleys were only passageways, a few feet wide. Refuse and ordure accumulated at the city's outskirts, inviting disease and multiplying the victims of the plague. The stereotyped, largely false image of the 'medieval town,' which many people who should know better still retain, would in fact be a true image for the growing cities of sixth- and fifth-century Greece, particularly in Attica and the Peloponnese. Certainly it applies with far more justice to these cities than to many towns in Western Europe in the thirteenth century A.D.

As long as the Greek town remained small, these primitive rural ways were not necessarily noisome or threatening to health: the sun is an efficient antiseptic, the open earth an acceptable compost heap, and the pig and the dog are eager scavengers. But there is plenty of evidence to show that filth of every description heaped up at the borders of the city; it was at such municipal dumps that unwanted babies in Athens were exposed and left to die. No wonder that Aristotle prescribed in his 'Politics' for official sanitary inspectors, to exercise supervision over the town's refuse; for the quantitative change from village to city had also produced a qualitative change that neither nature nor the old village ways could cope with.

Fortunately, the village pattern was not suddenly disrupted, for most Greek cities in their formative days did not aspire to large numbers or large domains. Cities with only a few thousand inhabitants would send out colonies long before they were overcrowded within. Even if the city had sought a bigger population, the limits of arable land and a sufficient water supply would still have curbed its growth. Athens, though surrounded by relatively rich alluvial soil, probably did not harbor more than a hundred thousand inhabitants, including slaves, in the fifth century; and it is doubtful if Miletus or Corinth, to mention two prosperous capitals, could have embraced many more, at least until those cities had been reorganized by Roman engineers. Few cities, as R. E. Wycherley points out, had more than ten thousand people.

I shall go back to the problem of the size of the city, which was first rationally considered by the Greeks, at a later point. But if anything were needed to prove that the towns of Greece, from the seventh century B.C. to the fourth, were both small and relatively self-contained, largely dependent upon their local countryside for food and for building materials, the story of Greek colonization would be sufficient. For these Aegean cities sent out colonies in every direction, and in particular to Sicily and to Italy: they ranged from Marseille at the mouth of the Rhone to Naucratis in the delta of the Nile, and eastward to the shores of the Black Sea. In the Etruscan cities, whatever their remote origin, one finds an art and a style of life that closely unites this apparently independent culture with that of the Aegean.

The chief colonizing cities were great commercial centers like Rhodes and Miletus in Asia Minor: the latter city supposedly sent out seventy urban colonies. That fact proves both a steady increase of population, and an unwillingness, even after trade opened up distant supply lines, to alter the nature of the city by encouraging excessive growth. The limit was not simply lack of land for building space, though in many areas that must have counted. Water and food exerted positive controls on growth: even more, perhaps, the sense of family and village affiliation fostered a desire for an intimate unit.

Significantly, Athens, with its system of imperialist exploitation and overseas trade in pottery and oil, was not among the great colonizing cities. By keeping its citizens close to home, this city overpassed the limits of safe growth and increased its dependence upon war and tribute for its continued 'prosperity.' But even the boldest military conquerors had to acknowledge the natural limits of the city. When Alexander's chief architect offered to build him the largest city of all time, that leader, who understood logistics as well as strategy, peremptorily dismissed the idea: Impossible to provision such a city!

The transposition of the village into the polis, the place where people come together, not just by birth and habit, but consciously, in pursuit of a better life, takes place before our eyes in Greece. There must have been many potential centers where the power of the lord and the feudal aristocracy had become enfeebled, and where, it would seem, the villagers' hatred of war, so bitterly recorded by Hesiod, would be carried over into the constitution and daily practices of the city. Certainly, the Greek village asked only to be let alone in its self-contained environment: it wanted neither to conquer nor to be conquered. Could the city flourish—could it even exist—on the same terms? The fact that Athens, like many other cities, did not build any all-enclosing walls until after the first Persian invasion shows that urban centers, under the conditions that existed up to the fifth century, had a certain sense of internal security. And the early absence of walls may account for just those human qualities that at first distinguished the Aegean cities from those of the Near East: their freedom and open-mindedness. In Athens, the building of the wall came as an afterthought: almost to the end, Sparta rejected it, as unworthy of a fighting caste.

But from the village, be it noted, came certain negative traits: isolation, jealousy, suspicion of the stranger, parochialism—the darker face of self-reliance and self-sufficiency. This independence too easily became quarrelsomeness, opposition for the sake of opposition, a willingness to cut off one's nose to spite one's face. Even within the city it might have had a disruptive effect: it was not for nothing that Aristophanes devoted a whole comedy to mercilessly castigating the Athenian over-fondness for litigation. This village isolationism was classically illustrated by the fact that Greek cities, despite Delphi's efforts, never arrived at a common calendar. They even began their years at different times.

The incorrigible self-centeredness of the Greek village could be broken down only in time of danger, on the appearance of a visible enemy. Obviously such temporary political union is different from the kind of structural unification that was required in Mesopotamia and Egypt for the control of floods or the annual reapportionment of the land: what Mary Austin called the "collectivism of the indivisible utility" had no application in Greece. Topography and village custom served as barriers to unification, despite all that language, literature, art, and mythology did to bind the cities of Greece together.

But though parochialism began in the village, it had other sources as well; and one must not forget that it was in the era when all the cities of Greece were closest to their village origins, the biggest boasting only a few thousand inhabitants, that the Greeks instituted the Olympian games. That large scale circulation and meeting of the elite broke down, by pressure of human intention, the distance between human communities that natural conditions had seemed to impose. So, too, it was Hesiod, the villager, who hated and denounced war, while it was Plato, the urban philosopher, who praised war as essential for developing human virtues.

One final trait had its origin in the villages. From the peasant, surely, and not solely from the landed gentry, came the distrust of the trader and the banker, the commercial go-between, the lender of money and the holder of mortgages: in fact, all the busy people who, to extend trade and promote wealth, were creating the new money economy, so hostile to the old rural ways and the old Attic penury.

These traders and bankers, backed by manufacturers and craftsmen, were the new organizers of the city; after the sixth century they threatened the power of the original aristocrats and warriors. But the problem of incorporating these new commercial groups into the commonwealth, bringing them actively into its services and making them responsible, never seriously concerned the great minds of Greece. The constitution of even commercial towns treated business as if it were non-existent. A citizen, by definition, could have no part in commerce. If he wanted such a career, it was necessary for him to migrate, as a stranger, to another town. Only a few towns, like Aegina and Chios, permitted their citizens to take part in trade.

Yet it was from the commercial cities of Ionia, indeed from merchants in their own persons, like Thales, that a whole world of new ideas came forth. Though these ideas distinguished Greek scientists and philosophers from their priestly forerunners in Babylonia and Egypt, the forms and values of the city, until the fourth century, were not altered by this fact. When finally these new agents were absorbed, it was largely under the reactionary influence of the new emperors, 'divine kings,' self-styled 'saviors.'

At this late point quantification and organization had become ends in themselves, and the more precious attributes of the polis disappeared. The superstitions of power came back with the exercise of over-centralized military power itself. In the Hellenic polis' failure to widen sufficiently the village horizon lies some of the responsibility for its final downfall. Strangely, by no effort of thought did the great minds of Hellas transcend either their geographic or their cultural environment.

3: OLYMPIA, DELPHI, AND COS

As an organ of culture, the Greek city reached its maturity in the fifth century, before it had achieved a rich organization of physical form, except in the acropolis. At that point its civic purposes had emerged from its aboriginal municipal functions—and were far more highly developed. Upon its dual heritage—the post-Mycenaean stronghold and the mountain village—a new set of institutions, more universal in nature, more spontaneous in association, was laid; and more than once these freer institutions seemed on the point of creating a new kind of urban organization, less enclosed, less divisive, less rigid and oppressive, than that which had given form to the walled city. I purpose to examine these fresh components —more visible to us now perhaps than they ever were to the Greeks— before I describe the actual structure of the fifth-century city.

Pausanias, a late observer of Greek cities, dismissed a city of the

Phocians as hardly worthy to be called a city, because it had no government offices, no gymnasium, no theater, no market, no piped water supply.
For him it was these buildings and utilities that distinguished a city from
a mere huddle of village houses. But the germ of the Greek city was
already well-developed in the village: what had held true in the neolithic
transition was still true. What is the assembly of magistrates, in the
Prytaneum or Town Hall, but the urban form of the ancient Council of
Elders, probably the oldest of secular political institutions? What is the
formal marketplace (agora) but the same convenient open space where
the elders met, big enough for the whole village to gather in, where the
neighbors could, incidentally, spread out their surplus products for barter?
What is the piped fountain but a more reliable form of the sacred spring,
whose raised basin was not so likely to be contaminated by pissing dogs
or the muddy feet of men? As for the theater, that too existed in embryonic
form in the village fertility rites, for spring and harvest: the circular
threshing floor became the stage of the new theater, and the villagers
themselves separated out from the protagonists as chorus, no longer actors,
but still too active and loquacious to be called merely spectators.

By the eighth century, possibly, the Greek city had begun to acquire
a physiognomy of its own. Like other ancient centers, the Greek town
was from the beginning the home of a god. Though many cities might
claim the same divinity, especially colonization towns, which so often
migrated under the aegis of Apollo, the local deity would show some
special feature that linked him either to the old hearth gods or to some
decisive historic event. So much was stereotyped.

Yet as early as the sixth century, the time of Solon, a fresh wind
seems to blow through these cities, from the eastern Aegean to the northern reaches of the Mediterranean; but above all in Attica: fogs of confusion and superstition dissipate before the morning sun, and its rays
begin to penetrate the deepest cave. The mind, newly conscious of itself
and its powers, falls into a contemplation of its own image; and the smile
on the Greek statues, which too glibly is dismissed as an archaic convention, may truly reveal this inner confidence and illumination. However
rank the village life at the base of the city, he who climbed the acropolis
would see in the sharp-edged mountain slopes and the luminous skies the
reflection of a mind that had become the measure of all things, judging
old customs, habits, laws by an independent rule, open to reason. The
gods must now meet human standards.

For a century or two, as a result of this transformation, the Greek
polis, particularly Athens, became a symbol for all that was veritably
human. Natural life itself turned out to be more wonderful, in its measured
limitations, than the insolent magnifications and clotted confusions of

mythological fantasy. To be human was to be more godlike than the ancient gods. What forces effected this transformation?

The easy explanation of Hellenic urban culture would be that which identified its quick felicities with its democratic principles, contrasting the polis with the great overgrown capitals of the oriental despotisms. That contrast was a natural one for the Greeks to make, in the exultation of defeating the Persian invasion; but the evidence does not fully support this explanation.

If the Greeks were notably successful in throwing off the institution of kingship, which had hardly passed beyond the claims of the earliest tribal chieftains, their achievement of democracy remained slow, partial, fitful, never fully effective. Not merely did landed oligarchies and tyrannies long continue in power in many regions; but even where democracy finally prevailed, as it did in Athens, it retained the old principles of segregation and monopoly. Athenian democracy excluded the foreigner and the slave: no small part of the total population. (Ominously, the polis had need of twelve hundred Scythian archers to police the Assembly and law courts.) Although, after Pericles, craftsmen and tradesmen often rose to the highest offices in the city, both the freedom and the equality that Athenian democracy boasted were under many restrictions. We must look elsewhere for the forces of the mind that seemed ready to breach the invisible walls that had confined the new attributes of personality to the king and his nobles, and limited a general human development in the ancient city.

To find the special secret of the Greek city one must look outside the bigger centers. And if one wanted to sum up in three words what supremely distinguished Greek urban culture from that of its predecessors, one might say simply: Olympia, Delphi, Cos. It was the contribution of these centers that raised the whole ceiling of human achievement so high.

None of these places had any pretenses to being a great city. Each stands in fact for a specialized kind of town, with a power of attraction that drew men together, occasionally or seasonally, from the farthest regions of Magna Graecia, sending them back again, with their parochial limitations challenged, and with a salient aspect of their life renewed and lifted to a higher level.

What the transport and interchange of goods had done to stimulate the daily life of the Mesopotamian city, the personal visits to Olympia, Delphi, or Cos did for the religious, political, literary, and athletic development of the Greeks. The first was the home of the Olympian games; the second held the chief shrine and the sacred oracle of Apollo, the one great unifying civic and religious influence, comparable to that of the Vatican in Roman Catholic countries; while the third was one of the great health resorts and sanatoria, where a new group of physicians, the predecessors and followers of Hippocrates (460-375 B.C.), sought through a rational understanding of nature to cure disease and promote health.

From these three centers flowed currents of vital energy, transmitted by pilgrims and participants, faring on foot and by boat, which brought into every Greek city a whole stream of unifying and self-transcending ideas and norms of life. The characteristic work of each of these centers was carried on in many other cities: Cnidus and Epidauros, the original home of the Asclepius cult, rivalled Cos; and the Apollonian shrine at Delos turned that barren isle into both a pilgrims' refuge and a center of international banking and trade despite its treacherous approach by water. Similarly, once the inter-urban games were started, many other cities competed with Olympia. Through the influence of these institutions, the more adventurous members of the polis came into direct contact with other cities, other peoples, other ways; and the participants experienced that process of 'withdrawal-and-return' which both Patrick Geddes and Arnold Toynbee have demonstrated historically is an essential mode of human growth. These festivals and congregations challenged the ingrained parochialism of the polis. The four great Panhellenic festivals—the Olympian, the Pythian, the Isthmian, and the Nemean—drew Greeks together from every part of Hellas, along the sacred roads, where wayfarers were immune to attack at such seasons. Such mobilization and congregation forecast even freer movement in an even wider world.

Olympia stood for the body as the active physical expression, through disciplined play, of the human spirit. Whatever the later sins of Greek dualism, in the formative days of their culture, the classic Greeks never identified spiritual development with incorporeality, still less with a Porphyrean contempt for the body or a monkish masochistic pleasure in degrading it or courting disease. Delphi represented through its oracle the combination of the unconscious, in its depths, accessible through darkness, sleep, drugs, intoxication, with an open-eyed intelligence and a far-seeing providence: its twin gods, as Werner Jaeger reminds us, were Apollo *and* Dionysus, not just the orderly, clear-thinking Apollo alone, himself a symbol of both solar and spiritual illumination. Those who were put to sleep by the priestess at Delphi were visited by the god in their dreams: probably under the influence of hypnotism or a soporific, even perhaps an anesthetic; for there is a report from that center of the lifting of a cataract from a sufferer's eye during the night, unknown to the dreamer.

It was such a Delphic priestess, Diotima, who bade Socrates listen to his daimon; so that, at the moment rational thought left the temple to run the gauntlet of common experience in the marketplace, it was accompanied by a vivid reminder of its pre-rational cosmic beginnings in cave and grotto and animal rite. The masters of Greek tragedy never forgot that lesson. It was not for nothing that Delphi in Greek legend, like Jerusalem on medieval Christian maps, occupied the exact center of the earth. This was its precise position in the Greek mind. The original function of the Delphic priesthood was to determine the correct order of the religious festivals, and it is quite probable that Delphi as early as the seventh century sought, though unsuccessfully, to spread its recognition of a uniform type of calendar in the Greek world.

Finally, Cos was the great center from which a new concept of health radiated: at once a sanatorium, a hospital, a center of medical research, where, as George Sarton has pointed out, medical thought matured. But these centers were not just a collection of utilitarian buildings, half factory, half hotel, like most of our modern hospitals. They also possessed the calm attributes of the cloister: here, for perhaps the first time, the function of the cloister, of withdrawal and inner dedication, escaped the confines of the temple, even while the temple of Asclepius itself remained close at hand.

The physicians at Cos knew the healing qualities of seclusion and beauty, space and order: they set their sanatoria on a little island, famous for its grapes and mulberry trees, and its specially fine silk, with a wide view over the sea: a noble landscape freed from the clutter, the disorder, the smells and noises of the Greek city.

Perhaps no one has ever translated these ideals so effectively, if quite unconsciously, as Henry James did in his dream allegory, 'The Great Good Place.' People travelled hundreds of miles by land and by sea to be under the care of such dedicated physicians, bound by their noble oath, working in such a healing environment. By the very act of detachment through travel, the patient took his first step toward rehabilitation; and the psychosomatic discovery of the curative properties of a change of scene may have been a contribution of Hippocratic lore, based on improvements the physicians observed in newcomers even before they applied their positive remedies. Can one doubt that the order that came into the new cities of the fourth century registered, in collective form, some of the lessons that this great school of healers and hygienists applied to the individual patient? That sense of space and harmony, in nature and of nature and yet surpassing nature through man's own ordered effort, left its mark on later cities.

The Olympian games were founded in 776 B.C. and continued to be held for almost a thousand years. It was not altogether by accident that these games arose in little Olympia, home of the gods, rival to the mountain in the north where the Olympian family originated. Games and contests have a religious origin, if not always an immediate religious outlet: Herodotus tells us about an annual contest with clubs at the entrance to an Egyptian temple, which probably reflected a much more ancient rite staged between those who represented Osiris and those who represented Set. In Greece, funerary games, whose victors were given crowns of the sacred herb, parsley, certainly came before the Olympic games, to celebrate the life and death of a chieftain or hero. But the singular merit of the Olympic games was to establish, every four years, a state of political peace in which the inhabitants of all cities could travel freely under protection of Zeus, without fear of arrest or injury. To violate any such pilgrim was an act of sacrilege.

At Olympia the cities met, so to say, in person; and the contests were concerned with the body as an expression of the human spirit. These games brought together poets as well as athletes; and both were moved to give their utmost to the competition, since their audience was not merely their fellow-townsmen, but the assembled representatives of a larger commonwealth, wide-flung Hellas.

Under the impetus from these games, a new institution entered the Hellenic city, and a new place must be found for it: the palestra or wrestling ground. This in time developed further into the gymnasium, an enclosed sports-ground, often set in a grove of plane trees, for every manner of athletic competition or exhibition. Such a center would be equipped with baths, dressing rooms, and finally classrooms; for, following Olympic precedent, the mind was not left apathetic and idle by too violent physical exercise. Here is where the young and the old came together for friendly bouts of wrestling or boxing, for racing, for hurling the discus or the javelin. Out of three such sacred groves, already established in the sixth century, came three famous schools of learning, the Lyceum, the Academy, and the Cynosarges.

If the marketplace had been, perhaps, an improvised center for such activities before the sixth century, there was no room left there when the city started to grow. So we find the gymnasium on the outskirts of the city, where there was unbuilt-on land, sufficient for open-air activities. Everywhere in the city, but here especially, there were statues of the gods and heroes: these reminders of 'perfect athletes and the perfect mothers of athletes' set a public standard for bodily grace and vigor. This plastic art influenced the youth of Greek cities as photographs and advertisements of motion-picture stars set standards for feminine beauty in present-day civilization. At the moment of adolescence when narcissism and body-consciousness first appear, the influence of such models cannot be over-estimated. I can testify personally to the effect of even an inferior Roman work, of an athlete with a strigil, upon my own physical development.

In a century or two, with the growth of the mercantile spirit in Greek society, the religious and cultural purposes of the Olympic games were overshadowed by sordid professionalism and commercialism; this went

along with the installation of rival competitions in other cities. Mere physical prowess, like that of Milo of Croton, took the place of graceful
strength and fleetness and imperturbable fortitude; indeed prize winning
by professional athletes had become, as in our own day, an end in itself
by the fourth century B.C.; and Theagenes of Thasos boasted of winning
five hundred prizes.

But so ingrained was the sense of sportsmanship at first, that even
wars between cities sometimes took the manners of a sporting contest, for
honor rather than for more vicious stakes. Witness the 'war' between
Chalcis and Eretria, in the seventh century, held only as a contest, with
all hurled missiles, spears, slings, and arrows barred. These cities had
emerged from the barbarous depravity of total war and had sublimated
brutal aggression.

In moving into the city, urban dwellers had left behind many salutary
country pastimes and vigorous bodily occupations: so it was the mission
of the Olympic games to bring back these rural virtues as part of the
daily urban routine—detached and stylized exercises, cut out of the old
matrix of the farm, the pasture, and the woodland hunt.

The spiritual by-products of this new institution proved as important
as its gifts to health; for here the old and the young came into constant
companionship, not as parents and children, or even as teachers and students, but as partners in discussion, led by the older members, all the
more stimulating because of the differences in age and the escape from
purely parental authority. Sometimes this intimacy proved an encourage-
ment to a sterile homosexuality, in provoking passionate infatuations relieved of any threat of offspring; but it was also, as the Platonic dialogues
remind us, a contribution to higher education. Did an authoritative priesthood have anything of comparable value to offer by way of method?
And as long as the gymnasium invited physical exercise, it helped to
overcome the bodily slackness that too often was the price exacted for
adaptation to the constricted, sedentary urban environment.

The part played by the Delphic shrine is harder to describe, especially since the cult left behind no readable record other than its treasury
and its votive monuments. Though the cult of Dionysus may have come
from much farther afield, it was perhaps with the sanction of Delphi,
itself constantly bringing together Apollonian measure and clarity with
Dionysian darkness and ecstasy, that the drama captured the Greek city.
Here we may pause to take in the theater as an urban institution which
entered the Greek city at about the same time as the gymnasium, perhaps
first performing in the agora on improvised grandstands of wood, as
depicted in three early sixth-century vases. But soon, because of the
crowds attending in the growing town, the theater established itself on
the slope of a hill on the outskirts, under the open sky.

The festivals out of which the theater arose were religious festivals, long celebrated in the village; and the priests from the temple occupied the front row of the 'orchestra.' If the Attic comedy grew out of old fertility rites, rooted in the neolithic past, tragedy wrestled with the problems of human development opened up by the new urban order: fate, chance, free will. As the city itself developed, the drama sloughed off both sides of its religious heritage: mere cerebral amusement took the place of bawdy rites and horseplay as well as solemn edification. With this went a loss of cosmic perspective. At the very moment its pride and confidence became overweening, the human self began to shrivel. Cut off from its sense of the cosmic and the divine, it seemed more and more a prey to meaningless change and external caprice. In its own development, the drama thus symbolized the course of urban development, as the vulgar, the trivial, the sordid, the spectacular displaced the sacraments of birth, citizenship, vocation, marriage, death.

Yet in its post-tragic phase, when the religious connection was broken, the theater remained one of the distinguishing marks of the classic city, visible in the most distant of towns built for the colonizers and pensioners of Empire. Even today, on the hillside of Fiesole near Florence, the semicircle of stone benches looking over the valley that spreads below and the mountains that rise beyond, recaptures the all but universal form of the Greek theater, and exhales a faint breath of the original culture that produced it. The beauty of ordered space within an ordered cosmos.

If one mark of the end of the classic city is the termination of the Olympic games, the other is the abandonment of the theater. For it was in the theater that the Greek citizen saw himself and obeyed the Delphic maxim: Know Thyself. Best of all, the relentless comedies of Aristophanes tell us, he learned to see himself, wryly, as others saw him, chastened by their painful laughter. But at the same time he beheld, in the larger figures of heroes and gods, beckoning potential selves whose imitation in moments of crisis would help him overpass the mediocrity of the safe and the habitual. Self-consciousness and self-realization, even self-transcendence, became the new marks of the urban personality—or at least of an awakened minority.

But even more directly and practically, Delphi worked still another change in the development of the Greek city. Because the founding of the city was for the Greeks, as it had been for earlier cultures, primarily a religious act, Delphi naturally assumed charge of the new foundations; and especially in the early period of colonization, the Pythian Apollo gave specific advice that dispatched new colonies in every direction, under the aegis of Apollo himself. Few cities would undertake such an expedition without consulting the oracle. Thus at a moment when the growth of population might have led to congestion within the city, to random emigration, or to conflicts for arable land in the more densely populated regions, Delphi, willy-nilly, faced the population problem and conducted a program of organized dispersal.

Through this program, the keepers of that shrine lessened both the acerbic economic competition and the wars of conquest, while it spread Greek culture and the Greek polis to the thinly settled village communities on the perimeter. The control of city growth by orderly colonization, repeated as often as numbers demanded, was the first practical recognition of an organic limit to city growth. During the century when it was most widely practiced, when the norm was maintained, the Greek city proved an extremely favorable environment for human development. The Delphic doctrine of the golden mean held for cities as well as for men. Note that religious persuasion and voluntary action brought about this colonization movement: not centralized military control. The latter came under Alexander the Great, when religious authority had crumbled and civic norms had vanished.

Cos, Cnidus, and Epidauros were no less symbols of the Greek concern for wholeness and balance than the Olympic games or the Delphic shrine; and the lessons they taught played a part in later town planning, though they have not yet been fully assimilated even today.

One of the most famous of Hippocratic treatises is that on 'Air, Water, and Places'; a work which laid down the outlines of public hygiene in relation to the choice of sites and the planning of cities. If the Greek love for the concrete object led these keen physicians to neglect forces and organisms below the ordinary threshold of sight, so that they apparently never suspected that diseases might be transmitted by invisible agents, they nevertheless did full justice to matters more easily discovered and handled: the orientation of buildings and city streets to evade the summer sun and catch the cooling winds; the avoidance of marshy lands and insanitary surroundings; the procuring of pure sources of water, as a matter doubly necessary for the sick, to whom wine must usually be forbidden.

These prescriptions did not make headway quickly. It was easier for the wealthy and the leisured to visit a distant sanatorium when they were ill than for a municipality to provide the capital needed for great works of engineering that would bring pure water down from the hills, provide ample open spaces for recreation within the city, open up the crowded dwelling quarters and secure circulation of air, if not by lessening residential crowding, then by intersecting each building block, at frequent intervals, by streets and alleys. Paradoxically, the big cities, which possessed the capital needed for these outlays, were least able to 'afford' the necessary improvements, though their very numbers made the improvements in hygiene more urgent.

Hippocratic theory, accordingly, did not become urban practice until the new Hellenistic cities were built, first in Greece, then in Roman coloni-zation towns. But the reiteration of these principles by the Roman architect and planner Vitruvius, in the first century A.D., showed that they remained alive and operative, just as no small part of Hippocratic medicine remained alive in Galen.

The understanding of the importance of pure water not merely pro-vided an incentive to municipal improvement: it led to the exploration of the curative properties of mineral springs; so that out of the original centers of medical treatment came their lineal descendants, the health resorts that specialized in natural hot and cold baths and copious water drinking. Bath itself in England was such a Roman center; and a belief in baths, including an appreciation of salt-water bathing, came back in the eighteenth century as a direct outcome of the classic-romantic revival, a whole century before fresh air and sunlight came to be regarded as the natural scientifically established method of combating rickets and tuberculosis.

The Hippocratic emphasis on air, water, soil, and situation did not gain an easy victory; for an ancient tradition of close building, a toler-ance of filth and putrefaction, a greedy desire to use every bit of land available, worked to transmit without improvement the medical and hygienic misdemeanors of the early builders of cities. But gradually the Hippocratic injunctions would bring into the city pure water for drinking and bathing and spacious parks for exercise and spiritual rejuvenation. These were essential urban equivalents for the natural facilities that the city had turned its back on. One phase of hygiene is, however, strangely missing: the medical school left no text on public sanitation; and there are no references to the proper disposal of excreta.

Such then were the decisive contributions the wide-ranging Greek, assembling periodically in special centers, made to the culture of cities: the gymnasium, the sanatorium, the theater. Not merely did they remold the form of the city: each introduced, likewise, a motive for wider cir-culation and cultural interchange, by travel and pilgrimage. This was a Panhellenic influence. In the poems of Tyrtaeus recited at the Olympic games even surly Sparta made a contribution to the common literary culture.

The people who ventured forth, in trickles or in broad streams, to Olympia, Delphi, and Cos, and their sister cities, had temporarily de-tached themselves from the self-enclosed world of the polis. They became members of a larger unity, brought about, not by encirclement and en-closure, but by a vivid attraction. At the point of meeting, they overcame the particularism and parochialism of their native city and gazed on a wider horizon. The sacred roads that led from Elis to Olympia, or from many other places to Delphi, served as a visible bond of this unity.

Potentially, these practices had within themselves the basis for a new kind of urban polity, based on federated organization, operating over wider areas, not by centralized command, but through voluntary transactions and mutual services. If these efforts had been more thoroughly understood and more consciously appraised by the political thinkers of Greece, even as late as the fourth century, they might still have left their mark on the city. But Greek practice was far in advance of Greek theory: indeed, theory accentuated the separate, the particular, the static, the archaic, and neglected the new tendencies toward dynamic cultural intercourse and political federation. Aristotle examined the constitutions of 158 Greek cities, each sufficiently different to merit separate analysis; but there is no record of his paying attention to the efforts at creating a general league of cities, though this had begun as early as the sixth century, and before Rome had wiped out the last vestige of Greek freedom, Greece would produce some twenty such confederations.

The majority of these leagues, McDonald pertinently notes, got their start in a common religious festival, and in the organization needed to protect and supervise a special cult. And all too belatedly two new devices of urban government were introduced: the principle of isopolity, by which one city gave its citizenship to another city, while remaining separate and self-governing; and that of sympolity, by which a city became part of a co-operative group, under a co-ordinating authority, with each citizen professing a double loyalty. In a peaceful world, these efforts might have multiplied and come to fruition.

Even those whose knowledge of Greece is as exhaustive as that of Toynbee are inclined to attribute the divisiveness of the Greek cities to their topographical situation, to jealousy and rivalry, or to their narcissistic infatuation with their own image. That all of these played a part one cannot doubt: but the fact that so many efforts were made at federation demonstrates the existence of many counter-pressures. The earliest federal state in Greece for which J. A. O. Larsen finds an adequate description was the Boeotian Confederacy of the period 447-386 B.C. The appreciation of that effort dates only from the discovery of the Hellenic Oxyrhynchus papyrus in 1908.

Perhaps this innovation was favored by the absence of mountain barriers and strong cities in that wide fertile plain; but despite its Attic reputation for thick-wittedness, Boeotia had in fact created a well-organized federal system, with a board of magistrates, a large representative council, a treasury and a command of an income, even a federal court or courts; and it was strong enough to impose uniform local governments upon the member cities. In all, a brilliant innovation.

This achievement of representative federal government, with its combination of union and local autonomy, was a political development of no little magnitude. What caused it to fail was not the inveterate particularism of Greek cities, something fatally inherent in their character and constitution: on the contrary, this federal system was overthrown by a brutal specific act, namely the 'King's Peace' of 386, which stipulated that Greek cities were to be 'free.' Under Spartan rule, this meant that they were *not* free to join together in a federal union. All this occurred before Demosthenes sought to rally the cowed cities confronting Philip of Macedon. Had Boeotian federalism prevailed against Spartan isolationism the cities of Hellas might have fended off the fatal blow at Chaeronea.

If the force and self-confidence of the Greek cities had not been wrecked by the series of wars that began among themselves, their later efforts at federation, born largely of desperation, might have given them a better chance against the empires that finally swept over them. But the larger concept of a federated urban polity, which would have rectified the failures of both urban isolationism and imperialistic political and cultural expansion, never had a career long enough to create a radically new pattern of civic life. War dragged the polis back to the more regressive pattern of the earliest king-centered cities, and finally wiped out all but a vestige of their independence and autonomy. So it was as conquered refugees, subjects, and slaves, not as free citizens, that the Greeks ultimately carried the lessons of Olympia, Delphi, and Cos to the rest of the world.

4: THE OLD TEMPLE AND THE NEW GOD

We have approached the Greek city from without; for it was on the outskirts of the city that the new institutions, which set it off from ancient types, found a home. But at the center of the Greek city, when it finally took form in the fifth century, were the characteristic institutions of the old citadel, almost unchanged. Here was the Temple that kept alive the old cult, with its nearby quarters for priests and priestesses. Here, too, was the old Palace, which was turned into a Town Hall when royal power was divided among the elective magistrates with a war lord, a law lord, and a shrine lord—though, Robert J. Bonner reminds us, the religious head of the state was still known as *archon basileus,* or chief king. As for the village meeting place, the agora, or market, it was often situated at the base of the citadel; but the growth of the marketing function would, when a city was extended or rebuilt after wartime destruction, often lead to its removal to the water's edge, for convenience in trans-shipment, exchange, and storage.

The daily activities of a Greek town were performed outdoors, often under a radiant sky, sometimes under the bleak condition of rainy autumn or snowy winter. This inurement to outdoor life offset some of the constrictions of domestic living quarters, especially for the male members of the community. Partial enclosure came in as one of the new luxuries of the Hellenistic period: when citizens lost their freedom, they consoled themselves with physical comforts, as people in our own quasi-totalitarian society do again today. But the acropolis remained the spiritual center of the polis; and, after the seventh century, its crowning structure was no longer the castle but the temple.

As the house of the city's god, the temple took the form of the traditional palatial mansion, a great hall with an anteroom and a front portico: a barnlike structure with a gabled roof whose wooden uprights would be translated, at length, into sturdy Doric or Ionic columns of marble. This building usually housed the sculptured image of the god or goddess, covered with gold, perhaps with ivory head and jewelled eyes, as in Phidias' famous image of Athene; while outside the sculptures and the geometric decoration would be painted in strong brilliant hues, all carrying a heavy supercharge of symbolic meaning. The great temple would be but one of many smaller temples and shrines disposed about the city, on sites not chosen so much for their esthetic importance as for the sacred events or associations that gave the spot a special sanctity. Both logical progression and esthetic order were secondary to time-encrusted religious sentiments.

In the larger cities, unlike those of the Christian Middle Ages, the temple was never big enough to house at one time any considerable part of the community: that was far from its purpose. For the chief rites and ceremonies were conducted outside this building, though within the sacred precincts. By the time the great temples were built in the fifth and the fourth centuries B.C., the gods themselves had undergone a transformation: no longer were they the superhuman image of the lords and ladies of the citadel, beheld from afar; rather, they had become incarnations of special human qualities or virtues, incarnations of justice, wisdom, or sexual passion. This was part of that emancipation from 'silly nonsense' which Herodotus regarded, along with Greek intelligence, as the mark that distinguished the Hellenes from the barbarians.

Even as early as the fifth century B.C. there was an element of conscious make-believe in Greek religion. In the course of Pericles' whole oration commemorating the Athenian dead there is not a single reference to the gods. Would that died-in-the-wool conservative Aristophanes have dared to picture, even in fun, the blockade of Heaven by the birds, had the traditional beliefs in the Olympian deities in fact not been corroded? True, Socrates, later than this, was condemned to death for supposedly alienating the young of Athens from the old gods. But this was done in an outbreak of democratic suspicion and resentment, in the midst of a losing war, in much the same spirit as an American Senate investigating committee, if the United States had been defeated by the Nazis, might have condemned Charles Beard for undermining popular faith in the fathers of the Constitution, or John Dewey for altering the rote teaching of the three R's.

The fact is that by the sixth century a new god had captured the Acropolis, and had, by an imperceptible passage, merged with the original deity. This new god was the polis itself; for the people who built these great temples were seized with an ecstasy of collective self-worship: they never noticed, perhaps, that it was their own image of order and beauty and wisdom that they had set high upon a hill, and that to achieve the means of creating such structures, they would often show exorbitant pride and shocking moral callousness. This situation called for humble and sharp-eyed self-examination, if the city were to be saved. One of the greatest of these buildings, the Parthenon, was the public-works project of Pericles himself: made possible by mounting acts of flagrant injustice and calculated terrorism, perpetrated by Athens upon her weaker neighbors and allies. This culminated in the wholesale extermination of the males of Melos, even after the surrender of its inhabitants. Such elaborate public works perhaps kept the surplus population of Athens in employment; but the money that made them possible was blood money, which degraded the taker.

Pericles' funeral oration tells a different story from that Greek scholars often have drawn from it, once one escapes the hypnosis of Thucydides' rhetoric. Covered by an affable mask of modesty and moderation, that speech is in fact a hymn of complacent self-worship: in it ideals still only partly realized were treated as if they were solid actualities, and injustices all too palpably realized were hardly even glanced at, still less repented of.

If one needed further proof of this insidious inflation of the collective ego, the Parthenon itself presented it: the moral weakness is not less visible because it had materialized in a flawless esthetic image. For what is the Panathenaic frieze but an idealized presentation of the actual procession that wound about the narrow streets of the city and climbed upward into the temenos of Athene, the members beholding themselves in the sculptured figures before them at the same time that, emerging onto the open hillside below the steps, they did reverence to their guardian of wisdom, with their common totem bird, the owl. So the self looked admiringly upon the self that looked upon the self: a state of enraptured narcissism. This infatuation with their own image deepened among the Athenians, no doubt, by reason of the final triumph over the Persians, which led to the restoration of the shrine the Persians had destroyed in 480 B.C. Even in 336 B.C., two years after the fatal defeat of Chaeronea, the citizens of Athens inscribed a stele with the text of a law against tyranny: and the accompanying relief represents democracy crowning the Demos of Athens!

For a time the Greeks' pride in their unfettered humanity possibly had a humanizing effect upon religion: it resulted, as Gilbert Murray pointed out, in a moralization of Olympus, in an effort to bring the gods up to at least a human level of conduct, and to cover over, as unworthy of godhead, the scandalous amours and knavish tricks that the members of the Greek pantheon had carried over from the cosmic delinquents of an earlier day. Olympus itself must be turned into a polis of respectable citizens. So the least godlike of the gods, Hephaestus the blacksmith, found a temple built for him, to celebrate his solid craftsmanlike virtues, hard by the old quarters of the potters and smiths below the Acropolis, while Prometheus, he whom Hesiod had characterized as 'sly,' became, in Aeschylus' drama, the moral superior of Zeus. Though Athens offers most of the ready examples of the deification of the polis, the spirit itself prevailed everywhere. God, city, and citizens became one compact manifestation of ego.

This worship of the polis, enthroned in myth and legend, wrought in costly architectural works, replenished in a succession of enchanting rituals, had an insidious effect upon the city. What began as collective self-respect, confident of powers tested under external pressure, turned into the worship of a frozen image of the communal self. In the end the polis was undermined and met destruction by its overcommitment to the arts and rituals that had fortified it in defeat and had celebrated its successes. Well did Plato observe in 'The Laws' that the greatest plague of the city was "not faction but rather distraction."

By the fourth century, which ushered in a great period of urban extensions and civic embellishments, the Athenians, typically enough, insisted on spending for their public games and festivals the funds they badly needed for the rebuilding of their navy, to keep off the conquering Macedonians. Demosthenes' oration 'On the Naval Boards' was in fact a counter-funeral oration. It was not the soldiers who had died in battle that Demosthenes mourned: rather the proud city that was dying in fatuous peace. But alas! it was the waxen corpse of the city, rouged and perfumed, that he sought to restore to life. Demosthenes' anguish over his fun-loving, responsibility-evading contemporaries is the final comment on Pericles' boasts. They were too enamored of their habitual excitements and distractions—their sports, their games and shows, and their new interest in fine cooking, revealed to us by Aulus Gellius—to be willing to confront the life-and-death realities that called for sacrifice.

Once again, the solid physical structure concealed the possibility of the spiritual decay behind it. In magnifying all that wealth and military power can bring, the Athenians had forgotten the essentially symbiotic and co-operative associations of the city, which flourish only when they are both internally balanced and in equilibrium within a wider environment. For it was not the finished perfections of the post-Periclean era, but the unfinished potentialities of the period between Solon and Pericles that had made Athens so great—that pregnant moment when buildings had not yet taken the place of men. Then a spirit of brilliant improvisation and creativity had affected every urban function.

In its great temples and monuments, the Greek city was not unique: Karnak and Heliopolis; Babylon and Nineveh, surely had as much to say. The Greek city's real strength was of another order: being neither too small nor too big, neither too rich nor too poor, it kept the human personality from being dwarfed by its own collective products, whilst fully utilizing all the urban agents of co-operation and communion. Never had any city, no matter how big, harbored and fostered such a multitude of creative personalities as were drawn together in Athens for perhaps a century. That is the most important fact about it; but if we lacked the written documents, the stones of Athens would not tell the story.

5: TOWN HALL AND MARKETPLACE

We now come to the dynamic center of the Greek city: the agora. The separation of the agora from the temple precinct, the lowly meeting place for secular transactions from the lofty meeting place dedicated to sacrifice and prayer to the gods, had been going on almost from the beginning. In Greece this separation came quicker than in Mesopotamia, for in post-Homeric times at least the trades and crafts had never been carried on under the direct command of the temple. So far from an early theological state-capitalism's arising out of a royal concentration of power, just the opposite happened: the voluntary contribution of gifts to a shrine like that of Apollo at Delos turned that barren isle into a thriving banking center, which played an important part in Hellenistic commercial development. If in the fifth-century economy the agora can be properly called a marketplace, its oldest and most persistent function was that of a communal meeting place. As usual, the market was a by-product of the coming together of consumers who had many other reasons for assembling than merely doing business.

Like so many other manifestations of the early Greek polis, one finds the agora described in the 'Iliad,' in the first adequate description of the daily round of a Greek community, namely, that which Homer concentrated in gold and silver images on the fabulous shield of Achilles. The agora is here a "place of assembly," where "the town folk were gathered," and the purpose of the gathering in this context was to decide whether a murderer had paid an adequate blood fine to the kin of the murdered man. The elders, "seated on polished stones in the midst of the hallowed circle," gave their decision.

Even the most primitive community must handle its common affairs and face its common difficulties, breaking unbearable tensions of anger, fear, suspicion, restoring the social equilibrium upset by assault and revenge, by robbery and arbitrary reparation. Such a place for forgathering, possibly under a sacred tree or by a spring, must have long existed in the village: an area large enough so that village dances or games might be held there, too. All these functions of the agora would pass into the city, to assume more differentiated forms in the complex urban pattern. But in its primitive state, the agora was above all a place for palaver; and there is probably no urban marketplace where the interchange of news and opinions did not, at least in the past, play almost as important a part as the interchange of goods.

Not indeed until the automatism and the impersonality of the supermarket were introduced in the United States in the mid-twentieth century were the functions of the market as a center of personal transactions and social entertainment entirely lost. And even here that social loss has been only partly offset by the development of the larger shopping center where, in the characteristic style of our over-mechanized age, various media of mass communication at least serve as a vicarious substitute—under the sly control of the guardians of the market, the advertisers—for direct face-to-face (two-way) communications between buyer and seller, neighbor and fellow-marketer.

The early agora had an amorphous and irregular form. If it was sometimes an open square, in a town like Thera it might be little more than the widening of the main street, a Broad Way, just as it was, to choose only one out of a hundred examples, in the English town of High Wycombe. Primarily the agora is an open space, publicly held and occupiable for public purposes, but not necessarily enclosed. Often the adjoining buildings are thrown about in irregular order, here a temple, there a statue to a hero, or a fountain; or perhaps, in a row, a group of craftsmen's workshops, open to the passer-by; while in the middle the temporary stalls or stands might indicate the market day when the peasant brought his garlic, greens, or olives to the town, and picked up a pot or got his shoes mended by the cobbler.

From the seventh century on, however, with the introduction of gold and silver stamped coins, as the new medium of exchange, commerce became a more important element in the city's life, and the economic functions of the agora continued to expand. Now an increasing group of people, largely in export and in wholesale operations, began to work, not for a better living alone, but for abstract riches: they sought to become as rich as the famous Lydian king, Croesus, without being prudently daunted by the fact that he came to a bad end. These new economic functions, indeed, pressed so hard against the political and legal offices of the agora that at the end of the sixth century, at least in Athens, the popular assembly, needing space, left the agora for the Pnyx.

Still, even in the time of Solon, the Ceramics Agora was laid out deliberately to serve alike as market, as place of assembly, and as festival place; and though one part of the agora was often reserved for housewives, the agora was pre-eminently a man's precinct. The agora indeed served as a sort of informal club where, if one waited around long enough, one would meet one's friends and cronies. But even in the fifth century, Aristophanes noted in 'The Clouds,' the landed gentry preferred to loaf in the gymnasium, where they would meet only their own kind.

This social function of the open place has persisted in the Latin countries: plaza, campo, piazza, *grand' place,* descend directly from the agora; for it is in the open place, with its surrounding cafés and restaurants, that spontaneous and face-to-face meetings, conversations, encounters, and flirtations take place, unformalized even when habitual. Even the sports and dramatic functions of the original agora never wholly disappeared: knightly tournaments were still held in the marketplace at the end of the Middle Ages in northern Europe, and were followed in the seventeenth century by military exhibitions. At Elis the agora indeed was called a Hippodrome; and horse races, similar to those that once took place there, still are run annually in the famous Palio at Siena which reaches its climax in the piazza before the Town Hall. Since the agora combined so many important urban functions—law, government, commerce, industry, religion, sociability—it is hardly any wonder, as Wycherley observes, that the agora continued to gain at the expense of the acropolis, until in the end it became the most vital and distinctive element in the city. In the Hellenistic town indeed, it even captured, in the new temple or the neighboring theater, some of the ancient occupants of the acropolis.

The agora in time became an indiscriminate container, not greatly different from the later Roman forum. The fourth-century Greek poet Eubolus observed that "You will find everything sold together in the same place at Athens: figs, witnesses to summonses, bunches of grapes, turnips, pears, apples, givers of evidence, roses, medlars, porridge, honeycombs, chick-peas, law suits . . . allotment machines, irises, lamps, water-clocks, laws, indictments." There a temple or a shrine would hold its place in a huddle of workshops, and the peasant with his donkey might jostle a philosopher pausing, as Plato must often have paused, to watch a potter or a carpenter at work before his open shop, just as one may still watch the corresponding craftsmen in Athens today.

But though the continued expansion of the agora measures the shift in the Greek economy, from neighborly rural trading to an overseas traffic, one singular fact about this growth must be noted, for it discloses a radical flaw in the constitution of the polis. That flaw did almost as much as its bellicose activities to undermine this whole urban civilization. Apart from the craftsmen, who might be either citizens of low degree, free foreigners, or slaves, the expanding mercantile facilities of the agora were in the hands of foreigners, 'metics,' as they were called. These people were denied, except under unusual circumstances, the privileges of citizenship: they could not help to make the laws, hand down legal decisions, possess landed property, or even, if non-Greek, intermarry with citizens. In short, they were a politically excluded minority, whose sole occupation was money-making: people who by necessity spent all their energies on getting money and the things that money could buy.

Business and industry were, unfortunately, outside the pale of Greek education or *paideia*: indeed, as Herodotus noted, the Greeks "hold in less honour than their other citizens those who learn any art . . . but deem such to be noble as abstain from handicrafts." This contrasted with the spirit of Solon's age, when, according to Plutarch, a " 'work was a shame to none,' nor was a distinction made with respect to trade, but the merchant's was a noble calling." Except in the commercial cities of Ionia, which had thrown off the aristocratic customs of Homeric Greece, and no longer equated the highest goods of life with those derived from the hunt and war, the Greek citizens rejected trade as a possible mode of the good life. Thieving and cheating, if we may judge from Homer, were not incompatible with the aristocratic virtues: but plain dealing, on the basis of value given and received, was treated as more ignoble than one-sided expropriation by forceful means. The Corinthians alone were sufficiently proud of their success as merchants to be exempt from this prejudice. This de-moralized money-making paved the way for other forms of demoralization.

The Greek contempt for trade was self-defeating: the good faith and reciprocity needed in all forms of long-distance commerce, dependent upon credit, never spread from business to politics; indeed, just the opposite happened, for Athens turned herself into a ruthless exploiter of the helpless, and the systematic enemy of her economic rivals, at a moment when her own growth of population demanded a widening of the whole field of joint effort for the common good. In building up her empire, Athens used the strong-arm methods of the nobility, with an extra twist of civilized brutality, in order to claim exclusively as her own the surplus that should have enriched all of Hellas.

In his biographic sketch of Pericles, Plutarch attempted to defend the public-works policy of that statesman, in much the same terms as people later defended that of Napoleon III and Haussmann. Since the city was provided with "all things necessary for the war, they could convert the overplus of its wealth to such undertakings as would hereafter, when completed, give them eternal honor, and for the present, while in process, freely supply all the inhabitants with plenty." He dwelt on the varied materials that went into the temple—stone, brass, ivory, gold, ebony, cypress wood—the various trades that fashioned them, the activities of merchants and mariners, who conveyed them, not to speak of "cartwrights, cattle breeders, waggoners, rope-makers, flax workers, shoemakers, leather-dressers, roadmakers, miners." Thus, he concluded, "the occasion and services of the public works distributed plenty through every age and condition."

All this, of course, was pyramid-building, both in the Egyptian and the later Keynesian sense of the words—if they were not interchangeable, indeed, from the beginning. And it says something for the moral decency of a large body of Athenian citizens that, despite the hugeness and far-reachingness of this bribe—continuous employment! an expanding economy! we never had it so good!—no part of his policy was more bitterly criticized in the popular assemblies. Pericles' enemies pointed out that Athens had besmirched its reputation by financing this huge program through removing from the Isle of Delos the common treasury of the Greeks, and appropriating it for the advantage of Athens alone. Compared with this kind of one-sided expropriation, even the sharpest kind of trading had moral advantages. Not adept at federation or representative government, not skilled like Miletus and Rhodes in colonization, Athens sought to monopolize both economic and cultural advantages, instead of using her vast talents in etherializing them and widely distributing them. No wonder coarse-minded Sparta had Delphi on its side.

As the number of foreign traders grew in proportion to the financial prosperity of the polis, the number of inhabitants who had no direct stake in its life grew along with it. These were the people who, if they sought education, would get it for a fee, quickly, from those wandering scholars, the Sophists: teachers whose chief sin was that they professed to be able to teach in a few short lessons, for pay, what the Hellenic city, with all its institutions co-operating, actually took a whole lifetime to give to its citizens.

Even when the Greek city became a 'democracy,' therefore, its citizens were a class apart, a 'dominant minority.' The greater the economic activities of the expanding fifth-century metropolis became, the more surely the gap between the citizens and the non-citizens widened. The imported handicraft workers, no less than the merchants, might come from lands unused to self-government and unable to value the freedom and autonomy of the polis: Aristophanes even mentions Egyptian bricklayers. They might be 'free,' but they could not assume active citizenship.

Many of the citizens of Athens lacked the means to live the leisured aristocratic life that their constitution presupposed. In order to get the leisure needed for performing his functions as legislator and juror, the Athenian citizen was forced to demand public support from the treasury for the period of his office. When Pericles introduced pay for such services, the old landed families, living on rent and estate-grown products, regarded this pay as little better than a dole or a bribe; but what was really scandalous was that it made the citizenry dependent for their freedom upon the enslavement of weaker communities.

Trade remained for the Greek citizen an unwelcome intruder in the ideal polis: it contrasted with both the aristocratic and the agricultural way of life. That animus was carried over to Romans like Cicero who, in 'De Civitate,' railed against those that were tempted far from home by "soaring hopes and dreams" of commercial profit; indeed he attributed the downfall of Corinth and Carthage to their "lust for trafficking" and the scattering and dispersion of their citizens. Meanwhile, the men of business became increasingly indifferent to the form of government, so long as it permitted them to carry on their enterprises and make profits. This indifference must have exercised an insidious influence over those who still sought to practice self-government. Economic power, though it may be hidden, cannot be ignored. By the end of the fourth century, the economic center of gravity had shifted decisively from land to commerce; from the old frugal self-contained oligarchy to canny traders, parading their gains, with whom an absolute ruler could do business.

The foreign trader in the fifth-century Greek economy played a part not dissimilar to that which the Jew played in the Christian economy of the medieval town: he was needed but not wanted. The best estimate of the population of the Greek city that scholars can make today reveals the weakness of this narrowed form of citizen participation. Athens at its height, according to Wycherley, had 40,000 full-fledged citizens (male), possibly 150,000 free people (metics, women, and children), and perhaps 100,000 slaves. The proportions are probably correct though the numbers are almost surely too high. In other words, less than one in seven of its inhabitants were citizens, with all the privileges of citizenship; and even among these citizens, a growing proportion were craftsmen and tradesmen who lacked the sense of public obligation that the landed families, not unlike the English landed gentry, encouraged among their members. The political leaders who followed Pericles were, successively, a hemp dealer, a sheep dealer, a leather dealer, and a sausage dealer: men without either the pride of the old aristocracy or the educated competence of the new maritime commercial class.

The failure to moralize trade and bring its goods, under suitable restraint, into the province of the good life was perhaps as serious a source of the Hellenic disintegration as the spread of slavery or the failure to cope with the successive assaults of swollen empires. Almost from the moment of creating the polis, the Greek had never been able to rectify his image of a noble, leisured life as essentially that pursued by the Homeric aristocracy. This image left out the trader, the banker, the handworker, the shopkeeper, all in fact who were needed to produce the economic surplus by other means than naked exploitation and robbery. Without that surplus, neither leisure nor democracy could flourish.

By failing to turn the businessman into a citizen, the Greek eventually turned the citizen into something worse than a businessman: first the insolent conqueror and exploiter, then the subservient subject, the cringing pedagogue, the cadger and bootlicker, the refined parasite, whose name became a byword of contempt among the Romans, much as they admired and copied the classic Greeks.

Yet if the commercial functions of the agora multiplied from the seventh century on, this does not necessarily mean that the political activities of the city ceased to take place there. The prime mark of democratization, in cities whose descendants demanded a wider distribution of political power, was the disappearance of the original palace, such as that which King Erectheus had built at Athens on the Acropolis.

This separation of political power from religious power was a turning point in the Hellenic city. And it is significant that the Town Hall, as one may translate *prytaneion,* kept on the modest scale of the later Greek cities, some of the original features of both palace and temple: it was still treated as the home of the king, and the sacred fire, dedicated to Hestia, was kept burning there. Here, too, was the place where foreign emissaries would be entertained or where a state banquet would be held. Naturally, the earliest documents on political and civil matters were kept in the *prytaneion.* Often the Council House (*bouleuterion*), a fairly big place where citizens served in mass, would remain in or near the agora.

This mixture of functions, characteristic though it was of the Hellenic city, seems to have disturbed the tidy classifying mind of Aristotle: he advocated the building of a separate political agora, well insulated by space from the commercial agora, not merely to segregate the political functions formally, but to keep non-citizens out, even as chance spectators.

Various Greek cities made an effort to apply democracy to government on a large scale; and their efforts should be as instructive to our age as they were to the authors of the 'Federalist Papers.' For the Greeks attempted to bring back to the complex organization of the city the sense of direct citizen responsibility and participation that had existed in village government. The Ephebic Oath of Athens expressed with no little beauty that periodic effort at civic dedication. On the theory that all citizens were equal, they distributed the lower offices by lot, and rotated them annually, or for shorter periods, for service in the town council or jury duty. Since the major consultation and judgment was done by people who addressed each other directly, face to face, eloquence became a major instrument of politics, and the ability to sway an audience became more important for political leadership than the ability to do a job. Those who did their job too well, like Themistocles or Aristides, were often suspect.

Nothing like a skilled civil service or an independent judiciary could spring up under these conditions. The Town Council, as W. Warde Fowler pointed out, was simply a large committee of the whole people, elected afresh every year; and it in turn prepared all the business for the still larger Ecclesia, or mass assembly. Functions that required practical or professional skill, the control of the army, the management of finance, the building and maintenance of docks, were entrusted to boards, somewhat the way in which the United States Senate entrusts these duties to standing committees.

This system was effective in undermining the influence of the landed families with their unfortunate habit of utilizing public power for family advancement. But it was equally a conspiracy against the aristocracy of talent; for it was only by accident that those with special abilities were placed in positions that utilized them; and even if they proved their merit, the odds were against their remaining in office. As a result, the demotion or exile of their more able leaders was one of the chronic weaknesses of Athenian politics. Even Pericles himself was not exempt from the popular tendency to offer up the leader as a scapegoat when things went wrong. The trial of Socrates reveals the same animus against those whose abilities awakened the opposition of envious and spiteful mediocrity.

As the population of the city increased, and as the complexities of economic and political life increased with it, the limitations of democracy as an exclusive system of government were likewise revealed. Pure democracy requires the intimacy of face-to-face meeting, possible only in small numbers; plus the traditional restraints and orderly procedures. Even Plato recognized the advantages of such closeness, for in 'The Laws' he observed that "There is no greater good in a state than that the citizens should be known to each other." In large numbers democracy is obviously unworkable, except in the limited sense of a popular referendum. Now as the population of the Hellenic city grew, not merely was there a growing proportion of non-voters to voters, but even the small body of privileged citizens became too big and lost direct contact with each other. As a result, clubs, parties, factions developed, all of which limited the direct influence of one mind on another.

Probably the greatest political failure of the Greek cities was their inability to pass from direct democracy to representative government: this left them the poor choice between irresponsible oligarchies or tyrannies, and relatively responsible but incompetent and overburdened democracies. Even in the Boeotian confederation, the Federal Council contained 660 members. Not merely was there a hesitation, apparently, to delegate authority; but the Greeks, in all their large popular assemblies, seemed to try to recapture the appearance, at least, of a village meeting in which everyone took part.

For all their gifts in logical abstraction, the Greeks did not willingly trust power to anyone out of their sight. Perhaps this is another indication of their love of the concretely perceptible and definable, which Spengler called attention to. But it also had behind it, possibly, a sense that the essential attributes of man cannot be delegated, and that all important functions must be fulfilled in person, as kings journeyed to Delphi themselves to learn the god's will. Did that limitation keep the Greek cities from maintaining active political relations even with their own colonies?

The problem of numbers plagued the great theorists of politics, Plato and Aristotle; and it is significant that Aristotle, who wisely believed in a mixed system of government, nevertheless tried to solve this problem by limiting the size of the city. His reasoning was excellent: but it could not be applied to cities like Athens and Corinth, which had grown far beyond the number he thought favorable, without effecting radical constitutional and structural changes. There Aristotle showed he had as little sense of the political wisdom of Delphi's urban dispersal policy as he had of the innovations of the Boeotian confederation. The first valid approach to this problem was not made till Ebenezer Howard broached it at the end of the nineteenth century in the book that became 'Garden Cities of Tomorrow.'

Anything like an adequate answer does not merely demand limitation: it also requires a new method of reorganizing and redistributing the population, when it expands beyond the desired norm—decentralization and regional federation. Now the Greeks sometimes liquidated small units to form a larger polis, as Theseus supposedly did with the scattered villages and towns of Attica to create greater Athens; and as the Phocians did in founding Megalopolis in the fourth century. But they went no farther. So when democracy grew weak, faction-ridden, incompetent, they knew no cure but to cling to congestion and call in a tyrant or emperor who would act in his own person for the muddled whole, and impose an outward unity.

Doubtless the failure of Greek democracy went deeper than its failure to handle large numbers. But the history of later communities shows how difficult it is to get leaders to accept heavy responsibility without their demanding both an extension of authority and an increase of tangible rewards; still less will officers attend to the dull minutiae of government day by day, unless they have professional status as paid officials. It was Athens' glory—and perhaps the secret of her two centuries of intense creativity—that she sought to maintain a large body of citizens who drew no civic distinction from either their family status, their wealth, or their professional roles. In order to perform his many roles as a citizen— military service, political deliberation, jury duty, public ceremonies, sing- ing, or acting—the Athenian avoided both the penalties and the perfec- tions of vocational specialization.

The Greek system then had its own special virtues. The very distaste for the specialized intelligence and competence which so roused Socrates' scorn accounts for a certain suppleness and readiness to cope with the moment: qualities that again bind the Greek gentleman-citizen to his admiring counterparts in latterday England. But the long-term activities of the city demanded long-term assignment of powers, capable of seeing a program through. So it was notably under the tyrants that economic capital was advanced, in the sixth century, for planting olive groves: an investment that does not yield even a partial return for twenty years or a full one for forty. And as the city grew, a larger amount of systematic repetitious effort, with reports and exact accounts, was necessary to keep it going. The latter duties were largely left to slaves. If the cities of Greece had been in fact democracies in the sense of including all their adult inhabitants, the whole organization would have bogged down that much sooner, by sheer weight of numbers.

The possibilities and difficulties of urban democracy under pressure of population-expansion were explored in fifth-century Athens. But the contradictions between political profession, military policy, and economic need were too great to be bridged. In the very act of seeking a secure supply of grain for her many mouths, Athens became an imperialist ex- ploiter. These aspects of life tightened into a gordian knot; and the sword that finally severed it undid the whole community.

CHAPTER SIX

Citizen Versus Ideal City

1: CITY AND CITIZEN

By the end of the sixth century the Hellenic city had begun to take form; but the form achieved was still rustic, often crude, and the life it contained was more significant than the container. Until the fourth century the proudest of Greek cities in Attica, if not in Asia Minor, was little better than a country town both in street layout and in buildings. Only when toward the end of the century one raised one's eye to the Acropolis and beheld the columned peristyle and the sculptured pediment of the new Parthenon could one believe that something else was happening here: mind was dawning once more on chaos.

The picture of the actual Hellenic city, which comes to us with a certain amplitude of literary evidence from Athens, contrasts with the white splendor that J. J. Winckelmann and his successors tended to read into the whole scene; for the Hellenophiles endowed the physical town with a marmoreal chastity, a purity and a rationality, that was displayed perhaps in the mathematics of Pythagoras or the logic of Parmenides, but which never characterized even the sacred quarters of the ancient polis. Like the much admired Laocöon, these were third-century virtues. The fifth century contrasts likewise with our own residual picture of the Greek mind at this period if we overemphasize its inner order, its love of abstract perfection, and forget all the violent, irrational, tormented aspects of Greek life one finds in the tragic dramatists, or in the rude horseplay and farmyard smut one encounters in Aristophanes.

Yes, the visible, tangible city was full of imperfections: the disorders of growth, the fermentations and secretions of life, the unburied refuse of outlived forms, not yet decently removed, the relics of rural ways not yet adjusted to the continued ordeals and challenges of urban life. Such a city might present momentary concentrations of significant form, as one climbed the steep path up the Acropolis at Athens and at last beheld the wide plain from an elevation of half a thousand feet; but one could not hope for prolonged order or sustained harmonies. Yet the inner carol of delight one might feel, when the rocks of the Acropolis fell away and one finally beheld the Parthenon itself, was perhaps all the keener for its contrast with the casual jumble and sprawl of the town below. No pallid esthetes, no mousy bureaucrats, produced these violent visual contrasts, or these high intensities of color that survive today only in rock and sky and sea. Athens was the work of men, "ready," as Alcaeus said, "to use their every resource."

The nearest equivalent to the architectural form of the Hellenic city would not be the surviving structures themselves but Plato's 'Banquet.' There a rational framework, articulated and logical, held in check the laughing challenges and the high-flown words, the passionate declarations and the reeling abandon of drink: only to allow the esthetic tension to collapse at the end, as it collapsed in the city as one descended from the Acropolis to the marketplace, or picked one's way, more by instinct than by any visible guides, through the tangle of walled alleys and blind streets that took one to one's destination.

Is the city of Parmenides and Plato, the city of beautiful-goodness, in which mind, as Anaxagoras said, "sets things in order," and the forms of art mirror a super-mundane perfection—is all this then an illusion? Did the forms of Phidias rise on this barnyard scattering of workshops and booths and cattle-pens and shrines and fountains, mid these mud-walled huts, hardly to be dignified with the name of houses? Is there no counterpart in the outer city to the order and clarity of the Greek mind?

There is no better place to confront the paradoxical relation between the mind and the body through which it expresses itself, the social body that becomes a humanized landscape or a city, than in the Greek polis, above all in Athens. One aspect of the order we find in the Greek mind was indeed passed on to the city during the later Hellenistic Age; but what we find in the city of the fifth century was something more deeply organic, closer to the quick core of human existence. That order had emerged as idea in the seventh and sixth centuries, a wild union of opposites, restriction and exuberance, Apollonian discipline and Dionysian delirium, rational intelligence and blind intuition, skyward flight and muddy tumble: the very opposite of all that one would now characterize as classical. The highest product of that experience was not a new type of city, but a new kind of man.

For little more than a generation—between 480 and 430 B.C., I should roughly place it—the polis for the first time assumed an ideal form that distinguished it from all earlier villages and cities: an ideal form not primarily in stone but in flesh and blood. In a great succession of citizens the new urban order, the ideal city, became visible, transcending its archaic outlines, its blind routines, its complacent fixations. For the Greeks added a new component to the city, all but unknown to earlier cultures, dangerous to any system of arbitrary power or secret authority: they brought forth the free citizen. Like Sophocles' lonely heroes, he was a king if not a god in his own right: acting alone and seeking by the exercise of his intelligence to "hold a hand uplifted over fate."

Whatever the city possessed the citizen considered his own birthright: between citizens as between friends there were to be no secrets, no professional walls, no presumption of inequality. The freeborn citizen owed nothing to princely favor or to his economic or official function: he resumed the place he had once had in village culture, that of being first of all a man, endowed with every human dimension, to whom every part of life was open and accessible. This at least was the ideal. And it is by its capacity to formulate that ideal—not by its failure to achieve it—that we still properly measure the Greek polis.

2: THE FORM OF THE HELLENIC CITY

Before we examine the ideal citizen in person, let us look more intently at the far-from-ideal city that helped to bring him into existence. Such an examination may change our preconceptions as to what constitutes a favorable environment for human growth. We shall discover, perhaps, that the kind of finished perfection we commonly look upon as favorable may be in fact a device for obstructing or halting that growth.

The core of the city, the center of its most valued activities, the essence of its total existence, was the acropolis; for the acropolis was above all the home of the city's gods, and here were all the holy offices derived from nature and history. Too exclusively has the image of the Athenian Acropolis been confined to its crowning buildings, above all to the Erectheum and the Parthenon; but beneath these buildings was a source of both their esthetic power and their activities: the mighty rock that raised these buildings to the sky, a rock whose blue and pink tints contrast with the marble above, and whose craggy outlines, even when capped by a sheer wall, contrast with the sublime geometry of the temples.

This was a holy mountain indeed, and its original primitive attributes helped to make it so: the caves, the graves, the grottoes, the springs, no less than the later shrines, sacred enclosures, fountains. Even before the first temple or palace was built, the Acropolis swarmed with gods and nymphs, the same chthonic gods, gods of the earthly and the human underworld, that marked Delphi as a sacred spot and have not yet entirely lost their magic power or their mystery. To confront the Acropolis at night, under the moon, or to take in the steep slopes of Delphi, from the topmost stadium down through the olive groves to the sea, even in daylight, is a religious experience that transcends any conscious formulation.

Here, gathered together on the Acropolis, are the true sources of the ancient city, from paleolithic spring and cave to neolithic wall and sacred enclosure, from royal palace and fortress to cosmic temple, from protected camp and village to the proud and powerful city. This combination of natural advantages and man-wrought artifacts does not lend itself to imitation: not everywhere did the image of the city leave such a deep impress on the mind as in Athens. The same form of temple, massively wrought in the Doric style, as in sixth-century Paestum, does not by itself, even when it is multiplied and better preserved than those on the Athenian Acropolis, produce a similar impression; for Paestum lies on a plain and the mountains that might have lent it their magic arise only in the background.

Paestum must, from the beginning, have been more of one piece than Athens ever was, even in its later Hellenistic days; but for that reason it lacked just those contacts with its more primitive foundations that Athens always retained and made the fullest use of, alike in the myths of the tragic dramas and the architectural order of the Acropolis, where the aboriginal rocks show no sign of having ever been covered over, except by buildings. Thus the deepest primitive sources and the highest esthetic expressions were united on the Acropolis, as they are united in the crypts, the gargoyles, and the soaring vaults of a Gothic cathedral. This explains in no little degree both the life of the city, and the form that this life gave to its buildings—even the formlessness in the residential quarters, which, like the huddle of a neolithic village, escaped this higher order. A complex but archetypal formation.

Let us climb the steep slopes of the Acropolis and observe the disposition of its original open spaces and buildings—though so much has by now been defaced or destroyed.

Its rocky sides were apt for defense rather than for building; so the task of the architect was not to weaken its contours or to facilitate movement, but to exploit the chance advantages of ledges and platforms, arranging buildings and monuments with no effort to achieve visual coherence or a climactic sequence except in the siting of the most important temple at the top. No axis, no continuity, no visual progression: no attempt at symmetry, either, except in the individual building, open to view and finished on all four sides, changing in form with the changing angle of approach. Divers sacred enclosures often interfered with the passage upward: sometimes enfolding an altar within, sometimes a statue of a god or a hero, sometimes a little building like the Choragic monument. For long these structures would resist removal, even when they stood in the way of some more importunate use of the area. Not till Hellenistic town-planning ideas prevailed and some of the old piety had faded, would they be removed with antiquarian respect, stone by stone, to another site. The Choragic monument of Lysicrates (334 B.C.) is now in fact enshrined in a little park at the eastern base of the Acropolis.

That—within the bounds set by tradition—there was some sort of conscious intention in the placement and design of the buildings on the Acropolis one can hardly doubt. Perhaps, as has been suggested recently, there was even a sophisticated exploitation of the visual possibilities of a devious, irregular approach. But the geometric form of the buildings themselves, circular or rectangular in plan, was not carried through in any systematic general way: each structure, rather, was self-contained, self-sufficient, equal and independent, not subordinate in any hierarchic kind of order. That in itself was in no small degree symbolic.

While these central structures on Athens' Acropolis were still, at the end of the sixth century, extremely simple, often doubtless crude, even when built of stone, one must read an even greater simplicity and roughness into the stalls, booths, and workshops of the agora below, where the sausage seller and the silversmith, the spice merchant and the potter and the money changer held forth. If the acropolis represents the city in depth, down to its deepest primeval sources, the agora represents it in extension, reaching out beyond its visible spatial limits. Except for the openness itself, the agora expressed no unity: almost any function might be performed there; almost any kind of building might be found there. The beginnings of a more formal order, with a new criterion of spaciousness and beauty of setting and indeed a new consciousness of delight in these very qualities, took place only on the outskirts of the city. There the new gymnasium found a home; and there a truly urban order dawned, not mid clutter, but in arbored spaciousness.

These newer structures, especially the theater, began as simple modifications of the earth forms: the theater turned the scooped-out slope of a hill into a semicircular amphitheater, with a smoothed circle in front of the banked spectators creating the stage where the dancers or actors could perform. All this had come quickly: Thespis introduced the first actor in a theater at Ikria in the first half of the sixth century; and the drama, in an interplay of formal invention and spiritual creativity had reached its pinnacle of expression in a century. Sophocles alone wrote a hundred plays, and in the course of the century that ended in 406 B.C., twelve hundred plays were written and produced. The multiplication of gymnasia was equally rapid. Once these functions had broken loose, religion and politics retained the central sites of the city; but the presence of historic mementoes and traditional uses hampered their free exploitation of the site. Though a building for getting ready for the processions was reported by Pausanias at the base, there was only one entrance to the Acropolis, and the great Panathenaic way was so narrow only five people could walk abreast on it.

If the layout of the Acropolis expressed an accumulation of traditional relationships, rather than a fresh, all-embracing order, what shall one say of the rubble of houses that sprawled at its base—houses built of unbaked brick, with tiled roofs, or even of mud and wattle with thatched roofs, still stamped with village crudeness? These made up the major portion of the city, right into the fourth century and even later, for somewhere between the second and the first century B.C., Dicaearchus could observe: "The road to Athens is a pleasant one, running between cultivated fields the whole way. The city is dry and ill-supplied with water. The streets are nothing but miserable old lanes, the houses mean, with a few better ones among them. On his first arrival a stranger would hardly believe that this is the Athens of which he has heard so much."

The best one can say of the housing situation in Athens is that the quarters of the rich and the poor were side by side, and that except perhaps in size and inner furnishings, were scarcely distinguishable: in the fifth century, noble poverty was more esteemed than ignoble riches, and public honors and family repute counted for more than private wealth. The houses, one story high, with low-pitched roofs, must have made the residential quarters like those of an unprogressive Mediterranean town today; but probably lacking even the whitewash.

Nothing that could be called a coherent street system characterized the residential district of these early towns: to a modern eye they would look as oriental as the seclusion of their womenfolk, which the Athenians also practiced. The lanes would be wide enough perhaps for a man with a donkey or a market basket; but one had to know one's quarter in order to find one's way about it. This very absence of system and orientation was prized as a means of defense in case the enemy penetrated the outer wall, advocated by Aristotle, praised later by Plutarch, who saw the advantages of thus causing confusion to the enemy, even in the Hellenistic Age.

But there was no paving to keep down the mud in spring or the dust in summer; in the central area there were no inner gardens or tree-lined parks, and only the beginnings of arcaded public promenades. In the bigger cities of the fifth century the spottiness, if not the downright lack, of sanitary facilities was scandalous, almost suicidal: a fact that the great plague during the Peloponnesian War, which had crowded Athens with refugees, emphasized. By 432 Athens was so overbuilt indeed that refugees were forced to encamp on the Acropolis, in defiance of sound warnings against this foul concentration issued from Delphi itself.

As long as towns remained relatively small, with open fields right at hand, their sanitary infelicities could be tolerated. Town sites of forty to a hundred acres, towns of from two to five thousand population, could afford a measure of rural laxity in matters like the disposal of garbage and human waste. Urban growth called for stricter care. Yet even in big cities there were, apparently, no public latrines.

On the matter of private latrines, the testimony of the spade and the word is contradictory and even the word is somewhat ambiguous. Modern excavators have dug up no indications of sanitary conveniences within the Hellenic house. This would seem to be backed by a passage in the 'Ecclesiasuzae.' Here Aristophanes shows an urban householder, on being roused from sleep, looking around for a suitable place to relieve himself, and actually squatting to evacuate, with various scabrous comic remarks about the process itself, in full sight of the audience. This reveals both a lack of elementary apparatus and any feeling of bodily shame; and the latter is confirmed again by Xenophon's notes on the Persians' special refinement and modesty, in their avoiding public display of the excretory functions.

This combination of negative and positive evidence might seem decisive if it were not for contra-indications, in particular another passage from Aristophanes' 'Peace,' where Trygaeus says: "Command all men to keep silence, to close down their drains and privies with new tiles and to stop their own vent holes." This would indicate that at least some of the houses had private sanitary provisions, though nowhere have I found any references to the further disposal of the dung. The subject itself was certainly not remote from Athenian consciousness, for the whole play I have quoted from revolves around a symbolic dung beetle on a farmyard dunghill; and in a further passage there is a reference to "a man emptying his belly in the Piraeus, close to the house where the bad girls are," so there is no doubt as to carelessness as well as shamelessness in performing such bodily functions.

As to baths, the testimony is equally difficult to interpret. Bathrooms have been discovered in Olynthus, a town of but 15,000 inhabitants. If private baths had been common, only the Greek desire for sociability would have given rise to public baths, which existed in Athens. Yet it is doubtful if the secluded and sheltered Athenian woman would have gone to such public baths—leaving her husband to take advantage of her absence by kissing the pretty Thracian serving maid, as one of Aristophanes' characters does—if tubs had been common at home. Still, private bathtubs must have been available, for again in 'Peace,' Trygaeus commands: "But hurry up, show this young girl into my house, clean out the bath, heat some water, and prepare the nuptial couch for herself and me." This makes the private bath seem a rite reserved for special occasions, as would be natural in a water-poor community, without a piped private supply, where all the water would be transported by hand, probably from a fountain. In general, it would seem that whatever the hygienic and sanitary facilities of the fifth-century city, they were limited and low grade.

This seems like a sorry picture of a great city, until we remember that we are dealing with a people unfettered by many other standard requirements of civilization, freed in an unusual degree from the busy routines of getting and spending: not given to guzzling and overdrinking, not making undue effort to secure comforts and luxuries, furnishings and upholstery: living an athletic, indeed abstemious life, conducting all their affairs under the open sky. Beauty was cheap and the best goods of this life, above all the city itself, were there for the asking.

3: THE POLIS INCARNATE

To understand the full achievement of the Hellenic polis, one must take one's eyes off the buildings, then, and look more closely at the citizen. For all the crudeness of the urban setting, as late as the fifth century, the Greek citizen had mastered Emerson's great secret: Save on the low levels and spend on the high ones. What we regard too glibly as an unfortunate handicap may in fact be partly responsible for the greatness of Athens.

The Greek citizen was poor in comforts and convenience; but he was rich in a wide variety of experiences, precisely because he had succeeded in by-passing so many of the life-defeating routines and materialistic compulsions of civilization. Partly he had done this by throwing a large share of the physical burden on slaves; but even more by cutting down on his own purely physical demands, and expanding the province of the mind. If he did not see the dirt around him, it was because beauty held his eye and charmed his ear. In Athens at least the muses had a home.

What distinguished the Greek polis in its developing phase was the fact that no part of its life was out of sight or out of mind. Not merely was every part of existence within view; only the most servile mechanical activities were denied to the citizen: in most occupations, the free man worked side by side with the slave, and the physician received the same rate of pay as a craftsman. All that men did was open to inspection, alike in the market, the workshop, the law court, the council, the gymnasium; and whatever was natural was acceptable, so that the naked body would be proudly shown in athletic contests, and even its most repulsive physiological processes were not excluded from consciousness. In that sense the Greek had a completely open mind. Until Pericles, the intimate human scale was maintained in every quarter; and the whole network of urban activities had visible form and relationship: even their occasional confusion stimulated the intelligence and promoted a fresh search for order.

For a brief generation in Athens, the ways of the gods, the ways of nature, and the ways of men came close to a common point: it seemed as if the arrests and fixations, the aberrations and perversions embedded almost from the beginning in the very stones of the ancient city might be overcome. And it was not merely in the figures of Phidias or Polygnotus that a new ideal of the human form, indeed of the fully developed personality at each of the climactic stages of life, had taken shape: that was but the crystallization of a more living moment that life itself had held in solution. In the generation that had thrown back the Persian invasion, a new idea of human wholeness took possession of this society and pervaded every life. In the activities of the polis, if not in all its architectural furniture, human nature suddenly rose to fuller stature.

In two men whose overlapping lives span the fifth century, the new ideal of wholeness, balance, symmetry, self-discipline became incarnate: Sophocles and Socrates. And not by accident was each in his own way a master of the dialogue; for it was by struggle and by opposition, not merely by symmetrical growth, that they rose to their fullest stature.

Sophocles, the older, handsome in body and face, the leader of the dance, skilled in warfare as a general, carrying on through his tragedies the new form of the drama, itself suddenly released from ancient village ritual—here was such a man as Solon had first foreshadowed, in his detachment from all the jealous preoccupations of power. Sophocles was the opposite of the archetypal specialist, the crippled, fragmentary man, molded by civilization to fill his little role and to serve with blind antlike devotion the needs of the hive. Just the contrary, here was a personality capable of facing life in all its dimensions, even in its furious irrationalities and obscure compulsions: at home in every environment, equal to every occasion, ready to assume moral responsibility for his choices, though the whole community might oppose him. "Single-handed or with the support of all."

Alongside Sophocles stands the contrasting figure of Socrates, likened in his old age to a Silenus, snub nosed, far from handsome, but with a magnificent physical frame and a constitution impervious to the rigors of war or climatic extremes; cool-headed in the midst of fighting, clear-headed in his cups, when others were reeling drunk: introvert and extrovert: capable of both solitary mental rapture and endless conversational inquiry. Like many other freemen, he was a stonecutter by training, and the son of two working people, a stonecutter and a midwife, but entirely at home in every part of the polis: an athlete among athletes, a soldier among soldiers, a thinker among thinkers.

These men were but two outstanding representatives of the new city, the city that was latent as an idea but was never adequately realized in brick or marble. They were not alone, for they were surrounded by people of similar dimensions, figures like Aristides and Aeschylus, Themistocles, Thucydides, Euripides, Plato. By their very existence these spirits gave evidence of that sudden mutation which produced, among a few million people, within a space of less than two centuries, a far richer efflorescence of human genius than history anywhere else records, except perhaps in renascence Florence.

Not least of Athens' achievements was its establishment of a golden mean between public and private life, and with this came a large-scale transfer of authority from paid officers, in the service of the King or the Tyrant, to the shoulders of the common citizen, taking his turn in office. He not merely performed military service at call, contributing his own equipment, but he served in the assembly and the law courts, and if he did not become a contestant in one or another of the games, if he did not act in the theater or sing in the chorus, he would at least have a place, in his turn, in the great Panathenaic procession. Almost every male Athenian, at one time or another, had to take part in public business, as a member of the ecclesia or assembly, and in seeing that its decisions were properly carried out. As Fowler emphasizes, work now done by executives, permanent secretaries, inspectors, and magistrates, was done by ordinary Athenians, rotating in sections of fifty.

Participation in the arts was as much a part of the citizen's activities as service on the council or in the law courts, with their six thousand judges. Each spring festival brought a contest between tragic dramatists: this called for twelve new plays annually, with the participation of one hundred and eighty choral singers and dancers; while each contest in comedies demanded sixteen new plays yearly and a hundred and forty-four choral singers and dancers. In the hundred years of the Empire, Ferguson tells us, two thousand plays of picked quality were written and staged in Athens, while six thousand new musical compositions were created and presented.

These esthetic activities demanded participation on an even greater scale than in the mystery pageants and miracle plays of the Middle Ages: every year something like two thousand Athenians, it has been estimated, had to memorize the words and practice the music and dance figures of a lyric or a dramatic chorus. This was an intellectual discipline as well as an esthetic experience of the highest order; and as an incidental result no small part of the audience consisted of ex-performers, expert judges and critics as well as enthralled spectators.

Thus the public life of the Athenian citizen demanded his constant attention and participation, and these activities, so far from confining him to an office or a limited quarter, took him from the temple to the Pnyx, from the agora to the theater, from the gymnasium to the harbor of the Pireaus, where matters that concerned trade or the navy would be settled on the spot. Not merely by cold reflection and contemplation, as the philosophers erroneously counselled, by action and participation, spurred by strong emotions, but by close observation and direct face-to-face intercourse, did these Athenians conduct their lives.

That open, perpetually varied and animated world produced a correspondingly unfettered mind. Both in the arts and in politics, Athens had largely overcome the original vices of the city, its one-man rule, its segregation of activities, its occupational narrowness, and worse, its bureaucratization—and they had done this for at least a generation without forfeiting skill or lowering the standard of excellence. For a while, city and citizen were one, and no part of life seemed to lie outside their formative, self-molding activities. This education of the whole man, this 'Paideia,' as Jaeger has called it, to delimit it from a narrower pedagogy, has never been equalled in another community so large.

Between the forthright Solon, who cast off, as if it were a soiled garment, the political power he had gathered into his hands, and the devious Pericles, who used words woven out of the deeds of free men to conceal a policy of 'colonial' exploitation, enslavement, and merciless extermination—between these polar opposites there was less than the span of a century. But in that brief period Athens was rich in citizens as no city had ever been rich before.

When this moment was over, buildings began to take the place of men. The secret of creating such citizens as the polis had briefly produced was eagerly sought by philosophers and educators, from Plato to Isocrates; but it was never successfully analyzed or revealed, and much of it doubtless still eludes us. By the time Plato was ready to put this question, the original synergy had turned partly into a concentration of stone, and part of it was dispersed in the wastage of war: Plato's own answer to the problem showed only the courage of desperation.

At all events, the potential city that was incarnated in Socrates and Sophocles was never brought to a further stage of communal realization. Those who planned and built the late Hellenic and post-Hellenic city did not succeed in developing the usages, the manners, the laws, the new urban forms that would have passed on the experience of Athens' golden day, and perfected an environment capable of molding the new personality. What Plato never suspected, apparently, was that the Athens of Solon and Themistocles was itself a greater school than any imaginary commonwealth he was capable of creating in his mind. It was the city itself that had formed and transformed these men, not alone in a special school or academy, but in every activity, every public duty, in every meeting place and encounter.

As a result, the philosophers who followed Plato and Aristotle, if they still sought balance and fullness of life, no longer dared to seek it in the city. They betrayed their own creed by dodging their civic responsibilities or by turning to an idealized empire or a purely heavenly polity for confirmation; whereas those who took on the burdens of commerce, politics, and war had no place in their muddy routine for the highest possibilities of personal development. The monuments of Greek art, which we now prize, were valid expressions of this life at its loftiest moments. But in part they were likewise material substitutes for a spirit that, had it known the secret of its own perpetuation, might have made an even more valuable contribution both to urbanism and to human development.

Never had the life of men in cities been so significantly animated, so varied and rewarding, never had it been so little blighted by external mechanisms and compulsions, as during the period I have sought briefly to characterize. Work and leisure, theory and practice, private life and public life were in rhythmic interplay, as art, gymnastic, music, conversation, speculation, politics, love, adventure, and even war, opened every aspect of existence and brought it within the compass of the city itself. One part of life flowed into another: no phase was segregated, monopolized, set apart. Or so at least it must have seemed to the full-fledged citizens, however doubtful the proposition might appear to their slaves or their womenfolk.

In such a human constellation, temple ritual might turn into tragedy and the boisterous bantering and the rude horseplay of the marketplace might become satiric comedy; while the gymnasium, at first a meeting place for athletes, would become in the Academy of Plato, in the Lyceum of Aristotle, or the Cynosarges of Antisthenes, the gathering place of a new kind of school, a true university, wherein learning became socially responsible, linked to a moral system that had become self-critical and rational. But that inner unification never quite produced an outward form that reflected and sustained in equal degree the life that had brought it into existence.

The role of the polis was admirable: every part of the city had come to life in the person of the citizen. But the worship of that institution and that role was an obstacle to further development, for however great the goods Athens achieved, they could not remain transfixed into a static image of perfection. No human institution, be it polis or papacy, can claim in its own being any ultimate perfection, worthy of worship. Growth and death will take their toll. In the division that had taken place during the sixth century between natural philosophy, which considered the cosmos as a thing or a process apart from man, and humanistic wisdom, which considered man capable of existing in a self-contained world outside the cosmos, the older insights into man's condition, truer if more confused, had been largely lost.

Even in Socrates, at least in Plato's Socrates, the limitations of the worship of the polis became patent, just at the point where they should have disappeared, in response to criticism. For exclusive preoccupation with the polis further widened the distance between the understanding of the natural world and the control of human affairs. In the 'Phaedrus,' Socrates declares that the stars, the stones, the trees could teach him nothing: he could learn what he sought only from the behavior of "men in the city." That was a cockney illusion: a forgetfulness of the city's visible dependence upon the country, not only for food, but for a thousand other manifestations of organic life, equally nourishing to the mind; and not less, we know now, of man's further dependence upon a wide network of ecological relations that connect his life with creatures as obscure and seemingly as remote as bacteria, the viruses, and the molds; and ultimately with sources of energy as remote as the radiations from distant stars. Babylonian superstition was closer to the truth in its erroneous associations of the planets' movements and human events than was Greek rationalism in its progressive dissociation of man and nature, polis and cosmos. To know oneself, as Socrates advised, is to know that one is not a disembodied mind or a walled-in city dweller, but an integral part of an enveloping cosmos, glimmering at last with self-consciousness.

Neither the Greek polis nor the Greek cosmos took the full measure of man: both were conceived in a static image that allowed for neither time nor organic development. By making the city their god, the Greeks generally, and the Athenians particularly, lost hold of the greatest gift of divinity—that of transcending natural limitations, and pointing to goals beyond any immediate fulfillment. Though the years from Peisistratus to Pericles had witnessed an extraordinary burgeoning of human powers, the fifth-century citizen did not find a way of producing a city capable of continuing the process itself: he sought only to fit the mold already achieved. But the polis could not become a cosmos, and a cosmos that did not allow for change, for transcendence and transformation, could not produce a higher order in the city.

We have here perhaps an explanation of why the Greek idea of wholeness and beautiful-goodness, incarnated in great personalities who flourished during and immediately after the Persian War, never fully created a city in its own image. What took the place of such an image was the Hellenistic city: sanitary, orderly, well-organized, esthetically unified; but grossly inferior in its capacity for fostering creative activity. From the fourth century on buildings began to displace men.

4: REGRESSION TO UTOPIA

There were many signs, even before the debacle of the Peloponnesian War, that the Greek cities were reaching an impasse in their development. They could not colonize farther afield without risking bloody conflicts, and they could not protect themselves against the threatening empires that surrounded them without forming a close political union, and continuing, on a basis of mutual aid, to feed a larger population. Mountains could no longer serve as walls, whilst midget dimensions and topographical obscurity were not enough to keep a city from being noticed by stronger states and wiped out.

Though the Greek cities had largely escaped by the very accidents of birth and topography many of the paralyzing fixations and regimentations of the oriental empires, there was something radically wrong with the polis, for it had no ideal goal that transcended its own limited existence. Socrates put some of the difficulty in a passage in 'The Gorgias': "You praise the men who feasted the citizen and satisfied their desires, and people say that they have made the city great, not seeing that the swollen and ulcerated condition of the state is to be attributed to these elder statesmen; for they have filled the city full of harbors and docks and walls and revenues and all that, and have left no room for justice and temperance."

The reaction against this state did not at first take the form of suicidal despair, as in Egypt and Babylonia. It showed itself, rather, in a movement toward withdrawal by the elite. Instead of detaching a whole colony to found a new city, an intellectual leader like Pythagoras would draw together a band of like-minded people and attempt, in a sort of polis within the polis, to establish a new regimen and a new discipline. Under the influence of Buddhist monasticism, linked to Greece by Alexander's conquests, that impulse would one day widen.

The other sign of this urban blockage is the appearance of a new kind of literature: that which attempted to outline the nature of an ideal commonwealth. Up to this time, the actual city had been idealized: now an effort was made—twice in fact by Plato in Syracuse—to actualize an ideal city. In part this effort marks a confidence that the processes of reason could impose measure and order on every human activity: never since the days of primitive magic had the human mind been so sure of the powers it commanded. Could not the city itself be treated as a work of art, subject to design and deliberate reconstruction? Utopia was nothing more than a new exercise in solid geometry, assuming that all rational men were willing to be such social geometricians. Meton, the surveyor and planner whom Aristophanes jibes at in 'The Birds,' is in fact the archetypal planner, from Hippodamos to Haussmann: regimenters of human functions and urban space.

"With the straight ruler," says Meton, "I set to work to inscribe a square within this circle; in its center will be the market-place, into which all straight streets will lead, converging to this center like a star, which . . . sends forth its rays in a straight line from all sides." We have no ancient record of this kind of planning anywhere, but that wild joke of Aristophanes became the characteristic mode of baroque thought two thousand years later.

In part, the essays in utopia marked a certain detachment from the dominant values of the polis, and a disillusion over current achievements. For a while this new literature, contrasting the actual with the possible or the abstractly ideal, seems to have been a common form, for Aristophanes made mock of it in more than one satire, as he did of the various socialist proposals that were then, apparently, in the air. And it is not without significance that the first exponent of this new mode of thinking, according to Aristotle, was Hippodamos, a professional town-planner.

Aristotle imputed to Hippodamos a capacity for innovation in practical planning that he can in fact lay no claim to: for though he may have popularized the gridiron type of layout, hitherto unfashionable in conservative Attica, this form had been common in Ionia since the seventh century. More likely, as Lavedan suggests, Hippodamos may have introduced the formal, enclosed agora in planning the Piraeus. His true innovation consisted in realizing that the form of the city was the form of its social order, and that to remold one it is necessary to introduce appropriate changes in the other. He seems, too, to have realized that town planning should have not merely an immediate practical aim, but an ideal goal of larger dimensions; and he thought of his art as a means of formally embodying and clarifying a more rational social order.

What that order was to be Aristotle informs us all too briefly in his 'Politics.' Apparently it had a mathematical basis, springing out of Hippodamos' belief in triads; but neither literary allusions nor achaeological remains suggest any fresh experimentation with the grouping of buildings or the laying out of quarters or streets in groups of threes. His city, Aristotle observes, "was composed of 10,000 citizens divided into three parts

—one of artisans, one of husbandmen, and a third of armed defenders of the state. He also divided the land into three parts, one sacred, one public, the third private: the first was set apart to maintain the customary worship of the gods, the second was to support the warriors, the third was the property of the husbandmen." A moment's reflection should have demonstrated to Hippodamos that the working classes would exist in grinding poverty if called to support in idleness a third of the population and hand over two-thirds of the wealth.

Not merely was Hippodamos an indifferent economist, but the division of society into three classes does not suggest any originality in his analysis of social functions. And the fact that one of these classes was the archaic warrior caste perhaps indicates nothing so much as the hold the old Mycenaean and Dorian stereotypes still had on the emancipated Greek mind, even at a moment of deliberate innovation. Aristotle himself admits as much; for he pointed out that "it is no new or recent discovery of political philosophers that the state ought to be divided into classes, and that the warriors should be separated from the husbandmen. This system has continued in Egypt and Crete to this day."

If we have no book of Hippodamos' to guide us, Plato's various excursions into utopia are enlightening. But they are dismaying, too, for they show that one of the greatest minds that ever flourished, a spirit that was both profound and playful, was unable to understand the source of his own great qualities. Still less did Plato appreciate, with any approximation to justice, the values that his forefathers and predecessors had created, or those his contemporaries might, with wiser guidance, have still brought forth.

While Pericles was surely a little self-hypnotized in his praise of the Athenians as "lovers of beauty without extravagance and lovers of wisdom without unmanliness," Plato was equally blind in reverse. When he disparaged the arts of Athens and held up the Cretan and Spartan virtues, exemplified in the grim Laws of Lycurgus, he condemned some of the chief sources of his own admirable qualities; for whether one loves Plato or hates him—and I share both feelings!—one thing is sure: only the opportunities offered by Athens could have enabled such a mind, far-ranging, beautiful even in its perversity, even while bent on coming to its cramped conclusions, to reach full maturity.

The weakness of Plato's understanding of the positive role of the city came out in the first book of 'The Republic,' and stayed with his thought, unmodified, until he wrote 'The Laws' in his old age, with all the tedious explicitness of a final testament. This is all the more noteworthy because he began his sociological analysis with an account, simplified but historically valid, of the limited but self-contained and basically tranquil life of the agricultural village commune, founded on an economy of needs.

He traced the development of the city, with its competitive ways and aggressive warlike aims back to the desire for luxuries not found in the immediate countryside, and with the growing lust for power. Thus he never succumbed to our baseless contemporary illusion that war is brought on by the demand of the 'have-nots' for the wealth that the 'haves' possess. He knew that pride and greed, excess, not poverty and envy, were at the bottom of it, if war could be explained on rational terms at all.

In the development of the community Plato noted that the inequality of native abilities and skills gave a basis for vocational specialization which made for interdependence. All prospered when the shoemaker confined his efforts to making shoes, the smith to beating metal, the peasant to minding his crops. From the fact of nature that men were different, Plato jumped to the gratuitous conclusion that they should stay that way, and even deepen their original differences by a lifetime of occupational specialization.

Since specialization ensured perfection in function, justice according to Plato demands that each member of the community be trained to perform the particular function that corresponds to this natural disposition, and be kept to that task. This conclusion seemed to him so inevitable that he never bothered to examine it critically; certainly he never even considered, as Dr. C. G. Jung has done in our time, that it might be in the interests of a better life to develop the weaker functions and not push an asymmetrical development into a deeper kind of organic disharmony. For Plato, wholeness and balance were not to be found in individual men, only in the hive. For the sake of the polis he was ready to sacrifice the life of the citizen: indeed, he was ready to sacrifice in the individual personality the admirable qualities that had begun to emerge from its life— harmony, moderation, poise, symmetry, organic balance.

Plato could not, theoretically, conceive of achieving perfection without such a sacrifice. Still less was he sufficiently detached to ask himself whether the perfection he sought was in fact an attribute of organic life. The image of the city that captivated him was a geometric absolute. Though in arriving at it he sought by his logic to emancipate himself from the accidents of history, he was in fact clinging to the archetypal historic container; and in one of the few passages where he gives any vivid concrete image of the city, in his description of the founding of Atlantis, it is obvious that his ideal is entirely a retrospective one.

If Pericles worshipped without due misgivings the living polis that was already beginning to disintegrate, Plato worshipped a dead one that was stillborn in his own mind. The embalmed image of the second was no better than the dynamic corruption of the first. Plainly, the world of art, the world of painted images and static structures enjoys a perfection no living being can achieve. But a living being has a thousand potentialities that no work of art possesses, including the potentiality for re-producing other human beings and for creating other works of art.

Now, Plato's insistence on the principle of functional perfection, through the division of labor and the splitting up of social roles, was a denial of all that fifth-century Athens might have taught him. With a singular unawareness of what he was doing, he put into the mouth of Socrates a paean to an 'ideal' social order. Unfortunately, that social order would have prevented Socrates himself from coming into existence! If Plato's sociology were sound, Socrates, once he had been apprenticed to the art of the stonecutter, should have remained a stonecutter all his life; in addition, he should have turned his period of active military serv-ice as citizen soldier over to a lifetime professional substitute, trained from boyhood to do nothing else; and finally, he should never have dared to match his wits against the best minds of his day, in a pedagogical role so different from that of a stonecutter.

On Socrates' own analysis, the only sound knowledge he possessed was that of stone cutting: this gave him no license even to ask questions about any other human concern. The choice is simple: either Socrates stands convicted of self-contradiction and stultification out of his own mouth, or Plato himself was completely refuted by his master's living example—happily so contrary to Plato's archaic conceptions. The wisdom of Socrates would never have found utterance if he had lived his life in accordance with Plato's philosophy.

When Plato turned his back on the disorder and confusion of Athens, to rearrange the social functions of the city on an obsolete primitive pat-tern, he also turned his back, unfortunately, on the essential life of the city itself, with its power to crossbreed, to intermingle, to reconcile oppo-sites, to create new syntheses, to elicit new purposes not predetermined by the petrified structure itself. In short, he rejected the potentiality—not unrelated to what Plato would have regarded as inadmissible confusion—of transcending race and caste and overcoming vocational limitations. He saw no way of unifying the divided selves of man without freezing them into so many fixed, graded, and classified parts of the polis.

So strictly did Plato sort out the classes in his ideal city, the phil-osophers, the warriors, the craftsmen, and the husbandmen, that he re-turned to the order of an insect community, whose social adaptations are sealed in biological structures that have remained unchanged for tens of millions of years. What he did not suspect apparently was that this geo-metric heaven might, in terms of man's suppressed potentialities, turn out to be a living hell.

Till now mankind has been saved from Plato's dream by its tech-nological innocence—and impotence. But we today, who have the means of achieving Plato's ambition without yet having plumbed its horrible implications, would do well to pause and examine the prospect. If we continue in science and technology along the lines we are now following, without changing our direction, lowering our rate of speed, and re-orienting our mechanisms toward more valid human goals, the end is already in sight. Cybernetics, medical psychiatry, artificial insemination, surgery and chemotherapy have given the rulers of men the power to create obedient automatons, under remote control, with just enough mind left to replace the machine when its cost would be prohibitive. The polite name for this creature is 'man-in-space,' but the correct phrase is 'man out of his mind.'

Another century of such 'progress' may work irreparable damage upon the human race. Instead of deliberately creating an environment more effective than the ancient city, in order to bring out the maximum number of human potentialities and the maximum amount of significant complexity, our present methods would smooth out differences and reduce potentialities, to create a state of mindless unconsciousness, in which most of man's characteristic activities would be performed only by machines. Even if the infamous nuclear and bacteriological weapons that already threaten wholesale extermination remained unused, historic man, he who lives in cultural time and space, who remembers and anticipates and makes choices, would disappear.

5 : THE CHALLENGE OF GREEK
DIALECTIC

Plato's polis might be described as a walled prison without room for the true activities of the city within its prison-yard. Yet Plato more than once corrected his bald premises and his naïve conclusions: the red-faced protests of Socrates' interlocutors, indeed the recourse to dialogue, were themselves a kind of admission of Plato's own reservations, though his inflexible logic makes him repeatedly over-ride common sense, in cheap, disingenuous verbal triumphs. What could be more preposterous, for example, than Socrates' demonstration that the political leaders of the past in Athens did not know their business, since they were by definition shepherds of men, and if their flock turned upon them, or if the dogs they had trained bit their hands, it was a sign that their government had failed?

All that this argument demonstrated was the failure of Plato to understand human character: a failure as deep as that of the old-fashioned behaviorist psychologists today, equally confident that they know how to condition men. It is precisely the psychological distance between men and dogs, between political leaders and dog-trainers, that turns every despotic system of conditioning, sooner or later, into a mockery, as some of the leaders of Russian communism, with far greater resources at their command than Plato's Guardians, by now perhaps begin to realize. The fact is that doglike obedience is not compatible with human growth, or even, over any long period, with human existence. Freedom for self-direction is necessary for growth, though this brings with it the possibility of sin, error, crime, imperfection, failure: the price that the living must pay for breaking the civil bonds that would keep them safely undeveloped —easy to handle and shape.

Here, too, Plato's perceptive mind opposed his own theoretic rigidity and his archaic sentiments. He was aware that good men might turn up anywhere; indeed, in his old age he remarked that "there are always a few inspired men whose acquaintance is beyond price, and who spring up quite as much in ill-ordered as in well-ordered cities." If Plato had followed that observation farther, he would have discovered the dynamics of true maturation, and with it a firmer morality than that based upon a fixed and unalterable apportionment of human functions.

Plato mistook ideal compass points for actual destinations. For him the good and the bad were eternal ideas, immutable and separate: once installed they need never change. By wise laws, by strict censorship, by firm discipline, by totalitarian controls insulated by secrecy, he proposed to remove the bad and maintain the good. He little realized that the very instruments he chose would reverse this process. What he did not understand, further, was that though good and bad are fixed points on the moral compass, the currents of life itself often reverse their polarity. "Evil will bless," as Emerson says, "and ice will burn." A good pursued too inflexibly may turn into a granite evil, setting a limit to further development; while error and mischief, when recognized and challenged, may in the very recoil provide energy for a forward movement.

Like a button-molder, Plato sought to cast life into a prepared mold: the gold in one, the bronze in another, the base lead in a third. He had in him nothing of the gardener or the experimental biologist, selecting the seed, planting it in the right soil, with the right exposure, weeding and mulching around the plant; providing it with nutriment the soil may lack; in short, co-operating with nature while seeking to improve its wild forms for human consumption—not looking for perfection in a mechanical substitute, arbitrarily measured and shaped.

Plato undervalued the vital stimuli and challenges to growth: variety, disorder, conflict, tension, weakness, and even temporary failure. Each of these, if it does not harden into a fixed pattern, may produce a far more desirable community than any mode of conformity, whether that conformity be imposed by the philistine executives of a modern government agency or business corporation aided by electronic computers, or by the greatest thinker and writer that Athens had helped to produce. This dialectic opposition of good and evil is not—*pace* the Zoroastrians and the Marxians!—the whole of life: there are processes of physiological change and maturation, of psychal disruption and eruption, that have little to do with it. But to overlook the place of dialectic in the polis is to overlook the city's main function: the enlargement in human consciousness of the drama of life itself, through whose enactment existence discloses fresh meanings, not given by any momentary analysis or repetitious statistical order.

Between the sixth and the fourth centuries, the Greek cities found themselves in the throes of two severe conflicts: first, an attempt to define the limits of law and justice and mutual aid, as against the claims of hearth and kindred; second, not unrelated to this, an effort to free the intellect itself through logic, mathematics, and rational morality, from the savage presentations of the unconscious. As we see plainly in the tragedies, they sought to do away with human sacrifice, the blood revenge, the sexual orgy, and their even more perverse civilized counterparts. They aimed boldly at overcoming the devouring serpent and the cloven-hoofed satyr, while yet giving due place to the dark elements in life that run counter to reason and conscious desire: the Fates and the Furies and blind chance (Tyche), which may strike down the virtuous and enshrine the wicked.

But note: the only drama that Plato allowed for in either 'The Republic' or 'The Laws' was the drama of war. With that too-generous allowance, he reinstated into the essential life of the governing class the oldest institution of the citadel, war itself, not as a ritual game but as a deadly grapple with other cities, aiming at their destruction. Yet, though his whole concept of the ideal city was a self-isolating one, it was only in war that Plato could dream of any kind of federation or union of Greek cities: there, too, his premises were effete.

We come at last to the physical embodiment of Plato's city, about which little may be said, because less was written. Though his dialogues are full of all sorts of vivid images drawn from daily life, his vision of the polis itself lacks architectural body. When he describes the ancient city of Atlantis, he is not in fact describing the Platonic polis, but the new Hellenistic city, with its gardens and gymnasia and race courses, its hot and cold water, its canals, with its royal palace next to the habitation of the god, the citadel guarded by water, and the city itself surrounded by a wall. His own polis makes no pretense to these sumptuous furnishings or large dimensions. The chief conditions for it are that it must be small, isolated, self-contained, enclosed like other Greek cities in a sheltered valley, living with puritanic rigor on the products of its own soil.

In 'The Laws' Plato goes a little farther, but vaguely: "The city should be placed as nearly as possible in the center of the country, we should choose a place which possesses what is suitable for a city, and this may be easily imagined and described" (alas! that he took for granted precisely what we should like to know) . . . "then we will divide the city into twelve portions, first founding temples to Hestia, to Zeus, and to Athene, in a spot which we will call an Acropolis, and surround with a circular wall, making the division of the center city and country radiate from this point. The twelve sections shall be equalized by the provision that those which are good land shall be smaller, while those of inferior quality shall be larger. The number of the lots shall be 5040, and each of them shall be divided into two, and every allotment shall be composed of two such sections, one of land near the city, the other of land at a distance. . . . After this they shall assign twelve lots to twelve Gods and call them by their names and dedicate to each god several portions. . . . And they shall distribute the twelve divisions of the city in the same way, in which they divide the country, and every man shall have two habitations, one in the center of the country, the other at the extremity."

Still later Plato adds a few details about the civic center: "The temples are to be placed all round the agora, and the whole city built on the heights in a circle, for the sake of defense and for the sake of purity." Though Plato in this passage rejects the wall around the city, it is notable that he kept it earlier around the old sacred precinct. But in the end, he grudgingly allows the wall a municipal function, saying: "If men must have walls, the private houses ought to be so arranged that the whole city may be one wall, having all the houses capable of defense by reason of their uniformity and equality toward the streets. The form of the city being that of a single dwelling will have an agreeable aspect and being easily guarded will be infinitely better for security."

All in all, Plato, in his last words about the city, departs very little from the traditional concrete image, already familiar; and when he adds, at the end, a provision not merely for the agora, but for "the gymnasia, the places of instruction, and the theatres . . . all ready for scholars and spectators," one sees that despite his radical challenges, all he wished to do was to confine the Spartan military life and discipline within the shell of the Athenian polis.

The only point that seems out of keeping with this Athenian-Spartan hybrid is his praise of colonization, for he said that nothing tended more to the improvement of mankind than war and colonization. His chief objection to hiving off in colonies, indeed, was that colonies which are of this homogeneous sort, based on friendship and the community of race, language, and laws, are likely to rebel against any form of constitution differing from that they had at home—and this presumably was a formidable obstacle to the ideal legislator, as Plato conceived himself, for he was eager to lay down radically different laws and customs and rituals for a new community. Though Plato disliked the Athenian demos who presumptuously made new laws without having dedicated a whole life to their study, he shared their faith in the law-making process itself as the chief means, apart from education, of social improvement. In this, he implicitly carried on the old conviction of kingship.

The number of citizens in The Republic was limited to 5,040. These, presumably, are members of the Guardian class, in which men and women seem to stand on an equal basis as in Sparta. This number would leave only a very small band of warriors, around a thousand, to protect the unwalled city; and it would provide a total population of, at most, between twenty-five or thirty thousand souls—oddly enough the number later chosen by Leonardo da Vinci and Ebenezer Howard for their ideal cities. Now five thousand citizens were perhaps the largest number that could be addressed in a suitable theater by a single orator. But in a state governed, not by popular vote, but by the wisdom of a small group of Guardians presided over by a Philosopher-King, often acting in felonious secrecy like the actual Council of Ten in medieval Venice, the reduction of the population to the size needed for direct face-to-face encounter and for democratic voting hardly seems a necessity. Perhaps Plato feared that a larger population would be harder to keep under strict control. Possibly he was right, though large numbers lend themselves to despotic suppression. Possibly it was the desire to keep population low enough to live off the local food supply, without depending upon overseas grain, that prompted Plato to advance this figure.

What Plato never asked was a question that a philosopher, if not an economist, might well have put to himself: How large a portion of Greek culture, with its immense productivity in every department of art and thought, could be kept in existence in such a small isolated community?

While Plato set a strict limit to the size of his city, he did not show how it was to be kept within bounds, whether by colonization, by infanticide and abortion, by late marriages, or by some other method. There is even some doubt as to whether communal marriage is for the Guardians alone or for the whole population, though the communal nurseries seem to have been intended for all classes, if only to allow a freer choice of the 'best' infants. Most of the concrete suggestions in both 'The Laws' and 'The Republic' are of a negative kind: no poets, no passionate music, no marital attachments, no parental solicitudes, no mixing of vocations, no luxury, no foreign intercourse. Restrictive, puritanic, authoritarian: such was his ideal. No city could have shrunk into the form that Plato desired without ceasing to be a city. Given his way, he would have turned the urban dialogue into the sterile monologue of totalitarian power, though those who begin by talking only to themselves end up by having nothing to say.

Yet Plato was right in thinking that the basic constitution of the city needed to be re-examined and altered. To take the city's political and economic life for granted, to seek to do better something that should not perhaps be done at all, is the oft-repeated error of political reformers and planners. He even had the good sense to see that the radical change he contemplated would take place more easily under the pressure of misfortune or colonization.

If the functions of the city were not to miscarry, the principle of aristocracy must be invoked: not merely to over-ride mediocrity but to subdue brute power: the power of arms, money, numbers. There again he was right. Plato's mistake lay in misconceiving the nature of the aristocratic principle, as the exclusive possession of a class or a profession. What was needed rather, was an infusion of responsible talent and dedicated service even in the humblest offices of daily life.

Plato's true disciples in the spirit came almost a thousand years later: the Benedictine monks. But when Benedict created their monastic utopia, he had the insight to reverse all of Plato's precepts, replacing war by peace and non-resistance, and tempering the austere wisdom and daily sanctification of the monastery with the discipline of daily work, thus uniting, in each according to his capacity, all the functions of life Plato had so carefully set apart. In addition, the Benedictine system gathered strength, not in isolation, but in forming a chain of similar communities, interchanging their products, across Europe.

One marvels at Plato's blindness. Greek culture had in his time reached a point of development that made it necessary to challenge the archaic forms so far embodied in the city: above all, it must confront the slavery and one-sided exploitation on which so much of its economic life had come to depend. These were the dawning insights in the great minds of the fifth century. Plato played no part in this re-evaluation of the traditional "Greek way of life." Rejecting the conventions of private property and the preoccupations of business, he despised them too heartily to seek to infuse them with the aristocratic principle.

Instead of moralizing the merchant, Plato sought to abandon trade itself. Citizens, like friends, should hold all things in common: even wives. His morality, like his rationality, was meant for upper-class use alone. The rest of the population was to be trained and subdued, made into harmless submissives like other domesticated animals. In his ideal house, he had no use for fresh air from outdoors: instead, he contrived a windowless chamber into which he could pump artificially purified air, under strict control. In that sense he anticipated the absurdities of a certain type of modern mind by twenty-four hundred years.

So, though Plato was willing to make the most radical changes in property, sexual and marital relations, and education, he left the primitive institutions of the citadel intact; indeed, he expanded all their evil possibilities. Economic exploitation, slavery, war, specialized life-time labor—all these were left untouched. Plato's polis relied for daily meat and drink on these sacred but diseased cows. Incredibly, despite his emancipation, through logic and mathematics, from vulgar beliefs, Plato retained all the superstitions of his own class, including the belief that manual occupations are by nature base. That prejudice long delayed the development of the natural sciences, until late medieval doctrine and practice finally overcame this sacerdotal dualism.

These fixations kept Plato from having an inkling into the real plight of the city: its premature crystallization in the archaic forms of the citadel. All that his effort came to was an attempt to make the citadel itself more secure, against the encroaching democratic city, by restoring its ancient monopoly of religion, science, and military power, backed by secrecy and infamous prevarication. An ideal city indeed!

CHAPTER SEVEN

Hellenistic Absolutism and Urbanity

1: THE ARISTOTELIAN TRANSITION

The transition from the Hellenic polis to the Hellenistic metropolis, and thence to the Alexandrian megalopolis, was marked by no sudden changes; for the institutions and forms of the latter had already been prefigured in the commercial cities of Asia Minor, and until Rome put a final quietus upon the struggle, the polis fought a long, desperate, rear-guard action, which continued even after Demosthenes' defeat, to preserve its existence and restore the values that had made it great.

Both aspects of Hellenistic life become visible in the life and work of the greatest mind that studied under Plato: Aristotle. The fact that he accepted the summons to the court of Philip of Macedon and served as the teacher of the prodigious youth who became Alexander the Great makes him typical of his period. His interest in the natural sciences equalled his concern for the humanities: yet the two fields largely remained separate in his mind, as they were to remain, with unfortunate results for both, for the next two millennia. But though Aristotle served the rulers of an expanding empire, he never fully understood that human growth demanded a widening as well as a deepening of the whole process of association: so he never broke through the inner divisions of the polis, of slave, foreigner, trader, citizen, nor did he remove the invisible wall that separated Greek from barbarian.

Aristotle's discussion of ideal cities nevertheless went farther in many directions than Plato's; for he was enough of a naturalist to accept with more grace than Plato the need for variety and plurality. But his political differences from his master were not so radical as they seemed to the younger man or to many of his later interpreters. Apart from sensibly rejecting the community of wives and pointing out the ambiguities in Plato's disposition of the classes, he merely systematized Plato's thought and brought it somewhat closer to actual practice. He even shared Plato's distrust of change; for though he admitted that changes in the other arts and sciences had been beneficial, as in medicine, and that many actual improvements had taken place by departing from barbarous old customs, he was reluctant to consider such improvements in politics.

Yet just because Aristotle's philosophy was basically that of a biologist, rather than a mathematician, he brought to the discussion of cities something that Plato lacked: a knowledge of the immense variety of species and an appreciation of the endless creative manifestations of life itself. With this came an understanding of the teleological, goal-seeking, self-actualizing nature of all organisms, and of the natural limits that define normal growth. For Aristotle, the ideal was not a rationally abstract form to be arbitrarily imposed on the community: it was rather a form already potential in the very nature of the species, needing only to be brought out and developed.

Aristotle was not handicapped by the restricted conception of causality that seventeenth-century physics imposed upon modern thought, in order to keep all changes on the plane of the external and the observable. He realized, as a later generation will perhaps again realize, that 'purpose' is engrained in all natural processes, not superimposed by man, though purpose no more admits of ulterior explanation than does causality. But in his time the nature of the teleological process was so obscure and so far beyond the resources of scientific description that he was forced to use an abstract noun, entelechy, to describe the form-determining elements: thus he turned an observable process into an extraneous and unobservable entity. But Aristotle's static terminology should not lead one to overlook the familiar facts that it points to. To use the word 'mechanism' when faced with the need for recognizing a teleological process is to overlook the fact that machines are themselves exquisite examples of purpose.

Aristotle properly applied to human fabrications like the city the important lesson he had learned from the organic world: the lesson of controlled growth. In every biological species, there is a limit to size; and he points out this is equally true of human artifacts. If a boat is too small it cannot perform the functions of a boat, that is, carry passengers or cargo; if too big, it cannot be handled or moved. There is a range of sizes, then, proper to the art of navigation. So with the constitution of cities. If a town is too small, no matter what its architectural pretensions or its legal status, it is still a village. If it overpasses the bounds of growth, absorbing more people than it can properly house, feed, govern, or educate, then it is no longer a city; for its ensuing disorganization keeps it from carrying on a city's functions.

True: Aristotle objected to the size of Plato's citizen population not because it was too small to give sufficient variety, but because it would require "territory as large as Babylon, or some other huge city, if so many people are to be supported in idleness." But in general Aristotle's position is not only sounder than Plato's: it is sounder than that of most of our present-day planners, who have not yet arrived at a functional definition of a city, and who do not realize that size and area cannot be increased indefinitely without either destroying the city or bringing about a new kind of urban organization, for which both an adequate small scale form and large scale pattern of life must be found.

Mere increase in size no more signifies improvement, or even adaptation, than technological expansion ensures a good life. The very dynamism of growth, as in the change from hand weapons to the hydrogen bomb, only increases the area of possible destruction.

Plainly it would have been easy for Aristotle to have clinched his definition of size by falling back upon the visible definition of the city wall; but he avoided that snare. "When," he asks, "are men living in the same place to be regarded as a single city—what is the limit? Certainly not the wall of the city, for you might surround all Peloponnese with a wall. Like this, we may say, is Babylon—and every city that has the compass of a nation rather than a city; Babylon they say, had been taken for three days before some part of its inhabitants became aware of the fact." What makes the city in fact one is the common interest in justice and the common aim, that of pursuing the good life. In "size and extent it should be such as may enable the inhabitants to live at once temperately and liberally in the enjoyment of leisure."

The Greeks had empirically reached this conclusion long before Aristotle: no one can define the Greek city in the early Hellenic period better than by saying that it was a community that was determined for its own good to remain small. Natural limitations helped to push the citizens to this conclusion; but even trading cities like Miletus, which could have met the problem of growth by extending the range of their exports and grain buying, did not take that course. The good life, as they understood it and practiced it, depended upon intimacy and small numbers. When the polis sent out a colony, it made no effort, it would seem, to extend either its territorial or its economic dominion: it sought only to reproduce conditions similar to those of the mother city. As between growth by accretion, which became socially inorganic and ultimately led to disintegration, and growth by colonization, which maintained integrity and purpose, the Greeks chose colonization, as the little towns of New England did in the seventeenth century. They had mastered the art of reproducing cities. If only they had succeeded equally in the art of uniting them. . . .

Aristotle brings forth many reasons. practical and metaphysical, for limiting the size of the city; but the final limit is that taken from political experience. "For both the governors and the governed," he observes, "have duties to perform; the special functions of a governor are to command and to judge. But if the citizens of a state are to judge and distribute offices according to merit, they must know each other's characters; where they do not possess this knowledge, both the election to offices and the decision of lawsuits will go wrong. When the population is very large, they are manifestly settled at haphazard, which clearly ought not to be. . . . The best limit of the population of a city, then, is the largest number which suffices for the purposes of life, and can be taken in at a single view."

At a single view: here is both an esthetic and a political conception of urban unity. This synoptic or over-all view, which enabled the citizen, from the height of the acropolis, to behold his whole city as readily as he might take in the form and character of a single person, was the essential Greek note. This differentiated the Hellenic city, however cluttered, from the limitless spreading of the overgrown megalopolis, which had preceded it in Mesopotamia and followed it in Italy, Africa, and Asia Minor.

So much for the valid contribution of Aristotle. But in his prejudice against artisans and merchants, Aristotle was as hidebound as Plato. When Aristotle defined the polis, not just as a community of living beings, but as a community of equals, aiming at the best life possible, he deliberately excluded the life of "mechanics or tradesmen, for such a life is ignoble and inimical to virtue": indeed, these classes cannot even hold a priestly office, "for the gods should receive honor from citizens only." The notion that the whole community must share the active life of the city, as all the peasants had shared the life of the village, did not occur to Aristotle any more than to Plato. The good life could be found only in noble leisure; and noble leisure meant that someone else must do the work.

This exclusion of a large portion of city dwellers from citizenship partly accounts for the debacle of the Greek city. By keeping the majority of its inhabitants outside politics, the area of full citizenship, the polis gave them a license to be irresponsible. What was equally bad, it gave them no other occupation than self-promoting economic activity, and relieved that of any moral end or obligation even in those affairs they could govern. Thus it prompted the traders, in Plato's words, "to seek inordinate gains, and having people at their mercy, to take advantage of them."

So the movement that had begun in fact with Socrates and his lower-class follower, Antisthenes, to open up the best life possible even to the handicraft worker and give him the full benefits of spiritual growth, halted in thought as it halted in action. Though Antisthenes got as far as starting a poor man's gymnasium, the Cynosarges, he could have no hope of reclaiming the whole polis or of seeing a day when the upper and lower classes would meet on common ground, on the basis of their common interests and equal capabilities.

Fortunately, Aristotle had one special quality that Plato lacked. He translated his principles into the physical structure of the city; and here the old mingled with the new. He provided for the orientation of the city, to promote health: we know indeed from Xenophon that orientation had become an important consideration, for he represents his Socrates correctly advocating a southern exposure as the most advantageous one, a bit of practical wisdom that the people of the Northern Hemisphere have repeatedly lost and rediscovered over thousands of years. Aristotle insisted, too, upon the importance of an abundance of springs and fountains; or, failing that, on reservoirs and cisterns for collecting rain water. The maxims of the Hippocratic school were here at last consciously applied to town planning.

Though some Greek towns still boasted of having no need for walls, that seemed to Aristotle a piece of military folly; indeed, he was so conscious of the need for resisting invasion that he sought to combine the new fashion of laying out streets in rectangular blocks with the more antiquated irregular mode of building, with twisting streets that followed contours or old footpaths; for the latter layout made it difficult for thieving strangers to get out of town or for assailants to find their way in. Perhaps he recalled the experience of the Thebans who penetrated Plataea, Thucydides tells us, and so completely lost their way that they were easily made prisoners. "The whole town," Aristotle pointed out, "should not be laid out in straight lines, but only certain quarters and regions: thus security and beauty will be combined."

In other matters, Aristotle was equally conservative. So he desired to set the agora as marketplace apart from the agora as political forum. The second he would establish after the example of Thessaly, as a freeman's agora, from which all trades and tradesmen would be excluded, unless summoned by the magistrates. He thought it would be charming if the gymnastic exercises of the older men were performed there: thus he sought to bring at least part of the gymnasium from the suburbs back into the heart of town.

Here, as elsewhere, though Aristotle was supposedly discussing an ideal city, it is plain that he found it hard not to treat the ancient city, with its strong class divisions, as an ideal. Both in him and in Plato what seem innovations are often reversions to the more primitive urban community of the Cretans, the Spartans, and even the Carthaginians; while with both philosophers, most of the social processes and functions of a later date, which conflicted with the ancient military pattern, were looked upon as so much unpleasant social refuse—to be diminished in amount and removed from sight as far as possible.

What Lavedan has said of the influence of Plato and Aristotle on later city planning and municipal order errs, I fear, on the generous side. "It consisted in preparing the mind to accept a certain number of restrictions dictated by the collective interest." But the fact is that they were not, by anticipation, either apologists or publicists for the new order, which shaped the growing Hellenistic cities without their help, and with little respect for their beliefs. Neither Plato nor Aristotle had any just insight into the happy moment that Athens, and in some degree all other Greek cities, had lived through, from the time of Solon to that of Pericles: therefore their ideal cities made no provision for continuing and strengthening these creative forces. They had no vision of a wider polis, incorporating the ideal principles of Cos, Delphi, and Olympia and working them into the generous complexities of an open society. Their ideal city was still just a small static container, under the grim direction of the citadel: for support, it had only a self-contained economy, supported, at least for Aristotle, by a robust middle class. The cultural center of gravity of such a city fell within its own base; but on such terms the burgeoning mind of the actual polis would have withered and wilted.

"It needs a whole society to give the symmetry we seek," observed Emerson. Aristotle and Plato sought this symmetry in less than half a society—not even a full polis but a class segment frozen in an archaic image. Not Athens or Corinth, alone, not Sparta or Delos, could flourish apart from its neighbors. Nor indeed could any of the cities of Hellas embody the Greek ideal of life without calling upon men and ideas and institutions that no one of them could appropriate exclusively for itself. Still less could any single class achieve the noble symmetry these philosophers sought. As a result, the growing polis, in its flux and disorder, swelling beyond all previous bounds, did more justice to the ideal possibilities of urban society than did these utopian projections, for all their crystalline perfection.

This failure to understand the dynamics of human development as a key to urban form was not overcome by any further progress in the natural sciences after Aristotle. Under tyrannous rulers it is safer to pursue the physical sciences than to study human nature and society. The Hellenic polis was arrested by another weakness: inability to understand the human contribution of the slave, the industrial worker, the foreigner, and the barbarian: that is to say, the rest of mankind. The goods that the Greeks had imagined and created were human goods, not limited in their origin or their destination to the Greeks alone. Plato might recognize, after his travels to Egypt, that the Egyptian priesthood had funded esoteric knowledge that surpassed any he had access to; but

the fact is that other peoples—the Jews, the Persians, the Babylonians—
had much to contribute to the Greeks, and it should have been possible
to embrace this otherness without being looked upon as a renegade or a
traitor. That the Greeks never repaired the error of slavery, that some of
their best minds could not even admit that it was an error, shows how
easily they submitted to arrest, how far they fell short even in their concept of democracy of the generically human.

By making the city, the artifact they themselves had created, into
their god, the Greeks lost hold of the greatest gift of divine experience—
the impulse and the capacity to transcend natural limitations. The invisible city, as yet only incarnated in a handful of great citizens, whose
new lines of magnetic force had issued from Olympia, Delphi, and Cos,
never assumed a more effective political and physical structure. While
that city was still in fluid form, it had nurtured men of larger stature, of
higher potentialities, than had ever before gathered in such numbers, among
such a small population. But when the moment to pass from individual
ideation and incarnation to collective embodiment took place, the city,
self-infatuated, returned to an earlier form, highly organized and ordered,
sanitary, wealthy, even sumptuously beautiful; but sadly inferior to the
inchoate polis of the fifth century in its capacity for creation.

Except in the physical sciences, in the more quantitative scholarly
disciplines, and in the production of material goods, nothing prospered
in the post-Hellenic city. For as technological organization and wealth
increased, the ideal purposes of the city no longer found expression in
the daily life. Even the mind was starved, not for lack of food, but by
its being overstuffed with depleted and sterile nutriment. The museum and
the library took precedence over life and experience: academicism replaced the organic balance of the original academy: collection and classification became the chief avenues of intellectual activity. The proliferation
of devitalized knowledge, knowledge treated as a substitute for responsible
action, not as an instrument of life, properly takes its name from the
great metropolis of Alexander. 'Alexandrianism' brought such knowledge
to heights rivalled only by the suavely empty productions fostered by the
great educational foundations of our own time. This sterile, academic
knowledge, like a dangerous virus prudently killed and diluted, must, if
we can judge by present experience, often give complete immunity against
original thought or fresh experience for a whole lifetime. Yet, as with
various other features of the Hellenistic city, something permanently
valuable—a patience, an order, a discipline, an ability to cope mechanically with large quantities—was passed on through the devious channels
of classical scholarship to later cities in Western Europe.

But quantitative expansion was not confined to the market or the
museum: every part of the city underwent the same process. The streets

grew longer and wider, the buildings bigger, the external regimentation
became more oppressively evident. But the more effectively the centralized controls and beneficent handouts of the great empires worked, the
more plainly did the Greek city depart from its original premises and—
what is more important—its original promise. Whatever it was, after
300 B.C. the polis no longer was internally strong enough to challenge,
even in thought, the political oppressions, the class divisions, and the irrational sacrifices, the futile war and pillage and destruction, that characterized the ancient city.

2: FROM SUPPLE 'DISORDER' TO
REGIMENTED ELEGANCE

From the seventh century on, the Greek cities developed along two different lines: largely spontaneous, irregular, 'organic' on the Greek mainland and its islands, more or less systematic and rigorous in the Asia
Minor poleis of Ionia. In the first, the spirit of the acropolis dominated:
in the second, that of the agora. One clung to the old pieties, only to be
overwhelmed by forces, internal and external, that it neither understood
nor knew how to control. The other organized a new mode of life, in
which agriculture was secondary to commerce. Yet both were perpetually
undermined and disintegrated by war and conquest.

During this early period of growth, the Ionian cities were repeatedly
destroyed by assault and rebuilt: the early history of Troy was told over
again and again. Though these new cities may at first have showed many
residual traits brought over from an earlier period of military and religious
rule, their new town plans were the direct expression of an essentially
mercantile society. The leading philosopher of the sixth century, Thales
of Miletus, one of the original seven sages of Greece, was perhaps the
first systematic student of nature with no religious tradition behind his
thought, the archetypal physicist. But he was admiringly known to his
fellow citizens as an astute trader who, observing one season a singularly heavy crop of olives, made a corner of the oil-presses before
harvest, and so became rich.

The foundations of the Hellenistic city, which flourished everywhere
from the fourth century on, were laid in Asia Minor during the sixth
century; perhaps, indeed, as early as the seventh, for the new trading
colony of Naucratis in Egypt showed a characteristic regularity and order

in its layout. If the slow organic growth of the cities of Attica was due to their topographical limitations and their economic poverty, the swift development of the cities of the East was due, not only to their richer hinterland, which multiplied economic resources and opportunities, but to a transfer of interest from military conquest and outright piracy to the manipulations and speculative excitements of trade itself.

This situation produced a thriving middle class, accustomed to physical comforts and luxuries the cities of Attica and Italy long lacked. Their habit of life became universal in the more prosperous cities of Greece after the fourth century: the contemporaries of Menander had lost the coarse village ways, and demanded perfumes, little objects of art like the exquisite Tanagra figurines, and a refined voluminous cuisine, as Aulus Gellius bears witness. They looked for small elegances to console them for a politically empty life. Increasingly they lost both the will to struggle for freedom and the incentives that would have made that struggle meaningful; and they covered over their vacuity, moral inertness, and anxiety by demanding more of the goods that money would buy. Those who were sufficiently prosperous and idle ended up with insomnia, for reasons that were obvious even to a contemporary dramatist. "Insomnia? I dare say—and here's the reason. How do you live? A stroll around the market and back you come all tired. Then a nice warm bath. Food when you feel like eating. Sleep? Your life's a sleep." This was a new version of the best life possible, less familiar to the Greeks than to those of us today in America who are rocked to sleep by an economy of misdirected abundance.

But in the sixth century this gilded cage of mercantile prosperity had not been put together: its bars still glittered because they were not yet tightly closed. Here in Ionia around the seventh century, two new inventions were put into circulation: coined money, which may have come from Assyria or Lydia, and the written alphabet. Those refinements of number and writing were prime tools of the mind, though they had first developed as essential notations in long-distance trading and commercial accountancy.

Even apart from their aptitude for commerce, the cities of Ionia must have been influenced, if only at third hand, by the municipal heritage of the Hittite, Assyrian, and Babylonian empires, to say nothing of Crete, before the Medes and Persians rose to power. The new type of planning that appeared in this area was in fact the ancient type we find in Mesopotamia; and since it would be erroneous to call this Hippodamian planning, I shall follow Roland Martin and call it Milesian, after Miletus, the chief point of origin.

We must associate this Milesian layout with a new regularity and system in commercial affairs. That order was by no means confined to

Asia Minor, since Cryne, founded in 630-624 in Lydia, boasted straight streets, crossing at right angles; while Naples and Paestum, Greek colonies planted in Italy in the sixth century, actually exhibit a checkerboard plan throughout. This Milesian planning introduced, almost automatically, two other elements: streets of uniform width and city blocks of fairly uniform dimensions. The city itself was composed of such standardized block units: their rectangular open spaces, used for agora or temple, were in turn simply empty blocks. If this formal order was broken by the presence of a hill or a curved bay, there was no effort at adaptation by a change of the pattern. With this plan goes a clarification of functions and a respect for convenience: so the agora shifted toward the waterfront, to be near the incoming ships and warehouses.

Geometric order, once established in the general plan of the city, penetrated its architectural conceptions as well. From Miletus, possibly through the work of Hippodamos, came the new type of agora, a formal rectangle, surrounded by a wall of shops on at least three sides. This geometric plan was not an easy one to apply to sites with an irregular topography; but it had one advantage that gave it currency in the sixth century and made it universal once more in the third century B.C.: it provided a simple and equitable method of dividing the land in a new city formed by colonization.

That virtue belonged to no particular age or culture. If the architects of Alexander the Great used it in his seventy urban foundations, so did the Romans in establishing their own colonization settlements for army veterans: indeed, it was the basis on which they laid out their temporary camps. This layout was used later in the building of garrison towns (bastides) in southern France in the fourteenth century A.D., and in Ireland in the seventeenth century; further, it was on the basis of the gridiron plan, with an open plaza in the middle, that the Spaniards laid out their colonial towns in the New World. Finally, the same type of plan, already more than two thousand years in use in Western Europe, became the basis of North American town planning and town extension, from the founding of Philadelphia, New Haven, and Savannah onward.

The standard gridiron plan in fact was an essential part of the kit of tools a colonist brought with him for immediate use. The colonist had little time to get the lay of the land or explore the resources of a site: by simplifying his spatial order, he provided for a swift and roughly equal distribution of building lots.

The very weakness of the Milesian plan—its indifference to the contours of the land, to springs, rivers, shore lines, clumps of trees—only made it that much more admirable in providing a minimum basis of order on a site that colonists would not, for long, have the means fully to exploit. Within the shortest possible time, everything was brought under control. This minimal order not merely put everyone on a parity: above all, it made strangers as much at home as the oldest inhabitants. In a trading city, always filled with sailors and foreign merchants, this ease of orientation and identification was no small asset. No wonder that even conservative Athens, when it sought to rebuild its port, called in Hippodamus to lay it out on the Milesian plan.

All this was something more than an abstract exercise in surveying and plotting, though there was a close affiliation between thought and practice here; for in addition to the general outlines, the placing of the agora, the docks, the warehouses, demanded professional knowledge; and when matters requiring judgment in these departments were before the Town Council, they would adjourn to the water front and come to a decision on the spot. With the habit, further, of laying out the whole town as a unit, in this mode, even the meanest of the new Greek cities would be provided from the beginning with adequate public spaces for public structures; and their placement within the gridiron broke up the monotony of a single kind of block, indefinitely repeated. It is not the monotony of the plan itself, but the later absence of this functional differentiation and emphasis, that gave the rectangular plan, in the nineteenth century, such a needlessly bad reputation.

The geometric order provided by the Milesian plan had still another use: that of dividing the city into definite neighborhoods, or at least giving that definition visible boundary lines. In the new plan of Thurium (443 B.C.), founded with the help of Pericles as a Panhellenic gesture of reconciliation with the communities that Athens had wronged, this Milesian influence predated the wider Hellenistic habit of a later period. Thurium was divided by four longitudinal and three transverse arteries into ten neighborhood units or superblocks, each dedicated to the component tribes: with one to the old inhabitants of Sybaris, for whom the new city was made—theirs had been destroyed by Croton in 510—and one for public buildings.

This incidentally is, I believe, the first historic example of a deliberately fabricated neighborhood unit, though there is plenty of evidence to show that natural neighborhoods, formed around a shrine or a temple, had existed from the earliest times. But it is a somewhat unfortunate demonstration of the principle, since, like the earlier division of Naucratis into a Greek and an Egyptian quarter, it was based on the principle of social segregation. With blocks so big, one can hardly doubt that, as in Philadelphia after the seventeenth century, a minor system of alleys must have developed to provide quicker passage for the pedestrian.

With the application of the gridiron plan, the street began to exist in its own right, not as before a devious passage grudgingly left over between a more or less disordered heap of buildings. Once the street assumed this degree of detachment, the notion of widening it to accommodate larger bodies of people would follow naturally, without any pressure from vehicular traffic. From the Maya and Inca cities, we now have independent evidence to show that broad streets and even highways are not a mere by-product of wheeled chariots or carriages. Religious processions and military parades both have need for them. Such widening of the streets took place in the Hellenistic cities of the third century, even when they were uninfluenced by the Roman religious system of orienting the main streets by the points of the compass. The military need was so evident to a contemporary that the historian Polybius actually compared the Hellenistic town to the camp of a Roman legion, with two main streets crossing at right angles.

The same sense of order and visual continuity made its way into the agora. This resulted, especially after the fourth century, in the building of stoas—colonnades or covered porches—sometimes to screen the shops from the sun, sometimes to serve the pedestrian. One side might be formed by a wall, which provided surface for mural paintings, such as one still finds by happy accident in Etrurian cities, or by inscriptions, recording conquests, donations, the laws of the city, or even a philosophic doctrine, as in the benign, pithy message that Diogenes of Oenoanda, an Epicurean, incised on the wall of a portico in Cappadocia (around A.D. 200) for the passer-by to read: a message Gilbert Murray reproduced in 'Five Stages of Greek Religion.'

The stoa itself may have originated at a much earlier period. There seems to be a Minoan example at Hagia Triada, with shops behind it, in true 'Hellenistic' style. But it became common in the Hellenistic cities, with their general effort to improve urban comfort. It was in the shade of the stoa that Zeno of Citium and the other stoic philosophers of the third century and later held forth. Their philosophy of universal law, of fixed unalterable order, of inflexible devotion to duty, come what may, corresponds ideologically with the new esthetic of the town plan, equally bent on order, equally undeviating.

The formal continuity thus achieved in the agora spread, with the development of the Hellenistic city, into other parts of the urban scene: the long avenue and the continuous open arcade were expressions of it: sometimes with grouped columns forming a terminal point for the eye, at the great cross streets, in somewhat the same fashion that obelisks were used later in the baroque city. One could find such arcades in Turin (Augusta Taurinorum) or Bologna as early as the third and second centuries B.C.; and this feature has remained one of the great esthetic delights of the Mediterranean city: even the modern arcades of Turin, to say nothing of the late renascence arcades of Genoa, count among the masterpieces of town planning, by reason not merely of their usefulness but of their noble scale.

Not the least service of the street in the Hellenistic plan was one it also served later in the American gridiron plan: it provided a bare minimum ration of open public space—open if arid—in the otherwise too closely built-up residential quarters. The street thus played a part that public parks and gardens were later to play, though rarely on a scale that corresponded with the need for them. Even quite late Hellenistic cities show no open courts between the houses in the residential quarters; and anything like the generous gardens that stretched behind the medieval row house in northern Europe was conspicuously absent. Perhaps the desire for light and air as well as free movement was responsible for the widening of the main streets. That re-enforced the demand due to the more frequent use of wheeled vehicles and palanquins, and the presence of ever denser crowds of people.

Already, in the Alexandrian city, the old Greek street width of twelve or thirteen feet was increased: probably the width in Alexandria itself, eighteen or nineteen feet, became common, while the main thoroughfare, Canopic Street, was a hundred feet wide; at that time a colossal dimension. But in fact the scale of all urban structures increased during the Hellenistic period, as the Pergamon altar in Berlin reminds us: this was part of a general quantitative expansion that affected both the area of the city and the heights of buildings. Two story buildings, even three story buildings, relatively unknown since Knossos, arose. With the increase in bulk—as later with the ballooning of the Dome—a building could dominate the city without being placed on a hill: so the great temples and law courts were usually set on level ground, in or near the agora, not on the heights.

But while allowing for other needs, one must not neglect the increasing place of circulation in the city plan. This was due not merely to the transport of merchandise and food for larger numbers of people, but also to the requirements of large armies of occupation, no longer a dispersed citizen force. With ordered movement came two architectural features that the Hellenic city showed hardly any awareness of: perspective and the long axis. Instead of getting an over-all view of the city by penetrating it, bit by bit, rambling around it, ascending the acropolis in zigzag fashion and thus taking it in from every direction and at every level, the avenue gives one a uniform slice of the city in cross section on a single level. The continuous façade: porticoes or buildings of equal height: the repeating columns of the fronts repeated the whole length of the avenue, produce precisely the same esthetic impression at any point. By walking farther one only gets more of the same thing.

One approached the monuments and temples of the acropolis from many angles, by varied movements, as one approaches a piece of sculpture, seeing a succession of faces and profiles. But the Hellenistic public building must be approached by a main avenue: even if it closes that avenue, it can be taken in standing still, at a respectful distance: as one comes nearer, it changes in size, but not in any quality but the details, which themselves are invariable too. With this kind of planning the Hellenistic city took on a Roman aspect even before the Romans had actually conquered greater Greece. From the standpoint of abstract form, indeed, it is hard to distinguish between the Hellenistic and the Roman town: it is chiefly in the social and ornamental contents, the effect of earlier traditions and habits, that the difference shows itself. As Wycherley points out, the new cities founded by the Seleucid monarchs in Mesopotamia—like Dura-Europos on the Euphrates—were standardized for export: a sort of mass-production polis.

Urban life had begun in Greece as an animated conversation and had degenerated into a crude agon or physical struggle. Under a succession of royal and imperial conquerors, the conversation ceased—it is the slave's lot, observed Euripides, "not to speak one's thought." With that the struggle likewise came to an end. What was left of the old urban drama was a mere spectacle, a show staged before a passive audience, with professional freaks, contortionists, and dwarfs usurping the place once occupied by self-respecting citizens.

Certainly the proportion of spectators to actors was altered under the more servile system of government; and this radical change expressed itself in the forms of the city. In the old polis every citizen had an active part to play: in the new municipality, the citizen took orders and did what he was told, while the active business of government was in the hands of professionals, tempted by loot or hired for pay, often reaching for both, as with the notorious Roman tax farmers and publicans. Even where the forms of self-government were preserved by the Romans, they applied only to an hereditary oligarchy.

The city thus ceased to be a stage for a significant drama in which everyone had a role, with lines to speak: it became, rather, a pompous show place for power; and its streets properly presented only two-dimensional façades that served as a mask for a pervasive system of regimentation and exploitation. What paraded as town planning in the Hellenistic Age was not unrelated to the kind of smooth lies and insidious perversions that go under the name of public relations and advertising in the American economy today.

We may trace this elegant petrifaction of the Hellenistic city through Miletus and its allied urban communities to the cities that fell under the various centralized states that eventually dominated the Aegean and

Mediterranean area: the Macedonian, the Seleucid, the Pergamene, and the Ptolemaic absolutisms. In following this evolution of both architecture and urbanism, we find ourselves face to face with one of the most puzzling contradictions in human development: the oft-repeated disharmony, not to say the rude conflict, between esthetic order and moral order.

As the inner life of the Greek city disintegrated, the outer aspect of the city showed a far higher degree of formal order and coherence. Certainly, the Hellenistic city was more sanitary, and often more prosperous, than the Hellenic city. If it was more severely regimented it was also, to a superficial eye at least, more beautiful. Not the city of the sixth and fifth centuries, but that of the third century, would be the modern town planner's dream: not the city of culture but the city of commerce and political exploitation: not the city of free men but the city of insolent power and ostentatious wealth. Even Marcel Poëte praised Hellenistic urbanism as 'modern.'

Is this a reflection on the art and politics of the Hellenic city? In some degree, yes: for it shows a partial failure to understand and successfully direct the forces of urban development. One cannot conceal the weaknesses of early municipal housekeeping. But perhaps it is the conventional town planner's dream that deserves even more to come under severe critical examination; for too often the perfected physical shell is the final expression of a frustrated and spiritually enfeebled civic organism.

No city of the fifth century, not even Periclean Athens, was able to spend as lavishly on public works as these rapacious and highly organized kingdoms and empires, drawing on a far ampler economic base. Though these new states squandered human vitality and economic wealth on the arts of war, they would often crown their success in commanding slave power and garnering tribute by lavishing money on costly public works of every kind. Democracies are often too stingy in spending money for public purposes, for its citizens feel that the money is theirs. Monarchies and tyrannies can be generous, because they dip their hands freely into other people's pockets.

This easy largesse was marked by an increase in the scale, as well as the mass, of public building, and by a delight in bigness for its own imposing sake: witness the Colossus of Rhodes, one of the seven wonders of the ancient world, a sculptured figure that dominated the harbor. What goes so lavishly into space rockets in our time went, with perhaps a little more visible reward, into equally monumental architecture almost equally empty of human benefit. In both cases, paranoid power learned to 'rationalize' the expression of its irrationality by its homage to art or science.

The Hellenistic city, then, became a showplace where the power of the rulers, dynastic or mercantile, was put on display, both to awe and to entertain their subjects. Perhaps to heal the deep wound caused by the Greek city's loss of effective political freedom and cultural creativity, the new rulers provided beauty, as a kind of balm, or analgesic; and the city as a whole exhibited a comeliness which, if it fell short of the best examples of Hellenic architectural order, nevertheless achieved a general level that Athens under Pericles never even aspired to. Athens herself was not the least to profit: the Kings of Pergamene were particularly kind to Athens.

Given these opportunities, the architects and planners of the Hellenistic Age made the most of them. They deliberately worked to achieve magnificent esthetic effects, not just in single buildings, but in the closer inter-relation of buildings both with each other and with the site. In the arrangement of long unbroken vistas, the apparent diminution in the height of the uniform columns as they receded in the distance gave the charm of perspective, mathematically ordered. Is it an accident that this esthetic order, which we first encounter in the processional ways to the temple in ancient Egypt, and will meet again in seventeenth-century Europe, came into existence along with absolute monarchy and large-scale bureaucratic supervision? Bureaucrats are professionally inured to monotony. The Medici, Pope Sixtus V, Louis XIV, and Napoleon III meet their ancient counterparts on common ground. Yet some of the engines of order and power have their uses or purposes other than those that may originally have caused them to be invented: that is the old lesson of the container. So the visible order of the Hellenistic city remained an incentive to urban design long after the tyrannous edicts and the arbitrary acts of conquest passed into nothingness.

If urban esthetic unity, on the Hellenistic scale, was an achievement that despotism might well, with due modifications, hand on to more sensible systems of government, one must escape the traditional hypnosis exercised on generations of scholars by all Greek achievements, in order to appraise it adequately. And to do this order justice, one should perhaps remember that the despot himself was an instrument in a larger movement of civilization: his arbitrary desires, or even those of his bureaucratic agents, were not the sole determinants of the new plan.

By the blindest and clumsiest means, moving toward ends that only the rarest of rulers, like Asoka or Marcus Aurelius, would ever become fully conscious of, these spreading empires were actually breaking down the stultifying parochialisms of traditional urban societies. The very migrations of prisoners, slaves, refugees, displaced persons, all widened the bonds of human association. Through that act, communities that had no interlinking civic bond fabricated, to their common advantage, a personal bond that transcended the polis; and in the same moment of the spirit a great part of what had once been secret and sacred knowledge was absorbed into the secular enterprises of the sciences, open to all who had the leisure and ability to pursue them. In this anti-civic situation, the mind, detached from political responsibilities, relieved of military duties, worked energetically at its private tasks as never before; and the city subtly reflected this new dispensation, in its very uniformity and anonymity and external order.

The Hellenistic period has won many admirers among scholars in our time, not least from the German savants who worshipfully identified the ruthlessness of Alexander and other absolute rulers with that of their own leaders, and denigrated those who, like Demosthenes, were bold enough to oppose them, as mere sentimentalists. Each age tends to flatter the part of the past that sends back its own image; and in that sense Pergamene Greece is closer to our contemporaries than Solon's age. Like our own day, this period was richer in science than in wisdom; for this was the time of Euclid, Archimedes, Hero of Alexandria, the mathematicians and physicists whose theorems and experiments laid the foundation for the scientific and technical structure that was not actually reared until the seventeenth century A.D.

Beyond that, it was a period of organizers and classifiers in all departments of thought: these encyclopedic minds came together in the great Library at Alexandria. Knowledge, once assimilated chiefly by direct contact from master to pupil—Plato, if the letter that tells this is genuine, never committed his deepest insights to writing—was now externalized in libraries and museums, almost freed from the hieratic order of the temple. Yet so strong was the original association between the academy and the temple, that when Ptolemy Philadelphus founded the museum at Alexandria he made it part of the palace, supported by a grant from the treasury, and placed under the direction of a priest nominated by the king.

Without system and order no one could have utilized these vast accumulations of economic and intellectual capital, unless justice and love had altered the whole scheme of distribution. Lacking such a radical transformation, the Hellenistic city perfected its busy, orderly, but inwardly anxious and unbalanced life, with its intellectual branches proliferating in every direction, its arts flowering in many vivid colors—and its deeper human roots drying up. In quantitative terms, all these improvements were immense, indeed staggering. The new scale applied alike to political power, to intellectual ability, to superficial esthetic attractiveness: but it framed a social and personal emptiness that mere numbers could not fill.

Monumentalism was the dominant esthetic attribute of the Hellenistic city; and the expansion of this monumentalism was, as Roland Martin has justly observed, the "fait du prince." This was the tie uniting the town-planning efforts of the sixth-century tyrants with those of the third-century political 'saviors,' as more than one Emperor styled himself. One might say, without too much injustice or depreciation, that the new despots helped maintain their particular kind of public embezzlement by a fresh species of esthetic bedazzlement: or rather, they revived an old kind, only too well known in Egypt, Assyria, and Persia. The very extent of their public-works projects, which gave employment to such varied kinds of labor on a large scale, served perhaps in some degree to allay popular discontent. Fat contractors and lean laborers made common cause. The Hellenistic town, with its systematic network of streets, its successive additions of theaters and fountain houses, its better water supply, often piped from the hills, had lifted the general physical level of the population.

This was no mean gift, and it would be foolish to disparage it. Nor were fresh innovations in planning lacking, apart from those that made for the flow of traffic from port to warehouse and unrolled the red carpet of power. To compensate for the spread of the town, which made the surrounding countryside ever less accessible, trees were planted within the built-up area; and pots of plants were even used as a form of street decoration. That mode continues in many European towns today. What we call 'street furniture,' if it was not entirely the invention of the Hellenistic city, was at all events now assiduously provided.

There was, moreover, a steady accumulation of temples, shrines, fountains, votive offerings, associated with both the living and the dead: everywhere these memorials served as repositories of memory and sentiment, recalling benefactions, victories, or the transitory presence of greatness; so that Pausanias' later travels in Greece are not so much a guidebook to buildings as a 'Recherche du Temps Perdu.' This was doubly valuable in a culture that, for no small part of the population, was remote from books. Victor Hugo's definition of the cathedral as the stone book of mankind applied even more to the ancient city.

The tie with our own day derives less from these details than from the common outlook of a power-centered culture. The increased open space provided by the larger agora and the wider and longer streets gave the Hellenistic city a 'modern' appearance. Canopic Street in Alexandria, founded in 331 B.C., was more than five times wider than the usual thoroughfare and four miles long. Under this dispensation every city would boast, at least in its newer quarters, a Plataea or Broad Way.

No doubt the Hellenistic city performed its commercial functions more efficiently, or at least more systematically, than the Hellenic city: it was above all an 'emporium.' But perhaps its greatest function was to serve as an arena for massive shows: a container for spectators. This emphasis

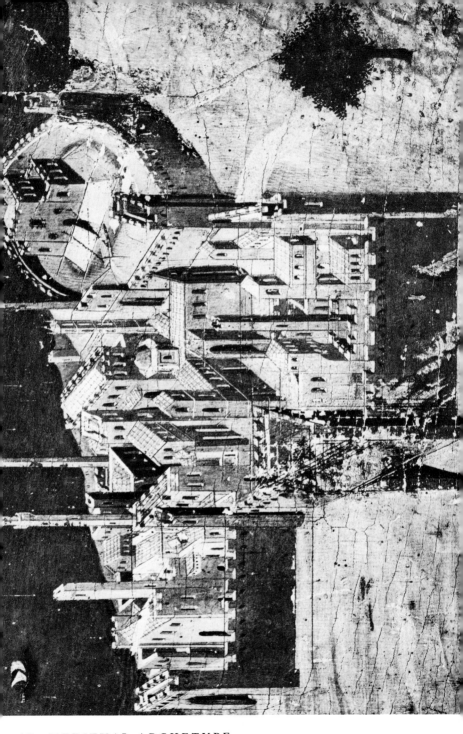

17: MEDIEVAL ARCHETYPE

18: MONASTIC ORDER

19: 'MEDIEVAL' OXFORD

20: DOMINANCE AND ENCLOSURE

21: THE STONES OF VENICE

22: CEREMONY AND PLAY

23: CHRISTIAN IDEALS

24: FLORENCE

25: RENASCENCE COMPOSURE

26: THRICE USABLE SPACE

27: BAROQUE DYNAMISM

28: BAROQUE FORMALISM

29: THE COURTLY LIFE

30: ARISTOCRATIC OPENNESS

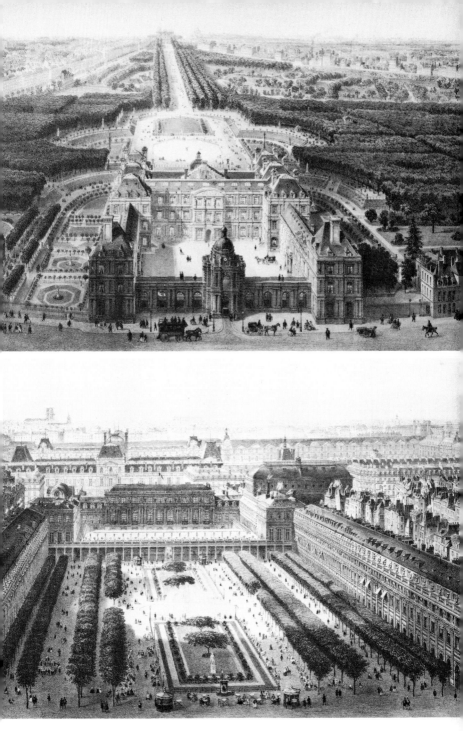

31: PALATIAL PERSPECTIVES

32: EXTENSION AND ENCYSTMENT

17 : MEDIEVAL ARCHETYPE

Lorenzetti di Ambroggio's painting at Siena presents the archetypal medieval (Italian) town. Except in the specific character of the buildings, with their emphasis on verticality, this is the archetypal historic city of all ages, complete with its fortified citadel, its town-encircling wall, and its great portals. The artist, by reducing the number of buildings and foreshortening the horizontal plane, has emphasized not only the towers but the general effect of verticality, thus losing any sense of inner gardens or places: so that it is almost prophetic of later changes. Both the Florence and the Siena Town Halls show many views of cities, including the famous allegory of Good and Bad Government in Siena. The frequent depiction of cities in medieval art, both in intimate glimpses and in panoramic views long before the great sixteenth century atlases and guides, or later prints, indicates an affectionate concern with the city as a deliberate work of art.

Photo by courtesy of Istituto Fotocromo Italiano S.A.—Firenze.

18 : MONASTIC ORDER

The monastery after the twelfth century made its presence felt in every quarter, as the plan of Valenciennes (Plate 32) shows. Since few medieval monasteries escaped destruction, dislocation, or 'improvement' after the sixteenth century, even in Italy, I have chosen to reproduce a later Carthusian example in Antwerp, which shows, as many such 'baroque' plans do, how little the traditional medieval plan was affected at first by the new open spatial order, though the ornamental and structural details both were quickly altered. The old view of St. Thomas's Hospital shows a similar combination of innerness and openness. These enclosed quadrangles may well have suggested the residential squares that came forth in the seventeenth century; but the introduction of wheeled traffic into those squares sacrificed their peace and quiet to movement and show. Inner space did not return until the radically new and improved design of Ladbroke Grove in London in the mid-nineteenth century: one of the high points of Victorian residential planning and the lineal ancestor of one main aspect of the Radburn plan: the continuous inner greenbelt.

[Upper] Carthusian Monastery. [Lower] St. Thomas's Hospital. From 'The Vanished City,' by Robert Carrier. London: Hutchinson & Co.

19 : 'MEDIEVAL' OXFORD

Even in Duns Scotus' day, Oxford, though not so beautiful as in the seventeenth century, must have been a "towery city and branchy between towers; cuckoo-echoing, bell-swarméd, lark-charméd, rook-racked, river rounded." *Much of the greenery remains, though threatened by incontinent motor roads and a too-thriving motor works, which latter seeks to return in the form of research endowments and buildings what its "base and brickish skirt" has robbed from the environment. The far view shows both the old and the new, from the Victorian gas tank (bottom), to Christ Church Meadow and distant Magdalen College Tower (upper right). The self-governing Oxford colleges, typically a complex of buildings forming a series of inter-connecting quadrangles, cloisterlike around open greens or gardens, create a group of superblocks, free only to walkers, except under special circumstances. The college precinct broke with the block dimensions established by the Milesian and Roman planners and freed the buildings from their rigid lineup along the corridor street. This is the historic prototype of both the superblock and precinct planning. Where it has been carried forward into a later day, as in the great Inns of Court in London, or as in Harvard College Yard, its insulation from traffic and noise and its freedom to effect a functional disposition of the buildings, prove a highly satisfactory adaptation to modern needs. The notion that urbanity is identical with close building, or with the absence of trees and gardens, is based on either a limited acquaintance with cities or a limited definition of urbanity. Both Cambridge and Oxford, like medieval Venice, have demonstrated a superior method of planning and grouping highly individualized urban quarters.*

[Upper] Photograph: Aerofilms and Aero Pictorial, Ltd., London. [Lower] Photograph: Aerofilms, Ltd., London.

20 : DOMINANCE AND ENCLOSURE

The Cathedral of Segovia dates from the beginning of the sixteenth century, though its wall dates back to the eleventh century. But in the great height of its tower, 345 feet, and its relationship to the rest of the town, it exemplifies to perfection the medieval relationship of the Church and the community. Note that the orientation of medieval sacred buildings is a cosmic-religious one, with the nave running east and west, no matter what the orientation of the other blocks and buildings. Though the sacred edifice is superbly dominant, it is almost never mathematically central: centrality is a baroque attribute. The resources that produced a Segovia or a Chartres, if applied to economic activities and fairly distributed, would have given everyone in the community a few pounds more of meat per year. The members of the Butchers' Guild, who so generously contributed to the building of the Cathedral at Chartres, might thus have become fatter and been more extravagantly clothed had they kept their money for private uses. But the Cathedral enlarged all the dimensions of communal life, even for the poor, long after the lifetimes of the builders and donors. The Beguines' Home in Amsterdam, the work of a lay order with many foundations throughout the Low Countries—there is a particularly fine one in Bruges—illustrates another facet of medieval enclosure, with the generous open spaces that usually went with such corporate building. The human scale of medieval hospitals and old people's homes contrasts favorably with the gardenless barracks so characteristic of the nineteenth century, and even later. Note that the chapel is an integral part of the design.

[Upper] Segovia. Photograph: Ewing Galloway. [Lower] Beguinage. Amsterdam.

21: THE STONES OF VENICE

At its height, between the completion of the Ducal Palace and the building of the Old Procurator's Hall, Venice was one of the most beautiful cities in the world, rivalled only perhaps by Peiping. The Grand Canal, as it sweeps between the one-time palaces to the west, and the Santa Maria della Salute and the old Customs House, is not merely a waterway but an enchanting mirror. Medieval Venice also brilliantly anticipated the best inventions of twentieth century planning. The present separation of fast moving bulky boat traffic on the Grand Canal from slower moving traffic on the network of minor canals, along with the network of footways, anticipated the Radburn plan: a magnificent innovation. The lagoons between the islands serve as the watery equivalent of open 'greenbelts.' The major traffic way, the Grand Canal, which forms the U in the upper picture, shows the ideal relation of such an artery to the city—tangential or peripheral, never approaching the delicate interior organs of the city except through frequent minor arteries and capillaries. (See Benton Mac-Kaye's masterly analysis (1929) of the complementary structure of the Townless Highway and the Highwayless Town.) The flouting of this rational principle of design by 'progressive' highway engineers has brought disorder and ruin to the cities that have been the victims of their complacent malpractices. The nearer view of St. Mark's Place demonstrates the organic order that prevails there, with each age making its highly individualized contribution to an urban whole that is improved rather than disrupted by this historic variety. The architectural quality established here does not stand alone: it is repeated, with minor variations, in the campo (neighborhood place) of the parish or the 'sixth,' with its tall campanile, its church, sometimes its scuola or guild hall, its one-time fountain or well, its local market, and its trattoria or cafe. Each neighborhood or parish reproduces on a smaller scale the essential organs of the bigger all-embracing city, with the maximum possibilities for meeting and association on every human level, all within walking distance of the center. The campi are easily identifiable even on this foreshortened air view by the church towers or the open spaces, which latter alone alleviate the now far too heavy density of the housing. The basin of water and the sheds directly above the campanile of St. Mark's belong to the

Arsenal quarter: the first specialized industrial zone, not greatly altered from that shown centuries earlier on Plate 34. To overcome its present overcrowding, without forfeiting all the values that make it pre-eminent as a magnificent collective work of art, Venice needs, not wholesale re-building, but what Patrick Geddes called 'conservative surgery': removing dead urban tissue, replacing it with modern structures on the same scale, and above all opening up internal spaces. Further growth around this still active commercial and industrial center demands the building of satellite cities on a co-ordinated regional plan. The municipality has wisely com-missioned the design of the first such 'New Town.'

Photographs by courtesy of the Municipality of Venice.

22: CEREMONY AND PLAY

Venice was a festive city, whose color and vitality and music, impossible to convey in print, still pervade every quarter; and its greatest artists, like Giovanni Bellini and Tintoretto have left a full record of the ceremonial splendors whose perfume still faintly pervades the empty banqueting hall in the Doge's Palace. Two of these pictures by Giovanni Bellini, show-ing the canals, the bridges, the quays, as they were when constantly in use will tell the reader more about the quality of that life than any com-ment of mine, or even Ruskin's. The painting [lower right] by an eight-eenth century artist reminds us of another facet of Venice's life—the spon-taneous, improvised popular Commedia dell' Arte whose literary transfor-mation by Goldoni produced the final dialogue, as it were, of this dying city, which "once had held the gorgeous East in fee." The darker side of this picture, the hellish prison reached by the Bridge of Sighs, in which the victims of the Inquisition were imprisoned and tortured, is still open to inspection. See also the great models of the Venetian galleys in the Arsenal Museum, which faithfully convey the grim horror of the galley slaves who manned the insolent fleets of Venice. But the painting, the architecture, and the music of Venice were not merely expressions of its effulgent sensual vitality: Tintoretto has depths that anticipate Rembrandt, and Palladio's Church on the islet of San Giorgio has a purity in its in-terior almost without rival. For all its vanity and its villainy, life touched some of its highest moments in Venice. If the civic virtues of Venice had been understood and imitated, later cities would have been better planned.

Photographs by courtesy of the Accademia and the Municipality of Venice.

23: CHRISTIAN IDEALS

Alkmaar, redoubtable center of cheese production, claims our attention, if only because its regular gridiron plan, like that of Middelburg or Delft, shows that this ancient layout was not confined in the Middle Ages to fortified frontier towns. But the unknown Master of Alkmaar, no mean painter, has left us precious architectural glimpses of the medieval city: burgher houses with their admirably functional windows, kept up with the trimness and tidiness one finds later in Vermeer and de Hoogh. These four examples from his 'Seven Works of Mercy' in the Rijksmuseum (Amsterdam) likewise show the medieval city's more saintly Christian intentions, the feeding of the hungry, the care of the injured and the sick, acts of charity that became more imperative from the fifteenth century on, with the sharper division of classes and the growth of a commercial and industrial proletariat no longer able to retreat to the country. Note the well-made bed and the open fire in the hospital: quite the equivalent of that which Carpaccio illustrated in St. Ursula's dream.

Photographs by courtesy of the Rijksmuseum, Amsterdam.

24: FLORENCE

Despite the enormous growth of industrial enterprise in its outskirts, Florence retains at its core the same mass of buildings revealed in this eighteenth century print. The dome of the Cathedral still dominates the landscape, as one approaches the city from afar, especially from the heights of Fiesole, and no profiteering high-rise buildings, such as have captured the area around Milan's great gothic edifice, have as yet been permitted. In no other city that I know is so much of the 'usable past' still actively being used, not in a spirit of pious conformity, but as a continuing function of daily life. As a result, the men marching in renascence costume on St. John's day, from the Santa Maria Novella to the Signory, have the same faces one sees in the renascence pictures, and wear their costumes without self-consciousness, as if they had never discarded them. Yet the brawling confusion and murderous imbecility of medieval Florence, attacking its neighbors and gnawing its own flesh, like that horrible creature in Dante's Inferno, left its mark on the grim palaces: examples of renascence brutalism. Except for the foreground, this is pretty much the Florence one beholds today, from across the river, for the inner city, still exhibiting its ancient Roman street plan in the core, has resisted the corrosions of time far better than London or Paris. The Signoria, the Bargello, and the Loggia dei Lanzi still connect us with the city of Dante and Giotto, whose tower rises before the Cathedral; but the city here presented, as depicted in the eighteenth century, is essentially that which Michelangelo and Leonardo da Vinci knew. While the hills are exaggerated, they show the extent of the suburban movement long indulged by the upper classes, even though, as a city plan of 1783 reveals, there was still considerable open space on the outskirts of the town within the walls: actually an internal greenbelt that began back of Santa Maria Novella.

25 : RENASCENCE COMPOSURE

As a setting for public buildings, the Piazza SS. Annunziata [upper] remains a classic example of three-dimensional city design. Some of its lessons have still to be adequately digested. Here two distinguished architects face each other on each side of the place as one approaches the church: Brunelleschi sets the example of order in his Children's Hospital; San Gallo, with the urbanity of renascence manners, conforms to the same lines in his orphanage. Michelozzo's church at the end of the place is perhaps lower and less distinguished than it should be, for even its arches are not quite as wide. But the fact that these little differences were not systematically ironed out, that the approaching streets do not, except for the main one, give an axial approach, is still evidence of medieval freedom in handling such matters. In one respect this square, like the Uffizi buildings [lower] sets a happy precedent that would have singular value today. These buildings are placed above the public way, on pedestals of their own. Neither traffic nor parked cars mar the esthetic aspect or outlook of the loggia itself. Similarly, the sunken space before the Uffizi, now used as a car-park, frees the building from the cars' presence, as a walk at ground level would not. To see how much is thus gained one need only compare this to the concealment of the Place Vendôme in Paris today by the ranks of motor cars at eye level (Plate 30). The Piazza SS. Annunziata is not a flawless composition, for the long façade of the church itself, which does not sufficiently hide the inharmonious rear, could only have been saved by being put on an even higher pedestal than the other two buildings. But the other dimensions of both elevation and open space are admirable. As for the Uffizi, the vista through the round arch, that true early renascence motive, repeated on many minor works of decoration, shows the new conception of space at its human best in Florence, before it became over-standardized and oppressive.

26 : THRICE USABLE SPACE

The Piazza Navona [left] got its shape from an ancient Roman race course, and its openness survived the dilapidation and the disappearance of the original structure. (As late as the eighteenth century, a drawing by Giuseppe Zocchi shows a piazza in Florence used as a race course, too, around an obelisk at each end.) Bernini's church and fountains brought it esthetically to life; but that life, as this eighteenth century print indicates, remained a many sided one: a place for lovers to stroll, a marketplace, a playground for the children of the neighborhood, with sidewalk restaurants on both sides of the place, where whole families can dine and gossip and drink, all three generations together. Today we have so specialized the simple functions of life that a planner would hardly dare to suggest a playground so encumbered with other facilities, or any similar amateurish combination of simple undifferentiated space and functions. Yet this superposition of human activities serving divers purposes is characteristic of the classic city and remains one of its greatest contributions, not least because of its spatial economy. Lacking such adaptable humanized space, planners now take refuge in extravagant absurdities like those shown on Plate 48. The open space around the Duomo in Florence [right] shown with Giotto's tower and the baptistry, had a major use for great religious processions, such as are shown here. But this again was one of many functions provided for in the church squares and townhall market squares: such as secular pageants and theatrical performances, to say nothing, alas! of public executions. As a final esthetic note, observe that the obelisk at the further end of the Piazza Navona serves as the equivalent of a tower in the middle distance, showing that the baroque eye still felt the need for slim medieval vertical accents.

27 : BAROQUE DYNAMISM

Bernini's colonnade for St. Peter's: baroque planning at its magnificent best. By its sweep and scale and order the colonnade effaces the confused environment around it and presents the Cathedral not only with a fitting approach but a stage to contain the crowds that participate in its open air ceremonies. The present photograph [upper] was taken before the removal of the buildings that once blocked the axis and the widening of the square before the colonnade. Instead of a sudden opening up of the space, the whole Cathedral is now visible from the Tiber approach: but those who regret the older medieval contrast of closure and openness should be consoled by the fact that the new avenue once more reveals Michelangelo's dome, which the lengthening of the nave, in defiance of his design, had concealed from this approach. The Spanish Steps [lower] is an equally decisive example of the same principle of planning: moreover it shows that by concentration and esthetic vitality a relatively small space may evoke uses and enjoyments that a much larger area, esthetically underdeveloped, would not afford. Baroque planning was usually at its best when it had most to contend with, in crowded neighboring buildings or irregular topography; and it too easily became pompous and empty when the planner had limitless resources and no natural or human obstacles to overcome.

[Upper] Photograph by Burton Holmes from Ewing Galloway. [Lower] Photograph by Alinari.

28 : BAROQUE FORMALISM

The Piazza San Carlo in Turin [upper] is one of the most perfect examples of baroque planning, and happily is still intact. Yet when compared with the Piazza SS. Annunziata in Florence one sees that there has been loss as well as gain, for the mathematical order of the design, with no break in the roofline, no alteration in the repeating elements, no change in the dimensions, has brought perfection at the expense of life: a sacrifice justifiable only for some transcendent religious purpose. The climax of baroque formalism, here, as in the Piazza del Popolo in Rome, is the provision of two identical churches on either side of the axis, purely for symmetry. Baroque taste reaches its peak of defiance of the organic in the clipping of hedges and even alleys of trees to transform them into formal architectural façades, as at Versailles. In the interests of uniformity the baroque despots put uniforms on everything: buildings, streets, trees, men. This regimentation would have been intolerable but for the other side of baroque life: its sexual exuberance and sensual ecstasy, symbolized by the characteristic spiral column and spiral staircases, by its superb display of the nude in painting and statuary, not least by the fountains of Bernini. The Academies of Science or Letters and the Art Gallery represented these two poles of the baroque city: the mechanical and the sensuous, regimentation and playful riot. But the palatial art gallery [bottom] indicates that again the frame had become as important as the picture.

29: THE COURTLY LIFE

The baroque scheme of life needed space for maneuver and display, whether for dashing equipages or marching men. Under the influence of the court the spectacular and the spectatorial arts flourished. Not merely the theater, but the new baroque art, the opera, which characteristically introduced the solo performer, the prima donna. The pleasure garden demanded space that the nineteenth century city begrudged except on its distant outskirts; but the sumptuous pavilion in Ranelagh Gardens was repeated, with many variations. The final vulgarization was the fun fair and pleasure resort: Coney Island.

[Top] Inner Court of the Louvre, in typical daily scene. [Middle Left] A theatrical performance at court, not yet completely formalized. [Middle Right] Teatro San Carlo at Naples, famous for its operas, with typical horseshoe seating arrangement. [Bottom] Rotunda at Ranelagh Gardens: note the truly central heating.

30: ARISTOCRATIC OPENNESS

The Place Royale, now the Place des Vosges [upper left], was a true residential square: but the view that the inhabitants once had of each other's houses is now blocked by rows of trees and a central clump. Victor Hugo's house here, now a museum, gives the visitor access to the domestic milieu of the original square. The derivation of this type of square from the open but bare inner courtyards of the great palaces becomes plain in the air view of the Louvre [upper right] and the fur-

ther development of the square into a little cité like the Palais Royal at the top of this photograph demonstrates a desirable next step—insulation from street noises, dust, and wheeled vehicles—which was never sufficiently imitated. (See Plate 31.) The third French gambit was the Place Vendôme [lower left]: originally designed for upper class residences, but now turned to more luxurious commercial uses. Haussmann's plan for the Avenue de l'Opéra [lower right], was worthy of Garnier's magnificent building: perhaps the freshest and most colorful work of baroque architecture the nineteenth century can show; but he nullified Garnier's intentions by opening up the other sides of the Place de l'Opera to traffic: a contribution to neither architecture nor music.

31: PALATIAL PERSPECTIVES

After the worst has been said about baroque formalism, one must still remember two, at least two, wonderful exceptions: the Boboli Gardens in Florence and the Jardin du Luxembourg in Paris [upper]. This view, terminating in the Avenue de l'Observatoire, is as beguiling on foot as when seen from the air: or rather much more so, because the central open space provides one of the most joyous urban settings for relaxation. Here the strictest kind of esthetic order encourages the greatest degree of playful spontaneity and visual delight: a fact that perhaps should be digested by 'progressive' educators and 'advanced' artists who have made play boring and creativity aimless by abolishing the rules and lifting all restrictions. As for the Palais Royal [lower] it has had its ups and downs, like the Place des Vosges, but it has never sunk so low as the great mansions still standing in the now slummy Marais quarter around St. Gervais to the east, which did not retain sufficient open space to protect themselves collectively. The trees and fountains still miraculously remain, in fact the whole design remains sound and charming, though no longer teeming with the life it had in Diderot's day.

32: EXTENSION AND ENCYSTMENT

The plan of Nice [upper] shows three classic stages in town building; though if an equally clear print had been available I should have preferred to present Edinburgh, for in the trough between the Old Town and the New Town, Edinburgh presents a fourth stage—the smoky waste of the railroad age. The castle on top of the hill is the typical acropolis formation, with the steep cliff itself serving as a protective wall: the town below shows the natural, block by block extension of the port community, with its artificial harbor and its esplanade and its irregular street system becoming by degrees more orderly. Baroque design comes forth in the planner's regular and almost symmetrical extension, with radial avenues, spearheaded bastions, and canals repeating the pattern of the new citadel layout on the heights. Compare this last with the even greater proliferation of ovals and squares in Edinburgh's New Town. As planned, these fortifications allowed ample growth. Contrast this with Valenciennes [lower] a medieval town encrusted in fortifications and commanded by a citadel equally elaborate. Under these circumstances, town growth was constricted. The reader provided with a magnifying glass will find that a typical new baroque structure has entered this town: les casernes, or the military barracks. In addition to those in the citadel there are three others. Note also the space for drill in the Place d'Armes before the citadel, much larger than the chief place bordered by the Town Hall in the middle, the cattle market at the bottom, or the fish market not far from the Town Hall on the canal. At other points in the plan, marked by clusters of squares, there are at least eight friaries and convents, with their ample open spaces and gardens. The plan with its blocks of different sizes and shapes, and its equally differentiated and complex street system cut by a meandering canal, betrays a slow organic growth; though unpresentable on this small scale, the large blocks doubtless had big interior gardens, to judge by many other contemporary plans, like that of Romilly. Already a suburban movement had begun outside the fortifications, to the left: the Faubourg Notre Dame, above, strewn along a road and forming a long oblong with well defined rectangular gardens, and the Faubourg de Cambrai, a smaller settlement apparently scattered in an open field. In short, a perfect picture of a medieval town encased in a baroque corset. Though the new fortifications do not control the plan of the town as in Vauban's chef-d'oeuvre, Neuf Brisach, the citadel at Valenciennes was designed by him. The whole system here constitutes one of the last classic examples of this elaborate but quickly exhausted art; albeit its military effectiveness in Valenciennes was proved as late as 1793 when it took 43 days' bombardment by an allied force of 140,000 soldiers with 400 cannon to make a surviving garrison of 3000 surrender.

on the spectator, this treatment of life itself as a spectacle, was a chronic weakness of the old leisure-class notion of culture, as something that was incompatible with work and would be soiled even by action. This was no mere aberration of a later decadent culture for it had been enunciated in the heyday of Greek society, before Plato. Had not Pythagoras compared life itself to the Great Games, "where some went to compete for the prizes and others went with wares to sell, but the best as spectators." In the Hellenistic city the role of the spectator was uppermost: rich and poor, noble and low, were now united in that role.

Consider the kind of urban 'arena' necessary for the coronation of Ptolemy Philadelphus, a not untypical monarch of the period at its best. To mount that spectacle there were 57,000 infantrymen, 23,000 cavalry, innumerable chariots, of which 400 bore vessels of silver, 800 were filled with perfumes; a gigantic chariot of Silenus, drawn by 300 men, was followed by chariots drawn by antelopes, buffaloes, ostriches, and zebras. What later circus could compare with this prototype? Such a parade could not have found its way through the streets of fifth-century Athens even in broken order.

Probably, indeed, this procession itself occupied more traffic space than the entire population of Athens would have used a few centuries before. It needed the whole length and breadth of the broadest avenues to serve as the frame for such a mounting of power, even as it must have needed a large swathe of grounds beyond the city's walls to marshal such an army in due order. It is in terms of such public pageants and parades, variously staged and often repeated, rather than as a response to practical requirements, that the main outlines of the Hellenistic city must be understood. Impressive bigness was what ruler and planner both sought.

Once this order was established in the big city, it would be imitated in smaller centers. How general the pattern was we know from such an undistinguished and commonplace little town as Priene, ironically lifted out of its natural obscurity by its accessibility to the archaeologist's spade —its very smallness, its lack of historic importance, making it just that much more complete as a specimen. Midway in its foundation between the Ionic cities and the Pergamene cities, it displays all the common elements except magnitude and extension.

Doubtless the physical structure of the Hellenistic town improved as technological facility increased: Archimedes' feat of destroying the enemy's ships by using the sun and a mirror to set fire to their sails may serve as a symbol of the kind of ingenious activity that began to pervade this fading classic culture, whilst it kept repeating the old myths and going through the old motions, ever more empty, for a full thousand years. But as to the vacancy and triviality of the life there is little doubt. The old polis was dead. Nightmarish fears and superstitious auguries overwhelmed men at the very moment the sciences were becoming more rigorous in their method and ever larger parts of the physical world seemed 'under control.' We have seen the same dark fantasies rising under similar conditions in our own time.

3 : BENEATH THE URBAN SURFACE

The outward form of the Hellenistic town hardly betrayed a hint of what was going on below the surface of its life. For a counter-movement of the spirit, challenging all the assumptions of civilized power, had been gathering headway from at least the sixth century. This movement arose in the classes that the old polis had excluded from citizenship; that is, among women, slaves, and foreigners, to say nothing of disaffected and alienated citizens. As the common life of the polis, apart from spectacles, became emptier—and perhaps the 'spectacle' was itself the emptiest of all manifestations—a new life sprang up, private, hidden, in clubs, friendly societies, burial groups, fraternities: above all in those secret congregations that met together for the worship of Bacchus, god of the corn and the vine, and Orpheus, god of the lyre, or later still, the more ancient Phrygian goddess of sex and fertility, the Great Mother herself, a carry-over from matriarchal days. Most of these clubs, according to W. W. Tarn, were small, a membership of even a hundred was uncommon; they were usually grouped around a small temple, and were apparently, after 200 B.C., often family associations, to perpetuate the family memory. With the polis in dissolution, these clubs formed, as it were, a private polis that served the needs of excluded foreigners and even sometimes of slaves.

The old shrines and temples with their daylight rituals and their bloody sacrifices were not for these new cults. The mystery religions, at first no doubt houseless, meeting far outside the city on the wooded slopes of mountains, finally brought into existence a new urban form, an enclosed hall, whose darkness corresponded to the darkness of the underworld from whence Bacchus was reborn, where Orpheus sought Eurydice. This was no longer a temple, maintained by a priesthood, but a meeting house (synagogue) built to enclose a congregation. Those who were purified, and who believed in the new god, were inducted into the mysteries and were saved: that is, they formed a new polis, more universal than any empire, but a polis not 'of this world.' No matter how hard life pressed on the believers now, they had the promise of a life beyond the grave, a real life, not as leaden shadows in a Plutonian realm.

Thus the participants in the mysteries seem to have escaped the limitations of the old polis: each found himself the member of a wider society that recognized neither temporal nor geographic boundaries. A political wisdom that the wisest members of the ancient city lacked, a wisdom unknown to Thucydides or Aristotle, to Socrates or to Plato, became the working creed of the mystery religions. The classes and groups that had been rejected by the polis became the leading members of the Great Society. But apart from their formal meeting places, like the great Telesterion, or 'Hall of the Mysteries,' in Eleusis, the home of one of the new cults, the new polis existed only in the mind. Those who sought salvation renounced the earthly city: they put behind them the transitory and corrupt body of the polis, courting only those moments of ecstasy or illumination that might offset a lifetime of frustration.

After the sixth century B.C. this new spirit began to express itself everywhere, in new religions and new philosophies, alike in China, India, Persia, the Near East, and the West: whatever their individual accents, these axial ideologies revealed a profound disillusion with the fundamental premises of civilization: its over-emphasis on power and material goods; its acceptance of grade and rank and vocational division as eternal categories; and along with this, the injustice, the hatred, the hostility and the perpetual violence and destructiveness of its dominant class-structured institutions.

But those who sought to reverse the polarities of civilized life could not do so and yet remain within the city that had first contained and increased the potential of all these destructive powers. To achieve a new life, the holders of the new vision must desert the city: they must either establish themselves in the rural hinterland, in lonely forest or hillside cave, or at least on the outskirts of the city, in gymnasia or in garden colonies, a few dozen or a few hundred, hardly enough to form even a village. Witness Pythagoras and Epicurus, witness the followers of Lao-tse, of the Buddha, of the Master of Righteousness. If they enter the city, they must form a secret society and go underground, in order to survive.

The movement that resulted in the creation of these new religions and cults must be interpreted, I submit, as a profound revolt against civilization itself: against its lust for power and wealth, its materialistic expansion and repletion, its degradation of life to the servitude of the body, its destruction of spontaneity by vacant routine, and the misappropriation of the higher goods of life by a dominant minority.

All this began far earlier than the sixth century B.C., for the emptiness of civilization that had no other goals than its own existence had become visible, as I have pointed out, long before: Vanity of vanities, all is vanity under the sun. The spirit expressed in the new religions had found utterance as early as the Assyrian tablet on Utnapishtim, Noah's alter ego:

> Give up possessions, seek thou life:
> Forswear [worldly] goods and keep the soul alive.

Since the new fraternities and religious groups had no part in the city and could not keep either their possessions or their city secure, they were driven, in compensation, to make the soul their chief object and to retain only so much of the city as would serve their cult. The polis, now shrunk to a church, at last could in the great dispersion of emigrants, refugees, colonists, expand beyond the city's walls.

Many centuries must pass, indeed, before the new religions could overcome their original alienation from the city and all its works. And an even longer time must pass before they seek even in theory to overcome the dualism between body and spirit, between the earthly and the heavenly city, which lay at the bottom of both this alienation and this special system of salvation.

So before the prophetic religions and mysteries leave their imprint on the city, the scene shifts. Rome conquers the Hellenistic conquerors, and overcomes the surviving free or semi-free cities of the Mediterranean and the Aegean Seas. In the Roman world the principles of Hellenistic town planning were carried further, and mingled with other urban elements derived from remoter municipalities in Africa and Asia. The muscular-cerebral culture of the Greeks gave way to the massively visceral culture of the Romans: the lean Attic diet was replaced by daily feasts on the most colossal scale. What the oral Greeks lacked almost entirely in their cities in the best Hellenic days, the anal Romans acquired in suffocating abundance. What the Greeks originally had in abundance, the gifts of improvisation and spontaneous creativity, qualities as visible in the small dimensions of an epigram or a tombstone as in an epic or a temple, the costive Romans could hardly show at all, at least after the death of the Republic, except by vulgar imitation and inflation.

CHAPTER EIGHT

Megalopolis into Necropolis

1: ROME'S FOREIGN INHERITANCE

When one thinks of the ancient city of Rome one thinks at once of its empire: Rome with its symbols of visible power, its aqueducts and its viaducts and its paved roads, cutting unswervingly across hill and dale, leaping over river and swamp, moving in unbroken formation like a victorious Roman legion. This Rome was held together by a loose administrative organization, using an arithmetical notation far too clumsy for efficient accountancy; but it partly offset its lack of abstract mathematical skill by its capacity for handling solid objects, and by its more generalized aptitude in the standardization and regimentation of large masses. Above all, the Romans had an empirical respect for any established order, even when it contradicted their own: a trait that served another race of Empire-builders, the British.

The Roman Empire, the product of a single expanding urban power center, was itself a vast city-building enterprise: it left the imprint of Rome on every part of Europe, Northern Africa, and Asia Minor, altering the way of life in old cities and establishing its special kind of order, from the ground up, in hundreds of new foundations, 'colonial' towns, 'free' towns, towns under Roman municipal law, 'tributary' towns: each with a different status if not a different form. In a general account of the Roman state just before it fell into ruin, the writer treated it as made up of separate civic bodies, to the number of 5,627. Even after the city of Rome had been sacked in the fifth century, the poet Rutilius Namatianus could say, with undiminished admiration: "A city of the far-flung earth you made."

That tribute was well-earned by Rome; for at the height of its protective power, old walls fell into disrepair or were disregarded in the further building of its cities, while new cities were built without walls. Under the Empire, for perhaps the first time since the foundation of cities, Western mankind had a brief glimpse of what it would be like to live in a completely open world, in which law and order everywhere prevailed, and citizenship, in every sense, was the common human heritage.

The same method and discipline that originally made Rome itself powerful, brought to its constituent municipalities the same principle of order. Indeed, the Roman virtues were more conspicuous in the freshly built colonial cities than in the old capital itself; for the order that Rome distilled for distant consumption and poured into fresh bottles, was mixed in the old container itself with lees and orts that had never been emptied out.

The foundation stones of the Roman town were quarried mainly from two other cultures, the Etruscan and the Hellenic. From the Etruscans, that still enigmatic people who civilized the north of Italy, came the religious and superstitious parts of Roman urban development. The acropolis of the Etruscan city was, as in the Aegean, always situated on a hill: it was there that the sacred auguries were made, before a city could be founded. The Romans, according to Varro, carried out Etruscan rites in founding new cities: not merely did they begin with an augury, to make sure of the favor of the gods, but the tracing of the outlines of the city was done by a priest, who guided the plow.

Unlike the Greek city, where the wall was often an afterthought, the Roman city began with such a wall; and the city, partly for religious, partly for utilitarian, reasons, took the form of a rectangle, setting the standard pattern for the overnight camp the Roman legionary later dug for himself. From this religious definition of the city possibly sprang another feature, the pomerium, a sacred belt inside and outside the wall, where no buildings might be placed. The military advantage of this practice for the defenders of the city may have added extra force to the religious sanction.

This rectangular layout was part of a much older tradition that had taken hold in northern Italy and may well date from early neolithic times. The pile villages of the Po Valley were planned like a later Roman castrum, if only because tree trunks and poles, being long and straight, yield themselves to, indeed practically demand, a strict rectangular arrangement. But, apart from the nature of the landscape itself, it is doubtful if there is any direct connection between the *terremare* settlements and the Roman towns. Indeed the representation of a small town, surrounded by a wooden stockade, on Trajan's column might suggest that there were other sources for the Roman city, still remembered or visible. The Roman talent for engineering seems, however, to owe a direct debt to the Etruscans, though the Italian peasant, still a doughty man with pick and spade, made this tradition everywhere his own. But in addition to its sacred outline, the Roman city was oriented to harmonize with cosmic order. The typical mark that distinguished it from Hellenistic cities of the same general character was the layout of its two principal streets, the *cardo,* running north and south, and the *decumannus,* running east and west.

This axial type of town, with its two main streets crossing at right angles near the center, is an old form: Badawy finds the earliest recorded examples in the fortresses built on rocky islands or banks of the Nile during the Twelfth Dynasty. Fortress, camp, and city have a common base in military regimentation.

The main streets were designed to cross in the middle of the city; there a foundation would be dug for the sacred relics, and there was the usual—or at least the ideal—place for the Forum, the Roman equivalent of acropolis and agora, conceived as one. While the principle of orientation had a religious origin, it would be modified by topography and by accidents of an earlier usage, as the gridiron plan, which went with it, would also be modified; yet it continued in existence, as a kind of fossil of an earlier culture, long after it had lost most of its cosmic significance. By the time of Vitruvius, a regard for hygiene and comfort further modified the layout of the Roman town so that he even suggested that minor streets or alleys be oriented to shut out the unpleasant cold winds and the 'infectious' hot ones. But as so often has happened, the religious practice had called attention to the principle of orientation itself.

From the Hellenistic town the Roman received a pattern of esthetic order that rested on a practical base; and to each of the great institutions of Milesian planning—the formally enclosed agora, with its continuous structures, the broad unbroken street lined with buildings, and the theater —the Roman gave a characteristic turn of his own, outdoing the original in ornateness and magnificence. The places where these two streams of influence came together in the Roman mind were in the African and Syrian towns, often greatly developed as specialized manufacturing towns and trade centers, or in military colonization towns, founded to serve as holding points for the Empire, permanently stocked with legionaries who could be called back into action. They did duty, too, as urban rest homes where the veteran of Rome's wars of conquest might retire on his allotment, to engage in business, and to enjoy in his years of leisure the results of conquest and pillage.

Timgad, which has been exhumed in recent times, is an example of the Roman planning art in all its latterday graces. Being a small town, like Priene, planned and built within a limited period, it has the same diagrammatic simplicity, unmarred by later displacements and renovations that busier towns subject to the pressures of growth would show. The regular checkerboard layout within a rectangular boundary, the arcaded walks, the forum, the theater, the arena, the baths, the public lavatories (over-costly, over-decorated) were standard equipment. All these are to be found in Timgad. Similar forms were repeated from one end of the empire to the other: from Chester in western England, which still has an elevated and covered 'Roman' shopping street, to Antioch and Ephesus in Asia Minor. The new marketplaces at Coventry and Harlow, with their upper tiers of shops and offices, are, no less than the early nineteenth-century shopping arcade at Providence, R. I., only a recovery of the admirable Roman multi-level plan.

Except for the elaborateness of the public baths and the over-sized arena (which even in a small town might hold twenty thousand people), none of these facilities was new. What Rome did was to universalize them—making them, as we would say today in somewhat Roman terms, 'standard equipment.' But as in Thomas More's description of the cities of Utopia, he who knows one of their towns knows all of them. Rome was the great sausage grinder that turned other cultures, in all their variety of form and content, into its own uniform links. Where the Romans left a measure of municipal freedom, it was not to promote variety but to maintain long-established distrust and jealousy among neighboring cities, to make sure, through their own continued division, of Rome's undivided rule.

Here again, as so often in city development, one must make a distinction between the container and the contents. In Roman cities, above all in Rome itself, as we shall see, the contents were often revolting, sometimes a veritable cesspool of human debasement and iniquity. But the container, esthetically speaking, was often a marvel of formal dignity and masterful composure. During the third and second centuries B.C., Rome left her characteristic marks on a series of new settlements for Roman and regional emigrants. From the original twelve cities of Tuscany, and the thirty cities of Latium, the Roman state, by the Augustan period, had seeded a further three hundred and fifty towns in peninsular Italy and another eighty in northern Italy.

These towns were cut to the new pattern, modest in scale, simple in layout: almost the exact opposite of the sprawling disorderly mother city itself. Hygenus, the Roman architect, considered "the ideal . . . town should be 2,400 by 1,600 feet, since any greater length might endanger defense by indistinct signals along its walls." Turin and Aosta both fill these requirements, the first almost exactly; though the areas in fact varied from 12 acres for Basle, about 50 acres for Strasbourg and Orléans, to 330 for London, 494 for Autun, and 660 for Nîmes. Though Vitruvius cast his vote for a circular wall to make defense easier, that prescription flew too flatly against precedent and habit to be followed.

Not enough has yet been made of the new towns that were built in the early days of the Empire, as holding points in the conquered lands. Strangely, even those who have appreciated their merits as examples of orderly town planning have ignored their systematic multiplication. Yet the very scale of their construction implies the existence of what, drawing on England's contemporary pioneering, one may call a governmental, 'New Towns' policy. Perhaps because Rome still wanted to proclaim its own uniqueness and its own dominance, it made no effort to establish a second Rome, until Byzantium was nominated as the eastern capital, and the whole center of gravity in the Roman state shifted to the eastern provinces. But the purpose of these colonial foundations remained a practical one: Cicero called Narbonne in southern Gaul (c. 118 B.C.) "a colony of Roman citizens, a watch tower of the Roman people, a bulwark against the wild tribes of Gaul."

The new towns seem all to have been planned for a limited population, around fifty thousand. That must have been the convenient limit of population. Placentia (Piacenza) and Cremona were settled in the same year with six thousand families each. This would come, with slaves, to something like the standard population—itself, incidentally, no small feat of building and organized emigration. Even the thriving seaport of Ostia probably did not exceed 50,000; and the highest estimate for Ostia would not do more than double the figure. Bologna probably contained fewer people in Roman times than in the Middle Ages. So though the empire could show many historic cities that had swollen, through manufactures and foreign commerce, to a larger size, the new foundations remained modest. Many new towns never, indeed, held as many as fifty thousand people; and the total population of all of them together may not have reached 17,500,000. Had there not been a deliberate policy of wide dispersal, in subordination to Rome, that population might have formed a dozen Romes. But note: at the very moment that Rome itself was approaching the upper limits of congestion and disorganization, the republic's practice of local urban dispersal was arrested. The establishment of coloniae in Italy itself almost ceased after A.D. 68.

To have established these new towns was a more valuable social achievement than any benefits Rome conferred on herself by her rapacious monopolies. What the new towns lacked in size, they gained in quality, and incidentally in self-sufficiency, for in normal times, in Gaul or Aquitaine, these towns could draw most of their food from the surrounding region: so they maintained the urban-rural balance that bigger places, by their very growth, upset. In many regions colonization was accompanied by a similar order in planning the landscape, mapping out roads and dividing fields into long rectangular parcels that are still visible from the air and respected in daily use. This system of 'centuriation' characterizes large parts of lowland Italy, Dalmatia, and Africa.

Certainly even if we lack the written evidence of it, there must have been forethought and conscious policy behind the founding of these Roman new towns. All the institutions and all the arts that Rome boasted were at hand in these places: even the gory rituals of the arena were made available by local philanthropists, seeking to earn a public monument to their generosity and wealth. Everything desirable in urban life was there except Rome's immensity, its variety, its concentration into a few square miles of the resources of a whole empire, from the Nile to the North Sea.

For the upper-class Roman, it would seem, the provincial towns did not exist: Rome's prestige held them, as London and Paris hold similar groups today. To live well, he must dwell in Rome, or when residence there became temporarily unendurable, because of plague or the fatigues of the social season, he must leave Rome for some country villa. But he certainly had no impulse to settle down to the less demanding routines and the less contradictory benefits, of the little provincial towns. Does one not, perhaps, detect in the silence of Latin writers with respect to the new towns—in so many ways more livable and more humanly desirable than Rome—something of the same fashionable snobbishness one finds in similar circles in England over the New Towns that now dot the landscape around London? They had rather be found dead in Rome than alive in Turin or Pavia. (Read Harlow or Crawley!)

But in the literature of the fifth and sixth centuries A.D. one may follow a different tale. By this time the raw new towns had mellowed, and each had acquired a character of its own that comes only with successive generations and the subtly colored deposits left by historic events. Out of their accepted limitations they had created the thriving provincial life one catches more than one happy glimpse of in the contemporary poems of Ausonius of Bordeaux. These towns kept alive what was precious in the old culture of the polis, just as towns like Aix-en-Provence, to this day, keep alive Gallic qualities, still animate in the eighteenth century, which have been stuffed into glass cases in Paris museums, but are no longer visible on its crowded avenues.

But Rome never had the imagination to apply the principles of limitation, restraint, orderly arrangement, and balance to its own urban and imperial existence; and it failed dismally to lay the foundations for the stable economy and the equitable political system, with every group effectively represented, that would have made a better life for the great city possible. Its best efforts to establish a universal commonwealth succeeded only in achieving a balance of privileges and corruptions.

One may still trace the imprint of Rome on a whole series of towns in Italy and elsewhere: Naples, Bologna, Parma, Piacenza, and Ostia were among the early foundations of the Republic, while, in the first century A.D., Como, Pavia, Verona, and Florence followed. All of these cities were designed as units, with blocks around 250 feet square, and with their open spaces and public buildings duly sited at the beginning, in relation to the main thoroughfares. Though Rome itself, with its seven hills, was an 'acropolis town,' formed out of a union of its own villages, each originally inhabited by a different tribe, it is notable that in the new towns, even where a hill was relatively handy across the river as at Turin, the town would be set on a level site by the river, for free circulation and a more regular layout.

The piazzas and campos and arcaded streets of the later Italian town were a direct issue of Roman planning; and though the medieval market-places differed functionally and architecturally from the Roman forum, it would be foolish to think of them as an altogether independent innovation. The open spaces of the town did not in fact assume a radically new form until the seventeenth century.

With Rome's skill in highway-building in mind, one turns to the new towns to see if it produced any modifications in the standard Milesian plan: all the more because traffic jams became the subject for municipal regulation, first in Rome in the first century B.C., then in the provinces. One might have thought that experience would have suggested the need for a sharp differentiation between main avenues and minor service streets, or even that the Roman engineers, aware of Rome's traffic congestion, which was spreading to the provincial towns, would have anticipated Leonardo da Vinci's proposals for separating wheeled traffic routes from pedestrian ways, carrying them on another level. But there was, as far as can yet be discovered, no bold departure from Greek precedent: the *cardo* and the *decumannus,* joined to the cross-country highroads, brought the main traffic to a meeting point in the center of the city, instead of touching the street network at a tangent on the outskirts, or at least forming a large hollow square free from traffic near the center, to one side of the avenue. Thus the old-fashioned crossing at the center produced a maximum amount of needless congestion. And though the town might be divided into *vici* —neighborhoods or quarters, with their own minor centers and markets— there was nothing in the street network itself that served to identify this unit or make its life more cohesive.

For certain developments in Roman planning, neither the unplanned metropolis nor the well-planned new towns offer an example; one must go rather to remoter towns in Syria and Asia Minor, some of which in the later days of the Empire rivalled Rome itself in population and in social complexity. What happened in Palmyra, Gerasa, and Phillipopolis, or at Antioch and Ephesus, probably had little or no effect on the further course of town planning in Western Europe. Yet some of the features visible in these towns at a late date are worth noting here, if only because they anticipated the spirit and form of the 'modern'—that is the commercial and bureaucratic—city, even more closely than the Hellenistic examples that impressed Poëte.

For one thing, the wide shopping street, stretching indefinitely toward the horizon, with its length often accentuated by colonnades, was a typical feature of these towns. This takes the place of the concentrated open market, apparently for the first time, though the main avenue, as in Palmyra, may expand into a circular plaza. Such shopping avenues existed at Damascus—"the street which is called straight," referred to in The Acts of the New Testament—and at Jerusalem; and they may even go back to the 'Broad Way,' sometimes translated as Boulevard in the Sumerian texts. Their length was usually broken, visually, by four-way arches at the crossing points of the main streets. As for Antioch— according to Libanius, in his oration on Antioch around A.D. 360— that city had sixteen miles of colonnaded streets, with the same sort of mixture of private and public buildings as one finds today on Piccadilly or Fifth Avenue. Libanius was conscious of the value of such thoroughfares; for he puts the case for them in so many words:

"As you walk along them you find a succession of private houses with public buildings distributed among them at intervals, here a temple, there a bath establishment, at such distances that they are handy for each quarter and in each case the entrance is in the colonnade. What does that mean, and what is the bearing of this lengthy description? Well, it seems to me that the pleasantest, yes, and most profitable side of city life is society and human intercourse, and that, by Zeus, is truly a city where these are most found. It is good to talk and better to listen, and best of all to give advice, to sympathize with one's friends' experiences, sharing their joys and sorrows and getting like sympathy from them—these and countless other blessings come of a man's meeting his fellows. People in other cities who have no colonnades before their houses are kept apart by bad weather; nominally, they live in the same town, but in fact they are as remote from each other as if they lived in different towns. . . . Whereas people in cities lose the habit of intimacy the further they live apart, with us, on the other hand, the habit of friendship is matured by constant intercourse and develops here as much as it diminishes there."

There is so little direct testimony as to what life was like in ancient cities, outside Athens and Rome, even in poems and novels set in an urban environment, that Libanius' observations are precious: all the more because, just as much as Aristotle before him, he puts the social function of the city above its subsidiary utilitarian needs and services.

But something else, equally 'modern,' characterized Antioch and distinguished it from Rome, where even at the height of the Empire the streets were dark at night and people ventured forth only at the risk of their lives, exposed to lower-class cut-throats and roistering upper-class hoodlums, as in eighteenth-century London. This distinction was street lighting. In Ephesus in the fifth century A.D. Arcadius Street was lighted with fifty lights, "as far as the Wild Boar Monument," but according to Ammianus, even in the middle of the fourth century "the brilliancy of the lamps at night often equalled the light of day." Libanius completes the testimony: he boasts that the citizens of Antioch "have shaken off the tyranny of sleep; here the lamp of the sun is succeeded by other lamps, surpassing the illumination of the Egyptians; with us night differs from day only in the kind of lighting. Trades go on as before; some ply their handicrafts, while others give themselves to laughter and song."

What does this mean? Perhaps nothing more than that the commercial spirit produces its own characteristic forms, without respect to other features in the cultural pattern, just as the military spirit, as expressed mechanically in a Sumerian or Macedonian phalanx, is still easily understood, and was carried over in similar forms in an eighteenth-century army, using radically different weapons. For one notes that it is with the multiplication of street lights and show-window lighting that the new commercial spirit announced itself in London early in the nineteenth century. This was so marked a change that the fatuous Prince von Pückler-Muscau could imagine, as he passed through London the night of his arrival, that a special illumination had been ordered in his honor. In short, the day-and-night market almost automatically produced the Gay White Way. Did such night lighting first encourage the mid-afternoon siesta in the hot southern city, or did it merely impose longer hours on the proletariat?

Regrettably we have no equivalent pictures of industrial towns in the Roman Empire, though Rutilius, going back home to Gaul early in the fifth century, noted sighting Elba, "famous for its mining, as rich as Noricum with its iron stores or Biturex where steel is tempered." Our picture of classic order might well be modified if we were acquainted with either the layout or the human contents of these places. Not until our Middle Ages do we behold industry clearly as an integral and acknowledged part of the city.

2: CLOACA AND AQUEDUCT

So far we have dealt with those aspects of the Roman town that the Romans derived mainly from the peoples they conquered and crushed; for up to 751 B.C., when according to Cicero Rome was founded, the Romans themselves had been only villagers. Even the 'New Towns' policy was not an innovation: what was it indeed but the Ionic practice of growth by colonization, more systematically carried out, yet more jealously restricted.

In the smaller towns of Gaul, just because of their modest scale, towns like Marseille, Narbonne, or Orange in southern France, with their independent foundations in Hellenic culture dating back many centuries, the Greek tradition must have dominated both politically and architecturally. The special Roman contribution to planning was chiefly a matter of sturdy engineering and flatulent exhibitionism: the taste of *nouveaux riches,* proud of their pillaged bric-a-brac, their numerous statues and obelisks, stolen or meticulously copied, their imitative acquisitions, their expensive newly commissioned decorations. But in the Greek provinces, whether in Gaul or Sicily, the Greek refinements of taste and style would not be lacking. Certainly the famous Maison Carée at Nîmes, beloved of Thomas Jefferson, is as exquisite a production as Attic art could have encouraged in its best period. Even when fresh this building must have seemed fragile, just as today, in its fragility, it seems curiously fresh.

But it is not by its derivative works, or by its pompous inflation of the classic orders, that Rome left its impress on urbanism. To find what Rome stood for, at both its physical best and its human worst, one must center attention on the city of Rome itself. Here is where the new scale was established: here is where the soldier and the engineer joined forces, not just to create walls and moats, but embankments and reservoirs, on a cyclopean scale. Here is where, in its great public structures, Rome attempted, not merely to cope with the large quantities of people it had brought together, but to give to its otherwise degraded mass culture an appropriate urban guise, reflecting imperial magnificence.

To investigate this contribution one must fortify oneself for an ordeal: to enjoy it, one must keep one's eyes open, but learn to close one's nose to the stench, one's ears to the screams of anguish and terror, one's gullet to the retching of one's own stomach. Above all, one must keep one's heart on ice and check any impulse to tenderness and pity, with a truly Roman stolidity. All the magnitudes will be stretched in Rome: not least the magnitude of debasement and evil. Only one symbol can do justice to the contents of that life: an open sewer. And it is with the sewer that we shall begin.

Surely it is no accident that the oldest monument of Roman engineering is the Cloaca Maxima, the great sewer, constructed in the sixth century on a scale so gigantic that either its builders must have clairvoyantly seen, at the earliest moment, that this heap of villages would become a metropolis of a million inhabitants, or else they must have taken for granted that the chief business and ultimate end of life is the physiological process of evacuation. So sound was the stone construction, so ample the dimensions, that this sewer is still in use today. With its record of continuous service for more than twenty-five hundred years, that structure proves that in the planning of cities low first costs do not necessarily denote economy; for if the utility needed has been soundly conceived and built, the final costs, extended over its whole prospective lifetime, are what really matter. On these terms, the Cloaca Maxima has turned out to be one of the cheapest pieces of engineering on record, though it is rivalled by some of the later viaducts and bridges that are still in use, not least by the magnificent Pont du Gard in Provence.

The Greek geographer Strabo remarked that while the Greeks attended chiefly to beauty and fortification, to harbors and to fertile soil, in planning their cities, the Romans were conspicuous for the pavement of streets, the water supply, and the sewers. This trait was fully established, then, by the first century A.D. Dionysius of Halicarnassus confirms this observation in almost the same words, and that consensus has lasted. Rome's capital achievements in more than one department might be summed up with words once used by a great scientist about a flatulent architectural interpretation of his highly revolutionary concepts of space and time: "Poorly digested but splendidly evacuated."

The Cloaca Maxima antedated the piping of water from distant springs and streams, perhaps because the local water supply from wells remained adequate till 109 A.D., when the Trajan aqueduct brought water for the first time to the right bank of the Tiber to satisfy the thirst of a growing population. Street paving came in even before the water mains; but it was applied to the roads outside the city before it was used on any scale within the city itself, for Rome was still wallowing in mud, on its marshy lowland soil, when, in 312 B.C., Appius Claudius constructed the first veritable Roman road, the Via Appia. The satires of Juvenal show, indeed, that paving could not have been universal in Rome, even in the time of the Empire, though there is no doubt that it was widely used, like many other innovations in whose employment Rome herself lagged, in the newer, smaller cities. The pedestrian had even an elevated sidewalk and stepping-stones across the traffic thoroughfare in Pompeii.

In all three examples, sewers, water mains, and paved roads, royal engineering innovations not unknown in more ancient towns and regions were converted into great collective forms, serving the urban masses. But as frequently happens in the vulgar applications of engineering, the physical benefits were limited by a certain poverty of imagination in carrying them through. The superabundant engineering was inadequate because— as in so much imposing American highway construction today—the human end in view was too dimly perceived or too reluctantly accepted as a final guide. Thus just as our expressways are not articulated with the local street system, so the great sewers of Rome were not connected with water-closets above the first floor. Even worse, they were not connected to the crowded tenements at all.

In short where the need was greatest, the mechanical facilities were least. Though the mass of the population might by day patronize at a small fee the public toilets in the neighborhood, they deposited their domestic ordure in covered cisterns at the bottom of the stair wells of their crowded tenements, from which it would be periodically removed by the dung-farmers and scavengers. Even punctual nightly removal would hardly lessen the foul odor that must have pervaded the buildings. (Urine, collected in special jars, was used by fullers in working up cloth.) In contrast with water removal, this dung-farming had the advantage of replenishing the soil of the surrounding farms with valuable nitrogenous compost, for then as now, flush toilets both wasted potential fertilizer and polluted the streams. But the load of excrement from this vast slum population must have been greater than the nearby land could bear; for there are records of open sewers and cess trenches in residential quarters, which were finally covered over, though not removed, at a later day.

The same uneconomic combination of refined technical devices and primitive social planning applied to the water supply. The public sources of water were ample, so much so that the vast volumes used for the baths apparently did not overtax it. But the private bath was a luxury of the rich; and the buildings exhumed in Rome show no pipes that would indicate the use of water above the first floor, though such a convenience sometimes existed in a little provincial town like Pompeii. Water and slops, in other words, had to be transported by hand, the first upwards, the second downwards, in the high tenements of Rome, just as they were transported in the equally high tenements of seventeenth-century Edinburgh. In this respect, Rome, for all its engineering skill and wealth, failed miserably in the rudiments of municipal hygiene. As a result, the danger of having a chamberpot emptied on one's head was as great, again, as in Edinburgh (Gardy-lo!), though the Roman courts exercised themselves to detect and punish the culprits in such cases as were brought to their attention by the municipal police.

In sum, in the great feats of engineering where Rome stood supreme, in the aqueducts, the underground sewers, and the paved ways, their total application was absurdly spotty and inefficient. By its very bigness and its rapacity, Rome defeated itself and never caught up with its own needs. There seems little doubt that the smaller provincial cities were better managed in these departments, just because they had not overpassed the human measure.

One cannot leave the subject of sewage disposal without noting another feature that casts serious doubt on the intelligence and competence of the municipal officials of Rome, for it records a low point in sanitation and hygiene that more primitive communities never descended to. The most elementary precautions against disease were lacking in the disposal of the great mass of refuse and garbage that accumulates in a big city; and Rome, in the heyday of the empire, must have numbered around a million human beings, give or take a few hundred thousand. If the disposal of fecal matter in carts and in open trenches was a hygienic misdemeanor, what shall one say of the disposal of other forms of offal and ordure in open pits? Not least, the indiscriminate dumping of human corpses into such noisome holes, scattered on the outskirts of the city, forming as it were a *cordon malsanitaire*.

Even without this invitation to typhoid, typhus, and cholera, the prevalence of malaria had made Rome and the surrounding campagna one of the most unhealthy areas in the world, right through the nineteenth century, as the readers of Henry James' 'Daisy Miller' still have reason to know. To make up for lack of health-department statistics, a large number of altars and shrines dedicated to the Goddess of Fever testify to the chronic threat of malarial infection; while the repeated onslaught of plagues, virulent and devastating, is on the record, with thousands dying in a single day. Is it any wonder that Rome, even in the palmiest days of imperial glory, was visited by a succession of desolating plagues—23 B.C. and A.D. 65, 79, and 162?

As an emergency measure to meet such mass inhumations, there might have been some justification for these pits; but as a matter of everyday practice they testify to Rome's chronic contempt for life. The quantity of dead matter that was thus dumped every day might indeed have frightened an even better technical organization than the Romans ever developed; for when the great gladiatorial spectacles were put on, as many as five thousand animals, including creatures as large as the elephant and the water buffalo, might be slaughtered in a single day, to say nothing of the hundreds of human beings who were likewise done to death in the arena. So incredible is the evidence that I prefer to quote directly one of the scholars who examined it first hand, the archaeologist, Rodolfo Lanciani.

"It is hard," says Lanciani, "to conceive the idea of a Roman carnarium, an assemblage of pits into which men and beasts, bodies and carcasses, and any kind of unmentionable refuse, were thrown in disorder. Imagine what must have been the conditions of these dreadful districts in times of plague, when the pits (puticuli) were kept open by night and day. And when the pits became filled, up to the mouth, the moat which skirted the wall of Servius Tullius, between the Colline and the Esquiline gates, was filled with corpses, thrown in as if they were carrion, until the level of the adjacent streets was reached."

In his excavations, Lanciani found about seventy-five pits or vaults, twelve feet square, thirty deep, filled with a "uniform mass of black, viscid, unctuous matter," and he remembered that on the day of finding the third pit, he was "obliged to relieve my gang of workmen from time to time, because the stench from that putrid mound, turned up after a lapse of twenty centuries, was unbearable, even for men inured to every kind of hardship, as were my excavators."

Under the provident Augustus, at the beginning of the Empire, a partial reform, which resulted in the substitution of cremation for inhumation —one could scarcely call it decent burial—took place. But this did not solve the other serious problem, that of garbage disposal.

If the sewage and water supply of the city of Rome, however grand the superficial impression of their engineering, do not stand up well under close inspection, the same applies also to the street system, which, over great areas, bore the traces of primitive footways and cartways, never sufficiently widened to accommodate wheeled traffic. Again, it was only in the small provincial and colonial cities that Roman order truly prevailed. There one discovers generous sidewalks for pedestrians, a convenience which, though known in Rome, never became common in every part of the city, for shops kept on spilling into the public ways of minor thoroughfares. Under the republic, according to Jerome Carcopino, only two streets could claim the name of 'viae,' that is, streets wide enough for two carts to pass—the Via Sacra, which was a processional way, and the Via Nova, whose very name indicates that it was an innovation. One of them crossed, the other flanked, the Forum Romanum. Roman roads varied from twelve to as much as twenty-four feet wide on parts of the great trunk highways; but about fifteen feet was the standard width. In other words, the two great avenues of Rome were no more than a prolongation of the great highroads; and the same system did not penetrate into the rest of the city.

As soon as the increase of population created a demand for wheeled traffic in Rome, the congestion became intolerable. One of Julius Caesar's first acts on seizing power was to ban wheeled traffic from the center of Rome during the day. The effect of this, of course, was to create such a noise at night, with wood or iron-shod cartwheels rumbling over the stone paving blocks, that the racket tormented sleep: at a much later date, it drove the poet Juvenal into insomnia. Just as motor car congestion now affects small towns as well as big ones, so the increase of animal-drawn vehicles impeded circulation everywhere. Hence Claudius extended Caesar's prohibition to the municipalities of Italy; and Marcus Aurelius, still later, applied it without regard to their municipal status to every town in the Empire; while, to complete the picture, Hadrian (A.D. 117-138) limited the number of the teams and loads of carts permitted to enter the city—cutting down even the night-time traffic at source. In a century and a half, traffic congestion had gone from bad to worse.

The fact that these regulations applied even in new cities, with their relatively commodious straight streets, indicates that it was in the nature of this new urban order to generate more traffic than the street network could cope with. And the reason for this disability was precisely the same reason that makes present-day traffic regulations, with the widening and multiplication of traffic arteries, so futile and inept: namely, no attempt was made to control the congestion of the land itself, or to reduce the density of population housed in its buildings. Absurdly, the factors that generate traffic remained outside the scheme of control. As if high building densities were not enough, poverty and lack of rentable space, according to Martial (A.D. 92), caused many streets to be cluttered with the stands and stalls of butchers, publicans, barbers, and tradesmen.

So far from arriving at a just proportion between roadways and buildings, between traffic densities and housing densities, Rome did just the opposite. The municipality permitted, indeed by its continued neglect it even encouraged, the housing of the vast mass of its population in over-crowded tenements, forming huge blocks called insulae or islands. These insulae contend with Rome's refuse pits as classic examples of vile municipal housekeeping.

Rome shows in diagrammatic contrast the relation of an exploiting ruling class to a depressed proletariat, and, as Petronius Arbiter well put it in the 'Satyricon,' "The little people came off badly; for the jaws of the upper classes are always keeping carnival." While a handful of patricians, about eighteen hundred families, occupied large private mansions, often with ample gardens and houses big enough to contain a whole retinue of free servants and slaves, many of the houses veritable palaces, the members of the middle classes, including officials, merchants, small industrial employers, probably lived in apartment houses such as those that have been excavated at the neighboring seaport of Ostia. These quarters were decent, perhaps, but the occupants paid a rent in Caesar's time, according to Ludwig Friedländer, about four times that of other towns in Italy. The great mass of the proletariat, in dire contrast, lived in some forty-six thousand tenement houses, which must have contained, on the average, close to two hundred people each.

These tenement houses bore the same relation to the spacious palaces and baths of the city as the open cess trenches did to the Cloaca Maxima. The building of these insulae, like the building of the tenements of New York, was a speculative enterprise in which the greatest profits were made by both the dishonest contractors, putting together flimsy structures that would barely hold up, and profiteering landlords, who learned how to subdivide old quarters into even narrower cells to accommodate even poorer artisans at a higher return of rent per un.t. (One notes, not without a cynical smile, that the one kind of wheeled traffic permitted by day in Rome was that of the building contractors.)

Crassus, who made a fabulous fortune in tenement house properties, boasted that he never spent money in building: it was more profitable to buy partly damaged old properties at fire sales and rent them with meager repairs. Such systematic slum clearance projects as Nero's great fire naturally increased the housing shortage and tightened the hold of the rapacious landlords. Thus the traditional slave's diet, the meagerest ration that would keep his body alive, was matched by the equally depressing slave's shelter—crowded, ramshackle, noisome. Such were the accommodations provided for the 'free citizens' of Rome.

Even in the crudest neolithic village, the house was always more than mere shelter for the physical body: it was the meeting place of a household; its hearth was a center of religious ceremony as well as an aid to cooking; it was the home of the household god and the locus of a family's being, a repository of moral values not measurable in money. All these associations and traditions were stripped away from the Roman insula: to squeeze maximum profit out of shoddy building and congested space, bare shelter sufficed; and to have recognized any other values would have been to diminish the possibilities of extortion. All the pious household usages, all the sentimental values attached to the family itself by writers like Cicero, applied only to the households of patricians. No one pretended that the denizens of Rome's slums had such favoring guardian spirits or could participate in ceremonial meals and family rites. Well did Tiberius Gracchus say, according to Plutarch: "The beasts of the field and the birds of the air have their holes and their hiding places, but the men who fight and die for Italy enjoy but the blessings of light and air." Under the Empire, even light and air were lacking in Rome. The floors were piled on top of each other, as they had never, in historic record, been piled before. Juvenal, writing in the second century A.D., exclaimed:

> Behold the mansion's towering size
> Where floors on floors to the tenth story rise.

The houses of the patricians, spacious, airy, sanitary, equipped with bathrooms and water closets, heated in winter by hypocausts, which carried hot air through chambers in the floors, were perhaps the most commodious and comfortable houses built for a temperate climate anywhere until the twentieth century: a triumph of domestic architecture. But the tenements of Rome easily take the prize for being the most crowded and insanitary buildings produced in Western Europe until the sixteenth century, when site over-filling and room over-crowding became common, from Naples to Edinburgh, and even Elizabethan London for a while succumbed to the same speculative misdemeanors. Not only were these buildings unheated, unprovided with waste pipes or water closets, unadapted to cooking; not merely did they contain an undue number of airless rooms, indecently over-crowded: though poor in all the facilities that make for decent daily living, they were in addition so badly built and so high that they offered no means of safe exit from the frequent fires that occurred. And if their tenants escaped typhoid, typhus, fire, they might easily meet their death in the collapse of the whole structure. Such accidents were all too frequent. So badly were the insulae clapped together that, in Juvenal's words, they "shook with every gust of wind that blew." That was hardly a poetic exaggeration.

These buildings and their people constituted the core of imperial Rome, and that core was rotten. As Rome grew and its system of exploitation turned more and more parasitic, the rot ate into ever larger masses of urban tissue. The main population of the city that boasted its world conquests lived in cramped, noisy, airless, foul-smelling, infected quarters, paying extortionate rents to merciless landlords, undergoing daily indignities and terrors that coarsened and brutalized them, and in turn demanded compensatory outlets. These outlets carried the brutalization even further, in a continuous carnival of sadism and death.

But before examining the chief recreations of the proletariat, by which they relieved their own sufferings by lasciviously gloating on people made to endure even worse tortures and degradations, let us behold Rome at its best. For Rome had more human attributes; and to the masses it exploited, it presented, even in its worst moments, astonishing glimpses of civic beauty and order, seemingly untainted by violence and greed.

3 : FORUM, VOMITORIUM, AND BATH

According to tradition, Rome was constituted by the union of various foreign tribes of the neighboring hills, under the leadership of the Romans themselves, perched on the Palatine. The symbol of this union, as Lavedan reminds us, was the foundation of a common marketplace (the Forum), with a place of assembly or comitium, which was also used in the early days for athletic and gladiatorial contests. Doubtless a temple was an essential and original part of the Forum, for the 'market peace,' so necessary to free exchange, was preserved by making the area itself sacred.

The forum was not simply an open square. As it developed in Rome, it was rather a whole precinct, complex in layout, in which shrines and temples, the halls of justice and council houses, and open spaces framed by stately colonnades played a part. Within these open spaces orators could address large crowds; while for inclement weather large halls, basilicas, served in many capacities. As August Mau observes about Pompeii, whatever took place in the market square might take place in the basilica, though it was chiefly devoted to business transactions and the administration of justice. The simplicity of the forum itself lent it to a variety of purposes: not least, finally, to that of a religious congregation.

The transformation of mere open space into the complete enclosure of the Forum began at an early date. Rome, according to Friedländer, was slowly ceasing to look like an overgrown country town even before 310 B.C., for the wooden booths of the butchers in the Forum had given way to money-changers' bureaux, while the food markets themselves became more copious and more specialized. As early as 179 Cato the Censor gave Rome a large central market for food, with a domed slaughter-house in the middle and shops radiating from it. By the time Vitruvius began to codify current practice, he prescribed that the treasury, the prison, and the council house ought to adjoin the Forum.

As succeeding emperors added directly to the Forum or, like Julius Caesar, founded a new one in the vicinity, ever larger crowds would be drawn to the center for shopping, for worship, for gossip, for taking part, as spectators or actors, in public affairs or in private lawsuits. The new road that passed through the Forum, the Argiletum, which connected it to the quarters of the artisans and merchants, was transformed into a monumental passage, the Forum of Nerva, when it entered the precinct.

Vitruvius had very definite ideas about its ideal size, which anticipated the principles so admirably expressed by Winston Churchill in his prescription for the design for rebuilding the British House of Commons. "The dimensions of the Forum," Vitruvius notes, "ought to be adjusted to the audience, lest the space be cramped for use, or else, owing to a scanty attendance, the Forum should seem too large. Now let the breadth be so determined that when the length is divided into three parts, two are assigned to the breadth. For so the plan will be oblong, and the arrangement will be adapted to the purpose of spectacles."

Here in the Forum Romanum was the center of public life not merely for Rome itself, but for the Empire—though there were naturally similar but subordinate centers in other parts of the city. Here between the Capitoline Hill and the site of Nero's Golden Palace or the later Colosseum, was the great place of assembly. Here vast crowds came together to witness the passage of their military leaders, in chariots, parading their trophies or their royal captives, bound to their chariot wheels, passing under triumphal arches, which served as framed, formal entrances to what was, in fact, an unwalled precinct. Monumental scale and spatial order prevailed here, with just that extra living touch which the accidents of time or topography might introduce.

Here, then, the new Rome of aggressive fact and reality, the Rome of looting soldiers, cringing slaves, and crass land speculators was concealed beneath the toga of the traditional Rome of patriotic aspiration and Stoic dream. Who could doubt here the reality of that ideal Rome, under whose enfolding law and peace, order was order, justice was justice, efficiency was efficiency, not masks for rapacity, greed, lust, and cruelty on a gigantic collective scale. In the Forum one might remember, without ironic reserves, indeed with honest admiration, the moral meditations and the duty-bound activities of a Cicero or a Marcus Aurelius. Here, too, one might easily forget the stinking pits of the carnarium or the orgy of torture that daily took place in the nearby arenas.

Since the Roman forum was, in effect, a combination of agora and acropolis, it did not present any radically new features that one would not have been able to identify in its Hellenistic prototype. What one finds, perhaps, is a greater concentration of varied activities, a higher degree of formal order, an expansion and magnification of the themes already present elsewhere in the Hellenistic town.

This new order, once established at the center, spread everywhere, particularly in the magnificent porticoes and colonnades with which Augustus delighted to enrich the city; for in less than twenty years the Campus Martius, the site of the Flavian amphitheater, was covered with colonnades, which stretched from the foot of the hills to the river itself, colonnades not merely of stone but of high walls of boxwood, setting off pools of open space where one might rest, to take in the sculptured figures or the gallery of wall paintings, or even, in the Portico of the Septa, a huge museum of curiosities, antiquities, and manufactures of the extreme East. Under Augustus, it has been estimated, the total number of colonnaded streets came to over thirteen miles. These porticoes remained in existence until the ninth century A.D.: streamlets and pools of esthetic refreshment bordered by grass and rubble.

With the axial plan went a tendency to organize buildings symmetrically in relation to the axis, even when this disposition was as effectively hidden as the apses in the Forum of Trajan were hidden by the colonnades in front of them. This general spatial clarification was what must have impressed the visitor in the center of the city. Over a great part of the growing metropolis the streets remained a jumble of narrow passages, cluttered with the disorderly contents of the shops and taverns that lined them, overshadowed by the high tenements on each side; and here only an occasional patch of urban design, a temple, a fountain, a portico, and a garden would awaken a noble echo from the center of the city. But where public munificence and municipal land ownership left the architect free to operate on his own terms, the Roman mind rose to the challenge of numbers and established a scale, and a method of handling the goings and comings of crowds, that probably had few rivals in any earlier type of city.

While Rome knew better than more modest provincial towns the indignities of overcrowding, it also knew the luxury of public space, generously carved into great structures: without the latter, indeed, the first might well have been insufferable. In the elaboration of the ancient Egyptian and Syrian dome and vault, the Romans rose to a new architectural height. The sky was not so much their limit as their model. They gave to the bath or the basilica, at the moment of its most crowded use, a quality that made the presence of so many bodies inoffensive; for the space above lifted the pressure of the masses below. Looking upward, one could both breathe and see freely. Even today, a building modelled on the Roman baths, like Pennsylvania Station in New York, retains this noble quality— or did until that structure was converted by its thoughtful guardians into a vast jukebox, disguised as a ticket counter, thus destroying at one vandal blow its esthetic form and its capacity to handle crowds effectively.

The architectural element that embodied this new command of urban space for mass assembly and mass movement was a special Roman contribution. To this feature the Romans gave a name peculiarly apt in its reflection of their own character and practices: the vomitorium. 'Vomitorium' stands for two things in the Latin lexicon: privately, it was a special room, adjoining the dining hall, where gluttonous eaters who had swilled too much rich and exotic food might throw up the contents of their stomach in order to return to their couches empty enough to enjoy the pleasures of still more food. The business of providing for the hasty emptying out of food was symbolically transferred to the great openings and passages in an amphitheater, through which the sated crowds could make a reasonably quick exit without trampling on each other.

The scale of the public vomitorium, necessarily a gigantic one, established the dimensions for the other parts of the building. It was in dealing with swarming masses, counted in thousands and tens of thousands, that the Roman imagination was stirred to an almost poetic splendor that was all too often lost when it handled details. In beholding today the dismantled ruins of a great Roman building, like the Baths of Caracalla, or the Colosseum itself, we have an advantage, it is true, that the Romans did not fully enjoy: we behold these structures in their naked severity, stripped of most of their costly, ostentatious clothing. (Some of this primitive austerity came back again, possibly for the sake of economy, in the times of Diocletian and Constantine.)

That nakedness may have still been close to the Rome of Scipio Africanus: but as Romans grew wealthy they no more enjoyed it than they enjoyed the Greek practice of nudity in the Olympic games. Nakedness for the Roman was either an accompaniment of defecation or a prelude to lust: they preferred every manner of decorative embellishment. Costly marbles and onyxes, intricate moldings, the Corinthian order rather than the Doric or Tuscan, complicated ornamental patterns in the mosaic of the pavement, and, above all, gilt, gilt in vast quantities, gilt sufficient in one instance to roof a whole arena. Perhaps only those of us who remember the Roman Catholic Cathedral at Westminster as it was a generation ago, before the brick walls of its serene romanesque interior were covered by decoration, can have a sufficiently vivid notion of the difference between the chaste straightforwardness of Roman engineering and the voluptuous appearance of the finished structures. Augustus' dying boast of finding a city clothed in brick and leaving it in marble may have been more hollow than he realized.

In Roman public architecture the scale, then, was everything: the Roman architect found a mass form for all the collective occasions of life, in the market, the amphitheater, the bath, the racecourse; and some of those forms were passed over to the city more than a thousand years later, as in the form of the oblong racecourse with sharp turns that became the Piazza Navona. But the open spaces of Rome, too, probably played a larger part than they did in most earlier cities. The parks around the Imperial palaces, though originally meant for private use, count among the earliest of open spaces devoted to spontaneous recreation *within* the city—though naturally this had always been available outside the city's walls. Caesar's bequest of his own gardens to the public is one of the earliest records of such a private privilege being turned over to the commonalty. Unfortunately Rome never caught up with the need for such pleasances in the slum districts, where they were most sorely needed.

Perhaps Rome's most characteristic contribution both to urban hygiene and to urban form was the Bath. In the history of the great baths one reads the condensed story of Rome itself. This people began as a nation of sturdy farmers, close to the earth, abstemious, hard-working, strong-muscled delvers and hewers, becoming through their very capacity for enduring hardship and taking blows the strongest people in antiquity. But their very strength and their unflagging industry turned them into a nation of grabbers and cadgers, living off their neighbors, converting their mother city into a gigantic mouth and stomach, sucking in foods, booty, works of art, slaves, religions, gods, scraps of knowledge, turning every refinement of culture, every decency of daily life, into something at once lurid and brutal, sensational and disgusting, pretentious and meaningless.

The bath, as it was known to Scipio Africanus, was a pool of water in a sheltered place where the sweaty farmer made himself clean. Seneca wistfully recalled that moment, before sunbathing and the general coddling of the flesh became fashionable. But as early as the second century B.C. the habit of going to the public baths was established in Rome; and by 33 B.C. Agrippa introduced free public baths in the form that this institution was finally to take: a vast enclosure, holding a great concourse of people, one monumental hall leading to another, with hot baths, tepid baths, cold baths, rooms for massage and rooms for lolling about and partaking of food, with gymnasia and playfields attached, to serve those who sought active exercise, and libraries as well, for the more reflective or more indolent.

In its grand scale and in its combination of different facilities, if in no other fashion, the Roman bath compares with the modern American shopping center, though not particularly to the latter's advantage. But whereas life for the everyday American, under a compulsive economy of expansion, is essentially a gadget-ridden, goods-stuffed emptiness puffed up for profit, in Rome acquisition was largely restricted to the upper classes and their financial agents, while for the majority life was largely a matter of finding surrogates and compensations at public expense. What began as a farmer's necessity of hygiene became a ceremonious ritual for filling the vacuity of an idle day. Though the Romans inflated the theological currency by inventing a special god for every occasion in life, the one supreme god that they really worshipped was the body. As to this, more than one tombstone bears witness with its boasts of the gluttonous eating and drinking of the occupant of the grave, as his chief claim to being piously remembered by his equally worthy successors. The religion of the body was as near as the Romans ever got to religion, once they lost their original Lares and Penates; and the public bath was its temple. An ideal environment for lollers, spongers, voyeurs, exhibitionists—body coddlers all.

The buildings themselves proclaim this fact: architecturally they rank among the supreme achievements of Rome; and only the Pantheon can be counted as a rival. Wherever the Roman went, he carried the idea of the public bath with him: on the busy Boulevard Saint Michel in Paris, the remains of such an ancient bath still remind one of those older occupants of Lutetia. Certainly the ritual had a practical side: this habit of cleaning the body thoroughly possibly helped to diminish the hygienic and sanitary misdemeanors of the city in other quarters, while the spatial magnificence of these buildings in itself was an aid to psychological composure, which offset in some degree the drab huddle and muddle of domestic existence.

But despite these beneficial side effects, so elevating to the spirit, the ritual of the bath occupied a disproportionate segment of the day, and directed too large a quantity of human energy toward the service of the body, treated as an end in itself. That there was probably a recognized difference between the religious and esthetic ritual of the bath and its practical hygienic uses, the existence of numerous private baths throughout the city seems to testify.

The relation of the bath to the sexual life of Rome must not, however, be overlooked. In the bath, the patron got over the debauch of the night before and made ready for the coming one. And though some effort was made, according to Carcopino, to separate men and women bathers by assigning special hours to each sex, these regulations broke down. By the time of Saint Jerome, even under official Christianity, he warned women against the lustful exposure and voyeurism of the baths, as a serious danger to the soul. Certainly, the baths were favorite places for making assignations: thus they anticipated one of the practices that brought the bath-houses of the late Middle Ages into disrepute. Even in modern times, the last vestige of the Roman bath, the so-called Turkish bath, maintained its ancient association with drunkenness and sexual debauchery.

4: DEATH IN THE AFTERNOON

Those who built up the power of Rome were driven to widen the frontiers of the Empire: their fears of invasion as well as their mounting commitments to protect their supply lines and their sources of food and raw materials encouraged a dream of a universal political order. Under the Pax Romana, that dream endured for about two centuries. To the extent that this peace was real, the conquests could be partly justified, even to the conquered; for a universal society, free from war or the menace of war, based on justice, not oppression and terrorism, had never yet been achieved among men. It was for this that thousands of good Romans had plotted and schemed, had fought battles, had held distant frontier posts, had endured voluntary exile, and had filled their days with the chores of public office: administrative regulations, legal codes, tax lists, property records. These Roman officials did their duty despite hardship and boredom, remembering in their dying hours the cold but comforting thoughts of Zeno of Citium, or Terence, or Virgil. . . . *I am human and nothing human is foreign to me.*

As an empire, Rome had succeeded better than Athens, which had never been strong enough to protect, even for a generation, the areas it exploited. Yet Rome had not in fact succeeded. For the city of Scipio's and Cicero's dreams vanished even before the sleepers awoke: in fact, it had never existed. Rome's order, Rome's justice, Rome's peace were all built on a savage exploitation and suppression. At its highest point, Rome was an oak whose wide-spreading branches hid the rottenness that was eating from within at the base of the trunk: the pigs might snout for truffles, which flourish best under diseased oaks, in the nearby earth, but more nourishing kind of food would not grow beneath those branches. The empire, which had pushed back the barbarous tribes that threatened its borders, had erected a greater barbarism at the very heart of its dominion, in Rome itself. Here the prospect of wholesale destruction and extermination from which the city had largely escaped, thanks to Roman arms, came back in the acting out of even more pathological fantasies. Predatory success underwrote a sickening parasitic failure.

The very name 'parasite' was a necessary Roman invention to describe a human relationship that had never before taken such a recognizable, indubitably pathological form. The Roman patricians had for long boasted of a procession of clients, who waited on them and bolstered up their egos: originally, the client was the self-supporting, presumably self-respecting tenant farmer or share cropper of a big landlord, dependent only for his allotment of land, but quite capable of earning his own living. The parasite had sunk much lower: he no longer had any positive economic relation to his patron: he was the fawning hanger-on, the inveterate sponger, who had no other means of livelihood than the bounties and favors of his host. By fastening himself on a rich man, he lost any possibility of independent locomotion or independent support. There are many precedents for this in the animal world.

In nature, this parasitism is often as ruinous to the host as it is to the creature that battens on him: if the latter loses the capacity for free movement or self-maintenance, the host, in turn, becomes dependent and must exert himself further to keep the seemingly weaker creature going. The rich and powerful often found themselves in this position: the decent living that they refused to give the lower classes on economic terms, they were forced to yield in outbursts of indiscriminate public largesse. Now Rome's parasitism was at first brought on and literally fed by Rome's very success in predatory conquest; and it ended by producing in a more general form the same functionless, empty, and dependent life for rich and poor alike, filled with unappeasable appetites and unresolvable anxieties.

In Rome, a whole population, numbering hundreds of thousands, took on the parasitic role for a whole lifetime; and the spreading empire was turned into an apparatus for ensuring their continued existence, supporting them 'in the state to which they were accustomed,' by shamelessly bribing the army that alone guaranteed the flow of tribute, slaves, captives, and wild beasts, which poured incessantly into the maw of this insatiable city.

So vital are the autonomous activities of the organism, so necessary are they for keeping it whole, that any surrender of independence has deep psychological repercussions. Particularly, the infantile feeling of dependence, prolonged into adulthood, awakens self-distrust and self-hatred, which exacts a suicidal desire for revenge. The impotent develop a craving for virtual, if not active, power while those who have not lived their own lives experience a violent desire to impose a humiliating death on others. To atone for the limitations of a parasitic existence, the parasite himself transposes the values of life, so that all his acts take a negative form. The hatred the parasite feels for himself he projects upon suitable victims and scapegoats, covering them with his own despair, his own self-loathing, his own desire for death.

By giving a municipal form to its parasitism, indeed by giving it a solid collective basis in the dual handout of bread and circuses, Rome solidified the fatal errors of its political exploitation of other lands and cities. Ironically, in yielding to parasitism it forfeited at the same time the predatory vitalities that had made it possible. Sinking under the soporific illusions of the Pax Romana, the old patrician leaders lost their grip. Even outside Rome, self-government gradually disappeared under the Empire: the once autonomous municipalities were governed by local magnates, representing the landed or the commercial interests, nominally servants to the state, who kept themselves and their kin in power by the same brazen methods that had been evolved in Rome. The peace and justice that the Romans boasted had about the same degree of reality as the 'competition' that operates under the current monopolistic control and forced consumption imposed by American business. It was a cold sham. The very pretense of law and order was repeatedly undermined by the murderous court plots, the rapacious blackmail, and the army uprisings that attended the choice of each successive emperor. The Praetorian Guard so greatly preferred a debauched dog like Commodus to his dignified and honorable successor, Pertinax, that they promptly murdered the latter.

The existence of a parasitic economy and a predatory political system produced a typically Roman urban institution that embraced both aspects of its life and gave them a dramatic setting: the old practice of the religious blood sacrifice was given a new secular form in the arena.

Roman life, for all its claims of peace, centered more and more on the imposing rituals of extermination. In the pursuit of sensations sufficiently sharp to cover momentarily the emptiness and meaninglessness of their parasitic existence, the Romans took to staging chariot races, spectacular naval battles set in an artificial lake, theatrical pantomimes in which the strip tease and lewder sexual acts were performed in public. But sensations need constant whipping as people become inured to them: so the whole effort reached a pinnacle in the gladiatorial spectacles, where the agents of this regime applied a diabolic inventiveness to human torture and human extermination.

The inhabitants of modern metropolises are not psychologically too remote from Rome to be unable to appreciate this new form. We have our own equivalent in the daily doses of sadism that follow, like contaminated vitamin capsules, our deficient commonplace food: the newspaper accounts, the radio reports, the television programs, the novels, the dramas, all devoted to portraying as graphically as possible every variety of violence, perversion, bestiality, criminal delinquency, and nihilistic despair. So, to recover the bare sensation of being alive, the Roman populace, high and low, governors and governed, flocked to the great arenas to participate in person in similar entertainments, more vividly staged, more intimately presented. Every day, in the arena, the Romans witnessed in person acts of vicious torture and wholesale extermination, such as those that Hitler and his agents later devised and vicariously participated in—but apparently lacked the stomach to enjoy regularly in person.

Even before Rome had changed from Republic to Empire, that city had become a vast collective torture chamber. There, at first under the guise of witnessing the just punishment of criminals, the whole population, as Seneca remarked, daily punished itself. So thoroughly was Rome committed to this evil that even the adoption of Christianity as the official religion of the State did not do away with the practice. When the Vandals were hammering at the gates of Hippo, Augustine's city, the groans of the dying defenders on the wall mingled with the roar of the spectators in the circus, more concerned with their day's enjoyment than with even their ultimate personal safety.

With their taste for extermination so deeply developed over many centuries, it is no wonder that the Romans thought Greek athletics a little effeminate and uninteresting: there was not enough blood, agony, and frightfulness in mere sporting contests. The life that had taken form in Rome after the suppression of the slaves' rebellion under the Gracchi and the vanquishment of its great commercial rival, Carthage, after the second Punic War, had internally rotted. From the first century B.C. Rome entered those stages of urban existence that Patrick Geddes characterized as 'parasitopolis' and 'patholopolis': the city of parasites and the city of diseases. Thus Rome became a container of negative life: life turning against itself in perverse and destructive activities. In this, Rome perpetuated and enlarged the evils to which all civilizations seem to expose themselves; for it found an architectural form and a public ritual that favored the constant expression of these negations. Like our own preparations for nuclear and bacterial extermination, this form gave an acceptable 'normal' outlet to what were otherwise unspeakable and privately inexpressible psychotic acts. In a disintegrating civilization the sanction of numbers makes madness and criminality 'normal.' Affliction with the universal disease then becomes the criterion for health.

The economic basis of this sadistic ritual was the fact that the proletariat of the city of Rome was supported by a dole: that is, by regular handouts to about 200,000 people of bread issued from public storehouses in various parts of the city. The temptation to lead an industrious life, with the hope of improvement in economic status, was weakened, especially in favored Rome itself, by the fact that the chief needs of existence, like bread and circuses, were available gratis, or in the case of baths, nearly gratis, to the populace.

To make attendance at these spectacles even easier, as early as the reign of Claudius, 159 days were marked as public holidays, and as many as 93, a quarter of the whole year, were devoted to games at the public expense. Vast fortunes were spent on staging even a single one of these events. This was the popular justification for the rapacity of the rich and the rapine of the military leaders. Here again the Roman way of life, like that in America today, knew no quantitative limits. One of the marks of imperial indulgence was the unexpected creation of new holidays to celebrate a victory, and so far from this habit's being curbed when Roman power began to fail, the number of red-letter days steadily increased. By A.D. 354 there were 175 days of games, almost twice the number as under Claudius, while the total number of public holidays came to two hundred, or more than half the year.

No body of citizens, not even the Athenians at the height of their empire, ever had such an abundance of idle time to fill with idiotic occupations. Even mechanized United States, with the five-day week, cannot compare with Rome; for after the hour of noon, in addition, the Roman workers, who had doubtless risen at daybreak, suffered no further demand on their time. The transformation of the active, useful life of the early Republican city into the passive and parasitic life that finally dominated it took centuries. But in the end, attendance at public spectacles, terrestrial and nautical, human and animal, became the principal occupation of their existence; and all other activities fed directly or indirectly into it.

Just as today 'real' life, for the millions, exists only on the television screen, and all immediate manifestations of life are subordinate, accessory, almost meaningless, so for the Roman the whole routine of the spectacle became a compulsive one: *The show must go on!* Not to be present at the show was to be deprived of life, liberty, and happiness. Seneca, the teacher and companion of young Nero, regarded his own presence at the gladiatorial games as nothing less than an affliction to the soul; but he went. The habit of resorting to the spectacles regularly was something that even the most sadly sane of Roman emperors, Marcus Aurelius, could not break, without fear of hostile public response. It was dangerous for the Emperor to show, even by his absence, his personal distaste.

The need for such mass entertainments became imperative in proportion to the futility of the rest of existence. Even the intellectual life of

Rome, never as acute as that of the Greek cities, betrayed a similar inanity and emptiness. Though Rome did not go so far as to invent the quiz show beloved by television audiences, people became interested in the same kind of vacuous questions: How many men rowed in Aeneas' galley? or what kind of food did Scipio have for breakfast before he conquered the Carthaginians?

We come, then, to a new urban form, the circus: a banked enclosure, open to the sky, where tens of thousands of Romans gathered to view the spectacles, some to pass the whole day there, for the performance would begin in the morning. It was here that the Roman mastery of engineering problems perhaps reached its height: it was here that the Roman delight in quantitative achievement conceived an architectural form whose very success depends upon mass and scale, with the spectators ranged, tier upon tier, in a steeply angled ascent.

The new form lent itself to many different purposes. The spectacle was so deeply ingrained in Roman life that even the theater departed from its original semi-circular plan, to a complete circle. With that change, the old drama in the Greek style gave way to a form of opera, dependent upon spectacular effects, and the opera evolved into a pantomime—doubtless necessary for an audience too big to hear words clearly in the open air.

Rome had become the arena of arenas, where the usual activities of a city were subordinated to the mass production of violent sensations derived from lust, torture, and murder. The most innocent of all these performances were the chariot races, though the possibility of the chariot being overturned and the driver trampled upon must have sated the illicit craving for blood, as the same possibility does in motor car races today. But the supreme performance of the arena, the one that gave a special stamp to the city in its characteristic degeneracy was the gladiatorial spectacle.

The gladiatorial games were first introduced into Rome in 264 B.C. by the consul Decimus Junius Brutus on the occasion of his father's funeral; but the Romans gave them a more utilitarian turn by employing the deadly contests as a popular means for the public punishment of criminals, at first presumably as much for an admonitory deterrent as an enjoyment. Too soon, unfortunately, the ordeal of the prisoner became the welcome amusement of the spectator; and even the emptying of the jails did not provide a sufficient number of victims to meet the popular demand. As with the religious sacrifices of the Aztecs, military expeditions were directed toward supplying a sufficient number of victims, human and animal. Here in the arena both degraded professionals, thoroughly trained for their occupation, and wholly innocent men and women were tortured with every imaginable body-maiming and fear-producing device for public delight. And here wild animals were butchered, without being eaten, as if they were only men.

The characteristic institutions that helped make the Hellenic city memorable, the gymnasium and the theater, derived ultimately from a religious source, the funerary games, the springtime and harvest rituals. One may say the same of Rome, but with a difference. In Rome, tragic death, religiously conceived, evoking pity and sober introspection, turned into mass murder, spewing unlimited terror without a saving touch of pity; while, by the same token, the healthy bawdiness of the old Attic comedy, with all its coarse sexual humor, became an obscene toying with the collective genitalia, in which impotence resorted to sadism to counterfeit and exacerbate sexual desire. In the Roman spectacle, even honest animal impulses were deformed and defiled.

The original excuse that justified substituting the gladiatorial games—with their chance of a reprieve—for the sullen execution of criminals was overwhelmed by the mass demand for inexorable murder, no matter who might be the victim. Not the least popular of these horrors was the chain killing, in which a single victim was appointed to be killed by another, who in turn was disarmed and killed, and so on down the line. The later use of Christian maidens as special offerings in the spectacle gave them an additional fillip: that of innocent virginity, being stripped naked before being thrown to the lions. In strict justice, let me add that it is on record that the crowd demanded the release of Androcles, when the lion from whose paw he had once extracted a thorn refused to eat him. Such an exhibition of sportsmanship was far too rare to be passed over even now.

The first of the great arenas, the Circus Flaminius, built in the Campus Martius, hard by the Tiber, in 221 B.C., was already a big structure. This early form was developed out of the simple flat racecourse, with seats for spectators on the neighboring hills, which dates back to the fourth century. But it was Julius Caesar who rebuilt the oldest and the largest of the circuses, the Circus Maximus—a structure that still mysteriously evades excavation—and this was so huge that it contained, according to one fourth-century authority, as many as 385,000 places for spectators, though Carcopino places it as 255,000 seats, and Curtius at "only" 80,000. But though horse racing persisted longer than the gladiatorial spectacles, if only because this became the chief form of contest acceptable to Christian Byzantium, it was in the theater meant for mass torture that the architectural form reached its highest development. The Colosseum, started by Vespasian, completed by Titus, and decorated by Diocletian, became a model for similar works in smaller cities—while its 45,000 places erected a standard of magnitude not surpassable except in Rome itself until our own day.

Even taking a low figure per unit, it would seem that almost half the population of Rome could be accommodated simultaneously in its circuses and theaters: a far higher proportion than was possible in other cities until electronic communication indefinitely extended the area of the performance and the number of spectators. Even in a small provincial town like

Pompeii, the amphitheater held twenty thousand people: probably more than half of its total adult population. The same inclusiveness characterized the baths, if one adds the hundreds of private institutions to the more gigantic public baths.

The arena and the bath were, in fact, the new Roman contribution to the urban heritage, one contaminating it, the other purifying it: both conceived as colossal structures for mass entertainment, at a time when mass organization demanded spatial compactness and high density of occupation. These two forms came into existence together and vanished together; and in their passage they absorbed interests and energies that might have gone, if they had been more beneficently directed, into the replenishment of the common life and the restoration of autonomous activity. What a grip the gladiatorial shows held one may gather from the fact that Constantine, who dared to make Christianity the official religion of the Roman state, did not abolish the spectacles, not even the gladiatorial games. At most, in 326, he terminated the throwing of criminals to the beasts; and it was not until 404, six years before the barbarian armies of Alaric sacked Rome, that gladiatorial combats were ended by Honorius.

By that time the old lights of the classic world, one by one, were going out. In 394, the last Olympic games were held; and in 537 water ceased to flow in the baths of Caracalla, though the cartloads of wood for heating the water had ceased to come in regularly for many years before. Even more significantly, the greatest contribution made by Greece to this otherwise over-corporealized life, the School of Athens, was closed in 529. So the old Hellenic culture of the well-minded body and the fully embodied mind, and the Roman culture of the largely mindless body, servile to its own sensations, parasitic upon its own power, both vanished together.

But the doom of the Roman way of life and the Roman urban heritage must have been visible in the great amphitheaters at a much earlier date, for those who had eyes to see. As daily life itself became more grim, as terror, suffering, and death could no longer be confined to the circus, those who were awake to its realities or sensitive to its evils must have shrunk from these ugly diversions. They would leave their vacant seats visible in the arena, with ever-widening gaps as the population itself diminished in number. Parasitopolis had become Patholopolis; and even further, Patholopolis had turned into Psycho-patholopolis, with a Nero or a Caligula as absolute ruler. That Patholopolis was beyond saving, even when it turned to Tyrannopolis, and sought to achieve security and continuity by fixed status and fixed residence. The mere momentum of habit, the inertia of numbers, increased the velocity of its downward descent. "Sauve qui peut!" Only one further stage of city development remained, and that came soon: Necropolis, the city of the dead.

By the fifth century the show was over at the center, though it went on for another thousand years on the eastern fringe of the Empire, where Byzantium, by an immense effort of will, sufficiently modified the contents of Roman life to preserve its institutions in a state of carefully arrested development—notable chiefly for improvements in the military arts. Some of that art and life still is visible in Rhodes.

But when the amphitheaters became only empty shells, the old performers did not suddenly disappear. You would find them straggling over the highways of this old Roman world, stopping at a barbarian court, drawing a crowd at a fair: the weight-lifter, the acrobat, the daring horseback rider, the man leading a bear. As an after-image in the European mind, perhaps in the living linkage of the flesh, from generation to generation, handing on their arts from parents to children, sometimes greatly venturesome, but no longer committed to death, the old circus folk perhaps continued their play. The monks' chronicles would not notice them, nor, if aware of their existence, even be able to identify them. But as shadow or substance, the circus remained in existence and eventually came back to life in the modern city. Expunged of their Roman sins, the surviving circuses and menageries still recall the Roman way of life. They remind one, too, that Rome itself was once upon a time 'the greatest show on earth.'

5: FOURTH-CENTURY URBAN INVENTORY

Rome, in its physical vastness and cumulative wealth resembled the empire it had conquered. To do justice to its possessions one must enumerate them and catalogue them. From the beginning everything in Rome had been colossal: that was the very genius of the city before it was much better than a village; for when King Servius laid out the first great wall, he encompassed over a thousand acres, as if to invite the growth that had not yet taken place. That wall was itself fifty feet broad, bigger than was needed to drive a couple of chariots abreast. Though, in view of the primitive military technology for assault, the thickness of Jericho's early walls is hard to explain, there is no rational explanation, either, for the thickness of Rome's.

The area and the population of Rome probably kept right on increasing through the third century A.D. After the enclosure by the Aurelian wall in A.D. 274, Rome covered 3,323 acres within, while the total building areas, including the built-up area immediately beyond the wall, was some 4,940 acres, according to Carcopino: a formidable city even in modern times.

The first comprehensive inventory of Rome's contents is unfortunately a late one, found in an official survey dated 312-315. Yet the mere listing of the contents helps to fill in the dim outlines of the surviving ruins. Here it is: 6 obelisks, 8 bridges, 11 public baths, 19 'water channels,' 2 circuses, 2 amphitheaters, 3 theaters, 28 libraries, 4 gladiatorial schools, 5 nautical spectacles for sea fights, 36 marble arches, 37 gates, 290 storehouses and warehouses, 254 public bakehouses, 1,790 palaces, 46,602 lodging-houses (tenements).

To this Lanciani would add 926 small privately conducted baths—at any minute, he reckoned, 62,800 citizens could use baths—18 fora or public squares, 8 campi or commons covered with grass throughout the year, used by the multitude, as Strabo notes, for "ball-playing, hoop-trundling, or wrestling"; likewise about 30 parks and gardens, first laid out by wealthy citizens for their private comfort but eventually absorbed into the public domains. This still leaves out of account the 700 public pools or basins and the 500 fountains, drawing their supply from 130 collecting heads or reservoirs that T. G. Tucker makes note of. The last, incidentally, are perhaps ancient Rome's most dazzling bequest to the modern city, as the Fontana di Trevi still bears witness.

Add to this city of the living another city of the dead. I speak not only of the cemeteries and the memorial monuments. There was in addition a vast throng of statues, 3,785 in bronze, and in all about 10,000 figures: so that Cassiodorus well observed that Rome held a second population of stone and bronze, in many respects better situated than the living. That tradition has been passed on. The parks of modern Rome are hardly behind the ancient city—and they are well ahead of any rival I know—in the number of portrait busts and statues they boast.

"To you," observed Aristides in his Laudation of Rome, "there comes from all lands and seas what the seasons bring forth and what the climates produce, what rivers and lakes and the handicraft of Hellene or barbarian make. Whoever, therefore, wishes to view all this, must either journey through the whole world or stay in this city. For the work and toil of other folks is ever here at hand, and in excess."

That is the classic apology for the overgrown city: by its public contents alone, this container was stretched, it would seem, to the bursting point, for it had made non-selectivity the very principle of its existence. Until the eighteenth-century metropolis invented the museum as its special form, the city itself served as museum.

But there is another way of describing this vast urban miscellany, where everything was either for show or for sale: that qualifying criticism comes from Lucian. "A man who loves wealth and is enthralled by gold and measures happiness by purple and power, who has not tasted liberty or tested free speech or contemplated truth, whose constant companions are flattery and servility, a man who has unreservedly committed his soul to pleasure and has resolved to serve none but her, fond of extravagant fare and fond of wine and women, full of trickery, deceit and falsehood" —such folk "should live in Rome, for every street and square is full of the things they value most."

After Rome's urban achievement has been taken in at its most extravagant best, it yet remains, in its vastness and confusion, the complete embodiment of purposeless materialism: a sort of super Victor Emmanuel monument, long before that colossus of bad taste was erected. By its very size, it defied one to take it in as a whole, from any single hilltop, as one might take in Athens; by its almost sickening profusion it made selectivity and disciplined direction difficult. Even today its oldest collection of buildings in continued use, its greatest single collection of memorials and treasures —namely, the Vatican City—still is such a suffocating pile of structures as its great urban predecessor, though its congestion is made esthetically tolerable, in true Roman fashion, by Bernini's magnificent colonnade.

As a symbol of the maximum possibility of urban confusion, of the orderly and the accidental, the rational and the capricious, the ennobled and the debased, Rome has remained unique for more than two thousand years. Like London today, it had something for everybody; and perhaps like London, too, it was full of unexpected good things that have left no record behind.

Plainly Rome suffered from megalopolitan elephantiasis. Now, in discussing an organism afflicted with a grave disease, which has become chronic, one has a natural tendency to identify the pathological condition, whose effect is often pervasive, with the whole life of the organism itself. Obviously this is an error: as long as an organism remains alive, its major organs must be functioning more or less normally, or at least sufficiently well to maintain it. So it doubtless was with Rome. Though it contained a greater number of pathological cells than any healthy body should tolerate, the larger part of it could still function as a human community: lovers exchanged the gifts of love, parents protected and enjoyed and planned for their children, craftsmen, whether slave or free, performed the work of their callings with interest and fidelity, and not until, toward the end of the Empire, their vocations were turned into forced, hereditary occupations did they attempt to escape from the city and its grim regimen.

More than this: new institutions appeared to make up for the decay of civic institutions and family life. Even before the Mithraic, the Manichean, or the Christian Churches found their adherents, a new civic grouping, the college, came into existence. These colleges were the sociable successors of the eight original economic guilds—never greatly favored by public authority—and the forerunner of the craft guilds that emerged again in written record in the early Middle Ages. For though groups meeting regularly, especially if in secret, were looked upon with dire suspicion by the authorities, it became necessary in the second century A.D. to license colleges as social institutions which cherished the obligation to give a decent funeral to their dead members, and to provide a monthly collation for those alive.

Slaves were permitted to join these colleges: they thus supplied a bond of fellowship to overcome the anonymity—and the anomie, that is the spiritual rootlessness and loneliness of the overgrown city. These groups kept up, as it were, the old family ceremonials, whose very possibility had been eliminated by overcrowded housing. The inscriptions and monuments left by obscure craftsmen and tradesmen in every part of the Roman world indicate a satisfaction in their work, and a self-respect: the smith with his hammer, the cooper with his cask, were proud to have their effigies carved on their gravestones. Had this large foundation of sound, normal existence not remained, Rome would have crumbled away centuries before it did.

Yes: when the worst has been said about urban Rome, one further word must be added: to the end men loved her, even the saintly Jerome. When she was only a shadow of her former self, wrinkled and grizzled, like Rodin's old courtesan, they remembered still the immense vitality and charm of her matronhood, if not the blotched innocence of her youth. Nothing that men have once loved can be wholly vile; and what they have continued to love over the centuries must, in the face of all appearances, have been somewhat lovable.

What is more, the Christian inheritors of Rome, despite their searing memories of the arena and their grievous retreat in the catacombs, chose Rome as the cornerstone on which to build a new urban civilization. When the cults of Mithras and Manes had passed—they were both still alive in Augustine's day—and Christians undertook to place their whole life on a new foundation, they beheld in the dying city itself the center of a new world. Over the centuries Rome survived as a city, better than Hippo, Bethlehem, or Antioch. From Rome, ultimately, came the Christian brotherhoods that spiritually re-colonized the old empire and extended its earthly realm. Rome thus remained a human reservoir. Much purer fountains, like that of Iona, could not pipe their water so far, or dispatch their couriers over such well-built roads.

6: LIMITS OF URBAN GROWTH

Rome, then, is the classic example of what that perspicuous biologist W. M. Wheeler called 'Abbau,' or the de-building process. The disintegration of Rome was the ultimate result of its over-growth, which resulted in a lapse of function, and a loss of control over the economic factors and human agents that were essential to its continued existence. At some point, Roman organization should have become etherialized and been capable, by education, of maintaining order without resort to either overt force or seizure. But that point was never reached; for Rome became to others, not a desirable pattern of disciplined civic co-operation but a menacing example of uncontrolled expansion, unscrupulous exploitation, and materialistic repletion.

What was lacking in the Roman scheme was a built-in system of control, applied at the center no less than in the new colonial towns. If Rome had achieved such a system, and had exercised such a self-restraint, she might, with her great talent for law and system, have supplied a necessary universal element that the Ionic pattern of colonization had lacked. Failing this, Rome's chief contribution to city development is the negative lesson of her own pathological over-growth; a lesson that is apparently so hard to read that city after city has taken mere physical and economic expansion as a testimony to its prosperity and culture.

For this reason, I have dwelt on Rome's chaotic sanitation, its parasitic regimen of life, its compensatory rituals of extermination. In the repeated decay and breakdown of one civilization after another, after it has achieved power and centralized control, one may read the failure to reach an organic solution of the problem of quantity. Every overgrown megalopolitan center today, and every province outside that its life touches, exhibits the same symptoms of disorganization, accompanied by no less pathological symptoms of violence and demoralization. Those who close their eyes to these facts are repeating, with exquisite mimicry, the very words and acts, equally blind, of their Roman predecessors.

In looking about for a point at which Rome's growth might have been controlled, one realizes that the answer lay in the political system as a whole. For Rome's problem was essentially that of inventing a means for diffusing its power and order, so as to make the whole Empire a balanced, intercommunicating system, in which there would be two-way intercourse and co-operation between all the component urban and regional parts. There was, as I have pointed out, the beginning of this in the layout of the new colonization towns in Italy in the last years of the Republic, and perhaps equally in those of Africa.

Unfortunately this movement never reached the point of attempting to make either the towns or the provinces more democratically self-governing and more self-sufficient: for too much of their surplus was destined to flow back to the center, through the very leaky channels of tax-gatherers and military governors. The cities were often given some degree of independence within this scheme; but what was needed was a method of encouraging their inter-dependence and of giving their regions effective representation at the center. This possibility seems to have been beyond the Roman imagination, for all the lip-service to Zeno's conception of a united humanity. Their gods were brought back to Rome and enshrined in the Pantheon; but there was no place for their living representatives in the capitol.

Cicero, in 'The Laws,' observed that "all natives of Italian towns have two fatherlands," one by nature and birth; the other by citizenship. But these fatherlands were not on a parity, even in Italy; while beyond the Alps the Romans even forbade the natives in Cicero's day to plant the olive and the vine, "so that our own olive groves may be more valuable." Thus Rome continued the old monopolistic practices of the ancient citadel, practices that had proved over three thousand years even more inimical to a durable union and a co-operative polity than the particularism of the little Aegean city-states.

The secret of Rome's domination was Divide and Rule. To prevent the smaller cities from uniting against Rome, the dominant partner in fact encouraged rivalry, lest a whole province should join together and present its united strength against Rome. This would hardly have been necessary if the Roman system had been founded on justice and equal participation in responsibilities and benefits. In the case of distant members of the empire, like Rhodes, a considerable amount of self-government and cultural autonomy was indeed permitted: active aid was required only in war. But otherwise the relationship was one of one-sided control and submission; indeed, as the Roman economy became progressively more parasitic, hence more dependent upon distant fields and factories for its supplies of grains, metals, textiles, papyrus, pottery, the more one-sided and monopolistic the relation became. What was needed was, as W. E. Heitland pointed out, something quite different: a genuine "consolidation of its forces, enabling the Central Power and the detached parts to work together as a living whole."

This would not merely have meant urban self-government and regional autonomy: it would also have meant the termination of Rome's own unhealthy over-growth. Such a state seems to have been achieved in Gaul by the fifth century, aided by the same forces that were making Rome itself untenable; and the very struggle against Rome's undue power within the Christian church, in the rise of one heresy after another in the provinces, from England to Africa, may also be taken as an effort to express, through religious convictions, the independence that the Roman state had otherwise denied. But this challenge came too late. Rome lacked the basis for two-way intercourse, since at the end it had no equivalent to offer in exchange. And by making cities dependent for their charters of self-government on the central state, Rome involved them in the cumulative weaknesses of that state.

During the period of the Pax Romana these grave faults were partly concealed. New towns were built without walls and the old ones allowed their fortifications to lapse. But when the barbarians began to infiltrate the over-extended defense works—even in Horace's time the imperial armies were shamefully molested—the need for local walls became desperate. Then towns as near to Rome as Ostia were encouraged to build walls for their self-defense—though to do this it was necessary to tear down their temples in order to have a sufficient supply of quarried stone to meet the emergency promptly. This was autonomy with a vengeance: not a willing transfer of power to those best capable of utilizing it, but an unwilling confession of imperial impotence.

Rome never faced the problem of its own overgrowth, for to do so it would have had to challenge both the political and the economic basis of the whole imperial regime. Instead of strengthening the economic and military position of the smaller cities, particularly in Germany, England, and Gaul, Rome met the challenge of its own overgrowth by that act of fission which created two autonomous empires, in the West and the East. Under Constantine and his successors, the Eastern Rome, Byzantium, became a sophisticated, somewhat purified counterpart of the original, with a more industrialized group of craftsmen, a more disciplined army, a more formalized routine. For a thousand years it made a virtue of arrested development.

Those who still held in the fourth century that the Roman empire had yet another thousand years to live were right, insofar as they identified Rome with Constantine's new city. But Byzantium, in overcoming the parasitism and disorder of Rome, created a shell in which century after century the living creature diminished in size, and its movements became ever more constricted. In effect, the Eastern Empire shrank to a province: the province to an urban region: in the end that region itself contracted to the limits of the city, within whose walls, on empty lots, food was again grown to feed the last remnants of its population, before they surrendered to the Turks. Much that was precious in Rome was kept in existence in Byzantium in a state of elegant fossilization: the Pandects of Justinian, the Greek Anthology, the art of mosaic painting. Ravenna and Torcello still reveal the glow in the dark embers of that dying fire.

With sufficient consciousness of its actual position, with sufficient intelligence to act on that consciousness, Rome might have done for the whole Mediterranean world what Lysias had urged Alexander to do for Greece. Rome might have maintained and diffused the economy of the autonomous city, while bringing these cities and regions into a larger circle of political union and economic interchange. That indeed was the way in which the Empire seemed ready to go at the beginning, until the ferocity of the second Punic War brought about a general demoralization of its leadership. But the Romans never came to grips with these cultural and civic realities: more and more they sought power, and the material emblems of power as values in themselves; and indeed in the pursuit of the second they lost even the rugged virtues that supported the first.

From the standpoint of both politics and urbanism, Rome remains a significant lesson of what to avoid: its history presents a series of classic danger signals to warn one when life is moving in the wrong direction. Wherever crowds gather in suffocating numbers, wherever rents rise steeply and housing conditions deteriorate, wherever a one-sided exploitation of distant territories removes the pressure to achieve balance and harmony nearer at hand, there the precedents of Roman building almost automatically revive, as they have come back today: the arena, the tall tenement, the mass contests and exhibitions, the football matches, the international beauty contests, the strip-tease made ubiquitous by advertisement, the constant titillation of the senses by sex, liquor, and violence—all in true Roman style. So, too, the multiplication of bathrooms and the over-expenditure on broadly paved motor roads, and above all, the massive collective concentration on glib ephemeralities of all kinds, performed with supreme technical audacity. These are symptoms of the end: magnifications of demoralized power, minifications of life. When these signs multiply, Necropolis is near, though not a stone has yet crumbled. For the barbarian has already captured the city from within. Come, hangman! Come, vulture!

CHAPTER NINE

Cloister and Community

1: THE HEAVENLY CITY

By the fifth century the life-blood was ebbing from the opened veins of Rome and the hands that had once grasped an empire could no longer keep any part of it securely in their hold. As the fingers relaxed, the parts fell away.

But the dying was a slow process, and in the midst of the urban decay fresh life was sprouting, like the seeds from garbage on a compost heap. The new religious vision that made this life possible gave a positive value to all the negations and defeats that the Romanized peoples had experienced: it converted physical illness into spiritual health, the pressure of starvation into the voluntary act of fasting, the loss of worldly goods into increased prospects for heavenly salvation. Even sin offered a path to salvation.

By renouncing all that the pagan world had coveted and striven for, the Christian took the first steps toward building up a new fabric out of the wreckage. Christian Rome found a new capital, the Heavenly City; and a new civic bond, the communion of the saints. Here was the invisible prototype of the new city.

Many reasons have been assigned for the triumph of Christianity; but the plainest of them is that the Christian expectation of radical evil—sin, pain, illness, weakness, and death—was closer to the realities of this disintegrating civilization than any creed based on the old images of "Life, Prosperity, and Health." The whole drama of life for the Christian derived from his method of encountering negations. Whereas in all the older civilizations, men had been freely sacrificed to their gods, with Christianity its god had taken human form and had accepted sacrifice in order to redeem sinful man and free him from the anxiety and guilt that issued forth from his condition.

Instead of evading the ugly realities of his time, the Christian embraced them. By doing willingly what pagans sedulously avoided, he both neutralized and in some measure overcame the forces that threatened him. He visited the sick; he comforted the widow and the orphan; he redeemed the ignominies of starvation, sickness, and squalor by making them an occasion for fellowship and love. Instead of clinging for security and comfort to the presence of large crowds, he accepted their dispersal and looked for solace in a more intimate union when only two or three were gathered together in the name of Christ: indeed, the holiest withdrew altogether, seeking solitude and silence.

All these inner transformations left their imprint, during the next thousand years, on the cities of Western Europe. But even before Rome fell, by the third century in fact, the Christian sect had begun to anticipate the worst; and their members, threatened with persecution and butchery, had begun to establish a new life for themselves in the caves that honeycomb the hills of Rome, where the Christians gave their fellow communicants a Christian burial, carving out subterranean chapels and altars, as well as tombstones. The new sense of fellowship first expressed in the Greek mystery religions now found a fuller expression.

Throughout the Empire Christianity had long been an underground movement: regarded officially, until A.D. 313, as a subversive activity. So it is no accident that in Trier and Metz it was in the old Roman walls and underground chambers of the circuses that the Christians first set up their chapels. In Metz, the first Christian Church stood inside the old amphitheater. Here was a new kind of ecclesia or assembly, for which neither the classic temple nor the Forum itself provided an appropriate urban form.

Not merely were the old Roman buildings spiritually detestable, with their pagan images and symbols: many of them became functionally worthless, like the theater, the arena, and bath, because they contradicted the whole Christian way of life. Only the old basilicas and temples, built to hold many people, were easily converted into shelters for Christian congregations: thus the temple of Antoninus and Faustina in Rome became the Church of St. Lorenzo, and the Senate House, the Church of St. Adriano; and by the fourteenth century A.D. nearly half of the thousand or more churches of Rome still indicated, by their name or their visible structure, their pagan origin. But the baths were no longer used as baths, nor the arenas as arenas. Their emptiness foretold their eventual dilapidation.

Rome certainly did not meet sudden death, nor did the cities of the empire quickly crumble away and become uninhabitable. The barbarian invasions had actually begun in the third century, and in a sense they went on, sporadically, for more than a thousand years. Even as late as the twentieth century, an Italian archaeologist would explain the difficulties of the Italian Army's fending off the Austrians and the Germans on the Piave by remembering that this was the opening through which the Goths and the Huns had poured long before. Actually, cities are like trees: once established, they must be destroyed to the roots before they cease to live: otherwise, even when the main stem is cut down, shoots will form about the base, as happened in Jerusalem even after its complete destruction in A.D. 70. What Lavedan calls the "law of the persistence of the plan" might even be widened into the "persistence of the individual urban archetype."

So with Rome and the cities it had colonized or governed: the population within them shrank; their activities became constricted; their lives were more and more subject to invasions they could no longer protect themselves against; the very highroads that had once brought them security and wealth now only made easier the path of barbarian conquest. With an invading army, a broken viaduct, a series of poor local crops, the remaining population would take to the hills. All this spelled the end of Roman urbanism, repeating the sad tale that Pausanias told when he visited the wasted and deserted regions of Greece whose cities had become broken shells. As urban life deteriorated for lack of manpower to keep up its usual routines, the old buildings would be ransacked for oddments of furniture and equipment, as a needy family, once wealthy, will pawn off its old possessions, one by one. But a hide-out in the country was worth a palace in town.

Within the city of Rome itself one could follow a change that was taking place everywhere. One of the first indications of the new medieval city was the transfer of the market, between the eighth and twelfth centuries, from the Forum to the more defensible Capitoline Hill. With the market went the municipal government itself, so that long before 1145, when it was almost entirely rebuilt, the latter was established on that steep hill. Yet old habits clung fast, too. As life became more insecure, the shopfronts would be bricked-in, too, for protection; but the older type, fully open to the street, and the new walled-in type were both carried into the Middle Ages in Italy, just as the fourteenth-century tenements of Florence preserved the form of the Roman insulae. Neither the Roman way of life nor the Roman forms altogether vanished, as Axel Boëthius has demonstrated. As late as the fifteenth century, the butchers were installed in the Forum of Nerva and under the lower arcades of the theater of Marcellus.

Over the first five hundred years, the changes in habits, custom, law were more conspicuous than those in the environing structures: the latter were marked, less by new buildings than by the invasion of grass and bushes, the crumbling of stones, the heaping up of rubbish, the soiling over of pavements. Doubtless the countryside showed the same effects even more rapidly than the cities. For if a cleared parcel of land at the English agricultural experiment station at Rothamsted could become a wilding forest in a century, the same return of pasture and woodland must have gone on throughout Western Europe, especially after the seventh century. By the eleventh century there was a serious problem of land clearance: the draining of fens, the cutting down of forests, the building of bridges, called for a new crop of pioneers. Here as elsewhere the disciplined monastic orders took the lead.

One lacks a clue to the new urban form if one overlooks the role of monasticism: it was a formative influence. For the most profound retreat from Rome was not that of the refugees who sought to save their bodies: it was above all a retreat of the devout who wished to save their souls. The great spirits who led this retreat were not unconscious of all the joys and virtues they were leaving behind: both Augustine and Jerome were honest enough to confess that, at least in sleep, they were allured and teased by sensuous images of Rome. But in the third century the retreat had passed into a collective stage: groups of hermits, sharing their solitude and developing a new routine of life, banded together, first on the edge of a great city like Alexandria, facing the desert, then far away, on rocky hilltops, like Monte Cassino or Mount Athos, or, later, on lofty Monte Senario near Florence (A.D. 1233), where the fragrant air of the pines is still sweeter than any incense.

The monastery was in fact a new kind of polis: an association, or rather, a close brotherhood of likeminded people, not coming together just for occasional ceremonies, but for permanent cohabitation, in an effort to achieve on earth a Christian life, addressed solely and singlemindedly to the service of God. Augustine, the Bishop of Hippo, founded such an order in the fourth century, and by the sixth, Benedict of Nursia gave it the form that was to influence, by direct impact or by indirect stimulus and challenge, every succeeding monastic order.

Here was the nodal point of a new kind of religious culture. This culture sought to transcend the limitations of earlier civilizations by withdrawing from their typical institutions: in principle it denied property, prestige, power. Those who accepted poverty as a form of life reduced the whole physical apparatus for bodily sustenance and ennobled work by making it a moral obligation.

The monastic colony became in fact the new citadel: a religious holding point that kept the general retreat from turning into a rout. But it was a citadel of the soul, and its palace was the Abbey Church. This parallel is not inexact. If it was in the royal palace that the secular instruments of urban civilization first took shape, it was in the monastery that the ideal purposes of the city were sorted out, kept alive, and eventually renewed.

It was here, too, that the practical value of restraint, order, regularity, honesty, inner discipline was established, before these qualities were passed over to the medieval town and post-medieval capitalism, in the form of inventions and business practices: the clock, the account book, the ordered day.

Whatever the confusions of the outer world, the monastery established, within its walls, a pool of order and serenity. No one doubted that the essential values of a Christian life were embodied there, though not all men were qualified to live at such a pitch of concentration and dedication: not even, as it turned out, the more prosperous monks themselves. So attractive were these manifestations of the Christian life that Joachim of Floris, in the twelfth century, looked forward to a final period of human development, the period of the Holy Ghost, when all mankind would be united, as monastic brethren and sisters, in the Monastery Universal. To Bernard of Clairvaux, in the same century, the cloister was a stronghold of paradise: he even coined the term *paradisus claustralis*.

The closest link between the classic city and the medieval city was that formed, then, not by the surviving buildings and customs, but by the monastery. It was in the monastery that the books of the classic literatures were transferred from crumbling papyrus to tough parchment; it was here that the Latin language was spoken in daily conversation, and escaped some of the diversification and mutual unintelligibility of Italian, Spanish, French, Roumanian, and their countless regional dialects and village variants; it was here, in the Benedictine Abbeys at least, that the advanced practices of Roman agriculture and Greek medicine were maintained, with a corresponding rise in productivity and health.

The secular Church was entangled in earthly responsibilities, at the mercy of worldly rulers, tempted to compromise with pagan beliefs and institutions, as in the cult of the Saints. Threatened with anarchy the Bishops were driven to exercise political authority and even to assume military leadership, when other powers failed. As municipal governors, the bishops united the offices of priest and ruler in ancient Roman fashion.

But the monasteries kept alive the image of the Heavenly City. As the new urban communities took form after the tenth century, the monastery made an even deeper imprint on their life at first than did the market. Here was the peace and order, the quietness and inwardness, beloved by Christian men. Westminster Abbey, the Abbeys of Clairvaux and St. Denis, Monte Cassino and Fulda exercised a command over urban life, even over its architectural forms, out of all proportion to their numbers. When Hrabanus, the famous Abbot of Fulda, referred to "the common life" as a characteristic of cities, he was transferring to the town the special office of the monastery. Actually the monastery, in its ideal form, was Aristotle's society of equals aiming at the best life possible. That common life was feasible in poverty, and even attractive. Would it be equally viable in prosperity?

2: NEED FOR PROTECTION

Before a new life could shape itself in the Middle Ages, it was necessary for the old life to disintegrate even further. But we must not picture this change as either sudden or uniform.

That life in general, throughout Europe, became more crude and chaotic, there is little doubt; and that the formative forces were no longer 'Roman' had been true, even before the empire disintegrated. At one moment, the ships bringing papyrus from Egypt would be cut off by pirates; at another, the postal service would go out of existence; or again, an old Roman patrician, on his way to becoming the most important civil officer in Rome, would disappear, and turn up after four years of silence in a Spanish monastery. Famine and disease reduced the population as a whole; probably the birth rate dropped—how much it is hard to say. Certainly, fewer people were left in the cities; and the old towns ceased to function as centers of production and trade.

Because of a wealth of literary evidence, we have a better picture of what went on in Gaul than elsewhere. And there is no doubt that the cities that managed to fortify themselves against the barbarians occupied a much smaller area than they had previously spread over. Bordeaux was reduced by its walls to a third of its previous size, and Autun, founded by Augustus, shrank from a town of five hundred acres to a village of twenty-five.

We have an even fuller picture of what happened from Nîmes and Arles, in Provence. In Nîmes the old amphitheater was transformed by the Visigoths into a little town, with two thousand inhabitants and two churches: after closing the entrances to the theater, the heavy masonry walls served as ramparts. And though the walls of Arles had been re-built by Theodoric, they were ruined again in the struggle between Charles Martel and the Arabs: after which the amphitheater at Arles, too, served as fortress, and a small medieval town grew up within it, more crowded than most, as a seventeenth-century print still shows us; for the buildings of this little settlement were not destroyed till the beginning of the nine-teenth century.

The new Christian culture that arose under these circumstances did not assume an urban form until the eleventh century. But the seeds of it were already planted in the church and the monastery; for the surviving architecture expresses the needs of this troubled age, with its emphasis upon enclosure, protection, security, durability, and continuity. Witness San Stefano Rotundo, Albi, Durham.

Yet between the sixth and eleventh centuries, when at last the cities of the West sprang to life and began to grow and multiply, there lies a 'Romanesque' period whose contradictory aspects need to be understood. The clouds driving over the landscape were dark and turbulent; but patches of light broke through them from time to time, as in the great monastic creativity of Ireland, particularly at Iona. But from the eighth century to the eleventh, the darkness thickened; and the early period of violence, paralysis, and terror worsened with the Saracen and the Viking invasions. Everyone sought security. When every chance might be a mischance, when every moment might be one's last moment, the need for protection dominated every other concern. Isolation no longer guaranteed safety. If the monastery had conducted the retreat, the city led the counter-attack.

Now in Italy and France the old ways never entirely disappeared, though they lapsed. Hence the pagan undercurrents in that life, under-currents so profound that the black and white Venuses known to the Roman world were later repeated in the black and white images of the Virgin Mary. What has been called the twelfth-century Renascence was rather the coming back into full consciousness of something that had never been completely displaced or forgotten. Did not John of Salisbury quote Plato centuries before the Platonists returned to Italy?

What is the twelfth-century Campo Santo at Pisa but a group of de-tached public buildings, standing within their own spacious precinct, more acropolis or forum than medieval marketplace. True, the architects, ac-cording to Vasari, derived some of their inspiration from the antiquities and sarcophagi that the Pisan fleet had brought home from the East. But this admiration for the ancient Roman work was no product of a later humanism: it was rather the piecing together of a living heritage that had, through unfortunate accidents, been deprived of its best local ex-amples. Does not the Baptistry itself derive partly from the Roman bath, a purified and etherialized bath for a ceremonial ablution; but equally noble in scale? Perhaps it is no accident that the Baptistry attains singular magnitude as a separate building chiefly in the land that originally pro-duced the secular Roman prototype.

But even where the old life remained, like some seemingly dead peren-nial, blackened by the winter frost, one cannot deny the general diminish-ment of energy and creativity. Life went down hill toward a subsistence level; for bodily security, no more, one was glad to place oneself under the protection of some barbarian chief; indeed, as the city disintegrated, its various original parts reappeared separately: so the old chieftain with his war band, in his fortified stronghold, ruling a nest of villages, comes back again. Urban developments that one can only speculate about with cautious reservations in Palestine and Mesopotamia can now be documented on the site all over Europe.

If the Saracen encirclement of the Mediterranean hastened the passage from the uniform imperial organization to an economy of local production and barter, with a crazy-quilt of local customs, local laws, conflicting jurisdictions, the final blow came from the other end of Europe in the invasions of the Norsemen in the ninth century. The final blow—and the first move toward recovery. These berserk raids were conducted in small boats that pierced to the heart of the countryside between Brittany and the Elbe; no district was immune to their sacking, burning, slaying. Apprehension over such forays may have created a new bond of interest between the feudal chieftain and his tributary peasants. But it also showed the technical inferiority of the scattered local war bands rallying on foot in opposing attacks carried out by swift-moving sea lords, specialized in war.

Sheer necessity led to the rediscovery of that ancient urban safeguard, the wall. Against sudden raids a wall, on guard at all hours, was more useful than any amount of military courage. The strength and security of a stronghold perched on a steep rock could be reproduced even in the lowlands, provided the inhabitants of a village built a masonry wall, or even a wooden palisade. We have surviving evidence of such wooden palisades from Poland, probably as early as the fifth century B.C., though whether this was mainly to keep in cattle and children or keep out marauding men may well be in doubt. But a heavy stone wall, particularly when surrounded by a moat, kept the attacker at bay.

In terror of the invaders, the inhabitants of Mainz, for example, at last restored their broken Roman walls. And under commissions from the German Emperor, Henry I, walls were built even around monasteries and nunneries to guard them from pagan attack. Twice in the ninth century, in 860 and 878, the monastery of St. Omer had been devastated by the Norsemen. But when these Vikings returned in 891, they found that the Abbey had at last erected walls and could defy them. So successful indeed was this renewed mode of achieving security that, by the tenth century, the monastery of St. Omer had become a town.

As early as 913 the 'Anglo-Saxon Chronicle' reports further that the building of fortresses and of walls around settlements was one of the chief activities of the King's army. Here is still further evidence, if any be needed, of the role of kings as city builders, through their ability to mobilize extra labor. But even as early as 885 the 'Chronicle' shows, Rochester was walled and successfully defended by its burghers; while a year later

King Alfred himself fortified the city of London. Military service became a necessity of citizenship, and it is even possible that the ability to provide a permanent army and to repair walls around a town was, as Frederick William Maitland suggests, one of the qualifications for corporate urban franchise.

The walled enclosure not merely gave protection from outside invasion: it had a new political function, for it proved a double-edged instrument. Reversing the ancient city's precedent, the wall could be used to maintain freedom within. By means of the wall, a little town, once helpless before even a small armed force, would become a stronghold. People would flock to such blessed islands of peace, as originally they had submitted in desperation to feudal gangleaders, becoming their vassals and serfs in return for a bit of land and security—or had given up all hopes of domestic felicity to find a sterile sanctuary in a monastery or a nunnery.

There was safety, once the wall was erected, in numbers. Life in the isolated countryside, even under the shadow of a nearby castle, now ceased to be as attractive as life in the populated town. Labor on the wall itself was a cheap price to pay for such security and regularity in trade and work. Though the right to build walls remained, significantly, a royal prerogative, the Peace of Constance, in 1184, yielded this right to the free cities of Italy.

Note the sequence. First the cowering countryside, with its local production and its mainly local barter. Only the abbeys and the royal estates would exchange their wine, their grain, their oil, over great distances. What trade came to a town from a distance was fitful and unreliable. But once a town was encircled by a wall, other normal attributes of urban life would appear: the container, re-established, became also a magnet. The extension of the wall from the castle or the abbey to the neighboring village often marked the physical beginning of a town, though the full legal privileges of an active municipal corporation could be obtained only by hard bargaining with the Bishop or the feudal proprietor who held the land.

The greatest economic privilege, that of holding a regular market once a week, assembling for exchange the neighboring peasants, fishermen, craftsmen, depended upon both physical security and legal sanctuary. So, as in ancient Greece, those who came to market were protected, during the marketing hours, by the Market Peace, now symbolized by the market cross of the marketplace. Here a new class got protection against theft and arbitrary tribute, and began to settle down permanently, at first just outside the walls: the merchants. When they became permanent members of the town corporation, a new era began, which helped reopen the old highways and waterways.

The fact that the merchants represented a new class can be deduced from their topographic position in the newly laid out 'suburb' just outside the walls. If at first the castle or the monastery was the town center, after the eleventh century the fresh activities of the community began to shift toward the marketplace, and the incorporation of merchants and crafts-men, as free citizens, would be marked in more than one place by the extension of the wall around their suburb. It is significant to note that, as Hegel points out, the *new* quarter in Regensburg in the eleventh century —as distinguished from the royal and clerical quarters—was that of the traders.

In the medieval town these powers, the spiritual and the temporal, with their vocational orders, the warrior, the merchant, the priest, the monk, the bard, the scholar, the craftsman and tradesman, achieved some-thing like an equilibrium. That balance remained delicate and uncertain; but the effort to maintain it was constant and the effect real, because each social component was weighted, each duly represented. Until the close of the Middle Ages—this indeed is one of the signs of the close—no one element was strong enough to establish permanently its own command over all the others. As a result, both physically and politically, the medie-val city, though it recapitulated many of the features of the earliest urban order, was in some respects an original creation. Freedom, corporate equality, democratic participation, autonomy, were never fully achieved in any medieval town; but there was perhaps a greater measure of these qualities there than had ever been exhibited before, even in Greece. For a brief while 'communitas' triumphed over 'dominium.'

The practice of granting freedom to cities from the eleventh to the fourteenth centuries was in fact a renunciation, on the part of the masters of the citadel, of the very tributes and exactions that originally had brought the city into existence. Though the castle often towered grimly above the city, always threatening to resume its original prerogatives, in the free cities feudal lordship took a place as just another semi-corporate entity: first among equals—though a few centuries later, through the growth of centralized absolutisms, princes regained the territory they had lost, and even greatly enlarged it. How complete the original renunciation might be, however, one discovers in the grant of freedom to Barcelona, wherein the king decreed that no toll-gatherer or tax-gatherer or any other official might impede or detain the movement of any citizens, their officials, or their messengers, or their goods, or their merchandise.

This urban movement, which arose out of the insecurity and disorder of romanesque Europe, had a chequered existence: it marched under various banners, issued out of different circumstances, and produced di-verse results.

Sometimes urbanization was deliberately promoted by feudal lords, seeking to increase their income by utilizing urban ground rents, taking a share of the tolls at the local market, making use of a big body of consumers to increase the value of the products of their own estates, not consumable on the premises. Often the demand by the towns for independence was opposed by the feudal proprietors: particularly by the Bishops, who were more formidable than war-chiefs because they were agents of a wide-flung institution, commanding both material and spiritual resources of an unusual kind. In some countries, as in England and France, municipal freedom was promoted by a temporary coalition with the central power, as a means of weakening the feudal nobles who challenged the king's dominion. But, opposed or helped, the population flowed into these protected centers, built and rebuilt them, and brought neglected parts of their life to a new pitch of activity and productiveness. In a few centuries, the cities of Europe recaptured much of the ground the disintegration of the Roman Empire had lost.

3: INCREASE OF POPULATION AND WEALTH

The revival of trade is often taken, even by excellent scholars like Pirenne, as the direct cause of the city building and civilizing activities that took place in the eleventh century. But before this could happen, a surplus of rural products and a surplus of population were necessary, to provide both goods for trade and customers to purchase them. If the merchants themselves had been the chief occupants of the new cities, they would have had to take in each other's washing.

As the barbarian populations of northern and central Europe became amenable to Christianity, lured more perhaps by its dazzling myths and superstitions than its insights into the human condition, the part played by the Church continued to increase. The protection offered by the Bishops rivalled that of the feudal counts, and the expansion of the Church's own economic power, as a land-holding proprietor, through purchase and pious bequests, gave her a position that even kings had to respect. In making the most of these conditions of distress and opportunity, the monastic orders served as pioneers: in fact, they led the whole urban advance, offering sanctuary to the refugees and hospitable shelter to the weary traveller, building bridges, establishing markets. At an early date, the nunnery of Gernrode in Germany was called *Kloster und Burg;* and many another convent served equally as a twofold place of refuge.

Happily, the holding of a regular market in a protected place worked to the advantage of the feudal lord or monastic proprietor. Considerably before the grand revival of trade in the eleventh century, one finds under Otto II (973-983) that permission was given to the widow Imma, who was founding a cloister in Kärnten, to provide a market and a mint, and to draw taxes therefrom: typical provisions in much later charters for new cities. In the time of Otto, Hegel further notes, most of the market privileges were granted to religious proprietors, rather than to temporal lords.

In Lombardy, where cities were already in existence, all the properties and appurtenances of the old municipalities with the rights of jurisdiction, were transferred automatically to the Bishopric, whose Bishop actually took over the old duties of municipal prefect. Such a grant was made at Modena in 892 and at Bergamo in 904. It was only with great reluctance that the Church, which had taken the lead in providing security and order, consented to transfer its municipal functions, in turn, to the guilds of merchants and craftsmen.

The market peace could not be broken without suffering heavy penalties. That peace had been recognized as essential to trade as early as Homer, indeed probably long before: and in countries under the royal aegis, a special market law, applying to fairs and markets, with a special court having jurisdiction over traders, came into existence. In England this was called the Court of Pie Powder—anglicized Norman for 'dusty feet.' Thus the various forms of security offered by religion, by jurisprudence, by standard economic practice, no less than by architectural engineering, united to assist in the foundation of medieval towns.

But note: the regular market, held once or sometimes twice a week, under the protection of Bishop or Abbot, was an instrument of local life, not of international trade. So it should be no surprise that as early as 833, when long-distance trade was mostly in abeyance, Lewis the Pious in Germany gave a monastery permission to erect a mint for a market already in existence. The revival of trade in the eleventh century, then, was not the critical event that laid the foundations of the new medieval type of city: as I have shown, many new urban foundations antedate that fact, and more evidence could be added. Commercial zeal was rather a symptom of a more inclusive revival that was taking place in Western civilization; and that was partly a mark of the new sense of security that the walled town itself had helped to bring into existence.

Though trade is one symptom of that revival, the political unification of Normany, Flanders, Aquitaine, and Brandenburg is another; the land reclamations and forest clearance of the monastic orders, such as the Cistercians (founded in 1098) is a third; and the immense building program that covered Europe with a "white robe of churches"—buildings are not articles of commerce—must count as a fourth. The over-emphasis of the role of the market as a generator of towns derives partly from the fact that historians have read present motives and incentives back into past situations; and partly it comes from their failure to distinguish the different roles of local, regional, and international markets. This whole development was misconstrued by Pirenne because he refused the title of city to an urban community that did not foster long-distance trade and harbor a large mercantile middle class—a quite arbitrary definition.

International markets have little effect upon the founding of towns. Great international fairs in the Middle Ages often took place at the time of a religious festival, when pilgrims from many parts of the country would flock to a holy shrine: it was the concourse of pilgrims that would draw travelling merchants temporarily to such a spot. But such fairs occurred, at most, only four times a year; and when the pilgrims went away, the merchants departed, too. Such international trade was too limited to keep a city going throughout a year: indeed, we know from the late example of Nizhni Novgorod that the city that mushroomed around the fair would be almost deserted the rest of the year. International trade did not produce medieval cities: but it promoted their growth, as at Venice, Genoa, Milan, Arras, Bruges, after they had been established for other purposes.

In general, the reason for the trader's secondary role should be plain: trade revival on capitalistic lines was confined to luxury wares, drawn from every part of Europe and even, after the Crusades, from the East. But the town itself was a place of exchange for local agricultural and handicraft production: so that even at a later period than the eleventh century, the merchants with their retainers accounted, according to Georg von Below, for only a small part of the town's population. However important commerce became, it was the producers in the medieval town that composed about four-fifths of the inhabitants, as compared with perhaps one-fifth or less in the present-day city.

Doubtless cities like Chartres, with its ten thousand inhabitants and its famous cathedral, offered facilities that attracted both pilgrims and traders, and thus gave it some of the status of an international fair. The extra profits made by this temporary invasion—as from a big convention or congress in a modern city—benefited the butchers, the bakers, the wine merchants, no less than the makers of sacred tunics; and this enabled these guilds, as von Simson reminds us, to provide the five great windows in the *chevet* that honor the Virgin.

The truth, then, lies in just the opposite interpretation to Pirenne's: it was the revival of the protected town that helped the reopening of the regional and international trade routes, and led to the trans-European circulation of surplus commodities, particularly those luxuries that could be sold at a high profit to the princes and magnates, or those articles in sufficiently short local supply to command good prices: fine wool from England, wine from the Rhine, spices and silks from the East, armor from Lombardy, saffron and quicksilver from Spain, leather from Pomerania, finished textiles from Flanders, not least religious icons and devotional objects from various art centers.

Cities formed the stepping-stones in this march of goods: from Byzantium to Venice, from Venice to Augsburg, and over the Rhine; and so, too, from Marseille and Bordeaux to Lyons and Paris, or from the Baltic towns like Dantzig and Stralsund down to the Mediterranean. The famous marzipan of Lübeck testifies by both its name (St. Mark's Bread) and its composition (almonds and rose water) to this relationship with Venice and the East. With this passage of goods, cities established first on a basis of local production grew in population and wealth; and the merchant population naturally grew with them.

Once the food supply was more plentiful, once urban settlements had become more secure, commerce served in still another way as a stimulus to growth: one must pay for foreign luxuries in money. As the demand for finery grew, and as more money was needed for the equipment of the feudal soldiery, particularly for the knights themselves in their expensive armor, the feudal lords had a special incentive to transform their rural holdings into urban areas which brought in a far larger cash return in rent. Urban rents may not have exclusively provided the funds for capitalist enterprise, but capitalist enterprise certainly stimulated the desire for urban rents. Such enterprise burgeoned after the Crusades, beginning at the end of the eleventh century, and roused an appetite for oriental luxuries, hitherto almost unknown in a largely manorial economy.

This need gave the feudal landlord an ambivalent attitude toward the city. As power ceased to be represented in his mind in purely military terms, he was tempted to part with a modicum of control over his individual tenants and dependents, in order to have their responsible collective contribution in the form of cash payments and urban rents: demands that the land-bound serf could not meet out of his poverty. That was an important secondary motive for the building of new towns and the granting of new privileges to the centers that were springing up, through sheer population growth, out of mere villages. The relative reluctance of the Bishops, on the other hand, to grant urban liberties may be explained as the result of their having an ample income without having to part with land or political control.

Early capitalism itself, however, proved a disruptive rather than an integrating force in the life of the medieval town. For capitalism precipitated the change from the old protective economy, based on function and status, aiming at security, moralized in some degree by religious precept and by a close sense of family ties and duties, to a new trading economy, based on individual enterprise, pricked by the desire for monetary gain. The economic history of the medieval town is largely a story of the transfer of power from a group of protected producers, earning a modest living, achieving a state of relative equality, to a small group of privileged wholesale merchants, the friends and rivals of princes, engaged in large scale transactions, often over long distances, for the sake of immense gains. With this transfer went the elevation of a new hierarchy, with rank and station based mainly on money, and the power money can command.

In turn, the attitude of protection and submission, which ideally characterized superior and inferior under the feudal regime, gave way to hostile expropriation on one side, with seething revolt and counter-challenge on the other: in short, the class war, in which no quarter was expected or given—precisely in the classic sense that would have gratified Karl Marx.

For a while, perhaps two or three centuries, the two orders mingled in the same towns, sometimes with grievous results on their economic life, as when in Flanders, in 1336, Louis de Nevers, out of loyalty to his French suzerain, ordered the arrest of the English representatives, and provoked a retaliation on the part of the English which ruined the textile trade that provided the count with his income. The action, furthermore, provoked an uprising of the guilds of Ghent, headed by Jacques Artevelde. But in the end, money everywhere prevailed, against both feudal and guild systems of protection. For money was capable of mobility, concentration, multiplication; power in other forms was fixed, hidebound, hard to assemble. Even the most powerful monarchs were held in an ever-tightening grip by the captains of finance.

This change from an economy of mutual protection to one of unilateral capitalist exploitation did not await, as Max Weber has unfortunately led many people to believe, the rise of sixteenth-century Protestantism: for Protestantism itself, on the contrary, had begun in the thirteenth century with the Waldensians—see 'The Condition of Man'—as a Christian protest *against* the new practices of capitalism. The capitalist economy was already well over the horizon when Chaucer wrote his wistful encomium on 'The Former Age,' when "ther lay no profit, ther was no richesse." By providing a nest in which the cuckoo bird of capitalism could lay her eggs, the walled town soon made it possible for her offspring to be crowded out by the boisterous newcomer it harbored.

Beneath the revival of industry and trade that took place between the eleventh and thirteenth centuries was a fact of more fundamental importance: the immense extension of arable land throughout Europe and the application to the land of more adequate methods of husbandry, including the systematic application of urban manure to the neighboring farmland.

In this respect, the concentration of an urban population may create a beneficent ecological pattern, providing soil renewal and crop improvement—if based on composting, not wasting. Wooded areas in Germany, a wilderness in the ninth century, gave way to plowland; the boggy Low Countries, which had supported only a handful of hardy fishermen, were transformed into one of the most productive soils in Europe. As early as 1150 the first polders, land reclaimed from marsh or sea by means of dykes, were created in Flanders. Free men, like the Friesian fishermen, voluntarily joined together in toil that had hitherto been done only under severe military compulsion and collective regimentation. Without the leadership of priest or king, with no other tools than the shovel, they built high dykes and great platforms of earth on which a whole town would stand. These feats of free labor served as prelude to the outburst of industrial energy that came to an almost explosive climax in the seventeenth century.

Agricultural irrigation was practiced in Milan as early as 1179; and near Rochefort du Gard in Provence, a whole lake was drained by the monks, to be turned into great vineyards. Along with this went the better breeding of horses, the invention of an improved harness and the use of iron horseshoes, the spread of water mills and wind mills. These improvements endowed the new urban communities with relatively vast sources of power and gave them an economic edge over the less favored countryside. Further mechanical inventions not merely transformed mining and metallurgy, and made glassmaking one of the leading arts: they likewise removed the need for servile labor, and provided a much greater surplus of power and goods than a slave economy could create under the lash of starvation. On that rising tide of effort, commerce, which had run aground during the romanesque period, floated once more and spread sails.

Here again, as Bertrand Gille has pointed out, the contribution of the monastery was a vital one. Just because the monks sought to do away with unnecessary labor, in order to have more time for study, meditation, and prayer, they took the lead in introducing mechanical sources of power and in inventing labor-saving devices. Cistercian regulations favored building monasteries near rivers that could supply water power; and how largely this counted can be seen in a description of Clairvaux Abbey, in Migne, at the time of Saint Bernard.

"The river enters the abbey as much as the well acting as a check allows. It gushes first into the corn-mill, where it is very actively employed in grinding the grain under the weight of the wheels and in shaking the fine sieve which separates flour from bran. Thence it flows into the next building, and fills the boiler in which it is heated to prepare beer for the monks' drinking, should the vine's fruitfulness not reward the vintner's labour. But the river has not yet finished its work, for it is now drawn into the fulling-machines following the corn-mill. In the mill it has prepared the brothers' food and its duty is now to serve in making their clothing. . . . Thus it raises and alternately lowers the heavy hammers and mallets . . . of the fulling-machines. . . . Now the river enters the tannery where it devotes much care and labour to preparing the necessary materials for the monks' footwear; then it divides into many small branches and, in its busy course, passes through various departments, seeking everywhere for those who require its services for any purpose whatsoever, whether for cooking, rotating, crushing, watering, washing, or grinding. . . . At last, to earn full thanks and to leave nothing undone, it carries away the refuse and leaves all clean."

This mechanical equipment was not unusual in monasteries; but it took time and capital to introduce it even in a more disjointed fashion into the medieval town. What the monastery might already boast by the eleventh century, the town could do only in the thirteenth and fourteenth centuries.

In the course of three centuries, the Europe we know today was opened or re-opened for settlement. This feat compares exactly with the opening of the North American continent between the seventeenth and twentieth centuries. One may, indeed, regard the American conquest as a continuation of the original process of settlement on a new soil, for the colonization of New England, at all events, was on medieval urban lines, as that of Cavalier Virginia and Dutch New York was on an even older feudal pattern of a manorial economy, with slaves and indentured servants (temporary serfs).

This extension of the agricultural base, this increase in physical power, were what in turn made possible the increase of population. According to Prosper Boissonade's estimate, the region between the Rhine and the Moselle increased its population tenfold between the tenth and thirteenth centuries. The English counties, which had numbered 1,200,000 souls in 1086—an exact figure supplied by the 'Domesday Book'—reached a total of 2,355,000 toward 1340. Everywhere, if the birth rate was not higher, the number of people who survived and lived long enough to reproduce was certainly greater.

This increase was not confined to the newly opened territories in the North. Italy had made such progress in its agricultural economy as to number at least 10,000,000 souls by the fourteenth century. Better established on its ancient base, closer to the higher civilizations of the East, Italy was the natural leader in the urban revival. In the thirteenth century, Venice was a highly organized municipality; at that time Venice and Milan each had probably over 100,000 people. Though most of these population figures are rough and untrustworthy, there is little doubt about the direction of the population curve, up to the Black Plague in the fourteenth century.

The Germanic cities, with perhaps the exception of the old Roman border town of Vienna, averaged a much lower population. But there was no lack of energy in the German colonization movement, or in the process of urbanization. For in the course of four centuries, 2,500 cities were founded; and the municipal framework then laid out lasted substantially until the nineteenth century: the original outlines of the territory often remained unaltered, though in the meanwhile the town had filled up its normal agricultural belt.

During the peak years of the movement, not merely did the number of cities multiply, but the rate of population growth, as far as it can be estimated, was roughly comparable with that of the nineteenth century in Europe. At the end of the twelfth century, for example, Paris had about 100,000 inhabitants; and at the end of the thirteenth, something like 240,000. In 1280, Florence had 45,000 inhabitants, and in 1339, around 90,000; while in the Low Countries, Bruges and Ghent showed comparable figures. The statistics on the increase of urban occupation by area are just as impressive. As for the twenty-year spread of the Black Death, which sometimes killed off half the population of a town, it caused only a temporary recession.

Trade, industrial production, mechanization, organization, capital accumulation—all these activities helped the building and extension of cities. But these institutions do not account for the feeding of the hungry mouths, nor yet for the high sense of physical vitality that accompanied this whole effort. People do not live on air, even though "city air makes people free," as the German saying went. The thriving life of these towns was rooted in the agricultural improvement of the countryside: it is nothing less than a cockney illusion to separate the town's prosperity from the land's.

Even though the relation of urban merchant families to the peasants who rented their land outside might remain suspicious and one-sided, not to say mutually hostile—the 'Chronicles of a Florentine Family' offer testimony on this score—the relationship was close and constant. The terraced vineyards, the trim fields protected by windbreaks, the traffic of fruit and vegetables to the city, the carting out and composting of refuse and dung, including the woolen wastes of Florence—all this gave the city, even an overgrown city like Florence, a stake in the countryside. This was so close, in some Italian cities, that each neighborhood would 'adopt' a particular village that lay outside as its own rural province.

In smaller towns, as we know from the marvelous urban atlases of the sixteenth and seventeenth centuries—Blaeu, Merian, Speed—the agri-

cultural improvements and rural charms of the countryside were transported into the heart of the city: witness the internal gardens, the cultivated
open spaces, and even the common fields, within or just without the walls.
The typical medieval city, excluding the few overgrown metropolises of
Italy, which were far from typical, was not merely in the country but of
the country; and as in ancient Mesopotamia, some food was grown, if
only to ward off starvation under siege, within the walls.

Indeed, agriculture and rural pursuits like fowling and fishing formed
a part of the daily life of the city. As late as the fourteenth century in
England, the urban burghers were required by law without distinction of
class to assist at harvest time in the gathering of the crops. The summer
exodus of the East Londoners to the hopyards of Kent is perhaps the last
survival of that medieval custom. Many small centers in France and
Switzerland, arrested in their growth long ago, still show these open
spaces, never built upon, and still used as gardens, as in that charming
little town on Lake Leman, Nyon. Even in crowded towns like Paris,
where high rents resulted in the continued covering over of the original
open spaces, the convents and monasteries and the hotels of the aristocracy
preserved large areas of garden and orchard.

4: CHARTERED TOWNS, COLONIAL
STRONGHOLDS

If the new or renewed methods of military protection—the wall and the
citizen army—ensured fresh popularity for cities as places for residence
and socially protected work, a special set of economic motives nevertheless
existed, which accounts for the headway this movement made. The liberation of towns was a step toward the efficient ordering of economic life: the
replacement of barter by money exchange, and of life service by urban
piecework or seasonal hire. In short, to use Sir Henry Maine's old distinction, from status to contract.

The eighteenth-century myth of the social contract was a rationalization of the political basis of the medieval town, whose survival in Geneva,
Citizen Jean-Jacques Rousseau knew, and whose independence and self-
respect he valued. For the corporate town was often in fact based upon
a social contract between the landed proprietor and the settlers or inhabitants: it came as a result of a bargain, for value given and received on
both sides, not primarily as the result of military conquest, as in the most

ancient examples. This, if I am not mistaken, was another new fact in urban history. Corporateness itself, as F. W. Maitland observed, "came with urban life."

The cities movement, from the tenth century on, is a tale of old urban settlements becoming more or less self-governing cities, and of new settlements being made under the auspices of the feudal lord, endowed with privileges and rights that served to attract permanent groups of crafts-men and merchants. The city charter, bestowed on both types of city, was a social contract; the free city had legal as well as military security, and to live in a corporate town for a year and a day removed the obliga-tions of serfdom. Hence the medieval city became a selective environ-ment, gathering to itself the more skilled, the more adventurous, the more upstanding—probably therefore the more intelligent—part of the rural population. Citizenship itself, free association, replaced the ancient ties of blood and soil, of family and feudal allegiance. The specialized voca-tional group now supplemented, in a new set of relationships and duties, the primary family and neighborhood groups: all had a place in the new city.

Political interest in the medieval period usually centers on the struggle for power between the urban bourgeoisie and its overlords, the counts, the bishops, the kings. This tends to neglect the part that feudalism itself took in encouraging the growth of cities. Many of the conflicts in the old centers came from attempts to drive a hard bargain with the new citizens, rather than from absolute resistance to granting any privileges whatever. For new towns were founded on a great scale throughout Europe, par-ticularly on the borderlands, by the great proprietors. Though many a village, achieving prematurely the legal status of town, never grew suffi-ciently to justify the title, what is even more surprising is the number of towns that started from scratch. J. M. Houston, in a paper on the Scottish Burgh, notes that the evidence does not show a gradual evolution from agricultural communities to towns: the charters of Ayr, Dumbarton, the Cannongate, and St. Andrew imply that the privileges of burghers were conditional on settlement on the land within the burgh. This was a sort of urban plantation system. Again the city was "un fait du prince." Many of the new towns were frontier posts, as in Gascony, Wales, Pomerania: and they resembled in their mode of occupation much later foundations in America, in that they enabled people discontented with conditions in the more settled parts of Europe to make a clean break and a fresh start.

On the political side, I shall quote Thomas Frederick Tout, whose study of medieval town planning was a landmark in English in this field. "The political necessity for town making arose earlier than the economic need. In the humble beginnings of the new towns of the Middle Ages, military considerations were always paramount. A strong ruler conquered a district adjacent to his old dominions, or wished to defend his frontier against a neighboring enemy. He built rude fortresses, and encouraged his subjects to live in them, so that they might undertake the responsibility for their permanent defense."

In a sense, these towns—as in the Roman military colonies—were a cheap substitute for a standing army. By giving the new burgher a right to bear arms, the ruler avoided the necessity for otherwise paying for their use. Since the serf, after all, had a permanent claim to the land he was tied to, it needed some extra bait to move him two or three hundred miles away. For the first time he had bargaining power, and the proprietor was forced to meet the demands of the prospective settler half way. In general, membership in the corporate urban community, even in such an insignificant little town as Lorris in France (which got no general right of self-government), meant freedom from forced payments and from feudal military service, as well as freedom to sell one's possessions and go elsewhere. Citizenship gave its possessor mobility of person. Need I emphasize how indispensable this was for the rise of a trading class, as well as for craftsmen, perfecting their art by working as journeymen under different masters in other cities?

By fighting, by bargaining, by outright purchase, or by some combination of these means the towns won the right to hold a regular market, the right to be subject to a special market law, the right to coin money and establish weights and measures, the right of citizens to be tried in their local courts, under their local laws and ordinances, and not least, as before noted, the right to bear arms. These powers, which had once been pre-empted by the citadel, now belonged to the city, and each citizen bore a responsibility for exercising them.

Probably the citizen's right of bearing arms did far more to curtail the power of the feudal nobility than the invention of gunpowder: did not the burghers of Flanders defeat the flower of French chivalry in open battle, without benefit of gunpowder? One finds the last echo of that special note in urban freedom, in the Constitutional provision in the United States that the citizen's right to bear arms shall not be abridged, though it is in democratic Switzerland, with its sturdier municipal tradition, that this right is still substantiated by the practice of giving to each member of the army reserve, on return home, his gun and his equipment. As for the charter itself, it led to the legal fiction, still piously preserved, that the town itself is a creature of the state and exists by sufferance. In plain fact the historic cities of Europe today are all older than the state that legally claims these rights, and had an independent existence before their right to exist was recognized!

All of these rights might or might not lead to complete local autonomy, free from any sort of interference, as in the great Hansa towns of Hamburg, Bremen, and Lübeck, which proudly functioned as free cities up to the time of Bismarck. But at all events they endowed the local community with most of the marks of what is now called a sovereign state; and by the same token they passed on eventually to the larger national entities that swallowed them, the provincialities, the jealousies, the bellicosities that marked the walled town.

When a feudal lord desired money to equip an army, join the Crusades, or indulge the new luxuries that seeped into Europe, he had one main economic source of wealth: his land. Under feudal custom, he might not alienate the land or sell it off; but by dividing it up, by encouraging the growth of old towns through grants of autonomy, and by founding new centers, he could increase his annual rents. Even though, with the customary long leases, rents might rise slowly for the original proprietor, his heirs would nevertheless in the course of time benefit from the unearned increment of the city's growth and prosperity. One must not forget that even in London, down to the present day, a few feudal proprietors, the Duke of Bedford, the Duke of Westminster, and the Crown, have held title to the most heavily exploited areas. In Germanic law, land was placed in a special category that set it apart from building and personal property; and once land itself became an object of commerce, to be bought and sold like any other commodity, the medieval town, as a corporate institution, was doomed.

Almost as important as the rent of the land itself in urban centers were special sources of urban income in which the proprietor of the land had a share: tolls at the bridges and the local market, customs imposts and fines from the court, all of which multiplied as the town itself increased in population. Some of these old dues lasted in Europe—like the tax on incoming carts and vehicles—right into the twentieth century, even in metropolitan Paris. Originally, in a pioneer town, it might be necessary to remit taxes to the newcomer provided he built a house: tax exemption to promote housing is a very old dodge.

As with all speculative enterprises, some towns might more than justify their landlord's hopes; and others, like many of the fortified towns (bastides) in southern France, might remain economically as well as socially torpid. Aigues Mortes, the once busy embarkation port for the Crusades, lingers on only as a museum piece. But town building itself was one of the major industrial enterprises of the early Middle Ages.

Now we can perhaps understand feudalism's ambivalent attitude toward this movement. The free city was a new source of wealth; but the challenging self-confidence and independence of the people who rallied to the Commune was a threat to the entire feudal regime. The town concentrated manpower and economic power and weapons of defense: its citizen armies, far more than the serfs who only served their master, had something to fight for—the freedom they had earned, the homes they had built, the town they had helped to create. While the battlefield and the tournament and the chase were the focal points of feudal life, the town offered economic and cultural resources that even the greatest castle could not afford. In Italy the opportunities for civil life attracted the nobles and smaller landowners to the town: if they did not take up urban residence willingly, they sometimes did so under municipal compulsion, so that the burghers could keep an eye on them. But in northern Europe this class for long held aloof, clinging to the bear hunt and the "brittling of the deer," the open-air life, and the smoky manorial hall, remaining themselves more akin to the peasants they oppressed than to the townsmen they had freed.

Even in Italy, the gap between these two aspects of the environment widened. As urban occupations, by their very success, drove farther afield the rural ones the city had still harbored, the antagonism between town and country sharpened. For the city was an exclusive society, based on voluntary association for a common purpose. Every townsman, in relation to the countryfolk born to the land, was something of a snob with such snobbery as only the upstart and the *nouveau riche* achieve. This fact was eventually to contribute to the undoing of urban freedom and self-government. By excluding the countryside from its privileges, the town found itself, from the sixteenth century on, confronted by an economic competitor, whose very lack of protection and regulation invited new economic enterprise and a disorderly kind of urban development.

5: DOMINANCE OF THE CHURCH

The ideas and institutions of medieval civilization concern us here only as they affected the structure of cities and the development of the organs of their cultural life. But unless one understands these ideas, the preponderance of great civic structures devoted to religious offices must remain unexplained.

In Western Europe, after the fall of the Roman Empire, the one powerful and universal association was the Church. Membership in that association was theoretically voluntary and practically obligatory. To be cut off from its communion was so great a punishment that, until the sixteenth century, even kings trembled before the threat of excommunication. From the smallest village with its parish church to the greatest city with its Cathedral, its many churches, its monasteries and shrines, the Church

was visibly present in every community: its spires were the first object
the traveller saw on the horizon and its cross was the last symbol held
before the eyes of the dying.

In a culture marked by bewildering diversities of dialect, law, cuisine,
weights and measures, coinage, the Church offered a common home, indeed a universal haven: the same credo, the same offices, the same masses,
performed with the same gestures, in the same order, for the same purpose, from one end of Europe to another. Never did strict Roman uniformity better serve mankind than during this period. In the most
important offices of life the meanest village stood on the level of a
metropolis. The Church Universal gave all communities, big and small, a
common purpose; but the unity so achieved fostered rather than suppressed their diversity and individuality.

The fundamental political divisions of society, underlying all other ties
and allegiances, were the parish and the diocese: no abstract areas marked
on a map, but each having, as its center, a common habitation for worship, and an appointed spiritual authority who represented the Pope. In
England, according to G. G. Coulton, there was one parish church to
every hundred families, and there were many villages and towns where
much fewer than a hundred families had a church. The universal form
of taxation was the tithe, a tenth of the annual income, which went to
the support of the great establishment of Rome, partly for upkeep, partly
for extensive investment.

Naturally the resident officers of the church, apart from those in
monasteries, formed no small part of the community. In 1314 the little
town of Cirencester in England numbered 105 acolytes, 140 sub-deacons,
133 deacons, and 85 priests, some 463 in all. A good share of the economic activities of the community was devoted to the support of the clergy
and of those who waited on the clergy, while, similarly, a large portion of
its capital, diverted from other possible enterprises by the Church, went
into the construction and maintenance of ecclesiastical buildings—cathedrals, churches, monasteries, hospitals, almshouses, schools, with all their
rich furnishing of statues and icons and paintings.

The main business of this community was not trade, however eagerly
the merchants might, as individuals, be concerned in amassing a fortune:
its main business was the worship and glorification of God, and at the
point of death, if not in the midst of his proud, grasping, crafty, domineer-
ing life, both merchant and lord would remember that obligation in disposing of his property.

The Church itself was a many-sided institution; and the Church
building performed many functions that were later separated and assigned
to specialized secular institutions. But even at its humblest level in the
city parish the church was a neighborhood center, a focus of the daily

community life; and no neighborhood was so poor that it lacked such a church, even though at the center of the town there might be a vast cathedral big enough to enclose all its citizens on solemn or festive occasions.

By itself, the local church might often be a "museum of Christian faith," as well as a house of worship. The presence of a saintly hermit, walled up in his cell near its doors, or even the bones and relics of such a saint, would be an attraction to the pious: all the more if it had a reputation for possessing miraculous powers. Churches and monasteries that possessed such relics became the goal of pilgrimage: the bones of Thomas à Becket at Canterbury, the blood of Saint Januarius at Naples, these things drew men to cities, no less than the possibility of political freedom or profitable trade.

In a very definite sense, despite its manifold origins and its ambivalent results, the medieval city in Europe may be described as a collective structure whose main purpose was the living of a Christian life. That purpose even colored institutions that, like war, were in flagrant contradiction to the Christian spirit, and it curbed other practices, like usury, which could only be resorted to by subterfuge, and with a bad conscience. But above all, the Christian conception of life with its affirmation of suffering and its readiness to give succour, brought into existence agencies for which there is no evidence in earlier urban civilizations.

Hospitals, for the general care of the sick and ailing, were now provided on a remarkable scale. The sanatorium was no longer a health resort set apart from the city and catering mainly to those who could afford to travel, but a place in the heart of the city, near at hand, open to all who needed it, under the care of men and women willing to undertake all the repulsive offices demanded by sickness, wounds, and surgical operations. Both the hospital and the isolation ward were direct contributions of the monastery; and with them came a more general kind of hospitality for the healthy, in need of overnight rest and food. Through all the centuries when inns and hotels were lacking, when private lodging was meager and wretched, the monastic hospice provided decent free accommodation.

The provision of almshouses was likewise a medieval municipal institution, for the care of the poor and the destitute was an obligation of Christian charity, and not the least handsome buildings in the late medieval city were in fact the almshouses—though their existence shows that poverty kept pace with increasing wealth. Finally, for the first time again, institutions for the care of the aged flourished in the late medieval city: sometimes, as in Bruges, Amsterdam, Augsburg, forming little neighborhood units, with their common gardens and their chapel: pools of civic comeliness to this very day.

At no point were these urban institutions separated from the Church; but at no point was the Church itself separated or separable from the community, since it was out of both compulsory and voluntary contributions, drawn from the whole community, that the necessary structures were built. All that the territorial state now seeks to do on a wholesale scale was first done, in a more intimate way, often probably with more feeling for the human occasion, in the medieval town.

In the sixteenth century, one further institution joined these earlier ones, mainly the concern of a later monastic order, the Jesuits: this was the foundling asylum. No earlier type of town had ever made such provisions for the unfortunate, or had translated individual acts of succour into such handsome public buildings. With Hrabanus (ninth century), one might describe the medieval city as a union of Church and community in pursuit of the Holy Life. Even when it miserably fell short of the Christian ideal, this union nevertheless had produced both institutions and buildings designed to further it.

Though the Church was everywhere in its ministrations, the most important civic effect of its otherworldly concerns was, by habit if not by conscious intention, the fact that it universalized the monastery. The practice of abstention and prayerful withdrawal, the spirit of enfolding and protection, left its imprint on the whole structure of the medieval town. As long as the medieval complex was intact, a constant stream of disillusioned worldly men and women turned from the marketplace and the battlefield to seek the quiet contemplative round of the monastery and the convent. Even when the preaching orders brought the spirit of the cloister into the heart of the city, seeking actively to convert the urban sinner and to succour the needy by the daily example of their poverty and their humility, this 'return,' too, soon took the old form and settled down in handsome buildings. Thus the new freedom brought a rural spaciousness into the heart of the city at the moment when the pressure of population in the more active trade centers was eating up the open spaces behind the private houses. The walled gardens of the new friaries sweetened the air of the most crowded town.

Daily concentration on the inner life had its compensatory effects: the vulgar daylight perceptions were illumined by the impassioned hallucinations of dream; the figures on the inner eye were as real as those that fell peripherally upon the retina. And though Protestantism in the sixteenth century brought in a distrust of the wanton eye, it preserved for private use the habits of the cloister: repeated prayer and inner communion, in a private 'closet.'

In the past half century architecture has turned from enclosure to exposure: a virtual replacement of the wall by the window. Even in the dwelling house, as Henry James was quick to note on his visit to the United States in 1905, all sense of intimacy and privacy was being forfeited by throwing one room into another, to create a kind of exposed public space for every moment and for every function. This movement has perhaps now reached the natural terminus of every such arbitrary interpretation of human needs. In opening our buildings to the untempered glare of daylight and the outdoors, we have forgotten, at our peril and to our loss, the coordinate need for contrast, for quiet, for darkness, for privacy, for an inner retreat.

This lesson needs application to the plans of cities not less than to buildings. The cloister, in both its public and its private form, has a constant function in the life of men in cities; and it was not the least contribution of the medieval city to demonstrate that fact. Without formal opportunities for isolation and contemplation, opportunities that require enclosed space, free from prying eyes and extraneous distractions, even the most extroverted life must eventually suffer. The home without such cells is but a barracks; the city that does not possess them is only a camp. In the medieval city the spirit had organized shelters and accepted forms of escape from worldly importunity in chapel or convent; one might withdraw for an hour or withdraw for a month. Today, the degradation of the inner life is symbolized by the fact that the only place sacred from intrusion is the private toilet.

6: SERVICE OF THE GUILD

While the Universal Church was concerned with the individual soul, the medieval community was based on classes and ranks, within a limited and local order, feudal or municipal. The unattached individual during the Middle Ages was one condemned either to excommunication or to exile: close to death. To exist one had to belong to an association—a household, manor, monastery, or guild. There was no security except through group protection and no freedom that did not recognize the constant obligations of a corporate life. One lived and died in the identifiable style of one's class and one's corporation.

Outside the Church, the most widespread representative of the corporate life was the guild: the two bases for fellowship, common work and a common faith, were united in the medieval town. When one first encounters the guild in England in Anglo-Saxon times (before 892), it is primarily a religious fraternity under the patronage of a saint, meeting for brotherly comfort and cheer, insuring its members against the dire accidents of life, and providing a decent burial. It thus incorporated features strikingly like those of its predecessor, if not its lineal ancestor, the

Roman funerary college, and at many removes it passed on those features to similar recent institutions, the English Friendly Society and the Order of Freemasons, or the American Elks and Odd Fellows; with their mingling of sociability and insurance.

The guild never lost this religious color. It remained a convivial brotherhood, adapted to specific economic tasks and trade responsibilities, but not wholly engrossed in them. In many towns the *conjuratio,* the oath to stand by each other for mutual succour, was an essential element of association. (No wonder Kropotkin drew so heavily on the medieval town for examples of Mutual Aid.) The brothers ate and drank together on regular occasions; they formulated ordinances for the conduct of their craft; they planned and paid for and enacted their mystery plays, for the edification of their fellow townsmen. In periods of prosperity they built chapels, endowed chantries, founded grammar schools—the first lay schools since the end of antiquity—and at the height of their power built guild halls, not seldom as magnificent as the Cloth Hall of Ypres. With their craft as a center, they fabricated a whole life, in friendly rivalry with other guilds; and as brothers, they manned the walls adjacent to their quarter, to meet the enemy.

Such unions and brotherhoods had existed, we have seen, among urban craftsmen of the Roman Empire, indeed even earlier in third-century Greece; and they lingered on in Byzantium. Though the connections remain obscure for lack of written documents, we know that the memory of a remote event, Alexander's spectacular conquests, remained alive in popular myth among the illiterate during the long Romanesque inter-regnum; and the idea, even the example, of such craft brotherhoods may not have quite vanished. The fact that the earliest German example of guild organization, the royal charters of Worms (897-904), mention transport workers as members, would point to a connection with the older Roman guilds. Apart from this, the first guilds of which there are records in Germany, besides burial associations, are those of the weavers of Mainz, in 1099, while even earlier Pavia boasted a guild by 1010, and St. Omer in France, a guild by 1050.

If the growth of the merchant guild in general anticipated by half a century or so the growth of the craft guilds, it must be remembered that, except in international trade, the line between craftsman and merchant was not closely drawn; for the craftsman who made goods to order might also sell his surplus. During the early period, craftsmen, according to Charles Gross, were admitted to merchant guilds and probably constituted the majority of members; just as later members of the feudal order, or scholars who wished to enter the government of the city, had to become a member of a guild like the apothecaries or the painters, in order to hold office.

The merchant guild was a general body, organizing and controlling the economic life of the town as a whole: regulating conditions of sale, protecting the consumer from extortion and the honest craftsman from unfair compe ition, protecting the traders of the town from the disorganization of their market by outside influences. The craft guild, on the other hand, was an association of masters working up their own products banded together to regulate production and establish standards of fine workmanship. In time, each of these institutions found its expression in the city: the first in the Town Hall or Market Hall, the second in the Guild Hall, sometimes built by a single guild, as in Venice's numerous small halls, sometimes a great edifice built by joint effort. Probably the early guild buildings were modest houses or rented rooms, long since destroyed, as it was with the ancient colleges, of which we have some record. But those that have been preserved often vie in their magnificence with the town hall or the cathedral. W. J. Ashley notes that the cost of these buildings was "one of the circumstances which led to and seemed to justify the demand for heavy entrance fees"; this in turn led to the restriction of the membership to the more wealthy members of the community. Not the first or the last time in which the pomp of a great architectural shell has destroyed the creature who burdened himself with its creation. . . .

The large function played by the guild in the medieval city up to the fifteenth century indicates a general elevation of the status of work, particularly manual work, and this again was largely one of the great achievements of the Church, partly in giving status to the occupations of the poor and the lowly, but even more, in the Benedictine order, in accepting manual toil as an essential component of a good life: "to labor is to pray." The shame of labor, that grievous heritage of servile cultures, gradually disappeared; and the frequent prowess of these urban guildsmen in war confounded the pretensions of the feudal classes, who despised all forms of toil, except those of the hunt and the battlefield. A city that could boast that the majority of its members were free citizens, working side by side on a parity, without an underlayer of slaves, was, I repeat, a new fact in urban history. With this went an application of intelligence to technical processes on a scale that no slave systems had ever encouraged. Medieval precept and practice had thus supplied the essential condition whose absence wrecked the restricted, slave-supported 'democratic' polity of Greece.

Note the difference, further, between the medieval community and the modern city. In industry, since the eighteenth century, it is the organization of the economic process that has taken definite corporate form in the factory, the business corporation, the chain store, the co-operative organization. Political associations, such as Chambers of Commerce, Manufacturers' Associations, and Trade Unions for long had no integral part in the economic organization: they sprang up on the outskirts belatedly, included only a part of the population concerned, and in no case, not even that of the trade union, did they pretend to cover any large part of the cultural life of their members.

In the medieval town, the actual organization of industry was simple and direct, between master and journeyman in the workshop, seller and buyer in the marketplace. But the primary fact was association. In fulfillment of its social purposes, the Guild became, through self-help, a health and old-age insurance society, a dramatic group, and an educational foundation. It is only during the last half century, in an effort to provide economic security, that many trade unions have begun to recapture some of the social interests and facilities of the medieval guild. Unfortunately, the same principle of protection, applied by the management of big industries to their works, providing theaters, sports fields, bowling alleys, medical clinics, now likewise threatens to introduce a new kind of commercial feudalism. Under this regime the tie to the factory, or at least to the great financial enterprise that runs it, becomes almost as binding as the serf's tie to his land—if only so that the invisibly chained worker may reap its benefits in old-age benefits. However difficult it was for laissez faire economists in the nineteenth century to understand the principles of guild society, there should be no psychological obstacle to our understanding them today.

Once the economic motive isolated itself and became the all-engrossing end of the guild's activities, the institution decayed: a patriciate of wealthy masters rose within it to hand on their privileges to their sons, and by requiring large entrance fees, to work to the exclusion and disadvantage of the poorer craftsman and the growing proletariat. By the time the religious dissensions of the sixteenth century broke up the brotherhood itself in Northern Europe, its co-operative economic nature had already been undermined: the fat people once more were battening upon the lean people.

If the guild in fact rose with the medieval city, by the same token it fell with it: the guilds were only the city in its economic aspect as the city was the guilds in their social and political aspect. Both the physical shell itself and the practices of the guild lingered on, hardly altered, until the eighteenth century, whose "enlightenment" was so largely devoted to their demolition. Even in the New World, the Carpenters' Company of Philadelphia operated as a medieval guild, along with many other such survivals, and medieval regulations of the market lingered everywhere, in some degree, till the end of that century. The use of the word medieval as a term of obloquy, for that which is barbarous and ignorant, was a coinage of the eighteenth century. People who are backward in their history often continue to interpret the Middle Ages in terms of that defamatory eighteenth-century stereotype.

The center of the municipality's activities was the Town Hall, which sometimes also served as Market Hall. In the beginning, the town hall was a free-standing building in the marketplace, usually of two stories, containing two halls, that on the lower floor being originally used for the finer wares which needed protection from the weather not afforded by booths that lined the marketplace itself. Often, as in the market hall still standing in Milan, the structure would be supported on columns that left the ground floor entirely open, an example of building 'en pilotis' for a sensible reason, centuries before Le Corbusier used it as a sort of vulgar trade mark for modern form, whether functionally needed or not.

The builders of the Middle Ages usually kept more practical matters firmly in mind: one of the great markets in Bruges, the commercial center of the north before the fifteenth century, was the Wasserhalle, so-called because it spanned a canal and brought the cargoes by barge directly into the market *from beneath*. The upper room of the town hall would be used for the meeting of the mayor and the council, for the administration of justice, for the reception of ambassadors, and for periodic feasts and drinking bouts. The remains of the latter, incidentally, linger on in modern London, along with the ghosts of the old Livery Companies, in the famous feast at the Guildhall that follows the annual election of the new Lord Mayor, and the pageantry of the Lord Mayor's parade.

In the town hall, too, toward the close of the Middle Ages, the leading families, drawn chiefly from the wealthier circle of the wholesale merchants, might—to the envy of the rest of the population—hold their dances and routs. In fact, it became a sort of collective palace for the patriciate: hence it was often called a "theatrum" or playhouse. Here marriages could be celebrated with due pomp. This provision has survived, with genuflections toward democracy, down to the present day. Note the acknowledgement of the older regime in the two special marriage chambers, first and second class, in the Hilversum Town Hall in Holland. Thomas Mann, in 'Buddenbrooks,' has given us a last faltering glimpse of that patrician burgher life.

By membership in the municipality one escaped direct feudal dues: one assumed burgher responsibilities. Not merely was military service imposed on males who were not officers of the Church, but the police forces of the town were originally selected by rotation from among the burghers: the duty of Watch and Ward. Night watches for cities and boroughs were decreed by Henry III in 1253; and Stow records two kinds of watch in Queen Elizabeth's day: a "standing watch" for serious duties, and a "marching watch" for celebrations. Modern communities have imposed such service only for war or for some sudden disaster; but the medieval city carried it into daily routines. And it is a serious question whether the leaving of such functions of protection completely in the hands of a professional police has not both weakened responsibility and done away with an effective means of civic education.

As late as 1693, by an act of the Common Council of London, provision was made that more than one thousand watchers should be constantly on duty in the City of London from sunset to sunrise, and that every inhabitant should take part. To maintain such a corps, one must inculcate a high sense of civic duty, and constantly replenish it by special examples of devotion and special awards: lacking these, the act lapsed in the eighteenth century. But the fire fighters and the ambulance workers who performed such heroic services in London—and in many other cities —during the Second World War were only resuming an ancient medieval liberty. Many of them have personally testified that the fellowship promoted by that duty more than made up for the harrowing experiences they underwent: so that they count those nights among their finest memories.

Here, as in most other departments, there existed a great difference between conditions in the tenth or eleventh century, still bare, constricted, precarious, and those in the sixteenth century, when wealth had poured into the more prosperous European towns. At the beginning the city was striving, as a new social unit, to establish its very existence: the constant insecurity promoted neighborly effort, even a general solidarity between the various ranks and occupations. They needed each other, and voluntary groups of neighbors formed spontaneously under that pressure, much as they form today in a New England village where the fire service and the hospital ambulance are still staffed by volunteers.

When the privileges had been won, great disparities in riches appeared between the 'successful' and the 'unsuccessful'; then wealth as well as station was inherited, and in turn created a new status, no less formidable because somewhat 'etherialized,' based on manners, breeding, accent. Then the invisible ha-ha between the classes, caused by an abrupt drop in the level, became more important than either the common concerns or the protective barrier that had once made the medieval city an organic social unit.

At the close of the Middle Ages, wealthy individuals began to endow schools, build asylums for the aged and the orphaned, taking over functions once performed by the guild, precisely as the new despots were taking over for the country as a whole the political privileges and regulations of the free cities, turning urban particularism into a national particularism and mercantilism. But when one attempts to generalize the period as a whole, one may still echo Gross, deeply though he was imbued with a Victorian distrust of the closed corporation and the protective policies of the guild, which put security above risk-taking and profit-making: "Exclusive of the inhabitants of the privileged *sokes* the . . . population was more homogeneous than that of towns existing at present; there were in the former fewer class distinctions, more equality of wealth, and more harmony of interests than in the latter."

As the words of one who was no admirer of the medieval economic system, this judgment carries double weight. And one may say all this without forgetting many dismal exceptions, like the servile state of the Flemish weavers in the thirteenth century, or the savage revolts that ensued, countered by savage repressions and exterminations inflicted by the ruling classes. Yes: violence and torture found a home within these walls, no less than security: some of the mutilated creatures in Breughel the Elder's paintings may have been the victims of the law, not merely of war or nature, as they would have been in ancient Babylon. But voluntary association and effort, voluntary aid and succour, had produced a political habit that would go far to challenge this savagery at a later day —though we know from the wholesale revival of torture and extermination in our own generation that this victory is never, or at least not yet, a permanent one.

The social activities of the medieval town did not shrink as the new capitalistic economy grew up: they rather shifted from self-help to alms-giving and foundational philanthropy, and finally, by necessity, to state aid. Outside the Church, one institution survived from the old guilds and even increased its power and influence: perhaps the most important single new institution produced by the medieval culture. With an instinctive recognition of its importance, the name of this institution was originally the common term for all guilds in the twelfth century: *universitas*.

The *universitas* became *the* guild. Like other forms of craft association, the aim of the university was to prepare for the practice of a vocation and to regulate the conditions under which its members performed their work. The new learning, Greek and Arabic medicine from Salerno, the new-formed corpus of Latin law, even the challenge to theology offered by Averroës, Avicenna, and above all, Aristotle, needed a new civic organ. Each of the great schools that originally formed the university, jurisprudence, medicine, and theology, was professional in character: though they had a system of general studies, their humanism lay in their life rather than in their specialized studies of ancient literature; indeed, the general 'humanistic' education that began to come in with the renascence college, particularly in England, was an upper-class graft on the original tree. To this day, it is the professional schools that help to differentiate the university from the college.

Beginning with Bologna in 1100, Paris in 1150, Cambridge in 1229, and Salamanca in 1243—though there were informal beginnings elsewhere in the cathedral schools of the twelfth century—the university laid down a co-operative organization of knowledge on an inter-regional basis. Scholars flocked to these centers from every part of Europe; and in turn, the masters studied and taught at distant centers, as they had done earlier in monastic and cathedral schools. The combination of sacred knowledge, scientific knowledge, and political knowledge, which the university offered in its faculties, had no exact parallel in any other culture.

Doubtless, the germs of the university had been latent in the Egyptian and Babylonian temples, as they were more plainly visible in Plato's academy and in the Library-School at Alexandria, or in the lecture system of the Roman municipalities. But in the university, the pursuit of knowledge was elevated into an enduring structure, which did not depend for its continuance upon any single group of priests, scholars, or texts. The system of knowledge was more important than the thing known. In the university, the functions of cultural storage, dissemination and interchange, and creative addition—perhaps the three most essential functions of the city—were adequately performed. And as the cloister and library of the monastery might be called a passive university, so the university might be termed an active cloister; for it made explicit, in its own right, as a secular function, one of the necessary activities of the city: the withdrawal from immediate practical responsibilities and the critical reappraisal and renewal of the cultural heritage, through the direct intercourse of master and student. In the original layout of the colleges in Oxford and Cambridge, medieval planning made its most original contributions to civic design: the superblock and the urban precinct divorced from the ancient network of alleys and streets.

Here was a social invention of the first order: for this alone the medieval corporation would stand out. The very independence of the university from the standards of the market and the city fostered the special sort of authority is exercised: the sanction of verifiable truth, ratified by the methods of logic and dialectic, authoritative scholarship, and scientific method, as these in turn have developed and accumulated from period to period. The vices of such an organization may be many; and its services during the intervening centuries have not been of uniform value, for the university shares to this day some of the exclusiveness and the professional conservatism of the guild system. Too often the major contributions to knowledge, from Newton to Einstein, from Gilbert to Faraday, have been made outside the university's walls. Nevertheless, the enlargement and transmission of the intellectual heritage would have been inconceivable, on the scale actually achieved since the thirteenth century, without the agency of the university. As the Church ceased to be the repository of new values, the university gradually took over some of this office. This fact has placed a premium upon the detached pursuit of truth, as the dominating life-value, and has ignored in large degree the realms of esthetics and morals. Thus the university has become a classic example of that over-specialization and limitation of function which now curbs human development and threatens even human survival.

7: PILGRIMAGE, PROCESSION, AND PAGEANT

In the new freedom of movement that sprang up with the corporate liberties claimed by the medieval town itself, life expressed itself as a pilgrimage: a lonely pilgrimage for Dante through Hell, Purgatory, and Heaven; a companionable pilgrimage for Chaucer en route to the shrine at Canterbury. Even in the very dregs of the medieval period, life is still seen under the image of a 'Pilgrim's Progress.'

Whatever the practical needs of the medieval town, it was above all things, in its busy turbulent life, a stage for the ceremonies of the Church. Therein lay its drama and its ideal consummation. Just as in the late industrial age, the imagination showed itself on the highest level in a railroad station or a bridge, in medieval culture practical achievement reached its peak, by an opposite movement, in the service of a great symbol of salvation. Men who had little to eat gave part of that little to say prayers and masses, light candles, and build a mighty fabric, in which legend, allegory, dogma, and knowledge crystallized in nave and altar, in screen and wall painting, in porch and rose window. On isolated occasions of great religious exaltation, such as Henry Adams described in 'Mont-Saint-Michel and Chartres,' they might even carry the very stones that were needed to the site, rich and poor alike.

No sedentary student, viewing this architecture in pictures, no superficial observer, taking up a position and attempting to plot out axes and formal relationships, is in a state to penetrate this urban setting even in its purely esthetic aspect. For the key to the visible city lies in the moving pageant or the procession: above all, in the great religious procession that winds about the streets and places before it finally debouches into the church or the cathedral for the great ceremony itself. Here is no static architecture. The masses suddenly expand and vanish, as one approaches them or draws away; a dozen paces may alter the relation of the foreground and background, or the lower and upper range of the line of vision. The profiles of the buildings, with their steep gables, their sharp roof lines, their pinnacles, their towers, their traceries, ripple and flow, break and solidify, rise and fall, with no less vitality than the structures themselves. As in a fine piece of sculpture, the outlines are often inexhaustible in their variety.

Within the general medieval pattern, deep changes in feeling took place across five centuries. Radically different life-experiences separate the confident sobriety of the great romanesque buildings, as solid as fortresses, as solemn as plain chant, from the humanism of the magnificent Lady Churches, audacious and lightheartedly experimental, where the walled tomb that symbolized acceptance of death turned into a heavenly lantern with its promise of resurrection; while the over-blown estheticism of the fifteenth and sixteenth centuries, with its riotous embroidery of ornament, tells still another story, of waning faith and waxing concern with the fripperies of daily life, or with overcompensating mortifications, such as Johan Huizinga recounts.

But through all these changes, the setting itself maintained its collective structure: it incorporated successive moments of the spirit without losing form. The towers of the churches and campaniles raised the eyes to heaven; their masses rose, in hierarchic rank, over all the lesser symbols of earthly wealth and power, indisputably the first, and through their rose windows the light burst in aureoles of pure color formed in abstract patterns. From almost any part of the city, the admonitory fingers of the spires, archangelic swords, tipped with gold, were visible: if hidden for a moment, they would suddenly appear as the roofs parted, with the force of a blast of trumpets. What had once been confined within the monastery's walls, was now visible within the whole medieval town.

The short approaches to the great buildings, the blocked vistas, increase the effect of verticality: one looks, not to right or left over a wide panorama, but skyward. This ambulatory enclosure was such an organic part of the processional movement and of the relation of the structures to each other that it did not need the extra emphasis the perpendicular Gothic of England actually gave it. Horizontal banks of windows were common in houses and horizontal string courses, boldly emphasized, break the vertical movement of the towers in Salisbury or Notre Dame de Paris, not less than in the Duomo in Florence. But, for all that, the usual movement of the eye is up and down, and the direction of the walker's movement, always changing, would constantly help to create dynamic, three-dimensional spatial forms through every farther passage, with a feeling of constriction in the narrow streets and of release as one suddenly came out into the parvis or the market place. Though the architectural details are so different in Lübeck, with its gables and pinnacles, and in Florence, with its low pitched or flat roofs and its wide overhangs, the total esthetic effect, produced by the plan of the town itself, is of the same order.

Those who walked about the city on their daily business, who marched in a guild pageant or in a martial parade or who joined in a religious procession, underwent these esthetic experiences, and, in the very twisting and turning of the procession could, as it were, see themselves in advance, as in a mirror, by observing the other parts of the procession: thus participant and spectator were one, as they can never be in a formal parade on a straight street.

Let us look at a medieval procession through the eyes of a late contemporary, who left behind a detailed picture of the occasion. Outside the pages of Stow, I know no description that gives one a more living sense of the medieval town. The time is early sixteenth century: the place is Antwerp: the witness is Albrecht Dürer.

"On Sunday after Our Dear Lady's Assumption, I saw the Great Procession from the Church of Our Lady at Antwerp, when the whole town of every craft and rank was assembled, each dressed in his best according to his rank. And all ranks and guilds had their signs, by which they might be known. In the intervals, great costly pole-candles were borne, and three long old Frankish trumpets of silver. There were also in the German fashion many pipers and drummers. All the instruments were loudly and noisily blown and beaten.

"I saw the Procession pass along the street, the people being arranged in rows, each man some distance from his neighbor, but the rows close behind the other. There were the Goldsmiths, the Painters, the Masons, the Broderers, the Sculptors, the Joiners, the Carpenters, the Sailors, the Fishermen, the Butchers, the Leatherers, the Clothmakers, the Bakers, the Tailors, the Cordwainers—indeed, workmen of all kinds, and many craftsmen and dealers who work for their livelihood. Likewise the shopkeepers and merchants and their assistants of all kinds were there. After these came the shooters with guns, bows, and crossbows, and the horsemen and foot-soldiers also. Then followed the watch of the Lord Magistrates. Then came a fine troop all in red, nobly and splendidly clad. Before them, however, went all the religious orders and the members of some foundations, very devoutly, all in their different robes.

"A very large company of widows also took part in the procession. They support themselves with their own hands and observe a special rule. They were all dressed from head to foot in white linen garments made expressly for the occasion, very sorrowful to see. Among them I saw some very stately persons. Last of all came the Chapter of Our Lady's Church, with all their clergy, scholars, and treasurers. Twenty persons bore the image of the Virgin Mary with the Lord Jesus, adorned in the costliest manner, to the honor of the Lord God.

"In this procession very many delightful things were shown, most splendidly got up. Wagons were drawn along with masques upon ships and other structures. Behind them came the Company of the Prophets in their order, and scenes from the New Testament, such as the Annunciation, the Three Holy Kings riding on great camels, and on other rare beasts, very well arranged. . . . From the beginning to end, the Procession lasted more than two hours before it was gone past our house."

Note the vast number of people arrayed in this procession. As in the church itself, the spectators were also communicants and participants: they engaged in the spectacle, watching it from within, not just from without: or rather, feeling it from within, acting in unison, not dismembered beings, reduced to a single specialized role. Prayer, mass, pageant, life-ceremony, baptism, marriage, or funeral—the city itself was stage for these separate scenes of the drama, and the citizen himself, even while acting his varied roles, was still a whole man, made one by the cosmic vision and held in tension by the human drama of the Church, imitating the divine drama of its founder. Once the unity of this social order was broken, everything about it was set in confusion: the great Church itself became a contentious, power-seeking sect, and the city became a battleground for conflicting cultures, dissonant ways of life.

CHAPTER TEN

Medieval Urban Housekeeping

1: THE DOMESTIC SCENE

In most aspects of medieval life, the closed corporation prevailed. But compared to modern life, the medieval urban family was a very open unit; for it included, as part of the normal household, not only relatives by blood but a group of industrial workers as well as domestics whose relation was that of secondary members of the family. This held for all classes, for young men from the upper classes got their knowledge of the world by serving as waiting men in a noble family: what they observed and overheard at mealtime was part of their education. Apprentices, and sometimes journeymen, lived as members of the master craftsman's family. If marriage was perhaps deferred longer for men than today, the advantages of home life were not entirely lacking even for the bachelor.

The workshop was a family; likewise the merchant's counting house. The members ate together at the same table, worked in the same rooms, slept in the same or common hall, converted at night into dormitories, joined in the family prayers, participated in the common amusements. Chastity and virginity were still the ideal states, as Saint Paul had proclaimed them, but the reader of Boccaccio or Chaucer will not exaggerate their prevalence. The guild itself was a sort of patriarchal family, which kept order in its own household, fining and penalizing smaller offenses against the brotherhood quite apart from the municipality. Even the prostitutes formed guilds: indeed, in Hamburg, Vienna, and Augsburg the brothels were under municipal protection. When one remembers that syphilis did not make its definite appearance, at least in virulent form, until the fifteenth century, even prostitution constituted a smaller threat to bodily health than it did in the following centuries.

The intimate union of domesticity and labor, surviving now in the city only in petty shops or in the household of an occasional painter, architect, or physician, dictated the major arrangements within the medieval dwelling house itself. Naturally, between the rude huts and bare stone enclosures of the tenth century and the elaborate merchant houses that were built from the eleventh to the sixteenth centuries, there was a difference as great as that between a seventeenth-century dwelling and a metropolitan apartment house today. Let us attempt, nevertheless, to single out certain common factors in this development. Some of them left a permanent imprint, down to the twentieth century.

Houses—only two or three stories high at the beginning—were usually built in continuous rows around the perimeter of their rear gardens; sometimes in large blocks they formed inner courts, with a private green, reached through a single gateway on the street. Freestanding houses, unduly exposed to the elements, wasteful of the land on each side, harder to heat, were relatively scarce; even farmhouses would be part of a solid block that included the stables, barns, granaries. The materials for the houses came out of the local soil, and they varied with the region, now wattle and daub, now stone or brick, now with thatched roofs (which were fire hazards), now with tile or slate. Continuous row houses forming the closed perimeter of a block, with guarded access on the ground floor, served as a domestic wall: a genuine protection against felonious entry in troubled times.

The earliest houses would have small window openings, with shutters to keep out the weather; then later, permanent windows of oiled cloth, paper, eventually glass. In the fifteenth century glass, hitherto so costly it was used only for public buildings, became more frequent, at first only in the upper part of the window. In the sixteenth-century painting of the Annunciation, by Joos van Cleve (Metropolitan Museum), one sees a double window, divided into three panels: the uppermost panel, fixed, is of diamond-paned glass; the next two panels have shutters that open inward; thus the amount of exposure to sunlight and air could be controlled, yet on inclement days, both sets of shutters could be closed, without altogether shutting out light. On any consideration of hygiene and ventilation this type of window, which was common in the Low Countries, was superior to the all-glass window that succeeded it, since glass excludes the bactericidal ultraviolet rays. Even more definitely, it was superior to the sealed glass wall which current architectural fashion has lately foisted on a supposedly enlightened age, in defiance of every scientific precept of hygiene or physiology.

By the sixteenth century glass had become cheap and widely available; so the popular saying in England about Hardwick Hall—"more glass than wall"—was equally true of the burgher houses. But strangely enough, in England ventilation was often inadequate. Did not Erasmus of Rotterdam suggest in a letter to Wolsey's physician that English health might be better if bedrooms had windows on two or three sides?

In the North Sea area a broad bank of windows would extend across the whole house at each story, front and rear, thus making up in effect for the tendency to deepen the house. But in the southern parts of Europe, the oppressive summer heat put a brake on this development, for all but the living room areas. Though medieval interiors, accordingly, were often subdued in lighting, if not dark, by our standards, their builders acted boldly to achieve light when they needed it: the old houses of the weavers, in Sudbury, England, have extra-large windows on the upper story, to give light to the loom; and when not enough light was available by that means, the workers would move outdoors, as the ancient lacemakers of Bruges still do, sitting by their doorsteps.

Heating arrangements steadily improved. This fact partly accounts for the outburst of human energy in the north; winter gradually ceased to be a period of stupefied hibernation. The open hearth in the middle of a stone floor, scarcely as effective as the arrangements in an Indian tepee, gave way to the fireplace and the chimney. Fireproofing went along with this development, for originally, lacking proper materials, the poorer burghers were tempted to experiment with wooden chimneys: an unduly optimistic practice repeated in the early settlements of New England and Virginia. In 1276 Lübeck passed an ordinance enforcing the use of fire-proof roofing and the fireproof party wall; and in London, after the severe fire in 1189, special privileges were given to people building in stone and tile; while in 1212 thatched roofs were ordered to be whitewashed, the better to resist fire.

As for the plan of the house, it varied with the region and the century; yet certain features remained common. Viollet-le-Duc has shown us the ground plan of a French house, with a shop on the ground floor, con-nected by an open gallery with the kitchen in the rear. The two formed a court, where the well occupied a corner. There was a chimney in the kitchen and in the living room, or *grande salle,* above the shop; from the latter there was access to the dormitories above. Moritz Heyne's plan of an old house in Nürnberg is not essentially different; but, as in the sur-viving houses of the seventeenth century, there are more interior rooms, a kitchen and a smaller room on the ground floor, a heatable room above the kitchen, and a number of chambers, with a toilet on the second floor directly above that on the first.

In Italy, a desire to be comfortable in summer, perhaps combined with an innate love of grandeur or a Roman sense of scale, raised the ceiling above any reasonable height, in Genoa or Florence, from the six-teenth century on; but the buildings that have survived from the thirteenth century, like Dante's dwelling, indicate more modest dimensions, better suited to year-round living. In the development of the house, rising man-made temperatures go along with an expansion of interior space and a raising of the ceilings, but heating rarely caught up with winter cold in Italy. The 'brutalist' scale of so many sixteenth and seventeenth century palaces was as brutal to the body as to the eye. The low-ceilinged serv-ants' floors must have been more comfortable, at least in winter, than the drafty masters' quarters.

The only form of modern hallway was the open gallery or the narrow, usually winding, stairs. The gallery was a common feature in dwelling houses, and it survives in the design of ancient inns, where a means of circulation was specially necessary, and the internal hall, because of the absence of artificial light, was not an attractive solution—until the whole inner court could be covered by a skylight, as in some nineteenth-century mansions and hotels. The main outlines of this type of house lasted right down through the seventeenth century, even later.

As one went downward in the economic scale, arrangements would be less differentiated and the space more constricted. The one-room apart-ment for a whole family in a multiple story dwelling, still common among the poor in many countries, possibly had its origin in the more industrial-ized cities of the later Middle Ages: even in the countryside, where there was no scarcity of land, Coulton records a family house for three people twenty-four feet long and only eleven feet wide. Both in city and country, the lack of space itself sprang from sheer poverty.

The fact that the burgher house served as workshop, store, and counting house prevented any municipal zoning between these functions. The competition for space between the domestic and the working quarters, as business grew and the scale of production expanded, was doubtless responsible for encroachment over the original back gardens by sheds, storage bins, and special workshops. But there is still a brewery in Bruges which now occupies almost one whole side of the Walplaats, built on the same scale as the residence alongside it: the loading is done in the courtyard behind. Here the storehouse, sheds, and garage have ample space—but are still on a medieval scale. Except where the industry was small and noisy, when it was often put at the edge of the town or outside the walls, this intimate connection of industrial and domestic life long remained normal: the exact antithesis of the segregated, legally sterilized residential quarter of today.

Mass production and the concentration of looms in great sheds was indeed known in Flanders in the fourteenth century, and operations like milling, glass-making, and iron-making required a more isolated type of workshop, sometimes surrounded by related workshops, as with fulling, dyeing, weaving, and shrinking. In these industries came the earliest break between domestic life and work, both in space and function. But at first the family pattern dominated industry, just as it dominated the organization of the Benedictine monastery. Survivals of this regime lingered on in every historic European city: the habit of 'living in,' long retained by London drapers, with the men and the women divided into dormitories, was a typical holdover from the Middle Ages.

In the disposition and the specialization of rooms in the Middle Ages, the ways of the aristocracy filtered down but slowly to the rest of the population. Comforts that were enjoyed by lords and ladies alone in the thirteenth century did not become popular privileges until the seventeenth century. One might see in this another instance of the "law of cultural seepage": the making of innovations by a favored minority and their slow infiltration over the centuries into the lower economic ranks. The first radical change, which was to alter the form of the medieval house, was the development of a sense of privacy. This meant, in effect, withdrawal at will from the common life and the common interests of one's fellows. Privacy in sleep; privacy in eating; privacy in religious and social ritual; finally, privacy in thought. This came about with a general clarification and separation of functions that even extended, by the seventeenth century, in France, to cookery.

In the castles of the thirteenth century, one notes the existence of a private bedroom for the noble owners; and one also finds, not far from it, perched over the moat, a private toilet: the first hint of the nineteenth-century luxury of a private toilet for every family, or the extravagant American demand for a private toilet for every bedroom. In 1362 Langland, in 'Piers Plowman,' chided the tendency of the Lord and Lady to withdraw from the common hall for private meals and for private entertainment. He must have foreseen the end of that reciprocal social relation between the stationary upper and lower ranks of the feudal regime: a relation that had mitigated its oppressions, since they shared the same quarters. The desire for privacy marked the beginning of that new alignment of classes which was to usher in the merciless class competition and individual self-assertion of a later day: for once consciences become tender, it is easier to practice inhumanity upon those you do not see.

The separation of the kitchen from the dining room is not characteristic, probably, of the majority of the houses in any country today: indeed, in America, thanks to the absence of domestic servants, the visual and functional union of these two parts is rapidly being restored. Such a separation had taken place in the monastery because of the scale of the preparations, and it was copied eventually in the manorial hall, the college, and the fine town house. But the common quarters offered this incentive to social living: they alone were usually heated. That the medieval house was cold in winter, hardly less in the south than in the north, perhaps accounts for the development of inner rooms, insulated from the outer walls by air, as it surely does for the development of the alcove for the bed, or of curtaining around the bed, to make the enclosed heat of the bodies warm the stale air.

Yet the cold could not have been unendurable, or else people would have worn nightdresses or kept on a shift, instead of "going to their naked bed," as numberless illustrations depict them. Privacy in bed came first in Italy among the upper classes: witness Carpaccio's 'Vision of St. Ursula,' in a bedroom one would still find adequate and charming today. But the desire for it seems to have developed almost as slowly as the means. Michelangelo, on occasion, slept with his workmen, four to a bed. As late as the seventeenth century, maidservants often slept in trundle beds (rolled under the big bed by day) at the foot of that of their master and mistress, while three centuries earlier, Thomas Hoccleve refers in a poem to an earl, a countess, their governess, and their daughter all sleeping in the same room.

Until the curtained bed was invented, sexual intercourse must have taken place for the most part under cover, and whether the bed was curtained or not, in darkness. Privacy in bed preceded the private bedroom; for even in seventeenth-century engravings of upper-middle-class life—and in France, a country of reputed refinement—the bed still often occupies a part of the living room. Under these circumstances, the erotic ritual must have been short and almost secretive, with little preliminary stirring through eye or voice or free movement. But sex had its open seasons, no doubt, especially spring; for the late medieval astrological calendars, which depict this awakening, show the lovers having intercourse in the open with their clothes on. In short, erotic passion was more attractive in the garden and the wood or under a hedge, despite stubble or insects, than it was in the house, on a mattress whose stale straw or down was never quite free from musty dampness or fleas.

For lovers in the medieval house, the winter months must have been a large wet blanket. But as against this somewhat unfavorable interpretation, one must, in honesty, quote the contrary judgment of the medieval poet François Villon:

> They boast of sleeping near the woodland tree.
> Doth not a chair-flanked bedstead better please?
> What say you? Does it need a longer plea?
> No treasure is like living at our ease.

To sum up the medieval dwelling, one may say that it was characterized by a general absence of functionally differentiated space. In the cities, however, this lack of internal specialization was offset by a completer development of domestic functions in public institutions. Though the house might lack a private bake-oven, there was a public one in the nearby baker's or the cook shop. Though it might lack a private bath-room, there was a municipal bath-house in the neighborhood. Though it might lack facilities for isolating and nursing a diseased member, there were numerous public hospitals: so that Thomas More, in his Utopia, could even conceive that in his ideal commonwealth people would prefer to be looked after in such an institution. And though lovers might lack a private bedroom, they could "lie between the acres of the rye," just out-side the city's walls—with a hey! and a ho! and a hey-nonny-no!

Plainly, the medieval house had scarcely an inkling of two important domestic requirements of the present day: privacy and comfort. And the tendency in the late Middle Ages to deepen the narrow house under the pressure of congestion progressively deprived those who stayed most steadily indoors, the mother, the domestics, the young children, of the necessary air and light which country dwellers in much cruder hovels could have.

Mark this paradox of prosperity. As long as conditions were rude—when people lived in the open, pissed freely in the garden or the street, bought and sold outdoors, opened their shutters and let in full sunlight—the biological defects of medieval housing were far less serious than they were later under a more refined regime. As for its virtues, the house by day was no sexual isolation ward: women had an intimate part in all family and business concerns, and woman's constant presence, if some-times distracting, probably had a humanizing influence on the working life: an influence raised to ideal heights in the thirteenth-century cult of the Virgin.

With motherhood itself valued and elevated, child care improved. It was no lack of concern for children that made the infant mortality records of the medieval period so black, so far as we may estimate them. The cradle, the hobby horse, and even the toddler, for the child who had not yet learned to walk, are depicted in sixteenth-century prints. These cherubs were treated with love: it was for a children's home in the Piazza SS. Annunziata in Florence that Andrea della Robbia did some of his most charming ceramic sculptures.

But the domestic environment, under the pressure of crowding and high rents at the end of the Middle Ages, became increasingly defective; and such diseases as are spread through either contact or respiration must have had a maximum opportunity for sweeping through the family in the late medieval house. The urban dwelling was, indeed, the weakest link in medieval sanitary arrangements, once the natural open spaces were pushed farther away with the growth of the town, and the inner ones got built over. In other respects, the standards were far more adequate than most Victorian commentators—and those who still echo their prejudices and blandly repeat their errors—believed.

2: AIR, SPACE, SANITATION

So much for domesticity: but what of the larger economy of the town? I shall begin with the field in which error and bias have been rife for more than two centuries: that of medieval sanitation.

As with every other characterization of the medieval town, sanitation is a difficult subject to handle on account of the wide variety that exists, not merely between countries, but between municipalities within a day's walk of each other. There are not merely marked differences between towns themselves during the same period, but in the same town at different periods. In addition, we must remember that practices that are quite innocuous in a small population surrounded by plenty of open land become filthy when the same number of people crowd together on a single street. Witness Cambridge where, according to Coulton, a pile of dung was allowed to accumulate in the public ways, carted away only at weekly intervals. Perhaps it was no accident that a parliament sitting in Cambridge in 1388 passed the first urban sanitary law in England.

In all probability, the early medieval village or town enjoyed healthier conditions, for all the crudeness of sanitary accommodation inside and outside the house, than its more prosperous sixteenth-century successor. Not merely was the town behind the walls sufficiently small to have quick access to the open land; but a good part of the population had private gardens behind their houses and practiced rural occupations within the city, just as they did in the typical American small town up to 1890, and still do in many places.

In addition, the burghers would have their own orchards and vineyards in the suburbs: and they would keep cows or sheep in the common fields, under the care of a municipal herdsman, even getting some of their wood supply from the town forest. Near the town, the fowler and the rabbit hunter could go after game. William Fitz Stephen noted that the citizens of London had the right of hunting in nearby Middlesex, Hertfordshire, the Chiltern Hundreds, and part of Kent: Epping Forest long remained a favorite haunt for them. And in the streams near the city, fishing was diligently pursued: Augsburg, for example, was noted for its trout, and until 1643 many of the city officials took their pay in trout.

This strong rural influence can be marked on the early city plans: the typical medieval town was nearer to what we should now call a village or a country town than to a crowded modern trading center. Many of the medieval towns that were arrested in their growth before the nineteenth century still show gardens and orchards in the heart of the community, just as one finds them in the sixteenth-century engravings. The standard of openness achieved in model housing estates like Bournville and Port Sunlight, late in the nineteenth century, was probably not more generous than that the middle classes enjoyed in many places. Goethe, in his 'Dichtung und Wahrheit,' describes such a fine rear garden in old Frankfurt, so favorable to family life.

Medieval people were used to outdoor living: they had shooting grounds and bowling grounds; they tossed the ball and kicked the football and ran races and practiced archery; all these opportunities were provided for by open spaces near at hand. When the open spaces filled up, Giovanni Botero notes, Francis I provided a meadow near the river for the scholars of the University of Paris—which proves that between the University on the Left Bank and the Ile de la Cité the land was far from being built up. The spirit of this hearty, informal play, incidentally, still pervades even today the merriest and perhaps the most beautiful of all formal urban parks, the Jardin du Luxembourg.

In sum, as far as usable open spaces go, the typical medieval town had at its foundation and through most of its existence a far higher standard for the mass of the population than any later form of town, down to the first romantic suburbs of the nineteenth century. Where these common open spaces were retained, as notably in Leicester, they formed the basis for public parks that rival the provisions made for royalty.

To form a notion of medieval standards of open space in building, one must turn to such surviving semi-public buildings as the Inns of Court in London, the colleges at Oxford or Cambridge, or the Homes for the Aged, such as one still finds in Holland, Belgium, and England. And one must not look at the narrow streets between the houses without remembering the open green or the neatly chequered gardens that usually stretched behind.

I lay emphasis upon the persistently rural character of the medieval town because the false contrary image has long established itself as a fixed idea, almost too firmly irrational to be removed by presentation of the actual evidence. People still mistake the cumulative decay that filled in the green spaces for the original structure, which was open and sound. As long as these open spaces remained, the crude sanitary arrangements of the small medieval town were not necessarily as offensive as they have been pictured. Complaints such as that made by the Preaching Friars at Beziers in 1345, on account of the bad odors issuing from a tannery, would hardly have been made if bad odors were constant and universal.

In time, the growing population, often unable to expand beyond the town walls, covered over the internal open spaces; and then grave hygienic misdemeanors were committed. How this happened one may learn through a typical instance from Stow. The Parish Church of St. Mary-le-Bow in London needed room in the churchyard for the burial of the dead. But by the middle of the fifteenth century, it was hemmed in by houses. John Rotham, in his will, gave a certain garden in Hosier's Lane to be a churchyard. After a hundred years, the over-crowded capital could not even afford open spaces for the dead: so this plot was built on. Garden: graveyard: houseplot—this was the succession. Finally, in the seventeenth century, the backyard might be built over, too, and the resultant insanitary mess, filled up with rubbish over the years, would then be regarded by an apostle of progress in the nineteenth century as "typical medieval overcrowding."

There is no doubt, however, that decayed corpses, subject to proper Christian burial, became a sanitary menace in the medieval town, as soon as they had a chance, by seepage, to contaminate the water supply. And as the population grew, the heaping up of the dead in the heart of the city increased the menace. It was naturally a convenience, both for burial and for further acts of pious remembrance, to have the dead within walking distance of the living: but this practice, in a town that relied upon wells and springs for drinking water, was one of the most serious hygienic misdemeanors of the medieval town.

As for the disposal of ordure, this has always been the bête noire of close urban settlements; and it still is. Most of the big cities today, throughout the world, have not yet showed sufficient technical resourcefulness in dealing with this problem; for in their reliance upon the flush toilet, they pollute their streams and waste the precious nitrogenous materials that might have enriched the soil. Where in earlier days the nearby farmers and market gardeners took advantage of the city's nearness, by systematically collecting human excrement for use on the land, both city and soil were the gainers: indeed, the bigger the city, the richer the land outside it, and the more profitable the activities of the market gardener.

The point to note, in coming to a judgment on medieval towns, is that crude sanitation is not necessarily bad sanitation; for a medieval farmhouse, in which the common dung pile was the only domestic privy, was not as great a menace to its inhabitants' health as the progressive pre-Pasteur town of the nineteenth century, blessed with refined water-closets in every middle-class dwelling, and cursed by a supply of drinking water drawn from the same river into which the sewage of the town above was emptied.

As early as 1388, the English parliament passed an act that forbade the throwing of filth and garbage into ditches, rivers, and waters. The poet Lydgate, in his 'Troy Book,' went even further; for he spoke of a river, "of fish ful plenteous," designed to carry off filth and ordure through *conduit pipes*:

> Whereby the town was utterly assured
> From engendyring of all corrupcioun,
> From wicked air and from infeccioun,
> That causen ofte by her violence
> Mortalitie and great pestilence.

Like the legislation, this passage both recognizes the existence of a serious evil and brings forth the remedy. By the sixteenth century, such special provisions for sanitary control and decency had become widespread. Thus Stow mentions an ordinance in London which commands that "no man shall bury any dung or goung within the liberties of the city" nor "carry any ordure till after nine o'clock in the night," that is, after bedtime. William Stubbs mentions that the first public sewage plant and water works were possessed by the city of Bunzlau in Silesia in 1543. While he notes, too, that the sewage was piped out to a disposal area, suggestive of a modern sewage farm, he does not explain how this puzzling innovation anticipated the English invention of the water closet in 1596. But Alberti, a full century earlier, in his chapter on 'Drains and Sewers,' distinguished between drains that carry away "the filth into some river, lake or sea" and those leading to a "deep hole dug in the ground." He added that "sinks for the reception of urine should be as far from the house as possible."

If we knew more about the incidence of infectious diseases in earlier periods we would have a better picture of medieval sanitation. But there is nothing to show that visitations of plague were more severe or more frequent than were repeated attacks of typhoid and cholera in American or European towns of the early nineteenth century: nor is there sufficient proof that poor sanitary arrangements were alone responsible for the origin or the virulence of medieval epidemics. But then, as now, lack of convenient washing facilities might explain dysentery through food contamination, and even the high infant death rate, about which there is no doubt. But the most prevalent offense against health was simply slatternly housekeeping: the widespread habit of covering floors with rushes, without renewing them frequently: a practice in England that Erasmus severely censured, with pointed reference to the accumulation of moldy straw, dirt, and bones, to say nothing of vomit and urine, and the droppings of domestic animals.

Yet even with much higher standards of municipal sanitation and domestic hygiene, modern cities are periodically swept by waves of influenza and poliomyelitis: indeed, the death rate from influenza in the great plague of 1918 equalled all but the worst of medieval plagues, the Black Death itself. If the medieval expectation of life at birth was low, a defective diet, especially a defective winter diet, must perhaps take almost as large a share of the blame as the erratic disposal of fecal matter; and the general lack of soap was possibly even more responsible for infant mortality.

On these matters, as Professor Lynn Thorndike pointed out, evidence favorable to many medieval cities is indisputable. He quotes Bruni's eulogy of Florence, in which Bruni remarks that "some towns are so dirty that whatever filth is made during the night is placed in the morning before men's eyes to be trodden under foot, than which it is impossible to imagine anything fouler. For even if there are thousands there, inexhaustible wealth, infinite multitudes of people, yet I will condemn so foul a city and never think much of it." Similarly, Leland, a later observer, in his journeys about England, made special mention of dirt whenever he came across it: evidently it was rare enough to deserve comment. Alberti observed that hillside Siena, which notably lacked drains, stank at all times of the day. In short, the evidence warrants neither a wholesale indictment nor a blanket absolution.

But a change for the worse certainly came about toward the *close* of the Middle Ages, despite sanitary regulations. This was due to the rise of the multi-story tenement house, often four and five stories high, sometimes many more in towns like Edinburgh. Such high dwellings discouraged the use of outdoor facilities: the very distance of the upper floors from the ground tempted people to carelessness and foulness in emptying their chamber pots. Here the lack of an adequate technical device became as monstrous as it had been in the ancient case of the Roman insulae. But this was a late development, a product of high rents and urban concentration. Until overcrowding began, the normal smells of a medieval town were probably no more offensive than those of a farmyard; and it was not for the nineteenth century, with its hideous sanitary misdemeanors, to reprove the earlier period. The open sewers of a "progressive center of civilization," such as Berlin, as Dr. William Osler found it in 1873, were probably as offensive to the nose and, as he noted, as dangerous to health.

What applies to human excreta applies also to garbage. Leftovers were eaten by the dogs, chickens, and pigs, which acted as town scavengers: a miniature of 1317, reproduced by Poëte, shows a sheep and a pig crossing a bridge in Paris, then the biggest metropolis in Europe. By the sixteenth century, in well-managed towns that had made provisions for street-cleaning, there was also a ban on keeping pigs in any part of the town, even in the gardens behind the houses. But in the early days, the pig was an active member of the local Board of Health. Like a great many other medieval institutions, he lingered on in more backward centers till the middle of the nineteenth century.

Non-edible waste was doubtless harder to dispose of: ashes, tannery offal, big bones; but certainly there was far less of this than in the modern city; for tins, iron, broken glass, bottles, and paper were scarce, or even non-existent. In the main, medieval refuse was organic matter, which decomposed and mingled with the earth. And in the final reckoning, one must not forget the ultimate municipal germicide: fire. In these nests of wooden buildings, particularly in the earlier centuries, there would be outbreaks of fire, famous in the annals of every town. This subjected whole streets and quarters to the most powerful of disinfectants. That function was not unrecognized. Stow notes that the custom of lighting bonfires on summer festival days not merely was an occasion for reconciliation with one's enemies, but had "the virtue that a great fire hath to purge the infection of the air." Thus it was the luxurious plating of the medieval towns in brick and stone that insidiously undermined the crude application of fire as germicide.

3: LUSTRATION AND THE FIVE SENSES

Two other matters closely connected with hygiene remain to be discussed: the bath and the supply of drinking water.

Even as early as the thirteenth century the private bath made its appearance. One of Boccaccio's ladies prepares a tub bath for her lover, and when he does not show up, thriftily takes it herself. Sometimes the bath came with a dressing room, as we learn from a sixteenth-century Nürnberg merchant's household book; while in the three room apartment described in Johann Andreae's ideal town, Christianopolis, a bath room counts as one of them, along with a kitchen and a sleeping compartment. In 1417, indeed, hot baths in private houses were specially authorized by the city of London. But if anything were needed to establish the medieval attitude toward cleanliness, the prevalence of public bath-houses should be sufficient.

Bath-houses were characteristic institutions in every North European city, and they could be found in every quarter. Complaint was even made by Guarinonius that children and young girls from ten to eighteen years of age ran shamelessly naked through the streets to a bathing establishment. Bathing was a family enjoyment. These bath-houses would sometimes be run by private individuals; more usually, perhaps, by the municipality. In Riga as early as the thirteenth century, bath-houses are mentioned, according to von Below; in the fourteenth century there were seven such establishments at Würzberg; and at the end of the Middle Ages there were eleven in Ulm, twelve in Nürnberg, fifteen in Frankfurt am Main, seventeen in Augsburg, and twenty-nine in Vienna. Frankfurt, indeed, had twenty-nine bath-house keepers as early as 1387. So widespread was bathing in the Middle Ages that the custom even spread back into the rural districts, whose inhabitants had been reproached by the writers of the early fabliaux as filthy swine. What is essentially the medieval bath has lingered in the Russian or Finnish village up to this day.

Public baths were for sweating and steaming, for almost antiseptic cleanliness. Such a purging of the epidermis was customary at least every fortnight, sometimes weekly. The very act of coming together in a bathhouse promoted sociability, as it had done in Roman times, without any embarrassment about bodily exposure, as Dürer plainly showed in one of his prints. The bath was a place where people gossiped and ate food, indeed, sometimes soaked sociably in a tub with a companion of the opposite sex; and in addition it served as a semi-medical resort where one attended to the more serious business of being cupped for pains or inflammatory conditions.

As bachelors multiplied in the growing city, and family life itself perhaps deteriorated, the bath-houses became the resort of loose women, looking for game, and of lecherous men, seeking sensual gratification. As early as 1438, Tafur, a Spanish nobleman visiting Bruges, was shocked by mixed bathing in bath-houses, "which they take to be as honest as church-going with us," for this spectacle was one of the titillating sights that strangers were taken to see. As a result, the medieval word for bathhouse, namely "stew," comes down to us in English as a synonym for brothel: it was so used as early as 'Piers Plowman.' Perhaps it is only poetic justice that many nineteenth-century cities, proud of all the ways in which they had progressed beyond the supposed dirt and disorder of medieval life, took the first step to make good their utter lack of bathing facilities in the poorer quarters by erecting public bath-houses. Doubtless their officials would have been shocked to learn that they were only following, on a pitifully reduced scale, a common medieval precedent.

The provision of drinking water was also a collective function of the town. First the guarding of a well or spring, in a suitable enclosure: then the provision of a fountain in the main public square, and of neighborhood springs and fountains, sometimes within the houseblock, sometimes in the public way. One of the first things that Pope Martin IV did in resuming the occupancy of the Vatican after the Great Schism was to restore one of the broken aqueducts of Rome, to provide water for its growing population. As numbers increased, it was often necessary to find new sources, as well as to distribute old ones over a wider territory. In 1236 a patent for a leaden conduit to convey water from Tyborne Brook to the city of London was granted; pipes were laid in Zittau in 1374; and in Breslau in 1479 water was pumped from the river and conducted by pipes through the city. Probably these pipes were such wooden pipes, of hollowed logs, as were illustrated in Dr. Georg Bauer's 'De Re Metallica,' and were used on Manhattan Island, for example, right down to the nineteenth century. As late as the fifteenth century, the provision of water conduits in London was a matter for private philanthropy, like hospitals and almshouses.

As with baths, the piping of water to public fountains whence it was distributed by hand to the houses, was not as convenient as the extension of a common system to all householders. But water piped from a distance by private companies did not begin to trickle in until the seventeenth century; and it was rarely in sufficient supply. To make up for its inconvenience, the fountain satisfied two important functions that tended to disappear later with an increase in technological efficiency: the public fountain was often a work of art, gratifying the eye as well as slaking the thirst, notably in the cities of Italy and Switzerland; and it was further a focus of sociability, providing an occasion for meeting and gossiping, since the fountain or pump, no less than the taproom of the tavern, served as the local newscaster for a quarter. Sanitarians and engineers today, seeking to spread their familiar mechanical benefits to backward countries by laying on water in every house in otherwise primitive villages, often grievously disrupt the social life of the community without offering sufficient compensation.

In one sense, the very inadequacy of the water supply of the medieval town was a source of its strength in defense, for it was at least self-sufficient. When after the seventeenth century growing cities were forced to look beyond their fortifications for water, they put themselves at the mercy of an army that could command the open country and cut off their supply: so their armies were finally driven into the open, too. But the big cities continued to grow more rapidly than either their technical or their capital resources; and this led either to accepting a meager water supply, or drawing freely upon sources polluted by sewage or poisoned by chemicals. This accounts in good part for the loss of cleanly medieval habits in the growing metropolises, and for the actual water famines that added to the other acute miseries of the new industrial towns of the nineteenth century.

Contrary to still current prejudice, many medieval towns, in their remedial and preventive measures for health, were far in advance of their Victorian successors. Public hospitals were one of the definite Christian contributions to the city. Jerome relates that in A.D. 360 Fabiola gave up his villa for the care of the needy sick, otherwise left to die wretchedly in the streets of Rome. From that time on, very rapidly after the eleventh century, the holy orders founded hospitals in almost every town: there would be at least two in most German towns, one for lepers, and one for other types of disease, according to Heil; while in "big" cities such as Breslau, with its 30,000 inhabitants in the fifteenth century, there would be as many as fifteen, or one for every two thousand people. What modern city can show anything like such adequate accommodations?

And note: these are the rule, rather than exceptions. Toulouse in 1262 had seven leproseries and thirteen hospitals; and one of these hospitals contained fifty-six beds; while Florence in the thirteenth century, Giovanni Villani records, with a population of about 90,000 people, had thirty hospitals with more than a thousand beds. Here, too, both in their number and in their modest domestic scale, the medieval town still has something to teach its elephantine, dehumanized successor.

Official municipal physicians made their appearance in the fourteenth century, even before the Black Death: in Constance as early as 1312. In Venice, a permanent health magistracy was created in 1485, to which in 1556 inspection and enforcement machinery were added that long served as a model to the rest of Europe. Contagious diseases, incidentally, were usually isolated outside city walls. The value of isolation wards, with separate toilets, had long been proved by the better equipped monasteries. Finally, the establishment of quarantine, for people passing in and out of cities from foreign parts, was one of the major innovations of medieval medicine. Much as travellers hated it, the practice was based on sound empiric observations, erring only on the side of caution, by allowing for almost three times the necessary incubation period.

The curtailment of infectious diseases and the gradual eradication of leprosy in Europe, thanks to the same policy of strict isolation, was nothing less than a triumph of preventive medicine. The rationalist physicians of the early nineteenth century, who confidently regarded contagion and infection without direct contact as superstitious figments of the medieval imagination, were not in fact as acute observers of cause and effect as their medieval predecessors.

In the main, then, the medieval town was not merely a stimulating social complex; it was likewise a more thriving biological environment than one might suspect from looking at its decayed remains. There were smoky rooms to endure; but there was also perfume in the garden behind the burghers' houses; for fragrant flowers and herbs were widely cultivated. There was the smell of the barnyard in the street, diminishing in the sixteenth century, except for the growing presence of horses and stables. But there would also be the odor of flowering orchards in the spring, or the scent of the new-mown grain, floating across the fields in early summer.

Cockneys may wrinkle their noses at this combination of rankness and fragrance, but no lover of country ways will be put off by the smell of cow or horse dung. Is the reek of gasoline exhaust, the sour smell of a subway crowd, the pervasive odor of a garbage dump, the sulphurous fumes of a chemical works, the carbolated rankness of a public lavatory, for that matter, the chlorinated exudation from a glass of ordinary drinking water more gratifying? Even in the matter of smells, sweetness is not entirely on the side of the modern town; but since the smells are *our* smells, many of us blandly fail to notice them.

As for the eye and the ear, there is no doubt where the balance of advantage goes. The majority of medieval towns in these respects were immensely superior to those erected during the last two centuries: is it not mainly for their beauty, indeed, that people still make pilgrimages to them? One awoke in a medieval town to the crowing of a cock, the chirping of birds nesting under the eaves, or to the tolling of the hour in the monastery on the outskirts, perhaps to the chime of bells in the new bell tower in the market square, to announce the beginning of the working day, or the opening of the market. Song rose easily on the lips, from the plain chant of the monks to the refrains of the ballad singer in the marketplace, or that of the apprentice and the house-maid at work. Singing, acting, dancing were still 'do-it-yourself' activities.

As late as the seventeenth century, the ability to hold a part in a domestic choral song was rated by Pepys as an indispensable quality in a new serving maid; and medieval music down to his time was composed mainly for the voice, addressed to the singers, rather than the listeners. In their polyphonic unison, each voice held its own, repeating the same melody in its own range, just as each guild and craft held its own within the city, one voice joining the next and going on with the tune, as one guild would join the procession after another, with its banners and its floats. In the daily routine, there were work songs, distinct for each craft, often composed to the rhythmic tapping or hammering or swaying of the craftsman himself.

Everywhere nature's noises mingled with man's. Fitz Stephen reported in the twelfth century that the sound of the water mill was a pleasant one amid the green fields of London. At night there would be complete silence, but for the stirring of animals and the calling of the hours by the town watch. Deep sleep was possible in the medieval town, immune from the ulcerating tensions of either human or mechanical noises.

If the ear was stirred, the eye was even more deeply delighted. Every part of the town, beginning with the walls themselves, was conceived and executed as a work of art: even parts of a sacred structure that might be unseen, were still finished as carefully as if they were fully visible, as Ruskin long ago noted: God at least would bear witness to the craftsman's faith and joy. The worker who had walked through the nearby fields or woods on a holiday came back to his stone carving, his wood working, his weaving or gold-smithing, with a rich harvest of impressions to be transferred to his work. The buildings, so far from being musty and 'quaint,' were as bright and clean as a medieval illumination, if only because they were usually whitewashed with lime, so that all the colors of the image-makers, in glass or polychromed wood, would dance in reflection on the walls, even as the shadows quivered like sprays of lilacs on the façades and the traceries of the more richly carved buildings.

Esthetic discipline might lack a name, for it was never separated from religious symbolism or practical requirements; but its fruits were everywhere visible. Nor was the desire for beauty unconscious: streets were extended, as Braunfels notes, "for the beauty of the city." Did not the citizens of Florence vote as to the type of column that was to be used on their Cathedral? Carved statues, painted walls, corbels, triptyches, and screens decorated alike the church, the guild-hall, and the burgher's house. Color and design were everywhere the normal accompaniment of the daily tasks. The array of goods in the open market added to the general visual excitement: velvets and brocades, copper and shining steel, tooled leather and brilliant glass, to say nothing of foods arranged in their panniers under the open sky.

Wander around the survivals of these medieval markets today! Whether they be as drab as the Sunday market in Whitechapel, as spacious as that on the Plain Palais at Geneva, or as handsomely enthroned as the Straw Market in Florence, they still have some of the human delight of their medieval prototypes. The plastic-coated automation of the American supermarket, with its ghastly fluorescent lighting, its meretricious packaging, its cunningly baited booby traps ('impulse buying'), its poisonous forms of preservative antisepsis, its frozen and flavorless foods, in their artfully arrested decay, presents a contrast that betrays both an esthetic and a physiological as well as a social loss.

This constant education of the senses is the elemental groundwork of all higher forms of education. When it exists in daily life, a community may spare itself the burden of arranging courses in art appreciation. And when it does not exist, such efforts are largely banal and self-defeating, for they deal chiefly in currently fashionable clichés, not in the underlying realities. Where such an environment is lacking, even the rational processes are half starved: verbal mastery, scientific accuracy, cannot make up for such sensory malnutrition. If this is a key, as Mme. Montessori long ago discovered, to the first stages of a child's education, it continues to be true even at a later period; for the city has a more constant effect than the formal school.

Life flourishes in this dilation of the senses. Without it, the beat of the pulse is slower, the tone of the muscles is lower, the posture lacks confidence, the finer discriminations of the eye and the touch are lacking, perhaps the will to live itself is defeated. To starve the eye, the ear, the skin, the nose is just as much to court death as to withhold food from the stomach. Though diet was often meager in the Middle Ages, though many comforts for the body were lacking even for those who did not impose penitential abstentions upon themselves, the most destitute or the most ascetic could not wholly close his eyes to beauty. The town itself was an ever-present work of art; and the very clothes of its citizens on festival days were like a flower garden in bloom. Today one can still capture some of that feeling by following the evening procession on Saint John's day in Florence, from Santa Maria Novella to the Piazza della Signoria.

4: PRINCIPLES OF MEDIEVAL

TOWN PLANNING

By the thirteenth century the main forms of the medieval city were fixed: what followed was an elaboration of detail. But the new institutions that began to dominate the town curtailed the older influence of the abbey and the castle, and the theme of the next three centuries was not authority, withdrawal, and security, but freedom, involvement, challenge, adventure. Crusades, missions, explorations opened up a wider world.

New dynamic elements entered the town, creating tensions and pressures that are well symbolized in the structure of the new Gothic cathedrals, which sacrificed the stability of the wall in order to throw open the interior to a flood of light. One would behold this dynamism on the periphery, in the batteries of windmills that surrounded the towns, and again, at the very center, as the new preaching orders and protestant laymen, oriented toward urban life, established their friaries and their *beguinages* in such open spaces as were left.

Let us take a look at the new contents of the town: a sample here and there will reveal the new social structure, and the new distribution of urban groups. In Carcassonne, in 1304, the population was about 9,500. This was divided into 43 noble households, 12 Lombard and 30 Jewish merchants, 63 notaries, 15 advocates, 40 soldiers, police, and messengers, 9 university-trained doctors, 9 priests, 250 clergy. In Florence, in the fourteenth century, with a population of 90,000, there were 25,000 men from fifteen to seventy years of age "fit to bear arms," 1,500 magnates, 75 knights, 1,500 foreigners, traders, and transients, 8 to 10 thousand boys and girls learning to read, 110 churches, 200 workshops of the Arte della Lana (woolen trades), 30,000 workers in textile trades, 80 money changers, 600 notaries, 60 physicians and surgeons.

Friar Bonvesin della Riva, in his panegyric on the 'Marvels of the City of Milan,' in 1288, reckoned that there were already two hundred thousand people in the city and its dependent area; and all his other figures support the description of a gigantic urban formation that had already, in its exuberance, passed beyond the medieval scale. The city was divided into some one hundred and fifteen parishes, a few of them having as many as between five hundred and a thousand families. "Outside the wall of the moat there are so many suburban houses that they alone would be enough to constitute a city." Pressure of population and poverty account, perhaps, for the volume of social services he describes, as follows:

"In the city, including the suburbs . . . there are ten hospitals for the sick, all properly endowed with sufficient temporal resources. The principal one of these is the Hospital of the Brolo, founded in 1145 by Goffredo de Bosero. . . . There are more than 500 poor bed patients and just as many more not lying down. All of these receive food at the expense of the hospital itself. Besides them, also, no less than 350 babies or more, placed with individual nurses after their birth. . . . Also the poor needing surgical care are diligently cared for by three surgeons, especially assigned to the task; the latter receive a salary from the Commune. . . .

"There are also houses of the Second Order of the Humiliati of each sex which in the city and the country reach the number of 220; inside them there is a copious number of persons living the religious life while working with their own hands." These lay orders, aiming at the practice of a Christian life in the heart of the city without the physical and spiritual withdrawal enjoined by the old monasteries, were part of an organized effort to infuse every aspect of existence with Christian principles. But far from welcoming this effort to achieve Christianopolis, the leaders of the Church saw in it a dangerous challenge to their vocational authority: so the movement was damned and conducted back into the older channels, backed by dominion and pride.

The great majority of medieval towns were closer to Carcassonne, in size, scale, and contents than to Milan; but small or big, they now held a great diversity of institutions and offered scope for a wide variety of special talents and aptitudes. These qualities were expressed both in their layouts and their buildings.

In general, there were three basic patterns of the medieval town, which corresponded to their historic origin, their geographic peculiarities, and their mode of development. Behind these urban patterns were still older rural ones, such as we find in the 'street' village, the cross-roads village, the commons village, and the round village, which could be represented graphically by =, +, #, and 0.

The towns that remained from Roman days usually retained their rectangular system of block platting, in the original center, modified by the building of a citadel or a monastery, which might alter the even parcelling out of the plots. Towns that grew by slow stages out of a village or a group of villages lying under a monastery or a castle would conform more closely to topography, changing slowly generation by generation, often preserving in their plan features that were products of historic accident rather than conscious choice.

This second kind of town is often regarded as the sole truly medieval type: some historians even deny the title of plan to its actual conformation. Those who refer to the winding streets of such a town as mere tracings of the cowpath do not realize that the cow's habit of following contours usually produces a more economical and sensible layout on hilly sites than any inflexible system of straight streets. Finally, many medieval towns were designed in advance for colonization: frequently, though not always, these would be laid out on a strict checkerboard plan, with a central place left open for the market and public assembly. All three modes were medieval. In separation or combination they produced an inexhaustible variety of forms.

At the very beginning of the Middle Ages one discovers, indeed, a certain partiality for the regular, geometric plan, with the rectangle as the basis of subdivision: see the ideal ground plan for the monastery of St. Gall in the ninth century. Kenneth Conant has shown, too, that the original buildings of Cluny were set in rectangular formation, within a three-hundred-foot square. Plainly Oswald Spengler's interpretation of the checkerboard plan as purely the product of the final hardening of a culture into a civilization is an unsupportable generalization. But though a geometric layout was more characteristic of freshly founded towns, it did not always follow that, as in the classic bastide of Montpazier, it would be coupled with a rectangular outline for the city as a whole. Sometimes the rectangles are placed within a circular bounding wall; sometimes, as at Montségur or Cordes in France, a basically rectangular plan was intelligently adapted to the contours and natural boundaries of the site.

I emphasize these points because the checkerboard or gridiron plan has been subject to a constant stream of misleading speculation and interpretation. Sometimes such plans are referred to as peculiarly American or New World types; sometimes, in the face of the brilliant precommunist Peiping, as a synonym for dullness. Even town-planning theorists have made such errors, largely because of their failure to grasp the difference, familiar to students of biology, between homologous and analogous forms. A similar form does not necessarily have a similar significance in a different culture; again, similar functions may produce quite different forms. As we have seen the rectangle meant one thing to an Etruscan priest, another to Hippodamos, a third to the Roman legionary, spading his camp for the night, and a fourth to the City Plan Commissioners for New York in 1811, seeking to provide in advance the maximum number of building lots. To the first, the rectangle might symbolize cosmic law; to the last, it meant simply the most favorable possibilities for real-estate speculation.

There is indeed a sound reason for thinking of medieval plans as usually more informal than regular. This was because rugged rocky sites were more frequently utilized, for they had decisive advantages for defense until effective cannon fire became possible in the sixteenth century. Since streets were not adapted to wheeled traffic and neither water pipes nor sewage drains needed to be provided for, it was more economical to follow nature's contours than to attempt to grade them down: note the tilt of the broad market place in Siena. By building on barren hilly sites, moreover, the thrifty citizens did not encroach on the richer agricultural bottom land.

In organic planning, one thing leads to another, and what began as the seizure of an accidental advantage may prompt a strong element in a design, which an a priori plan could not anticipate, and in all probability would overlook or rule out. Many of the surviving irregularities in medieval towns are due to streams that have been covered over, trees that were later cut down, old balks that once defined rural fields. Custom and property rights, once established in the form of lots, boundaries, permanent rights of way, are hard to efface.

Organic planning does not begin with a preconceived goal: it moves from need to need, from opportunity to opportunity, in a series of adaptations that themselves become increasingly coherent and purposeful, so that they generate a complex, final design, hardly less unified than a pre-formed geometric pattern. Towns like Siena illustrate this process to perfection. Though the last stage in such a process is not clearly present at the beginning, as it is in a more rational, non-historic order, this does not mean that rational considerations and deliberate forethought have not governed every feature of the plan, or that a deliberately unified and integrated design may not result.

Those who dismiss organic plans as unworthy of the name of plan confuse mere formalism and regularity with purposefulness, and irregularity with intellectual confusion or technical incompetence. The towns of the Middle Ages confute this formalistic illusion. For all their variety, they embody a universal pattern; and their very departures and irregularities are usually not merely sound, but often subtle, in their blending of practical need and esthetic insight.

Each medieval town grew out of a unique situation, presented a unique constellation of forces, and produced, in its plan, a unique solution. The consensus is so complete as to the purposes of town life that the variations in detail only confirm the pattern. That consensus makes it look, when one views a hundred medieval plans in succession, as if there were in fact a conscious theory that guided this townplanning. The agreement was deeper than that. But toward the close of the Middle Ages, the rationale of this planning was expressed by the highly reflective intelligence of Leone Battista Alberti, in his 'De Re Edificatori.'

Alberti was in many ways a typical medieval urbanist. In his concern for functionalism, the localization of business, curved streets, "he did no more," as Lavedan observes, "than register approval of what he saw under his eyes." Even when Alberti justifies the continuously curving street, with its gently blocked yet ever-changing vistas, he was only giving conscious expression to something his predecessors recognized and valued, too. The slow curve is the natural line of a footwalker, as anyone can observe if he looks back at his tracks in the snow across an open field, unless he has consciously tried to overcome this tendency. But the pleasure in that curve, once laid out by the pedestrian, is what gives character to medieval building, on such a consummate piece of late-medieval and renascence building as the High Street in Oxford. There a single tree whose branches jut out beyond the building line enriches the picture more than would a whole arcade of streets.

The other source of the organic curves in the medieval town was the emphasis on its central core. Lavedan goes so far as to say that "the essential fact of medieval urbanism is the constitution of the city in such a fashion that all the lines converge toward a center, and that the contour is usually circular: this is what contemporary theorists call the radio-concentric system." Unfortunately, the term radio-concentric calls to mind the spider web. What one finds, rather, in most towns, is a central quarter or core, surrounded by a series of irregular rings, which have the effect of enclosing and protecting the core, while, by devious passages, approaching more closely to it. Where there is something that approximates a continuous circular street, it is almost surely the indication of a wall that has been torn down. Even in a little town like Bergues, as seen in Blaeu's great Atlas, with its almost geometric precision in its central core, only three streets come together at the center. The resulting plan is generated by the two opposing forces of attraction and protection: the public buildings and open places find security behind a labyrinth of streets, through which the knowing foot nevertheless easily penetrates. It is only with the baroque planners who worked to overcome the medieval pattern that the street drives headlong into the town center, as in the asterisk plan — though Alberti himself, as it happens, anticipated this new scheme, which symbolized the collection of public power in a centralized institution or a despotic prince.

The determining elements in the medieval plan hold both for an old town on a Roman foundation, like Cologne, or for a new town like Salisbury. The wall, the gates, and the civic nucleus determine the main lines of circulation. As for the wall, with its outside moat, canal, or river, it made the town an island. The wall was valued as a symbol as much as the spires of the churches: not a mere military utility. The medieval mind took comfort in a universe of sharp definitions, solid walls, and limited views: even heaven and hell had their circular boundaries. Walls of custom bounded the economic classes and kept them in their place. Definition and classification were the very essence of medieval thinking: so that philosophic nominalism, which challenged the objective reality of classes, and presented a world of unrelated atoms and disconnected events, was as destructive to the medieval style of life as cannonballs proved to be to the walls of the town.

The psychological importance of the wall must not be forgotten. When the portcullis was drawn and the town gates were locked at sundown, the city was sealed off from the outside world. Such enclosure helps create a feeling of unity as well as security. It is significant — and a little disturbing — that in one of the rare modern communities where people have lived under analogous conditions, namely in the atomic-research community at Oak Ridge, the protected inhabitants of the town grew to value the 'secure' life within, free from any sort of foreign invasion or even unauthorized approach — though it meant that their own comings and goings were under constant military surveillance and control.

But once again, in the medieval community, the wall built up a fatal sense of insularity: all the more because the poor state of road transport increased the difficulties of communication between towns. As so often happened in urban history before, defensive unity and security reversed their polarity and passed over into anxiety, fear, hostility, and aggression, especially when it seemed that a neighboring city might prosper at its rival's expense. Recall Florence's shameless assaults on Pisa and Siena! This isolationism was in fact so self-defeating that it gave sanction to forces of exploitation and aggression, both in Church and in State, that sought at least to bring about some more inclusive unity, by turning the all too solid wall into a more etherialized frontier boundary, outlining a far wider province.

One may not leave the wall without noting the special function of the town gate: far more than a mere opening, it was a "meeting place of two worlds," the urban and the rural, the insider and the outsider. The main gate offered the first greeting to the trader, the pilgrim, or the common wayfarer; it was at once a customs house, a passport office and immigration control point, and a triumphal arch, its turrets and towers often vying, as in Lübeck, with those of the cathedral or town hall. Wherever the river of traffic slows down, it tends to deposit its load: so it would be usually near the gates that the storehouses would be built, and the inns and taverns congregate, and in the adjoining streets the craftsmen and merchants would set up their shops.

Thus the gate produced, without special zoning regulations, the economic quarters of the city; and since there was more than one gate, the very nature of traffic from different regions would tend to decentralize and differentiate the business areas. As a result of this organic disposition of functions, the inner area of the city was not burdened by any traffic except that which its own needs generated. The original meaning of 'port' derives from this portal; and the merchants who settled in this port were once called 'porters,' till they passed the name on to their menial helpers.

Finally, one must not forget an ancient function of the wall, which came back in the Middle Ages: it served as an open promenade for recreation, particularly in the summer. Even when the walls were no more than twenty feet high, they gave a point of vantage over the surrounding countryside, and permitted one to enjoy summer breezes that might not penetrate the city.

5: CIVIC NUCLEUS AND NEIGHBORHOOD

No town plan can be adequately described in terms of its two-dimensional pattern; for it is only in the third dimension, through movement in space, and in the fourth dimension, through transformation in time, that the functional and esthetic relationships come to life. This holds particularly for the medieval city; for the movement it generated led not merely through horizontal space, but upwards; and to understand the plan one must take in the mass and profile of its dominant structures: especially the disposition of the nuclear components, the Castle, the Abbey or Friary, the Cathedral, the Town Hall, the guild hall. But if one building may be taken as the key structure in the medieval town plan, it is the Cathedral; so much so that Braunfels even suggests that the master builders in charge of the Cathedral also, in fact, exercised a pervasive influence over other public buildings.

With certain notable exceptions, the dominant medieval buildings did not exist in empty spaces; still less did one approach them along a formal axis. That type of space came in with the sixteenth century, as in the approach to Santa Croce in Florence; and it was only with the nineteenth century that urban 'improvers' who were incapable of appreciating the medieval system of town planning removed the smaller structures that crowded around the great Cathedrals, to create a wide parklike area, like that in front of Notre Dame in Paris: bleak staring emptiness. This undermines the very essence of the medieval approach: the secrecy and the surprise, the sudden opening and the lift upwards, the richness of carved detail, meant to be viewed near at hand.

Esthetically, a medieval town is like a medieval tapestry: the eye, challenged by the rich intricacy of the design, roams back and forth over the entire fabric, captivated by a flower, an animal, a head, lingering where it pleases, retracing its path, taking in the whole only by assimilating the parts, not commanding the design at a single glance. For the baroque eye, that medieval form is tortuous and the effort to encompass it is tedious; for the medieval eye, on the other hand, the baroque form would be brutally direct and over-unified. There is no one 'right' way to approach a medieval building: the finest face of the Chartres cathedral is the southern one; and though perhaps the best view of Notre Dame is from across the Seine, in the rear, that view, with its engirdling green, was not opened up till the nineteenth century.

Yet there are exceptions. There is a handful of minsters—to say nothing of countless village churches—that are free-standing buildings, set in the midst of an open green, quite detached from the busy life of the town: Salisbury and Canterbury are almost suburban in their free use of space and greenery, while Pisa's Campo Santo is equally detached and open. Often an original graveyard accounts for such openness.

In the main, the great church is central to the town, in every sense but a geometric one; and since it drew to itself the largest crowds, it needed a forecourt to provide for the entrance and exit of the worshippers. With the theological orientation of the church, its altar pointing toward the East, the church would often be set at a non-conforming angle to a more regular pattern of streets. When one finds the marketplace either spreading in front of the cathedral, or opening a wedge or a square for itself nearby, one must not assign to these institutions the same values they have today: it was the market that was occasional, while it was the church whose services were constant and regular. As with the original growth of the city, the market settles close to the church because it is there that the inhabitants most frequently come together.

One must think of the church, indeed, as one would now think of a 'community center': not too holy to serve as a dining hall for a great festival, as a theater for a religious play, as a forum where the scholars in church schools might stage oratorical contests and learned disputes on a holiday, or even, in the early days, as a safe-deposit vault, behind whose high altar deeds or treasures might be deposited, safe from all but the incorrigibly wicked.

In one manner or another, a constant procession of people, alone, or by twenties or by thousands, wound through the streets to the portals of the church. Here is where one set out on one's journey; here is where one returned. If it were otherwise, how could one account for the riches lavished on the building of a Bamberg, a Durham, an Amiens, a Beauvais, an Assisi, in communities of ten thousand inhabitants or less. Such communities today, with all our mechanized facilities and capital accumulation, would find it hard to raise funds for a pre-fabricated parish house, bought at a discount.

As for the open places of the medieval city, even the big marketplaces and cathedral places were anything but formal squares. More often than not, in towns of organic growth, the marketplace would be an irregular figure, sometimes triangular, sometimes many-sided or oval, now sawtoothed, now curved, seemingly arbitrary in shape because the needs of the surrounding buildings came first and determined the disposition of the open space. Though sometimes the market may be but a widened street, there are other examples, in Brussels or Bremen, in Perugia or Siena, where the proportions of the place are ample: big enough not merely for many stalls, but for public gatherings and ceremonies. The marketplace recaptured, in fact, the function of the earliest forum or agora.

In the marketplace the guilds set up their stages for the performance of the mystery plays; here the savage punishment of criminals or heretics would take place, on the gallows or at the stake; it was here that at the end of the Middle Ages, when the serious occupations of feudalism were transformed into urban sports, that great tourneys would be held. Often one marketplace will open into another subordinate place, connected by a narrow passage: Parma is but one of many examples. The dry goods and hardware market was usually separated for very natural reasons from the provisions market. Many a square we now admire purely for its noble architectural frame, like the Piazzetta San Marco in Venice, originally was carved out for a utilitarian purpose—in this case a meat market.

Apart from the cathedral and, sometimes, the town hall, where mass and height were important symbolic attributes, the medieval builder tended to keep to modest human dimensions. Almshouses would be founded for seven or ten men; convents might begin with the apostolic dozen; and instead of building a single hospital for the entire town, it was commoner to provide a small one for every two or three thousand people. So, too, the parish churches multiplied throughout the growing town, instead of letting a few big edifices wax at the center. In London in the twelfth century, according to Fitz Stephen, there were 13 conventual and 126 smaller

churches, for a population of possibly 25,000 people; and Stow notes some
three centuries later from two to seven churches in each of the twenty-
six wards.

This decentralization of the essential social functions of the city not
merely prevented institutional overcrowding and needless circulation: it
kept the whole town in scale. The loss of this sense of scale, in the over-
sized burgher houses of the north, or in the crazily competitive fortress
towers of Bologna or San Gimignano was a symptom of social pathology.
Small structures, small numbers, intimate relations—these medieval attributes gave the town special qualitative attributes, as against large
numbers and mass organizations, that may help account for its creativity.

The street occupied in the medieval town a quite different place than
in an age of wheeled transportation. We usually think of urban houses
as being ranged along a line of pre-determined streets. But on less regular
medieval sites, it would be the other way about: groups of trades or institutional buildings would form self-contained quarters or 'islands,' with
the building disposed without relation to the public ways outside. Within
these islands, and often outside, the footways marked the daily goings and
comings of the inhabitants. The notion of a 'traffic network' was as absent
as constant wheeled traffic itself. 'Islands' formed by the castle, the monasteries or colleges, the specialized industrial section of the more advanced
towns, like the Arsenal at Venice, interrupted the closer pattern of small
scale residential blocks.

In medieval new towns, the charters often distinguished between traffic streets—traffic being mainly carts—and lesser streets; and in uniform
Montpazier, as centuries later in Philadelphia, the houses had a two-street
frontage, one on a broad street twenty-four feet wide and one on an alley
seven feet wide. But in general, the street was a line of communication for
pedestrians, and their utility for wheeled transport was secondary. Not
merely were the streets narrow and often irregular, but sharp turns and
closures were frequent. When the street was narrow and twisting, or when
it came to a dead end, the plan broke the force of the wind and reduced
the area of mud.

Not by accident did the medieval townsman, seeking protection against
winter wind, avoid creating such cruel wind-tunnels as the broad, straight
street. The very narrowness of medieval streets made their outdoor activities more comfortable in winter. But likewise, in the south, the narrow
street with broad overhangs protected the pedestrian against both rain
and the sun's direct glare. Small variations in height and building material
and rooftop profile, and variations in window openings and doorways
gave each street its own physiognomy.

Though Alberti favored straight and broad streets for noble and powerful cities, to increase their air of greatness and majesty, he wrote a most perceptive apology for the older medieval type of winding street. "Within the heart of the town," he observed, "it will be handsomer not to have them strait, but winding about several ways, backwards and forwards, like the course of a river. For thus, besides by appearing so much longer, they will add to the idea of the greatness of the town, they will likewise be a great security against all accidents and emergencies. Moreover, this winding of the streets will make the passenger at every step discover a new structure, and the front door of every house will directly face the middle of the street; and where as in larger towns even too much breadth is unhandsome and unhealthy, in a smaller town it will be both healthy and pleasant to have such an open view from every house by means of the turn of the street." No one, not even Camillo Sitte, has done better justice to the esthetics of medieval town planning.

The medieval town thus had a character in its residential quarters that the blank walls of a classic Greek city, for example, certainly lacked. But the town enjoyed still another happy feature, perhaps carried over from the ancient city: for frequently the street would be edged on each side with an arcade, which formed the open end of a shop. This gave better shelter than even a narrow open street, and one finds it not merely in France and Italy, where it might in fact be a conscious continuation or resumption of the classic portico, but in towns like Innsbruck in Austria, in the street leading up to Das Goldene Dachl. One must not forget how important physical protection against the weather was, for the stalls and booths of handicraftsmen and merchants were not generally put behind glass till the seventeenth century; in fact, the greater part of the business of life, even cooking, was conducted more or less outdoors. The closed narrow street, the arcaded front, and the exposed shop were in fact complementary. Not till cheap glass enclosed the second could new conceptions of town planning open up the first.

One further feature of the street must be noted: its paving. Some three centuries before wheeled vehicles became common, the street lost its natural underfooting. Paving for the pedestrian came in as early as 1185 in Paris, 1235 in Florence, and 1310 in Lübeck; indeed, by 1339 all of Florence was paved; while by the end of the fourteenth century even in somewhat backward England, William Langland could use the figure "as common as the pavement to every man that walketh." Often these early improvements applied only to a single important street, and the movement spread so slowly that it did not reach Landshut in Bavaria till 1494, though that other great technical innovation, window glass, was used by South Bavarian farmers, according to Heyne, in the thirteenth century. In the hands of the medieval pavior, paving became an art, often repeat-

ing in stone the pattern of the mower's scythe; while in Venice, the color
and line of the pavement adds to the magnificence of St. Mark's plaza
itself.

The provision and care of paving reminds one of another feature about
the management of the medieval town: here again it was association that
had a public basis, while physical organization was, more often than not,
on a private basis. Certainly this applies to paving, lighting, and the piped
water supply. By the sixteenth century the first two were usually mandatory; but they were carried out by the private householder for his particular private property. The cleaning of streets likewise remained for long
a private concern: a custom that lingered beyond the nineteenth century
in London, in the institution of the crossing sweeper, who disappeared
only with the banishment of the horse. (Medieval practice, curiously, still
usually applies to the building and maintenance of sidewalks.) Under
the paving act that prevailed in Northampton in 1431, the municipal
authorities had the power to order the owners of the property to pave
and keep in repair the street in front of their houses and adjoining property, but "no property owner was compelled to extend the pavement into
the street above thirty feet, so it became the duty of the town to pave the
market and similar wide places."

Note one more feature: the neighborhood unit and the functional
precinct. In a sense, the medieval city was a congeries of little cities, each
with a certain degree of autonomy and self-sufficiency, each formed so
naturally out of common needs and purposes that it only enriched and
supplemented the whole. The division of the town into quarters, each
with its church or churches, often with a local provision market, always
with its own local water supply, a well or a fountain, was a characteristic
feature; but as the town grew, the quarters might become sixths, or even
smaller fractions of the whole, without dissolving into the mass. Often,
as in Venice, the neighborhood unit would be identified with the parish
and get its name from the parish church: a division that remains to this
day.

This integration into primary residential units, composed of families
and neighbors, was complemented by another kind of division, into precincts, based on vocation and interest: thus both primary and secondary
groups, both *Gemeinschaft* and *Gesellschaft,* took on the same urban pattern. In Regensburg, as early as the eleventh century, the town was divided
into a clerical precinct, a royal precinct, and a merchant's precinct, corresponding thus to the chief vocations, while craftsmen and peasants must
have occupied the rest of the town. To this constellation, university towns,
like Toulouse or Oxford, would also add their college precincts, each
relatively self-contained; while as convents and nunneries were drawn into
the city, a movement that went on steadily from the thirteenth to the

eighteenth century, a scattering of conventual precincts, different from the cathedral precinct, would likewise follow, adding their gardens and open spaces, however private, to the sum total of open spaces in the city. In London, the Inns of Court, like The Temple, formed still another kind of enclosed precinct.

The significance of the functional precinct has been too tardily recognized, even by planning theorists: in fact, perhaps the first modern planners to have done justice either to the historic form or its modern variations were Henry Wright and Clarence Stein. But these precincts were the first translation of the spatial qualities of the sacred precinct of the original city into the vernacular of everyday life. At the present moment, when the very existence of the city today is threatened by the overexpansion of wheeled traffic, the tradition of the medieval precinct, released from the street and the major traffic artery, comes back as a new form at a higher point in the spiral of development.

One cannot leave the medieval city, in its unity and diversity, without asking a final question about its planning: how far was it pursued as a conscious effort to achieve order and beauty? In formulating an answer, it is easy to overestimate both spontaneity and accidental good looks, and to forget the rigor and system that were fundamental qualities in the education of both scholar and craftsman. The esthetic unity of the medieval town was not achieved any more than its other institutions without effort, struggle, supervision, and control.

No doubt most of the supervision was personal; most of the agreements probably came from face-to-face discussions of interested parties, which left no record behind. But we know that when the Town Hall of Siena was built in the fourteenth century, the municipal government ordered that the new buildings put up on the Piazza del Campo should have windows of the same type. And though much work remains to be done in medieval archives to bring out all the functions of the Town Architect, we know, too, that in Italy the office was an old one. We need not doubt Descartes in his 'Discourse on Method' when he observes that "there have been at all times certain officers whose duty it is to see that private buildings contributed to public ornament."

What the nineteenth-century admirer of medieval art regarded as the result of effortless spontaneity and artless unconsciousness was done in fact with method and conscious intention in urban planning, precisely as any other art is carried through. Lavedan, it is true, in his admirable appreciation of the medieval town, is inclined to regard its beauty as a mere by-product of its practical and symbolic concerns. But the city was no more innocent of intentional esthetic order than it was of geometric order, though its discipline was pliant enough to allow for the new, the spontaneous, the different.

As a result, the same 'medieval' town plan could, by the eighteenth century, hold together Romanesque, High Gothic, Florid, Renascence, and Baroque structures, often jostling together on the same street, without any dulling of the esthetic moment: indeed, with just the contrary effect. The esthetic mixture corresponded with the historic social complex. This was a mode of planning that met the requirements of life, and yielded to change and innovation without being shattered by it. In the deepest sense of the words it was both functional and purposeful, for the functions that mattered most were those of significance to man's higher life.

Under such a canon of planning, no one was tempted to deny either the old form that still served well, or the new form that represented a new purpose; and instead of wiping out buildings of different styles in order to make them over wholesale in the fashionable stereotype of the passing moment, the medieval builder worked the old and the new into an ever richer pattern. The bastard estheticism of a single uniform style, set within a rigid town plan, arbitrarily freezing the historic process at a given moment, was left for a later period, which valued uniformity more than universality, and visible power more than the invisible processes of life.

6: CONTROL OF GROWTH AND

EXPANSION

Many people think of medieval life as sluggish and the medieval town as static. But though the tempo was different from that of the twentieth century, whose dynamism is often disruptive and self-defeating, the Middle Ages was a period of constant, sometimes violent, change. Towns multiplied and grew, from the tenth century to the fifteenth. So we must ask: How did the medieval town accommodate its increasing population? And what if any were the limits of its growth?

The limit that originally defined the physical town was the wall. But as long as a simple wooden palisade or a masonry wall sufficed for military defense, the wall was no real obstacle to town extension. Technically, it was a simple matter to tear down the wall and extend the city's boundaries, to provide inner space; and the circular streets of many medieval towns testify, like the annual rings of trees, to the successive periods of growth, marked by extensions of the wall. Florence, for example, enlarged its wall circuit for the second time in 1172, and not more than a century later, built a third circuit that enclosed a still greater area. When the pressure of the overfilled belly became uncomfortable, the Florentine municipality, so to say, loosened its belt.

As the suburbs spread, the wall would engirdle them. This was common practice in growing towns up to the sixteenth century, when the new system of fortification made necessary by accurate artillery fire made such simple forms of town extension impossible. But even at its widest, no medieval town usually extended more than half a mile from the center; that is, every necessary institution, every friend, relative, associate, was in effect a close neighbor, within easy walking distance. So one was bound every day to encounter many people by coincidence whom one could not meet except by pre-arrangement and effort in a bigger city. The Historic Mile of Edinburgh stretched between the extreme limits of the castle top and the Holyrood Abbey at the outskirts. When these limits were overpassed, the medieval town, as a functioning organism, ceased almost by definition to exist; for the whole community structure was a system of limitations and boundaries; and their breakdown in the city revealed an even wider dismantling through the whole culture.

The restrictions on the medieval town's growth were due partly, of course, to natural and social conditions, rather than to the cincture of the wall: limitations of water supply and local food production; limitations by municipal ordinances and guild regulations, which prevented the uncontrolled settlement of outsiders; limitations of transport and communication, which were overcome only in advanced cities, such as those of the Low Countries, which had waterways instead of roadways for heavy traffic. For practical reasons alone, the limits of horizontal expansion were speedily reached. As a result, in the early centuries of medieval city development, the surplus population was cared for by building new communities, sometimes close by, but nevertheless independent and self-sufficient units. This practice was followed as late as the seventeenth century in New England. So Charleston threw off Woburn, Dedham Medfield, and Cambridge Belmont, each no mere scattering of houses, but a civil and religious community, with a central meeting house for religion and a local system of government. As late as the nineteenth century, Ipswich founded Marietta, Ohio.

In short, the limitation on area and population did not make the medieval town static: that is an illusion. Not merely were thousands of new urban foundations made during the early Middle Ages, but settled towns that found themselves physically hampered or inconveniently located moved boldly to better sites. Thus Lübeck changed its original site, in order to better its means of trade and defense, and Old Sarum left its wind-beaten, inconvenient hill-site, to settle at Salisbury, by the river. Town building was prosecuted, in general, with a ready expenditure of energy and constructive zeal for which there are few modern parallels outside devastated areas. But this vast urban movement was not governed by the covetousness of the modern real estate speculator, seeking quick and inordinate gains. Even for urban investments, long term security was of more concern than short term profits; and the feudal conception of land, as a stewardship and trust, in a different category from more mobile forms of property, was so deeply rooted that in Europe it has never altogether disappeared.

The general pattern of medieval town growth, then, was radically different from the period of concentration and consolidation around great political capitals, which immediately followed it. The medieval pattern was that of many small cities and subordinate villages in active association with their neighboring towns, distributed widely over the landscape. Elisée Reclus discovered, indeed, that the villages and towns of France could be plotted with amazing regularity, forming the pattern of a day's walk from the most distant point to and from the market. In other words, the pedestrian's needs dominated: he who could use his legs had access to a city. The urban pattern conformed to the economic one; and both favored the small unit and direct face-to-face communication.

As to population distribution, the facts are plain. The medieval town ranged in size from a few thousand to forty thousand, which was the size of London in the fifteenth century. Populations above a hundred thousand, achieved earlier by Paris, Venice, Milan, Florence, were highly exceptional until the seventeenth century. Toward the close of the period, Nürnberg, a thriving place, had about twenty thousand inhabitants, while Basel, no mean town, had around eight thousand. Even on the productive soils of the Lowlands, supported by the highly organized textile industries, under a rigorous system of capitalist exploitation, the same limitation holds: in 1412 Ypres had only 10,376 inhabitants, and Louvain and Brussels, in the middle of the same century, had between 25,000 and 40,000. Bruges, the biggest, may have held 70,000. As for Germany, town life there was concentrated in some 150 'large' cities, of which the largest did not have more than 35,000 inhabitants.

All these statistics, it is true, date from the century after the Black Death, which in some provinces carried off half the population. But even if one doubled the figures for the towns themselves, they would still remain, in terms of modern population massings, small and scattered. In Italy alone, partly because of the old Roman foundations and because capitalism there had an earlier start, these figures have to be enlarged. Overcrowding and overbuilding, with increasingly extortionate rents and increasingly constricted dwelling space—as well as suburban expansion and scatterment—did not become common until the capacity for building new cities had greatly diminished. What caused this recession of urban vigor I shall discuss in a later chapter.

CHAPTER ELEVEN

Medieval Disruptions, Modern Anticipations

1: CHRISTIANOPOLIS—SHADOW AND SUBSTANCE

The monastery, the guild, the church, served as formative elements of the medieval town. More effective than were Cos, Delphi, and Olympia in Hellas, they shaped every quarter of the city and molded a common life that promised to overcome the abortive institutions originally entrenched in the ancient citadel. Voluntary co-operation and contractual obligations and reciprocal duties partly replaced blind obedience and one-sided coercion. At the moment these new structures were visible, working side by side, one may say that the archetypal medieval town had taken form. This does not imply that all these institutions would be present in any particular town or carry equal weight: for the mercantile spirit was positively hostile to the university, and medieval towns like Bruges and Lübeck never boasted such an intellectual center, while others, like Venice or Bristol, long resisted this innovation.

In the early Middle Ages, even business and religion, however, were in organic relationship: so much so that business would copy the institutions of religion in the organization of its trading bases. The Hansa trading settlements, for example, were on monastic lines, and exacted the same kind of narrow devotion to pecuniary if not heavenly gain; while one of the chief functions of the Knights Templar was to serve as forwarding agents and bankers. But at the end of the Middle Ages—and this is one of the decisive signs of the end—even pious matters have a worldly tinge. Religion gave way to commerce, 'faith' to 'credit.'

But even the establishment of business activities on a capitalistic basis had a theological origin; for the doctrine of the Treasury of Salvation, as set forth by the Schoolmen, anticipated the theory of capitalistic savings toward future rewards, promising ultimate productive returns and huge profits; while the justification of profit itself, as opposed to an even *quid pro quo* in exchange, had been put forward by Vincent of Beauvais.

May one then speak of the medieval town as a Christian city, an embodiment in a corporate political scheme as well as in buildings of the Christian way of life? Was it a true City of Refuge—a haven from the contradictions and frustrations we have noted in every earlier urban culture? Unfortunately, the medieval town was no more the successful fulfillment of Christian hope that it sometimes seemed to pious advocates in the thirteenth century, than it was the unredeemed compound of ignorance, filth, brutality, and superstition that it seemed to many post-medieval commentators.

In appraising the medieval town we should avoid both errors. We must, of course, dismiss the charming tapestry of the Middle Ages composed by Pugin, Ruskin, Morris, and similar writers: they often treated intentions as if they were accomplished facts, and ideals as if they were realizations; for they readily attributed to the seething contents of medieval life all the beauty that is still visible in the container. But if we dismissed medieval culture as a whole, because of the torture chamber and the public burning of heretics and criminals, we should also wipe out all pretensions to civilization in our own period. Has not our enlightened age restored civil and military torture, invented the extermination camp, and incinerated or blasted the inhabitants of whole cities? The contradictions of medieval life were minor compared to those we conceal in our own breasts.

In certain respects, the medieval town had succeeded as no previous urban culture had done. For the first time, the majority of the inhabitants of a city were free men: except for special groups, like the Jews, city dweller and citizen were now synonymous terms. External control had now become internal control, involving self-regulation and self-discipline, as practiced among members of each guild and corporation. Dominium and communitas, organization and association, dissolved one into the other. Never since the great dynasties of Egypt had there been such a religious unity of purpose under such a diversity of local interests and projects. Though the social structure of the town remained a hierarchical one, the fact that a serf might become a free citizen had destroyed any biological segregation of classes and brought about an increasing measure of social mobility.

These were great achievements; but the faith and dogma that had made them possible stood in the way of further developments that challenged its authority and its all-too-worldly goals. The truth is that while the Church, through its universal presence and mission, dominated every aspect of medieval life, the very success of this institution embrangled it in the affairs of this world. As the price of its own continued ministry, the Church accepted the same fatal commitments that had pushed every earlier urban civilization, whether under an Assurbanipal or a Pericles, to its final ruin. The Church's ideal concern for the Hereafter, the only realm over which it professed full authority, was undermined by its own materialization, which caused it to seek a visible counterpart of its favored holy estate, more magnificent than any earthly rival could afford. This self-betrayal was denounced by one medieval Church Father after another, from Bernard of Clairvaux to Francis of Assisi. More than one saint pointed out that the building too easily served as substitute for the spirit it supposedly harbored. At the time Notre-Dame de Paris was built, around 1180, Pierre le Chantre wrote, in his 'Summa Ecclesiastica': "The chevets of our churches should be more humble than their bodies, because of the Mystery they symbolize; for Christ, who is at our head—the head of his church, is more humble than his church." Instead, he notes, the chevets "are built higher and higher."

What was involved in a realization of the Christian city? Nothing less, I submit, than a thoroughgoing rejection of the original basis on which the city had been founded: the renunciation of the long-maintained monopoly of power and knowledge; the reorganization of laws and property rights in the interests of justice, free from coercion, the abolition of slavery and of compulsory labor for the benefit of a ruling minority, and the elimination of gross economic inequalities between class and class. On those terms, the citizens might find on earth at least a measure of that charity and justice that were promised to them, on their repentance, in heaven. In the Christian city, one would suppose, citizens would have the opportunity to live together in brotherhood and mutual assistance, without quailing before arbitrary power, or constantly anticipating external violence and sudden death. The rejection of the old order imposed originally by the citadel was the minimal basis of Christian peace and order.

From the very moment the Church became the official religion of the Roman state, in A.D. 313, that program was in jeopardy, and the City of God drew ever farther away. Patches of Christian peace and order remained visible in the monastery; and not a little of that spirit entered the city through the brotherly offices of the guild. But the Christian idea flourished best in adversity, and with success it met with a series of reverses that culminated in the thirteenth century. So long as life itself was oriented to death and suffering, no small measure of the Christian intention found an outlet in acts of compassion and charity, which took their appropriate institutional form in the city. In no previous urban culture was there anything like the large scale provision for the sick, the aged, the suffering, the poor that there was in the medieval town. But these philanthropic achievements were somewhat like the intellectual achievements of the Schoolmen: the structure seemed unshakable provided that one did not scrutinize the groundwork.

All too soon, the Church rendered to Caesar not merely the things that are Caesar's, but also the things that are God's. Not alone did the Church refrain from touching the ancient foundations of political and military power, private property, and intellectual monopoly. So far from rejecting these counterclaims to the holy life, the Church accepted them and took them for her own; when necessary, she sought to achieve by threat and force what she could not obtain by willing allegiance and free gift. By the time of Dante, supposedly the height of the medieval synthesis, he dreamed of an emperor to rule Christendom, who would be able to rescue the world from the claims of an iniquitous and rapacious Pope.

Because the Church expected human suffering and was inured to it, its clergy handled without quailing life's denials and frustrations, its miscarriages and tragedies. But when life flowed back into this whole culture, as trade prospered and wealth accumulated, the Church began increasingly to utilize for its own pride and power all the prevailing un-Christian or anti-Christian practices, so that even her most reputable dogmas often took on a superstitious form. If the Church protected the human corpse against violation by physicians seeking to gain medical knowledge of the body through anatomic dissection, she graciously allowed the bodies of the living to be fiendishly mutilated in punishment, in execution of her own judgment of heretics. Once the Inquisition was started in the thirteenth century, she even invented ingenious mechanical devices of her own to perform torture on suspected heretics, in order to enforce confession.

By the thirteenth century, the wealth, luxury, and worldly power embodied in the leading medieval cities had undermined the radical postulates of Christianity: namely, poverty, chastity, non-resistance, humility, obedience to a divine mandate that transcends all considerations of bodily security or material satisfaction. The Church itself, as the wealthiest institution in Christendom, was the very scene of this sordid revolution. No matter how many individual saints she might continue to bring forth, her own worldly example was not such as to chasten those who sought for wealth in ever larger quantities in the market place, for power on the battlefield, or for loot and treasure in a conquered city. This perhaps explains why Christianity did not create a Christianopolis.

The climax of both Gothic architecture and medieval culture came in the thirteenth century. By the following century, it became plain that the forces that might have reclaimed the medieval town for a Christian way of life would meet their most serious opposition, not at first in the market place, but within the Church itself. The great symbol of the effort to restore the original Christian spirit—and of its decisive defeat, too—

33: THE URBANE VILLAGE

34: COMMERCE COMMANDS

35: GETTING AND SPENDING

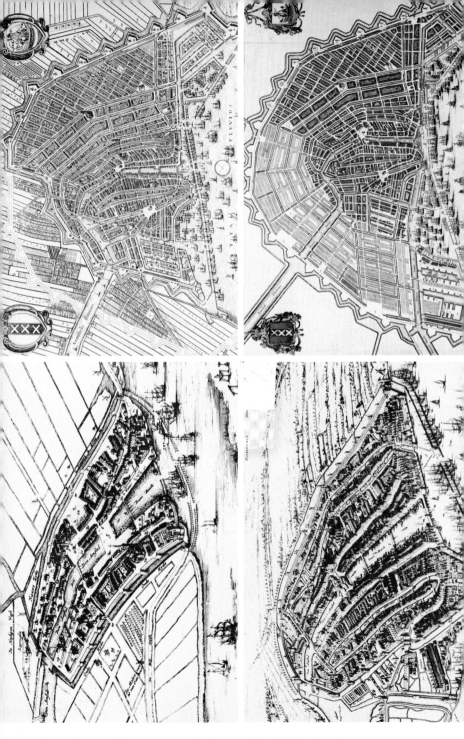

36: ORGANIC PLANNING: AMSTERDAM

37: PRIDE OF BATH

38: UNDER ONE ROOF

39: INDUSTRIAL COKETOWN

40: PALEOTECHNIC INFERNO

41: MODEL INDUSTRIAL VILLAGE

42: GREEN COUNTRY TOWNS

43: CONQUEST OF SUBURBIA

44: BLOOMSBURY AND HAMPSTEAD GARDEN

45: BELATED BAROQUE: WASHINGTON

46: STANDARDIZED CHAOS

47: URBAN DEVASTATION

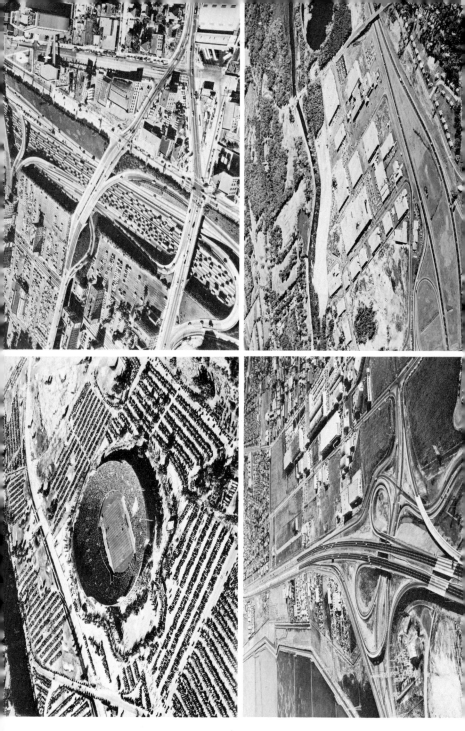

48: THE SPACE EATERS

33: THE URBANE VILLAGE

Some of the finest examples of late medieval planning and building are in Cotswold villages like Chipping Camden and Burford, though their equivalents can be found in many other regions. Chipping Camden, shown here, is a perfect example of the 'street village,' widening in the center for a marketplace. The long narrow lots, also typical, led to the extension of the building area by side shoots, which in time, without a further development of blocks, led to site overcrowding. The street picture [upper] demonstrates that row houses, when not mechanically stamped out, need not be monotonous: note that merely placing the ground floor window above eye level, in the second panel of windows, gives full internal privacy without a long front garden. William Morris regarded Bybury, another Cotswold village, as the most beautiful in England: it has examples of site planning and house grouping that set both an esthetic and social standard for architects like Ashbee, Voysey, Unwin, and Parker. From these villages the suburban architects of the late nineteenth century had much to learn in combining urbanity with openness, but they missed the lesson by concentrating on picturesque accidents of gable, oriel, and bay, too often overlooking more essential elements.

[Lower] Photograph: Aerofilms, Ltd., London.

34: COMMERCE COMMANDS

Large scale overseas trade began again with the Venetian and Genoese penetration of the Levant; but it did not become a dominant factor in city development until the seventeenth century, or produce such vast port cities as London, Liverpool, Hamburg, Rotterdam, Marseille, and New York until the nineteenth century. The competitive animus and laissez-faire ideology of the trading classes after the seventeenth century delayed the building of great collective utilities on an adequate and coherent plan: curiously the classic examples of a well-planned port precinct, with facilities for ship-building, repair, chandlery, lading, and storage, were the earliest: the Arsenal quarter in Venice [upper] founded in 1104, and after that, those in Amsterdam. The building of the dock facilities and the mole for the harbor at Dunkirk [lower] serves as a reminder of similar activities in many other ports, culminating in the great Port of London, whose immense organization incited Hippolyte Taine's superb description in his 'History of English Literature': a passage that only lack of space prevents me from quoting in full. The need for more coherent planning and development finally, through a typical stroke of British political genius, promoted a new form of public authority, which combined the virtues of private enterprise with public guidance and responsibility: the Port of London Authority, in 1908. This type of corporation, imitated elsewhere, was a model for the British New Towns development authorities, and suggests the possibility of creating regional planning authorities on similar legal and administrative lines.

[Upper] The Arsenal in Venice: note wall, building sheds, dry dock, etc.—a classic example of a well-planned industrial quarter. [Lower] Dunkirk in the eighteenth century, with new mole, port facilities, and fortifications.

35 : GETTING AND SPENDING

The courtyard of the Royal Exchange, London, [top] might be called a cloister of commerce: another witness to the persistence of medieval forms for un-medieval purposes. The building of Bourses in the sixteenth century signalized the change from a goods economy facilitated by money to a money economy only secondarily concerned with goods. Adventurous speculation and rapid turnover became the key to great wealth. When Wren put forth his plan for the City of London after the great fire, he placed the Bank of England, not St. Paul's, at the center: this was organic planning in terms of the new capitalism. The spacious interior shown here [middle] served as model for later institutions: the great national banks were, as it were, the religious cult centers of capitalism. The shopping parade [bottom] made buying an engrossing daily function, and the new wide window with its open display of goods under glass promoted 'window-shopping.' The combination of shopping with wheeled traffic tended to turn every avenue into a shopping avenue. That elongated form, seen at its worst in Oxford Street, London, brought commerce into every quarter of the city, instead of concentrating it in market squares and in short narrow streets. This introduced confusion and blight into the domestic quarters, and as the streets lengthened, heedlessly increased the amount of competitive commercial space without regard to service or even to profit. In the end, the sole drama of the commercial city is getting and spending: except for these purposes all the cultural functions of the city were progressively devaluated.

36 : ORGANIC PLANNING : AMSTERDAM

Stage One [upper left]: The fishing and shipping town at the mouth of the Amstel: a site not dissimilar to that of Geneva or Zurich. The banking and bridging of the Amstel already begun: a canal and wall protect the town on three sides. Stage Two [lower left]: Further utilization of the canal as a means of urban transportation: extension of narrow blocks parallel to main water artery, with growth of shipping facilities and mul-

tiplication of windmills on outskirts. Overcrowding blots out gardens in original town though they are maintained in the new blocks. Stage Three [upper right]: Establishment of central place (the Dam, seat of the Palace) to the left, with new streets leading toward it in non-conformity to original pattern. Building of worker's quarters (the Jordaan) in small blocks with narrow streets, again non-conforming, but following the original line of fields. This unhappily prevented the symmetrical completion of the plan in the poorer area. Stage Four [lower right]: Despite original confusion and lopsided development, a bold spiderweb plan creates a semi-circular system of interconnected canals, with water routes and tree-lined streets both converging toward the harbor. The emergence of this geometric form from Stage Three represents a fusion of organic growth and mechanical form, in which both are brought to a higher degree of perfection. What town planner could have plotted this result at Stage One? With a unified but varied traffic system, with canals that preserved openness, with comely row houses and gardens, and continuous tree-lined arcades, Amsterdam rivalled Versailles in beauty without sacrifice of utility. As with most historic cities, this great urban work of art is now clogged and befouled by motor traffic that has turned its pleasances into parking spaces and reduced all traffic to a pedestrian gait without restoring any amenities to the pedestrian. The extension of Amsterdam, from the nineteenth century on, made no provision for a decentralization of business and industry into equally organic sub-centers: this is mainly responsible for Amsterdam's present troubles; for there is a congestion of even bicycle traffic. Though rightly praised for its comprehensive municipal housing since 1920, too little of the later planning and building in Amsterdam has been of the masterful quality that created the seventeenth century city.

37: PRIDE OF BATH

Spas and baths as health resorts had never entirely fallen out of existence, but in the eighteenth century these places took on a new life as the upper classes flocked to them, prompted perhaps by the winter excesses of food and strong liquors. Whereas the medieval pilgrim visited religious shrines, in the interest of his spiritual health, his baroque counterpart visited baths in the hope of restoring his physical health. The baths, purgatives, and curative waters were an excellent pretext for another kind of life. Here all the typical baroque pleasures were available: gambling, dress, flirtation, liaisons, dances, music, sometimes the theater. In effect a minor court, ruled by a self-elected prince, specialist in dress and manners, despot of fashion—the 'dandy,' historically personified in two fig-

ures, Beau Nash and Beau Brummel. By consensus the most beautiful of all these cities is Bath, established long ago by the Romans. Set back from the right angle bend of the river Avon, the Roman town with its small blocks in checkerboard pattern had grown up around the baths themselves. Close to that site, the medieval abbey had been planted. In the eighteenth century, following the patronage of Charles II, fashionable people went to Bath for the waters. This prompted a series of piecemeal improvements in the old town, which led the landowners of the neighborhood to engage in a series of bolder plans for laying out residential neighborhoods. Here, in three great spinal extensions, Gay Street, the Circle, and the Royal Crescent, with the adjacent Queen Square at the south end of Queen Street, one has, in miniature, the new order of planning at its captivating best. Even now, after a century and a half of change, the heart of Bath has qualities of design that even the best examples in Paris, Nancy, London, or Edinburgh do not surpass. The excellence of Bath shows the advantage of a strict discipline, when it is supple enough to adapt itself to challenging realities, geographic and historic. The placing of the Royal Crescent on a height that commands the whole valley, protected by the park that spreads below, shows that it was no mere application of an arbitrary geometric figure; and while nothing in the rest of the eighteenth century city reaches this level of planning, the further building of Bath, right through the Regency, never fell too short of its standard. Not less notable than the preservation of the parklike environs was the generous allotment for gardens in the rear: gardens visible through their iron gates, spacious and richly textured, as shown in the plan of 1786, and still often handsomely kept up today. This is a superior example of open planning, combined with a close urbane relationship of the buildings, which are treated as elements in a continuous composition. In short, Bath's eighteenth century town planning was as stimulating and as restorative as the waters, and the money invested has brought far higher returns in life, health, and even income than similar amounts sunk into more sordid quarters. But the standards of Bath did not survive the baroque pattern of life. Eventually all-too-astute business men displaced the landed proprietors whose public spirit and esthetic command made possible the noble planning of Bloomsbury, the New Town in Edinburgh, and Bath.

[Upper] Bath in relation to its landscape. The fine view of the hills from the Royal Crescent, at the bottom is now hidden by the trees in the foreground, but originally was responsible for the semicircular plan. [Lower] The nearer view of Bath shows the ample individual gardens behind both the Royal Crescent and the Circle, as well as the park areas that set off and enhance the urbane streets. Photographs: Aerofilms, Ltd., London.

38: UNDER ONE ROOF

Just as 'from door to door' and 'without being stopped by a red light' represent the ultimate ideals and unconditional demands of current motordom, regardless of what happens to landscape and city in pursuing them, so 'under one roof' was the ideal expression of the paleotechnic planner in the nineteenth century. Steel and glass had a hypnotic effect upon 'progressive' nineteenth century minds, and still has on their successors. This ideal form derived from the hothouse and was put to good purpose there originally by Joseph Paxton, the designer of the marvellous Crystal Palace [upper right] where the great exhibition of 1851 was held. The glass enclosed arcade, like that of Milan's famous meeting place [left] led to the design of the early department stores where even more goods were put under one roof, at first with a glassed-in overhead light in the central court. In Les Halles in Paris [lower right] the hothouse form was again put to rational use, in contrast to the contemporary glass-enveloped train-sheds which unfortunately retained and concentrated the acrid smoke of the steam locomotives. The desire to make such enclosures universal springs in most cases from an insistent technological itch rather than from any specifically civic or humane purpose. Current proposals for putting a whole city under a glass or plastic dome would blot out, as if they were worthless, all the stimulating changes in sky and weather, in the passages from indoors to outdoors, from darkness to light, and not least in architectural expression, that make the city such an enlivening environment. 'All under one roof' may prove just a mock-up for the terminal form of the anti-city: 'all in one underground shelter.' This would be environmental control with a vengeance—a biological and psychological vengeance. For the ultimate projection of this brave new world in a sterilized super-dimensional '1984' see Plate 64.

[Upper Right] Photograph: Ewing Galloway.

39: INDUSTRIAL COKETOWN

When Schinkel visited Manchester, he hailed the stark architecture of its great brick factories as the primitive form of a new order of building: an insight that was confirmed not only in many mills and factories, but in the extension of the same esthetic and utilitarian principles to the great Chicago steel-skeleton skyscraper primitives of the eighteen-eighties— and their belated rediscovery and restatement by Loos, Gropius, and Le Corbusier a generation later. The cotton factories [upper] with the gas tanks at the right, show the new dominants in the industrial town: the nearby workers' housing represents the new minimum of order and hygienic decency introduced gradually in the second half of the nineteenth century: likewise the overcrowding, with its wasteful multiplication of expensive paved streets and avenues. The clarity of the photograph, which gives no hint of the prevailing smoke and dirt, probably indicates a work stoppage. This is far from the worst example of the paleotechnic disrespect for life: see another demonstration left from an earlier day: the undertaker's delight, Plate 41 [top]. The American steel town [lower] shows the typical pre-emption of the river front by the railroad and the great steel mill, the pollution of the air by smoke and effluvia. Attention to the placement of noxious industries with respect to prevailing winds, their insulation from residential quarters, and methods of refuse disposal that would avoid cluttering the landscape or befouling the streams, played no part in the layout of early industrial towns. (For better neotechnic layouts see Plates 53 and 48, lower right.) Despite these serious defects, the confinement of steel towns to the often narrow valley bottoms along the Monongahela and the Allegheny kept the hills wooded and accessible to these small communities, and provided natural recreation areas for fishing and hunting that bigger towns like Pittsburgh and Cleveland, by their very growth, overran and destroyed.

Photographs: Ewing Galloway.

40: PALEOTECHNIC INFERNO

Perhaps only those who have been in combat have had any experience comparable to the realities of the nineteenth century industrial town prior to the transformations effected by the trade union movement, the cooperative movement, collective sanitary facilities and regulations, and social welfare legislation. The civic and religious life of these centers was carried on in ugly brick chapels, grim Mechanics' Halls, and even more sordid trade union headquarters, hardly identifiable until the end of the nineteenth century by any outward architectural grace. The only enlivening drama was provided by the struggles of national politics and the even more dramatic violence of the lockout and the strike. The rally of the Striking Gas Workers' Union in the eighteen-eighties typifies this moment. So great was the terror of working class uprising on the part of their exploiters that army barracks were deliberately scattered over the industrial towns in England: an army of occupation. The similar building of militia armories in heavily defensive buildings took place in the United States from the seventies to the nineties. In this environment a chronic blindness to beauty was almost as conspicuous as its general absence: perhaps a protective anesthesia. On that matter, William Morris had a gleam of

*demonic inspiration, writing to Mrs. George Howard in August 1874:
"Neither do I grudge the triumph that the modern mind finds in having
made the world (or a small corner of it) quieter and less violent, but I
think that this blindness to beauty will draw down a kind of revenge
one day: who knows? Years ago men's minds were full of art and the
dignified shows of life, and they had little time for justice and peace;
and the vengeance on them was not the increase of violence they did
not heed but destruction of the art they heeded. So perhaps the Gods
are preparing troubles and terrors for the world (or our small corner of
it) again, so that it may become beautiful and dramatic withal."*

[Upper] Outdoor strike meeting. [Lower] London slum and public market: two of
a series of interpretations of the paleotechnic Inferno that called forth Gustav Doré's
best powers. All pictures from the Illustrated London News.

41: MODEL INDUSTRIAL VILLAGE

*Neither municipal authorities nor industrial leaders felt adequate to cope
with the industrial town as a whole: hence philanthropic enterprisers went
back to a simpler village pattern. Some of the early factory housing in
Lowell, Mass., and Manchester, N. H., set a standard of human decency
and architectural order in these eotechnic (water power) industries that
was rarely met in bigger towns. The original leader in the communal housing movement was Robert Owen, whose success as a manufacturer was
not, unfortunately, confirmed by his communal experiments. In France, the
utopian influence of Fourier, equally marked, resulted in the actual building of at least one phalanstery by the ironmaster Godin, at Guise: an
early, more modest form of Le Corbusier's Unity House, a sort of 'village in the air,' with all the drawbacks of a small community and few
of the advantages. To the drastic need for improvements, the top photograph bears witness: for the houses in the foreground are built back to
back, with half the house destitute of light, fresh air, or outlook. I withhold the name of the town because similar degraded housing (and cellar
occupation) can be found in many other industrial areas. The first practical leader in better planning and housing was Sir Titus Salt, the founder
in 1851 of Saltaire. The reader may find it hard to distinguish this model
housing, in the upper left corner [middle] from that shown in Plate 39.
But note the park and playing fields to the right, bordered by the canal
and the River Aire. These were provided from the beginning and are
still maintained, though in the light of later purposes this area should not
have been so completely separated from the housing quarter: some of its
acreage might well have been spared in order to create bigger domestic
gardens. Saltaire was remarkable not only for its three-bedroomed houses,*

but for the provision of bathhouses, washhouses, and even almshouses for the aged. Salt's initiative was followed by other far-sighted manufacturers at Bournville, Port Sunlight, Earswick, Essen, Pullman, and many other points. The great improvement in housing layout of the first three over Saltaire had a beneficial effect upon the later provision of workers' houses. Port Sunlight, near Birkenhead, [bottom] despite its village scale shows with almost comic precision, in its outmoded baroque approach to the civic center, the influence of princely absolutism even under an industrial disguise. But note the generous size of the residential block interiors, which are divided up into allotment gardens, unfortunately with a complete sacrifice of the private garden as outdoor room.

[Top] Industrial town in England. Photograph: Aerofilms, Ltd., London. [Middle] Factory and housing at Saltaire. Photograph: Aerofilms, Ltd., London. [Bottom] Port Sunlight. Photograph by courtesy of Unilever, Ltd.

42: GREEN COUNTRY TOWNS

Near view of Chipping Camden [upper] already presented in Plate 33 shows the same combination of open spaces, gardens, and parkland later identified as suburban, but better described as the 'open plan.' What was called by the romantics a 'return to nature,' was often in fact only a return to the country town. The British upper classes, with their country houses near such a village and their town houses close to St. James's or Green Park, had the best of both worlds—which partly accounts, perhaps, for their success both in breeding and governing. Great Malvern [lower] exhibits the painless transition from the original country town growing up around a Benedictine priory (its church shows plainly near the center), to the late eighteenth century Spa, specializing in the then popular water cure. The 'Victorian gothic' mansions, built between 1840 and 1900, were set in open spaces as ample as those of any contemporary suburb, and perhaps re-enforced the growing taste for such a mode of living. The same motives had an effect on the design of 'model villages,' as the previous plate shows. Both the country town and the health resort erected a positive qualitative standard for water, sunlight, garden and recreation space, that could not be permanently confined to the upper classes or to the countryside. By this new standard the hygienic and esthetic misdemeanors of both industrial town and commercial metropolis could be judged. Even as early as 1685, when William Penn planned Philadelphia, this rural image served as desired model, for he specified that the new city was to be "a green country town."

Photographs: Aerofilms, Ltd., London.

43: CONQUEST OF SUBURBIA

Bronxville [upper] presents a classic picture of the last half century of suburban development. It began as a 'greenbelt suburb' with a handsome shopping center conveniently around the railroad station (center), in contrast to the insulated over-extended shopping centers that were to come a generation or more later. The original one-family houses, embowered in trees, set back from tree-lined streets and roads, represent the romantic ideal in its purity, and parts of the natural greenbelt may still be seen at the outskirts. But it had a new feature that enhanced its advantages: the green strip curving from the bottom upward, under railroad and motorway, is the Bronx River Parkway, the first regional parkway, originally conceived as a means of embellishing the hitherto untidy and sometimes sordid banks of the Bronx River: primarily a handsome strip park, planned for pedestrian walking and picnicking with only the most modest kind of motor road to accompany it. Continuity of space and movement and insulation from buildings and cross traffic made this the prototype of later parkways and expressways, some as beautiful as the nearby Taconic Parkway, a masterpiece of highway and landscape design, planned to follow the ridgeways and avoid the settled bottom land. The rural virtues of the suburb meanwhile resulted in a pressure for further accommodation which increased land values and brought in bulky metropolitan apartment buildings. Without public control and regional planning on a scale far beyond the powers of local authorities this area in another generation will hardly be distinguishable from any other overcrowded portion of the conurbation. Paradoxically, it is only as the lopsided, socially segregated suburb becomes a balanced urban community with no small part of its population working within the neighboring area that the rural landscape, the pedestrian parkway, and the domestic garden can be recovered. Where the pressure of population remains high, the best way of meeting it is by reorganizing both city and suburb into more organic neighborhood units, such as that of Chatham Village, Pittsburgh, [lower] which combine compactness and urbanity with both domestic open spaces and local park areas. Since Chatham Village remains one of the high points in site planning and architectural layout of the last generation, its failure to excite even local imitation remains inexplicable—all the more because it has been from the beginning an unqualified financial success, with a long waiting list of would-be renters.

[Upper] Bronxville, N. Y. Photograph by Fairchild Aerial Surveys, Inc., New York.
[Lower] Chatham Village, Pittsburgh. Photograph by courtesy of Clarence S. Stein.

44: BLOOMSBURY AND HAMPSTEAD GARDEN

Bloomsbury [upper] was one of the great triumphs of English planning and building. So strong was its influence that even a nineteenth century commercial builder like Thomas Cubitt imitated the example of the great landlords. The succession of squares shown here, with Russell Square in the middle, again demonstrates the way in which well-planned open spaces serve as a preventive of blight and disorder. The university precinct, with the British Museum in the foreground as focal point, takes full advantage of this order and enhances it: the tower of the University of London, standing alone, properly dominates the area, though the over-building of towers and high-rise structures, now going on all over London, will eventually annul the spaciousness of such quarters by throwing too heavy a load of people on the squares and too much traffic on the streets. Hampstead Garden Suburb [lower] was the culmination of a century of open planning. Here Unwin and Parker, profiting by the mistakes made in designing Letchworth Garden City, produced a far more coherent scheme that nevertheless afforded a rich variety of architectural settings in generous private gardens, and much usable public space, both open playing fields and woods. Hampstead Garden Suburb carried on the innovations made by Olmsted in Riverside, Ill., and Roland Park, Md.: the superblock, the quiet cul-de-sac, even the strip park and the inner block common. It paved the way, too, for further innovations, by Ernst May in Frankfort, particularly in Frankfort-Römerstadt, and by Wright and Stein in the United States. In its avoidance of excessive street widths and front gardens, it is superior in compactness and urbanity to many of the New Towns built half a century later. In the design of Wythenshawe, near Manchester, Barry Parker added one further innovation, the parkway, which separated the neighborhoods yet favored the building of small shopping centers at their conjunction.

[Upper] Photograph: Aero Pictorial, Ltd., London. [Lower] By courtesy of the London County Council. Huntington Aerosurveys, Ltd., London.

45: BELATED BAROQUE: WASHINGTON

The magnificent sweep of the Washington plan is best seen from the air, which conceals the barbarous way in which L'Enfant's plan was mangled, first by uncomely buildings and now by the introduction of expressways into the heart of the city. These are only two of many errors that vitiated Washington's noble plan. The failure to provide sufficient office space for the growing bureaucracy on both sides of Pennsylvania Avenue, the failure to limit the height of business buildings, the failure to keep the railroad

yards and stations at the outskirts of the central area, showed how lack-
ing in either public spirit or economic understanding the 'practical' ex-
ecutors of L'Enfant's plan were. The partial redemption of his concep-
tions begun by the Macmillan commission, with the rehabilitation of the
Mall, the building of the Lincoln Memorial, and the exemplary parking
of the Potomac Basin, unfortunately reckoned without the blight of the
motor car. When in 1959 the Roosevelt Memorial Commission sought a
site that could be approached on foot, without risk of life, in a spot free
from the visual and auditory distractions of motor traffic, none could be
found.

[Upper] The Mall, with the Washington Monument and the Lincoln Memorial at
the end of the Axis. [Lower] Heart of Washington, with National Capitol in center,
the Union Station to the right, and the White House beyond the 'Triangle' to the
right of the Washington Monument. Photographs by Fairchild Aerial Surveys, Inc.,
New York.

46: STANDARDIZED CHAOS

Though the most significant technical and architectural developments of
the skyscraper took place in Chicago from the 1880's onward, the profits
of congestion were even more eagerly exploited in New York, both in
high apartment houses and office buildings. The traffic arteries of the city
were planned in 1811 to take care of a population housed mainly in two
and three story buildings as in the area to the left. The building of ten
to forty story skyscrapers in effect superimposed from three to a dozen
cities in the same area, so even had private wheeled traffic remained at
a pre-automobile level the streets would have been desperately clogged.
The tallest building (in deep shadow) toward the bottom [upper] is the
RCA building, the dominant feature of Rockefeller Center, whose mi-
nuscule Plaza with its sunken skating rink serves as one of Manhattan's
few focal points for informal meeting and lounging, comparable to the
Spanish Steps in Rome. The similar popular success of Mellon Square
in Pittsburgh, has proved the Lonely Crowd's hunger for such informal
gregariousness. Olmsted's magnificent Central Park (middle) with its mul-
tifold independent systems of circulation improved on Leonardo da Vinci's
early suggestion for Milan and anticipated the Radburn Plan, to say noth-
ing of Le Corbusier, by almost a century. The nineteenth century slum
tenements of New York fully equalled in congestion, bad sanitation, and
high rents the most sordid quarters of Berlin, Bombay, Glasgow, Genoa,
or Naples. These vile quarters are now being replaced by more orderly
housing precincts, with light, air, sanitary conveniences of a superior or-
der. The example in the foreground [lower], Stuyvesant Town, was built
by a private insurance company with generous aid by the State: but its

residential density of 393 per acre remains that of a slum. Despite its inner open spaces, this housing would require eighty additional acres to provide the park and playground space now regarded as desirable, nineteen more than the entire project without buildings. This fact is studiously ignored by those who confuse the visual open space provided by high-rise buildings with functional and usable open space, scaled to the number of people per acre. The multiplication of such formidable enclaves of congestion in every part of the city, sometimes privately exploited, sometimes public housing projects, always with government aid under 'urban renewal' legislation, cannot be justified as a contribution to a meaningful and valuable social life, or as a desirable pattern for human co-operation. A whole city built on this basis would be a bureaucratic nightmare of inefficiency and inhumanity.

Photographs: Ewing Galloway.

47: URBAN DEVASTATION

Currently the most popular and effective means of destroying a city is the introduction of multiple-lane expressways, especially elevated ones, into the central core. This came about immediately after elevated railways for passenger service were being demolished as public nuisances! Though Los Angeles presents the hugest example of large-scale urban demolition by incontinent expressway building, Boston is perhaps an even more pitiable victim, because it had more to lose, since it boasts a valuable historic core, where every facility is within walking distance, and a metropolitan transit system that, as far back as the eighteen-nineties, was a model of effective unification. As with current military plans based on nuclear extermination, Boston's planners are attempting to cover over their initial mistakes by repeating them on a wider scale. The ultimate outcome will be similar to that in Greensboro, North Carolina [bottom], nicknamed the 'Parking Lot City,' but unfairly so because every city is fast becoming a parking lot city, even Amsterdam and Paris, with all their space devoted to cars and none left for any other functions of the city. Thus the bombs that devasted the City of London in the Blitz [middle] did no more damage than the unrestricted planning of expressways and parking lots is now doing every day, abetted by a national highways program planned on the same assumptions of mono-transportation from 'door to door.' A single subordinate function of the city has been made the sole reason for its existence—or rather, the triumphant justification for its non-existence. With the motorways, as with the building of skyscrapers, we find superb technical skill in mechanical organization and practical design united to paralyzing social incompetence and cultural illiteracy.

[Top] Multiple-lane elevated highway in Boston, with built-in bottlenecks where it joins the street network. Photograph: Ewing Galloway. [Middle] Bombed out area around St. Paul's, London. Photograph: British Official. By courtesy of the British Office of Information. [Bottom] Greensboro, N. C. Photograph: Ewing Galloway.

48: THE SPACE EATERS

The essential facilities and functions of the city—co-operation, communication, and communion, meeting, mixture, and mobilization—call for a container where a great diversity of activities can simultaneously take place. Such a container, in order to be sufficiently economic of space, requires a diversified transportation network. When only one means of transportation is available, the activity itself must be pushed out of the city, even for such occasional mobilizations as that shown in the Pasadena Rose Bowl [upper left]. The notion that no American will willingly walk even a quarter of a mile is sardonically contradicted by the formidable distances they actually plow through in shopping centers and in parking lots. Needless to say, these paved deserts remain expensively idle and empty when no crowd activities take place. The freeway at Los Angeles [upper right] illustrates the cancer of mono-transportation in its most advanced stages: the multiple-lane expressway and parking lot have almost completely eaten away the living tissue of the city. In the interest of an unimpeded traffic flow highway engineers produce vast clover leaves [lower left] even in low density areas with limited cross traffic, where there is no reason whatever why the arterial flow should not be occasionally halted as in a city street. Saving time by squandering space is hardly a public economy in areas like the Bay Region of San Francisco that are threatened with serious shortages of agricultural and recreational land and huge excesses of unusable leisure time. Though the 'industrial park'—American equivalent of the English 'trading estate' [lower right]—is a superior example of neotechnic planning, admirably insulated from the neighboring community, effectively served by highways, the cheapness and convenience of one-story construction has encouraged loose planning and sprawl. Here building on stilts would have permitted the housing of motor cars beneath, protected against summer heat and winter snow, and would have freed space for a noon-hour recreation area, with beneficial results both to work and production. In such areas public authority might well place differential taxes favoring higher industrial building, economic of land, and discouraging low ones except for plants needing exceptionally heavy installations of machines. But in America space-eating has become almost a national pastime. The demands for space made by airports using jet transportation are so copious that they can only be satisfied in open country so far from the major cities that they nullify the jet plane's gain in speed, between cities as distant as New York and Chicago. The standards that Frank Lloyd Wright projected in 'The Disappearing City'—at least one acre of land per family—are taken as universally desirable even if not achievable. As a result the city itself is fast disappearing: its scattered parts "lost in space."

[Upper Left] Photograph by Fairchild Aerial Surveys, Inc., New York. [Upper Right and Lower Left] Photographs by courtesy of the State of California, Department of Public Works. [Lower Right] Photograph: Ewing Galloway.

is Francis of Assisi. It was Francis, himself a merchant's son, who sought
to substitute voluntary Christian service, a free exchange of gifts, for the
ordinary arrangements of hiring and buying. Those who sought to live like
the early Christians, Francis thought, would no longer withdraw from
life like the early monks, but would go among men, setting a smiling
example of Christian love, preaching by acts as much as by words, working for others, living in poverty without any permanent shelter, and taking no thought for the morrow. All labor was to become a labor of love:
life, instead of being encased in buildings and walls, was to be a 'Song of
the Open Road,' and its material requirements were to be improvised, as
Francis improvised the great meeting of Christian brothers and sisters at
Portiuncula, with a success in voluntary provisioning that astounded his
rival, Dominic.

In Francis' dream, this new order of brothers and sisters was to have
no building of its own, no permanent possessions to bind the spirit to
possessiveness itself. This was one more attempt, along the lines of Lao-tse
and Jesus, to break down the walls of the power-driven, wealth-encrusted
ego and dismantle, ultimately, the walled city, that ego's greatest collective expression. In a word, emancipation from the closed container: a
true and complete etherialization.

The Papacy put down this heresy as sternly as it stamped out that of
Peter Waldo (c. 1170), the pious merchant, who founded the first of the
great protestant sects for a similar purpose. Not without statesmanlike
cunning, the Pope insisted on making the Franciscan order an instrument
of Papal power, and he ensured its subordination, indeed its inner sub-
version, by encouraging a heavy investment in appropriate conventual
buildings, in the very birthplace of the new order; for there is no quicker
way of killing an idea than to 'materialize' it too soon. The glory of Giotto's
paintings in the Upper Church at Assisi conceals the betrayal of Francis,
who would have been at home only in the Lower Church. A short while
later, by a bull of Pope John XXII, the reawakened belief in Christian
communism, the notion that a sharing of possessions and the means of
life had been practiced by the early apostles, as related in the New Testament, was anathematized as a heresy.

Yet the desire to create a Christian city for long haunted the medieval
mind, from the time of Waldo and Langland to that of John Bunyan and
Johann Andreae. Heaven itself, we must remember, was an urban artifact:
a city where immortal souls met each other and beheld the ineffable
Presence throughout eternity. The longing for a Christian city kept crop-
ping out, shyly, despite papal frowns, in the orders of dedicated laymen,
like the Beguines, which took hold particularly in the Low Countries; and
it flared up, to the point of revolutionary effort, among the Anabaptists of
Münster and elsewhere. But the one power that might have made Chris-

tianopolis more than a utopian dream, the Church itself, was firmly set against it.

If at the beginning the medieval city was truly shaped by Christian needs and interests, it was never completely transformed by the Christian challenge: the ancient powers and principalities were all too firmly lodged behind its walls. The jealous gods who had presided over the birth of the city in Mesopotamia and Egypt were more persistent and persuasive than the new teacher from Palestine, who, like Buddha, had turned his back upon all symbols of material permanence and all self-estranging formalisms. The repetitive ritual of the old temple, the coercive violence of the old citadel, the hostile enclosures and isolations that gave ancient magical aberrations a permanent form—these institutions remained at the very core of the medieval town. Though repeatedly threatened by outside invasions, Huns, Saracens, Mongols, Turks, the worst damage inflicted on medieval towns was that which one Christian community perpetrated on another, in an endless round of savage, merciless urban wars. Over that scandal and shame, the voice of the Church remained monotonously silent. How could it be otherwise? Rome's own acts would have choked her admonitory words.

For this miscarriage of the medieval city, Christian theology had an answer: namely, the doctrine of original sin. This presupposes a radical flaw in the constitution of man, arising out of Adam's disobedience, which turned his original sin into an organic, hereditary ailment: a perverse tendency set aside God's purposes by putting his own selfish nature first. So inveterate is this tendency, according to Christian theology, that in the very act of combatting it, man may commit what he is trying to avoid; the only way out, therefore, is the acknowledgment of chronic failure and the hope for repentance and grace.

The fact is that sin had become the Church's principal source of worldly revenue. Only by enlarging this sphere and inflating these debits could the Church's monopoly of salvation yield sufficient profits. So, when the goods of civilization were replenished, from the tenth century onward, its evils were restored in due proportion, by the very institution that should have addressed itself to reducing them. By the sixteenth century Machiavelli would observe, not without justice, in his 'Discourses': "The nearer people are to the Church of Rome, which is the head of our religion, the less religious are they." By the time the Council of Trent addressed itself to this situation, it was too late to stay the disintegration of the medieval urban complex.

Whatever the medieval city might be, then, it remained only the pale simulacrum of Christianopolis. The outline of that city was strong enough to give one hope for a new urban order, based on the religious and social premises of the most widespread of all the axial religions. But in the very growth of the town the spiritual substance tended to disappear. Again we face the same paradox of static, one-sided materialization we first examined in the growth of the Greek city.

2: VENICE VERSUS UTOPIA

At the close of the Middle Ages, one city in Europe stood out above every other because of its beauty and its wealth. Red Siena, black and white Genoa, gray Paris, variegated Florence might all put in their claims as archetypal medieval cities, and certainly Florence rose above all the other cities of Europe, from the thirteenth to the sixteenth century by reason of the austere magnificence of its art and the vivacity of its intellectual life. But golden Venice has a special claim on our attention. No other city shows, in more diagrammatic form, the ideal components of the medieval urban structure. In addition, none gave a better indication in its own internal development of a new urban constellation that promised to transcend the walled container, as it had existed from the end of the neolithic phase.

The esthetic glories of Venice have never been forgotten or disparaged, except perhaps by her threadbare inhabitants in that sad period when the economic foundations of Venice were sapped and the whole edifice began to crumble. But the new example Venice set in city planning was never taken in, much less imitated by other cities. If people were aware of the uniqueness of Venice's plan, they treated it as a mere accident of nature, not as a series of bold adaptations which, though based on singular natural features, had a universal application. That is why I purpose to examine the plan of Venice here; for Venice pushed even further, right into our own age, the organization by neighborhoods and precincts whose recovery today, as an essential cellular unit of planning, is one of the fundamental steps toward re-establishing a new urban form.

Venice was the creation of a group of refugees from Padua in the fifth century A.D., fleeing across the lagoons from the invader. The shallow waters of the Adriatic took the place of the stone wall for protection, and the swamps and islands, connected only by water, suggested the dredging of canals to fill in the nearby lands and to establish channels of transportation. The gondola (mentioned as early as 1094) was the perfect technical adaptation to these narrow, shallow waterways. Though Venice had to develop cisterns for collecting rain water, to supplement the supply that came by boats from the mainland, she solved the ever-vexing problem

of sanitation more easily than her mainland rivals, by being able to dump
her sewage directly into the sea, where the action of salt and sunlight,
along with tidal movements, seems capable of neutralizing reasonable
concentrations of noxious bacteria.

At the core of Venice lies the Piazza San Marco: an open space in
front of its ancient Byzantine Church, originally the orchards of St. Mark's.
In 976, close to where the Campanile was first built in the twelfth century, a lodging house for pilgrims to the Holy Land was established. This
was the beginning of the later hotel quarter. As early as the twelfth century,
a piazza, filled with market stalls, was taking shape here, for in 1172
the place was widened. The buildings that are now standing around the
place record a continuous development that began with the rebuilding of
St. Mark's itself, in 1176, the erection of the old Campanile in 1180, the
beginning of the Ducal Palace in 1300, and the old Procurator's Hall in
1520. This was followed by the building that closes up one side of the
piazetta, the Library, designed by Sansovino in 1536, on the site of the
old bakeries. But note: the final addition to the present square, which
made it an esthetic whole by completing the end opposite the Cathedral,
was not made till 1805.

Both the form and the contents of the Piazza were, in brief, the products of cumulative urban purposes, modified by circumstance, function,
and time: organic products that no single human genius could produce
in a few months over a drafting board. Gradually, the political and social
functions of the piazza pushed back the original rural and marketing functions; and the latter were, step by step, transferred to other parishes of
the city, leaving only restaurants, cafés, shops, and hotels near the site of
the first hostelry for pilgrims.

In short, the plan of Venice was no static design, embodying the needs
of a single generation, arbitrarily ruling out the possibilities of growth,
re-adaptation, change: rather, here was continuity in change, and unity
emerging from a complex order. Significantly, in a city ruled by an iron-
handed patriciate, ruthless in its centralization of power and responsibility,
the members of the Council of 480 were decentralized: they were compelled to reside in the parishes they represented. By the same token, the
Magistrates of the Arsenal had their residences in that specialized industrial quarter of the town. This prevented that over-concentration of upper-
class housing that so often leads to the toleration of urban disorder in the
remoter districts of a town. If the great palaces occupy the airy sites on
the Grand Canal, facing the sea-breezes, they also have their attachments
to the quarter behind.

What the casual tourist often does not always realize is that the pattern of St. Mark's is repeated on a smaller scale in each of the parishes

of Venice. Each has its campo or square, often of an odd trapezoidal shape, with its fountain, its church, its school, often its own guildhall; for the city was originally divided into six neighborhoods, each harboring one of the six guilds of the city. The canals, now some 177 in all, serve as the boundaries of these neighborhoods, as well as connecting links: they are both waterbelts and arterial highways, functioning like the greenbelts and through motor ways of a well-designed modern town, though not so reckless of urban space as American highways or the neighborhood greenbelts of English New Towns frequently are. Around the city, the great lagoons serve as inviting water promenade and 'park' in one, with townscape and water replacing landscape. No other city from the fifteenth century on has tempted more painters to reproduce its image.

Many of these characteristics of Venice can be matched in other medieval cities. What was never so clearly expressed elsewhere was the system of functional zoning: a system established more easily here, because of the disposition of the greater and lesser islands around the central city. Venice turned this seeming handicap into an opportunity.

According to its situation and size, each of Venice's islands found its appropriate function: not least that dedicated to the convent of San Georgio, close to St. Mark's. The first functional precinct was that of Torcello: a church and a cemetery islet seven miles away, where the dead were buried. The next precinct was an industrial quarter, that of the Arsenal, erected in 1104, enlarged in 1473 and again in the sixteenth century: a shipyard, provisioning center for vessels, and a munitions works, which in the fifteenth century employed 16,000 workmen and harbored 36,000 seamen. Another principal industry of Venice, its glass industry, was established by an act of the Grand Council on the separate island of Murano by 1255.

Now these were the first large scale industrial areas to be set apart from the mixed uses of the ordinary medieval city. Had there been eyes to see and intelligence to appraise, Venice might have set the pattern for the development of heavy industries in growing urban centers after the sixteenth century; and as rapid transport facilities increased, the nuclear but open plan of Venice would, if imitated, have overcome the tendency to provide for extension by solid massing and overcrowding and sprawling, in the fashion of other expanding cities.

By making the most of their opportunities, in other words, the Venetians, no doubt inadvertently, invented a new type of city, based on the differentiation and zoning of urban functions, separated by traffic ways and open spaces. This was zoning on the grandest scale, practiced in a rational manner, which recognized the integrity of neighborhoods and which minimized the wasteful 'journey to work.' So native to the city was this system, that it was carried on even in the nineteenth century, when the island of Lido became a seashore pleasure resort: a recreation precinct.

The neighborhoods and industrial zones of Venice, so far from destroying the unity of the city, served only to keep the central quarter from being unduly congested. But on days of public holiday, like the magnificent water festival which celebrated the marriage of the city and the Adriatic, the Piazza San Marco, the Piazzetta, and the nearby quays brought the whole city together, with the Ducal Palace itself, perhaps the most beautiful example of municipal architecture in the world, forming the dominant setting in the collective ritual.

The political order of Venice was based on an ultimately demoralizing combination of violence and secrecy: its rulers used private informers and secret assassination as a commonplace weapon of control. This system must have hampered every variety of honest work, candid judgment, and trustful collaboration, causing those at the center to be stultified, like the members of any totalitarian system today, by their own morbid fantasies and hallucinations. We have seen, even under our own formally democratic government in America, that any group that operates in secret, be it an Atomic Energy Commission or a National Security Council or a Central Intelligence Agency, loses touch with reality by the very terms on which it operates. What begins as the suppression of a critical opposition ends with the suppression of truth and the elimination of any alternative to the accepted policy, however patent its errors, however psychotic its plans, however fatal its commitments.

Actually, the political state of Venice was less successful than its makers supposed, despite its prosperity and continuity. But the urban community was kept in some degree of balance because its ruling group at least paid the price for their system, as totalitarian states do today, by trading security for freedom: thus they provided over many centuries for steady industrial employment, social services of many sorts, and dazzling public festivals. So, typically, it was not the workers, but rival members of the ruling classes, that usually threatened treason or revolt.

But the physical order created by the Republic of Venice was even better than its makers knew: they had in fact, without any apparent consciousness of their achievement, devised a new type of urban container, marked by the etherialization of the wall. Even its decayed and overcrowded remains today point to a radically different urban organization than the ancient, still-persistent, stone-age image and pattern. What Venice could achieve in a city that never, in its palmiest days, numbered more than two hundred thousand people, a modern municipality, with our facilities for rapid communication and transport, might do for a community ten times that number. Strangely, it needed the invention of the

Radburn plan in 1928 before even an occasional town planner's eye opened sufficiently to take in the innovations that Venice had fully consummated five centuries before. But the striking similarity, the separation of the pedestrian from other modes of traffic and transport—though it was completed in Venice long before Leonardo da Vinci made the same proposal to cure the traffic congestion of Milan—is only a small part of the total contribution that Venice made to the art of town planning.

Venice itself had grown out of the grim realities of forced immigration, war, conflict, piracy, and trade. Though it commanded men's allegiances, over the generations, by its splendor and order, it made no pretenses to being an ideal city: it was merely the best that a succession of energetic merchants and industrialists, who courted money and power, and the luxuries that money and power will buy, were able to conceive. Let us contrast it then with a city whose fabricator sought, in fact, to present an ideal pattern: namely, with Amaurote, the capital of Sir Thomas More's 'Utopia,' a book published in 1516, just at the turning point of Venice's own fortunes.

Amaurote, situated in the center of the Island of Utopia, is one of 54 cities or country towns, none of which is less than 24 miles from the next, though "none is so isolated that you cannot go from it to another in a day's journey on foot." Amaurote itself, the capital, is four-square in plan, on a tidal river, like London, to bring the boats in from the sea. The streets, twenty feet wide, "are well laid out both for traffic and to avoid the winds," and every house has both a street door and a garden door; indeed their zeal for gardening "is increased not merely by the pleasure afforded them, but by the keen competition between streets, which shall have the best kept gardens." This outer green belt and this inner spaciousness are re-enforced by two years of country living, mandatory under the law, for every inhabitant. Thus More makes sure of his garden city by educating garden-citizens.

Each Utopian city is divided into four quarters. In the middle of each quarter is a marketplace, with shops and stores about it. But the more intimate organization, the neighborhood, is based on the family. Each thirty families selects a magistrate, while the whole body of magistrates selects the Mayor, and all the cities send representatives to the Utopian legislature. The basis of this whole system of representative government is the thirty neighborhood families, whose members dine together regularly in one of the spacious dining halls that line the street. There the chief magistrate and his wife preside at High Table.

Perhaps this innovation of More's was not altogether lost: it foreshadows that of the Amana communities in Iowa, with their common dining halls, now used as public restaurants. Along with More's grouping of households goes a common nursery: even in a day when house servants were usual, More did not ignore the advantages of such occasional relief from family care. Thus the primary form of organization is not the guild, but the family and the neighborhood; or rather, what the French planner, Gaston Bardet, has called the "patriarchal echelon." In the communal institutions More restores the sharing and largesse that were common in simple communities before the introduction of a money economy.

More's greatest innovation, perhaps, was to give institutional support for the medieval townsman's love of country life and sports. He decreed that agriculture should be the one common pursuit, for both men and women: they are all instructed in it from their early years, partly by regular teaching in school, partly by being taken out into land adjacent to the city, as if for amusement, where they do not merely look on rural activities, but, as opportunity arises, do the actual work.

Since participation in work is universal, the Utopians work only six hours a day. This gives them both an economy of abundance and a fullness of leisure; and they devote the latter chiefly, through both private study and public lectures, to learning. The idle rich, the swashbuckling retainers, and the lusty beggars have no place in More's Utopia: neither have the "great and idle company of priests and the so-called religious." A devout man himself, ready to die at the stake for his honor and his Church, More well knew the hollowness of much of the ostentatious religious devotion of the late medieval city.

In some ways, it would seem, More's imaginary city is not merely a great advance over Venice, but in its desire for equality, in its effort to spread both goods and leisure, in its conversion of work into a form of play, and both into a means of sustaining the mind, it anticipates the social potentialities our own period has begun to outline. In Amaurote, collective service and friendly association have softened the rigid forms of power. Here, in faint outline at least, is the social city of the future, as Venice, in much bolder and clearer form, possibly pre-figures the future physical city. Toward both goals, the great cities of the world have still a long way to go.

But precisely at the point where More must translate his social improvements into material forms, his imagination halts, as Plato's had halted before him. Or rather, More's images freeze into the forms of his own time, which were just beginning to come forth out of the medieval order. Thus his scale is no longer the medieval pedestrian scale: the city is roughly two miles square; and the distribution of people, with ten to sixteen adults in a family, six thousand families in all, brings the total population up well over one hundred thousand. At this point, it is true, he sets a limit; for after filling up deficient population in such cities as are below this level, More provides for colonization outside the country.

Along with this new spatial scale goes a new uniformity, yes, and a new drabness and monotony. "He who knows one of the cities," he ob-serves, "will know them all, so exactly alike are they, except where the nature of the ground prevents." The same language, the same manners, customs, laws. The same similarity in appearance: no variety in urban form. No variety in costume: no variety in color. This was the new note: the note of standardization, regimentation, and collective control: Quaker drab or prison drab. Is this Eutopia—the 'good place'?

Was More attuned in advance to the coming age of despots, ready though he was to challenge the nearest despot in person? What caused him to look upon the absence of variety and choice as in any sense an ideal requirement? Did he, even more intuitively, suspect the price that our own age would have to pay eventually for its mechanized production and its economy of abundance? And was he therefore prepared, in the name of abstract justice, to pay that price, heavy though it might be in terms of other goods, equally essential to human life? He has left us no clue to the answer.

In some respects, the reader will note, More's Utopia struck at the radical defects and shortcomings of the medieval town: the preponder-ance of private riches, the over-specialization of the crafts and professions into a strict, hierarchic, often mutually hostile, non-communicating order. By giving the urban citizens a country education and a period of com-pulsory agricultural service, he sought to break down the disparities and the latent hostilities that existed between the two realms. So too, he restored and extended the urban garden, as an essential part of the town plan, at the moment when it had begun to be cramped, and in places had already disappeared.

More's desire for inner spaciousness was repeated, incidentally, in the large blocks provided in William Penn's plan for Philadelphia in 1688; but by the eighteenth century, as Elfreth's Alley and many similar alleys still remind us, the generous original blocks were subdivided by streets and alleys that reduced the living quarters to doll's-house size, with open spaces correspondingly cribbed and cabined. Above all, it would seem, More consciously tried to "withdraw as much time as pos-sible from the service of the body and devote it to the freedom and cul-ture of the mind," not just for a class but for a whole community. And yet, even in the seemingly untrammeled dreams of this humane man, he still was fastened to the ancient walls of the citadel: slaves, in punish-ment for their crimes, performed the viler labors of the community, and war, though hateful to the Utopians, remained an integral part of their institutional life. In fact, Utopians were experts at propaganda and sub-version as an instrument of warfare, and used physical blows only for the *coup de grâce*. Is this, again, Eutopia?

If Venice was the highest product of medieval practice, Utopia was perhaps, with regard to the constitution and organization of urban communities, the fullest example of late medieval thought. But who would exchange Venice for the dreary regimentation and uniformity of Amaurote? And yet who would exchange the civic decencies of Amaurote for the secretive tyranny, the festering suspicions and hatreds, the assassinations of character, the felonious assaults and murders that underlay the prosperous trade and the festive art of Venice? The flaw that had been handed on from civilization to civilization, through the urban container, was still visible in both cities. When we admire the surviving outward form, we must not forget the persistence of the inner trauma—the trauma of civilization itself, the association of mastery and slavery, of power and human sacrifice.

3: MEDIEVAL SURVIVALS AND MUTATIONS

The best examples of a culture are not always the most characteristic ones; for what is most typical is what is most time-bound and limited. Dekker and Chapman are part and parcel of late medieval London, while Shakespeare, though he shared this milieu, transcended it at a hundred points. This holds likewise for the culture of cities. In the sixteenth and seventeenth centuries certain fresh urban forms came into existence: they characterized neither the receding Middle Ages nor the oncoming mercantile economy and absolutist government. And these new urban forms were not 'transitional,' since they led only in their own direction, toward their own further goals. But they have more significance for us today than the dominant specimens of the period, which I shall treat under the general heading of the Baroque.

While many older medieval centers, deserted by overseas trade, were drying up like a river in drought, leaving only the bed carved by the once rushing waters, and while militarism and mercantilism were imposing a more mechanical pattern of growth, the countryside was undergoing an organic improvement and rejuvenation. The institutions of the medieval city at last flowed back into the countryside and produced villages and country towns whose urbanity was heightened by their rural setting. This improvement was expressed most happily in the villages of central and northern Europe, from Bavaria to the Netherlands and thence over to England, right into the western counties. It resulted in the transformation

of the frowsty little settlements of medieval times, often a collection of
hovels, pinched in size, done in scrap materials—still visible in many
seventeenth-century prints—into smart, compact, well-ordered little communities, built of stone or brick, whose little guildhall or market hall
would be duly embellished with painting or sculpture not greatly inferior
to that in the great urban centers: a medieval town in miniature, again
with ample gardens behind the row houses.

Some of the finest villages in England—Burford, Bybury, Chipping
Camden—date in their final form from the period between the sixteenth
and the eighteenth century: a time that must, within the bigger corporate
towns, be described as one mainly of decay. The reason for this renewal
of the village was probably, at bottom, an economic one: the gradual
escape of the crafts from the over-protected and over-controlled corporate
town, and the growing parity of the rural craftsman, who had a garden
to supplement his wages, with the urban worker, living in congested quarters, with high rents and little effective guild protection, especially in the
new industries. The increased efficiency of agricultural production from
the sixteenth century on no doubt played a part, too, especially in the
Low Countries where mixed farming, with cows, horses, and pigs to furnish manure, raised horticulture to a level that had been reached, perhaps,
only in China.

The disappearance of the three-field system and the unification of
scattered strips into larger parcels paralleled the unification of the feudal
system into large national entities; and it created the more unified landscape of post-medieval Europe, sometimes with definite boundary marks
and hedges, as in England, sometimes in the older open forms, as in
Bavaria, Switzerland, and Holland. The once-feudal village, stimulated
by the fresh infusion of hand industry and by a more plentiful food supply, got almost its first opportunity to trade with the city on an even level,
and so to command goods from the outside world.

From these surviving villages today one can get one's best notions of
the layout of the original medieval towns, now hopelessly confused in their
formations with the debris of half a dozen different cultural epochs. In
places like Bybury, one even comes upon departures from the row house,
in little groupings that anticipated—and indeed helped to form—the
finest efforts of Raymond Unwin and Barry Parker. Nor did mechanized
production upset this new order: rather, it furthered it, for the wider use
of the water mill and the wind mill gave the village a source of power that
often enough, through the very fact of urban growth, had become insufficient in the crowded center.

In these fresh departures in vernacular form, the Dutch contributions
were particularly significant. Their influence, like that of the advanced
horticulturists with their glass houses, was felt throughout Europe, for the

Dutch farm and the Dutch garden became models for progressive agriculture. And this command of water was registered within the city as well as on the polders, for the two were in constant intercourse: this gave the ordinary Dutch country town or canal village, no less than Amsterdam, not merely a clean façade and a frame of verdure, but a super-clean interior, such as would be established with the aid of sand or holystone and sea water on the most shipshape of vessels. The big windows of the seventeenth-century small house in Holland, repeated more than two hundred years later, alike in the architecture of the radical Oud and that of the conservative Grandpré-Molière, brought into the dwelling an amount of sunlight and fresh air that corresponded to that which Johann Andreae had pictured in his ideal city of Christianopolis, itself no bigger than a village.

In general, the layout and amenities of the Dutch brick cottage of this period were not merely in advance of its contemporary upper-class housing in other countries: they are still above the level that has so far been reached in most places by contemporary reformers of housing. The result was not wholly ideal, as we shall see when we discuss Amsterdam, but both the democratization of the medieval city and the decentralization of industry moved in the right direction, favoring local decisions, human control, the human scale.

A similar change took place in the New World, for it was there that the medieval order renewed itself, as it were, by colonization. In South America, the new colonial towns were laid out in advance, in accordance with principles laid down in the Laws of the Indies, codified in 1523, at the time of the conquest of Mexico. But these new towns looked backward, not forward—for they followed the standard Bastide pattern, and carried that standardization further by providing for a forum, or plaza, ideally 400 by 600 feet, in the center of the town, with a church dominating one side, leaving the plaza itself open. The house blocks were strictly rectangular in form and the streets wide: so much so, according to Robert Smith, that the Italian bishop Geradini, on his arrival at Santo Domingo in 1520, commended the streets as broader and straighter than those of his native Florence. Though the Portuguese colonial towns were often more irregularly carried out, and were closer to the more organic medieval pattern, nowhere does one find anything that corresponds to such an ideal baroque scheme as Palma Nuova.

If the Spanish colonial town in the New World was a military survival, the New England village was a happy mutation. In the settlement of the Back Bay colony, the Puritan adventurers, though they were more familiar with trade and handicraft than farming, easily resisted the temptation to pile up their population in the port of Boston. Fortunately, they were dependent at the beginning upon agriculture, and this forced them to risk spreading their plantations thinly, in order to occupy the land. The heart of their new towns and villages was the Common: an open area, often larger than the Spanish plaza, where their sheep and cattle might safely graze, under the eye of a municipal official, the cattle reeve. Around the common, from the very outset, the public buildings were erected: the meeting house, the town hall, and later the school. These institutions served as a rallying point for the community, and the Common did duty as drill ground for the local militia: another medieval institution. The medieval ideal of self-government, so imperfectly fulfilled in Europe on account of the persistent opposition by lords, bishops, bourgeois magnates, here came into full flower, for the protestant congregation had control of the church as well as the town.

Each member of the community at the beginning was allotted his share of the land: usually from half an acre to an acre within the village, though the parson might have as much as ten acres, while the farm allotments lay in the outskirts, beyond the early stockades, sometimes far enough to justify the erection of a summer house, as in the medieval city. In the early regulations, according to William Weeden, no one was permitted to live more than half a mile from the meeting house lest, in the rigors of a New England winter, he should evade his social obligations as a member of the Church.

Sometimes the common was a wide strip of a hundred and fifty or two hundred feet, running the length of the village, as in Sharon, Connecticut, sometimes an oblong or a square. Around this area, from the eighteenth century on, were set the separate houses, with white clapboards and green shutters, free standing, decently separated from their neighbors, with deep rear gardens large enough for a small orchard and a stable, as well as a vegetable plot. Tall elm trees or maples on each side of the road furnished shade from the torrid summer sun and partial windbreaks against the winter wind; their leafy arcade unified the scattered houses: a perfect unison of man and nature. As late as the nineteenth century, in the layout of some of the early villages of Ohio, like Gallipolis, these admirable features were preserved. Only in the suburbs of the upper middle classes in the nineteenth century was any approximation to the order and beauty of this open layout achieved.

At a time when the medieval town was being encysted, when people swarmed behind massive fortifications, accepting a city without trees or gardens or even single-family dwellings, as the normal environment of town life, here in America the more open order of the medieval city was kept in being—indeed, amplified and enriched: a princely spaciousness for democratic purposes. This order was based on the fact that the New England town deliberately refused to grow beyond the possibility of socializing and assimilating its members: it thus brought into existence, and in many places kept going for two centuries, a balance between rural and urban occupations, as well as an internal balance of population and usable land.

When the allotted area was fully occupied, and crowding threatened, the surplus members of the community would select a new pastor and move off to a new plantation, to erect a new meeting house, enclose a new common, form a new village, and lay out fresh fields. Hiving off to new centers discouraged congestion in the old ones; and the further dividing of the land in the new communities among all its members, in terms of family need as well as wealth and rank, gave a rough equality to the members, or at least guaranteed a basic minimum of existence to the diligent and the thrifty. Each family had its rights in the common land; each family had fields on the outskirts, as well as gardens nearer their homes; each male had the duty of participating in the political affairs of the town through the annual town meeting. A democratic polity—and the most healthy and comely kind of environment, as long as it remained on a small scale. In every fiber this renewed medieval form contrasted not merely with its own authoritarian past, but with all the anti-democratic assumptions of the new baroque order.

The continued growth of the New England town by division of the central social nucleus into new cells, having an independent life of their own, recalled the earlier pattern of Greece. But the New England towns added a new feature that has never been sufficiently appreciated nor as widely copied as it deserved: the township. The township is a political organization which encloses a group of towns, villages, hamlets, along with the open country area that surrounds them: it performs the functions of local government, including the provision of schools and the care of local roads, without accepting the long-established division between town and country. Within the limits of the township—sometimes covering an area of a dozen or more miles in each direction—its inhabitants recognized the need for decentralized facilities, in the one room primary school house or the country general store. In the township pattern, the growth of population and social facilities was not confined to a single center: something like a balance was achieved locally, within a regional pattern equally balanced.

The political importance of this new form must not be under-rated, though the failure to grasp it and to continue it—indeed to incorporate it in both the Federal and the State Constitutions—was one of the tragic over-sights of post-revolutionary political development. Thus the abstract polit-ical system of democracy lacked concrete organs. No one assessed the importance of the township system better than Emerson, writing in his 'Journal' in 1853: "The town is the unit of the Republic. The New England States founded their constitutions on towns and not on communities, which districting leads us to. And thus are the politics the school of the people, the game which everyone of them learns to play. And therefore they are all skillful in California, or on Robinson Crusoe's Island, instantly to erect a working government, as French and Germans are not. In the Western States and in New York and Pennsylvania, the town system is not the base, and therefore the expenditure of the legislature is not economic but prodigal. By district, or whatever throws the election into the hands of committees, men are re-elected who could not get the votes of those to whom they are known."

Yet this example was not altogether lost in the establishment of later communities. The scattering of the population in villages and towns within the open country persisted in Ohio and Wisconsin on much the same pattern as in New England; and this wide diffusion lessened the tendency to funnel population into a few big centers, as in present-day Australia or the Pacific Northwest.

After the eighteenth century, the social features of the New England village and mill town would be repeated only in utopian communities: most notably in the Amana villages of Iowa, a 'true inspiration' that throve for almost a century. The Amana community embraced some twenty-five thousand acres of land, and was made up of seven agricultural villages, each with its own church and school, its bakery, its dairy, its wine cellar, its post office, and its general store. These communities were from a mile and a half to four miles apart; but all were within a radius of six miles from old Amana.

The villages themselves, consisting of a cluster of forty to a hundred houses, were arranged in the manner of a German street village, with one long straggling street and several irregular offshoots. At one end of the village were barns and sheds; at the other end, the factories and workshops; on either side lay the orchards, the vineyards, and the gardens; while in the areas between the communities carefully planted forests provided a large part of the lumber needed for their furniture-making industry, once as famous as Amana blankets and Amana bacon and ham, and the Amana freezer. The architecture of these villages, and their general layout, a comely, straightforward brick vernacular, was superior to the usual run of buildings in the second half of the nineteenth century: it vied with that of the earlier Shaker communities in everything but architectural inventiveness.

These practical common-sense advances in urban development, though on a village scale, were in fact just as important for their potential contribution to city building as to their actual success in their own rural setting. Their nuclear growth within an open but unified pattern was exemplary. Both were part of a general culture which, partly by good luck and a favoring chain of circumstances, partly by conscious planning, had achieved a balanced economy.

This eotechnic culture was incorporated in a multitude of small towns and villages, connected by a network of canals and dirt roads, supplemented after the middle of the nineteenth century by short line railroads, not yet connected up into a few trunk systems meant only to augment the power of the big cities. With wind and water power for local production needs, this was a balanced economy; and had its balance been maintained, had balance indeed been consciously sought, a new general pattern of urban development might have emerged. But this possibility was burked by the prevailing ideology, which favored intensive specialization and the centralization of economic power in a few big centers, to which small urban units would be subservient.

In 'Technics and Civilization' I pointed out how the earlier invention of more efficient prime movers, Fourneyron's water turbine and the turbine windmill, could perhaps have provided the coal mine and the iron mine with serious technical competitors that might have kept this decentralized regime long enough in existence to take advantage of the discovery of electricity and the production of the light metals. With the coordinate development of science, this might have led directly into the more humane integration of 'Fields, Factories, and Workshops' that Peter Kropotkin was to outline, once more, in the eighteen-nineties. While it is useless to linger over these vanished possibilities, one would be blind to ignore the fact they once existed, and remained available over a much longer period than most people realize. In countries that are still industrially underdeveloped, the possibility of carrying out this superior pattern is still open; but unfortunately their Western advisers, whether capitalist or communist, are wedded to centralized mass organization for production, and lack both the technical insight and the historic perspective to promote a more humanly responsive economy.

Today one looks with a fresh eye on all these mutations: especially the seventeenth-century Dutch village and New England village: both expressions of a new kind of dynamic ecological balance, superior to either the urban monopolies of the Middle Ages or the unregulated sprawl, industrial or suburban, that followed. As in the penetrating psychology of a Spinoza or a Rembrandt we find a spirit more available for the future than in the sharp mechanical analysis of a Descartes or the more typical portraiture of the court painters like van Dyck, so in these urban forms we find an early empirical anticipation of the pattern for a dynamically balanced environment, urban and rural, like that we must eventually create in terms of our own culture, for a whole civilization.

Is it not clear that the Dutch town architects and village councillors, like the governors and preachers of New England, had a far more significant understanding of the life of men in cities than the baroque princes, who sought only a mirror for their vanity? Their synthesis was a more inclusive and organic one; and in terms of real life, it is Louis XIV and Le Nôtre whom we must now consider provincials. Versailles was essentially a spoiled child's gigantic toy, precisely as their dynastic politics was, realistically considered, child's play. Louis XIV's love of playing with soldiers—in his old age he confessed, a little apologetically, to an overfondness for war —would have been more dignified if he had indulged himself with leaden soldiers, instead of with flesh and blood. What was this statecraft but adult infantilism, parading as national interest and disguised by architectural magnificence? The planners who have reclaimed the Zuyder Zee, extended Amsterdam and rebuilt Rotterdam, the architects who have built a multitude of well-knit modern communities over the face of that great garden which is Holland, follow a sturdier tradition.

4: DISRUPTION AND FOSSILIZATION

As the nineteenth-century idea of unceasing change and 'progress' raises for us today the problem of stabilization and equilibrium, so the medieval idea of security raised, from the fourteenth century onward, the problem of how life, growth, and movement were to take place in a world governed by the ideas of fixed custom and inherited privilege. Must the wall be torn down? Must the armor be removed? Or did this civilization have the capacity to continue growth from its own center and so to arrive, without disintegration, at a wider synthesis? That was a problem for both its central institution, the Church, and for the medieval city: but neither could solve it without transcending its inherited limitations.

About the ensuing facts, there is little occasion for dispute. Both institutions failed, and modern civilization paid the penalty for that failure. After the sixteenth century, the medieval town tended to become a shell: the better the shell was preserved, the less life was left in it. That is the history of Carcassonne or Rothenburg-an-der-Tauber, among others. Where the external form was rapidly altered by pressure of population and new measures of economic enterprise, the inner spirit was transformed, too. Sometimes the old town sought to mirror the new life by a purely outward adaptation, a change of façade: right through the eighteenth century, the gabled roofs and richly textured brick faces of the old burgher houses would often be coated with plaster, sometimes with an enlargement of the windows or a touch of classic decoration for cornice, lintel, or doorway. The elegant quarter of Bruges, the Ridderstraat, whose very name reveals its aristocratic nature, still presents such a face. But the old forms, even with minor inner changes, did not express the new life: so the medieval town became in effect a museum of the past; and its inhabitants, if not reduced to being curators, had only a restricted part to play in the new culture. Such puddles of medieval life, sometimes dried up, sometimes rank with decay, are still scattered over Europe.

The protected economy of the medieval corporation was, in origin, based on the corporate superiority of the walled town over the barbarous, insecure life of the open country. So great were its advantages in the training of men for orderly economic effort, fostering skill by every variety of emulation and gain, that industry for long was not tempted to seek the low wages of the country, or accept the low standards and the clumsy technical equipment of the rural craftsman. Municipal restrictions might be onerous to the more speculative enterprisers; but they were easier to endure than feudal exactions, and since they rested on common consent, expressed in law, they were less capricious. Even the nobility appreciated these urban advantages: life and the goods of life, with all the spice of variety and the challenge of the unexpected, were concentrated in cities.

By the sixteenth century the disparity between city and country, politically speaking, had been partly removed. Improvements in transport by water had lessened the distance between city and countryside; and since feudal dues, even in rural districts, had been converted into money payments in many regions, people could remain in the open country or go back and forth without a risk of falling into the status of serfs or liegemen. One evidence of this equalization is the number of dialogues gentlemen wrote in the sixteenth century, weighing the advantages of the two environments: the two modes were at least near enough to be compared and chosen.

This new parity was abetted by the fact that security was gradually established in the open country through the rise of a central authority in the newly consolidated states. When the kings put down the warring nobles, industry could prosper outside organized municipalities. Protected by the symbolic might of the national government, industry might spring up even in non-enfranchised villages, beyond the pale of any older municipal government. Merchants with capital enough to purchase raw materials and the instruments of production—knitting machines for instance—could farm their work out in the countryside, paying subsistence wages instead of town rates, escaping regulations as to employment and quality made by the guilds, cutting under the urban standard of living, and in general playing the devil with the regulated market. Under this regime, infant labor came in. As early as the seventeenth century in the 'progressive' Netherlands, John Evelyn noted that five-year-old children were put to useful work. The protected town economy could not hold its own against such cut-throat competition.

Moreover, toward the close of the Middle Ages the mining and glass industries played a far larger part than they had played in the beginning. These industries, with their rubbish and dirt, their demand for timber and ample storage space, were usually placed outside the limits of the earlier settlements. From the first they had taken on most of the features of later capitalistic industry for the same reasons that were decisive later: the machinery of production was too expensive to be purchased by a single man or worked by a family unit; and the methods themselves required the hiring and organization of whole gangs who were usually employed as wage laborers, and who could be hired only by an employer with enough working capital to tide himself over between the season of production and the moment when sales were finally made. Proportionately, a larger part of the industrial population came to get its livelihood outside the incorporated municipalities. Even if these industries gave rise to new urban settlements, they did not foster municipal 'liberties' and they remained competitors with the guild-protected centers.

The old monopolies had been achieved by the co-operative action of the burghers for the benefit of the town. From the sixteenth century on, the new monopolies issued in England and France were not town monopolies but trade monopolies: they worked for the benefit of privileged individuals who controlled the trade, no matter where they were scattered. For those producing monopolies, the whole country was a province; and their promoters, like Sir Richard Maunsell, the English glass manufacturer, were either drawn from the nobility or speedily elevated to it. Big industry, investment banking, and wholesale trade were not on a single town basis: they reached everywhere, through marriages, partnerships, and agents. Even within the incorporated municipalities, the old guilds and corporations crumbled, first in Italy, then elsewhere, before the attack of financially more powerful groups that often usurped the functions of town government, overthrowing the elected officers, through their ability to hire mercenaries.

The growing inportance of international commerce from the fifteenth century on took advantage of weaknesses that were inherent in the craft guild and the walled town. The first weakness is that they were both on a purely local basis. To exercise monopolistic control within their walls, it was essential that they should be able to govern the realm outside, too: this meant a policy of harmonizing their own interests with those of the countryside, and eventually, of bringing about a federated organization of city regions.

But the actual policies pursued by the most potent and dynamic medieval cities were set aggressively in the opposite direction. Venice forced the inhabitants of the mainland on whom she depended for food, up to Bergamo, to supply exclusively the Venetian market. Florence, which had dealt in a reasonable way with Pistoia and gained its friendship, attacked Lucca, Pisa, and Siena in the most savage fashion, and turned them into bitter permanent enemies. Now and then the guilds of one town might help those of another, as the guilds in the neighborhood of Colmar supported the Colmar guild of bakers on a ten-year strike. But on the whole, the guild was able to exercise its authority only over those who actually came to practice within the walls of the town; and the towns themselves were governed by chronic jealousy and shortsightedness in their dealings with each other.

Behind the weaknesses of the guilds was this deeper defect in medieval urban policy. The medieval town was a burgher stronghold, and though originally composed of peasants and craftsmen who had fled the country-side, it ironically turned into a tyrannous mechanism for exploiting those who were left on the farms and in the villages. The burghers literally cut the ground from under their own feet. Ecologically speaking, the city and countryside are a single unit. If one can do without the other, it is the country, not the city; the farmer, not the burgher.

But the triumphs of art and invention in the city made the city doubly contemptuous of its backward rural neighbors: the country was treated as a half-witted dependent, or what was worse, as a foreigner. In Italy, the municipalities denied the peasants the privileges of citizenship, and in Germany the Bannmeilenrecht compelled the nearby peasants to supply the city with both food and the necessities of industry. Instead of creating allies in the open country, who could have helped strike at the roots of feudal power, they created a sullen wall of enemies; and the behavior of their armies, on their expeditions against other cities, probably did not make them more welcome.

All these facts point to the overthrow of a protective town economy, with its accepted economic limitations and its security, and the institution of an expanding economy, which concentrated privilege, rewarded those who did not over-prize security, and broke the state of hierarchical tension between groups into an open class war. The medieval system, based on graded social ranks, of course knew no economic equality. But in the earlier part of the medieval period, when urban land was fairly evenly divided and the means of production were largely individual tools and skills, the mobility of the trained worker, once his apprenticeship was over, insured him against victimization. Since he owned his tools, he could command his livelihood. This was not the least guarantee of medieval freedom and autonomy, for it prevented too wide a spread between upper and lower ranks, as long as skilled labor was not too plentiful.

In the textile industry of Flanders and northern Italy, the characteristic breach between workers and masters appeared as early as the thirteenth century. The newly introduced spinning wheel and the draw loom exercised an influence comparable to that of the spinning jenny and the power loom five centuries later. In Cologne, the weavers temporarily succeeded in overthrowing the patriciate in 1370-71; and the same happened in Ghent under the leadership of Artevelde. But the odds were against the guilds:

their victories were brief. While they operated on a local basis, their opponents, through family marriages and alliances, princely and royal and espiscopal, were united on a European basis. Hence the ruling classes could bring many forms of pressure and authority to bear at a single point.

As a result, the power of the feudal aristocracies and the princely dynasties, though challenged, was never successfully displaced over any considerable period by any combination of cities in Europe. When the cities joined forces with the king, in order to lessen the impositions of the nobles or ecclesiastics, they succeeded only in displacing a local tyrant by a more ubiquitous, although often a more lenient one. Soon they found themselves the subject of the all-powerful state they had helped to create. Only cities as great and wealthy as London were able to meet their royal master on anything like equal terms, and indeed, when pushed to it, were capable of removing him. The chief difficulty was that the political unit, the economic unit, and the religious unit were not, in medieval society, in a symmetrical relationship, and were not unified by any common framework other than the dynastic state.

Power, privilege, ancient custom, had made the political map of Europe a crazy quilt of conflicting jurisdictions, divergent allegiances, and meaningless particularisms. Though implicit in medieval political theory—as Gierke pointed out—there was the concept of a visible unity of mankind in Church and Empire, this unity was "neither absolute nor exclusive": it was rather "a manifold and graduated system of partial bodies, each of which, though itself a whole, necessarily demands connexion with a larger whole."

Unfortunately for the working out of this theory, the parts were never consistently articulated: hence, as Gierke again points out, "As time goes on we see that just this federalistic construction of the Social Whole was more and more exposed to attacks which proceeded from a centralizing tendency. This we may see happening first in the ecclesiastical and then in the temporal sphere." When this centralizing process imposed a new pattern, medieval localism and autonomy were eliminated. And when protection was restored, it came into effect as the mercantilism of the absolute monarchies, creating state monopolies to feed the central exchequer.

Various attempts at confederation were made, indeed, between related cities. In addition to the enterprising and relatively enduring union of Hansa cities, there was a League of Swabian Cities in 1376 and a Rhenish League in 1381, while England had the Union of Cinque Ports. But the weakness of these confederacies, like that of the Greek cities, served as warning to the astute writers of the 'Federalist Papers.' In general, the movement toward unity did not come from the free cities, nor was it firm enough and generous enough in intention to prevail. In Italy, during the fourteenth century, Lombardy, the Romagna, Tuscany, Umbria, and the

Marches were partitioned among 80 city-states, or, as Toynbee puts it, in one half of Italy in A.D. 1300 there were more self-governing states than could be counted in the whole world in 1933. But the self that did the governing was too narrow, too insulated a self. During the next two centuries, unification reduced these Italian municipalities to ten political units: because the cities themselves had not taken the initiative in effecting a federal union, this necessary process was accompanied by a loss of freedom, autonomy, and power.

It was in Switzerland and Holland that the problem of the federal unification of the corporate towns and the countryside was actually solved without undermining the political integrity of the urban unit; and it is to the Swiss and Dutch cities that one must turn for perhaps the most successful examples of the transition from the medieval to the modern order. That the Swiss achieved unity without despotism or submission to the arbitrary forms of centralized authority shows that the feat was technically possible: moreover, it gives color to the notion that it was humanly practicable on a wider European basis, since the three language groups in Switzerland, with their mountain barriers to transportation and intercourse, gave the country almost as many obstacles to unity as the most diverse territories of Europe as a whole. The proof was genuine, but the example was not infectious. Actual life in other regions took a different political course.

Now, territorial unification, internal peace, and freedom of movement were all highly necessary conditions for the new system of capitalistic industry. Centralized power developed in states like England and France, with at least the passive connivance of the underlying corporations and communities, because of the tangible benefits that flowed from the establishment of the King's Peace, the King's Justice, and the King's Protection, which insured safe travel on the King's Highway. From the standpoint of trade, transportation, and travel, conditions had actually been worsening since the twelfth century: a fact that contradicts the glib Victorian assumption of automatic progress. Along the Rhine, for example, there had been only nineteen toll stations at the end of the twelfth century; in the thirteenth, twenty-five more were added, and in the fourteenth, another twenty, so that by the *end* of the Middle Ages, the total was something over sixty. The stoppages and the burdensome fees might occur as often as every six miles: an intolerable condition.

Road tolls, bridge tolls, river tolls, town tolls—these economic exactions had been multiplying precisely at the moment when the routes of trade were lengthening, and when the constant flow of goods was becoming more important to a stable economic market. In addition, the lack of uniform coinage, combined with the dubious inflationary policies of this or that needy ruler or town, offered another handicap to commerce. Except in the provinces mentioned, the cities of Europe proved too parochial-minded, too jealous of their special privileges, to solve these problems by common measures. Here external conformity, enforced by the military power of the state, stepped in to perform the task where co-operative methods were not tried, or were given but a partial, grudging trial and had failed. Inept self-government, short-sighted fiscal policies leading to bank-ruptcy, often provided an opportunity for the central authority to step in and set matters straight—at the sacrifice of urban liberties, as in France.

We who live in a world still corroded by a similar folly, now embracing the planet rather than the continent of Europe, can without any sense of ironic superiority understand this fatal impasse. The medieval corpora-tions vainly sought to solve within the walls of the town problems that could be handled only by breaking down the walls and deliberately pooling their sovereignty and their control in a wider unity. Every aspect of Euro-pean life was involved in that reorientation. It was not simply a question, as Dante thought, of putting a Pope or an Emperor at the head of the temporal realm. Forerunner in so many political departments of the Sov-ereign National State, the medieval town handed on to the state all its own limitations, magnified many diameters. By displacing the city, by refusing to make use of its corporate functions, the State in turn helped to weaken and debase municipal life.

The sealed urban container proved the impossibility of meeting the situation by local adjustments, directed toward self-sufficiency, as the Na-tional States of our own day, however large, must likewise discover. The walled states of today are courting universal chaos and destruction for the same reasons that destroyed the medieval town. Autonomous bodies cannot thrive without fostering the unifying and universal processes, and actively participating in them.

Only one institution was, in the Middle Ages, capable of transcending this narrow parochialism and these futile monopolistic efforts: that was the Universal Church. But the diminishing universalism of the Church, its ten-dency to shrink into its ancient Roman shell, emphasizing its own authori-tarianism and absolutism, its custom of being staffed mainly by Italians in the upper ranks of the hierarchy, a custom favored by the uxorious nepotism of the renascence popes, was organically a phase of the general disease that undermined medieval culture. From the thirteenth century on, the Church, if it did not lose immediately in spiritual authority, gained in worldly estate—and that is the surest way of undermining spiritual authority. The rich dignitaries of the Church, whose magnificent scale of expenditure put secular princes in the shade, likewise eclipsed and mocked their own Prince, whose kingdom was not of this world. By the fifteenth century, there was often more ascetic renunciation in the counting house than in the monastery—and a higher standard of personal conduct and economic probity as well.

Had the Church remained economically disinterested, it could perhaps have joined forces with the cities and provided a framework for their union. But though the Dominican and Franciscan orders had arisen in the thirteenth century and had quickly made their way into the city, the Church itself remained rooted in the feudal mode of the past, and abandoned it only to take on the power of the new Caesars. When it transcended the feudal mode, it succumbed to the very forces and ways of life that its essential teachings condemned. So by the sixteenth century, indeed even as early as the fourteenth, the authority of the Church was seriously undermined from within: here was no lofty arbiter, no universal force making for righteousness. Corruption had become a stench in Rome no less than in other despotic municipalities and dukedoms; and in the sixteenth century, the very blessing of the Church, the indulgence, was farmed out on a share basis to the leading investment banker of the time, Jacob Fugger.

For a final judgment on the whole regime with which the Church was deeply involved, I turn to the contemporary testimony of Thomas More, now a canonized saint of this same Church: "When I consider and turn over in my mind the state of all flourishing commonwealths today, so help me God, I can see nothing but a conspiracy of the rich, who are aiming at their own advantage under the name and title of the commonwealth. They invent and devise all ways and means by which they may keep without fear of losing all they have amassed by evil practices, and next to that may purchase as cheaply as possible and misuse the labour and toil of the poor."

If the international religious order of Christendom was incapable of preserving the medieval regime by renewal from within, Protestantism, which rested on a national basis and issued in a state-supported Church was even less capable of serving the needs of cities. With the rise of latterday Protestantism, the old fellowship weakened: cleavages in matters of religious observance increased the economic disruption and further weakened, particularly in the North, the possibility of restoring a universal community of purpose. Even in protestant communities, the continued proliferation of dissident sects, the Quakers, the Unitarians, the Anabaptists, created heresies within heresies, and further division among the divided. Behind identical house-fronts in the old cities one might find bitter religious enemies, living side by side: more hostile in that neighborly relation than before, when they had lived leagues apart. At that moment the neighborhood ceased to be a tolerable form of association: only private life flourished.

In the end, with the validity of the Universal Church challenged and the reality of the group denied, only the atomic individual was left, seeking by his individual effort either salvation or profit, if possible a little of both, at the expense, if necessary, of his fellow citizens.

This debacle was summed up in the caustic lines of Robert Crowley, writing in the sixteenth century:

> And this is a city
>   In name but in deed
> It is a pack of people
>   That seek after meed [profit].
> For officers and all
>   Do seek their own gain
> But for the wealth of the Commons
>   Not one taketh pain.
> And hell without order
>   I may it well call
> Where every man is for himself
>   And no man for all.

What Langland had predicted in the fourteenth century in his long harangue on the wiles and perversities of Lady Meed had in two centuries finally come to pass throughout European society. The city had almost ceased to be a common enterprise for the common good; and neither the local authority of the municipal corporation nor the universal authority of the Church was sufficient to direct for the benefit of the commonwealth the new forces that were making headway throughout European civilization.

When new towns came to be built in the nineteenth century, the last precedent anyone would have thought of was that of the medieval city. Slowly, the life of the old towns dried up, their walls hollow shells, harboring institutions that were also hollow shells. Today it is only, as it were, by holding the shell quietly to one's ear, as with a sea shell, that one can catch in the ensuing pause the dim roar of the old life that was once lived, with dramatic conviction and solemn purpose, within its walls.

CHAPTER TWELVE

The Structure of Baroque Power

1: MEDIEVAL DISSOLUTION

Human cultures do not die at a given moment, like biological organisms. Though they often seem to form a unified whole, their parts may have had an independent existence before they entered the whole, and by the same token may still be capable of continuing in existence after the whole in which they once flourished no longer functions. So it was with the medieval city. The habits and forms of medieval life were still active at least three centuries after its 'close'—if one takes the sixteenth century as that decisive point. Even today, the Church of Rome, which dominated Western Europe for a thousand years, with its peculiar combination of authoritarian centralization, Roman absolutism, local autonomy, political resilience, and theoretic moral rigor, remains in operation on the dogmatic basis of the theology of Thomas Aquinas, within the political framework of Gregory the Great: still holding itself the sole repository of a truth and a faith essential to human salvation.

Some medieval institutions in fact renewed themselves in the sixteenth century by adopting the style of their time: thus monasticism took on a new life by reorganization on military lines, with absolute obedience to the head of the order, appropriately called the Director General, in the Society of Jesus, and this society, no longer content merely to set an example of piety or to preach, met the new demands of education by establishing a new kind of school, the secondary school, intermediate between the grammar school and the university. As for the architectural content, there was no real break between gothic building and neo-gothic building. The English provincial builder carried into the eighteenth century traditional modes of construction that educated gentlemen, ignorant of the life outside their circle, were beginning to revive once more as decoration and amusement, as at Walpole's Strawberry Hill. Is Wren's Tom Tower at Oxford Gothic or Neo-Gothic? One can assign equally good reasons for calling it either.

This mingling of the old and the new is visible everywhere in Europe. A good part of the new building, even in the seventeenth century, practically all of the 'renascence' building before this century, took place on medieval street plans, within the walls of essentially medieval cities, erected by crafts and guilds still organized on medieval lines. Rabelais' Abbey of Thelema, with its mixture of the old monastery and the new aristocratic country house, had its counterpart in the city. Even in the New World the older medieval laws of the market remained in force in the towns during the eighteenth century. So it was only in the newly founded towns, created for princely residence or colonization, that the post-medieval institutions created a strict, logical order wholly their own.

2 : THE NEW URBAN COMPLEX

Between the fifteenth and the eighteenth century, a new complex of cultural traits took shape in Europe. Both the form and the contents of urban life were, in consequence, radically altered. The new pattern of existence sprang out of a new economy, that of mercantilist capitalism; a new political framework, mainly that of a centralized despotism or oligarchy, usually embodied in a national state; and a new ideological form, that derived from mechanistic physics, whose underlying postulates had been laid down, long before, in the army and the monastery.

Until the seventeenth century all these changes were confused and tentative, restricted to a minority, effective only in patches. In the seventeenth century the focus suddenly sharpened. At this point, the medieval order began to break up through sheer inner corruption; and thenceforth religion, trade, and politics went their separate ways.

In order to understand the post-medieval town, one must be on guard against the still fashionable interpretation of the Renascence as a movement toward freedom and the re-establishment of the dignity of man. For the real renascence of European culture, the great age of city building and intellectual triumph, was that which began in the twelfth century and had achieved a symbolic apotheosis in the work of an Aquinas, an Albertus Magnus, a Dante, a Giotto. Between that revival and the classical revival of the fifteenth century a great natural disaster had taken place: the Black Death of the fourteenth century, which wiped out between a third and a half of the population, according to the most conservative estimates. By the sixteenth century, these losses had been repaired; but the breach in continuity that resulted from the plague was accentuated by a lowering of communal vitality, like that which comes after an exhausting war.

In the social disorganization that followed, power came into the hands of those who controlled armies, trade routes, and great accumulations of capital. With the rise of military despotisms, came the suppression of academic freedom in the universities, and the studious suppression of the independence of the spiritual powers, in the interests of the temporal rulers. All this has a familiar ring today: it parallels what went on in Russia, Germany, Italy, and various other parts of Europe after the First World War, and what went on, even in the physically remote United States, after the Second World War. The transformation of the medieval universities from international associations of scholars to nationalistic organizations, servile to the new despots, impervious to 'dangerous thoughts,' bound by loyalty oaths, went on steadily; and it had its parallels in the Church and the city.

Within a few centuries, all the older medieval institutions gave evidence of their profound demoralization. Huizinga, in 'The Waning of the Middle Ages,' has documented this change with a wealth of examples. In the fifteenth century, according to von Below, there was the beginning of organized gambling in Germany in houses provided by the municipality. And the same tendencies appeared in the Church: not merely the buying of offices and the sale of blessings, but the general recrudescence of superstition. Belief in witchcraft, rejected by Saint Boniface in the eighth century, was given final sanction of the Church in 1484: perhaps because there had been in fact a recrudescence of earlier pagan earth cults that inverted Christian morality. And it was in the seventeenth century, marked by the appearance of the exact methods of the physical sciences, that the persecution of witches became popular. Some of the most vicious offenders in this respect were the new scientists and philosophers themselves: people like Joseph Glanvill who almost in the same breath were predicting the complete transformation of the physical world by science and technics.

But the very shock of the Black Death also produced a quite different reaction: a tremendous concentration of energies, not on death, eternity, security, stability, but on all that human audacity might seize and master within the limits of a single lifetime. Overnight, six of the seven deadly sins turned into cardinal virtues; and the worst sin of all, the sin of pride, became the mark of the new leaders of society, alike in the counting house and on the battlefield. To produce and display wealth, to seize and extend power, became the universal imperatives: they had long been practiced, but they were now openly avowed, as guiding principles for a whole society.

From medieval universality to baroque uniformity: from medieval localism to baroque centralism: from the absolutism of God and the Holy Catholic Church to the absolutism of the temporal sovereign and the national state, as both a source of authority and an objective of collective worship—there was a passage of four or five centuries between the old and the new constellations. Let us not obscure the essential nature of this change by referring only to its esthetic accompaniments. The unearthing and the measurement of classical monuments, the discovery of Plato and Vitruvius, the reverence for the Five Orders in Architecture, the sensuous delight in antique ornaments and in newly unburied statues—all this threw a garment of esthetic decency over the tyrannies and debaucheries of the ruling powers. Connoisseurs like Hippolito Vitellesco might embrace and talk to his classic statues—John Evelyn reported—as if they were alive: but living men were being turned into automatons, obedient only to external command: a recrudescence of the earliest practices of King-centered cities.

The underlying tendency of this new order did not become fully visible until the seventeenth century: then every aspect of life departed from the medieval pole and re-united under a new sign, the sign of the Prince. Machiavelli's work on 'The Prince' provides more than one clue to both the politics and the plan of the new city, and Descartes, coming later, will re-interpret the world of science in terms of the unified order of the baroque city. In the seventeenth century the intuitions of precursors like Alberti were finally realized in the baroque style of life, the baroque plan, the baroque garden, and the baroque city. Right into the middle of the nineteenth century, new urban quarters were being planned for the middle classes, with seedy elegance, on the aristocratic baroque pattern. What is now mainly the boarding house and hotel quarter of South Kensington in London is the dying Victorian exhalation of that fresh breath of power and order.

3: OPENNESS AND CLARIFICATION

Before baroque organization had gained control of almost every aspect of the scene, there was an intermediate stage in which the new and the old mingled and reciprocally gained by their very contrast and opposition. This phase still unfortunately is called "the" renascence: a term too solidly established to be discarded easily, yet almost as misleading in its connotations as "the" industrial revolution. At this point in urban building, the now-meaningless enclosure, and the disorder and clutter that often characterized the late medieval city, had become intolerable. Even on practical grounds, crooked streets and dark alleyways had become suspect as abettors of crime: King Ferrante of Naples in 1475 characterized narrow streets as a danger to the State.

In order to breathe once more, the new planners and builders pushed aside the crowded walls, tearing down sheds, booths, old houses, piercing through the crooked alleys to build a straight street or an open rectangular square. In many cities, people must have had the sense of the shutters being suddenly opened in a musty room hung with cobwebs.

But to call these fifteenth- and sixteenth-century changes a 're-birth' is to misunderstand both the impulse and the result. We are dealing rather with a kind of geometric clarification of the spirit that had been going on for many generations, and that sought, not a wholesale change, but a piecemeal modification of the historic city. In cities like Florence and Turin, whose original Roman outlines were still visible, the new style was so deeply organic that it seems a continuation of its own past, rather than a renunciation of it. The Loggia dei Lanzi in Florence, for example, was completed in 1387. Though by the calendar it belongs to the Middle Ages, in form it is definitely 'renascence'—open, serene, with its three round arches and its classic columns. A rebirth? No: a purification, an attempt to get back to the starting point, as a painter might paint over the smudged colors and confused forms of his canvas to recover the lines of his original sketch.

If one uses the term precisely, there is no renascence city. But there are patches of renascence order, openings and clarifications, that beautifully modify the structure of the medieval city. If the new buildings, with their impersonal gravity and decorous regularity break up the harmony of the medieval pattern, they established a contrapuntal relationship which brings out, by contrast, otherwise unregarded, often invisible, esthetic qualities in the older streets and buildings. The theme itself remained medieval; but new instruments were added to the orchestra and both the tempo and the tonal color of the city were changed.

The symbols of this new movement are the straight street, the unbroken horizontal roof line, the round arch, and the repetition of uniform elements, cornice, lintel, window, and column, on the façade. Alberti suggested that streets "will be rendered much more noble if the doors are built all after the same model, and the houses on each side stand on even line, and none higher than the other." This clarity and simplicity was enhanced by the two-dimensional façade and the frontal approach; but the new order, while it was still alive, never was carried through with any over-riding consistence, such as the seventeenth century introduced, with its strict rules of composition, its endless avenues, and its uniform legal regulations. It is, indeed, just in this pliancy, in this avoidance of regimentation, that the new renascence builders prove their debt to the medieval order. The height of Sansovino's new library in the Piazza San Marco is not exactly that of the Ducal Palace; so, too, the height of the buildings around the Piazza Santissima Annunziata in Florence is only roughly the same. However strict the order of the renascence street, it does not go far enough to be rigid or oppressive.

One of the first of these new streets, that built by the Big Four in Genoa, was actually called the Strada Nuova: it was designed, Vasari tells us, by Galeazzo Alessi of Perugia, for the purpose of being the most magnificent street in Italy; and it was lined with enormous palaces, freestanding, also designed by him, with hillside gardens behind them, big enough to house a private army—and with correspondingly high rooms. But this bold new street, if wider than the old lanes and alleys, is still only twenty feet across; and it is less than seven hundred feet in length. Thus in the beginning the pattern of the old city was not substantially altered, even at the command of ruthless and powerful magnates. Most of the renascence palaces in Florence were erected on narrow Roman and medieval streets: one of the great exceptions is the Pitti Palace across the river —a suburban site, yet still close to the old via Romana.

Not merely were the ambitions of the new urban planners of the sixteenth century still limited and modest: it was this very modesty that brought out what was best in the old order as well as the new. There was no attempt by the new planners to harmonize their design with old medieval patterns: that would have been self-defeating. But because so much of the old was still standing, the new buildings created a rich, complex order, often more satisfying esthetically than the uniform, single-minded compositions of a later period. The classic example of this visual achievement is the straight, narrow street formed by the two sides of the Uffizi in renascence Florence. They are a sort of diagrammatic illustration of the new order. The classic composition of these buildings, with their repeating motifs and their converging horizontal lines would soon become dull, if they did not promptly reveal a different kind of building: the tower of the old Palace of the Signory in the Piazza beyond.

Once the planner was free to design an entire city on the same principles as the Strada Nuova or the Uffizi, the esthetic limitations of this wholesale regimentation of space, and this equally wholesale disregard for the variety of human functions, became manifest. In the first case, order was still an instrument of life; in the second, life had become an instrument of order. But in small measures the new order of the renascence design often added to the beauty of the medieval city, giving it, as in the Piazza Santissima Annunziata, some of the inner spatial repose of the monastic cloister. At a later stage, we shall examine the extension of the principle of such open spaces to residential building, where it contributed a fresh element to the vocabulary of the planner.

Up to the seventeenth century the new tradition in building, using old classic forms again to express new intuitions and feelings, produced a fresh sense of openness, clarity, and formal order. Visual disarray that had been tolerated in the ancient city gave way to a formal costume. Raw, eroded sites like the Capitoline Hill in Rome were plated with stone, and the steep goat path turned into a grand flight of stairs. Not the least contribution of the renascence tradition, indeed, was its street furniture: stone and brick paving, stone stairs, sculptured fountains, memorial statues. In its sense of vertical movement, the upward play of the fountain and the ascent of the steps, these innovations added a spatial liveliness to the functions they served. The Spanish Steps in Rome, at once a flower market, an arena, and a penitential approach to the Trinitá above, perform a service of liberation that must be measured not by the area occupied but by intensity of use.

Some of this spirit lingered in the best work of the baroque period: particularly in the sculptured fountains and squares by Bernini in Rome. But these patches of beauty and order gain not a little by the contrasting clutter around them. As soon as baroque order became widespread, uniform, and absolute, when neither contrast nor evasion was possible, its weaknesses lay revealed. Clarification gave place to regimentation, openness to emptiness, greatness to grandiosity. The solo voice of the planner might be amplified many volumes; but it could never take the place of all the singers in a civic chorus, each holding his own part, while following the contrapuntal score.

Within the shuttered world of specialist art criticism, and even of city design, these changes from renascence to baroque are often interpreted as changes in taste or esthetic insight alone: but what gave them the influence they have actually exerted on the planning of cities is the fact that they were supported at every point by profound political and economic transformations. The forces that had originally brought the royal cities of the ancient world into existence reappeared once more, with scarcely a change, except perhaps that the new engines of power were even more effective, and the resultant city plans even more ruthless, one-sided, noncooperative; even more indifferent to the slow, complex interactions, the patient adjustments and modifications, through trial and selection, which mark more organic methods of city development. To understand the baroque plan that took shape finally toward the end of the seventeenth century, creating new urban quarters and even new residential cities for royalty, one must follow the shifts in authority and power that took place at the end of the Middle Ages.

Because all these tendencies finally came to a head in the baroque city, I long ago chose to use this term—originally contemptuous—as one of social description, not of limited architectural reference. The concept of the baroque, as it shaped itself in the seventeenth century, is particularly useful because it holds in itself the two contradictory elements of the age. First, the abstract mathematical and methodical side, expressed to perfection in its rigorous street plans, its formal city layouts, and in its geometrically ordered gardens and landscape designs. And at the same time, in the painting and sculpture of the period, it embraces the sensuous, rebellious, extravagant, anti-classical, anti-mechanical side, expressed in its clothes and its sexual life and its religious fanaticism and its crazy statecraft. Between the sixteenth and the nineteenth century, these two elements existed together: sometimes acting separately, sometimes held in tension within a larger whole.

In this respect, one might regard the early renascence forms, in their purity, as proto-baroque, and the neo-classic forms, from Versailles to St. Petersburg, as 'late' baroque: while even the careless uncontrolled romanticism of the eighteenth-century gothic revivalists might be considered, paradoxically, as a phase of baroque caprice. None of this makes sense if one thinks of the baroque as a single moment in the development of architectural style. But the widening of the term has gone on steadily during the last generation; and a certain original vagueness and contradictoriness in the epithet adds sanction to this more generalized use. In terms of the city, the renascence forms are the mutants, baroque forms are the dominants, and neo-classic forms are the persistents in this complex cultural transformation.

4: TERRITORY AND CITY

From the beginning of the Middle Ages two powers had been jockeying for leadership in Western Europe: one was royal, the other municipal. Even in the great days of the Free Cities there were parts of Europe where the royal power had consolidated more swiftly and had kept the cities themselves in a state of feudal vassalage: England, Aquitaine, Sicily, Austria. Where royal and imperial power was weakest, as in northern Italy, the city achieved its fullest independence as a political entity. But even where it was strong, as in Aragon, royal power was far from absolute: witness the oath sworn by the subjects of the King of Aragon: "We, who are as good as you, swear to you, who are not better than we, to accept you as our king and sovereign lord, provided that you observe all our liberties and laws; but if not, then not."

The consolidation of dispersed feudal estates and the creation of continuous fields of political administration within a clearly defined frame were important for the welfare of the communities concerned. The real question was whether this consolidation was to be undertaken on behalf of a small privileged class, or whether it was to be achieved through a free union of cities and regions. Unfortunately the cities themselves, as we have seen, were not immune to the temptations of a predatory and parasitic life, made possible by the command of military weapons: they undertook exploitation by force both in home territories and in more distant imperialistic ventures: alternately repeating the political mistakes of the Spartans and the Athenians, if not the Romans.

The more powerful cities often sought to conquer their weaker neighbors, if for no better purpose than to suppress a rival market: and in times of war, from the end of the twelfth century on, they would in Italy transfer a great measure of executive power to a special officer, the Podesta, who in the emergency was released from the bondage of law. Sometimes the cities employed professional mercenaries to assert their mastery over their rivals: the Pisans were among the first to hire professional soldiers in war against Florence; and their success was so humiliating that the latter city began to lose faith in its boasted citizen army. Florence, a free city, contracted to surrender its freedom a second time, in 1322, to the King of Naples, in return for his protection.

Under military adversity, the municipalities of Italy were the first to reverse the process of achieving freedom; and though they hopefully regarded the employment of feudal or hired professionals as a temporary measure, they too often found that the new Condottiere, as the price of victory, would become ruler of the town whose liberty he had been hired to protect. Soon the image of the Man on Horseback, the new princely tyrant, would stand alone in the market place: symbol of the new technique and the new power—though, except for the horse, almost as old as the city itself.

There was a further internal weakness in the medieval democratic polity, not unlike that encountered in Athens. The wide division of power and responsibility put heavy demands upon each citizen's time; and though rapid rotation in office—six Priors of Florence served terms of only two months, the others for only a year—was a safeguard against corruption, it also undermined efficiency and was a handicap in developing a long-term policy. Braunfels has estimated that about a thousand people a year were called into the service of Florence under the guild and party system; and in smaller cities like Siena, Pisa, (20,000), or Pistoia and Arezzo,

(10,000), an even larger proportion would be needed. In the thirteenth century the Great Council in Lucca, with a population of fifteen thousand people, numbered 550 members.

While the city remained restricted in population, the democratic system was workable. But with urban growth came irresponsibility, inefficiency, division of interests, political lethargy—all of which opened the way for a tyrannous dictator who would gather all power in his own hands. When the amateur walks out on the job, the professional steps in.

In short, to achieve despotic power over their neighbors, the cities consented, step by step, to the loss of their own internal freedom: what is more, they lost the moral case against other forms of despotism. The only parts of Europe where the civic corporations and the territorial state were unified without loss of civic liberty were, as I have indicated, the Swiss Cantonal Confederation and The Netherlands.

In the early Middle Ages, the great feudal lords had succeeded in feeding their retainers, collecting their rents, and securing a modicum of peace and order in their domains only by being in continual movement from one estate to another. The court was a mobile camp: vigilance and movement were the price of power. This held for kings as well as lesser nobles. The royal ministers, the royal judges, the whole apparatus of government and fiscal control, was essentially a mobile one: authority was maintained by personal supervision. During the fourteenth century in the great monarchies of England and France, this process came to an actual halt. The records of the courts, the rolls, the registers, the archives, the correspondence, not to mention the officials themselves, had become too numerous and bulky to move. As population and territory increased in size, direct personal supervision became impossible: impersonal administration and delegated authority became necessary.

Though the popular movement for parliamentary control did not maintain itself very successfully except in England, the modern state began to shape itself in the fourteenth century. Its marks are a permanent bureaucracy, permanent courts of justice, permanent archives and records, and permanent buildings, more or less centrally located, for conducting the official business. The process was well described by Tout. "By Henry II's reign," he observes, "the English king had centralized so much authority under his immediate jurisdiction that all men of substance had frequent occasion to seek justice or to request favors at court." This movement, or rather, this *settlement,* took place first in financial administration, which had its special seat at Westminster: it was gradually extended to all the other offices of State. And the process itself was a reciprocal one: the centralization of authority necessitated the creation of the capital city, while the capital city, commanding the main routes of trade and military movement, was a powerful contribution to the unification of the state.

This transfer of power was accompanied by the rise of an official bureaucracy. The wandering ruler of the early Middle Ages, often absent from his castle or his capital, fighting or crusading, had now settled down: strong enough to compel his most powerful vassals to come to him. With the establishment of archives, deeds, tax records, in the capital city, came a regiment of clerks and permanent officials, the functionaries of the new 'Circumlocution Office,' not subject to municipal election.

Under despotic organization nothing could be done within the municipality without special license; and both the making and the breaking of rules were a source of profit to the prince. The collection of taxes, the imposition of fines, the promulgation of rules and regulations, not least the issuance of passports—all this was grist to the bureaucratic mill. By the fourteenth century a passport system was established in Padua; and in Ferrara the Duke inspected personally the daily list of travellers which the innkeepers were ordered to present. This Byzantine regulation, which actually originated in Constantinople, soon became universal. Punishment, that necessary arm of arbitrary power, itself became a source of income: an Italian prince, according to Jacob Burckhardt, said that the quarrels of his subjects netted him more than twelve thousand ducats in fines.

To house all these new bureaucratic functions a new type of building must be erected: the office building. The original model for this structure is that designed by Vasari in Florence, the Uffizi (the Offices), whose interior was once crowned with an open top floor loggia. Here is the original cliché of bureaucratic architecture at its best, fortunately modest in scale, dull but not formidable, destined to be reproduced with minor variations on a monumental scale, with grinding monotony, in the bureaucratic purlieus of Paris, St. Petersburg, Berlin, Washington, and their imitators. The repetitions and regimentations of the bureaucratic system left an even deeper mark on the city than did the new army. Under this regime, there was perhaps often some immediate gain in municipal efficiency; but there was always a loss in autonomy. Today, with the triumph of the managerial hierarchy, both structure and function have the nightmarish quality depicted by Kafka in 'The Trial.'

Mark that the capital city had a social as well as a political role to play. In the capital, provincial habits, customs, and dialects were melted down and recast in the image of the royal court: this became the so-called national image, national by prescription and imitative fashion rather than in origin. Centuries were needed to effect a unification even in such extra-personal activities as the regulation of weights and measures: it was not until 1665 that Colbert proposed to "bring the whole of his majesty's kingdom within the same statutes and within the same system of weights and measures." Even security of life and property did not follow very swiftly in every corner of the new national realm: as late as 1553 in the

'Guide des Chemins de France' there were notations in the open spaces between towns of 'brigandage' or 'dangerous Forest.'

The consolidation of power in the political capital was accompanied by a loss of power and initiative in the smaller centers: national prestige meant the death of local municipal freedom. The national territory itself became the connecting link between diverse groups, corporations, cities: the nation was an all-embracing society one entered at birth. The new theorists of law, as Gierke pointed out, were driven to deny that local communities and corporate bodies had an existence of their own: the family was the sole group, outside the state, whose existence was looked upon as self-validated, the only group that did not need the gracious permission of the sovereign to exercise its natural functions.

Once political power had been thus consolidated, economic privileges were obtained by individuals, not from the city, but from the prince; and they could be exercised, as a rule, anywhere in the realm. After the sixteenth century, accordingly, the cities that increased most rapidly in population and area and wealth were those that harbored a royal court: the fountainhead of economic power. About a dozen towns quickly reached a size not attained in the Middle Ages even by a bare handful: in a little while London had 250,000 inhabitants, Naples 240,000, Milan over 200,000, Palermo and Rome, 100,000, Lisbon, port of a great monarchy, over 100,000; similarly, Seville, Antwerp, and Amsterdam; while Paris in 1594 had 180,000.

As the great states of the modern world took shape, the capitals continued to monopolize population. In the eighteenth century the cities with over 200,000 included Moscow, Vienna, St. Petersburg, and Palermo, while already in the 100,000 class were Warsaw, Berlin, and Copenhagen. Toward the end of the eighteenth century Naples had 433,930 inhabitants, Paris around 670,000, and London over 800,000; while the trading cities like Bristol and Norwich, or the industrial cities like Leeds, Manchester, Iserlohn, and Paderborn for the most part remained small in size: that is, with less than 50,000 inhabitants.

The trading town of Hamburg and the industrial town of Lyons, both with secure medieval foundations and a continuing economic life, are the main exceptions; for they both had over 100,000 inhabitants at the beginning of the nineteenth century; but up to then they did not represent the dominant forms of political and financial power. The increase of size and scale in financial and political operations spread to other departments: Rome boasted a hospital with accommodations for 450 foundlings, 500 girls, and 1,000 beds for patients in a single apartment: a total loss of the human scale, with a corresponding mechanization of personal relations.

In contrast to the medieval regime, power and population were no longer scattered and decentralized. Only in the Germanic countries did the older type of municipal economy effectively linger on; and the consolidation of Brandenburg-Prussia in the seventeenth century changed the shape of things even there. The state grew at the expense of the component parts: the capital city grew out of all proportion to the provincial cities, and in no small measure at their expense. As the municipalities became important, local control needed to be supplemented by national legislation, and finally nothing could be done without the help and sanction of the central authority. Though natural capitals were usually situated at points of special advantage for trade and military defense—these being elements that entered originally into their selection—the baroque rulers brought all the powers of the state to bear to confirm these advantages. Where a natural center was lacking, they imitated at a distance Peter the Great's colossal willfulness in the founding of St. Petersburg.

In short, the multiplication of cities ceased, or at least that activity was largely transferred between the sixteenth and the nineteenth century to the New World. City building was no longer, for a rising class of small craftsmen and merchants, a means of achieving freedom and security. It was rather a means of consolidating political power in a single national center directly under the royal eye and preventing such a challenge to the central authority from arising elsewhere, in scattered centers, more difficult to control. The age of free cities, with their widely diffused culture and their relatively democratic modes of association, gave way to the age of absolute cities: a few centers that grew inordinately, leaving other towns either to accept stagnation or to stultify themselves in hopeless gestures of subservient imitation.

5: INSTRUMENTS OF COERCION

In the growth of the modern state, capitalism and technics and warfare play a decisive part; but it is impossible to assign a prior role to one or the other. Each developed through internal pressures and in response to a common milieu; and the state developed along with them.

How did the modern doctrines of absolute political power arise? Why did the political despot emerge so easily out of the concentrations of economic capital and political authority that took place in the fourteenth-century Italian city, with more than one guild, more than one family, contending for the position? How did the fashion of despotism, creating big despots like the Tudors and midget despots like the minor rulers of German states, spread over Europe—despots who have their counterparts, sometimes their origins, in the new business men and financiers? There is another name for this growing belief in absolute power: one might call it the illusion of gunpowder.

The old saw that gunpowder brought about the ruin of feudalism is far from being true. Although feudal independence could not resist the centralization of power in national monarchies, gunpowder had the effect of giving the feudal aristocrats a new lease on life, rescuing them from the pressure of the walled towns; for gunpowder increased the range, power, and mobility of the professional soldiers—and arms was the age-old profession of the feudal leader. In a very real sense, however, the introduction of gunpowder early in the fourteenth century, that century which undermined so many medieval institutions, sounded the death knell of the free cities.

Up to this time security had rested mainly on the simple moat and wall: sufficient defense against raiding warriors who carried no heavy instruments of assault. A well-fortified city was virtually impregnable: even as late as Machiavelli's day he remarked that the "cities of Germany . . . are fortified in such a manner that . . . to reduce them would be tedious and difficult, for they all have the necessary moats and bastions, sufficient artillery, and always keep in the public storehouses food and drink and fuel for one year."

Down to the fifteenth century, defense had the upper hand over assault. Alberti's advanced treatise on city planning (1485) did not reckon with cannon, and the new art of fortification played but a minor role. Indeed, artillery was so imperfect and was used with so little skill at first that, as Guicciardini remarks, the besieging of towns was slow and uncertain; and until the French invasion of Italy under Charles VIII, with an unprecedented number of troops, 60,000, and with iron cannonballs instead of stone, all moving at a hitherto unheard-of speed—until this happened cities were on equal terms, or rather more than equal terms, with the attacking parties. Thereafter, conditions were reversed: while a non-explosive stone or iron ball, which the defender's cannon could employ, did but little harm when dropped among companies of men, it could do great damage when used in assault for breaking open a wall or dropping through a roof. The new artillery of the late fifteenth century made cities vulnerable; and their old form of defense, on inaccessible hill or crag, just made them more conspicuous targets: so the 'impregnable' town of the early Middle Ages was even easier to reduce than its fortified successor.

In the attempt to equalize military conditions, the towns from this point on were compelled to abandon their old system of simple walls, defended for the most part by a citizen soldiery. They were forced to hire soldiers, so that they might sally forth and engage the enemy in open battle; and after the successful defense of Milan by Prospero Colonna in

1521 they were forced to adopt the new methods of fortification that had been worked out there by the Italian military engineers. Perugia, with its projecting towers "like the fingers of a man's hand," had set the example, according to Alberti.

These new fortifications were far more elaborate than the old walls: they had outworks, salients, bastions, in spearhead forms which permitted both the artillery and the armed infantry to rake the ranks of the attacking forces, from whatever side they might approach. By bringing the muskets of the defenders to the outmost positions they could theoretically put the city itself, whose circumference would be many hundred yards behind, beyond the reach of the enemy's most powerful gun. For barely two centuries these ingenious defenses seemed to promise security: but like so many other forms of military protection, they cast a dreadful social burden upon the protected population, and were ultimately responsible, in many cities, for those vile crowded conditions for which the *medieval* town has been so often reproached.

Instead of the simple masonry wall, which an ordinary house mason might plan or build, it was necessary now to create a complicated system of defense that called for great engineering knowledge and a vast expenditure of money. These fortifications, difficult to build, were even more difficult to alter except at a prohibitive cost. The old walls could be extended to include a suburb: they did not handicap natural growth and adaptation. But the new fortifications prevented lateral expansion. In the sixteenth- and seventeenth-century cities, fortification must have had the same effect upon finances that the building of subways and expressways so often has had on the modern metropolis: they put an intolerable burden on the municipality and exposed it to the exorbitant aid of the financier.

Even under a centralized regime, as in France, the inhabitants of Metz offered their services gratis, so that they might accomplish at an expenditure of 25,000 livres work that would otherwise have cost 50,000: a voluntary effort to escape heavy financial impositions. Despite the frequent use of forced labor in France, the social cost was no slight one. Unproductive capital expenditures, diverting energy from the production of consumable goods, drain a people's resources even when the cost is not expressed in terms of money. Perhaps one of the great advantages of the English towns after the sixteenth century, which aided England in the race for commercial supremacy, was that they alone were free from this tax on their resources.

No less disastrous than the financial costs of construction were the direct results upon the population itself. While the old-fashioned city was divided into blocks and squares and then surrounded by a wall, the newly fortified city was planned primarily as fortification, and the city was fitted into this strait-jacket. The space occupied by the new fortifications was usually greater than that occupied by the whole town. In Strasbourg during the Middle Ages, according to Eberstadt, no less than four extensions of the city wall had been made between 1200 and 1450. But the population increased three times between 1580 and 1870 without any change in its layout. Whether old or new, its opportunities for expansion were over. New growth could take place only vertically; and no prudent burgher would build his house outside the walls in a possible no-man's-land. Administrators like Richelieu indeed ordered every building razed in the territory surrounding a fortified town: the city lay, as Paris did until but the other day, in the midst of a waste of non-building land, subject to artillery fire.

Not alone did the new fortifications remove the suburbs and gardens and orchards too far from the city to be reached conveniently except by the wealthier classes who could afford horses: open spaces within were rapidly built over as population was driven from the outlying land by fear and disaster, or by pressure of enclosure and land-monopoly. This new congestion led to the destruction of medieval standards of building space even in some of the cities that kept their medieval form and had preserved them longest. Overcrowding had in fact begun in the capital cities even before the seventeenth century. Stow notes that in London stone buildings were being replaced by wooden-framed ones to save space taken up by the heavier stone walls, and four and five story buildings were taking the place of two story ones. (The change from masonry to steel cage construction took place in the late nineteenth-century American city for the same reason.) But in the seventeenth century these practices became universal: the systematic building of high tenements began —five or six stories high in old Geneva or in Paris, sometimes eight, ten or more in Edinburgh.

This pressure of competition for space forced up land values in the political capitals. High land values, as in Berlin from the time of Frederick the Great on, hardened into a bad pattern for housing: overcrowding of the land, absence of play areas for children, lack of light, air, interior accommodation: high rents. Slum housing for a large part of the population, not simply for beggars, thieves, casual laborers and other outcasts, became the characteristic mode of the growing seventeenth century city. The existence of those slums defiled the high esthetic principles of the architects and builders in the same way that the frequent use of the corridors in Versailles as common urinals defiled the exorbitant esthetic pretensions of that court.

By the sixteenth century the practices of the Italian engineers dominated city building. Dürer's treatise on urban fortification gives only scant attention to the city proper; and in most of the other books and plans on the subject the city is treated as a mere appendage to the military form: it is, so to say, the 'unoccupied' space that is left. Leonardo da Vinci, like Palladio, dealt in his notebooks with the city proper, suggested the separation of pedestrian ways from heavy traffic arteries, and went so far as to urge upon the Duke of Milan the standardized mass production of workers' houses. But despite these pregnant suggestions, his contributions to the art of city building remain meager and incidental compared with his extraordinary zeal in improving the art of fortification and assault. It is easy to see where both opportunity and creative energy lay.

Eventually the new movement reached its summit in the types of fortification devised in the seventeenth century under the great engineer, Sébastien Vauban—a layout so formidable that it required a new corps of the army, the miners and sappers, also organized by Vauban, to undermine and demolish it. Although the art of fortification had entailed endless sacrifices, it collapsed soon after it had evolved this final form. The new spy-glass improved the fire of artillery; and the increased mobility of supplies, through canals and roads and the organization of a responsible commissariat, gave an impetus to the mobile army. Meanwhile the territorial state itself had become the 'City' that was to be defended. The economic waste of this military perversion remained unrivalled till the insensate nuclear bomb and rocket development of our own period.

6: WAR AS CITY-BUILDER

The development of the art of fortification shifted the emphasis in building from architecture to engineering, from esthetic design to material calculations of weight, number, and position: prelude to the wider technics of the machine. But especially it altered the urban picture from the short-range world of the medieval city, with its walking distances, its closed vistas, its patchwork space, to the long-range world of baroque politics, with its long-distance gunfire and its wheeled vehicles and its increasing desire to conquer space and make itself felt at the other side of the world.

In the old medieval scheme, the city grew horizontally: fortifications were vertical. In the baroque order, the city, confined by its fortifications, could only grow upward in tall tenements, after filling in its rear gardens: it was the fortification that continued to expand, the more because the military engineers had discovered after a little experience that cannon fire with non-explosive projectiles can be countered best, not by stone or brick, but by a yielding substance like the earth: so the outworks counted for more than the traditional rampart, bastion, and moat. Whereas in earlier baroque fortifications, the distance from the bottom of the talus to the outside of the glacis was 260 feet, in Vauban's classic fort of Neuf-Brisach it was 702 feet. This unusable perimeter was not merely wasteful of precious urban land: it was a spatial obstacle to reaching the open country easily for a breath of fresh air. Thus this horizontal expansion was an organic expression of both the wastefulness and the indifference to health that characterized the whole regime.

A good part of the new tactics of life sprang from an impulse toward destruction: long-range destruction. Christian piety and capitalist cupidity combined to thrust the new conquistadors across the seas to plunder India, Mexico, and Peru; while the new type of fortification, the new type of army, the new type of industrial workshop, best exemplified in the vast arsenals and arms factories, conspired to upset the relatively co-operative ways of the protected town and destroy its scale. Protection gave way to ruthless exploitation: instead of security, men sought adventurous expansion and conquest. And the proletariat at home was subject to a form of government no less ruthless and autocratic than that which ground the barbaric civilizations of North and South America into pulp.

War hastened all these transformations; it set the pace for every other institution. The new standing armies, vast and powerful and awe-inspiring in peace time no less than in war, transformed war itself from a spasmodic to a continuous activity. The need for more costly sinews of war put the cities into the hands of usurious oligarchies that financed the ruler's mischievous policies, lived sumptuously on the profits and loot, and sought to entrench their positions by backing the ensuing despotism. In an economic crisis the guns of the hired soldiery could be turned, at the first signs of revolt, upon the miserable subjects. (The English, like the Dutch, escaped the baroque pattern earlier than other countries by turning tables on their despotic ruler.)

In the Middle Ages the soldier had been forced to share his power with the craftsman, the merchant, the priest. Now, in the politics of the absolute states, all law had in effect become martial law. Whoever could finance the army and the arsenal was capable of becoming master of the city. Shooting simplified the art of government: it was a quick way of ending an embarrassing argument. Instead of accepting the ordinary accommodations that ensure the healthy expression of diversities of temperament, interest, and belief, the ruling classes could dispense with such give-and-take methods: their vocabulary recognized only 'take.'

The gun, the cannon, the standing army helped produce a race of rulers who recognized no other law than that of their own will and caprice —that fine race of despots, sometimes imbecile, sometimes talented, who elevated the suspicions and delusions of the paranoid state into a ritual of compulsion. Their totalitarian and quasi-totalitarian imitators today, with no smaller delusions but with greater capacities for destruction, now threaten the very existence of the human race.

The transformation of the art of war gave the national rulers a powerful advantage over the real corporations and groups that compose a community. It did more than any other single force to alter the constitution of the city. Power became synonymous with numbers. "The greatness of a city," Botero observed, "is said to be, not the largeness of the site or the circuit of the walls, but the multitude and number of inhabitants and their power." The army, recruited for permanent warfare, became a new factor in the state and in the life of the capital city. In Paris and Berlin, and other lesser centers, these standing armies created a demand for special forms of housing, since soldiers could not be permanently quartered on the population without provoking a sense of grievance.

The army barracks have almost the same place in the baroque order that the monastery had in the medieval one; and the Parade Grounds—the new Champ de Mars in Paris, for instance—were as conspicuous in the new cities as Mars himself was in renascence painting. Turning out the guard, drilling, parading, became one of the great mass spectacles for the increasingly servile populace: the blare of the bugle, the tattoo of the drum, were as characteristic a sound for this new phase of urban life as the tolling of the bells had been for the medieval town. The laying out of great *Viae Triumphales,* avenues where a victorious army could march with the maximum effect upon the spectator, was an inevitable step in the replanning of the new capitals: notably in Paris and Berlin. Both symbolically and practically, the design established that everything was 'under control.'

Along with the barracks and drill grounds, which occupy such large sites in the big capitals, go the arsenals. In the sixteenth century an extraordinary number of such buildings were erected. By 1540 Francis I had erected eleven arsenals and magazines: this went on, at a keener or slower pace, in all the other capitals. Soldiers, as Sombart has pointed out, are pure consumers, even as in action they are negative producers. Their demand for dwelling quarters was accompanied by a demand for provisions and drink and clothes on a similar scale. Hence the ranks of public houses and the army of tailors around the barracks quarters; indeed, a second standing army of shopkeepers, tailors, publicans, and whores springs up—the more miserable members of which owe their plight, perhaps, to the effect of the never-ending succession of military conflicts that agitated Europe and reached a climax in the eighteenth century. (See Pitirim Sorokin's able statistical summary in his 'Social and Cultural Dynamics.')

Do not underestimate the presence of a garrison as a city-building agent. A standing army is a body of consumers making a mass demand.

In 1740 the military population of Berlin numbered 21,309 out of a total of about 90,000 people: almost a quarter. The presence of this mass of mechanized and obedience-conditioned human beings necessarily touched every other aspect of life. The army supplied the model in its discipline for other forms of political coercion: people got into the habit of accepting the aggressive bark of the drill sergeant and the arrogant brutal manners of the upper classes: they were copied by the new industrialists, who governed their factories like absolute despots. Hutton in his history of Birmingham relates how the lord of the manor in "1728 . . . seized a public building called the Leather-Hall and converted it to his private uses. . . . The constable summoned the inhabitants to vindicate their rights, but none appearing, the Lord smiled at their supineness and kept the property." Beneath the superficial polish of baroque upper-class manners there is the constant threat of an ugly, coercive discipline. These two qualities thread through every aspect of baroque life, even its luxury and folly.

7: THE IDEOLOGY OF POWER

The two arms of this new system are the army and the bureaucracy: they are the temporal and spiritual support of a centralized despotism. Both agents owed no small part of their influence to a larger and more pervasive power, that of capitalist industry and finance. One must remember, with Max Weber, that the rational administration of taxation was an accomplishment of the Italian cities in the period *after* the loss of their freedom. The new Italian oligarchy was the first political power to order its finances in accordance with the principles of mercantile bookkeeping— and presently the fine Italian hand of the tax-expert and financial administrator could be observed in every European capital.

The change from a goods economy to a money economy greatly widened the resources of the state. The monopoly of rent, the booty from piracy and brigandage, the loot of conquest, the monopoly of special privileges in production and sale through patents granted by the state, the application of this last system to technical inventions—all these resources swelled the coffers of the sovereign. To increase the boundaries of the state was to increase the taxable population: to increase the population of the capital city was to increase the rent of land. Both forms of increase could be translated ultimately into terms of money pouring into the central exchequer. Not merely did the royal governments become capitalistic in their workings, founding industries of their own, in arms, porcelain, tapestry: but they sought, under the notion of a 'favorable balance of trade,' to create a system of exploitation in which every sovereign state would receive more in exchange, in measure of gold, than what it had given: classic colonial economics.

Capitalism in its turn became militaristic: it relied on the arms of the state when it could no longer bargain to advantage without them: the foundations of colonial exploitation and imperialism. Above all, the development of capitalism brought into every department secular habits of thought and matter-of-fact methods of appraisal: this was the warp, exact, orderly, superficially efficient, upon which the complicated and effulgent patterns of baroque life were worked out. The new merchant and banking classes emphasized method, order, routine, power, mobility, all habits that tended to increase effective practical command. Jacob Fugger the Elder even had a specially designed travelling set made for himself, containing a compact, efficiently organized dining service: nothing was left to chance.

The uniformity of the die that stamped the coin at the National Mint became a symbol of these emergent qualities in the new order. Florence gained international fame and special commercial status by coining its gold florin in honest uniform weight. Interests that were later sublimated and widened in physical science first disclosed themselves in the counting house: the merchant's emphasis upon mathematics and literacy—both so necessary to long-distance trade through paid agents acting on written instructions—became the fundamental ingredient in the new education of the grammar schools. It was not by accident that Newton, the physicist, became master of the mint, or that the merchants of London helped found the Royal Society and conducted experiments in physics. These mechanical disciplines were in effect interchangeable.

Behind the immediate interests of the new capitalism, with its abstract love of money and power, a change in the entire conceptual framework took place. And first: a new conception of space. It was one of the great triumphs of the baroque mind to organize space, make it continuous, reduce it to measure and order, and to extend the limits of magnitude, embracing the extremely distant and the extremely minute; finally, to associate space with motion and time.

These changes were first formulated by the painters and architects and scene painters, beginning with Alberti, Brunelleschi, Uccello, and Serlio. While the Flemish realists, working in the medium of the advanced spinning industries, had accurate perceptions of space, it remained for the Italians of the fifteenth century to organize space on mathematical lines, within two planes, the foreground-frame, and that of the horizon line. They not merely correlated distance with intensity of color and quality of light, but with the movement of bodies through the projected third dimension. This putting together of hitherto unrelated lines and solids within the rectangular baroque frame—as distinguished from the often irregular boundaries of a medieval painting—was contemporary with the political consolidation of territory into the coherent frame of the state. But the development of the straight line and the uniform building line, as a means of expressing uniform motion, took place at least a century before the building of actual façades on visually limitless avenues.

Similarly, the study of perspective demolished the closed vista, lengthened the distance toward the horizon, and centered attention on the receding planes, long before the wall was abolished as a feature of town planning. This was an esthetic preface to the grand avenues of baroque design, which at most have an obelisk, an arch, or a single building to terminate the converging rays of the cornice lines and the pavement edges. The long approach and the vista into seemingly unbounded space—those typical marks of the baroque plan—were first discovered by the painter. The act of passage is more important than the object reached: there is keener interest in the foreground of the Farnese Palace than in the gawky façade that caps the hill. The new renascence window is definitely a picture frame, and the renascence painting is an imaginary window which, in the city, makes one forget the dull courtyard that an actual opening would reveal.

If the earlier painters demonstrated Cartesian mathematics before Descartes, on their system of co-ordinates, the general sense of time likewise became more mathematical. From the sixteenth century on the domestic clock was widespread in upper-class households. But whereas baroque space invited movement, travel, conquest by speed—witness the early sail-wagons and velocipedes and the later *promenades aériennes* or chute-the-chutes—baroque time lacked dimensions: it was a moment-to-moment continuum. Time no longer expressed itself as cumulative and continuous (durée), but as quanta of seconds and minutes: it ceased to be life-time. The social mode of baroque time is fashion, which changes every year; and in the world of fashion a new sin was invented—that of being out of date. Its practical instrument was the newspaper, which deals with scattered, logically incoherent 'events' from day to day: no underlying connection except contemporaneity. If in spatial order repeating patterns take on a new meaning—columns on the façades of buildings, ranks of men on parade—in time the emphasis rests on the novel and non-repetitive. As for the archaeological cult of the past, it was plainly not a recovery of history but a denial of history. Real history cannot be recovered except by its entering into a fresh life in a new form.

The abstractions of money, spatial perspective, and mechanical time provided the enclosing frame of the new life. Experience was progressively reduced to just those elements that were capable of being split off from the whole and measured separately: conventional counters took the place of organisms. What was real was that part of experience which left no murky residues; and anything that could not be expressed in terms of visual sensations and mechanical order was not worth expressing. In art, perspective and anatomy; in morals, the systematic casuistry of the Jesuits; in architecture, axial symmetry, formalistic repetition, the fixed proportions of the Five Orders, and in city building, the elaborate geometrical plan. These are the new forms.

Do not misunderstand me. The age of abstract analysis was an age of brilliant intellectual clarification. The new system of dealing with mathematically analyzable fragments instead of with wholes gave the first intelligible collective means of approaching such wholes: as useful an instrument of order as double-entry bookkeeping in commerce. In the natural sciences, the method of analytic abstraction led to the discovery of units that could be investigated swiftly and accurately *just because* they were dismembered, fragmentary, incomplete. The gain in the power of systematic thought and in the accurate prediction of physical events was to justify itself in the nineteenth century in a series of mighty advances in technics.

But in society the habit of thinking in terms of abstractions worked out disastrously. The new order established in the physical sciences was far too limited to describe or interpret social facts, and until the nineteenth century even the legitimate development of statistical analysis played little part in sociological thought. Real men and women, real corporations and cities, were treated in law and government as if they were imaginary bodies; whilst artful pragmatic fictions, like Divine Right, Absolute Rule, the State, Sovereignty, were treated as if they were realities. Freed from his sense of dependence upon corporation and neighborhood, the 'emancipated individual' was dissociated and delocalized: an atom of power, ruthlessly seeking whatever power can command. With the quest for financial and political power, the notion of limits disappeared—limits on numbers, limits on wealth, limits on population growth, limits on urban expansion: on the contrary, quantitative expansion became predominant. The merchant cannot be too rich; the state cannot possess too much territory; the city cannot become too big. Success in life was identified with expansion. This superstition still retains its hold in the notion of an indefinitely expanding economy.

Botero, contemporary with this development, noted its implications. "The founders of cities," he said, "considering that laws and civil discipline could not be easily conserved and kept where a mighty multitude of people swarmed (for multitudes do breed and bring confusion) they limited the number of citizens beyond which they supposed the form and order of government they sought to hold within their cities could not else be maintained. But the Romans, supposing power (without which, a city cannot long be maintained) consisteth for the most part in the multitude of people, endeavored all the ways and means they might to make their country great." That says everything.

In the desire for more subjects—that is, for more cannon fodder, more milch-cows for taxation and rent—the desires of the Prince coincided with those of the capitalists who were looking for larger and more concentrated markets filled with insatiable customers. Power politics and power economics reinforced each other. Cities grew; consumers multiplied; rents rose; taxes increased. None of these results was accidental.

Law, order, uniformity—all these then are special products of the baroque capital: but the law exists to confirm the status and secure the position of the privileged classes; the order is a mechanical order, based not upon blood or neighborhood or kindred purposes and affections but upon subjection to the ruling Prince; and as for the uniformity—it is the uniformity of the bureaucrat, with his pigeonholes, his dossiers, his red tape, his numerous devices for regulating and systematizing the collection of taxes. The external means of enforcing this pattern of life lies in the army; its economic arm is mercantile capitalist policy; and its most typical institutions are the standing army, the bourse, the bureaucracy, and the court.

Thus the baroque rulers reinstated all the institutions of the original urban implosion, even in some cases the union of sacred and temporal powers in a state church presided over by a king under divine appointment. The old god of the city now became a national deity, as the old city walls became the 'national frontiers.' That god renewed the original demands for tribute and human blood. 'Le Roi Soleil' was as near as Christian theology permitted to being a veritable Sun God.

8 : MOVEMENT AND THE AVENUE

Since I am dealing with an age of abstractions, I purpose to follow its style. I shall treat of the part before I discuss the whole. First the avenue: then the separate institutions and buildings: only after that the city, as an esthetic if not a complete social unit.

The avenue is the most important symbol and the main fact about the baroque city. Not always was it possible to design a whole new city in the baroque mode; but in the layout of half a dozen new avenues, or in a new quarter, its character could be re-defined. In the linear evolution of the city plan, the movement of wheeled vehicles played a critical part; and the general geometrizing of space, so characteristic of the period, would have been altogether functionless had it not facilitated the movement of traffic and transport, at the same time that it served as an expression of the dominant sense of life. It was during the sixteenth century that carts and wagons came into more general use within cities. This was partly the result of technical improvements that replaced the old-fashioned solid wheel with one built of separate parts, hub, rim, spoke, and added a fifth wheel, to facilitate turning.

The introduction of wheeled vehicles was resisted, precisely as that of the railroad was resisted three centuries later. Plainly the streets of the medieval city were not adapted either in size or in articulation to such traffic. In England, Thomas tells us, vigorous protests were made, and it was asserted that if brewers' carts were permitted in the streets the pavement could not be maintained; while in France, parliament begged the king in 1563 to prohibit vehicles from the streets of Paris—and the same impulse even showed itself once more in the eighteenth century. Nevertheless, the new spirit in society was on the side of rapid transportation. The hastening of movement and the conquest of space, the feverish desire to 'get somewhere,' were manifestations of the pervasive will-to-power. "The world," as Stow remarked when the fashion was taking hold in London, "runs on wheels." Mass, velocity, and time were categories of social effort before Newton's law was formulated.

Movement in a straight line along an avenue was not merely an economy but a special pleasure: it brought into the city the stimulus and exhilaration of swift motion, which hitherto only the horseman had known galloping over the fields or through the hunting forest. It was possible to increase this pleasure esthetically by the regular setting of buildings, with regular façades and even cornices, whose horizontal lines tended toward the same vanishing point as that toward which the carriage itself was rolling. In walking, the eye courts variety, but above this gait, movement demands repetition of the units that are to be seen: it is only so that the individual part, as it flashes by, can be recovered and pieced together. What would be monotony for a fixed position or even in a procession, becomes a necessary counterpoise to the pace of fast-moving horses.

In emphasizing the demands of wheeled traffic, which became urgent in the seventeenth century, I do not wish to neglect a characteristic need that disclosed itself at an even earlier period: the need of avenues for military movement. To cite Alberti again, he distinguished between main and subordinate streets. The first he called—and the name is important—viae militares, or military streets: he required that these should be straight. Anyone who has ever led a company of men through an irregularly planned city knows the difficulty of conducting them in martial order through its windings and twistings, particularly when the streets themselves are ungraded: inevitably, the individual falls out of alignment and the ranks present a disorderly appearance. To achieve the maximum appearance of order and power on parade, it is necessary to provide a body of soldiers either with an open square or a long unbroken avenue.

The new town planners had the needs of the army constantly in mind: Palladio seconded Alberti. In addition to observing that the ways will be short and convenient if planned in a straight line, and so large that horses and coaches be no hindrance to each other when they meet, Palladio says that "the ways will be more convenient if they are made everywhere equal; that is to say, that there be no place in them where armies may not easily march." This uniform oversized street, which was to become such a blight in the development of neighborhoods in new cities, and which was to add so greatly to the expenses, had purely a military basis.

Palladio's further definition of the new military avenue is equally significant: he distinguished it from the non-military kind by pointing out that they pass through the midst of the city and lead from one city to another, and that they "serve for the common use of all passengers for carriages to drive or armies to march." Accordingly Palladio dealt with the military streets alone because non-military streets ought to be regulated according to the same principle as military ways, and the more alike they are the *more commendable they will be.*" In view of the importance of the army to the ruling classes, it is no wonder that military traffic was the determining factor in the new city plan, from the first mutation in Alberti to the final survival in the laying down of Haussmann's boulevards in Paris.

The esthetic effect of the regular ranks and the straight line of soldiers is increased by the regularity of the avenue: the unswerving line of march greatly contributes to the display of power, and a regiment moving thus gives the impression that it would break through a solid wall without losing a beat. That, of course, is exactly the belief that the soldier and the Prince desire to inculcate in the populace: it helps keep them in order without coming to an actual trial of strength, which always carries the bare possibility that the army might be worsted. Moreover, on irregular streets, poorly paved, with plenty of loose cobblestones and places of concealment, the spontaneous formations of untrained people have an advantage over a drilled soldiery: soldiers cannot fire around corners, nor can they protect themselves from bricks heaved from chimney tops immediately overhead: they need space to maneuver in. Were not the ancient medieval streets of Paris one of the last refuges of urban liberties? No wonder that Napoleon III sanctioned the breaking through of narrow streets and cul-de-sacs and the razing of whole quarters to provide wide boulevards: this was the best possible protection against assault from within. To rule merely by coercion, without affectionate consent, one must have the appropriate urban background.

In the new city, or in the formal additions made to old centers, the building forms a setting for the avenue, and the avenue is essentially a parade ground: a place where spectators may gather, on the sidewalks or in the windows, to review the evolutions and exercises and triumphal marches of the army—and be duly awed and intimidated. The buildings stand on each side, stiff and uniform, like soldiers at attention: the uniformed soldiers march down the avenue, erect, formalized, repetitive: a classic building in motion. The spectator remains fixed. Life marches before him, without his leave, without his assistance: he may use his eyes, but if he wishes to open his mouth or leave his place, he had better ask for permission first.

In the medieval town the upper classes and the lower classes had jostled together on the street, in the marketplace, as they did in the cathedral: the rich might ride on horseback, but they must wait for the poor man with his bundle or the blind beggar groping with his stick to get out of the way. Now, with the development of the wide avenue, the dissociation of the upper and the lower classes achieves form in the city itself. The rich drive; the poor walk. The rich roll along the axis of the grand avenue; the poor are off-center, in the gutter; and eventually a special strip is provided for the ordinary pedestrian, the sidewalk. The rich stare; the poor gape: insolence battens on servility.

The daily parade of the powerful becomes one of the principal dramas of the baroque city: a vicarious life of dash and glitter and expense is thus offered to the butcher's boy with a basket on his head, to the retired merchant out for a stroll, to the fashionable housewife, shopping for bargains and novelties, to the idle mob of hangers-on in all degrees of shabby gentility and downright misery—corresponding to the clients of imperial Rome.

"Mind the carriages!" cried Mercier in his eighteenth-century 'Tableau de Paris.' "Here comes the black-coated physician in his chariot, the dancing master in his *cabriolet,* the fencing master in his *diable*—and the Prince behind six horses at the gallop as if he were in the open country. . . . The threatening wheels of the overbearing rich drive as rapidly as ever over stones stained with the blood of their unhappy victims." Do not fancy the danger was exaggerated: in France the stage-coach, introduced in the seventeenth century, killed more people annually than the railroad that followed it. This increase in the tempo of life, this rapid motion, these superficial excitements and dangers, were the psychological sweetening of the bitter pill of autocratic political discipline. In the baroque city one might say, "The carriages move swiftly," just as people once said, to justify fascism in Italy, "The trains run on time."

There was only one desirable station in this despotism; it was that of the rich. It was for them that the avenue was made and the pavement smoothed out and springs and cushions added to the wheeled vehicle: it was to protect them that the soldiers marched. To keep a horse and carriage was an indispensable mark of commercial and social success; to keep a whole stable was a sign of affluence. In the eighteenth century the stables and mews crept into the less savory quarters of the capitals, behind the wide avenues and the sumptuous squares, carrying there the faint healthy smell of straw and manure. If the fowls no longer cackled at dawn, the restless stomp of a high-bred horse might be heard at night from rear windows: the man on horseback had taken possession of the city.

9: THE NEW DIVINITY

The breakup of the medieval church set free the 'ions' that were re-polarized in the baroque city. One may seize the process in a concrete figure if one considers how each element in the old structure was appropriated by a special institution, sect, or group. Follow the dismemberment: the protestants captured the preacher's rostrum and made it the core of their new chapels, where no graven image competed with the speaker's face, and no rich ceremonial distracted attention from his urgent voice. The aristocracy commanded the painter and the architect: art was carried away to special halls and galleries, and to make the process easier, the new easel picture took the place of the wall fresco. Angels and saints became Bacchuses and Graces: first, secular faces of popes, courtiers, business men surrounded the Holy Image: finally they displaced it.

So with the other parts of the edifice. The choir, which once chanted hymns to God, was removed to the concert hall or to a balcony of the ballroom: the religious festival became the court masque, to celebrate a mundane birthday or a wedding; while the drama, leaving the porches of the church, where the clergy and guildsmen had once enacted their mysteries and moralities, was turned over to professional actors under the patronage of the nobility: their first raffish quarters are on the outskirts of the city. The chapter-house, with its complement of at least formally celibate clergy, became the aristocratic men's club of the nineteenth century: exclusive, monastic, even if ostentatiously sybaritic: the Carlton, the Reform, the Jockey Club, the Herrenclub, and their imitators.

Finally the nave, the bare assembly place, became the bourse. Do not fancy that the latter is a faked parallel: in the seventeenth century the brokers plied their trade in the nave of St. Paul's, and the money changers all but drove the representatives of Christ from the temple—till at last the stench became too great for even a venal Church to endure. Wren's unused plan for the reconstruction of London after the fire handsomely recognized this new order of life. He did not give the dominating site to St. Paul's: he planned the new avenues so as to give this honor to the Royal Stock Exchange.

This analytical decomposition of the Church gave each institution a special opportunity to flourish in its own right. On the positive side, this was another witness to the visual clarification and the intelligent specialization of functions that characterized baroque order. All these institutions had become detached from the Church because fresh life and growth were stifled there. There would have been no Shakespeare if the Church had kept control of the drama, and no great Rembrandt portraits if he had continued to paint the staple group portraits of the complacent worthies of the Guild. But these various fragments of art and culture were dispersed with respect to the population as a whole: dispersed and put out of their reach. It was only in the court of the Prince that the parts were united again to form a new whole for the exclusive benefit of those who wielded power.

We have seen what became of the medieval cathedral. But what became of its God? Here the transformation can be recorded only in terms of blasphemy. The absolute ruler by divine right usurped the place of the Deity and claimed his honors; he might even call himself Le Roi Soleil, superstitiously arrogating to himself the myth of a Pharaoh or an Alexander the Great. In the new cult, the part of the Virgin Mary, most powerful intercessor at the throne of heaven, was taken by the king's mistress. The powers and principalities of the new heaven, indispensable to its regimen, were the courtiers who crowded around the throne of the Monarch and proclaimed his glory. The parallel was not absent from even pious minds in the seventeenth century. "Whoever," said La Bruyère, "considers that the king's countenance is the courtier's supreme felicity, that he passes his life looking at it and within sight of it, will comprehend to some extent how to see God constitutes the glory and the happiness of the saints."

Learned flunkies wrote treatises to prove the despot's direct connection with heaven, to uphold his omnipotence, to admonish obedience to his divine commands. When their rationalizations fell short of his own exorbitant claims he might even, like James I of England, take a hand in writing the necessary eulogium himself. "The prince," according to Castiglione, who wrote the classic treatise on 'The Courtier,' "ought to be very generous and splendid, and give to all men without reserve, because God, as the saying runs, is the treasurer of generous princes." Fortune's cornucopia must indeed be inexhaustible at the rate it was drained at court: Avenel reports that one of the great ballets at Versailles, in which one hundred and fifty people took part, came to a hundred thousand francs. There was nothing exceptional in this. "In 1618," Allardyce Nicoll observes in his study of renascence masques, "James, by no means the most financially reckless of monarchs, devoted four thousand pounds, a sum to be valued now at forty thousand, on a single production, while in 1633 the Inns of Court, preparing a vast entertainment, succeeded in spending over twenty-one thousand pounds, or two hundred thousand pounds in our money." The most talented painters and architects of the time labored to make memorable productions that would vanish with a single performance.

Luxury spread from dress and amusements to eating, and from eating in the palace to eating in similar fashion on the battlefield. "Speaking of dinners," observed the Duc de Saint-Simon in his memoirs, "the luxury of the Court and Town has spread to the army, to such a degree that delicacies were found there which were formerly unknown in the most peaceful places. Hot meals were served at every halt during marches, and repasts carried to the trenches during a siege were like feasts, with several courses, fruits and ices; and all kinds of wine in profusion." This concentrated triviality had a discouraging effect on good minds. Francis Bacon, imaginatively picturing the new world of science, could not resist the courtly impulse to describe the elaborate costumes in which the experimenters in the New Atlantis performed their scientific labors.

The demand for unlimited funds infected every rank in society; and it was the key to the economic policies of the absolute state. When taxation did not supply sufficient means for the prince and his favorites, he resorted to pillage: distant kingdoms in the case of Philip of Spain, or nearer monasteries for Henry VIII: when these did not suffice, he robbed the poor man of his pennies in order to bestow gold on those already rich. Hence the whole policy of licenses and patents: one needed a special permission, to be obtained at a price, even to build a house.

The constant growth of a bureaucracy to superintend these exactions and further the distribution of privilege added to the burden on the community: the Circumlocution Office was a convenient means of taking care of retainers and their younger sons: from St. Petersburg to Whitehall it was an inevitable appanage of upper-class society. "Never was bureaucracy carried to such a point of exaggeration, extravagance, and tiresomeness," wrote Mercier: "Never did business so drag since the creation of this army of clerks who are in business what footmen are in service. References, regulations, registrations, formalities of all kinds have multiplied with such profusion and so little discernment."

It finally came down to this: a whole country was run for the benefit of a few dozen families, or a few hundred, who owned a good share of the land—almost half in France in the eighteenth century—and who battened on the unearned increments from industry, trade, and urban rents.

CHAPTER THIRTEEN

Court, Parade, and Capital

1: POSITION OF THE PALACE

Baroque city building, in the formal sense, was an embodiment of the prevalent drama and ritual that shaped itself in the court: in effect, a collective embellishment of the ways and gestures of the palace. The palace faced two ways. From the urban side came rent, tribute, taxes, command of the army, and control of the organs of state; from the rural side came the well-built, well-exercised, well-fed, well-sexed men and women who formed the body of the court and who received honors, emoluments, and the perquisites the king magnanimously bestowed. Power and pleasure, a dry abstract order and an effulgent sensuality, were the two poles of this life. Mars and Venus were the presiding deities, until Vulcan finally cast his cunning iron net of utilitarianism over their concupiscent forms.

The court was a world in itself; but a world in which all the harsh realities of life were shown in a diminishing glass, and all its frivolities magnified. Pleasure was a duty, idleness a service, and honest work the lowest form of degradation. To become acceptable to the baroque court, it was necessary that an object or a function should bear the marks of exquisite uselessness. The most powerful water wheels of the seventeenth century at Marly—still in operation—and the great hydraulic pumps that counted among its chief technical advances were used merely to work the fountains in the Gardens of Versailles. Fischer von Erlach's steam pump, the first used in Austria, was not applied to a mine, but to the fountains in the gardens of the Belvedere Palace in Vienna; and that significant agent of production, the automatic power-machine, achieved its first great success applied to buttons (the stamping machine), to ribbons (the narrow automatic loom), and to army uniforms (the first sewing machine).

The ritual of the court was an attempt to confirm the make-believe of absolute power by a special drama. I know no better picture of the environment, no more fulsome demonstration of its narcotic illusions, than the panegyric uttered by Nicholas Breton:

"Oh, the gallant life of the Court, where so many are the choices of contentment, as if on earth it were the Paradise of the World: the majesty of the sovereign, the wisdom of the Council, the honour of the Lords, the beauty of the Ladies, the care of the officers, the courtesy of the gentlemen, the divine services of the morning and evening, the witty, learned, noble, and pleasant discourses all day, the variety of wits and the depth of judgements, the dainty fare, sweetly dressed and neatly served, the delicate wines and rare fruits, with excellent music and adorable voices, masques, and plays, dancing and riding; diversity of games, delightful to the game-ster's purposes; and riddles, questions, and answers; poems, histories, and strange inventions of wit, to startle the brain of good understanding; rich apparel, precious jewels, fine proportions, and high spirits, princely coaches, stately horses, royal buildings and rare architecture, sweet crea-tures and civil pleasure; and in the course of love such carriage of con-tent as sets the spirit in the lap of pleasure, that if I should talk of the praise of it all day, I should be short of the worth of it at night."

One need not underscore the counter-accents of actuality: the inane conversation that passed for wit, the unwanted babies that got past the barriers of the fashionable contraceptives known from the sixteenth cen-tury on to the upper classes of France and Italy, the politely ruthless competition for place and preferment. There was still enough plausibility in the mellifluous composition even when the sour notes were accounted for. The motto written over the door of Rabelais' Abbey of Thelema was: "Do as You Please." Over the palace gates there was an extra proviso: "As long as It Pleases the Prince." One must however add one fact that is too often left out of the conception of this ceremonious and sensuous baroque life. Its ritual was so tedious that it veritably bored people to distraction. The daily routine of Prince and courtier was comparable to that of an auto worker in an assembly plant: every detail of it laid out and fixed, as much for the sovereign as for his entourage. From the moment the Prince's eyes opened to the last moment when his mistress left his bedchamber, he was, so to say, on the assembly line.

Perhaps this pervasive tedium accounts not only for the effortful friv-olity, but for the element of sheer vagrant mischief, like the outbreak of schoolboys who have been kept under too strict confinement, in baroque state policy. Much of the intricate plotting and counterplotting was the work of bored virtuosos of diplomacy who liked nothing better than to prolong the game itself. Surely the eternal standing, waiting, bowing, scraping—of which Taine has given an unforgettable picture in his descrip-tion of 'The Ancient Regime'—must have run against the grain of well-fed men and women. Small wonder that spectacular amusements played such a large part in their lives.

Unfortunately, the very distractions of the court became duties. The 'performance of leisure' imposed new sacrifices. The dinner party, the ball, the formal visit, as worked out by the aristocracy and by those who, after the seventeenth century, aped them, gave satisfaction only to those for whom form is more important than content. To be 'seen,' to be 'recognized,' to be 'accepted' were the supreme social duties, indeed the work of a whole lifetime. In its final dismal vulgarization, in reports in contemporary gossip columns, this is the part still performed in night clubs and theatrical openings. No small part of the life described in 'Vanity Fair' and 'The Red and the Black' at one end of the nineteenth century, and by Proust at the other end, consisted of visiting and 'paying court': empty formalities. Proust noted that it was at the time of Louis XIV that a serious change had come about in the life of the aristocracy, which had once had active responsibilities, grave duties, serious interests: the only questions treated with moral earnestness were those which concerned manners.

As in so many other departments of life the baroque court here anticipated the ritual and the psychal reaction of the twentieth-century metropolis. A similar grind: a similar boredom: a similar attempt to take refuge in 'distractions' from the tyrannical oppression that had become a routine and from the routine that had become an overwhelming oppression.

2: INFLUENCE OF THE PALACE ON

THE CITY

The baroque court had a direct influence upon the town in nearly every aspect of life: it is even the parent of many new institutions democracy later claimed for its own. There was no parallel domination of the castle even in the medieval Italian town: if anything, the forces flowed in a contrary direction and the feudal gentry became more urbane. In time, at many removes, the democratic ideal would be massively perverted under capitalism in an effort to popularize the image of courtly life as the desirable consummation of human existence and the final cachet of 'success': suffocating luxury, conspicuous expenditure, extravagant waste, a glut of novelties and sensations, organized into a carnival of triviality for the sole purpose of keeping an expanding economy in operation.

The ultimate price of such an expanding economy, both at court and in the goods-devouring households of our contemporary democracy, is a contracting life: that of the swollen parasite, helpless, dependent, enslaved to its host.

One must not think of the dominance of the palace in terms of a single building with its courtly functions: the palatial style of life spread everywhere; indeed, the word palazzo, first in Italy, signifies any magnificent building, such as a lord or a merchant prince might occupy. Palatial, in baroque terms, stands for spaciousness and self-sufficient power. The desire for self-sufficiency had indeed appeared in another form in the fourteenth century, in the forest of competitive towers, spindly and four-square, that turned the skylines of Lucca, Bologna, or San Gimignano into so many bristling urban pin-cushions. There the new spirit took a wholly medieval form to express dominance. But from the fifteenth century on, horizontal spaciousness was emphasized: power spread itself. Lacking space in the city, it would escape to the suburbs, as Louis XIV, remembering how he had been forced to flee Paris before a popular uprising in his youth, took refuge in Versailles: a suburban capital.

So commodious were the interiors of the new palaces that an equally new upper-class institution, the hotel, not merely takes its name from the urban palace in France, but performs one of its main functions, that of offering seemingly unstinted hospitality—though at a price. The very formality and anonymity of the plan gave the palace a certain flexibility of accommodation, all the more because it was designed to house large numbers of servants and courtiers. To this day, many of the best luxury hotels in Rome are old palaces. Rome and Padua were in fact the first cities to build new hotels for commercial use on a palatial model. That in Padua (around 1450) had stables for two hundred horses. The alternate later use of these old palaces as art galleries, museums, academies, and office buildings shows the organic relation between the baroque style of life and its typical institutions.

Thanks especially to aristocratic patronage, the theater took its modern form in London, Paris, and minor cities: a modification of the old Greek and Roman form. Under the lead of Palladio's Teatro Olimpico at Vicenza, the theater was now a covered hall, in which the audience was seated according to rank and ability to pay, and in which, from their fixed position, they became the passive spectators of a drama seen, as it were, through a transparent show window. So deeply was the theater in the style of this age that anatomy dissections were annual public performances, performed in 'theaters,' as such halls are still sometimes called.

The new baroque spatial perspective first manifested itself, not in the actual city, but in a painted street scene in the theater (Serlio); and it was not an accident that the new city planners, like Servandoni, Inigo

Jones, and Bernini were likewise scenic designers. The new city itself was in fact an essay in formal scenic design: a backdrop for absolute power. When the royal finances were inadequate to perform sufficiently grandiose feats of building in marble, the appearance would be counterfeited in paint and plaster, or a monumental façade would pretentiously mask the insignificant building behind it.

Pre-eminently, it was on the side of pleasure and recreation, of theatrical display and showmanship, that the influence of the palace was most potent. The pleasure garden, such as Ranelagh Gardens in London in the seventeenth century, and Vauxhall and Cremorne Gardens in the eighteenth and early nineteenth, were attempts to supply the more lascivious pleasures of the court to the commonalty at a reasonable price per head. The later French equivalent was the Bal Masqué, and the German parallel, the more domestic and orderly beer garden. Such pleasure gardens were popular everywhere that court life was visibly on parade: the famous Tivoli Gardens in Copenhagen still bears witness to this fact, though the beer gardens New York boasted for half a century after the Civil War have now disappeared. These gardens consisted of a large central building, often gaudily decorated, where dances and routs could be held, and where great feasts could be given; surrounded by gardens with recessed arbors and woods where people might roam on a fine evening, eating, drinking, flirting, copulating, watching fireworks or lantern displays: the gaiety and license of the carnival, offered daily. Oliver Goldsmith in 'A Party at Vauxhall Gardens' left good descriptions of both scene and mood.

Swings and roundabouts made their appearance in these pleasure gardens. Likewise, at the beginning of the nineteenth century, the aristocratic love of speed came out in the more popular chute-the-chutes. As for the merry-go-round, with its circular whirl of wooden horses, its French name, carrousel, plainly reveals its aristocratic origin: for the carrousel was the daily display of horseflesh and carriages, for which circles and roundpoints or wide plazas were originally framed. With wooden horses, the hoi-polloi could taste the same pleasures. During the nineteenth century the older baroque elegance disappeared: beginning first, perhaps in international fairs, more rowdy forms of amusement and more breathtaking distractions, like the Ferris Wheel, came to the front, and finally only the tawdry glitter remained, as at Coney Island. We may well recall Rainer Maria Rilke's remarks on Capri: "Have you ever seen, when men acted or let themselves go in the direction of pleasure, relaxation, or enjoyment that they came by any pleasant results?"

But the point of origin in baroque urban culture is as plain as the downward path itself: pleasure, for the masses in every great city or in its remotest outlying roadhouse and dance hall, is still baroque pleasure:

show, glitter, expense, visual titillations with erotic conquests or sub-erotic possibilities, all duly paid for, accompanied by eating and drinking in necessarily expensive restaurants and cafés. And when the special pleasure garden disappeared with the expansion and congestion of the city, the same element re-entered the city in appropriate quarters, such as Broadway, Piccadilly, Soho, Montmartre, the Rembrandtplein.

If the pleasure garden grew on one stem of the palatial baroque life, the museum grew even closer to the main trunk: a product of the economy of limitless acquisition, as the first was of limitless consumption. At first, doubtless, the museum proceeded from the motives of scientific curiosity, as in Aristotle's collections; while in the medieval period, under the influence of Christian theology, the museum took the form of a collection of religious relics—a saint's tooth, a phial of blood, a splinter of the true cross, housed naturally in churches. But the museum in the modern sense began again with the collection of coins and inscriptions, a practice that had become common as early as the fifteenth century in Italy. These collections anticipated by a few years the natural history collections of a von Netteshyn, a Paracelsus, or an Agricola. The writings of the latter were indeed instrumental in causing the Elector Augustus of Saxony to form the collections that have since developed into the museums of Dresden.

In time, the purpose of these museum collections widened. Mercier, writing in 'L'An 2000' (1770), a utopian picture of the future, foresaw a museum where "all the different sorts of animals, vegetables, and minerals were placed under the four wings and were visible by one glance of the eye." On the façade of this building was written: "An Abridgement of the Universe." The ambition was admirable; but the result, we have sadly learned, may be an invitation to indigestion, as long as baroque standards of limitless acquisition and consumption and display are respected.

At the beginning, the love of ancient art and of newly found curiosities and monstrosities seemed equally eager. Evelyn described a Venetian palace, filled with Roman statues, but also containing "things petrified, walnuts, eggs in which the yolk rattled, a pear, a piece of beef with the bones in it, a whole hedge-hog." This too was the style of the time. Everywhere a random search for buried art treasures and natural wonders took place: a sort of primitive 'collection economy' of the mind, before organized cultivation was achieved.

As a result of the princely desire to bring home loot from foreign conquests, and to acquire by purchase or patronage what could not be obtained by superiority in arms, the great collections of art that form the Vatican Museum, the Louvre, the National Gallery, the British Museum, and similar institutions were formed. Here again the court and the aristocracy played a leading part. Yet the opening of the British Museum in

1759 after Sir Hans Sloane's bequest was a landmark in *popular* culture; for when display ceased to be merely a private gratification of the possessor, it had the possibility of becoming a means of public education. The very growth of the collection hastened this changeover.

As for the art gallery, to serve as a setting for art was in the very nature of the palace. One had only to remove the domestic offices and appoint a bureaucratic custodian to effect the transformation. Sometimes this change occurred in sheer self-defense. Raphael's 'Galateo,' for instance, was painted for the dining room of the banker, Agostino Chigi. But so many people came to see the picture that, under this pressure, the room was converted into an art gallery during the owner's lifetime. By the end of the nineteenth century, when Mrs. Jack Gardner in Boston, or Mr. Henry Frick in New York, built palatial mansions for themselves, they already anticipated such a final use of their collections: from the beginning they served only as interim custodians of a public building.

Halfway between pleasure and curiosity stands one last bequest of the palace: the zoological garden. The keeping of wild animals, especially the more ferocious or exotic ones, was still an attribute of kings in the Middle Ages, though the practice goes back to the remotest evidences of kingship. The extension of these collections of living animals, with a provision of permanent quarters and exhibition grounds, was part of the same general movement as that which promoted the museum. Like the museum, the zoo furnished a suitable destination for the explorer's finds and the hunter's trophies. The divinely appointed King still enacted in play his archetypal hunter's role, handed on from his late stone age ancestors.

Here was a fresh contribution to the city: a reminder of that feral state which urban man, in his illusion that he has successfully conquered nature, too easily forgets. The playful antics of the monkey, the imperturbability of the hippopotamus, the gay sleek motions of the seals—all these examples of nature's inexhaustible creativity, if they did not bring the city dweller into contact with nature, at least had a relaxing effect upon the overstrained urban ego. They not merely gave pleasure to the child but kept the child alive in the adult. Even such motheaten baroque relics as the dancing bear or the organ-grinder's monkey often brought a touch of animal gaiety into the drab gutters of the nineteenth century street. Is it by accident that these vestigial emblems of baroque court life were usually presided over by an Italian?

One by one, these palatial institutions registered their presence on the new city plan. Sometimes they came under private auspices; sometimes with royal or municipal support; always in the gilded image bearing the original stamp of the court and the palace. But I have kept the finest contribution to the last. This was the opening of the royal park: a feature all the more necessary because of the building over of the smaller pleasure grounds and playing fields that had once engirdled the medieval city. The doing over and extension of the broad landscape park in the heart of the city was perhaps the most felicitous contribution the palace made to urban life. Nothing has done more to keep the centers of London, Paris, and Berlin from stifling congestion and ultimate disintegration than St. James's Park, Green Park, the Tuileries, the Tiergarten. Though the space occupied by these parks might perhaps have been better apportioned throughout the city, if they had been planned, not for the king's convenience, but for the commons, they at least kept in constant view the aristocratic concept of space and verdure, as an essential part of urban life: not to be covered over without biological impairment, as well as esthetic dreariness and depression.

But even in the matter of providing parks, the spirit of the age eventually asserted itself. When the Crown planned Regent's Park in London, the Park itself was valued openly as a device for increasing the ground values of the neighboring properties held by the Crown. Yet even that lesson was lost on the commercial speculators who so largely dominated building during the nineteenth century: they retained the baroque desire for gain, without doing justice to the baroque love of pleasure and beauty, which might have both modified their rapacity and given greater security and durability to their investment. In the long run, the extravagant aristocratic landlords proved better business men—and even better citizens.

3: BEDROOM AND SALON

If the influence of the court was effective in the city at large, it was no less so in the household: at all events, in the houses of the middle classes and their economic superiors. Here the habits of the court, both for good and bad, eventually prevailed. For bad in that a new domestic despotism grew up, which had its source in the vast number of disfranchised people who crowded into the capitals to sell their services for a pittance. The good side was the esthetic improvement in manners, perhaps not altogether unaffected by the increased knowledge of the bland and perfect forms of Chinese civilization; and above all, the spread of privacy within the home: a fact which gave rise to a new code of sexual manners, embroidering the preliminaries of sexual intercourse, and tending to lengthen the period of amatory youth for both sexes. The very word courtship, for that preliminary play which includes the display of wit and charm as well as physical passion, shows how much our erotic life owes to the practice of the court: it is a late sixteenth-century coinage.

The change in the constitution of the household manifested itself in various ways. First, by the gradual divorce of the home, henceforth a place for eating, for entertaining, and in a secondary way for rearing children, from the workplace. The three functions of producing, selling, and consuming were now separated in three different institutions, three different sets of buildings, three distinct parts of the city. Transportation to and from the place of work was first of all a privilege of the rich merchants in the big cities: it was only in the nineteenth century that it filtered down to the other classes in the city, and, instead of being a privilege, became a grievous burden. As the result of the household's becoming exclusively a consumer's organization, the housewife lost her touch with the affairs of the outside world: she became either a specialist in domesticity or a specialist in sex, something of a drudge, something of a courtesan, more often perhaps a little of both. Therewith the 'private house' comes into existence: *private from business,* and spatially separated from any visible means of support. Every part of life came increasingly to share this privacy.

This growth of domesticity partly signified the weakening of public interest among the middle-class citizens. Especially among the banned and excluded religious sects there was a natural tendency to substitute private life for public affairs. Deprived of his old liberties, unable often even to vote for his municipal officers or take part in the official business of his town unless appointed by the Prince, it was natural that the citizen's interest should shift to purely selfish concerns. If he were a member of a banned religious sect, as many among the merchant classes were, the incentive was even greater. The excluded groups rejected the public interests and activities of the larger community. Both citizenship and neighborliness tended to lapse. The city was nobody's business.

To make up for lack of effective domestic work, a new type of housework was invented that took up the slack and enriched the ritual of conspicuous consumption. I mean the care of furniture. The fixtures of the medieval household were equipment: chairs to sit on, beds to sleep in: icons to pray before: so much and no more. Furniture is really a re-invention of the baroque period: for by furniture one means useless or super-refined equipment, delicate vases to dust, inlays and precious woods to polish, metal work to keep shiny, curtains to be shaken and cleaned, bric-a-brac and curios to be washed.

Display outstripped use; and the care of furniture commanded time that once went to the weaving of tapestries, the embroidery of garments, the making of useful household preserves, perfumes, and simples. These new burdens were inflicted upon housewives and domestics at the very moment that the form of the house itself had changed, multiplying the number of private chambers to be supplied with wood, coal, water, and raising the height of dwellings from two flights of stairs to five, one below ground.

Up to the seventeenth century, at least in the North, building and heating had hardly advanced far enough to permit the arrangement of a series of private rooms in the dwelling. But now a separation of functions took place within the house as well as within the city as a whole. Space became specialized, room by room. In England, following the pattern of the great houses, the kitchen was broken off from the scullery, where the dirty work was done; and the various social functions of the kitchen were taken over by the living room and the parlor. The "use of the common dinner table for the household," Holm tells us, "died out in the early years of the seventeenth century, and the servants thenceforward took their meals below stairs."

So wide did the gap become between classes that even the humane Emerson, seeking to restore this democratic form, met rebellion on the part of his servants and was forced to abandon the practice. The dining room could no longer be treated as a sleeping apartment, too; and though in the seventeenth century a lady's bedroom still served as a reception room for her guests, whether or not the bed stood in an alcove, in the eighteenth a special room for meeting and conversation, the drawing room, the salon, came into existence. And the rooms no longer opened into each other: they were grouped along the corridor, like houses on its public counterpart, the new corridor street. The need for privacy produced this special organ for public circulation.

Privacy was the new luxury of the well-to-do; only gradually did the servants and the shopkeepers' assistants and the industrial workers have a trace of it. Even in the fine houses of the nineteenth century, the domestics often slept in the kitchen or in a bunk adjacent to it, or in dormitories. Now, privacy had been reserved, in the medieval period, for solitaries, for holy persons who sought refuge from the sins and distractions of the outside world: only lords and ladies might dream of it otherwise. In the seventeenth century it went with the satisfaction of the individual ego. The lady's chamber became a boudoir, literally a 'sulking place'; the gentleman had his office or his library, equally inviolate; and in Paris he might even have his own bedroom, too, as husband and wife pursued their separate erotic adventures. For the first time not merely a curtain but a door separated each individual member of the household from every other member.

Privacy, mirrors, heated rooms: these things transformed full-blown love-making from a seasonal to a year-round occupation: another example of baroque regularity. In the heated room, the body need not cower under a blanket: visual erethism added to the effect of tactile stimuli: the pleasure of the naked body, symbolized by Titian and Rubens and Fragonard, was part of that dilation of the senses which accompanied the more generous dietary, the freer use of wines and strong liquors, the more extravagant dresses and perfumes of the period.

Flirtation and courtship created those movements of suspense and uncertainty, of blandishment and withdrawal, that serve as safeguards against satiety: a counterpoise to the regimentation of habit. These lusty men and women were never so much at home as when they were in bed. Ladies received callers in bed; statesmen dictated their correspondence in bed; an undercurrent of erotic interest thus permeated the household, sometimes bawdy, sometimes brutal, sometimes romantic, sometimes tender —every shade from the bedroom of Juliet to that in which Joseph Andrews almost lost his virtue. The private needs of the bedroom even penetrated the garden: the summer house, the temple of love, or the more aristocratic maze, composed of high box hedges: places remote from the prying eyes and admonitory footsteps of even the servants.

4: DISAPPEARANCE OF THE BATH

Meanwhile other technical changes haltingly entered the dwelling house. The invention of the water-closet by Sir John Harington in 1596 made an important sanitary improvement in the house; but the fashion did not spread fast; for even the interior dry privy was introduced into France in the eighteenth century as an English novelty; while the Palace of Versailles, built regardless of expense, did not have even the conveniences of a medieval castle: portable commodes on wheels were used. Before the invention of the trap and the ventilating stack for the water-closet, the backing up of sewer gas into the dwelling house almost counterbalanced the advantages of the new improvement: note the British concern during the nineteenth century with 'bad drains.' With the eotechnic device of the water-closet came another practice directly derived from the Chinese: the use of toilet paper: more important for domestic hygiene than the wallpaper that came in more or less simultaneously.

With all its luxurious display, the baroque city will not bear close inspection in the matter of hygienic and sanitary standards: the typical medieval town was more salubrious. Much though the body was now celebrated in poesy and painting, or systematically investigated in physiology, the people of the period neglected to clean it as thoroughly as the preceding culture had done. Probably in order to limit the dangers of contracting syphilis by contact, the medieval bath had begun to fall out of use in the sixteenth century. Even among the Jews, who might have been expected in their ghettos to preserve medieval habits so thoroughly in harmony with Mosaic sanitation, the ritual bath that used to take place in the Synagogue—the Mikveh—was given up during the Renascence. The new Baptists might insist upon total immersion; but one experience seems to have lasted them a lifetime.

Doubtless the rising price of hot water had something to do with this lapse, among the common people at least: it would follow upon the scarcity of wood fuel in the immediate neighborhood of the bigger cities. But the fact itself is beyond doubt. In 1387 there were 29 bathmen in Frankfurt; in 1530, none. In the seventeenth century, after a breach, the bath was re-introduced as a foreign importation, a luxury, a means of renovating the body after a debauch: the so-called Turkish or Russian bath. But almost immediately these baths became pleasure haunts and houses of assignation: bagnio again meant brothel. Dirt diseases, such as smallpox, flourished in this period; and with the crowding of the cities the volume of water that had been sufficient when the mains were installed in the sixteenth century proved altogether inadequate. Since these mains were often neither renewed nor extended, the inhabitants of the town would have a much smaller quantity of water per capita in the eighteenth century than they had had two or three centuries before. When the bathroom finally made its way into the house in the nineteenth century, to the chants of mechanical progress that then arose, only a belated antiquary might possibly recognize that Johann Andreae had assigned such a room *to each three room apartment* in his ideal city, Christianopolis, and that such rooms had been common, in the better burgher houses in Germany, in the Middle Ages.

5: BAROQUE DOMINANCE AND DISPLAY

Apart from overseas colonization, the chief new cities built from the sixteenth to the nineteenth century were 'residence cities' for kings and princes, like Versailles, Karlsruhe, and Potsdam, or garrison towns, residences of royal power *in absentia,* like Londonderry, Philippeville, and Christiansand. Only in such towns could the baroque theory of planning be carried out fully in every department: Christopher Wren's attempt to do so in London after the great fire of 1670 was foiled by tenacious mercantile habits and jealous property rights.

Whether as a citadel for his army or as a permanent home for the prince and his court, the baroque city was in fact a 'command perform-ance.' The town extensions that were done on new lines were usually built in capital cities like Naples or Munich, or in aristocratic towns like Nancy (1588) or Edinburgh (1765). In cities like Edinburgh and London, the new bourgeoisie had themselves achieved almost aristocratic pretensions and scope.

This original sponsorship gave town planning itself an association with arbitrary power that partly accounts, perhaps, for the democratic distrust of the whole planning process during the nineteenth century: the doctrine of laissez faire meant not only freedom from guild regulation and mo-nopoly, but likewise freedom from central regulation and control of any kind, including that of the town planner. The methods of town planning itself, as practiced by high-handed agents of the prince, were responsible for not a little of this antagonism. In 1492, for example, Ludovico the Moor ordered the inhabitants of Vigevano to tear down their old market place and to rebuild it after the plans of his engineer, Ambrogio de Curtis. Except for the new cathedral, the whole job was done in two years, with a ruthless expedition that would have done honor to a Baron Haussmann. The bias of the military engineer was visible in both the plans and the methods. So one need not be surprised to find the chief baroque treatises on town planning were composed by such engineers: Martini, Perret, Speckle. So, too, the most original suggestions in planning, those for sep-arating traffic streets from pedestrian ways, and decentralizing overgrown cities into smaller units of 30,000 people, likewise came from a genius who also practiced military engineering: Leonardo da Vinci.

Long before the invention of bulldozers, the Italian military engineer developed, through his professional specialization in destruction, a bull-dozing habit of mind: one that sought to clear the ground of encum-brances, so as to make a clean beginning on his own inflexible mathe-matical lines. Often these 'encumbrances' were human households, shops, churches, neighborhoods, treasured memorials, the basis of a whole tissue of habits and social relations. The wholesale removal of the buildings embodying these forms of life would wipe out the co-operations and fidelities of a lifetime, often many lifetimes. That in making a 'clean job' the planner would have to destroy precious social organs that could not be replaced as easily as streets can be paved and houses built did not seem important to the early military engineer any more than it seems so to his twentieth-century successors, in charge of 'slum clearance projects' or highway designs.

In the interest of mechanical efficiency and outward esthetic con-formity, the engineer ignored the social structure of the city, and in his effort to accelerate traffic, he impeded the meeting and co-operation of those whom the traffic supposedly served. Thus Baron Haussmann, in the course of building the Boulevard Saint-Michel, that bleak, noisy thorough-fare, tore through the heart of the ancient Latin Quarter, which had been an almost autonomous entity since the Middle Ages. And he took the simplest of all methods of improving one portion of it: he wiped it out. He not merely cleared the area surrounding the Schools, but in a side-swipe even cut off part of the Gardens of the Palais du Luxembourg, sac-rificing to straight lines, broad avenues, unimpeded vehicular movement the specific historic character of the quarter and all the complex human needs and purposes it served.

These baroque clichés of power, hardly even with the decency of a disguise, lingered right into the twentieth century: witness the plowing of the Seventh Avenue extension through the one historic quarter of New York that had integrity and character, or the similar, even more grandiose effacement created by the misconceived Benjamin Franklin Boulevard in Philadelphia—the latter a brutal gash from which the city has not yet recovered in more than thirty years. Where the original baroque terms still prevailed, this type of planning might still have some justification: thus a short and symbolically appropriate avenue connects the Admiralty Arch with Buckingham Palace in London, whilst the crest above is lined by foreign embassies. But elsewhere such plans, which their administrators still innocently supposed to be 'modern,' merely repeat with faithful mo-notony the social ineptitudes of princely power. These errors go as far back as Bramante; for a contemporary pamphlet, denouncing Bramante as a maker of ruins and the terror of old Rome, pictures him as suggesting to Saint Peter that he replace the proverbially narrow and difficult path to Heaven by a wide avenue, straight and well paved.

Given this despotic, military approach, the new plan distinguished itself from the older medieval informality by the use of straight lines and regular block units, as far as possible of uniform dimensions, except where diagonal streets changed the blocks into irregular polygons. The new order was definitely an extroverted one: characterized by the open place or round point, with its radiating streets and avenues cutting im-partially through old tangles or new gridirons, moving toward the bound-less horizon. No inner space there! The asterisk plan was, in fact, an origi-nal baroque contribution, though as I pointed out earlier it first occurred as a satiric suggestion in Aristophanes. The baroque town planner turned that forgotten conceit into a solemn fact. But he had his professional rea-sons. From such a central point, artillery could command every approach. The ideal prototype of the new plan was based upon military considera-tions that go back as far as Francesco Martini's octagonal layouts, with streets radiating from the center, around 1500. In 1593 the Republic of Venice founded such a new town, Palma Nuova; and a Dutch planner built its counterpart in Coeworden only four years later, which again was followed by Glückstadt on the Elbe, about forty miles from Hamburg, in 1616.

Both the ideal plans for miniature towns, and the concrete forms derived from them, transposed into larger schemes, must be considered mainly as exercises in military esthetics: toy models for the parade of power. Though the minuscule towns that were built completely on such an enclosed pattern were, by their own physical definition, incapable of growth, they set a pattern of thinking that had a widespread influence. The three great avenues that radiate from the Piazza del Popolo in Rome, the conception of Pope Sixtus V, were designed to make it easy for the pilgrim to find his way to the various churches and holy spots; yet they were conceived in the same undeviating military manner; and it is not by accident that one of them, the Corso, became the principal shopping street of Rome, open to the 'carriage trade.'

The forerunner of the asterisk type of avenue plan was, as one might expect from a hunting aristocracy, the royal hunting park itself. Here the long lanes, cut through the trees, enabled the mounted hunters to rally at a central point and go galloping off in every direction. Hunting and the breakneck riding that accompanies it remain to this day the privileged sport of what survives of aristocracy in every country. The central meeting point, the roundpoint, was originally the seat of the hunting lodge. When the plan for Versailles was laid down, the new palace itself was set on the site of the old hunting lodge where Louis XIV had first wooed his mistress, Mme. de la Vallière. But in the plan of a royal capital, the meeting place now served another purpose: the palace gathered to itself the new avenues of the city as the ruler himself gathered the political power that had once been dispersed among a multitude of feudal families and municipal corporations. All the main avenues would lead to the palace. And when one raised one's eyes in the street, the palace, as often as not, would close the vista. The axial approach served as a spotlight to focus attention on the prince.

In Latin countries, particularly, the asterisk plan remained for three centuries the hallmark of elegant urban design. This type left its mark, not merely on Versailles, but on such suburban districts as Garches and Meudon. As late as 1859, the first prize for a plan for the extension of Barcelona was awarded to a plan whose diagonals converged toward the historic core of the old city. Still later, in 1911 in fact, a new residential quarter was laid out in Rome with an imitative but now purposeless central plaza as a spacious point of origin for radiating streets. Even in the frontier (English) territory of Upper Canada, in 1829, the little town of Goderich was planned with a marketplace as hub—now handsomely filled with trees—and eight spokes wide enough to carry today's traffic. This type of plan was in fact imitated over an area as wide as Western Civilization itself, in places as far apart as Samarkand and Washington. The plan of Samarkand, as it stood at the end of the nineteenth century, was indeed classic in every respect, indeed an archetypal example of the baroque mode. In the middle a citadel; to the east the old city spread out. Raying outward from the citadel were the streets and boulevards of the new town, moving westward. Was it a coincidence that these boulevards terminated, north and south, in a barracks and a military hospital?

For the asterisk plan there was, however, another parallel point of origin. In the early starlike schemes of fortification, the city proper, set within it, became a regular polygon, usually eight-sided; and the main streets were either divided in the form of a cross or placed so as to converge in the center from each of the angles of the octagon. When this type of fortification lost its value, the main effect of the new pattern was to make the city itself, or the quarter, a sector of the original spiderweb, with the other avenues radiating out into a park or the open country, as in the royal town of Karlsruhe. We shall later examine the functional adaptation of that plan to the most lively and comely of all seventeenth-century cities, Amsterdam, whose form might never have approached its original perfection without precisely this geometric suggestion.

The scheme of central place, circles or open squares, dominated by monuments, flanked symmetrically by public buildings, with avenues spreading out from such centers, profoundly altered every dimension of building. Unlike the medieval town, which one must slowly walk through to appreciate its never ending transformations of mass and silhouette, its intricate and surprising details, one can take in a baroque town almost at a glance. Even what one does not see one can easily extrapolate in one's imagination, once the guiding lines are established. The avenue now became definitely the horizontal frame of the terminal buildings. Though these edifices might be capped by a dome or a towered cupola, the main effect of the plan itself was to increase the importance of the regulating horizontal lines, formed by the lintels, the string courses, and the cornices: for the first time all these parts were united in a perspective whose effect was intensified by the seemingly infinite length of the avenue.

Not merely did the domes of the dominant buildings seem to float: the buildings themselves, when established alone at the end of a broad avenue, likewise floated in space, and sometimes, like the buildings that frame the Place de la Concorde, were almost lost in it. If the medieval town with its insistence on enclosure might at its worst produce a sense of claustrophobia, the city of absolutism produced just the opposite effect, that of agoraphobia: a horror of emptiness, saved only by the fact that the space would be cut in tatters by the constant movement of vehicles.

The rapid movement of the spectator through this space, in a carriage or on horseback, was in fact essential to relieve the esthetic monotony of these uniform avenues, with their uniform buildings and, in the last stage, their all-too-uniform application of the classic orders. Only by tying the park and the alley of trees very close to the new urban street picture could a certain starkness of the architecture be overcome. By the use of such verdure, the Avenue de l'Observatoire and the Champs Elysées have a gracious quality that was not altogether absent even in the speculative boulevards of Haussmann's Paris.

Whatever else the baroque plan stood for it signified the military conquest of space: the human results were not taken into account, except in so far as they conspired to the advantage of the upper classes. But once the constraining fortification was gone, the indefinite length of the new avenue proved a handicap; for it belittled the king as well as his subjects.

Herein lies the paradox of power. Centralized political power takes its origin from the sheer force and capability of a dominant personality: it reaches its negation when all these attributes and energies are absorbed by an official mechanism, whereby the original power is conveyed to a distant point through a bureaucratic and military organization. If tyranny is a consequence of democratic confusion and ineptitude, it is equally true that democratic vulgarization is an inevitable result of the final stage of tyranny: depersonalized efficiency. After a time, the mightiest of emperors, financial magnates, or dictators counts for no more than the man in the street: they are both cogs, caught in the same mechanism. The Pitti Palace, seen from across its courtyard, still seems formidable: but Versailles, beheld at a great distance, is no more formidable than a horizontal factory unit, built for the straight line assembly of puppets. These long avenues serve as a diminishing glass; in the long perspectives of Versailles or St. Petersburg, the central human figure, King or Czar, became ever smaller and soon reached his political vanishing point

6: URBAN FUNCTIONS AS LEFTOVERS

As I have indicated, the city was sacrificed to the traffic in the new plan: the street, not the neighborhood or quarter, became the unit of planning. The uniform avenue brought movement and confusion into parts of the town that had been quiet and self-contained; and it tended to stretch out the market along the lines of traffic, instead of providing local points of neighborly concentration where people could congregate and meet— though in cities like London, less under the sway of baroque ideas than most big capitals, neighborly concentration in a few short market streets would still prevail. Living space, in the baroque plan, was treated as a leftover, after the avenue itself determined the shape of the houseplot and the depth of the block.

With this neglect of urban functions other than traffic went an over-valuation of the geometric figure: a square like the new Freudenstadt, a nine-sided figure with radio-concentric streets, like Palma Nuova, a partial star like Karlsruhe. What does this mean? The abstract figure delimits the social contents, instead of being derived from them and in some degree conforming to them. The institutions of the city no longer generate the plan: the function of the plan is rather to bring about conformity to the prince's will in the institutions. There are, it is true, a few exceptions: but alas! they remained on paper. Filarète's ideal star plan was one exception: its central place was rectangular, with the cathedral and the palace on the short sides and the merchants' quarters and the food markets on the long sides. Likewise medieval in its respect for function is the fact that each of the sixteen radial streets is broken by secondary places, eight of these for parish churches, the other eight reserved for special markets, such as those for wood, straw, grain, wine. Such a plan, with its concern for the everyday life of the parish, was still medieval in spirit, if baroque in outline. One need hardly add that Filarète's ideal city was never built: this type of thinking now lacked authority and influence. The prince and his aides had other considerations in mind.

The subordination of the contents of urban life to the outward form was typical of the baroque mind; but its economic costs were almost as extravagant as its social losses. If the topography was irregular, the terrain must be evened out, at whatever cost in materials and manpower, merely in order to make the plan work: the avenue will not swerve in its course or alter its width by a few feet in order to save a fine tree or keep intact a precious building. In event of a conflict with human interests, traffic and geometry take precedence. So difficult is it to execute a baroque plan on irregular contours that most new city building took place on level sites. Sometimes, indeed, the projector retreated from his original plans when, as in the case of the avenues radiating from the Piazza del Popolo in Rome, one hillside proved to be too rugged to be penetrated by the pro-posed avenue. (It seems doubtful, in fact, if the planner could have con-descended to look at the site when he so projected it: a not uncommon negligence in this type of planning.)

Francesco Martini, it is true, varied his ideal plans by an ingenious application of spherical geometry to fit curved hillsides, with tolerable grades for streets, but even that essay in three-dimensional thinking re-quired that the curve of the solid whose contours he conformed to should be actually more regular than it usually is in nature. Not alone, then, did baroque indifference to topography add greatly to the expense of city development: in addition, the increase of wheeled vehicles added to the cost by entailing a heavier type of paving and more of it. The widening and lengthening of avenues added a further burden; and Pope Sixtus IV in 1480 wisely met this by imposing an extra charge on property owners who profited by improvements made in their neighborhood. Unfortunately this sound procedure, like his other remarkable innovation— the condemning of private land for such public purposes as street widening —was not taken up seriously by other municipalities till the end of the nineteenth century.

This is not to say that geometric order cannot play a useful part in planning: quite the contrary. An age like ours, which has succumbed to purely capricious and aimless 'free forms,' may soon have to recover an appreciation of a more rigorous discipline, with its intelligible simplification and order, and its reasonable constraints. The function of geometry in planning is to clarify and guide. Like every other type of useful abstraction, it must be conditioned by the concrete situation in its wholeness and its variety, and give way to specific needs when the latter point to some aspect of life that has escaped the formula. In a period when changes were rapid and when custom could no longer serve as sufficient guide, geometry might well serve as a temporary expedient to produce at least an outward conformity. Unfortunately, baroque planners tacitly assumed that their order was eternal. They not merely regimented space but they sought to congeal time. Their ruthlessness in clearing out the old was equalled only by their stubbornness in opposing the new: for only one order could harmonize with their kind of plan—namely, more of their own.

In short, a baroque plan was a block achievement. It must be laid out at a stroke, fixed and frozen forever, as if done overnight by Arabian Nights genii. Such a plan demands an architectural despot, working for an absolute ruler, who will live long enough to complete their own conceptions. To alter this type of plan, to introduce fresh elements of another style, is to break its esthetic backbone. Even the superficial contents of a baroque plan can be preserved only by severe administrative regulations. Where these were maintained, as in Paris, order might be preserved on the surface for many generations, even for centuries.

The seventeenth-century feeling for outward unity was perhaps best summed up by Descartes, who is one of the most representative thinkers of the period, not least because he was a soldier as well as a mathematical philosopher. "It is observable," said Descartes, "that the buildings which a single architect has planned and executed are generally more elegant and commodious than those which several have attempted to improve. . . . Thus, also, those ancient cities which from being at first only villages have become, in the course of time, large towns, are usually but ill laid out compared with the regularly constructed towns which a professional architect has freely planned on an open plain; so that although the several buildings of the former may often equal or surpass in beauty those of the latter, yet when one observes their indiscriminate juxtaposition, there a large and here a small, and the consequent crookedness and irregularity of the streets, one is disposed to allege that chance, rather than any human will guided by reason, must have led to such an arrangement. And if we consider that nevertheless there have been at all times certain officers whose duty was to see that private buildings contributed to public ornament, the difficulty of reaching high perfection with but the materials of others to operate on will be readily acknowledged."

There could be no sharper contrast between the two orders of thinking, the organic and the mechanical, than here: the first springs out of the total situation, the other simplifies the facts of life for the sake of an artful system of concepts, more dear to the mind than life itself. One works co-operatively with 'the materials of others,' perhaps guiding them, but first acknowledging their existence and understanding their purpose: the other, that of the baroque despot, insisting upon *his* law, *his* order, *his* society, is imposed by a single professional authority, working under his command. For those on the inside of baroque life, the courtier and the financier, this formal order was in effect organic: it represented the values they had created for themselves as a class. For those outside, it was a denial of reality.

The essence of this mode of thinking, the most representative symbol of baroque design in both its weakest and its most creative moments, is the seventeenth-century formal garden or park. This is a formal composition in space, in which the natural growths and efflorescences become merely subordinate patterns in a geometrical design: so much carpet and wall paper and ceiling decoration, artfully put together out of nature's foreign materials. The clipped alley in which the trees are turned into a smooth green wall: the clipped hedge: the deformation of life in the interests of an external pattern of order—here was something at once magnificent and preposterous, as if Procrustes had been given the imagination of a Poussin.

To understand the final limitations of the baroque plan, its failure to deal with any mode of existence except that derived from the court, one must ask: What provisions were made for the civic nucleus? In the neighborhood, none. The local market and the school were not given special sites on the plan; nor does the local park within the big square serve even as a minor playground for neighborhood children, save those who have legal access, by right of ownership, to the square. As for the civic institutions of the municipality, they were subordinate to the Prince's palace; and the theory of this civic nucleus was admirably set forth by Palladio.

"To return to the principal squares, to those that ought to be joined to the Prince's palace, or that for the meeting of the states, as the country is either a monarchy or a republic. The exchequer or the public treasury, where the money and treasure of the public is lodged, ought to join them likewise, as well as prisons. These latter were anciently of three sorts; one for such as were debauched or immodest . . . and which we now assign to fools or mad-folks; another was for Debtors . . . and the third was for traitors or wicked persons."

The palace: the exchequer: the prison: the mad-house—what four buildings could more completely sum up the new order or better symbolize the main features of its political life. These were the dominants. Between them stretched the blankly repetitive façades; and behind those façades the forgotten and denied parts of life somehow went on.

7: THE FORUM OF THE FASHIONABLE

In one place, however, baroque planning rose above its political and military premises; here it created a form independent of the purposes of the palace. This was in the conception of the residential square. The open square had never disappeared; but by the same token it had never, even in the Middle Ages, been used entirely for residential purposes, if only because the counting house and the shop were then part of the home. But in the seventeenth century, it reappeared in a new guise, or rather, it now performed a new urban purpose, that of bringing together, in full view of each other, a group of residences occupied by people of the same general calling and position. Dr. Mario Labó is right in regarding the Strada Nuova in Genoa, as more of a quarter than a street; but the new squares gave a fresh definition to this kind of class grouping.

In the older type of city, particularly on the Continent, the rich and the poor, the great and the humble had often mingled in the same quarter, and in Paris for instance, they long continued to occupy the same buildings, the wealthier on the ground floor, the poorest in the attic, five or six stories above. But now, beginning, it would seem, with the establishment of Gray's Inn in London in 1600, a new kind of square was formed: an open space surrounded solely by dwelling houses, without shops or public buildings, except perhaps a church. Gray's Inn, indeed, was a transitional form, between the medieval walled enclosure, with inner gardens, dedicated to a convent or a great lord's mansion, and the square, walled in only by its own houses, conceived as part of the new street pattern.

The earliest of the French squares, in Paris, the Place Royale (now called the Place des Vosges) was first conceived by Henri IV in 1604, as the site of a new carpet factory, one building of which was actually erected. But in 1605, this project was enlarged to include quarters uniform with the factory in which workers could be housed: seemingly a hopeful precedent for the new industrial order that was in process of assembly, in great weaving and pottery factories, under royal patronage. But in the same year this happy initiative was abandoned in favor of another kind of experiment: the square dedicated solely to upper-class residences. Thus this particular open space reverted in a sense to its original use, for one side of the site had been the old Royal Hôtel des Tournelles, with its tournament field for knightly games; and it returned for a moment to that festive use in 1612. In much the same fashion, it may be noted, St. Ovid's Fair, an old medieval institution, persisted in the Place Vendôme.

In London, the land for these new squares was provided by the great feudal estates that held large tracts of the city. Even in parishes, the feudal nobility had established, in the Paris suburb of Saint Germain for instance, country houses with spacious back gardens, like that which stretches behind the Musée Rodin; whose palatial dimensions derive from its original use. Celia Fiennes, in her 'English Journeys,' notes "there was formerly in the City several houses of the noblemen with large gardens and out houses and great entrances, but of late are pulled down and built into streets and squares and called by the names of the noblemen, and this is the practice of almost all."

The new squares, in fact, met a new upper class need, or rather a whole series of needs. They were originally built for aristocratic or merchant families with the same standards of living, the same habits of life. If the uniform façades of the square concealed differences of political opinion and religious faith, there was perhaps extra need in the seventeenth century for just this kind of arbitrary class cloak to conceal their emerging disparities, rivalries, and enmities: gentlefolk showed a common class front that politely concealed their ideological and party differences. Those who lived on a square had, by that very fact, achieved an extra distinction; and presumably they would be able to keep a coach and horses, an expenditure that even a rising civil servant, like Samuel Pepys, faced with some trepidation.

Architecturally, these squares were at the beginning somewhat bleak: they looked more like a parade ground than the little urban parks many of them became after the eighteenth century, when the romantic taste for landscape came back into the stony wastes of the town. The open spaces of the squares were not conceived, indeed, as places for strolling and relaxing in the open, as they are used now: they were rather parking lots for vehicles: places, as Evelyn noted in 'Londinum Redevivum,' where coaches may stand, and where no doubt the impatient horses on a cold day might be exercised from time to time while the coachman was waiting for his master or mistress. In these open squares, further, guests could be driven to a great party in carriages without causing an undue congestion. So, ironically, such squares as the Place Vendôme (1677-1701), which now serves as a car-park for automobiles, are in a sense only reverting to their original use: but with this difference—the old coaches were usually limited in number and many of them would be in motion, whereas the present occupants form a solid, immobile mass.

In the eighteenth century the transformation of the residential square went further. In the layout of most squares, insufficient space had been provided for back gardens; indeed, these turned all too quickly into paved utilitarian yards, where rugs would be beaten and clothes hung to dry. When this lack was sufficiently missed, the owners of the houses on the square made out of the blank open space a common garden or park. In Turgot's great perspective plan of Paris in 1737, the Place Royale is already enclosed by a fence with four gates and eight straight walks converging toward a mounted equestrian statue in the middle. In England, after a generation or two of planting, the trees and turf introduced a new beauty into the townscape, and sweetened the air. But the innerness of the old medieval gardens was gone: the new note was visual openness and social privacy. Class barriers now formed an invisible ha-ha.

Though the development of the residential square spanned two and a half centuries, the form, the architectural treatment, and the area of open space remained consistent, at least in London. Berkeley Square, with its five acres, perhaps strikes an average. More than two dozen squares were built in Central London before 1827, mainly in Bloomsbury, Mayfair, and Belgravia: they ranged from Covent Garden and Leicester Square (1630 and 1635) through Grosvenor (1695) and Bedford (1775) on to Boston Crescent and Belgrave Square (1820 and 1825). In time, they displayed a wide range of forms, oblongs like Torrington Square, semi-circles like Mornington Crescent, circles like the Place des Victoires in Paris, open ellipses like some of those in the New Town of Edinburgh. Even in quarters that finally succumbed to changed uses and impoverishment, these open spaces served to keep up a level of decency and order that contrasted favorably with the dingier side streets.

The example set by London and Paris was imitated in lesser cities. The Place Ducale in the townlet of Charléville is cut of the same cloth, architecturally, as the Place Royale in Paris; and in the squares and circles and crescents of Bath, as laid out by the Woods, they reached a higher pitch of perfection than elsewhere, perhaps, partly because of a truly magnificent exploitation of the irregular hilly sites in the new parts of the town. Unfortunately, since it is the buildings of the Royal Crescent that are usually photographed, not the view from them, those who have not

visited Bath may easily not realize that the wide sweep of the Crescent
is not an arbitrary form, but an imaginative response to the wide sweep
of landscape that the site commands: a view of the distant hills that must
have been even more striking before the intervening trees had grown
sufficiently to close it off. Here the baroque prodigality of space was
amply justified by the esthetic result—to say nothing of the salubrity
of such open planning. Architectural critics who recently have confused
urbanity with high population densities and tight building, stultify themselves by forgetting the openness of Bath: the most consistently urbane
of English cities, which in its best days boasted the population of a country
town and cultivated the polite airs of a metropolis.

How far this new order could go in a direction quite different from
the palatial baroque precedents, Craig's plan for the New Town of
Edinburgh in 1767 demonstrates. That order and unity were the result
of a unified attitude toward life, the unified ownership of the land, and the
unified control of the architect and builder. If the land had been first
broken up into individual parcels, sold to competitive private owners,
each proud of his own tastes, jealous of his own whims, ferocious in
defense of his own ideology, the result would have been the chaos that
too often prevailed in the late nineteenth-century street, urban or suburban. Here, in London, Bath, or Edinburgh, rather than in the palatial
residence cities of more famous example, like Versailles, the baroque
order was at its best: regimentation with a formal bow and a quiet smile.
The structural ingredients were simple, and they owed almost nothing
to a blind imitation of the past. The open space a simple geometric figure,
crescent, circle, oval, square, bounded by a rail that enclosed the greenery: a street on the periphery, for access. Common building materials,
brick, stone, or stucco, uniformly framed the sides of the square: likewise a common roof line, and common repeating elements, windows,
doors, columns.

The requirements were so fundamental, the method of treatment so
direct, that these houses still are livable quarters, one hundred to three
hundred years later: I can testify to that from experience. Their spaciousness, their very anonymity, their lack of "functional exactness," to
use Matthew Nowicki's term, have prolonged their life; for they serve
almost equally well as apartments, hotels, offices, studios, in fact for
almost every purpose except their original one of one-family residence.
At their meanest, both architecture and plan showed good manners: at
their best, they met all the requirements of an ostentatious but dignified
life, at a period when such show could be maintained by a generous
retinue of ill-paid servants. The length of time this form prevailed unchanged testifies to its merits: Thomas Cubitt was still building such
houses and squares in London in the first half of the nineteenth century

So much by way of just appreciation. But one must not look too close, even in upper-class quarters, behind the handsome classic front. They have both a front and a rear. The front, which was meant to be seen, is still handsome. The rear, which was meant to be hidden, was usually sordid, often downright disgraceful. Here the architecture mirrors the life: Hogarth's series on 'The Rake's Progress,' like Boswell's 'Diaries,' reveals much that the purely architectural engravings of the period conceal. Observe the backs of the fine houses in Charlotte Square, Edinburgh: they are barracks. Follow the alleys that lead off the square: you will find a slum, separated from the fine houses only by stables, occupied by the servants and the petty tradesmen. Where these buildings do not exist before the great square comes into being, they will eventually be provided as part of the development: the streets behind the somewhat overblown façades of Nash's Regent's Park were planned from the beginning, so to say, as built-in slums. Thoughtfully, the planners even provided a little quarter of smaller houses, designed for the convenient occupancy of mistresses and courtesans.

Definitely, such upper-class planning had almost nothing to contribute to the order of the rest of the city, whose population lived at a lower economic level, and was housed, as we shall see, in accord with a different principle, in which neither taste nor health nor family life was a consideration. The point was admirably illustrated in a sixteenth-century dialogue between a countryman and a city man. The former extols the advantages of the country and the sociable life he enjoys there with his honest neighbors—"graziers, butchers, farmers, drovers, carpenters, carvers, taylors, and such like men, very good and honest companions." That life, which had once existed in the city, too, had now disappeared; for his opponent answers: "And so I think, but not for you, being a gentleman." "What," exclaims the countryman, "would you have me live alone and solitary? That were worse than to be dead." To which the gentleman of the town replies: "Nay, neither, for if you did for the most live in court and city among the better sort, you would ever find company there, *fit for your estate and condition.*" Baroque planning, even at its best, remained on that narrow basis. It was meant for the better sort: it fitted their condition.

8 : REMNANTS OF BAROQUE ORDER

The baroque cult of power has been even more tenacious than the medieval ideology: it remained in being and extended its hold on other departments of life, creating Napoleons not merely in statecraft but in business and finance, though its regimentation progressively lost the lively feeling for esthetic expression that the great practitioners of its earlier phases actually had. Through the very workings of democracy, baroque absolutism tightened its hold upon society: we must not forget that military service for the entire male population, not for a few months every year, as under feudalism, but for years at a time, dates only from the French revolution. In modern times, no absolute prince dared impose such universal compulsion: it had hardly been possible, indeed, after the time of the Pyramid builders.

Armies, governments, capitalistic enterprises took the characteristic animus and form of this order, in all its inflated dimensions. Particularly in governmental planning, the baroque image remained dominant: though the 'new town' halls of nineteenth-century Europe might often be cast in the mode of the Middle Ages, from Vienna to Manchester, the houses of parliament (with the exception of that at Westminster) and the government offices would be in some dull and pompous version of the baroque, sometimes desiccated into the correctness of the neo-classical. Even the demented exponent of Nazism, with his deliberate regression to the savage gods of Germanism, cast his fantasies of dehumanized power into an appropriately classic extravagance of emptiness.

In Paris, Madrid, St. Petersburg, Vienna, and Berlin, the baroque style in both architecture and planning not merely lingered on, but found its greatest opportunities for large scale application. While royal residence cities ceased to be built after the eighteenth century, the great capitals in their growth and extension followed the same general lines, often with a ruthless disregard of the historic values one might expect to find preserved and piously furthered in national monuments and shrines. Some of the greatest successes in baroque planning were reserved, indeed, for nineteenth-century Paris: proof, incidentally, that an historic phase of urban culture creates a durable archetype that cannot be put neatly within the time boundaries of any single period, for reasons we have already explored.

In Paris the baroque approach served two imperial leaders, Napoleon I and Napoleon III. Each of these leaders carried out and enlarged plans for the improvement of Paris that their less adventurous predecessors had only toyed with. To the degree that these rulers exercised real power, the style itself retained more than a little of its old vitality. Whereas Colbert's plan for Paris in 1665 had stressed the *control* of building and expansion, these new rulers, more royalist than the old kings, were on the side of growth and expansion. Their animus served well the bankers and speculators who profited by the subsequent increase of ground rents and building gains.

Right on into the twentieth century urban planning itself, at least in the great metropolises, meant chiefly baroque planning: from Tokyo and New Delhi to San Francisco. The most grandiose of these projects was Burnham's and Bennett's plan for Chicago, with its parks and its parkways, its diagonal avenues, its elimination of industry and railroads from the river front. But here as elsewhere one must note the typically baroque failing: no concern for the neighborhood as an integral unit, no regard for family housing, no sufficient conception of the ordering of business and industry themselves as a necessary part of any larger achievement of urban order. In the same fashion, the San Francisco civic center was conceived, like those at Cleveland and Springfield, without any further control over the townscape that enveloped it—and that openly denied its esthetic pretensions.

Some of the best and some of the worst examples of baroque planning did not come forth until they had ceased, flagrantly, to be either symbolically or practically appropriate to the age that had constructed them. Without princely powers, stringent control of the surrounding area, heavy capital investments, baroque plans could not cope with the disorderly competitive enterprises of the expanding and towering city. For in baroque schemes half a loaf is actually worse than none: what remains undone or unaffected by the plan is itself a confession of its weakness.

Apart from the incongruity of baroque forms with the purposes and functions of a modern city, there was a further weakness that its later advocates never realized. Its very grandeur was based upon an innocence of, if not a contempt for, practical needs: even the needs of traffic. Thus its most imposing contribution, the long, straight, wide avenue served indeed to connect distant points quickly; but the very width of the avenue created a barrier between its opposite sides; and until a late date, when traffic lights were introduced, the crossing of such an avenue, even with the aid of pedestrian islands, was a hazard.

For the purpose of shopping, that great post-seventeenth-century pastime, it is the narrow streets, unreceptive to traffic, like Old and New Bond Street in London, the Calverstraat in Amsterdam, the Calle Florida in Buenos Aires, that flourish best. And if the avenue is a barrier, what shall we say to such wide, windy places as the Place de l'Etoile, whose circumnavigation on foot is nothing less than a pilgrimage? Such extravagances demand a heavy daily sacrifice, disproportionate to the benefits achieved.

What, then, is responsible for the active hold that the baroque plan has so long kept on the planner's mind? Why is so much superficially modern planning still carried out in the baroque spirit, with the same imperious extravagance and the same imperious contempt for human needs—though the grand avenue has turned into an 'expressway' and the great roundpoint has become a clover leaf? Behind all these modes are the assumptions—and superstitions—of unqualified power. The baroque prescription carries with it the same kind of authority that the old-fashioned physician exercised when he automatically prescribed a drastic purgative for his patient, no matter what the symptoms or the nature of the disease: it promised definite results, swift, visible, even striking.

If one compares the handsome geometry of a baroque plan with the kind of patient, piecemeal replacement and modification suggested in Rowland Nicholas' plans for the rebuilding of Manchester, one discovers the specious advantages of this administrative superficiality. It takes both knowledge and imagination to realize that the process the Manchester planner would set in motion would produce a far sounder city than a single impatient razing of a whole quarter, followed by a wholesale cutting through of new avenues and large-scale building projects, with a peremptory diversion of money and effort from other parts of the town equally in need of patient treatment, step by step. The showy decisiveness of the baroque style gives it an edge, in the beginning, over projects that take fuller account of the biological, social, and economic realities.

And yet, there was a measure of deep human insight in Daniel Burnham's famous observation: "Make no little plans, for they have no power to stir men's minds." And there are moments when the audacity of baroque esthetics, with its ruthless overriding of historic realities, provides an answer to what would be insuperable difficulties, if one sought a piecemeal solution. No one could accuse W. R. Lethaby, a medievalist by profession, an advocate for a functional modern vernacular, free from style-posturing, as being one who had an *a priori* fondness for baroque design: just the contrary. Yet, face to face with the indecisive sprawl of Central London, with its incurable tangle of mean streets, its lack of any intelligible order or visible purpose, as formless (he noted) as a London fog, he suggested the plan of the Golden Bow. The curve of the Thames gave the bend of the Bow, with St. Paul's at one end and Westminster Abbey at the other: the arrow was a new avenue, winging over Waterloo bridge straight into the heart of London, pointing at the British Museum.

Here was a bold solution, as happy as the Regent Street conceived and built by Nash to cut through a similar urban undergrowth. The Golden Bow did not suggest the creation of a wide-flung network of symmetrical streets and diagonal traffic avenues after the Parisian fashion of Haussmann: indeed Lethaby specified that the 'arrow,' which would open up the view of the river, should be a pedestrian mall, free from vehicles. But he applied this method to make a fresh cut through the urban debris, almost as a surgeon would cut out dead tissue in a festering wound. This was not, of course, the typically baroque approach: it was rather that of the renascence planner, applied with greater force, over greater distances, on the large scale to which the seventeenth-century designers had long acclimated the mind. But what happened to the baroque plan when applied as a whole to a modern city one may find by considering one of the greatest single examples of the method and the style: the plan of Washington.

9: THE LESSONS OF WASHINGTON

Only a century or so separates the design of Versailles, the greatest if not the biggest of the palatial 'new towns,' from Major Pierre Charles L'Enfant's plans for the building of Washington, submitted in 1791. In the meanwhile, the political order of Western society had been shaken to its foundations. Three revolutions, the English, the American, and the French, had disposed of the whole scheme of irrevocable, centralized power, incarnated in an absolute monarch, whose airs and pretensions had begun to rival his earliest Egyptian prototype. With the downfall of absolutism had gone the overthrow of the feudal estates, the secularization of the state, the removal of the restrictive regulations imposed by the guilds and municipalities; and along with that, the abolition of the guilds themselves, and the transformation of the city into a dependency whose powers had been granted by the state and might be taken away again.

If anything should have modified the baroque pattern, one might think that this wholesale reconstitution of political society would have accomplished that result. Particularly in the early days of the American republic, when the powers of the state were still nebulous and undetermined, limited by the prerogatives of provincial systems of government. But what do we find?

When the new capital was to be designed, as the seat of the Federal government, it was a French engineer who was called in to do the job. He was a remarkably competent man, far abler and more foresighted, than his patrons and colleagues ever realized: indeed considering his youth and limited experience, almost a genius. L'Enfant believed, in his own words, that the "mode of taking possession of, and improving, the whole district at first must leave to posterity a grand idea of the patriotic interest which promoted it": so even its squares were to be enshrined with sculptured figures "to invite the Youth of succeeding generations to tread in the paths of those sages or heroes whom their country thought proper to celebrate."

Despite L'Enfant's firm republican convictions, the design he brought forth for the new capital was in every respect what the architects and servants of despotism had originally conceived. He could only carry over into the new age the static image that had been dictated by centralized coercion and control. The sole feature that was lacking was the original sixteenth-century fortifications, since there was no apparent need for military defense. As it happened, this was an embarrassing oversight, for such works alone might have saved the new public buildings in Washington from their destruction by British raiders in the War of 1812. Apart from that, the plan was an exemplary adaptation of the standard baroque principles to a new situation.

Now L'Enfant, with true planner's insight, began, not with the street system, but with the principal buildings and squares. Between these cardinal points he devised "Lines or Avenues of direct communication," aimed not merely to promote traffic but to "preserve through the whole a reciprocity of sight at the same time," with special attention to convenience and pleasant prospects en route. Washington was thus planned as a series of interwoven traffic spider webs, with its main avenues as generous in their dimensions as the Champs Elysées. The principal avenues were 160 feet wide, with 10 feet of pavement on each side, 30 feet of gravel walk "planted with trees on each side," and 80 feet in the middle of the carriage way. Even the lesser avenues, like those leading to public buildings or markets, were 130 feet wide, while the remaining streets, 110 to 90 feet, vie with the largest crosstown streets provided in the 1811 plan for Manhattan, and surpass in generosity anything considered elsewhere in historic cities.

Doubtless it was the very absence of buildings that made L'Enfant's homage to the avenue so profound. But his gridiron pattern of streets was varied in size, not uniform in dimensions like those of Penn's plan for Philadelphia. Apart from the irregularity of the blocks formed by converging diagonals, the difference in their size corresponds to some need not fully explained by L'Enfant. The variations in both block and street dimensions shows that this was no simple drawing-board plan: in conceiving it L'Enfant was able to relate the elements of the plan to the daily functions they served.

While one pays due tribute to the quality of L'Enfant's imagination, one must observe that he was not able to escape the usual baroque sacrifice of all the other functions of the city to space, positional magnificence, and movement. Of the sixty-thousand-odd acres included in his plan, 3,606 were required for highways, while the land required for public buildings, for grounds or reservations, was only 541 acres. By any criterion that apportionment between dynamic and static space, between vehicles and buildings, was absurd. Only a modern highway engineer, with his extravagant intersections, could compete with L'Enfant in this reckless wastage of precious urban land.

As a result, only 1,964 acres, less than two-thirds of the amount required for streets and avenues, were left to be divided into building lots,
creating a total of 20,272 building lots. At the generous allowance of six
persons per dwelling house, this would not give accommodation to more
than a hundred and twenty thousand people, if every lot could in fact have
been used solely for residential purposes. The street system demanded a
city of at least half a million people to justify it: the plan permitted, on
its own original terms, something on the order of a hundred thousand.

This, too, shows the limitations, not so much of L'Enfant's imagination, as of the ideology he took for granted. And it is no justification of
the original allotment to note that both traffic and density of occupation
eventually caught up with L'Enfant and more than excused his extravagance. By the time that happened it had become plain that once wheeled
traffic is treated as the chief concern of planning, there will never be enough
space to keep it from becoming congested, or a high enough residential
density to provide taxes sufficient to cover its exorbitant demands.

On the surface, Washington had all the aspects of a superb baroque
plan: the siting of the public buildings, grand avenues, the axial approaches, the monumental scale, the enveloping greenery. With no single
big city, not even St. Petersburg, available to serve him as model, L'Enfant
had nevertheless succeeded in envisaging what a great capital, conceived
in baroque terms, might be. He had heeded Alberti's dictum that "the
city, or rather the region of the city, is the greatest and most important
among public buildings." And he had even made the most of what was,
before the hand of man touched it, a discouraging site: bottom land,
bordered by a swamp on the Potomac side, and dissected by a small river,
ironically called the Tiber, which soon became a sewer. The framework
was there, but the contents were absent. For one thing was lacking: the
power to execute the plan by building. The order existed on paper, but
not in fact.

The failure was all the more lamentable because no one since the
Woods in Bath had accepted more eagerly the challenge of a difficult
site. Instead of trying to remove these difficulties, L'Enfant sought to take
advantage of them. Thus his plan for a cascade flowing down Capitol
Hill, utilizing water from the Tiber, was worthy of Bernini himself.
L'Enfant began, adroitly, by siting the essential public buildings, in order
to establish the civic cores, the points of attraction, in the most commanding situations. Even his conception of the spinal relation of the Mall
and Pennsylvania Avenue, though sadly overblown, was of the same order
of thinking as Lethaby's Golden Bow. Only after he made the major dispositions of the buildings, did he proceed to fill up the interstices with
streets and blocks. Federal buildings, including a non-sectarian National
Church for public ceremonies, local building sites for schools and col-

leges, all were duly established by L'Enfant as determining elements in the plan.

Surely, a wise, foresighted government would not have overlooked these admirable suggestions or forfeited these sites: rather, it would have acquired the whole District of Columbia by purchase, and would have rented, not sold, the land essential to its development as a national capital. Without public control of the land itself, Major L'Enfant's plan was defeated before he had even come within sight of the opposing army.

Even today, after the partial recapture of L'Enfant's conception through the appreciative McMillan Commission of 1901, the reality of some of L'Enfant's grandest proposals has only been partly realized, while others, like the Mall, reveal the sterility of a purely visual approach to planning, when it has no foundations in the functions that it serves: the Mall is actually a greenbelt, at best a fire barrier, which keeps segregated and apart areas that should in fact be more closely joined. In the beginning, the infant city could not fill these adult breeches; and by the time it was ready to, the style of the age had irretrievably changed.

Even the government buildings themselves, with the executive and legislative branches at opposite ends of the grand axis, were too far apart to be effectively related by the eye. The domed Capitol alone, alike by its form, its bulk, and its position, escapes annihilation by L'Enfant's all-too-magnificent distances. In piously emulating the constitutional separation of powers, L'Enfant had gone too far; and even if from the beginning Pennsylvania Avenue in its entire length had been lined with uniform office buildings, like those belatedly introduced into the 'Triangle,' the result would have been deadly.

As for the Mall, which L'Enfant thought of as a proper place for ambassadorial residences—he reduced the proposed buildings to invisibility by the very breadth of the long green. Unfortunately, so strong is the image of baroque order even today that no one dares suggest that this is perhaps the only part of Washington that might be appropriately lined with ten or fifteen story buildings as the only way of redeeming this spatial desolation and saving the rest of Washington for a more human scale.

In its heyday, the strength of baroque planning lay in the fact that the surface plan and the three-dimensional structure of the city, or at least the façades of that structure, proceeded together. Planning and building, in Karlsruhe, Versailles, St. Petersburg, went hand in hand. Under the conditions that governed L'Enfant's work, the paper plan had no influence whatever over the contents: the forces that could make the plan come to life or kill it were not in the hands of either the planner or his client, the new United States government, impecunious, hesitant, committed to a laissez-faire philosophy that nullified the political assumptions that under-lay the plan.

There is no question as to what happened in Washington. L'Enfant's bold conception was brutally massacred; and as if that were not sufficient, it was, in time, visually disrupted and defiled by a wide scattering of un-kempt and irrelevant buildings. Even to this day, the area immediately around the Capitol is spotted by an outbreak of urban eczema that a baroque architect would at least have been able to hide behind a wall, if his patron lacked sufficient authority to demolish the buildings themselves. Plainly, the plan by itself could not generate the city of gleaming white limestone fronts and uniform roof lines that L'Enfant must have dreamed of. When Dickens visited Washington in 1842, he found it a city of "spacious avenues that begin in nothing and lead nowhere; streets a mile long that only want houses, roads, and inhabitants; public buildings that need only a public to be complete, and ornaments of great thoroughfares that need only great thoroughfares to ornament."

In conceiving the city as a whole, as it would be in its finished form, L'Enfant had dared greatly; and in terms of baroque assumptions and baroque purposes—done over, as in a painting by David, with classic republican symbols—he had planned superbly. But he forgot the strict limits of his assignment. He overlooked the fact that he himself could not build the city he had planned, nor had the political leaders of his generation that power, much though they might recall the classic figures in Plutarch. The country itself would need at least half a century of growth, prosperity, and unification, before it could even begin to fill out such a comprehensive outline; and in the meanwhile, the more modest beginnings which might have been made within a more appropriate frame would be obstructed rather than hindered by the very grandeur of the full-blown scheme.

L'Enfant forgot, in fact, that time is a fatal handicap to the baroque conception of the world: its mechanical order makes no allowances for growth, change, adaptation, and creative renewal. Such a command per-formance must be executed, once and for all, in its own day. Had L'Enfant respected these narrow limits, he might have achieved as much success in the siting of the main government buildings as Jefferson was to achieve in his University of Virginia campus; but by providing for everything, he lost even the little he might have achieved.

L'Enfant's plan was saved from total obliteration by two things alone. One was the work of Alexander Robey Shepherd, who carried out a series of major public improvements after the Civil War. This commissioner was known as Boss Shepherd: like his near contemporary, Haussmann, he had the proper dictatorial qualifications for carrying out a baroque plan. Fortunately, Shepherd also had enough imagination to undertake, at last, the planting of the wide streets and avenues with trees, as L'Enfant had specified. These trees gave the surface plan a stabilizing third dimension. That natural arcade, green for a large part of the year, mercifully hides some of Washington's worst architectural misdemeanors, without seriously obscuring the more comely buildings. But in the case of avenues that lack such embellishment, the sordor is often unrelieved.

The other fact that redeemed L'Enfant's original plan, though it did not add to its beauty, was the filling up of the overload of wide streets with sufficient wheeled traffic to justify their existence: this came in only with the motor car. Though motor traffic has now caught up with the plan, clogging the most extravagant arteries, and hiding the verdure behind a metallic wall of parked cars, Washington has proved a classic testing station for the question of whether a city dedicated wholeheartedly to traffic could sufficiently survive for any other purposes.

Already it is plain in Washington—and will become plainer as the city receives the inundation of new expressways, which recklessly spoil every view and defile every approach to its finest urban prospects—that when traffic takes precedence over all other urban functions, it can no longer perform its own role, that of facilitating meeting and intercourse. The assumed right of the private motor car to go to any place in the city and park anywhere is nothing less than a license to destroy the city. L'Enfant's plan, by its very invitation to traffic, has now proved its own worst enemy.

But note: the part of Washington that has become the favored area for residence is not the area that fronts on the grand traffic avenues, with their noise and their poisonous gases. Just the contrary; it is Georgetown, with its narrow streets and its more compact layout, modest enough to serve in the nineteenth century for the little dwellings of mechanics and tradesmen. This area has been converted, during the last generation, into an upper-class residential neighborhood. There one gratefully finds, not the monumental, but the domestic scale.

Yet when all is said, Washington must count as a classic example of baroque planning. If Washington could have been built in twenty years, parading suitable uniform structures, all occupied, it might have been a miracle of the solo town planner's art: a final period-piece to close the epoch. Failing this, its very sweep and grandeur invited disorder. Absolute power, republican discipline, and public spirit alike were absent. The fault lay not merely with L'Enfant but with those who had charge of the execution of L'Enfant's plan: beginning with President Washington, who had more respect for his fellow landowner, Daniel Carroll, the greatest landlord in the district, than he had for the integrity of L'Enfant's plan.

The dismissal of L'Enfant was a sign that the landowners and commercial speculators, not the government, were to exercise the major control over the development of the Capital. Though L'Enfant realized, in his own words, that the "capital city's nourishment, unlike that of other cities, would come out of its public buildings rather than out of its trade centers," it was the traders and speculators whose heedless feet trampled out the best features of L'Enfant's plan, leaving only the bleached outline. But except for his failure to hold at bay the actual forces that would overwhelm his plan, I know no other baroque town planners, not even those in Haussmann's *équipe,* who showed a better grasp of the interrelation of topography, traffic, monuments, and public buildings than L'Enfant did. What was lacking was a responsible form of political control, to replace the often extravagant and irresponsible commands of despotism. But that would in turn have altered the very character of the plan.

In this respect, the smudging of the great Washington plan symbolizes the fate of the whole baroque scheme, as it affected the life of men in cities. In a period of flux and change, the baroque insistence upon outward order and uniformity had at least imposed a common standard, and reminded the upper-class city dweller of the interdependences of the common life. In Europe, a series of building acts established standards of construction, limited heights, and imposed a measure of decency, which limited competition at lower levels. In England, and even more in the United States, these standards seemed irksome to the leaders of the nineteenth century. Thus the sensible English Building Act of 1774 became known as the 'Black Act,' a synonym for bureaucratic repression and drab monotony. In the name of freedom, the new leaders of commerce and industry, once they were freed from the restraints of baroque taste, invited speculative uncertainty and planless competition. As a result, the great tide of urbanization in the nineteenth century resulted in a strange phenomenon: the progressive submergence of the city. The landscape was filled, instead, with a spreading mass of urban flotsam and jetsam, cast overboard in the storm of capitalist enterprise.

CHAPTER FOURTEEN

Commercial Expansion
and Urban Dissolution

1: FROM MARKETPLACE TO MARKET
ECONOMY

Even before political centralization, in its most absolute form, had found expression in the baroque plan, the center of gravity had subtly begun to shift to a new constellation of economic forces. The state policy called mercantilism, which sought to transfer to the crown's centralized direction the protectionism and monopolistic control of the medieval town, proved only to be a transitional dodge. For the new forces favored expansion and dispersal in every direction, from overseas colonization to the building up of new industries, whose technological improvements simply cancelled out all medieval restrictions. The demolition of their urban walls was both practical and symbolic.

The institution that represented these new forces bears the classic name of 'capitalism,' and I deliberately resist the current American fashion of giving it a fresh name free from its many unpleasant historic associations. By the seventeenth century, capitalism had altered the whole balance of power. From this time on, the stimulus to urban expansion came mainly from the merchants, the financiers, and the landlords who served their needs. Only in the nineteenth century were these forces greatly augmented by the pressure of mechanical invention and large-scale industrialism.

Though there is a constant and intimate connection between the development of commerce and industry, in discussing the urban transformation it is convenient to separate out these two aspects of the new capitalist order. Not merely convenient, indeed, but historically accurate: for no small part of the effective inventions between the thirteenth and the eighteenth century was the work of the new commercial enterprisers or their servants: from double-entry book-keeping, commercial drafts, and the joint-stock company to the three-masted sailing ship, light-houses, docks, and canals. In the thriving port cities by river and sea, Bristol, Havre, Frankfurt-am-Main, Augsburg, London, Antwerp, Amsterdam, new standards and ideals were at work: calculations of profitability and rentability entered into every transaction.

The growth of the commercial city was a slow process, for it met with resistance in both the structure and the customs of the medieval town; and though it profited by baroque regularity, in fact was partly responsible for it, it had no use for the extravagances of princely display. But the final result of capitalism was to introduce the modes of the marketplace, in a universal form, into every quarter of the city: no part of it was immune to change, if this could be brought about at a profit. As we have seen, this change began in the medieval city, with the growth of long-distance trade. So well established was this new kind of commerce, outside the domain of individual guild regulations, that by 1293 the brokers or 'factors' of Bruges had established their claim to act as intermediaries in every wholesale transaction in Bruges. And so marked was this influence that, two centuries before Thomas Aquinas, Alain of Lille could say: "Not Caesar now, but money, is all."

With the extension of the wholesale market, engaged in long-distance operations by means of both money and credit, seeking large speculative profits, there grew up a new attitude toward life: a combination of ascetic regularity and speculative enterprise, of systematic avarice and presumptuous pride. If the presiding theme of the Middle Ages was protection and security, the new economy was founded on the principle of calculated risks. Under the medieval system the market had been controlled for the benefit of both producer and consumer; and the effects of any undue preoccupation with gain were offset, in the long run, by gifts, charities, deathbed restitutions, brotherly help to the needy. Though the church was the favored recipient of capital accumulations, it redistributed not a little of the collective gains in caring for the ill and the poverty-stricken but it made no effort at any more general reapportionment.

One of Adam Smith's great objections to such medieval trade regulations as still lingered in the eighteenth century was that those of the same trade would "tax themselves in order to provide for their poor, their sick, their widows and orphans." Capitalism removed this burden from production: nothing stood between the worker and starvation except a willingness to work, when and if called upon, on the stringent terms laid down by the new enterprisers. The lower the worker's standard of living could be pushed, the higher the profits to the capitalist enterpriser.

Within the nest of the medieval town, the egg of the capitalist cuckoo, though larger than the normal egg of the local trader, was still treated as a member of the same clutch: indeed, at first capitalism took on the very costume and manners of the period, professing to eschew usury, and to accept the concept of the just price, without regard for the eagerness of the buyer or the scarcity of the product. But time, very quickly indeed after the fourteenth century, gave the new enterprisers a preponderance of power, so that they not merely often became the heads of municipal governments and larger states, but their animus and habits of life were applied to the whole economy. These new disciples of Midas no longer dealt with commodities and men, with families and groups, but with abstract magnitudes. They were concerned almost exclusively with what Thomas Aquinas called artificial wealth, upon whose acquisition nature, as he pointed out, had placed no limits. This absence of limits became not the least significant mark of the commercial city: it partly accounts for the steady loss of form that went on after the eighteenth century.

With capitalist accountancy went the need for a secular bureaucracy: an army of clerks and paid agents to keep accounts, to attend to correspondence, even to furnish the news necessary in order to take advantage, if possible before anyone else, of changed conditions in the market. So perhaps the first visible entry of capitalism into the medieval town was made by the grammar school, where the elements of reading, writing, and arithmetic were the main objects of study. This advance was counterbalanced by the resistance of commercial cities to the new intellectual guild, the university, on its very belated appearance in Bruges, Lübeck, Lyons, Antwerp, London, Augsburg, Venice.

The control of paper, in both the French and the English meanings of the term control ('inspection' and 'exercise of power to dominate') became the mark of the new commercial bureaucracy, at first unobtrusively housed in the 'counting rooms' of the old medieval town houses and mansions. But the institution that marked the turning point in the development of the commercial town, its first decisive manifestation, was the Bourse: so named after the original Bruges banking house, De Beurze, which began to serve as a center for large scale commercial transactions in the thirteenth century.

The business of exchange, speculative buying and selling, and brokerage, was plied in the new bourses, and it was the cities that established such exchanges—first Bruges, then Antwerp in the sixteenth century, before the Spaniards razed it, then Amsterdam and London in the seventeenth century—that grew most quickly, and that established the new forms of life for the moneyed classes. The Bourse, the national bank, and the merchants' Exchange were the Cathedrals of the new capitalist order.

The transformation of the market from a protected component of the medieval town, limited to its special sphere, to an expanding institution that thrust its methods and its goals into every other part of the city, and demanded its share in every transaction, was not unimpeded. When Henri II submitted to the municipality of Paris a proposal to establish a bank of the Italian type, the very merchants of the town suggested that the question should be submitted to the theologians, since the proposed interest of eight per cent seemed to them nothing less than usury, contrary to the laws of God and subversive of good morals. Similarly the state itself, so far from being ready to destroy the protective institutions of the municipality, sought rather to bring them under a more comprehensive national control. This rear guard fight against the corrosive forces of capitalism continued within the city: thus Colbert's plan for Paris in 1665 stressed the limitation and control of building even more than Elizabethan statutes had done for London more than two generations earlier.

But liquid capital proved to be a chemical solvent: it cut through the cracked varnish that had long protected the medieval town and ate down to the raw wood, showing itself even more ruthless in its clearance of historic institutions and their buildings than the most reckless of absolute rulers. One might characterize this whole change as the replacement of the concrete market place of the medieval town by the abstract transnational market, which flourished wherever a profitable deal could be made. In the first, concrete goods changed hands between visible buyers and sellers, who accepted the same moral norms and met more or less on the same level: here security, equity, stability, were more important than profit, and the personal relations so established might continue through a lifetime, or even for generations.

In the abstract market, people who might never see each other engaged in monetary transactions for which the goods themselves served, rather, as counters: the purpose of such transactions was profit, and the accumulation of more capital, to be sunk in other enterprises of increasing magnitude. Customary morality, corporate standards, traditional evaluations all served as brakes upon speculative enterprise: so likewise was the heavy capital investment in ancient buildings, constructed to endure over the centuries. In order to have a free field for its typical interests, capitalism adopted two methods in relation to the existing urban structures: either it sought to escape to the suburbs beyond, free from all municipal restrictions, or alternately it sought either to demolish the old structures or to occupy them at a far higher density than that for which they had— in a supposedly poorer age—been designed. Urban demolition and replacement became one of the chief marks of the new economy. The more ephemeral the container, the more rapid the turnover.

In relation to the city, capitalism was from the beginning anti-historic; and as its forces have consolidated over the last four centuries, its destructive dynamism has increased. The human constants had no place in the capitalist scheme: or rather, the only constants it recognized were avarice, cupidity, and pride, the desire for money and power.

The condition of pecuniary success was to despise the past, because it was an accomplished fact, and to welcome the new, just because it was a departure, and therefore an opening for profitable enterprise. In the interest of expansion, capitalism was prepared to destroy the most satisfactory social equilibrium. Just as the new ideas of business resulted— gradually after the sixteenth century, rapidly after the eighteenth—in the suppression and destruction of the guilds, so these new ideas brought about the demolition of old buildings and the effacement of playing fields, market gardens, orchards, and villages that stood in the way of the growing city. No matter how venerable these old uses might be, or how salutary for the existence of the city itself, they would be sacrificed to fast-moving traffic or to financial gain.

2: THE NEW FREEDOM

Between the thirteenth and the eighteenth centuries, the innovations of capitalism consolidated as a body of doctrine and a rule of practice: habits of abstemiousness, abnegation, systematic order, the practice of postponing present pleasures for much greater future rewards, were transferred from religion to business, where they produced immense visible gains. The introduction of town clocks in the thirteenth and fourteenth centuries was but one symptom of the fact that business was no longer regulated by the sun and the powers of the human frame. In the large-scale textile factories at the end of the Middle Ages, diligence was enforced on workers by a stricter, more impersonal overseership than could be exercised in the loose intimate routine of the small workshop, with its intervals of gossip, its rude horseplay and playful inattention to business. The spirit of that older order still lingered in Elizabethan times in Dekker's play, 'The Shoemaker's Holiday.'

Capitalism, denying the holiness of poverty or the imaginative sustenance of art, sought solely to increase the amount of consumable goods and measurable gain. At the critical moment after the Black Death, when population was again beginning to increase with compensatory vigor that soon offset those great losses, capitalist enterprise and a growing technological resourcefulness sought to meet the challenge of numbers. They did so by giving to economic factors a degree of sustained effort they had never before achieved. The success of capitalist enterprise engendered confidence in the human powers; and in a period of religious schism and corruption, capitalism appeared as a healthy, liberating activity, whose private gains would ultimately work public benefit. Many of the practices introduced by capitalism were in fact salutary and of permanent profit to any humane economy; but the immediate effect of this new system, by the seventeenth century, was to transform the complex social order of the city into the over-simplified routines of the market. Its ultimate result was a money-making economy that had no definable ends or purposes other than its own further expansion.

Yet these new entrepreneurs needed the old cities, particularly the big capital cities or their provincial equivalents: for rents and profits were there at hand, avid for investment. In these well-established towns, large bodies of consumers were assembled, striving for place and favor by luxurious display, aping their aristocratic superiors; there, likewise, old structures, representing heavy capital investments, were still standing, capable of being turned to new uses without drawing off capital and labor from far more profitable new ventures.

The cities that offered the new municipal privilege of free trade and free deposit of goods, without entry tax, to encourage further business transactions, were the first to feel the stir of new enterprises and to further economic concentration. That is why Antwerp and Lyons flourished mightily in the sixteenth century. What the capitalist meant by 'freedom' was escape from protection, regulation, corporate privilege, municipal boundaries, legal restrictions, charitable obligations. Each individual enterprise was now a separate entity, claiming the right to be a law unto itself, in competition with other self-sufficient particles, which put the pursuit of profit over every social obligation.

In the Middle Ages 'freedom' had meant freedom from *feudal* restrictions, freedom *for* the corporate activities of the municipality, the guild, the religious order. In the new trading cities, or Handelstädte, freedom meant freedom from *municipal* restrictions: freedom for *private* investment, for private profit and private accumulation, without any reference to the welfare of the community as a whole. The apologists for this order, from Bernard Mandeville to Adam Smith, assumed that the pursuit of individual activities deriving from greed, avarice, and lust would produce the maximum amount of goods for the community as a whole. In the period when this creed was the prevailing orthodoxy—roughly up to the third quarter of the nineteenth century, when industrial and municipal regulations began timidly to mitigate the resultant filth and illth—the rich grew richer and the poor grew poorer. This fact was expressed, with diagrammatic clarity, in the contrast between the West End and the East End of more than one great city.

Now, as with the growth of the national state itself, the development of capitalism was, in part, a necessary effort to overcome the serious limitations of the medieval economy. In the effort to achieve a static security, the medieval corporations had resisted new inventions and new methods of work: they clung to their trade secrets, their esoteric formulae, their 'mysteries.' Their members sought, too, to keep guild privileges within families or self-limited groups, raising obstacles against the extension of citizenship to outsiders, even seeking by conspiracy and war to keep down the possible competition of urban neighbors. Instead of accepting the traditional products of the regional economy as relatively fixed and limited, the new merchant adventurers sought to expand production and widen the market: they furthered technological improvements like the knitting machine, and they drew widely on overseas areas alike for raw materials and for finished products. The shipment and interchange of these goods formed an increasingly large part of the activities of prosperous cities; and with this more and more of the economic life escaped the control of the municipalities.

Thus capitalism, by its very nature, undermined local autonomy as well as local self-sufficiency, and it introduced an element of instability, indeed of active corrosion into existing cities. In its emphasis on speculation, not security, upon profit-making innovations, rather than on value-conserving traditions and continuities, capitalism tended to dismantle the whole structure of urban life and place it upon a new impersonal basis: money and profit.

All this had a direct effect upon both old structures and new. The old became expendable: the new were conceived, almost from the beginning, as ephemeral. Capital, most adventurous when it was liquid and mobile, looked with distrust upon heavy investments in permanent equipment and buildings; and even after it had perfected a more fluid, transferable form in the joint-stock company, it tended to favor buildings of a utilitarian character, quick to construct, easy to replace—except when the need for public confidence in an institution's wealth and solidity justified a heavy investment in ostentatious masonry.

The result of this animus on the structure of cities was twofold. Moneyed interests progressively dominated landed interests in laying out and building the new quarters of the city. What is perhaps even more significant is that all land that had escaped feudal tenure and was subject to unlimited sale was considered, more and more, as a means of making money. Feudal land was leased for 99 or 999 years: at least three generations. This system favored continuity and it slowed the upward movement of prices. When land became a commodity, not a stewardship, it passed out of any kind of communal control.

There were many efforts to slow down the transfer of municipal and feudal land to individual proprietorship; but the change from feudal holdings, with reciprocal duties between landlord and tenant, and commercial proprietorship, with no obligations save the payment of taxes, went on steadily. Stow has given us a graphic description of the process: In Shoreditch there was "one row of proper small houses with gardens for poor decayed people, there placed by the prior of the said hospital [St. Mary Spittle] every one whereof paid one penny rent by the year at Christmas . . . but after the suppression of the hospital these houses, for want of reparations, in a few years were so decayed that it was called Rotten Row and the poor worn out . . . houses, for a small portion of money, were sold from Goddard to Russell, a draper, who new built them and let them out for rent enough, taking also large fines of the tenants, near as much as the houses cost him purchase and building."

As soon as the principles of capitalist conversion, divorced from any sense of social responsibility, were accepted, slum accommodations and slum housing received authorization. D'Avenel, he who wrote the classic historic treatise on 'Money and Prices,' marks the sixteenth century as a definite turning point. From then on in France, urban rents go higher and demand a disproportionate part of the urban worker's budget. The actual change must have come in many places, London for one, before the sixteenth century: how otherwise can we explain the indignant lines in 'Piers Plowman': "They buy houses, they become landlords, if they sold honestly they would not build so high." By the sixteenth century Robert Crowley confirmed this observation, in his verses on 'Rent Raisers':

> A man that had lands of ten pound by year
> Surveyed the same and let it out dear:
> So that of ten pound he made well a score
> More pounds by the year than other did before.

The new commercial centers, with their increasing populations, set the pace for intensified land uses; and the more limited the amount of land available, through natural constriction, as in hilly Genoa, or through private monopoly, as in Vienna or London, the higher were the rents and the greater the possibilities of gain from degraded and anti-social uses. What the steamship companies discovered in the nineteenth century in their exploitation of steerage passengers, the ground landlords discovered long before: maximum profits came, not from providing first class accommodations for those who could well afford them at a handsome fee, but from crowded slum accommodations, for those whose pennies were scarcer than the rich man's pounds.

There were many parts of London, New York, and Paris before the middle of the nineteenth century where one could say with confidence: the worse the dwelling, the higher the total rent of the property. The only limit to this happy achievement of wringing profit from the necessities of the poor came when the cost of crime, vice, and disease in the slum, reflected in taxes and poor rates, began to lessen the net gain from rents. This did not come about in London until Victorian times, when a wholesale slum clearance in the city of London was effected, partly to acquire new space for commercial expansion, but likewise to escape the growing parish poor-law charge.

The transformation of the more commodious older houses into clotted tenements, where a whole family—often more than one family—could be cooped into a single room, was not sufficient to accommodate the increasing population of the more 'prosperous' towns. New quarters must be built that would accept these depressed conditions as a standard from the beginning.

According to Roger North's autobiography, speculative building began on a large scale in London with Dr. Barbone's ventures after the Great Fire of 1666. The decrease in housing quarters then gave him a favorable opportunity. "He was the inventor of the new method of building by casting of ground into streets and small houses, and selling the ground to workmen by so much per front foot, and what he could not sell, built himself. This had made ground rents high for the sake of mortgaging, and others, following his steps, have refined and improved upon it, and made a superfoetation of houses around London."

Instead of being penalized for his anti-social exploitation of land, the slum landlord, on capitalist principles, was handsomely rewarded: for the values of his decayed properties, so far from being written off because of their age and disrepair, became embedded in the structure of land values and taxes. If a new use were proposed for the land, it could only be done profitably by maintaining a slum level of congestion, or by admitting even higher densities.

The more dense the occupation, the higher the income: the higher the income, the higher the capitalizable value of the land. Cities like London for long escaped the worse results of this vicious circle through the fact that so much of the land was in feudal holdings on long-term leases. But when Frederick the Great departed from Germanic custom and put the land on a Roman legal basis, with the same status as the structure, he opened the way for the untrammeled realty speculation that corrupted the planning and layout of Berlin until the end of the First World War when the municipality acquired large tracts of land for housing.

On the outskirts of the commercial town, this process went on at an accelerating rate. By dividing outlying farmsteads into building parcels, the piece by piece dismemberment of the corporate town was brought about. From the beginning of the nineteenth century, laissez-faire meant, municipally speaking, "Let him who will, speculate on a rise in land values and rents." With the military wall demolished, the social controls over the indefinite expansion and dispersion of the city disappeared: the acceleration of transportation, first private then public, increased the possibilities of turnover and hastened the pace of the whole urban transformation. Commercial speculation, social disintegration, and physical disorganization went hand in hand. At the very moment that cities were multiplying in numbers and increasing in size all through Western civilization, the nature and the purpose of the city had been completely forgotten: forms for social life that the most intelligent no longer understood, the most ignorant were prepared to build. Or rather, the ignorant were completely unprepared, but that did not prevent their building.

3: ORGANIZATION OF TRANSPORT
AND EXCHANGE

The mobilization of goods for their rapid interchange and distribution was the great achievement of the market economy: this antedated the technological exploits of the coal and iron age, and in no small degree made them possible. In this process, as in the development of the ancient city originally, the waterways served as the chief means of transportation and communication, not merely with distant territories, but within the city itself. As late as the beginning of the nineteenth century in London, thousands of watermen still carried passengers in their wherries on the Thames.

While older commercial centers like Florence and Bruges began to go downhill in the sixteenth century, the sea ports and river ports on the main trade routes flourished: witness Naples, Palermo, Lisbon, Frankfurt-am-Main, Liverpool. The building of canals spread from the Low Countries to the rest of Europe; and the Dutch skill in controlling and pumping water was utilized, further, in the development of the earliest water mains for the growing cities. The first regular canal boat transportation with hourly service took place between Delft and Rotterdam in the seventeenth century; but Grenoble, according to Blanchard, had public conveyances for passengers and goods to Lyons as early as 1623.

Docks, warehouses, and loading facilities followed by slow stages. Though the mechanical crane, worked by a squirrel-cage treadmill, had been used in Bruges in the Middle Ages, loading machinery developed slowly, probably because of the availability of a growing proletariat of casual workers, unprotected by any guild, around the great ports. The installation of lighthouses, likewise, came tardily; while port facilities comparable to those in the Arsenal at Venice, with materials for building, repairing, and stocking ships for distant voyages, were not built on any scale until the seventeenth century, when Amsterdam took the lead, followed in the eighteenth century by Liverpool. Though London's East India Company docks date from 1600, it was only in 1802 that the next great dock, that of the West India Company, was built.

In looking over the records of the trading cities before the nineteenth century, one is struck by the stingy and grudging nature of the technical improvements that were introduced in the cities themselves. The spirit of make-shift and make-do too often prevailed, as compared with the constructions of an earlier period, when commerce, instead of being treated as an end in itself, was integrated with other urban activities. The thirteenth-century salt warehouses of Lübeck still stood in the twentieth century: likewise similar warehouses of the seventeenth century in Amsterdam. But in the formative period of the later commercial city, there was relatively little investment in durable structures: one of the first departures came in the great docks and warehouses of Liverpool, classic monuments, utilizing cast-iron columns, designed on a noble scale; and only in the nineteenth century did London produce the great succession of warehouses and docks that line the waterfront, past the Tower to Tilbury.

Even the building of adequate roads and avenues to connect the port with the city came as an afterthought in most towns, though these facilities often proved congested and impassible. As for the provision of decent accommodations for the families of the longshoremen and sailors and truckers who served the port, this was left to the operations of the market, like the doss-houses, the brothels, and the taverns that surrounded the docks. The degradation of the stevedore, the porter, the navvy, and the sailor not merely infected the waterfront proper, but spread to other quarters of the city, probably increasing the incidence of plagues and certainly that of syphilis.

So general has been this degradation in port cities that it came to be treated as a normal aspect of a maritime city's existence. Perhaps the happiest effect of the wholesale destruction of cities during the Second World War was the opportunity it gave to the alert planning authorities of Marseille, Rotterdam, and London to make a fresh start in their long-festering waterfront areas.

As we shall find in other aspects of the capitalist urban economy, where the new spirit was modified by an older ideology, more concerned with social and esthetic norms, the results were conspicuously better: behold Havre, where Guyon le Roy was commissioned by Francis I to build the port he had made plans for. This was a speculative enterprise;

and though it bankrupted the original undertaker, who did not get a clear title to the land, it was the first of a series of government-sponsored public works that gave the French ports, in their comeliness and order, a clear lead over their muddled German and English rivals. The lighthouses and moles at Cherbourg still bear witness, not to business enterprise, but to the foresight and resourcefulness of the engineers of Napoleon Bonaparte.

Observe the striking contrast between the resourceful experimentalism of capitalism during its early days—with its double-entry bookkeeping, bills of exchange, limited liability investment—and the relative poverty of the structural changes it then effected in the new commercial quarters of the city. Perhaps one of the reasons for this backwardness, even in matters that would have furthered their own purposes, is that the bankers and merchants were interested in prompt immediate returns: they apparently feared any collective enterprise that might benefit themselves, lest it benefit their competitors even more. The commercial town was an agent for making money, and—in the interest of profit—decay, disorder, and structural inefficiency were tolerated or indeed even encouraged, as a means of lowering the overhead. Venice had already proved that beauty and order were no deterrents to financial prosperity, and Amsterdam, in the seventeenth century, was to prove it again. Both of these cities were organized by highly successful businessmen, of exemplary skill, intelligence, and cupidity, full of scrupulous unscrupulousness. Yet even those who professed to admire their achievements did not attempt to imitate them.

4: THE SPECULATIVE GROUND PLAN

The main attributes of the new commercial spirit, the emphasis on the regular and the calculable on one side, and of speculative adventure and audacious expansion on the other, found their ideal expression in the new city extensions. The pattern was an ancient and familiar one. But the resurgent capitalism of the seventeenth century treated the individual lot and the block, the street and the avenue, as abstract units for buying and selling, without respect for historic uses, for topographic conditions, or for social needs. Except where ancient feudal rights or royal prerogatives slowed down the process, the municipality lost control of the land needed for its own proper development.

If the layout of a town has no relation to human needs and activities other than business, the pattern of the city may be simplified: the ideal layout for the business man is that which can be most swiftly reduced to standard monetary units for purchase and sale. The fundamental unit is no longer the neighborhood or the precinct, but the individual building lot, whose value can be gauged in terms of front feet: this favors an oblong with a narrow frontage and great depth, which provides a minimum amount of light and air to the buildings, particularly the dwellings, that conform to it. Such units turned out equally advantageous for the land surveyor, the real estate speculator, the commercial builder, and the lawyer who drew up the deed of sale. In turn, the lots favored the rectangular building block, which again became the standard unit for extending the city.

No one who has followed the present history will make the common error of finding the original source of this type of planning in the United States. The only fact that makes it more conspicuous in America than in the old world is the absence, except for areas like the original settlements of Boston and New York, of earlier types of city planning. From the seventeenth century onward, Western city extensions, as in Stuttgart and Berlin, in London and Edinburgh, were made in the same fashion, except where ancient water courses, roads, or field boundaries had established lines that could not be lightly over-ridden.

The beauty of this new mechanical pattern, from a commercial standpoint, should be plain. This plan offers the engineer none of those special problems that irregular parcels and curved boundary lines present. An office boy could figure out the number of square feet involved in a street opening or in a sale of land: even a lawyer's clerk could write a description of the necessary deed of sale, merely by filling in with the proper dimensions the standard document. With a T-square and a triangle, finally, the municipal engineer could, without the slightest training as either an architect or a sociologist, 'plan' a metropolis, with its standard lots, its standard blocks, its standard street widths, in short, with its standardized, comparable, and replaceable parts.

Such plans fitted nothing but a quick parcelling of the land, a quick conversion of farmsteads into real estate, and a quick sale. The very absence of more specific adaptations to landscape or to human purpose only increased, by its very indefiniteness and designlessness, its general usefulness for exchange. Urban land, too, now became a mere commodity, like labor: its market value expressed its only value. Being conceived as a purely physical agglomeration of rentable buildings, the town planned on these lines could sprawl in any direction, limited only by gross physical obstacles and the need for rapid public transportation. Every street might become a traffic street; every section might become a business section.

To permit the progressive intensification of land use, with a corresponding rise in rent and realty values was, from the business point of view, one of the specific virtues of this inorganic type of plan. This was a new kind of urban order, in which business took precedence over every other kind of activity. But even from the most limited utilitarian point of view, the new gridiron plans were spectacular in their inefficiency and waste. By usually failing to discriminate sufficiently, in the first instance, between main traffic arteries and residential streets, the first were not made wide enough while the second were usually too wide for purely neighborhood functions. This excess threw the costs of extra paving and over-lengthy utilities lines and mains upon residential streets that could ill afford them.

The refined meanness of the English by-law street, after 1870, was an exception; but even in those very cramped layouts, as Raymond Unwin was to demonstrate in his 'Nothing Gained by Overcrowding,' money was thrown into excessive street acreage and expensive paving that could have been spent to better purpose by providing, with the same amount of public space, for internal park and play areas.

In paying no attention to topography, the gridiron planner opened the way for fat pieces of 'honest' municipal jobbery, in the grading and filling and paving of streets. On steep hilly sites, like that of San Francisco, the rectangular plan, by failing to respect the contours, placed a constant tax upon the time and energy of the inhabitants, and inflicted on them daily economic losses, measurable in tons of coal and gallons of gasoline wasted, to say nothing of undoing the major esthetic possibilities of a hillside that is intelligently platted.

In contrast the winding streets of medieval Siena respected the contours, but intersected them at intervals to open up a view, dropping steeply in flights of stairs, to serve as pedestrian shortcuts. This demonstrates admirably the esthetic and engineering superiority of an organic plan, carried out with other ends in view than the maximum number of saleable lots and the minimum exercise of imagination. As early as 1865, Frederick Law Olmsted had pointed out these advantages in San Francisco —only to have his advice cast aside.

With this blank formal layout, no thought was given to either the direction of the prevailing winds, the circumscription of industrial districts, the salubrity of the underlying soil, or any of the other vital factors that determine the proper utilization of an urban site. As for orientation of buildings for maximum exposure to winter sunlight, that ancient necessity, known to both the Greeks and the Chinese, was completely overlooked, until the principle was belatedly re-established by a series of independent investigators, notably by the French planner, Augustin Rey, early in the twentieth century. And one further lack must be noted: the absence of any functional differentiation between the residential, the industrial, the commercial, and the civic quarters—though if their requirements were respected each would demand blocks of different lengths and depths, with appropriate streets and avenues, to accord with their different loads of traffic, and their functionally different building layouts.

All this means that, in the gridiron plan, as applied in the commercial city, no section or precinct was suitably planned for its specific function: instead the only function considered was the progressive intensification of use, for the purpose of meeting expanding business needs and raising land values. Now the fact is that in urban planning, such bare surface order is no order at all. No city plan is anything but a paper pretense until it has established, as its minimal condition, a maximum coverage of land, a maximum density of occupation, in relation to projected functions and living standards, and a maximum height and bulk of building in relation to the need for open space and public movement: all framed within a timed sequence of renovations and replacements.

One further effect of the gridiron system must be noted. Once the land had been broken up into separate lots whose size had originally been determined by the traditional single-family residence, the assemblage of such lots into parcels suitable for larger buildings offered a new field for canny speculation and unscrupulous forestalling; while the assemblage of larger tracts, a whole block or a neighborhood within the occupied portions of a town remained a task beyond the largest private resources except when—as in the case of Rockefeller Center—the site had been owned as a unified parcel by some historic institution. Even when land was needed for public purposes, the buying out of the many separate owners became one of the great handicaps to good public management: a process that lent itself in many cities, not only to tedious delays, but to various forms of blackmail and graft.

The Lex Adickes, which permitted the assemblage of parcels and their pro-rata distribution on a better plan, to the individual owners, did not come in, even in Germany, until 1902; and it took the bombing out of the center of Rotterdam by the Nazis in 1940 to create sufficient public spirit in that city to have this system supplied on a sufficiently large scale to permit the bold re-planning that has actually gone on there since 1945.

On strictly commercial principles, the gridiron plan answered, as no other plans did, the shifting values, the accelerated expansion, the multiplying population, required by the capitalist regime. But the city planned on those principles was a failure for other human purposes; and any attempt to improve it without changing those principles was doomed to defeat. Planning is by nature a comprehensive process, involving the interplay of many needs, purposes, and functions: whereas such planning as was done by the individual enterpriser was a piecemeal effort for his own limited ends. Only one municipal activity, other than the extension of streets and blocks, was needed for his purposes: the building of transportation lines. In that sense, the gridiron plan reached its ideal culmination in Señor Soria y Mata's proposal for the Linear City. Himself a transportation engineer, he boldly proposed to make the new city a function of a spinal rapid-transit system, projecting a continuous urban belt parallel to the transportation lines, to connect the older historic centers. Motorized movement was all-controlling.

The extension of the speculative gridiron and the public transportation system were the two main activities that gave dominance to capitalist forms in the growing cities of the nineteenth century. Public stage coaches were followed by railroads, steam ferries, bridges, electric surface transit, subways, and elevateds, though not always in the same time order. Each further extension of the city, each new increment of population, could be justified as insurance against the over-investment in these utilities and as a further guarantee of the general increase of land values, not merely within the city's boundaries, but even in the unincorporated or unannexed territory lying outside. An expanding economy demanded an expanding population; and an expanding population demanded an expanding city. The sky and the horizon were the only limits. On purely commercial terms numerical growth was synonymous with improvement. The census of population was sufficient to establish a city's cultural rank. We shall soon witness the final results of this process in the formation of Megalopolis.

In estimating the need for new subways in New York, for example, almost half a century ago, the engineer of the Public Service Commission furnished the classic statement of these aims: "All lines must necessarily be laid to the objective point—Manhattan. Every transit line that brings people to Manhattan adds to its real estate value. The value of property on Manhattan Island on account of its geographic and commercial location must increase just so long as population in the surrounding territory increases." That the object of a good transit system might be the more even distribution of industrial and commercial opportunities, of good housing facilities, and even of land values, so that the whole process might have some other aim than enriching the holders of land in Manhattan at the expense of the rest of the metropolitan community, seems not to have occurred to this naïve agent.

As for its contribution to the permanent social functions of the city, the anonymous gridiron plan proved empty. In the United States, civic centers might sometimes be provided in the new towns of the nineteenth century, as they were in the plans for Cincinnati, St. Louis, and Chicago; but by the time the gambling fever had risen, these municipal sites would be sold to pay for their street expansion and street paving: even slow growing Savannah progressively forfeited the advantage that its old system of town squares had provided. When the need arose for sites for public buildings or parks, the appropriate parcels of land would have been already in individual ownership, sometimes already built upon, always advanced in price. Almost the only exception to this I have been able to find is Rochester, where a number of squares, originally laid out by speculators as an advertising feature in 1820, still remain part of the city plan—thanks perhaps to that provincial city's relatively slow growth as compared with terminal cities like Buffalo or New York.

That a city could not control its growth without controlling the development of its land, and that it could not even provide space for its own public buildings, in the right situation, unless it could at least acquire and hold land long before the actual need for it arose, had not even entered the new urban mind. The very notion of public control was from the outset taboo. Where profits were concerned, private interest was held superior, on classic capitalist theory, to public interest. True, the powers of the state or the municipality were never entirely rejected by capitalist enterprise. Capitalism greedily demanded large subventions and subsidies, vast outright gifts, like those that originally promoted the western railroads and that now, just as improvidently subsidize private air and motor transportation.

Thus the city, from the beginning of the nineteenth century on, was treated not as a public institution, but a private commercial venture to be carved up in any fashion that might increase the turnover and further the rise in land values. The analysis of this condition by Henry George, and its bold rectification by Ebenezer Howard in his proposal for the new Garden City, which would corporately hold all its land, marks a turning point in the conception of both municipal economics and municipal government.

5 : THE PRICE OF URBAN EXPANSION

The law of urban growth, as dictated by the capitalist economy, meant the inexorable wiping out of all the natural features that delight and fortify the human soul in its daily rounds. Rivers would be turned into running sewers—see William Morris' description of the desecration of the Wandle—waterfronts might be made inaccessible to the stroller, ancient trees might be slaughtered and venerable buildings torn down to speed traffic; but as long as the upper classes could go carriage driving in Central Park or have a morning canter on Rotten Row, the lack of recreation space and recreative beauty in the city at large would not be noticed.

No serious public recognition of the need for children's playgrounds came till after 1870, by which time the space needed could be acquired only at a colossal outlay. Hence the peculiar function of the over-developed street in the commercial plan: it was forced to take the place of the back garden and protected square of the medieval town, or of the open place and park of the baroque order. Thus this paved desert, adapted primarily to wheeled traffic, became also park, promenade, and playground: a grim park, a dusty promenade, a dangerous playground.

Even where overcrowding of the land did not exist—for example in many of the smaller towns of midland America—the broad street or avenue was valued as a symbol of progress: so that it was laid out with an amplitude that bore no functional relation to its present or its potential use, though the excessive cost of paving and upkeep would be reflected in increased taxes on the abutting properties. The value of such street planning, a sort of belated caricature of the baroque enlargement of space as an expression of princely command, was largely decorative: it was a symbol of possible traffic, possible commercial opportunity, possible conversion from residence into more extensive business use. The street itself thus provided an extra excuse for the fantastic land values that were sometimes optimistically tacked in advance onto rural properties that stood in the path of the advancing city. And the surviving civic traditions of New England were nowhere better shown than in the fact that towns like Pittsfield and New Bedford, though submitting to industrialization, kept conservatively to narrow streets, thirty to sixty feet in width, and thereby eased the taxes on adjacent houses and gardens. The town, even when planned on the gridiron pattern, thus kept some of the advantages that a new generation of planners was to discover in the planning of industrial garden villages at the end of the nineteenth century.

All over the Western World during the nineteenth century, new cities were founded and old ones extended along the lines I have just described. The first sign of a boom would be the extension of skeleton streets, consisting of curbstone and standpipes for the water systems. The multiplication of these streets prematurely extended the city and added to the amount of expensive pavement, expensive sewers and water mains forcing growth to take place in the most costly fashion possible, by scattered individual houses, spotted at random in time and space, instead of in compact settlements, built within a limited time. For any purpose but speculation, this system was extremely wasteful, and the cost of such premature exploitation fell back on the rest of the city.

These specious pecuniary criteria were recognized at an early date. In a report to the Commissioners of Woods and Forests in England, John Nash observed that "the artificial causes of the extension of the town are the speculations of builders encouraged and promoted by merchants dealing in the materials of building, and attorneys with monied clients, facilitating, and indeed putting into motion, the whole system; by disposing of improved ground rents, by numerous other devices, by which their clients make an advantageous use of their money; and the attorneys create to themselves lucrative business."

This belief in constant, unlimited growth was pervasive. In America urban enterprisers gambled on such growth, and then tried to put a bottom under their hopes by deliberately attracting business and industry and population away from competing towns: sometimes by gifts of land, even factory buildings, without ever demanding that the manufacturers who settled in the town guarantee a wage level high enough to keep the new workers from being a public liability. New York, indeed, not only built the Erie Canal to ensure a superior connection with the hinterland, but managed later, through imposing differential freight rates worked out at the expense of other cities, to maintain her monopoly of the oceanic and continental traffic routes.

The desire to utilize every square foot of rentable space dominated the owner, even when the building was for his private use and not designed for sheer pecuniary exploitation. In many cities during the nineteenth century, this reduced the rear garden to a backyard for drying clothes, and that in turn was reduced in space to such a point that many expensive residences off Fifth Avenue, in New York, were built almost back to back, like any lower-class slum, and lacked both outlook and ventilation. Again, capitalist enterprise, hypnotized by its own preoccupation with gain, over-reached itself; for an overcrowded plan does not necessarily bring the maximum return immediately, nor is it likely to remain sound and attractive enough to ensure profitable exploitation during a long period of years.

Spacious designs like those for the Place Vendôme or Russell Square, still flourishing after centuries of use, turned out to be far more economical than those that sought only to cover the maximum amount of rentable space. The high profits of the latter depend on a quick turnover. In municipal economics, as opposed to private, it is not the first costs of a project that count, but the final costs, as apportioned over its entire life span.

Not so much speculative profit by itself, as the preoccupation with such profit to the exclusion of any other human consideration, was the chief source of these evils in planning and design. The large scale building of the Woods in Bath was done under commercial incentives, but fortunately at a time when other motives, the sense of what is proper to one's rank and station, modified the commercial aim. Thus the Woods, like Robert Adam in Edinburgh, could work on the more generous baroque scale, think of the whole street front as a single unit, and treat the open space as an integral part of the whole design. Once these aristocratic ideals were trampled on by the rising philistines who built the nineteenth-century city, only the uniformity and repetition of baroque design was retained in the standardized row house of New York or London, or the standardized apartment houses of Napoleon III's Paris and Bismarck's Berlin.

6: THE TRAFFIC IN TRAFFIC

One further feature of the commercial plan was the corridor avenue itself: a linear thoroughfare designed mainly to further the circulation of wheeled vehicles. In the new plan, there was often hardly any differentiation between street and avenue, between neighborhood circulation and trans-urban circulation. Even those who could afford the finest residences established themselves on avenues, like Fifth Avenue in New York or Broad Street in Philadelphia, rather than on side streets with quiet interior quarters. So difficult is it to escape this pattern, when commercial principles dominate, that even today a new shopping center on a major highway in Long Island boasts the inconvenient fact that it is a mile long.

The sacrifice of the neighborhood to the traffic avenue went on all during the nineteenth century. Even in a residential suburb like Hampstead Garden in London—a beautiful plan with many admirable innovations—the planners placed the shopping area along a corridor avenue instead of creating a compact market center. The traffic generated by the commercial city was so formidable, that as early as the nineteenth century, in New York, traffic snarls were common, and the demand for faster modes of public transportation grew. Up to this time, in most cities, the major part of the population walked to work. This did not mean that their work necessarily remained in their own neighborhood; but that even where it did not, the worker or even the employer, might travel by foot two or three miles to his job, though in bad weather this was a serious handicap to underfed and poorly clothed pedestrians.

With the invention of the cheap stage coach, the railroad, and finally the tramway, mass transportation came into existence for the first time in history. Walking distance no longer set the limits of city growth; and the whole pace of the city extension was hastened, since it was no longer avenue by avenue, or block by block, but railroad line by railroad line, and suburb by suburb, raying out in every direction from the central district. In some respects, these supplementary forms of transportation, following routes that did not always coincide with the street network, offset the worst weaknesses of the street system of circulation; and in an era of cheap fares, it gave the poorer paid workers a degree of mobility that placed them on a parity with those who could afford private vehicles.

Unfortunately, the provision of public transportation went on under the same canons of speculative profit that governed the rest of the city: traffic speculation and land speculation played into each other's hands, often in the person of the same enterpriser. At the very moment this took place, the perceptive Emerson, as early as 1836, identified the great potentiality of the new scale of time and space: that it would turn roads into streets, and transform the regions into neighborhoods. But the ideal consummation of this possibility through the use of the region as the unit of development remained unfulfilled, for the increase of range of traffic was utilized as a means of increasing the perimeter of cities already too big for human advantage. Rapid public transportation, instead of reducing the time required for reaching the place of work, continued to increase the distance and the cost with no gain in time whatever.

What holds true for the horizontal extension of the commercial city in the nineteenth century and later, holds true equally for its vertical expansion by means of the elevator. The latter was at first confined to the bigger cities of the New World. But the radical mistakes that were first made in the promotion of skyscrapers are now universal, partly through a relaxation of over-stringent controls, partly through commercial pressure, partly through fashionable imitation, partly through the architect's desire to exploit new technological facilities. All the mistakes first made in American cities are being repeated on an equally horrendous scale in Europe and Asia. If fast transportation made the horizon the limit for urban sprawl, the new methods of construction made the "sky the limit," as gamblers loved to say. Apart from any functions it might better serve by piling one floor upon another, the high rise building became a status symbol of 'modernity.'

The combination of these two methods of expansion and congestion, horizontal and vertical, produced the maximum opportunities for profit: that was in fact the principal motivating force. But this purely mechanical system of growth becomes in the end self-limiting; for the disadvantages of crawling traffic, moving through the city at half the speed of horse-drawn vehicles fifty years ago, are the direct results of inordinate increases of urban density, residential and business, as well as the increase in the number of private motor cars. And the lack of space to move in is not diminished by the dedication of ever larger areas of the city to widened avenues, expressways, viaducts, parking lots, and garages: for the time is approaching in many cities when there will be every facility for moving about the city and no possible reason for going there. Even now, the befouled and poisonous air, the constricted housing at three or four hundred residents per acre, the demoralized social life, teeming with violence and crime, have led to a general exodus from the central areas of cities. In this sense the disease is a self-limiting one; but only because it must eventually destroy the organism that harbors it.

This criticism of the modes and ends of capitalism, as manifested in urban expansion, is not an effort to minimize the huge problems of growth the nineteenth-century city confronted, still less does it imply a failure to recognize the value of the new technical improvements that were now at the city's disposal, ready to supplement the footways and waterways that no longer sufficed the more dynamic and varied life of the modern city. Quite the contrary: the problem of growth must be handled by all corporate associations and organizations, no less than by organisms. Who would hope seriously for a solution to any of our urban problems by a return to a more primitive technological or social basis?

The mistake of the progressive commercial mind was to give undue importance to those modes of circulation that promised the highest financial return: this led the planner to overlook the role of the footwalker, and the need for retaining the flexibility of mass movements that only pedestrian circulation can ensure. At the same time it committed him later to the one-dimensional solution of private transportation by motor car, and to giving transportation itself priority over many other urban functions, quite as essential to a city's existence.

Thus the overgrowth of the traffic network, bent on increasing the profitable congestion of the center, produced in fact, even technically speaking, an exceedingly primitive solution. Except at its congested core, the resulting city lacked many of the happy amenities of social life, which much smaller and seemingly more backward cities still possessed.

7: THE REGIMENTATION OF CONGESTION

The new ground plan often produced on paper the appearance of order and spaciousness: but the new building in the mercantile city undermined the very pretense of these qualities by introducing hitherto unheard of degrees of congestion, making universal bad practices that in most cities before the seventeenth century had at worst only been occasional, almost accidental. This regimentation in time affected every part of the city: but first of all it affected the dwellings of the poor.

Urban congestion naturally takes place when too large a number of people begin to compete for a limited number of apartments and rooms; and as a commercial and industrial proletariat began to throng into the great capitals of Europe in the sixteenth century, these conditions became chronic. Urban improvement could have taken place only if the forces that were thrusting people into the city had been controlled at the source.

Competition for space by poor unprotected immigrants had the same effect on seventeenth-century Paris or Edinburgh as on eighteenth-century Manchester and nineteenth-century Liverpool and New York: the ground rents rose and the living quarters worsened. A hectare of land in Paris in the thirteenth century was worth 2,600 francs according to d'Avenel: in the twentieth century a hectare in the same district was worth 1,297,000 francs: even allowing for the different value of money, the rise was staggering. Who benefited by that advance? Not the occupants. Whose income kept pace with it? Not the workers'.

"The worker of the Middle Ages who had an annual income of a thousand francs, could pay without difficulty for a little house from one hundred to two hundred francs a year: his situation became still better when rents went immensely lower in the fifteenth century by reason of the abundance of empty dwellings, while wages had gone up to 1200 francs. But at the moment when the journeyman did not, from 1550 to the height of the eighteenth century, earn more than 675 francs per year, and when the poorest Parisian houses rented for 350 francs, one perceives why it was necessary for him to give up living under a separate roof."

With appropriate variations, this condition held throughout Europe, and in the more prosperous seaports of North America. From the standpoint of the working classes, the period was one of increasing exploitation, and with regard to their quarters, one of increasing dilapidation and constriction. One notes the newly lowered standards even in the typical works of philanthropy. Though by present housing standards the group housing for the aged in Augsburg, built by Jacob Fugger for the poor, is a remarkably handsome architectural group, the parallel rows of houses have only a minimum of open space for gardens, compared with the existing open spaces shown on a contemporary plan of Augsburg: even works of charity had become stingy in their utilization of land, for now space, like time, was money.

To understand the source of this congestion, apart from the desire for wringing profits out of the necessities of the poor, unable like their economic superiors to bargain and withhold acceptance, one must realize that by the seventeenth century destitution had been accepted as the normal lot in life for a considerable part of the population. Without the spur of poverty and famine, they could not be expected to work for starvation wages. Misery at the bottom was the foundation for the luxury at the top. As much as a quarter of the urban population in the bigger cities, it has

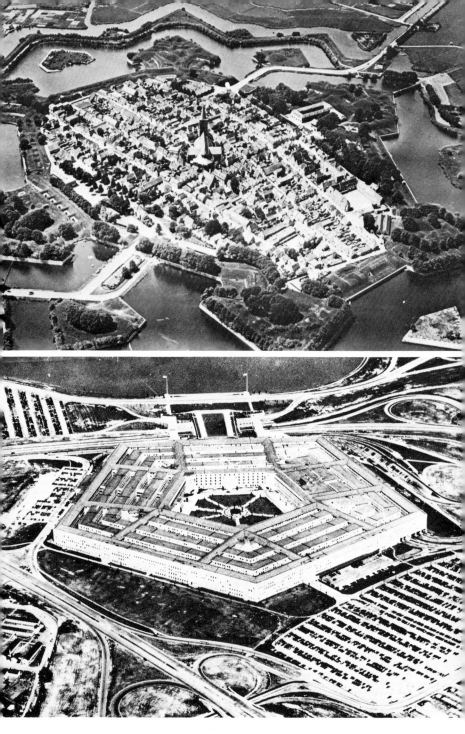

49: SUBLIMATION AND REGRESSION

50: PLUS ÇA CHANGE...

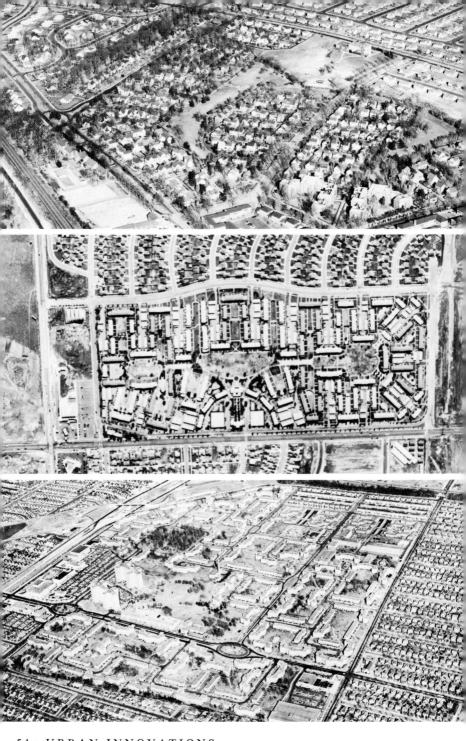

53: FUNCTIONAL ZONING

55: HISTORIC CORE

56: UNIVERSITY CITY

AGE I. 1840-1880

AGE II. 1880-1920
AGE III. 1920-1960

STAGE IV. 1960-2000 [?]

57: REGIONAL GRID

58: GREEN MATRIX

59: THE HUMAN SCALE

60: TOWARD 'SOCIAL CITIES'

61: THE CIVIC NUCLEUS

62: THROUGH TERROR TO TRIUMPH

63 : CIVIC RESURGENCE

64: HIVE OR CITY

49: SUBLIMATION AND REGRESSION

Naarden in The Netherlands [upper]. A military extravagance converted finally into a civic opportunity. Fortunately, the outer baroque fortification consisted largely of earthworks: hence their eventual removal in the nineteenth century often prompted their sublimation into a beautiful park girdle, not merely in Naarden but in Bremen, Cracow, and many other towns. The Pentagon in Alexandria, across the Potomac from Washington [lower]. An effete and worthless baroque conceit, resurrected in the nineteen-thirties by United States military engineers and magnified into an architectural catastrophe. Nuclear power has aggravated this error and turned its huge comic ineptitude into a tragic threat: for here the citadel has come back to life once more, with every ancient dimension magnified, every error raised to the tenth power. The Bronze Age fantasies of absolute power, the Bronze Age practice of unlimited human extermination, the uncontrolled obsessions, hatreds, and suspicions of Bronze Age gods and kings, have here taken root again in a fashion that imitates— and seeks to surpass—the Kremlin of Ivan the Terrible and his latterday successors. With this relapse, in less than a decade, have come one-way communication, the priestly monopoly of secret knowledge, the multiplication of secret agencies, the suppression of open discussion, and even the insulation of error against public criticism and exposure through a 'bi-partisan' military and foreign policy, which in practice nullifies public reaction and makes rational dissent the equivalent of patriotic disaffection, if not treason. The dismantling of this regressive citadel will prove a far harder task than the demolition of the earlier baroque fortifications. But on its performance all more extensive plans for urban and human development must wait.

[Upper] Photograph by courtesy of The Netherlands Information Office. [Bottom] Photograph: Ewing Galloway. For my more extensive criticism of the chronic psychopathology of our morally disoriented age, see 'The Morals of Extermination' in the Atlantic Monthly, October 1959: Also 'In the Name of Sanity.'

50: PLUS ÇA CHANGE . . .

[Upper left] Working class housing in the nineteenth century. Drab, repetitive, mechanically conceived, crowded, with all the space allotted to the street, none to garden or playground. [Lower left] Railroad transportation coordinately appropriated large swathes of land near the center and brought dirt and noise into the residential neighborhood. [Upper right] This twentieth century example of suburban housing is appreciably above the great mass of such housing around most American metropolitan centers: despite the bulldozer's operations, a few trees have been left,

there is more space around the houses, and even a swatch of public open space has been provided by the builder. Vestigial romanticism. But in view of the many superior precedents available in site planning and house grouping (see Plates 44, 51, 60) the result here only repeats the mistakes of the railroad age at a higher point in the spiral. As for the shopping center and its parking lot and the motor highway [lower right] these again display the standard paleotechnic vices, only slightly disguised: spatial desolation and civic disintegration, in the interest of speeding the technological and sales turnover. Mono-transportation produces mono-functional isolation. Meanwhile smoke from garbage incinerators and exhaust from motor cars and jet planes—to say nothing of coeval forms of industrial pollution—produces smog quite as deleterious to health as the older smoke pall.

[Upper Left] Manchester neighborhood. Photograph: Aerofilms, Ltd., London. [Lower Left] Railroad yards at Doncaster. Photograph: Aerofilms and Aero Pictorial Ltd., London. [Upper Right] Photograph by New York Times. [Lower Right] Garden State Plaza at Paramus, N. J. Photograph by Fairchild Aerial Surveys, Inc., New York.

51: URBAN INNOVATIONS

The Radburn Plan [top], the first major departure in city planning since Venice, was prompted by a suggestion from a layman, who conceived its new layout as a "town for the Motor Age." (See Clarence Stein's 'New Towns for America.') But adaptation to the motor car was only one of many distinguishing features: it utilized the separation of traffic by overpasses and underpasses, first demonstrated by Olmsted in Central Park; the suburban superblock, with a more systematic use of the cul-de-sac for privacy and quiet; the continuous strip park (also an invention of Olmsted's); the separation of neighborhood access roads from main traffic arteries, as outlined by Perry's neighborhood unit concept; and the school and swimming pool set in the park, as the civic nucleus of a neighborhood. These radical transformations were somewhat hidden by the retention of the conventional suburban house; but even on the photograph the difference between the basic Radburn unit and the conventional semi-suburban layout at the top is plain. Had Radburn become a fully developed greenbelt town, instead of being liquidated to meet the depression, it might have had an immediate effect comparable to that of Letchworth and Welwyn on the design of the British New Towns. A comparison with Plate 60 will bring out the special virtues of the Radburn Plan, which European planners have been slow to recognize. Le Corbusier's adoption of the same scheme, ready-made for him at Chandigarh by Mayer and Nowicki has finally given the cachet of his reputation to a plan that the uninformed may believe he invented. Baldwin Hills Village [middle] dem-

onstrates the virtue of 'precinct planning,' within a superblock insulated from through traffic, with the private garage kept at the periphery—the whole tract kept free from the superfluous streets visible in the ordinary commercial development, above. This is an outstanding example of good planning, for the inner park is for people, not cars. Here the density might have been tripled without marring the openness of the plan. Such superblocks contrast favorably with the windy bleakness of high-rise slabs with their esthetically unformed and usually ungardened open spaces. [Bottom] A residential neighborhood unit (Fresh Meadows, Long Island) skillfully planned to slow down motor traffic without effecting the complete separation achieved in Radburn. The ample open spaces, the retention of an oak woods at the middle left, the avoidance of needless streets, the provision of adequate nearby neighborhood markets as well as a general shopping center that draws on the whole area, the use of collective parking garages instead of individual hutches or wasteful parking lots, show that combination of openness and urbanity which should be characteristic of a well-planned city—in contrast to the economically wasteful and esthetically destitute standardization of the surrounding area. The weakest points in the whole design are the two poorly conceived and ill sited highrise apartment houses, whereas the three-story apartment houses are excellent. The London County Council's Roehampton Estate, with its mixture of tower apartments and lower houses and maisonettes, shows a better handling of big units.

[Top] Photograph by Fairchild Aerial Surveys, Inc., New York. [Middle] Photograph by courtesy of Clarence S. Stein. [Bottom] Photograph by courtesy of New York Life Insurance Company.

52: PRECINCT PLANNING

Precinct planning has survived into modern times in such happy examples as Harvard Yard [upper] which is also a superblock insulated from through traffic. The same orderly but varied layout of buildings would be equally applicable to a group of apartment houses. The value of Harvard Yard depends upon the exclusion of the motor car: the possibility of this, without forfeiting convenience, was proved not merely in Radburn, but in Sunnyside Gardens and Baldwin Hills. For lack of such control, many of Harvard's handsomest buildings, once surrounded by open greens, like Austin Hall, are now sinking mid a sea of motor cars. The Harvard Business School, on the other side of the Charles River [lower] is also a self-contained precinct: but it pays toll in space-eating motor cars. Incidentally, the heavy wooded area to the upper left indicates one of the most charming examples of spontaneous mid-nineteenth century suburban planning, with superblocks and cul-de-sacs, laid out before Olmsted practiced the art. As with the Oxford and Cambridge colleges, none of Harvard's piecemeal planning, not even the Graduate Center, has been either as handsome or as economically justifiable as that of the Yard. Today the only alternative left is that between disruptive congestion and well-directed colonization: new Harvards in related areas of New England, perhaps in other parts of the country. Will this and other great universities continue to follow Rome's erroneous example, or will they learn the lesson of Delphi, which the town of Cambridge itself followed in the seventeenth century?

[Upper] Harvard Yard. Photograph by Felt. By courtesy of Harvard University. [Lower] Photograph: Ewing Galloway.

53: FUNCTIONAL ZONING

The city is essentially a place for diversified and mixed activities; yet in the case of industries like cement and chemical works, steel plants and slaughter houses, spatial insulation is desirable and justifies relatively long journeys to work. Even in electrical works [middle] the need for railroad sidings and large-scale plant organization demands that the whole area be freed from the street pattern and separated by at least a park strip from the rest of the city. Such industrial zoning and corporate plant development has been one of the best features of the British New Towns, beginning with Welwyn Garden City. The separation of the steel plant [top] from the workers' housing contrasts happily with that shown on Plate 39: though the roadways are still wastefully wide, the gardens and playing greens, characteristic of most publicly aided housing in Britain since 1920, are a vital contribution to amenity and health. The trading estate (Industrial Park) at Slough [bottom], is one of a number that began in England with the huge Trafford Park estate in Manchester, in the eighteen-nineties. When planned as an integral part of a town or a group of towns, they are a valuable contribution to urban order. In the United States the use of zoning for non-functional purposes, particularly in residential areas, often produces architectural monotony, practical inconvenience, and social segregation. Functional mixing is on occasion as imperative as functional separation.

[Top and Middle] Photograph: Ewing Galloway. [Bottom] Photograph: Aerofilms, Ltd., London.

54: PRESERVATION AND RENOVATION

As leader in urban planning, Philadelphia now occupies the place that Boston did in the eighteen-nineties. The renewal of the historic core around Independence Hall has provided a stimulus that has spread over the adjacent oldtime residential quarter of Society Hill, and now promises to bring about the rehabilitation of the central commercial district. The recolonization of the historic precinct with residential housing in restored eighteenth and early nineteenth century structures has been combined with new apartment houses: unfortunately the dimensions of the latter reflect the commercial scale, based on high rents, rather than the domestic scale, based on human needs. The formalistic baroque approach to Independence Hall [upper left] shows how much easier it is to open up space than to enclose it in an organic form. But the little informal neighborhood parks and playgrounds [lower left] connected by pedestrian greenways, deserve the widest imitation in Philadelphia and elsewhere. The new appreciation of order and openness, first registered in the historic precinct, has now extended to the business quarter, where alert preparations by the City Planning Commission took advantage of the demolition of the railroad viaduct and its terminals to create a new business center and hotel quarter: a project in which private enterprise and public spirit happily joined. The mediocrity of the architectural form is partly redeemed by the open order and the sensitive use of the inner spaces. The civic nucleus of Philadelphia, though weakened by the suburban exodus, has begun, through the art museum, the library system, the universities, and not least through the historic precinct itself, to exert its attractive power throughout the Delaware Valley. This should lead, not merely to the inner renewal of the city, but to the maintenance of the green matrix and the changeover from the clotted conurbation of the past to the new urban and regional grid.

[Upper Left] Independence Hall, with new formal approach. [Upper Right] The historic core, showing Carpenters' Hall, a new world Guild Hall (with turret) in the middle, and beyond William Strickland's Second Bank of the United States (Greek Temple) the American Philosophical Society, and the tower of Independence Hall. [Bottom Left] Small neighborhood park, in the historic area, whose rehabilitation began with the setting out of gardens in old buildings used by insurance companies, still concentrated in this quarter. [Bottom Right] Penn Center: first outlined in plan and model by the City Planning Commission. All photographs by courtesy of the City Planning Commission, Edmund N. Bacon, Executive Director.

55: HISTORIC CORE

Partly because of the high land values, the diverse corporate ownerships, and the continued business needs of the City of London, its post-war planners did not seek, like the preservers of the historic core of Philadelphia, to turn the area around St. Paul's into a great park. But the temptation to treat the buildings immediately around St. Paul's as a formalistic baroque composition was present at the beginning and the same esthetic premises encouraged vehement opposition, later, to the better plan here shown. Instead of designing the quarter immediately around St. Paul's to 'harmonize' in outward details with the Cathedral, in the fashion too often followed in Philadelphia by commercial firms near Independence

Hall, Sir William Holford here suggested a setting that boldly contrasts with the architectural jewel it holds. He even avoided the temptation to impose uniform heights and regular façades: but achieved a great diversity in buildings, with hitherto unattainable open spaces, by varying heights in proportion to the amount of ground covered, producing a variety of approaches and a succession of open and blocked vistas, that honor London's gifts of complexity and surprise. Contrast this organic plan, with its functional suppleness and esthetic variety, its well-filled spaces and friendly enclosures, with the deadly uniformity, the visual bleakness, the inhuman scale, and even worse, the human irrelevance of the series of grandiose city plans that Le Corbusier put forward from the 'twenties onward. In this plan for the St. Paul's precinct, business needs and business interests have been accommodated to other human activities, whereas in the 'ideal cities' of Le Corbusier and his imitators (up to Chandigarh) a bureaucratic regimentation prevails throughout. Unfortunately, Le Corbusier's imagination, deeply in harmony with the negative tendencies at work in contemporary society, has for a whole generation been the most powerful single influence over architecture and city planning in every part of the world. Here, in contrast, what is valuable in Le Corbusier's thinking has been admirably assimilated and brought into organic relation to the full span of urban activities. Here, too, the preservation and enhancement of an historic monument has produced, not a series of stultifying fakes, but suggestions for a fresh order of planning and building applicable elsewhere.

[Left] Forecourt and entrance to St. Paul's. [Right] Side view from the east. Photographs of models by courtesy of the Town Planning Review. (See Holford in Bibliography.)

56: UNIVERSITY CITY

The most essential role of the city, apart from the daily drama itself— that of enlarging and transmitting the cultural heritage—is now being performed chiefly in university cities, of the order of Berkeley, shown here, and Cambridge. Berkeley—named after the great philosopher in memory of his poem 'On the Founding of an Institution of Learning in America'—was projected in 1858; in the mid-sixties F. L. Olmsted was invited to plan the campus. Unfortunately, money for the University's development was provided by the sale of lots adjacent to the University precinct: with the result that the town itself has now lost its physical identity by coalescence with its bigger neighbor, Oakland. Close inspection of the plate will show that the university and the town below offer an example of almost every cultural component of the historic city: temple, arena, gymnasium, campanile, theater, town hall, 'palace,' park, and even (in the dormitories!) the monastery. In the emerging economy, with its prospect of a surfeit of annually consumable goods and a surplus of dismally empty leisure, the University holds a key position: for the school sprang from the Greek polis' margin of leisure, and in the opening age, paideia, or education in the fullest sense, as used in Werner Jaeger's classic exposition, will become the essential business of life. With its long memory, its vital international affiliations, its disciplined devotion to intellectual communication and co-operation, the university has become the central nucleus in the new urban and cultural grid. But in carrying on the intellectual activities of the ancient temple, the university still bears the signs of its origin. Though it furthers scribal and scientific lore, the 'new learning' that came in with the ancient city, it has only begun to make a place for the older arts that predated the temple: painting, ritual, dance, music, religion itself. Further, by its concern with advancing systematic knowledge alone, the university has pushed to the point of caricature many of the worst aspects of the historic city: intense vocational compartmentalization, over-specialization, and hierarchic subordination under a pervasive bureaucratic discipline. Meanwhile the expanding universe of knowledge, subject to forces similar to those that have produced automatic technological expansion, has lost its central human point of reference: hence a failure to evaluate, assimilate, and put to wider human uses its own most valuable products. The result has been the obliteration of the whole man, and the progressive dehumanization of the fractional man, committed to a fractional contribution to knowledge, incapable of embracing a whole situation, or giving a whole response, with emotions, feelings, and imagination as disciplined as his intellectual reactions. As now constituted, even the greatest universities—and the University of California at Berkeley is one of the great ones—exhibit the current metropolitan vices of over-growth and congestion, dissociation and disorganization. If the University is to function as the organizing nucleus in the new urban implosion, it must not merely decentralize and reorganize its facilities on a regional basis, as many American state universities are now doing, but undergo an inner transformation: from pedagogy to paideia, from science to wisdom, from detachment to commitment. Out of this will spring a new system of learning, a new attitude toward every manifestation of life, as different from the science and technology founded by Galileo, Bacon, Descartes and Newton as they were from the theology of Thomas Aquinas. Without this Great Instauration our plans for city development will remain sterile and superficial.

Photograph: Fairchild Aerial Surveys, Inc., New York.

57: REGIONAL GRID

This analysis of the growth of urban communities in New York State, mainly the work of Henry Wright, begins with the culmination of the early settlement and colonization. The population pattern indicates state-

wide activity and intercourse, based on 900 miles of canals, 5,000 water wheels, 400 small industrial towns. Though the railroad supplemented canal and highroad, it, too, followed a regional pattern with many small cross-country lines. These lines were in time absorbed into a few trunk line railroads, but they remained in operation, though enfeebled, into the third decade of the twentieth century. The second period was one of concentration, along the main-line transportation routes that favored the metropolis and abetted its congestion. This began with the establishment of a regular shipping service between New York and Liverpool in 1816, and was promoted by the building of the Erie Canal along the Mohawk Valley, ending at Buffalo, which gave New York direct water connection with the Great Lakes and their hinterland. The railroad, following the same waterlevel route, largely replaced the canal by 1880. The steam railroad and electric trolley both promoted concentration within the bigger cities and began the suburban dispersal. In 1925 Wright pictured a possible distribution of cities shown here, with greater concentration than in the first period, less than in the second. Between 1920 and 1960 the actual setting aside of the Adirondack State Forest withdrew population from that area; but metropolitan congestion and blight continued more rapidly than ever in the New York and Buffalo areas. In picturing the concept of the urban and cultural grid, I have turned to Wright's diagram as the closest equivalent, though it naturally needs further development. This diagram indicates how regional balance might be achieved, through a planned distribution of population and industry into many smaller communities, of varying sizes and functions, such as that shown [lower] in the Mohawk Valley. By deliberate organization and association the smallest of these communities might have metropolitan advantages that the metropolis itself does not now enjoy, while preserving a more diversified environment, with richer opportunities for education and recreation.

[Upper] Henry Wright's historic diagnosis and plan for New York State. Final report of the New York State Housing and Regional Planning Commission. Albany: 1926. [Lower] Small town in Mohawk Valley. Photograph: Ewing Galloway.

58: GREEN MATRIX

The maintenance of the regional setting, the green matrix, is essential for the culture of cities. Where this setting has been defaced, despoiled, or obliterated, the deterioration of the city must follow, for the relationship is symbiotic. The difficulty of maintaining this balance has been temporarily increased, not merely by the incontinent spread of low-grade urban tissue everywhere, dribbling off into endless roadside stands, motels, garages, motor sales agencies, and building lots, but by the rapid indus-

trialization of farming itself, which has turned it from a way of life into a mechanical processing business no different in content or aim or outlook from any other metropolitan occupation. The re-occupation and replenishment of the landscape, as a source of essential values in a balanced life, is one of the most important conditions for urban renewal. The planner's supposed necessity to choose between greenbelts and green wedges is like the other current decision between high-rise flats for central cities and low single family dwellings for the peripheral communities: a gratuitous dilemma and a false alternative. What is vital is the preservation of the green matrix in which urban communities, big and small, are set: above all the necessity to prevent the uncontrolled growth of urban tissue from effacing this matrix and upsetting the entire ecological pattern of city and country. With the increase of leisure, it has become more important than ever to conserve the natural background, not merely by maintaining areas with rich soils for agriculture and horticulture, as well as areas with impressive topographic features for recreation and solitude, but to increase the opportunity for personal activities on an amateur level, in horticulture, landscape gardening, bird and animal breeding, and scientific observation. The Tennessee Valley Authority shared the weakness of the State regional planning surveys and reports that followed it in the nineteen-thirties in being almost exclusively oriented to stream control, power production, and soil conservation, with no urban policy whatever. Had the original directors paid more attention to the success of the small industrial town of Kingsport, Tennessee, planned in 1915 by John Nolen under the direction of private enterprise, they would have coordinated their superb regional improvements with the renewal and extension of the existing small communities, and the building of new ones —or at least called attention to the need of legislation working toward these ends. This failure is particularly vexing in relatively underdeveloped regions, like the Tennessee Valley and adjacent areas in North Carolina, where all the errors and absurdities that have produced the massive dissociated conurbations of the past are now being fatuously repeated.

[Top] Tennessee Valley Landscape. Photograph by courtesy of the Tennessee Valley Authority. [Middle] Facilities for water recreation. Courtesy, Museum of Modern Art, New York. [Bottom] Kingsport, Tenn., Fairchild Aerial Surveys, Inc., New York.

59: THE HUMAN SCALE

The human scale is never an absolute one: for it is determined, not alone by the normal dimensions of the human body, but by the functions that are facilitated and by the interests and purposes that are served. Thus a group of tall buildings [upper left] like the widely spaced apartment houses near the Centrum of Vällingby may still maintain the human scale, especially since the lower buildings in the foreground shopping center, the ridge of low apartments in the background, and the trees on the left, 'step down' the esthetic imposition of bigness, as a transformer steps down electric current to a usable local voltage. Vällingby, nine miles from central Stockholm, though not planned to have an industrial and commercial base for more than twenty-five per cent of its residents, is an exemplary step toward metropolitan decentralization and reintegration within a permanent green matrix. The center has a theater, cinema, meeting rooms, a town hall, a library, even a youth center, along with both high and low apartment buildings; while around it the more open residential areas are scattered in between parkland and forest. The offices and the shopping center are placed astride the electric rapid transit system, and though the center, here as in Rotterdam, has parking space for the private car, the planners have provided a whole transportation network, with due regard for rapid public traffic. The multi-level shopping center at Coventry [lower left] with its trees and banks of flowers, its sheltered walk and pleasant relationship of buildings is, by consensus, one of the finest built anywhere: but when first put forward in 1946 its best features, its enclosure and precinctual isolation, were opposed by the 'business interests' who mistook bad habits for good reasons. The housing to the right, two views of the same estate near Richmond, show how the human scale can be maintained at a considerably higher residential density than that favored in either suburbs or new towns, when the architect is freed from arbitrarily uniform prescriptions as to garden allotments, setbacks from roads, and obsolete street patterns; and once he frees himself from such formalistic images as the high-rise slab whose extravagant costs are not compensated for by either social or esthetic benefits.

[Upper Left] Vällingby Centrum. Photograph by Lennart af Petersens, Stockholm. [Lower Left] Coventry Shopping Center. Photograph by courtesy of the Department of Architecture and Planning, the City of Coventry, Arthur Ling, City Architect. [Upper and Lower Right] Parkleys, Ham Common, Surrey. Two and three story flats, residential density c. 80 persons per acre. Photograph by courtesy of Eric Lyons.

60: TOWARD 'SOCIAL CITIES'

Harlow, one of the handsomest of the British New Towns, is in more than one sense a dream fulfilled: Howard's dream of the Garden City, first realized in Letchworth and Welwyn Garden Cities, Unwin's dream of the open green town, with residential housing at twelve to fourteen families an acre, Clarence Perry's dream of urban reorganization by neighborhoods, not least Sir Patrick Abercrombie's dream for post-war Greater London. As the inserted picture shows, Abercrombie suggested the neighborhood shopping centers, though with more apartment houses than the

New Towns Corporations have found it expedient to build. The ample playing spaces in the New Towns are prescribed for British schools under the post-war education act, but the larger ones might well have been placed in the peripheral greenbelt. For urban purposes of accessibility and easy meeting, continuous strip parks, as in Radburn, would, I submit, have been preferable to the broad plats of green; while the more systematic use of the superblock and cul-de-sac would have produced greater compactness with even better residential privacy. But as in most New Towns the factory quarter is superb. Harlow is one of a cluster of cities that extend from Essex into Hertfordshire: an embryonic town cluster or 'social city' still to be given full political realization. The building of the fifteen New Towns under the difficult economic conditions that prevailed for a decade after 1945 was one of the high marks of British municipal statesmanship. For a brief while the needs of life, encouraged by wartime sacrifices, prevailed over the attractions and perversions of a money economy.

Harlow. Begun 1947. Population, 1960: almost 50,000. Planned maximum population: 80,000. Photograph by courtesy of the Harlow Development Corporation. [Inset] Section of a New Town, from Patrick Abercrombie's 'Greater London Plan.'

61: THE CIVIC NUCLEUS

Unlike the ancient city, the nucleus of the contemporary town is a mainly secular one: the reflection of the dominant technology and economy. But within this core, a new order and comeliness has begun to prevail, as these photographs from the Town Center of Harlow plainly reveal. Though the provisions for schools and playing fields in the New Towns has been as exemplary as the planning of New Town industrial zones, the failure to plant new technical schools, colleges, and universities in these communities, or to make any future provision for them, was a radical oversight. (See Plate 56). Nevertheless a fresh integration of the city's functions is going on, both in the neighborhood centers and in Town Center [top]. Witness the combination of shops, business and professional offices, and municipal buildings shown here, with an open plaza admirably designed—I speak as an eye witness—for staging public ceremonies. No isolated shopping centers can compare in either convenience, efficiency, or human interest with the complex activities of a genuine civic center. The planning of cities cannot be confined to 'housing, work, recreation, and circulation,' the standard planner's definition: the whole city must rather be conceived mainly as a theater for active citizenship, for education, and for a vivid and autonomous personal life.

[Top] Harlow. Town Center. [Middle and Bottom] Town Center, renewal of the pedestrian mall and the open plaza in contemporary style, closed to wheeled traffic. All photographs by courtesy of the Harlow Development Corporation. Frederick Gibberd, Town Planner.

62: THROUGH TERROR TO TRIUMPH

*Ossip Zadkine's sculpture [upper] placed on a plaza fronting the inner
Harbor of Rotterdam, symbolizes the agony of the city, whose inner core
was demolished, with the extermination of thirty thousand people, by
German bombs in May 1940. This barbarism was preceded by the destruction of Warsaw in 1939, and magnified and repeated many times in
the Nazi assaults on London, Coventry, Manchester, and Liverpool, only
to be brought to a quantitative climax by democracy's adoption of the
same methods in assaults on Berlin, Hamburg, Dresden, Tokyo, Hiroshima and Nagasaki, and many other cities, in a universal urban holo-
caust. Not every city rose to the challenge of its destruction as deter-
minedly and as skillfully as Rotterdam. By pooling the old properties, it
became possible to replan the center [lower] for both business and residential occupation. In front of the department store (The Beehive) in
the center of the picture stands Naum Gabo's magnificent constructivist
sculpture, itself a tribute to the skill and daring of the Rotterdam shipyard, where it was built, and to the imagination of the city planning director who demanded a visual interruption in the street picture at this
point. The long low group of buildings in the rear is part of the Lijnbaan
shopping mall. Behind this, a group of high-rise apartment houses whose
empty interior courts might have been improved by a freer precinctual
arrangement and an in-filling of lower structures. But the main purpose,
the restoration of the city as a meeting place, where a diversity of human functions are brought together, has been admirably carried through.*

[Upper] Zadkine's Rotterdam statue, with nearby waterfront, where the booms and
cranes in the distance echo the upraised arms. Foto Openbare Werken, Rotterdam.
[Lower] Commercial and political center of Rotterdam. Cornelius van Traa, City
Planner. Photograph by courtesy of The Netherlands Information Service. Aero-
photo 'Nederland.'

63: CIVIC RESURGENCE

*The word 'renewal' is a tame one to describe the resurgence of Rotter-
dam; but no photograph, indeed no single work of sculpture or building can adequately convey the energies focussed there. Zadkine's sculpture is here shown in its living context [top], with part of the great port
in the background. The monument itself, as is appropriate for a memorial
so charged with painful emotions, has been placed at a point a little inaccessible and remote, to be visited deliberately, not passed by daily and
ignored. The Lijnbaan [middle and bottom] done in modest materials
on a modest scale, meant to house a variety of smaller shops, restaurants,
and cinemas, is exemplary in almost every way: not least because one of
its malls terminates visually in the surviving Town Hall. The flowered*

plots and the benches [middle], along with the glass-enclosed outdoor cafe, emphasize its recreational and social values; while the narrow walk, like that of the Calverstraat in Amsterdam, makes shopping itself easy. Instead of hastening the flight from the city, the core of historic Rotterdam invites a return. But such cores can be kept alive only by dealing with all the factors that affect the city's life. Many pressing problems, however, like provision for population increase and preparations for peace, transcend the powers and functions of the city alone. High density building can no more solve the population problem than underground shelters can protect a city from nuclear and bacterial extermination.

[Upper] Plaza and waterfront. [Middle] Lijnbaan, designed by Bakema and van der Broek. Flower beds as integral part of pedestrian mall. [Lower] Mall with glassed-in outdoor cafe. Photographs by courtesy of The Netherlands Information Service.

64: HIVE OR CITY

Whether our scientific technology should be controlled and directed for the purposes of life, or whether life shall be regimented and repressed in order to promote the ceaseless expansion of technology is one of the main questions before mankind today. Without conscious deliberation, indeed almost automatically, Western civilization during the last half century has moved far along the second course. Its ultimate outcome must approach the sub-human hive, pictured here by a group of Japanese technicians as the "super-community of the twenty-fourth century," in which all the functions of the human organism and the human personality have been absorbed by a collective apparatus, functioning as an all-embracing super-organism, leaving human beings with an epiphenomenal and purposeless existence as floating cells. The 'Study Group for Life Apparatus' observes that the "control section of the super-mechanism creates a multi-dimensional mutual control ensuring that human life everywhere on the globe be full of warm solidarity and harmony." Yes indeed! Against this life-simulating man-heap, so ingeniously designed to bring the transformations of man to an end by a final suicidal leap into a super-mechanism operating in super-space, I would invoke the smiling spirit of 'Erewhon': for Samuel Butler was perhaps the first to perceive the ultimate destination of a dehumanized technology: a world in which man would function only as a machine's device for producing another machine. If life prevail, the city of the future will have, as but few contemporary cities have, the qualities shown in this Chinese painting of the Festival of Spring: with the endless permutations and combinations that varied landscapes, varied occupations, varied cultural activities, and the varied personal attributes of men make possible. Not the perfect hive, but the living city.

[Upper] Image of a Super-Community. Article published by the Study Group for Life Apparatus in the Kokusai-Kentiku. January, 1960. For an understanding of this thesis I am greatly indebted to a special translation made by Donald L. Philippi. [Lower] Plate from the Ch'ing Ming Scroll: Collection A. W. Bahr, Fletcher Fund, 1947; courtesy of The Metropolitan Museum of Art. For a critical analysis of the dominant technocratic myths and dogmas, see my 'Art and Technics,' and 'The Transformations of Man,' particularly in the latter the chapter on 'Post-historic Man.'

been estimated, consisted of casuals and beggars: it was this surplus that made for what was considered, by classic capitalism, to be a healthy labor market, in which the capitalist hired labor on his own terms, or dismissed workers at will, without notice, without bothering as to what happened to either the worker or the city under such inhuman conditions. In a memorandum dated 1684 the Chief of Police of Paris referred to the "frightful misery that afflicts the greater part of the population of this great city." Between forty and sixty-five thousand were reduced to outright beggary. There was nothing exceptional about Paris. When Herman Melville, as a boy, visited the prosperous city of Liverpool in the eighteen-thirties, he found, as he describes in 'Redburn,' a woman with two babes at her breast dying in a cellar opening under the sidewalk. Despite his efforts to obtain aid, no one would succour these creatures. They were removed only when their dead bodies stank.

But in the end, without any contrivance on their own part, the proletariat had their unpremeditated revenge: the standards that were first applied to the dwellings of the poor were, by the nineteenth century, progressively embodied in the homes of the middle and upper classes. The first multi-family tenement building was erected in New York, for the lowest income group, on Cherry Street in 1835: it covered ninety per cent of the lot and standardized airless and insanitary conditions. Within a generation this new kind of dwelling was offered to the well-to-do groups, as the smartest product of fashion, the Paris flat. There was undoubtedly a place in a city like New York for smaller quarters for the individual bachelor or small family, collectively managed: the flat itself with all the rooms on one floor is a convenient arrangement of a modest dwelling place. But the new flats were not created on the old shallow house plan, two rooms deep: like the dwellings of the poor they occupied the larger part of the plot, and instead of providing the amenity of collective open spaces and gardens, they offered, for most of the rooms, a mere air-shaft, or, with further building in the neighborhood, the rear wall of another flat, just as badly designed.

This indifference to the elementary necessities of hygiene or amenity characterized the development of the commercial town: hence the mordant commentary of Patrick Geddes, summing up the whole downward movement of building and housing during the nineteenth century, under this one-sided preoccupation with rent and profit: "Slum, semi-slum and super-slum, to this has come the Evolution of Cities." In the course of time the rate of return even for the quarters of the rich was almost as favorable from a commercial standpoint as the miserable madeover houses or tenements of the poor.

The final proof of this degradation of housing through the application of capitalist standards came, during the nineteenth century, from philanthropy: here the Victorian experience repeated the earlier demonstration of the Fuggerei. When the first model housing was introduced by a charitable group in New York, in the eighteen-fifties, the plan, as a matter of course, produced inside rooms that had no light except from a window opening on an outside room. Even in terms of the mean offerings to the underpaid workers then current, this model tenement proved so vile that it soon became the favored resort of thieves and prostitutes.

This caricature might seem an accident, had the same tale not been repeated in a respectable form in the model dwellings erected by George E. Peabody in London through the second part of the nineteenth century, and imitated widely by other groups and public bodies. The Peabody Buildings had a minimum of light, air, sanitation: but no more than a minimum; for instead of being two or three stories high, like the typical London dwelling in the poorer parts of the city, these model dwellings were four and five stories high: incorporating a density that corresponded, not to human needs, but to the cost of land. The court between the buildings was paved from wall to wall. This not only prohibited even the most pinched garden, but was protected further by a regulation that prevented children from using the meager space to play in.

Peabody's well-meaning efforts in turn set a pattern of blight for further housing for the lower-income groups. Even where visual open spaces are now provided in such 'model' schemes, with buildings covering only fifteen or twenty per cent of the area, the density of occupation, in structures ten to fifteen stories high, remains a slum density: from 300 to 450 people per acre. This produces a dearth of usable land for park and playground in the neighborhood almost as serious as it was in the vile and dirty quarters the new buildings replace. The fact that these buildings all too quickly turn into slums should surprise no one except their one-eyed planners, who have no insight into the nature of either a home or a neighborhood, nor yet a city.

8 : THE FORMS OF GETTING AND

SPENDING

With the coming of capitalist enterprise, the older forms of the market did not entirely disappear in the Western World; but they were henceforth restricted largely to provision merchants. Even in the New World such markets were often gathered together under one roof, sometimes actually imitating European market halls, as in New York, Philadelphia, Washington, and Baltimore; while Faneuil Hall in Boston may be considered a direct continuation of the old world market.

In general it was only in the poorer quarters that one could still buy a dress, a pair of trousers, or a stove from an open cart, though in Paris, more tenacious of medieval habits than would appear on the surface, the department stores were compelled to open up street-stands, at least in the lower middle-class neighborhoods. But market squares had no place in the new urban layout: neither the traffic circles of the baroque plan nor the endless corridor avenue of the commercial plan favored that kind of pedestrian concentration.

The open air shop, the outlet for the workroom in the rear, tended to disappear, too: the new type of shop took shape behind glass windows, greatly enlarged to cover the whole front and serve as a center of display. No effort was spared to decorate the interior smartly, particularly in the more modish commodities. To fit up a pastry-cook's shop with plate glass windows and pier glasses and glass lanterns and twenty-five sconces for candles and six large silver salvers, and to paint the ceiling and carve the columns and gild the lanterns, took a pretty sum. It is a modern custom, observes Daniel Defoe in 'The Compleat English Tradesman,' to "have tradesmen lay out two-thirds of their fortune in fitting up their shops. . . . 'Tis a small matter to lay out two or three, nay five hundred pounds."

The display market for goods already made, rather than produced on the order system, had already come into existence: from the seventeenth century on, it gradually encroached into one line after another, hastening the tempo of sale and placing a premium upon the visual enticement of the buyer. The special market day lingered on in rural neighborhoods; but in the commercial town every day was market day. Buying and selling became not merely an incidental traffic in the conveyance of goods from producer to consumer: it became one of the principal preoccupations of all classes. 'Marketing' rested on the basis of domestic needs: 'shopping' was a less urgent, a more frivolous occupation. Shopping furnished excitement: it afforded a special occasion for the lady of the house to dress up, to sally forth, to exhibit her own person.

"I have heard," said Defoe, still obviously shocked by the practice, "that some ladies, and these, too, persons of good note, have taken their coaches and spent a whole afternoon in Ludgate Street or Covent Garden, only to divert themselves in going from one mercer's shop to another, to look upon their fine silks and to rattle and banter the shopkeepers, having not so much as the least occasion, much less intention, to buy anything."

As the permanent market took form both producer and consumer tended to become more anonymous: it was the middleman who made a name for himself by anticipating the idiosyncrasies of the buyer or by manipulating his taste and judgment. To avoid striking in the dark, a new patron and purchaser assumed control of the market: Dame Fashion. Again I must quote the invaluable Defoe: "Every tailor invents new fashions, the mercer studies new patterns, the weavers weave them into beautiful and gay figures, and stores himself with a vast variety to allure the fancy; the coachmaker contrives new machines, chairs, Berlins, flies, etc., all to prompt the whimsies and unaccountable pride of the gentry. . . . The upholder [upholsterer] does the like in furniture, till he draws the gay ladies to such an excess of Folly that they must have their houses new furnished every year; everything that has been longer than a year must be called old, and to have their fine lodgings seen by a person of any figure above twice over, looks ordinary and mean."

Money was supreme: the customs of the market were not confined to the shops. Again le Vicomte d'Avenel, whose history of property gives invaluable documentation of goods and prices, has put the matter well. "It was in the past, under the ancient regime, from the end of the Middle Ages to the Revolution, when force did not exercise a great place and when public opinion counted for little, that money ruled in France. Almost everything could be bought, power and honors, civil and military employment, and the nobility itself, whose titles were inseparable from the ground upon which they rested. It was necessary to be rich to become somebody, and if the favor of a prince occasionally distinguished a poor man, it would at the same stroke make him rich, since riches were the ordinary consequence of power."

Life, even aristocratic life, expressed itself most easily in terms of trade and money. In a moral homily of the sixteenth century on serving men, note the figure of the very opening passage: "In this Bourse or Exchange of Human Affairs, which consisteth (as it were) altogether in merchandise, buying and selling, it is very meet that there should be all manner conditions and callings . . . summoned on forfeiture of ten pounds on Issues to appear, with money and ware always ready, to maintain the mundane market." Life was like that. By hook or crook, by trade or theft or public corruption or financial enterprise, one got hold of money: "rapine, avarice, expense," made life "mean handy-work of craftsman, cook, or groom!" Wordsworth's sonnet was a compact indictment.

In the great capital cities, too large for people to know their neighbors, the standards of the market came generally to prevail. People sought by overt display to make a decisive impression as to their station in life, their taste, their prosperity: every individual, every class, put on a front. Fashion is, so to say, the uniform of the day, and well-to-do people wore this uniform in the home or the street with the same discipline as the soldier on his military parade. Venice had set the pace in dictating personal fashions, thanks to the fabled charm of her courtesans; Paris took up these duties in the seventeenth century; and thereafter each national capital served as pattern for the rest of the country. Part of the economic use of the capital city, from the standpoint of the great factors and importers, was to discredit local goods, which varied in pattern, in color, in stuff, in texture, in decoration, in accordance with local traditions, and give circulation to those in use at the capital. Slick commercial frippery undermined the sobrieties of craftsmanship, even as it annulled the traditional preferences, or idiosyncrasies, of maker and customer.

Some hint of this state had already become plain in the sixteenth century; for Stow is at pains to "answer the accusation of those men, which charge *London* with the loss and decay of many (or most) of the ancient cities, corporate towns, and markets within this realm. . . . As for retailers thereof, and handicraftsmen, it is no marvel if they abandon country towns and resort to London; for not only the court, which is nowadays much greater and more gallant than in former times . . . but also by occasion thereof the gentlemen of all shires do fly and flock to the city, the younger sort of them to see and show vanity, and the elder to save the cost and charge of hospitality and housekeeping." Fashion competition, which was the life of trade, was also largely the death of the customary industries of the provincial towns. Eventually they were forced to produce for the anonymous distant market or lose their industries entirely. The effect of this is observable in our irregional system of production and distribution down to the present day.

In this economy, the centralization of the baroque capital, which involved costly wastes in transport, now became a special virtue. "The magnitude of the city of London adds very considerably to the Inland Trade, for as the City is the center of our trade, so all the manufactures are brought hither, and hence circulated again to all the country. . . ." "How many thousands," Defoe exclaims again in another place, "I might say how many hundreds of thousands of men and horses are employed in the carrying and re-carrying to and from London the growth of England and the importations of foreign countries; and how many of these would stand still and want business . . . if this great city was divided into fifteen cities . . . and they were situated in so many different places remote from one another, where the countryside within 20 or 30 miles round would be sufficient for them and able to supply them, and where every port would import its own goods from abroad."

This last passage is a succinct explanation of the difference between the medieval urban economy and the new commercial economy: no better could be offered. But in terms of social energetics and cultural life, what Defoe took for a eulogy is actually a damning indictment.

The expansion of the market has been one of the most characteristic attributes of the commercial regime: it is involved in the whole scheme of substituting vicarious satisfactions for direct ones, and money goods for life experiences. By the eighteenth century, the public markets and producers' shops of the medieval town were being converted into specialized shops under continuous operation. Even at this early date in Paris, in the reign of Louis XV, a banker named Kromm founded a department store with some two or three hundred employees. In 1844, a modern department store, the Ville de France, opened in Paris with a hundred and fifty employees on its staff.

If the vitality of an institution may be gauged by its architecture, the department store was one of the most vital institutions in this commercial regime. One of the first large buildings to employ iron columns instead of a masonry wall was the A. T. Stewart department store in New York; while Schinkel's design for a Berlin department store in the eighteen-thirties, though never executed, was far ahead of the labored traditionalism of Messel's overpraised Wertheim store in Berlin. Finally, one of the best utilitarian buildings of our period, a radical departure in design, was Sullivan's Schlesinger and Meyer Building (now Carson, Pirie, Scott, and Company) in Chicago.

The department store offered the buyer the greatest possible number of wares under one roof and diversified the temptations to buy at the same time as it concentrated the opportunity. Thus it became in effect a many-storied marketplace. Even more, it served as an immense World's Fair of art and industry in which all the exhibits were on sale.

But it is hardly surprising that the chief architectural forms produced by the commercial city were based on abstract units of space: the front foot and the cubic foot. With no essential structural re-arrangement the hotel, the apartment house, the department store, and the office building were convertible, one into the other. Where speculative profits from the sale of buildings proved sufficiently tempting, convertibility would give way, in the end, to replaceability: every part of the structure would be designed not with a view to long time service, but with a view to its being wrecked and replaced by an even higher and more profitable structure, within a single generation, sometimes even more quickly. Capitalism, in its effects upon cities, is like that aberration of human physiology known to medicine as the stomach that digests itself.

Commercial enterprise produced only one form during the nineteenth century that did not answer to its great criterion of convertibility and continued speculative increase; and this form, one notes without surprise, proved to be an abortive one, and for long ceased to be copied or improved. This was the glass-covered shopping arcade: an attempt to find a new structure, utilizing the new achievements in iron frames and glass walls that modern technology offered. In the early part of the nineteenth century, specimens of this kind of arcade established themselves in every commercial city, from those in Naples and Genoa to the Burlington Arcade (1819) in London. The shopping arcade in Brussels is one of the longest; while the most magnificent is that great cruciform structure in Milan, a generous concourse, with its shops, its cafés, its restaurants. These new structures had the special merit of taking shopping off the crowded street, with its confusion of vehicles and noise: an admirable example of functional planning. The idea of such an arcade was put forward, not merely by James Silk Buckingham, the projector of a model Victorian town, but also by Ebenezer Howard, in his first outline of the Garden City, where he wished to place the whole shopping area under glass. The projector of a 'model town,' Pullman, Illinois, actually built such an arcade; and curiously enough, one was even built in the little country town of Hitchin, near Howard's first Garden City, Letchworth.

Though most of these shopping arcades are still prosperously in existence, they have not been widely imitated; or rather, it is only with the creation of anti-urban shopping centers, built for the accommodation of motor traffic, that this conception has been brought back in a modified form. The real weakness of the shopping arcade, from the standpoint of commercial practice, was its functional exactitude: it was good for only its original purpose, and was, from its very nature, unconvertible. That violated the first canon of design for the commercial city.

9: AMSTERDAM'S EXEMPLARY
CONTRAST

There is one city that bears witness to the commercial spirit at its best, before it had completely dissociated itself from the customary controls and the collective commitments of its medieval prototype. That city is Amsterdam. The fact that it was not widely imitated shows that it was not capitalism alone, but a complex of institutions, personalities, and opportunities, coming together at a unique moment, that made that city one of the greatest examples of the town planner's art. Even so, it remains capitalism's one outstanding urban achievement, rivalled only by elegant Bath.

If one takes Amsterdam as the most important example of a city that effected the transition from protectionism to commercial competition without losing form, this is not to disparage the vitality of some of Amsterdam's rivals, like Delft and Haarlem. It is rather to show, by taking the hardest example, that with the most rapid commercial expansion and most rapid growth of population, the physical growth of the post-medieval city need not have raised insuperable obstacles to orderly design. Throughout its main period of expansion, Amsterdam did not lose its unity; and though its medieval quarter was allowed to fall into decay, the city as a whole did not deteriorate, except for a brief period in the nineteenth century when commercial rapacity and dismal taste produced quarters whose ugliness and human insufficiency rivalled those of more typical nineteenth-century industrial towns.

The technical development of the Dutch city was based on the marvellous control of water, not merely for communication and transport, but for the sculpture of the landscape. Long before the mechanical apparatus for digging and transporting earth was perfected, the Dutch, by dogged hand labor, had raised many of their cities on mounds, above the waters; and the same application of collective energy caused them to protect the land against flood. The control of both the sea and the inland waters had begun in a minor fashion, Gerald Burke relates, as far back as the eighth century; and though the Dutch needed the co-operation of the windmill to solve the problem of water control in their land, much of it below sea level, by the eleventh century, even before this pumping engine was introduced, the technics of dyke-building and drainage had been improved, and a considerable area of land reclaimed.

This work from the beginning required co-operative management, both in building and in maintaining the dykes: that need resulted in the creation of Water Catchment Boards, in the thirteenth century—independent authorities, still in operation today. Since the water is so close to the surface, the houses of Dutch cities must be built on piles: the difficulty of creating these foundations kept the Dutch cities from spreading at the random will of the property owner. Under municipal direction, the growing city was opened up, section by section, and supplied with collective services. Within this system of collective action and orderly restraint, the dynamic forces of capitalism operated, almost in spite of themselves, toward a public end. Amsterdam for this reason might be taken as a striking example of the value of a mixed economy, in which public and private enterprise complement each other.

Amsterdam began as a community with the diking or damming of the little river, the Amstel. The original urban core was contained within the crescent canal that surrounded the old city, not walled until 1482: but in Dutch cities the dyke, in fact, took the place of the wall in promoting cohesion and common effort. When trade shifted from the Baltic to the North Sea, following the unexplained migration of the herring, Amsterdam, which was reached by a long protected water route, not exposed either to storms or to piracy, began to gain as a port for trans-shipment of goods. So when Antwerp was disabled by the Spaniards in the sixteenth century, the Amsterdam Bourse became the center of the money market. Up to the end of that century Amsterdam's growth had been steadily impeded apparently by the struggle with Spain. But toward the end of it, a whole generation before the exodus of the Spaniards, Amsterdam's mercantile prowess was directed toward its own urban development.

Plainly, it was not for nothing that Amsterdam had absorbed all the commercial lessons the Italians could teach: wares consigned to Amsterdam, Violet Barbour informs us, could usually count on quick sale, prompt payment, and broad choice of opportunities to invest the proceeds. Here, too, storage facilities were ample and merchants who wished to store their goods till they got better prices could borrow money on the warehouse receipts; while money itself was so well managed that investors were happy to accept only a two per cent return in Amsterdam, as against many times that amount on exchanges where the capital might be lost.

Note the results: a chamber of assurance was set up in 1602, a new bourse in 1608, and a lending bank in 1614. Population more than quadrupled between 1567, when it was about 30,000, and 1630, when it was around 115,000. The necessary enlargement of the city provided the opportunity for a new order of planning; while the means for building was furnished by the prosperity of the ruling merchants. Even war was no obstacle to this growth: Amsterdam had become the chief market for grain, naval supplies, and munitions, the sinews of war: her capitalists even traded freely with the enemy, so that whoever lost on the battlefield, the Dutch would gain on the exchange.

The excellence of the new plan had its immediate foundation in the Building Ordinance of 1565: this proved so satisfactory in its workings that it remained in force till the early nineteenth century, when its abandonment was probably responsible for some of the sadder aspects of Amsterdam. This ordinance required, among other things, that the piling foundations had to be approved by municipal officers before the building could commence, that each plot should have its own privy, and that streets and footpaths laid out by the council had to be paid for by plot holders, the costs being in proportion to the width of frontage. This carried further the sanitary provisions enacted, in the face of multi-family overcrowding, in 1533, which made mandatory that drain pipes and sewers be open to inspection. In other words, this plan was not a surface improvement: it was the final expression of a more thoroughgoing attention to the conditions of health and social life.

The new plan had begun in 1585 with the laying out of the Heerrengracht, on the site of the removed Bastions, to the north: that canal, serving both for traffic and open space, set a new dimension for such planning: eighty feet wide. This beginning was enlarged by Hendrikje Staets, in the 'Plan of the Three Canals,' a plan approved by the municipality in 1607. Neither the first canal, nor the second, the Keisergracht (1593), had provided the spider-web system of canals that was finally built; but in the meanwhile the geometric plan of Coeworden, Amsterdam's bastion, may have impressed the planners. As the work proceeded, the carrying through of a system of concentric canals, traversed by canals and streets directed toward the old center, suggested itself. Though at one point, in the interests of creating a park, a plan was put forward that would have cut into this symmetrical arrangement and broken the transportation network, in the end the functional disposition and the geometric figure were perceived for what they were: a unity. In expressing that unity the whole inner city took final form.

The man largely responsible for carrying out the Plan of the Three Canals was Daniel Stolpaert, a surveyor-architect (1615-1676). He translated it from an image on paper to a many-dimensioned social reality: for it was he who allocated the frontages along the three monumental canals to large business houses and town houses for the merchants, buildings that were then of the same scale and dignity. It was he who assigned the building blocks formed by the radial and circumferential canals to lower middle-class and artisan dwellings. He preserved, too, the frontages in the harbor proper and along the Browersgracht for warehouses; while the new area to the west, the Jordaan, was zoned for industry and for certain charitable foundations. What distinguished this plan from the superficial and perniciously wholesale zoning of American cities in the present century was that the planning and the building were part of a single reciprocal operation.

But note: the carrying out of the plan was the task of private enterprise, undertaken by individuals and small groups, for profit, though sometimes by religious organizations to provide homes for the aged and the indigent, or by big commercial organizations seeking to provide sufficient housing for their employees: occasionally, if rarely, the work was undertaken by housing societies. It was this continuous application of planning and building that kept the rapid growth of Amsterdam from being as disastrous to good housing and municipal order as was the rapid growth of London. Not least important about this plan, which links it to L'Enfant's Washington, was the timely reservation of sites for local churches and marketplaces. If that example alone had been followed in later planning elsewhere, it would have both economized the costs and improved the character of new cities and city extensions.

The Plan of the Three Canals was a miracle of spaciousness, compactness, intelligible order. It accepted all that was valid in baroque planning, with just sufficient variation in the individual units, combined with the rich tracery of trees bordering the canals, to take the curse off the military regimentation of baroque classicism. The successive breaks in direction of the spider-web plan keep the distant vista from being empty and oppressive. The canals themselves were eighty to eighty-eight feet wide: set off by paved, tree-lined walks from the buildings that lined them. These buildings were based on lots that averaged twenty-six feet in width, thus giving rise to the ample, three-windowed façade, with far more opening than wall, which brought sunlight into the depths of the house. There was a minimum distance of 160 feet between the backs of buildings: and the garden space for each lot was therefore around 26 by 80 feet: a generous space for both lovers of gardens and those who sought outdoor repose. The maximum site coverage was fifty-six per cent. This plan brought the delights of the suburb, its open space, its gardens, its trees, within the closer compass of the inner city.

Here in the new quarters of Amsterdam was the esthetic culmination of five centuries of collective effort in commanding water and making land. Order had spread from polders to city. Nothing so thoroughly and uniformly good as Amsterdam had previously made its way into city design, on the same scale, anywhere. Even the Dutch themselves did not for long live up to the great example before them.

The order created by the Plan of the Three Canals remained in advance of any other urban planning, taken as a whole, for three centuries. It is only now that it is seriously threatened by the religion of the motor car, which is ready to sacrifice the utilities and delights of city life for the development of space-eating facilities for getting in and out of town—though the very multiplication of such facilities reduces the effective speed of the traffic it seeks to promote. Like the boulevards of Paris, the handsome arbored ways that line the great canals have been reduced to parking lots: a depressing spectacle.

To deal with this problem of maintaining the historic core would require a chapter in itself. Here I must qualify my admiration for the success of the Plan by calling attention to the place where commercial profits, not civic ends, controlled the development of Amsterdam and set a precedent that worsened with the advance of capitalism. This was in the Jordaan area, to the southwest of the city. Here, instead of creating a new quarter, on the same principles as the old city, the planners followed the quite different layout of the old fields, cutting in narrow diagonals across the new lines of established growth. And since the Council did not acquire this area, a group of merchants developed it as a speculation, with narrow canals, and narrow streets, not eighty feet wide, but something like eighteen. Worse still, the land is lower than the rest of the city, because the developers cheapened the operation by failing to build the surface up in the customary manner.

Into these cramped neighborhoods, on equally cramped plots, they crowded houses, where the poorest workers, or the immigrant French protestants, the Spanish and Portuguese Jews, found a minimal accommodation. Whereas the merchants' houses boasted a minimum 160 feet between the *backs,* the entire width of the workers' blocks was only 120 feet. While the standard density per net residential acre was usually not more than five houses to the acre in small Dutch towns, or twenty, at most, in big cities, the new workers' housing was many times higher. To have done better than this for the people housed, the builders would have had to forgo profit, or the municipality—the builders in their civic guise—would have had to provide a subsidy. Capitalism, almost by definition, had no answer to this problem: indeed, it refused to admit the possibility of any answer, even in non-capitalist terms, till the second half of the nineteenth century.

From the example of Amsterdam I am tempted to draw two contradictory conclusions. One is the very obvious one, that the benefits of capitalism were confined to those on the inside, the merchants, traders, financiers, investors; and that it was no part of a capitalist economy to provide urban quarters for the working classes except on terms that would furnish a handsome profit: that is to say, by overcrowding, skimping, niggardly provisions even for light and air, a general worsening of the whole urban environment. Where, however, the income of the householder sufficed, good accommodations might be produced, provided that profit were not the only motive behind the building. What made the merchants' quarters of Amsterdam so excellent, was the maintenance of corporate vigilance in planning the layout and supervising the whole ensemble with a view to the public good: this was a happy bequest left over from the old medieval economy. Responsible public direction working for well-conceived public ends is essential for the foundation and development of all urban communities.

The worst manifestations of capitalism in urban development came about when it became dominant and exclusive, parading itself in its brute nakedness, without historic clothes of any kind, except patched and tattered castoffs. At that point, commercial success showed itself for what it was and still largely is: civic destitution. From the standpoint of an expanding capitalist economy, indeed, capitalism's prospects of profits, which rested on continuous turnover, demanded the continued destruction of old urban structures, for the sake of their profitable replacement at ever higher rents. Heavy long term investments in buildings whose spacious surroundings would guarantee their continuity were not attractive to the capitalist investor, once he had emancipated himself from considerations of a safe return. In the poorer quarters, following the example of his great Roman progenitor Crassus, the capitalist even hastened the pace of destruction by begrudging the necessary investment for repair and renewal. For the twentieth century, unceasing destruction and replacement became the new rhythm of city development. In this, capitalism's role was to liquidate the container.

But during the two or three centuries in which capitalism mingled with older institutions and was colored by them, its dynamism brought about some of the best residential planning that any city had yet boasted; and in cities like Bath, this new order reached down even into humbler middle-class quarters. A great part of the elegant new building of London, Bath, Edinburgh, and lesser places during the eighteenth century was, in fact, speculative building; though some of the best of it, like Adams' Adelphi Terrace in London, and Bullfinch's similar terrace in Boston, were at first commercial failures.

Unfortunately, the original urban functions all ceased to have a significant place in the commercial city: older institutions were either pushed into the interstices left by business enterprise, or were forced to adopt the ways and methods native to such enterprise, transforming their traditional goods into abstract counters, giving to publicity, advertising, showmanship, numerical triumphs (attendance, enrollment, contributions, income) what they originally gave to the educational and cultural purposes that these by-products lamely referred to. In our time the ultimate fate of the commercial city is to become a backdrop for advertising: a fate well symbolized by the recent transformation of New York's two railroad stations from great public monuments to exhibition halls for a commercialism whose tawdriness by contrast gives almost a regal dignity to the financiers who originally conceived these stations with some sense of public obligation.

CHAPTER FIFTEEN

Paleotechnic Paradise: Coketown

1: THE BEGINNINGS OF COKETOWN

Up to the nineteenth century, there had been a rough balance of activities within the city. Though work and trade were always important, religion and art and play claimed their full share of the townsman's energies. But the tendency to concentrate on economic activities, and to regard as waste the time or effort spent on other functions, at least outside the home, had been growing steadily since the sixteenth century. If capitalism tended to expand the province of the marketplace and turn every part of the city into a negotiable commodity, the change from organized urban handicraft to large scale factory production transformed the industrial towns into dark hives, busily puffing, clanking, screeching, smoking for twelve and fourteen hours a day, sometimes going around the clock. The slavish routine of the mines, whose labor was an intentional punishment for criminals, became the normal environment of the new industrial worker. None of these towns heeded the old saw, 'All work and no play makes Jack a dull boy.' Coketown specialized in producing dull boys.

As witness to the immense productivity of the machine the slag heaps and rubbish heaps reached mountainous proportions, while the human beings whose labor made these achievements possible were crippled and killed almost as fast as they would have been on a battlefield. The new industrial city had many lessons to teach; but for the urbanist its chief lesson was in what to avoid. By reaction against industrialism's misdemeanors, the artists and reformers of the nineteenth century finally arrived at a better conception of human needs and urban possibilities. In the end the disease stimulated the antibodies needed to overcome it.

The generating agents of the new city were the mine, the factory, and the railroad. But their success in displacing every traditional concept of the city was due to the fact that the solidarity of the upper classes was visibly breaking up: the Court was becoming supernumerary, and even capitalist speculation turned from trade to industrial exploitation to achieve the greatest possibilities of financial aggrandizement. In every quarter, the older principles of aristocratic education and rural culture were replaced by a single-minded devotion to industrial power and pecuniary success, sometimes disguised as democracy.

The baroque dream of power and luxury had at least human outlets, human goals: the tangible pleasures of the hunt, the dinner table, the bed were always temptingly in view. The new conception of human destiny, as the utilitarians projected it, had little place for even sensual delights: it rested on a doctrine of productive exertion, consumptive avarice, and physiological denial; and it took the form of a wholesale disparagement of the joys of life, similar to that necessitated by war, during a siege. The new masters of society scornfully turned their backs on the past and all the accumulations of history and addressed themselves to creating a future, which, on their own theory of progress, would be just as contemptible once it, too, was past—and would be just as ruthlessly scrapped.

Between 1820 and 1900 the destruction and disorder within great cities is like that of a battlefield, proportionate to the very extent of their equipment and the strength of the forces employed. In the new provinces of city building, one must now keep one's eyes on the bankers, industrialists, and the mechanical inventors. They were responsible for most of what was good and almost all that was bad. In their own image, they created a new type of city: that which Dickens, in 'Hard Times,' called Coketown. In a greater or lesser degree, every city in the Western World was stamped with the archetypal characteristics of Coketown. Industrialism, the main creative force of the nineteenth century, produced the most degraded urban environment the world had yet seen; for even the quarters of the ruling classes were befouled and overcrowded.

The political base of this new type of urban aggregation rested on three main pillars: the abolition of the guilds and the creation of a state of permanent insecurity for the working classes: the establishment of the competitive open market for labor and for the sale of goods: the maintenance of foreign dependencies as source of raw materials, necessary to new industries, and as a ready market to absorb the surplus of mechanized industry. Its economic foundations were the exploitation of the coal mine, the vastly increased production of iron, and the use of a steady, reliable—if highly inefficient—source of mechanical power: the steam engine.

Actually, these technical advances depended socially upon the invention of new forms of corporate organization and administration. The joint stock company, the limited liability investment, the delegation of administrative authority under divided ownerships, and control of the process by budget and audit were all matters of co-operative political technique whose success was not due to the genius of any particular individual or group of individuals. This holds true, too, of the mechanical organization of factories, which greatly augmented the efficiency of production. But the basis of this system, in the ideology of the period, was thought to be the atomic individual: to guard his property, to protect his rights, to ensure his freedom of choice and freedom of enterprise, was the whole duty of government.

This myth of the untrammeled individual was in fact the democratization of the baroque conception of the despotic Prince: now every enterprising man sought to be a despot in his own right: emotional despots like the romantic poets: practical despots like the business men. Adam Smith in 'The Wealth of Nations' still had a comprehensive theory of political society: he had a correct conception of the economic basis of the city and valid insight into the non-profit-making economic functions. But his interest gave way, in practice, to the aggressive desire to increase the wealth of individuals: that was the be-all and the end-all of the new Malthusian struggle for existence.

Perhaps the most gigantic fact in the whole urban transition was the displacement of population that occurred over the whole planet. For this movement and resettlement was accompanied by another fact of colossal import: the astounding rise in the rate of population increase. This increase affected industrially backward countries like Russia, with a predominantly rural population and a high rate of births and deaths, quite as much as it affected progressive countries that were predominantly mechanized and de-ruralized. The general increase in numbers was accompanied by a drawing of the surplus into cities, and an immense enlargement of the area of the bigger centers. Urbanization increased in almost direct proportion to industrialization: in England and New England it finally came about that over eighty per cent of the entire population was living in centers with more than twenty-five hundred population.

Into the newly opened lands of the planet, originally peopled by military camps, trading posts, religious missions, small agricultural settlements, there came an inundation of immigrants from countries suffering from political oppression and economic poverty. This movement of people, this colonization of territory, had two forms: land pioneering and industry pioneering. The first filled the sparsely occupied regions of America, Africa, Australia, of Siberia and, later, Manchuria: the second brought the overplus into the new industrial villages and towns. In most cases, these types came in successive waves.

The extensive land migration in turn helped to bring to the European system of agriculture the resources of hitherto untapped parts of the world:

particularly a whole series of new energy crops, maize and potato—and that pungent agent of relaxation and social ceremony, the tobacco plant. Moreover the colonization of tropical and subtropical lands added a further energy crop now supplied to Europe for the first time on a grand scale—cane-sugar.

This enormous increase in the food supply was what made possible the increase of population. And the external colonization in new rural territories thus helped to create that surplus of men and women and children which went toward the internal colonization of the new industrial towns and commercial emporia. Villages expanded into towns; towns became metropolises. The number of urban centers multiplied; the number of cities with populations above five hundred thousand increased, too. Extraordinary changes of scale took place in the masses of buildings and the areas they covered: vast structures were erected almost overnight. Men built in haste, and had hardly time to repent of their mistakes before they tore down their original structures and built again, just as heedlessly. The newcomers, babies or immigrants, could not wait for new quarters: they crowded into whatever was offered. It was a period of vast urban improvisation: makeshift hastily piled upon makeshift.

Mark that the rapid growth of cities was no mere New World phenomenon. Indeed, the rate of city growth was swifter in Germany after 1870, when the paleotechnic revolution was in full swing there, than in new countries like the United States: this despite the fact that the United States was then steadily receiving immigrants. Though the nineteenth century was the first to rival the early Middle Ages in large scale land colonization and settlement, the premises upon which these enterprises were conducted were far more primitive than those of the eleventh century. Colonization by communities, except in the case of little idealistic groups, the most widely successful of which were the Mormons, was no longer the rule. Every man was for himself; and the Devil, if he did not take the hindmost, at least reserved for himself the privilege of building the cities.

Here in the new industrial centers was a chance to build on a firm foundation and make a fresh start: such a chance as democracy had in the eighteenth century claimed for itself in political government. Almost everywhere that opportunity was fumbled. In an age of technical progress the city, as a social and political unit, lay outside the circle of invention. Except for utilities such as gas mains, water pipes, and sanitary equipment, often belatedly introduced, often slipshod, always ill-distributed, the industrial city could claim no important improvements over the seventeenth-century town. Indeed, the most wealthy and 'progressive' metropolises often denied themselves elementary necessities of life like light and air that even backward villages still possessed. Until 1838 neither Manchester nor Birmingham even functioned politically as incorporated boroughs: they were man-heaps, machine-warrens, not agents of human association for the promotion of a better life.

2: MECHANIZATION AND *ABBAU*

Before we inquire how this vast flood of people found urban accommodation, let us examine the assumptions and attitudes that people brought to the new task of city building.

The leading philosophy of life was the offspring of two entirely dissimilar types of experience. One was the rigorous concept of mathematical order derived from the renewed study of the motions of the heavenly bodies: the highest pattern of mechanical regularity. The other was the physical process of breaking up, pulverizing, calcining, smelting, which the alchemists, working with the mechanically advanced mine workers of the late Middle Ages, had turned from a mere mechanical process into the routine of scientific investigation. As formulated by the new philosophers of nature, this new order had no place for organisms or social groups, still less for the human personality. Neither institutional patterns nor esthetic forms, neither history nor myth, derived from the external analysis of the 'physical world.' The machine alone could embody this order: only industrial capital boasted corporate form.

So immersed are we, even at this late date, in the surviving medium of paleotechnic beliefs that we are not sufficiently conscious of their profound abnormality. Few of us correctly evaluate the destructive imagery that the mine carried into every department of activity, sanctioning the anti-vital and the anti-organic. Before the nineteenth century the mine had, quantitatively speaking, only a subordinate part in man's industrial life. By the middle of the century it had come to underlie every part of it. And the spread of mining was accompanied by a general loss of form throughout society: a degradation of the landscape and a no less brutal disordering of the communal environment.

Agriculture creates a balance between wild nature and man's social needs. It restores deliberately what man subtracts from the earth; while the plowed field, the trim orchard, the serried vineyard, the vegetables, the grains, the flowers, are all examples of disciplined purpose, orderly growth, and beautiful form. The process of mining, on the other hand, is destructive: the immediate product of the mine is disorganized and inorganic; and what is once taken out of the quarry or the pithead cannot be replaced.

Add to this the fact that continued occupation in agriculture brings cumulative improvements to the landscape and a finer adaptation of it to human needs; while mines as a rule pass quickly from riches to exhaustion, from exhaustion to desertion, often within a few generations. Mining thus presents the very image of human discontinuity, here today and gone tomorrow, now feverish with gain, now depleted and vacant.

From the eighteen-thirties on, the environment of the mine, once restricted to the original site, was universalized by the railroad. Wherever the iron rails went, the mine and its debris went with them. Whereas the canals of the eotechnic phase, with their locks and bridges and tollhouses, with their trim banks and their gliding barges, had brought a new element of beauty into the rural landscape, the railroads of the paleotechnic phase made huge gashes: the cuts and embankments for the greater part long remained unplanted, and the wound in the earth was unhealed. The rushing locomotives brought noise, smoke, grit, into the hearts of the towns: more than one superb urban site, like Prince's Gardens in Edinburgh, was desecrated by the invasion of the railroad. And the factories that grew up alongside the railroad sidings mirrored the slatternly environment of the railroad itself. If it was in the mining town that the characteristic process of *Abbau*—mining or un-building—was seen at its purest, it was by means of the railroad that this process was extended by the third quarter of the nineteenth century to almost every industrial community.

The process of un-building, as William Morton Wheeler pointed out, is not unknown in the world of organisms. In un-building, a more advanced form of life loses its complex character, bringing about an evolution downward, toward simpler and less finely integrated organisms. "There is," observed Wheeler, "an evolution by atrophy as well as by increasing complication, and both processes may be going on simultaneously and at varying rates in the same organism."

This held precisely true of nineteenth-century society: it showed itself clearly in the organization of urban communities. A process of up-building, with increasing differentiation, integration, and social accommodation of the individual parts in relation to the whole was going on: an articulation within an ever-widening environment was taking place within the factory, and indeed within the entire economic order. Food-chains and production-chains of a complicated nature were being formed throughout the planet: ice travelled from Boston to Calcutta and tea journeyed from China to Ireland, whilst machinery and cotton goods and cutlery from Birmingham and Manchester found their way to the remotest corners of the earth. A universal postal service, fast locomotion, and almost instantaneous communication by telegraph and cable synchronized the activities of vast masses of men who had hitherto lacked the most rudimentary facilities for coordinating their tasks. This was accompanied by a steady differentiation of crafts, trades, organizations, and associations: mostly self-governing bodies, often legally incorporated. This significant communal development was masked by the fashionable theory of atomic individualism: so it rarely achieved an urban structure.

But at the same time, an *Abbau,* or un-building, was taking place, often at an even more rapid rate, in other parts of the environment: forests were slaughtered, soils were mined, whole animal species, such as the beaver, the bison, the wild pigeon, were practically wiped out, while the sperm whales and right whales were seriously decimated. Therewith the natural balance of organisms within their ecological regions was upset, and a lower and simpler biological order—sometimes marked by the complete extermination of the prevalent forms of life—followed Western man's ruthless exploitation of nature for the sake of his temporary and socially limited profit economy.

Above all, as we shall see, this un-building took place in the urban environment.

3: THE POSTULATES OF
UTILITARIANISM

In so far as there was any conscious political regulation of the growth and development of cities during the paleotechnic period, it was done in accord with the postulates of utilitarianism. The most fundamental of these postulates was a notion that the utilitarians had taken over, in apparent innocence, from the theologians: the belief that a divine providence ruled over economic activity and ensured, so long as man did not presumptuously interfere, the maximum public good through the dispersed and unregulated efforts of every private, self-seeking individual. The non-theological name for this pre-ordained harmony was laissez-faire.

To understand the uncouth disorder of the industrial town one must analyze the curious metaphysical preconceptions that dominated both the scientific and the practical life. 'Without design' was a laudatory term in the Victorian period. As in the decadent period of Greece, Chance had been elevated into a deity that was supposedly in control not only of human destiny, but of all natural processes as well. "The gist of Darwin's theory," wrote Ernst Haeckel, the biologist, "is this simple idea: that the struggle for existence in nature evolves new species *without design,* just as well as man produces new varieties in cultivation with design." It was by following what they presumed was nature's way that the industrialist and the municipal officer produced the new species of town, a blasted, de-natured man-heap adapted, not to the needs of life, but to the mythic 'struggle for existence'; an environment whose very deterioration bore witness to the ruthlessness and intensity of that struggle. There was no room for planning in the layout of these towns. Chaos does not have to be planned.

The historic justification for the laissez-faire reaction needs no demonstration now: it was an attempt to break through the network of stale privileges and franchises and trade regulations that the absolute State had imposed upon the decayed economic fabric and dwindling social morality of the medieval town. The new enterprisers had good reason to distrust the public spirit of a venal court or the social efficiency of the Circumlocution Offices of the growing taxation-bureaucracy. Hence the utilitarians sought to reduce governmental functions to a minimum: they wished to have a free hand in making investments, in building up industries, in buying land, in hiring and firing workers. Unfortunately, the pre-ordained harmony of the economic order turned out to be a superstition: the scramble for power remained a sordid scramble, and individual competition for ever-greater profits led the more successful to the unscrupulous practice of monopoly at the public expense. But design did not emerge.

In practice, the political equality that was slowly introduced into the Western polities from 1789 onward, and the freedom of initiative that was demanded by the industrialists were contradictory claims. To achieve political equality and personal freedom, strong economic limitations and political restraints were necessary. In countries where the experiment of equality was made without attempting to rectify annually the effects of the law of rent, the result was a stultification of the original purpose. In the United States, for example, the free bestowal of land upon settlers in 160-acre tracts under the Homestead Law did not lay the basis of a free polity: within a generation the unequal properties of the soil, the unequal talents of the users, had resulted in gross social inequalities. Without systematically removing the fundamental disparities that grew out of the private monopoly of land, the inheritance of large fortunes, the monopoly of patents, the only effect of laissez-faire was to supplement the old privileged classes with a new one.

The freedom demanded by the utilitarians was in reality freedom for unrestricted profits and private aggrandizement. Profits and rents were to be limited only by what the traffic would bear: decent customary rents and a just price were out of the question. Only hunger, distress, and poverty, Townsend observed in his commentary on the English Poor Laws, could prevail on the lower classes to accept the horrors of the sea and the battle-field; and only these same helpful stimuli would "spur and goad" them on to factory labor. The rulers, however, maintained an almost unbroken class front on any issue that concerned their pocketbooks as a class; and they never scrupled to act collectively when it was a question of beating down the working classes.

This theological belief in pre-ordained harmony had, however, an important result upon the organization of the paleotechnic town. It created the natural expectation that the whole enterprise should be conducted by private individuals, with a minimum amount of interference on the part of local or national governments. The location of factories, the building of quarters for the workers, even the supply of water and the collection of garbage, should be done exclusively by private enterprise seeking for private profit. Free competition was supposed to choose the correct location, provide the correct time-sequence in development, and create out of a thousand un-coordinated efforts a coherent social pattern. Or rather, none of these needs was regarded as worthy of rational appraisal and deliberate achievement.

Laissez-faire, even more than absolutism, destroyed the notion of a co-operative polity and a common plan. Did not the utilitarian expect the *effects* of rational design to appear from the unrestricted operation of conflicting random private interests? By giving rein to unrestricted competition, reason and co-operative order were to emerge: indeed rational planning, by preventing automatic adjustments, could, it was supposed, only interfere with the higher workings of a divine economic providence.

The main point to note now is that these doctrines undermined such municipal authority as had survived, and they discredited the city itself as anything more than a 'fortuitous concourse of atoms'—as the physics of the time erroneously described the universe—held together temporarily by motives of self-seeking and private profit. Even in the eighteenth century, before either the French Revolution or the coal-and-iron revolution had been consummated, it had become the fashion to discredit municipal authorities and to sneer at local interests. In the newly organized states, even those based on republican principles, only matters of national moment, organized by political parties, counted in men's hopes or dreams.

The time of the Enlightenment, as W. H. Riehl sharply said, was a period when people yearned for humanity and had no heart for their own people; when they philosophized about the state and forgot the community. "No period was more impoverished than the eighteenth century in the development of a common community spirit; the medieval community was dissolved and the modern was not yet ready. . . . In the satirical literature of the time, whoever wanted to portray a blockhead represented him as a Burgomaster, and if he wished to describe a meeting of Jackasses, he described a meeting of Town Councillors."

Urban growth had indeed begun, from industrial and commercial causes, even before the paleotechnic revolution was well started. In 1685, Manchester had about 6,000 people; in 1760, between 30,000 and 45,000. Birmingham had 4,000 at the first date and almost 30,000 in 1760. By 1801 Manchester's population was 72,275, and by 1851 it was 303,382. But once the concentration of factories abetted the growth of towns, the increase in the numbers became overwhelming. Since the increase produced extraordinary opportunities for profit making, there was nothing in the current traditions of society to curb this growth; or rather, there was everything to promote it.

4: THE TECHNICS OF AGGLOMERATION

The specialized industrial center originated as a spore, escaping from the corporate medieval town, either because of the nature of the industry— mining or glass-making—or because the monopolistic practices of the guilds prevented a new trade like machine knitting from springing up there. But by the sixteenth century, handicraft industry, too, was spreading through the countryside, particularly in England, in order to take advantage of cheap, unprotected cottage labor. So far had this practice gone that by 1554 an act to remedy the decay of corporate towns was passed, prohibiting anyone living in the country from disposing of his work by retail, except in fairs.

By the seventeenth century, even before the mechanization of spinning and weaving, the English cloth industries were dispersed in Shropshire and Worcestershire, with employers and workers both scattered in villages and market towns. Not merely did these industries escape from the town regulations: they escaped from the costly initiation fees and charitable dues of the guilds. With no customary wages, with no social security, the worker, as Adam Smith pointed out, was, under the discipline of starvation, fearful of losing his job. "If you would have your work tolerably executed, it must be done in the suburbs," he points out, "where the workmen, having no exclusive privilege, have nothing but their character to depend upon, and you must then smuggle it into town as best you can."

The increasing use of water power in production abetted the escape into upland regions where small, swift running streams, or rivers with falls, provided a head of water. Hence the textile industry tended to spread through the valleys of Yorkshire, or later along the Connecticut and the Merrimac in New England; and since the number of favorable sites in any one stretch was usually limited, relatively large plants, with factories four or five stories high, came in along with mechanization itself. A combination of cheap rural land, a docile, starvation-disciplined population, and a sufficient source of steady power filled the needs of the new industries.

But it took the better part of two centuries, from the sixteenth to the eighteenth, before all the agents of industrial agglomeration were developed in equal degree. Before this, the commercial advantages of the corporate town counterbalanced the industrial advantages of cheap power and cheap labor supplied by the factory village. Till the nineteenth century industry remained decentralized, in small workshops, scaled to agriculture: communities like Sudbury and country towns like Worcester in England.

Humanly speaking, some of the worst features of the factory system, the long hours, the monotonous work, the low wages, the systematic misappropriation of child labor, had been established under the decentralized eotechnic organization of production. Exploitation began at home. But water power and canal transportation did little damage to the landscape; and mining and smelting, as long as they remained small in scale and scattered, made scars that were easily healed. Even today, in the Forest of Dean, near the Severn, where the ancient practices of charcoal burning mingle with those of small scale mining, the mining villages are more comely than in more 'dynamic' areas, and both the mines and the slagheaps are easily hidden by trees or almost effaced by other vegetation. It was the change of scale, the unrestricted massing of populations and industries, that produced some of the most horrendous urban effects.

The use of Watt's steam engine as a prime mover, changed all this: particularly, it changed the scale and made feasible a far heavier concentration of both industries and workers, while it removed the worker himself farther from the rural base that gave the cottager with his garden an auxiliary supply of food and a touch of independence. The new fuel magnified the importance of the coal fields and fostered industry there or in places accessible by canal or railroad.

Steam worked most efficiently in big concentrated units, with the parts of the plant no more than a quarter of a mile from the power-center: every spinning machine or loom had to tap power from the belts and shafts worked by the central steam engine. The more units in a given area, the more efficient was the source of power: hence the tendency toward giantism. Big factories, such as those developed in Manchester, New Hampshire, from the eighteen-twenties onward—repeated in New Bedford and Fall River— could utilize the latest instruments of power production, whereas the smaller factories were at a technical disadvantage. A single factory might employ two hundred and fifty hands. A dozen such factories, with all the accessory instruments and services, were already the nucleus of a considerable town.

In their attempts to produce machine-made goods at low prices for consumption in the world market, the manufacturers cut costs at every point in order to increase profits. The most obvious place to begin this paring was in the wages of the workers. In the eighteenth century, as Robert Owen noted, even the most enlightened manufacturers made unsparing use of child labor and pauper labor: but when the age of child workers was legally regulated and the supply diminished, it became necessary to tap other sources. To have the necessary surplus of workers, to meet the extra demands in the busy seasons, it was important for industry to settle near a great center of population, for in a country village the support of the idle might fall directly upon the manufacturer himself, who often owned the cottages and might, during a shutdown, lose his rents.

It was the manic-depressive rhythm of the market, with its spurts and stoppages, that made the large urban center so important to industry. For it was by drawing at need on an underlayer of surplus labor, fitfully employed, that the new capitalists managed to depress wages and meet any sudden demand in production. Size, in other words, took the place of an efficiently organized labor market, with union wage standards and public employment exchanges. Topographical agglomeration was a substitute for a well-timed and humanely regulated mode of production, such as has been coming into existence the last half-century.

If the steam-powered factory, producing for the world market, was the first factor that tended to increase the area of urban congestion, the new railroad transportation system, after 1830, greatly abetted it.

Power was concentrated on the coal fields. Where coal could be mined or obtained by cheap means of transportation, industry could produce regularly throughout the year without stoppages through seasonal failure of power. In a business system based upon time-contracts and time-payments, this regularity was highly important. Coal and iron thus exercised a gravitational pull on many subsidiary and accessory industries: first by means of the canal, and after 1830, through the new railroads. A direct connection with the mining areas was a prime condition of urban concentration: until our own day the chief commodity carried by the railroads was coal for heat and power.

The dirt roads, the sail-power, the horse-power of the eotechnic transportation system had favored a dispersal of the population: within the region, there were many points of equal advantage. But the relative weakness of the steam locomotive, which could not easily climb a grade steeper than two feet in a hundred, tended to concentrate the new industrial centers on the coalbeds and in the connecting valleys: the Lille district in France, the Merseburg and Ruhr districts in Germany, the Black Country of England, the Allegheny-Great Lakes region and the Eastern Coastal Plain in the United States.

Population growth, then, during the paleotechnic regime, showed two characteristic patterns: a general massing on the coal areas, where the new heavy industries, iron and coal mining, smelting, cutlery, hardware production, glass manufacture, and machine-building flourished. And in addition a partly derivative thickening of population along the new railroad lines, with a definite clotting in the industrial centers along the great trunk lines and a further massing in the greater junction towns and export terminals. Along with this went a thinning out of population and a running down of activities in the back country: the falling off of local mines, quarries, and furnaces, and the diminishing use of highways, canals, small factories, local mills.

Most of the great earlier political and commercial capitals, at least in the Northern countries, shared in this growth. Not merely did they usually occupy geographically strategic positions: they had special resources of exploitation through their intimacy with the agents of political power and through the central banks and bourses that controlled the flow of investments. Moreover, they had the further advantage of having gathered, for centuries, a vast reserve of miserable people at the margin of subsistence: what was euphemistically called the Labor Supply. The fact that almost every great national capital became *ipso facto* a great industrial center served to give a further push to the policy of urban aggrandizement and congestion.

5: FACTORY, RAILROAD, AND SLUM

The main elements in the new urban complex were the factory, the railroad, and the slum. By themselves they constituted the industrial town: a word that described merely the fact that more than two thousand people were gathered in an area that could be designated with a proper name. Such urban clots could and did expand a hundred times without acquiring more than a shadow of the institutions that characterize a city in the mature sociological sense—that is, a place in which the social heritage is concentrated, and in which the possibilities of continuous social intercourse and interaction raise to a higher potential all the complex activities of men. Except in shrunken, residual forms, even the characteristic organs of the stone age city were lacking.

The factory became the nucleus of the new urban organism. Every other detail of life was subordinate to it. Even the utilities, such as the water supply, and the minimum of governmental offices that were necessary to a town's existence often, if they had not been built by an earlier generation, entered belatedly: an afterthought. It was not merely art and religion that were treated by the utilitarian as mere embellishments: intelligent political administration long remained in the same category. In the first scramble of exploitation, no provisions would be made for police and fire protection, water and food inspection, hospital care, or education.

The factory usually claimed the best sites: mainly, in the cotton industry, the chemical industries, and the iron industries, the sites near a waterfront; for large quantities of water were needed now in the processes of production, supplying the steam boilers, cooling hot surfaces, making the necessary chemical solutions and dyes. Above all, the river or canal had still another important function: it was the cheapest and most convenient dumping ground for all soluble or suspendable forms of waste. The transformation of the rivers into open sewers was a characteristic feat of the new economy. Result: poisoning of the aquatic life: destruction of food: befouling of water so it was unfit to bathe in.

For generations, the members of every 'progressive' urban community were forced to pay for the sordid convenience of the manufacturer, who often, it happened, consigned his precious by-products to the river, for lack of scientific knowledge or the empirical skill to use them. If the river was a liquid dump, great mounds of ashes, slag, rubbish, rusty iron, and even garbage blocked the horizon with their vision of misplaced and unusable matter. The rapidity of production was in part matched by the rapidity of consumption, and before a conservative policy of scrap metal utilization became profitable, the formless or deteriorated end-products were cast back over the surface of the landscape. In the Black Country of England, indeed, the huge slag heaps still look like geological formations: they decreased the available living space, cast a shadow on the land, and until recently presented an insoluble problem of either utilization or removal.

The testimony that substantiates this picture is voluminous; indeed, it is still open for inspection in the older industrial cities of the Western World, despite herculean efforts to cleanse the environment. Let me however quote from an early observer, Hugh Miller, the author of 'Old Red Sandstone': a man thoroughly in harmony with his age, but not insensitive to the actual qualities of the new environment. He is speaking of Manchester in 1862.

"Nothing seems more characteristic of the great manufacturing city, though disagreeably so, than the river Irwell, which runs through the place. . . . The hapless river—a pretty enough stream a few miles up, with trees overhanging its banks and fringes of green sedge set thick along its edges —loses caste as it gets among the mills and print works. There are myriads of dirty things given it to wash, and whole wagonloads of poisons from dye houses and bleachyards thrown into it to carry away; steam boilers discharge into it their seething contents, and drains and sewers their fetid impurities; till at length it rolls on—here between tall dingy walls, there under precipices of red sand-stone—considerably less a river than a flood of liquid manure."

Note the environmental effect of the *massing* of industries that the new regime tended to make universal. A single factory chimney, a single blast furnace, a single dye works may easily have its effluvia absorbed by the surrounding landscape: twenty of them in a narrow area effectively pollute the air or water beyond remedy. So that the unavoidably dirty industries became through urban concentration far more formidable than they were when they had existed on a smaller scale and were more widely dispersed about the countryside. At the same time clean industries, such as the making of blankets, which still goes on at Witney, in England, with bleaching and shrinking conducted out in the open air of a charming countryside, became impossible under the old rural methods in the new centers. There chlorine took the place of sunlight, and for the healthful outdoor work that often accompanied the older processes of manufacture, with changes of scene as well as process to renew the spirit of the worker, came the dull drudgery of work within a dirty building hemmed in by other dirty buildings. Such losses cannot be measured in merely pecuniary terms. We have no calculus for figuring how much the gains in production were offset by the brutal sacrifice of life and a living environment.

While factories were usually set near the rivers, or the railroad lines that paralleled the rivers (except where a level terrain invited diffusion), no authority was exercised to concentrate factories in a particular area, to segregate the more noxious or noisy industries that should be placed far from human habitations, or to insulate for domestic purposes the appropriate adjacent areas. 'Free competition' alone determined location, without thought of the possibility of functional planning: and the jumbling together of industrial, commercial, and domestic functions went on steadily in industrial cities.

In areas with a rough topography, such as the valleys of the Allegheny plateau, a certain amount of natural zoning might take place, since only the river bottoms would afford enough space for a big mill to spread— though this disposition ensured that the maximum amount of noxious effluvia would rise and spread over the homes on the hillsides above. Otherwise living quarters were often placed within the leftover spaces between the factories and sheds and the railroad yards. To pay attention to such matters as dirt, noise, vibration, was accounted an effeminate delicacy. Workers' houses, often those of the middle classes, too, would be built smack up against a steel works, a dye plant, a gas works, or a railroad cutting. They would be built, often enough, on land filled in with ashes and broken glass and rubbish, where even the grass could not take root; they might be on the edge of a dump or a vast permanent pile of coal and slag: day in and day out the stench of the refuse, the murky outpouring of chimneys, the noise of hammering or of whirring machinery, accompanied the household routine.

In this new scheme, the town itself consisted of the shattered fragments of land, with odd shapes and inconsequential streets and avenues, left over between the factories, the railroads, the freight yards and dump heaps. In lieu of any kind of over-all municipal regulation or planning, the railroad itself was called upon to define the character and project the limits of the town. Except in certain parts of Europe where old-fashioned bureaucratic regulations happily kept the railroad stations at the outskirts of the historic city, the railroad was permitted, or rather, was invited to plunge into the very heart of the town and to create in the most precious central portions of the city a waste of freight yards and marshalling yards, economically justifiable only in the open country. These yards severed the town's natural arteries and created an impassable barrier between large urban segments: sometimes, as in Philadelphia, a veritable Chinese wall.

Thus the railroad carried into the heart of the city not merely noise and soot but the industrial plants and the debased housing that alone could thrive in the environment it produced. Only the hypnotism of a new invention, in an age uncritically enamored of new inventions, could have prompted this wanton immolation under the wheels of the puffing Juggernaut. Every mistake in urban design that could be made was made by the new railroad engineers, for whom the movement of trains was more important than the human objects achieved by that movement. The wastage of space by railroad yards in the heart of the city only furthered its more rapid extension outward; and this in turn, since it produced more railroad traffic, gave the extra sanction of profits to the misdemeanors so committed.

So widespread was this deterioration of environment, so hardened have people in big cities become to it in the course of a century, that even the richer classes, who could presumably afford the best, to this day often indifferently embrace the worst. As for housing itself, the alternatives were simple. In the industrial towns that grew up on older foundations, the workers were first accommodated by turning old one-family houses into rent barracks. In these made-over houses, each separate room would now enclose a whole family: from Dublin and Glasgow to Bombay, the standard of one room per family long held. Bed overcrowding, with three to eight people of different ages sleeping on the same pallet, often aggravated room overcrowding in such human sties. By the beginning of the nineteenth century, according to a Dr. Willan, who wrote a book on the diseases of London, it had produced an incredible state of physical defilement among the poor. The other type of dwelling offered to the working class was, essentially, a standardization of these degraded conditions; but it had this further defect, that the plans of the new houses and the materials of construction usually had none of the original decency of the older burgher houses: they were meanly built from the ground up.

In both the old and the new quarters a pitch of foulness and filth was reached that the lowest serf's cottage scarcely achieved in medieval Europe. It is almost impossible to enumerate objectively the bare details of this housing without being suspected of perverse exaggeration. But those who speak glibly of urban improvements during this period, or of the alleged rise in the standards of living, fight shy of the actual facts: they generously impute to the town as a whole benefits which only the more favored middle-class minority enjoyed; and they read into the original conditions those improvements which three generations of active legislation and massive sanitary engineering have finally brought about.

In England, to begin with, thousands of the new workers' dwellings, in towns like Birmingham and Bradford, were built back to back. (Many still exist.) Two rooms out of four on each floor therefore had no direct daylight or ventilation. There were no open spaces except the bare passages between these doubled rows. While in the sixteenth century it was an offense in many English towns to throw rubbish into the streets, in these early industrial towns this was the regular method of disposal. The rubbish remained there, no matter how vile and filthy, "until the accumulation induced someone to carry it away for manure." Of this there was naturally no lack in the crowded new quarters of the town. The privies, foul beyond description, were usually in the cellars; it was a common practice to have pigsties under the houses, too, and the pigs roamed the streets once more, as they had not done for centuries in the larger towns. There was even a dire lack of toilets: the 'Report on the State of Large Towns and Populous Districts' (1845) states that "in one part of Manchester in 1843-44 the wants of upward 700 inhabitants were supplied by 33 necessaries only—that is, one toilet to every 212 people."

Even at such a low level of design, even with such foul accompaniments, not enough houses were built in many cities; and then far worse conditions prevailed. Cellars were used as dwelling places. In Liverpool, one-sixth of the population lived in "underground cellars," and most of the other port cities were not far behind: London and New York were close rivals to Liverpool: even in the nineteen-thirties, there were 20,000 basement dwellings in London medically marked as unfit for human occupation. This dirt and congestion, bad in themselves, brought other pests: the rats that carried bubonic plague, the bedbugs that infested the beds and tormented sleep, the lice that spread typhus, the flies that visited impartially the cellar privy and the infant's food. Moreover the combination of dark rooms and dank walls formed an almost ideal breeding medium for bacteria, especially since the overcrowded rooms afforded the maximum possibilities of transmission through breath and touch.

If the absence of plumbing and municipal sanitation created frightful stenches in these new urban quarters, and if the spread of exposed excrement, together with seepage into local wells, meant a corresponding spread of typhoid, the lack of water was even more sinister. It removed the very possibility of domestic cleanliness or personal hygiene. In the big capital cities, where some of the old municipal traditions still lingered, no adequate provision for water was made in many new areas. In 1809 when London's population was about a million, water was available over the greater part of the city only in the basements of houses. In some quarters, water could be turned on for only three days in a week. And though iron pipes made their appearance in 1746, they were not extensively used until a special act in England in 1817 required that all new mains be built of iron after ten years.

In the new industrial towns, the most elementary traditions of municipal service were absent. Whole quarters were sometimes without water even from local wells. On occasion, the poor would go from house to house in the middle-class sections, begging for water as they might beg for bread during a famine. With this lack of water for drinking and washing, it is no wonder that the filth accumulated. Open drains represented, despite their foulness, comparative municipal affluence. And if families were thus treated, one need scarcely turn to the documents to find out how the casual laborer fared. Deserted houses of uncertain title were used as lodging-houses, fifteen or twenty people in a single room. In Manchester, according to the police statistics of 1841, there were some 109 lodging-houses where people of both sexes slept indiscriminately; and there were 91 mendicant lodging-houses. "Playfair told the Health of Towns Commission in 1842 that in all Lancashire there was only one town, Preston, with a public park, and only one, Liverpool, with public baths."

This depression of living quarters was well-nigh universal among the workers in the new industrial towns, once the new industrial regime was fully established. Local conditions sometimes permitted an escape from the extreme of foulness I have been describing: the housing of the mill-workers at Manchester, New Hampshire, for example, was of a far superior order; and in the more rural industrial towns of America, particularly in the Middle West, there was at least a little free elbow room and garden space for the workers. But wherever one looks, the improvement was but one of degree: the *type* had definitely changed for the worse.

Not merely were the new cities as a whole bleak and ugly, environments hostile to human life even at its most elementary physiological level, but the standardized overcrowding of the poor was repeated in middle-class dwellings and in the barracks of the soldiers, classes that were not being directly exploited for the sake of profit. Mrs. Peel cites a sumptuous mid-Victorian mansion in which the kitchen, pantry, servants' hall, housekeeper's room, butler's and footmen's bedrooms were all placed in the cellar: two rooms in front and two rooms in the rear looked into a deep back basement: all the others were 'lighted' and 'ventilated' by panes of glass high up in the inner walls. Corresponding forms of degraded housing were worked out in Berlin, Vienna, New York, and Paris during the middle of the nineteenth century. The new apartment houses of the middle classes backed upon deep, airless courts that had most of the characteristics of cellars even when they were technically above ground. Only 'backward' towns escaped these infamies.

To judge by popular oratory, these defects were narrow in range, and, in any event, have been wiped out during the past century through the onward march of science and humanitarian legislation. Unfortunately, popular orators—and even historians and economists who supposedly deal with the same set of facts—have not formed the habit of making firsthand surveys of the environment: hence they ignore the existence of the clots of degraded paleotechnic housing that exist in only slightly modified form throughout the Western World today: even back-to-back houses, tenements with airless courts, and cellar-lodgings. These clots not merely include most of the workers' dwellings built before 1900; they include a great part of what has been done since, though they show improvements in sanitation. The surviving mass of housing that was built between 1830 and 1910 did not represent even the hygienic standards of its own day; and it was far below a standard framed in terms of present-day knowledge of sanitation, hygiene, and child care—to say nothing of domestic felicity.

"Slum, semi-slum, and super-slum—to this has come the evolution of cities." Yes: these mordant words of Patrick Geddes apply inexorably to the new environment. Even the most revolutionary of contemporary critics lacked genuine standards of building and living: they had no notion how far the environment of the upper classes themselves had become impoverished. Thus Friedrich Engels, in order to promote the resentment needful for revolution, not merely opposed all "palliative" measures to provide better housing for the working classes: he seems to have held that the problem would be solved eventually for the proletariat by a revolutionary seizure of the commodious quarters occupied by the bourgeoisie. This notion was qualitatively inept and quantitatively ridiculous. Socially speaking, it merely urged as a revolutionary measure the miserable process that had actually gone on in the older towns as the richer classes moved out of their original quarters and divided them up for the working class occupation. But above all the suggestion was naïve because it did not perceive that the standards embodied even in the more pretentious new residences were often *below* those desirable for human life at any economic level.

In other words, even this revolutionary critic was apparently unaware of the fact that the upper-class quarters were, more often than not, intolerable super-slums. The necessity for increasing the amount of housing, for expanding the space, for multiplying the equipment, for providing communal facilities, was far more revolutionary in its demands than any trifling expropriation of the quarters occupied by the rich would be. The latter notion was merely an impotent gesture of revenge: the former demanded a thoroughgoing reconstruction of the entire social environment —such a reconstruction as the world is perhaps on the brink of today, though even advanced countries, like England and Sweden and The Netherlands, have not as yet grasped all the dimensions of this urban change.

6: HOUSES OF ILL-FAME

Let us look more closely at these new houses of the working classes. Each country, each region, each population group had its own special pattern: tall tenements in Glasgow, Edinburgh, Paris, Berlin, Hamburg, Genoa, or two story buildings, with four, five, sometimes six rooms in London, Brooklyn, Philadelphia, Chicago: vast wooden firetraps called three-deckers in New England, happily blessed with open air porches, or narrow brick row houses, still clinging to an older Georgian row pattern, in Baltimore.

But in industrial housing there are certain common characteristics. Block after block repeats the same formation: there are the same dreary streets, the same shadowed, rubbish-filled alleys, the same absence of open spaces for children's play and gardens; the same lack of coherence and individuality to the local neighborhood. The windows are usually narrow; the interior light insufficient; no effort is made to orient the street pattern with respect to sunlight and winds. The painful grayish cleanliness of the more respectable quarters, where the better-paid artisans or clerks live, perhaps in a row, perhaps semi-detached, with a soiled pocket-handkerchief of grass before their houses, or a tree in a narrow courtyard in the rear—this respectability is almost as depressing as the outright slatternliness of the poorer quarters: more so indeed, because the latter often at least have a touch of color and life, a Punch-and-Judy show in the street, the chatter of the market stalls, the noisy camaraderie of the public house or bistro; in short, the more public and friendly life that is lived in the poorer streets.

The age of invention and mass production scarcely touched the worker's house or its utilities until the end of the nineteenth century. Iron piping came in; likewise the improved water closet; eventually the gas light and the gas stove, the stationary bathtub with attached water pipes and fixed outlets; a collective water system with running water available for every house, and a collective sewage system. All these improvements slowly became available to the middle and upper economic groups after 1830; within a generation of their introduction, they indeed became middle-class necessities. But at no point during the paleotechnic phase were these improvements made available to the mass of the population. The problem for the builder was to achieve a modicum of decency *without* these new expensive utilities.

This problem remained soluble only in terms of a primitive rural environment. Thus the original division of Muncie, Indiana, the 'Middletown' of Robert Lynd's survey, had houses eight to a block, each on a lot sixty-two and a half feet wide and a hundred and twenty-five feet deep. This certainly provided better conditions for the poorer workers than what followed when rising land values crowded the houses and narrowed the garden space and the play space, and one out of four houses still lacked running water. In general the congestion of the industrial town increased the difficulties in the way of good housing, and added to the cost of overcoming these difficulties.

As for the furnishings of the interiors, Gaskell's picture of the housing of the working classes in England struck the lowest level; but the sordor continued, despite minor improvements, in the century that followed. The effects of pecuniary poverty were in fact aggravated by a general falling off in taste, which accentuated the impoverishment of the environment, by offering barbarous wall paper, meretricious bric-a-brac, framed oleograph pictures, and furniture derived from the worst examples of stuffy middle-class taste: the dregs of the dregs.

In China a friend of mine reports seeing a miner, grimy, bent with toil, tenderly fondling a stalk of delphinium as he walked along the road; but in the Western World, down to the twentieth century, when the allotment garden began to have its beneficent effect, the same instinct for fresh vital form was destined to feed on the deliberate monstrosities that the manufacturer offered to the working classes under the guise of fashion and art. Even religious relics, in Catholic communities, reached an esthetic level so low as to be almost a profanation. In time, the taste for ugliness became ingrained: the worker was not willing to move from his older quarters unless he could carry a little of its familiar filth, confusion, noise, and overcrowding with him. Every move toward a better environment encountered that resistance: a real obstacle to decentralization.

A few such houses, a few such lapses into filth and ugliness, would have been a blot; but perhaps every period could show a certain number of houses of this description. Now, however, whole quarters and cities, acres, square miles, provinces, were filled with such dwellings, which mocked every boast of material success that the 'Century of Progress' uttered. In these new warrens, a race of defectives was created. Poverty and the environment of poverty produced organic modifications: rickets in children, due to the absence of sunlight, malformations of the bone structure and organs, defective functioning of the endocrines, through a vile diet; skin diseases for lack of the elementary hygiene of water; smallpox, typhoid, scarlet fever, septic sore throat, through dirt and excrement; tuberculosis, encouraged by a combination of bad diet, lack of sunshine, and room overcrowding, to say nothing of the occupational diseases, also partly environmental.

Chlorine, ammonia, carbon monoxide, phosphoric acid, fluorine, methane, not to add a long list of some two hundred cancer-producing chemicals, pervaded the atmosphere and sapped vitality: often in stagnant lethal concentrations, increasing the incidence of bronchitis and pneumonia, causing widespread death. Presently the recruiting sergeant was not able to use the children of this regime even as cannon fodder: the medical discovery of England's mistreatment of her workers, during the Boer War and the First World War, did perhaps as much as any one other factor to promote better housing there.

The crude results of all these conditions may be followed in the mortality tables for adults, in the disease rates for urban workers compared with agricultural workers, in the expectations of life enjoyed by the various occupational classes. Above all, perhaps the most sensitive barometer of the fitness of the social environment for human life is the infant mortality tables.

Wherever the comparison was made between country and city, between middle-class quarters and poor quarters, between a low density district and a high density district, the higher rate of disease and death usually fell in the latter class. Had other factors stayed the same, urbanization by itself would have been sufficient to lop off part of the potential gains in vitality. Farm laborers, though they remained throughout the nineteenth century a depressed class in England, showed—and still show—a much longer expectation of life than the higher grades of town mechanics, even after municipal sanitation and medical care had been introduced. Indeed, it was only by a continual influx of new life from the country that the cities so hostile to life could survive at all. The new towns were established in the mass by immigrants. In 1851, out of 3,336,000 people of twenty years and upward inhabiting London and 61 other English and Welsh towns, only 1,337,000 had been born in the town of their residence.

Taking the infant-mortality rate, the record is even more disgraceful. In New York City, for example, the mortality rate for infants in 1810 was between 120 and 145 per thousand live births; it rose to 180 per thousand by 1850, 220 in 1860, and 240 in 1870. This was accompanied by a steady depression in living conditions: for after 1835, the overcrowding was standardized in the newly built tenement houses. These recent calculations corroborate what is known about the infant mortality rate in England during the same period: there the rise took place after 1820 and fell most heavily on the towns. There are doubtless other factors responsible for these retrograde tendencies; but the new towns, as an expression of the entire social complex, conditioning hygiene, diet, working conditions, wages, child care, education, had an important part to play in the result.

There has been much unwarranted congratulation over improvements in urban health under industrialism because those who believed that progress automatically occurred in every department of life during the nineteenth century refused to face the harsh facts. They did not let themselves make comparative studies between town and country, between the mechanized and the unmechanized; and they assisted further in creating confusion by using crude mortality tables, not corrected according to age and sex groups, and not therefore allowing for the heavier distribution of adults in the cities and the larger incidence of children and old people, more subject to disease and death, in the countryside.

These statistics made town mortality rates look more favorable than they really were on close actuarial analysis. To this day scarcely the beginnings have been made toward a satisfactory analysis of births and deaths, health and disease, in relation to environment. By lumping urban and rural rates together in a 'national' figure the relatively poorer showings of the 'prosperous' industrialized and urban areas have been concealed.

Similar misleading analyses, disguised as objective research, continue to be made. Thus Mabel Buer attempted to vindicate the industrial revolution from the charge of creating urban blight by making a study of the decrease in the death rate that took place before 1815—that is, before overcrowding, bad sanitation, and the general urbanization of the population had produced their characteristic devitalizing results. There is no need to cast doubt upon this earlier improvement any more than one need forget the steady *general* drop in the death rate throughout the nineteenth century. But it fails to wipe out the equally indisputable fact of later deterioration.

Instead of giving credit for the early advance to the mechanization of industry, one should give due credit to quite another department—the increase of the food supply, which provided a better diet and helped raise resistance to disease. Still another factor may have had a part: the wider use of soap, made possible by the increased amount of available fats. The use of soap in personal hygiene may have extended from the washing of the nipples of the nursing mother to the child in her care: finally it passed by example from the feminine to the masculine half of society. That increased use of soap is not easily measurable in trade schedules; for soap was originally a commercial monopoly, and as such, a luxury article: ordinary soap was mainly produced and consumed within the household. The spread of the soap-and-water habit might well account for the lowering of infant mortality rates before the nineteenth century; even as the dearth of water and soap might account in part for the deplorable infant death rates of the paleotechnic town.

In the main, hygienic poverty was widespread. Lack of sunlight, lack of pure water, lack of untainted air, lack of a mixed diet—these lacks were so common that they amounted to a chronic starvation among the greater part of the population. Even the more prosperous classes succumbed: sometimes even prided themselves on their vital deficiencies. Herbert Spencer, who was a non-conformist even to his own creed of utilitarianism, was forced to preach the gospel of play and physical relaxation to his contemporaries; and in his 'Essays on Education' he went so far as to make a special plea to parents to permit their children to *eat fruit*.

7: A CLOSE-UP OF COKETOWN

One may grant that at the tempo at which industrialism was introduced into the Western World, the problem of building adequate cities was almost insoluble. The premises which made these operations possible also limited their human success. How build a coherent city out of the efforts of a thousand competing individualists who knew no law but their own sweet will? How integrate new mechanical functions in a new type of plan that could be laid out and speedily developed—if the very essence of such integration depended upon the firm control of public authorities who often did not exist, or who, when they did exist, exercised no powers except those specifically granted by the state, which put individual property rights at the top? How provide a multitude of new utilities and services for workers who could not afford to rent any but the most destitute types of shelter? How create a good physical plan for social functions that themselves remained abortive?

Cities that still contained vital residues of medieval tradition, like Ulm, sometimes managed, through the slow tempo of their growth and a bold policy of large-scale municipal land ownership, to effect the transition with relatively little loss. Where industry came in explosively, however, as in Nuremberg, the results were as vile as in towns that had no historic shell whatever. And in the New World, towns were built as late as 1906 (Gary, Indiana) with no regard for any physical features except the location of the industrial plant. As for still later industrial complexes like the motor car metropolis of Detroit, they learned nothing from the mistakes of the past: did not Henry Ford assert that history was bunk? So the plants they erected in accord with the most advanced engineering practice were set in the midst of an urban welter—classic models of municipal disorganization and technical incompetence. The very age that boasted its mechanical conquests and its scientific prescience left its social processes to chance, as if the scientific habit of mind had exhausted itself upon machines, and was not capable of coping with human realities. The torrent of energy that was tapped from the coal beds ran downhill with the least possible improvement of the environment: the mill-villages, the factory agglomerations, were socially more crude than the feudal villages of the Middle Ages.

The new urban emergent, the coal-agglomeration, which Patrick Geddes called the conurbation, was neither isolated in the country nor attached to an old historic core. It spread in a mass of relatively even density over scores and sometimes hundreds of square miles. There were no effective centers in this urban massing: no institutions capable of uniting its members into an active city life: no political organization capable of unifying its common activities. Only the sects, the fragments, the social debris of old institutions remained, left like the muddied debris scattered by a great river after the flood has subsided: a no-man's-land of social life. These new cities not merely failed for the most part to produce art, science, or culture: they failed at first even to import them from older centers. When a surplus was locally created it was promptly drained off elsewhere: the rentiers and financiers employed it upon personal luxuries, or upon philanthropies, like that of Carnegie's Music Hall in New York, which often benefited the capital cities long before any similar bequests were made to the region from which the riches were originally drawn.

Approach more closely the paleotechnic town: examine it with eye, ear, nose, touch. Present-day observers, because of the growing contrast with the emerging neotechnic environment, can at last see what only poets like Hugo or Ruskin or Morris saw a hundred years ago: a reality that the philistines, tangled in their utilitarian web of dreams, alternately denied as a sentimental exaggeration or greeted with enthusiasm as an indisputable mark of 'progress.'

Night spread over the coal-town: its prevailing color was black. Black clouds of smoke rolled out of the factory chimneys, and the railroad yards, which often cut clean into the town, mangling the very organism, spread soot and cinders everywhere. The invention of artificial illuminating gas was an indispensable aid to this spread: Murdock's invention dates back to the end of the eighteenth century, and during the next generation its use widened, first in factories, then in homes; first in big cities, later in small centers; for without its aid work would frequently have been stopped by smoke and fog. The manufacture of illuminating gas within the confines of the towns became a characteristic new feature: the huge gas tanks reared their bulk over the urban landscape, great structures, on the scale of a cathedral: indeed, their tracery of iron, against an occasional clear lemon-green sky at sunrise, was one of the most pleasant esthetic elements in the new order.

Such structures were not necessarily evil; indeed, with sufficient care in their segregation they might have been comely. What was atrocious was the fact that, like every other building in the new towns, they were dumped almost at random; the leakage of escaping gas scented the so-called gas-house districts, and not surprisingly these districts frequently became among the most degraded sections of the city. Towering above the town, polluting its air, the gas tanks symbolized the dominance of 'practical' interests over life-needs.

The poisonous pall of smoke had already come into the pottery districts in the eighteenth century, through the use of cheap salt glazes; now it closed in everywhere, in Sheffield and Birmingham, in Pittsburgh, Essen, and Lille. In this new environment black clothes were only a protective coloration, not a form of mourning; the black stovepipe hat was almost a functional design—an assertive symbol of steam power. The black dyes of Leeds, for example, turned its river into a dark poisonous sewer; while the oil smudges of soft coal spat everywhere; even those who washed their hands left a rim of undissolved grease around the side of the washbowl. Add to these constant smudges on flesh and clothing the finely divided particles of iron from the grinding and sharpening operations, the unused chlorine from the soda works, later, the clouds of acrid dust from the cement plant, the various by-products of other chemical industries: these things smarted the eyes, rasped the throat and lungs, lowered the general tone, even when they did not produce on contact any definite disease. As for the reek of coal itself, it is perhaps not a disagreeable one: man with his long savage past has become fond of musty odors: so perhaps its chief misdemeanor was that it suppressed or made people insensitive to pleasanter smells.

Under such conditions, one must have all one's senses blunted in order to be happy; and first of all, one must lose one's taste. This loss of taste had an effect upon diet: even well-to-do people began to eat canned goods and stale foods, when fresh ones were available, because they could no longer tell the difference. The enfeeblement of elementary taste-discrimination extended to other departments than food: color-discrimination became feeble, too: the darker tones, the soberer colors, the dingier mixtures, were preferred to pure bright colors, and both the Pre-Raphaelites and the Impressionist painters were reviled by the bourgeoisie because their pure colors were thought 'unnatural' and 'inartistic.' If an occasional touch of bright color was left, it was only in the signs on the hoardings— for Coleman's mustard or Reckitt's blue—paper surfaces that remained cheerful because they frequently had to be changed.

Dark, colorless, acrid, evil-smelling, this new environment was. All these qualities lowered human efficiency and required extra compensation in washing and bathing and sanitation—or at the last extreme, in medical treatment. The cash expenditure on cleaning alone was no small expenditure in the paleotechnic town, at least after the need for cleanliness itself was acknowledged. Take one item alone from a typical paleotechnic survival: Pittsburgh. Its smoke pollution began early, for a print in 1849 shows it in full blast. A generation ago the annual cost of keeping Pittsburgh cleaned was estimated at some $1,500,000 for extra laundry work, $750,000 for extra general cleaning, and $60,000 for extra curtain cleaning. This estimate, about $2,310,000 per year, did not count the losses due to the corrosion of buildings or the increased costs of painting woodwork, nor yet the extra costs of lighting during periods of smog.

Even after strenuous efforts to reduce smoke pollution, a single great steel plant in the heart of Pittsburgh still makes mock of these efforts at improvement—indeed, so heavy is the hold of paleotechnic tradition, that the municipal authorities only recently helpfully connived at the extension of this plant, instead of firmly demanding its removal. So much for pecuniary losses. But what of the incalculable losses through disease, through ill-health, through all the forms of psychological deterioration from apathy to outright neurosis? The fact that such losses do not lend themselves to objective measurement does not make them non-existent.

Indifference to these forms of devitalization during the paleotechnic period rested mainly on invincible ignorance. In 'Technics and Civilization' I quoted the indignation and surprise of a leading apologist for this civilization, Andrew Ure, over the testimony offered by the astute physicians called before Sadler's Factory Investigation Committee. These physicians referred to the experiments made by Dr. Edwards of Paris upon the growth of tadpoles, proving that sunlight was essential to their development. From this they concluded—we now know with complete justification—that it was equally necessary to the growth of children. Ure's proud answer was that the gas lighting of the factories was a sufficient substitute for the sun. So contemptuous were these utilitarians of nature and well-tried human custom that they brought up more than one generation upon a devitalized diet, based purely on the consumption of calories. That diet has been improved during the last generation by a fresh budget of scientific knowledge, only to be debased once more by the spreading use of poisonous insecticides and pesticides, food preservatives and additives, to say nothing of equally fatal radioactive poisons like Strontium 90. As for the paleotechnic environment, it still widely resists correction, and casts its blight over tens of millions of people.

Next to dirt, the new towns boasted another distinction, equally appalling to the senses. The baneful effects of this blight have been recognized only in recent years, thanks to advances in technics not unconnected with that typical biotechnic invention, the telephone. I refer to noise. Let me quote an ear-witness account of Birmingham in the middle of the nineteenth century.

"In no town in the world are the mechanical arts more noisy: hammerings incessantly on the anvil; there is an unending clang of engines; flame rustles, water hisses, steam roars, and from time to time, hoarse and hollow, rises the thunder of the proofing house [where firearms are tested]. The people live in an atmosphere vibrating with clamor; and it would seem as if their amusement had caught the general tone, and become noisy, like their inventions." The indifference to clang and racket was typical. Did not the manufacturers of England keep Watt from reducing the noise made by his reciprocating engine because they wanted auricular evidence of its power?

Today, numerous experiments have established the fact that noise can produce profound physiological changes: music can keep down the bacteria count in milk; and by the same token definite ailments, like stomach ulcers and high blood pressure, seem to be aggravated by the strain of living, say, within sound of a busy motorway or airport. The diminishment of working efficiency through noise has likewise been clearly established. Unfortunately, the paleotechnic environment seemed specially designed to create a maximum amount of noise: the early hoot of the factory whistle, the shriek of the locomotive, the clank and urge of the old-fashioned steam engine, the wheeze and screech of the shafts and belting, the click and whirr of the loom, the pounding of the drop hammer, the mutter and snuffle of the conveyor, the shouts of the workers who worked and 'rested' amid this varied clamor—all these sounds abetted the general assault on the senses.

When reckoning up the vital efficiency of the country as compared with the city, or the medieval town as opposed to the paleotechnic town, one must not forget this important factor in health. Nor have recent improvements in certain departments, the use of rubber heels and rubber tires, for instance, lessened the strength of the indictment. The noise of the gasoline driven motor cars and trucks in a busy city, as they start up, change gears, acquire speed, is a sign of their technical immaturity. Had the energy that has been put into styling car bodies gone into the design of a silent thermo-electric power unit, the modern city would not be as backward as its paleotechnic predecessor in the matter of noise and fumes.

Instead, the 'progressive' metropolises of motordom, like Los Angeles, exhibit, indeed magnify, all the urban evils of the paleotechnic period.

Experiments with sound made in the nineteen-thirties in Chicago show that if one grades noise by percentages up to one hundred per cent—which is the sound, like an artillery cannonade, that would drive one mad if continued over an extended period—the countryside has only from eight to ten per cent noise, the suburbs fifteen, the residential districts of the city twenty-five per cent, commercial districts thirty per cent, and industrial districts thirty-five. These broad lines would doubtless hold almost anywhere during the last century and a half, though perhaps the upper limits were higher. One must remember, too, that the paleotechnic towns made no effort to separate factories from workers' homes; so that in many towns noise was omnipresent, in the day and often in the night. The age of air transportation, whose noisy planes destroy the residential value of suburbs in the neighborhood of airports, now threatens to widen even further this assault on life and health.

Considering this new urban area on its lowest physical terms, without reference to its social facilities or its culture, it is plain that never before in recorded history had such vast masses of people lived in such a savagely deteriorated environment, ugly in form, debased in content. The galley slaves of the Orient, the wretched prisoners in the Athenian silver mines, the depressed proletariat in the insulae of Rome—these classes had known, no doubt, a comparable foulness; but never before had human blight so universally been accepted as normal: normal and inevitable.

8: THE COUNTER-ATTACK

Perhaps the greatest contribution made by the industrial town was the reaction it produced against its own greatest misdemeanors; and, to begin with, the art of sanitation or public hygiene. The original models for these evils were the pest-ridden prisons and hospitals of the eighteenth century: their improvement made them pilot plants, as it were, in the reform of the industrial town. Nineteenth-century achievements in molding large glazed drains and casting iron pipes, made possible the tapping of distant supplies of relatively pure water and the disposal, at least as far as a neighboring stream, of sewage; while the repeated outbreaks of malaria, cholera, typhoid, and distemper served as a stimulus to these innovations, since a succession of public health officers had no difficulty in establishing the relation of dirt and congestion, of befouled water and tainted food, to these conditions.

On the essential matter of urban deterioration, John Ruskin had spoken to the point. "Providing lodgements for [working people] means," he said, "a great deal of vigorous legislation and cutting down of vested interests that stand in the way; and after that, or before that, so far as we can get it, through sanitary and remedial action in the houses that we have, and then the building of more, strongly, beautifully, and in groups of limited extent, kept in proportion to their streams, and walled round, so that there may be no festering and wretched suburb anywhere, but clean and busy streets within, and the open country without, with a belt of beautiful garden and orchard round the walls, so that from any part of the city perfectly fresh air and grass and the sight of the far horizon may be reachable in a few minutes walk." That happy vision beckoned even the manufacturers who, here and there, in Port Sunlight and Bournville, began to build industrial villages that rivalled in comeliness the best of the later suburbs.

To bring back fresh air, pure water, green open space, and sunlight to the city became the first object of sound planning: the need was so pressing that despite his passion for urban beauty, Camillo Sitte insisted upon the *hygienic* function of the urban park, as a *sanitary green,* to use his own expression: the 'lungs' of the city, whose function became newly appreciated through their absence.

The cult of cleanliness had its origins before the paleotechnic era: it owes much to the Dutch cities of the seventeenth century, with their plentiful water supplies, their large house windows showing up every particle of dust inside, their tiled floors; so that the scrubbing and scouring of the Dutch housewife became proverbial. Cleanliness got new scientific reinforcements after 1870. As long as the body was dualistically separated from the mind, its systematic care might be slighted, as almost an indication of more spiritual preoccupations. But the new conception of the organism that grew up in the nineteenth century, with Johannes Müller and Claude Bernard, reunited the physiological and the psychological processes: thus the care of the body became once more a moral and esthetic discipline. By his researches in bacteriology Pasteur altered the conception of both the external and the internal environment of organisms: virulent microscopic organisms flourished in dirt and ordure, and largely disappeared before soap-and-water and sunlight. As a result, the farmer milking a cow today takes sanitary precautions that a mid-Victorian London surgeon did not trouble to take before performing a major operation, till Lister taught him better. The new standards for light, air, and cleanliness which Florence Nightingale established for hospitals she even carried into the white-walled living room of her own home—a true prelude to

Le Corbusier's admirably hygienic 'Esprit Nouveau' in modern architecture.

At last, the industrial town's indifference to darkness and dirt was exposed for what it was, a monstrous barbarism. Further advances in the biological sciences threw into relief the misdemeanors of the new environment with its smoke and fog and fumes. As our experimental knowledge of medicine increases, this list of evils lengthens: it now includes the two hundred-odd cancer-producing substances still usually found in the air of most industrial cities, to say nothing of the metallic and stone dusts and poisonous gases that raise the incidence and increase the fatality of diseases of the respiratory tract.

Though the pressure of scientific knowledge worked slowly to improve conditions in the city as a whole, it had a quicker effect on the educated and comfortable classes: they soon took the hint and fled from the city to an environment that was not so inimical to health. One of the reasons for this tardy application of modern hygiene to city design was the fact that individual improvements in the hygienic equipment of dwellings made a radical alteration in costs; and these costs were reflected in heavier municipal investments in collective utilities, and in heavier municipal taxes to keep them up.

Just as early industrialism had squeezed its profits not merely out of the economies of the machine, but out of the pauperism of the workers, so the crude factory town had maintained its low wages and taxes by depleting and pauperizing the environment. Hygiene demanded space and municipal equipment and natural resources that had hitherto been lacking. In time, this demand enforced municipal socialization, as a normal accompaniment to improved service. Neither a pure water supply, nor the collective disposal of garbage, waste, and sewage, could be left to the private conscience or attended to only if they could be provided for at a profit.

In smaller centers, private companies might be left with the privilege of maintaining one or more of these services, until some notorious outbreak of disease dictated public control; but in the bigger cities socialization was the price of safety; and so, despite the theoretic claims of laissez faire, the nineteenth century became, as Beatrice and Sidney Webb correctly pointed out, the century of municipal socialism. Each individual improvement within the building demanded its collectively owned and operated utility: watermains, water reservoirs, and aqueducts, pumping stations: sewage mains, sewage reduction plants, sewage farms. Only the public ownership of land for town extension, town protection, or town colonization was lacking. That step forward was one of the significant contributions of Ebenezer Howard's garden city.

Through this effective and widespread socialization, the general death rate and the infant mortality rate tended to fall after the eighteen-seventies; and so manifest were these improvements that the social investment of municipal capital in these utilities rose. But the main emphasis remained a negative one: the new quarters of the city did not express, in any positive way, the understanding of the interplay between the organism as a whole and the environment that the biological sciences brought in. Even today one would hardly gather from the fashionable pseudo-modern use of large sealed glass windows, that Downes and Blunt had established as early as 1877 the bactericidal properties of direct sunlight. That irrationality betrays how superficial the respect for science still is in many presumably educated people, even technicians.

For the first time, the sanitary improvements made originally in the Sumerian and Cretan palaces, and extended to the patrician families of Rome at a later date, were now made available to the entire population of the city. This was a triumph of democratic principles that even dictatorial regimes could not inhibit: indeed, one of the greatest public benefits conferred by the overthrower of the Second French Republic, was in the redoubtable cleaning up of Paris under Baron Haussmann, a service far more essential, indeed far more original, than any of his more famous acts of town planning proper.

New York was the first big city to achieve an ample supply of pure water, through the building of the Croton system of reservoirs and aqueducts, opened in 1842; but in time every big city was forced to follow this example. Sewage disposal remained a difficult matter, and except in cities small enough to have sewage farms capable of transforming all such waste, the problem has not yet been adequately solved. Nevertheless, the standard of one private, sanitary toilet per family—a water closet connected to public mains in closely built communities—was established by the end of the nineteenth century. As for garbage, the usual dumping or burning of this valuable agricultural compost remains one of the persistent sins of unscientific municipal housekeeping.

The cleaning of streets remained a more difficult problem, until Belgian blocks and asphalt became universal, the horse was eliminated, and the public water supply became plentiful; yet in the end it proved easier to handle than the cleansing of the air. Even today, the screening out of the ultraviolet rays, through excess of dust and smoke, remains one of the vitality-lowering attributes of the more congested urban centers, which the showy but technically antiquated motor car has increased rather than lessened, even adding the invisible poison of carbon monoxide. As a partial offset, the introduction of running water and baths into the dwelling house—and the intermediate stage of re-establishing public baths, abandoned after the Middle Ages—must have helped in reducing both disease generally and infant mortality in particular.

All in all, the work of the sanitary reformers and hygienists, a Chadwick, a Florence Nightingale, a Louis Pasteur, a Baron Haussmann, robbed urban life at its lower levels of some of its worst terrors and physical debasements. If the creative aspects of city life were diminished by industrialism, the evil effects of its waste-products and excrement were also in time reduced. Even the bodies of the dead contributed to the improvement: they formed a green ring of mortuary suburbs and parks around the growing city; and here, again, Haussmann's bold and masterly treatment of this problem must earn a respectful salute.

The new industrial environment was so glaringly lacking in the attributes of health, that it is hardly any wonder that the counter-movement of hygiene provided the most positive contributions to town planning during the nineteenth century. The new ideals were provisionally embodied in a Utopia, called 'Hygeia, or the City of Health,' brought forth by Dr. Benjamin Ward Richardson in 1875. Here one discovers unconscious holdovers that reject the accepted degree of overcrowding; for whereas, less than a generation later, Ebenezer Howard provided 6,000 acres to hold and encircle 32,000 people, Richardson proposed to put 100,000 people on 4,000 acres. In the new city, the railroads were to be underground, despite the coal-burning locomotives then current; but no cellars of any kind were to be permitted in houses, a prohibition that was given statutory backing in England. But the construction was to be of brick, inside and outside, capable of being hosed down—a recurrent masculine dream—and the chimneys were to be connected to central shafts, to convey the unburned carbon to a gas furnace where it would be consumed.

Archaic as some of these proposals now are, in many ways Dr. Richardson was not merely ahead of his own times: he was equally ahead of our own day. He proposed to abandon "the old idea of warehousing diseases on the largest possible scale," and advocated a small hospital for every 5,000 people. By the same token, the helpless, the aged, and the mentally infirm were to be housed in modest-sized buildings. Richardson's physical conceptions of the city are now dated: but his contributions to collective medical care are still, I submit, worth pondering. With ample rational justification he proposed to go back to the high medical and human standards of the medieval town.

9: THE UNDERGROUND CITY

Mainly, it was by the reactions that it produced, by the exodus that it prompted, that the paleotechnic regime had an effect upon future urban forms. These counter-attacks were abetted, from the eighteen-eighties on, by a transformation within industry itself, furthered by the applications of science directly to invention; for the new regime was based on electric energy and the lighter metals, like aluminum, magnesium, and copper, and on new synthetic materials, like rubber, bakelite, and the plastics. The inner improvement of the industrial town proceeded partly from these innovations, which we associate with the spread of the private bath-room, the telephone, the motor car, and radio communication; but the even deeper reaction to the classic pattern of Coketown was that embodied in the emerging concept of the Welfare State. There is no better witness to the impoverished or positively evil conditions brought in by the industrial town than the mass of legislation that has accumulated, in the last century, aimed at their correction: sanitary regulations, health services, free public schools, job security, minimum wage provisions, workers' housing, slum clearance, along with public parks and playgrounds, public libraries and museums. These improvements have yet to find their full expression in a new form of the city.

But the archetypal industrial town nevertheless left deep wounds in the environment; and some of its worst features have remained in exist-ence, only superficially improved by neotechnic means. Thus the auto-mobile has been polluting the air for more than half a century without its engineers making any serious effort to remove the highly toxic carbon monoxide gas from its exhaust, though a few breaths of it in pure form are fatal; nor have they eliminated the unburned hydrocarbons which help produce the smog that blankets such a motor-ridden conurbation as Los Angeles. So, too, the transportation and highway engineers who have recklessly driven their multiple-laned expressways into the heart of the city and have provided for mass parking lots and garages to store cars, have masterfully repeated and enlarged the worst errors of the railroad engineers. Indeed, at the very moment the elevated railroad for public transportation was being eliminated as a grave nuisance, these forgetful engineers re-installed the same kind of obsolete structure for the con-venience of the private motor car. Thus much of what appears brightly contemporary merely restores the archetypal form of Coketown under a chrome plating.

But there is one aspect of the modern city where the hold of Coke-town grips even tighter, and the final effects are even more inimical to life. This is in the knitting together of necessary underground utilities to produce a wholly gratuitous result: the underground city, conceived as an ideal. As one should expect of a regime whose key inventions came out of the mine, the tunnel and the subway were its unique contributions to urban form; and not uncharacteristically, both these utilities were direct derivatives of war, first in the ancient city, and later in the elaborate sapping and mining necessary to reduce the baroque fortification. Though the surface forms of Coketown's transportation and shelter have been widely replaced, its underground network has prospered and proliferated. The water main and the sewer, the gas main and the electric main, were all valuable contributions to the upper level city; and under certain limited conditions, the underground railroad, the motor car tunnel, and the underground lavatory could be justified. But these utilities have now been augmented by underground shops and stores, finally by the underground air raid shelter, as if the kind of environment that served the physical mechanisms and utilities of the city brought any real advantages to its inhabitants. Unfortunately, the underground city demands the constant attendance of living men, also kept underground; and that imposition is hardly less than a premature burial, or at least preparation for the encapsulated existence that alone will remain open to those who accept mechanical improvement as the chief justification of the human adventure.

The underground city is a new kind of environment: an extension and normalization of that forced upon the miner—severed from natural conditions, under mechanical control at every point, made possible by artificial light, artificial ventilation, and the artificial limitations of human responses to those that its organizers deem profitable or serviceable. This new environment coalesced gradually out of a series of empirical inventions: hence even in the most ambitious metropolises, only rarely have the streets or the underground utilities (like the great sewers of Paris) been designed with a view to their economic repair and connection with neighboring buildings, though it is plain that in the more crowded quarters of a city, a single tunnel, accessible at intervals, should serve as a collective artery, and would in the long run effect great economies.

In analyzing the costs of housing a generation ago, Henry Wright discovered that the cost of a whole room was buried in the street, in the various mechanical utilities necessary for the house's functioning. Since then, the relative cost of these underground pipes and wires and conduits has increased; while with every extension of the city, as with every increase of internal congestion, the cost of the whole system disproportionately increases, too.

Given the pressure to sink capital more extensively into the underground city, less money becomes available for space and architectural beauty above ground: indeed, the next step in the city's development, already taken in many American cities, is to extend the principle of the underground city even to the design of buildings that are visibly above ground, and so defeat art at every point. With air conditioning and all-day fluorescent lighting, the internal spaces in the new American skyscraper are little different from what they would be a hundred feet below the surface. No extravagance in mechanical equipment is too great to produce this uniform internal environment: though the technical ingenuity spent on fabricating sealed-in buildings cannot create the equivalent of an organic background for human functions and activities.

All this is merely by way of preparation. For the successor of the paleotechnic town has created instruments and conditions potentially far more lethal than those which wiped out so many lives in the town of Donora, Pennsylvania, through a concentration of toxic gases, or that which in December 1952 killed in one week an estimated five thousand extra of London's inhabitants. The exploitation of uranium to produce fissionable materials threatens, if continued, to poison the lithosphere, the atmosphere, the biosphere—to say nothing of the drinking water—in a fashion that will outdo the worst offenses of the early industrial town; for the pre-nuclear industrial processes could be halted, and the waste products be absorbed or covered over, without permanent blight.

Once fission takes place, however, the radioactivity released will remain throughout the life of the products, sometimes a life measured in many centuries or even millennia: it cannot be altered or disposed of without contaminating, ultimately, the area where it is dumped, be it the stratosphere or the bottom of the ocean. Meanwhile, the manufacture of these lethal materials goes on, without abatement, in preparation for collective military assaults aimed at exterminating whole populations. To make such criminally insane preparations tolerable, public authorities have sedulously conditioned their citizens to march meekly into cellars and subways for 'protection.' Only the staggering cost of creating a whole network of underground cities sufficient to house the entire population as yet prevents this perverse misuse of human energy.

The Victorian industrialist, exposing his fellow citizens to soot and smog, to vile sanitation and environmentally promoted disease, still nourished the belief that his work was contributing, ultimately, to 'peace and plenty.' But his heirs in the underground city have no such illusions— they are the prey of compulsive fears and corrupt fantasies whose ultimate outcome may be universal annihilation and extermination; and the more they devote themselves to adapting their urban environment to this possibility, the more surely they will bring on the unrestricted collective genocide many of them have justified in their minds as the necessary price of preserving 'freedom' and 'civilization.' The masters of the underground citadel are committed to a 'war' they cannot bring to an end, with weapons whose ultimate effects they cannot control, for purposes that they cannot accomplish. The underground city threatens in consequence to become the ultimate burial crypt of our incinerated civilization. Modern man's only alternative is to emerge once more into the light and have the courage, not to escape to the moon, but to return to his own human center—and to master the bellicose compulsions and irrationalities he shares with his rulers and mentors. He must not only unlearn the art of war, but acquire and master, as never before, the arts of life.

CHAPTER SIXTEEN

Suburbia — and Beyond

1 : THE HISTORIC SUBURB

Those who led the 'march of civilization' from the eighteenth century on were inclined to be contemptuous of the countryside, the home of backward farmers, shaggy yokels, or pleasure-seeking aristocrats living on their feudal rents, not on profits wrung from trade and manufacture. Yet even among the utilitarian leaders and beneficiaries the impulse to escape from their industrial environment was a common one: in fact to have enough wealth to escape it was a mark of success.

Well before the industrial town had taken form the notion of leaving behind the complexities of civilization had become attractive to the European mind once more, just as it had been during the decadence of Rome. For the restless and hardy, there was the conquest and colonization of new lands, mingled with the romantic call of the unspoiled wilderness; for more domestic, reflective souls, there was fishing, rambling, botanizing, going on family picnics or musing in solitude deep in the woods. Without waiting for Rousseau to prove that most of the ills of life were derived from the arid rituals of an over-refined civilization, many Europeans had begun to act on these premises. Country life seemed best; and the farther one got away from the city the more one gained in health, freedom, independence. Most of the salubrious features of the nineteenth-century suburb had in fact already been incorporated in the country town, with greater respect for social mixture and co-operation than it was possible to achieve in the one-class suburban community. The very life insurance tables established the superiority of the countryside in terms of animal vitality: in England the peasant and the country squire had the highest expectations of life.

Though the rise of the suburb brought about significant changes in both the social contents and the spatial order of the city, most of the interpreters of the city, until but yesterday, curiously passed it by; and even the few writers who have touched upon the planning of the suburb, notably Professor Christopher Tunnard, have treated it as a relatively recent phenomenon. But the fact is that the suburb becomes visible almost as early as the city itself, and perhaps explains the ability of the ancient town to survive the insanitary conditions that prevailed within its walls. (Woolley found evidences of suburban developments in 'Greater Ur' beyond the built-up area—scattered buildings as far as the temple of al'Ubaid, four miles away.) If we are in doubt as to the layout and inner core of the Egyptian city, both paintings and funerary models show us the suburban villa, with its spacious gardens. In Biblical times, we find mention of little huts that were built in the midst of the open fields or vineyards, perhaps to guard the crops overnight when they were ready to pick, but doubtless also to refresh the soul, weary of the baked bricks and the foul smells of the city itself. These frail shelters are still commemorated in the Jewish feast of the autumn harvest.

All through history, those who owned or rented land outside the city's walls valued having a place in the country, even if they did not actively perform agricultural labor: a cabin, a cottage, a vine-shaded shelter, built for temporary retreat if not for permanent occupancy. Early city dwellers did not wait for rapid transportation to take advantage of this rural surcease. As long as the city remained relatively compact and self-contained, it was possible to keep a balance between rural and urban occupations, yes, and between rural and urban pleasures: eating, drinking, dancing, athletic sports, love-making, every manner of relaxation had a special aura of festivity in a verdant, sunlit landscape. One of the chief penalties for continued urban growth was that it put this pleasurable setting at such a distance and confined it more and more to the ruling classes.

In earlier periods we have seen that new groups and institutions, with larger demands for space than the closely filled-in city could offer, necessarily settled on the outskirts, in little suburban enclaves. Not merely did the Aesclepium at Cos lie outside the city, as Sarton tells us, but the gymnasium and even the academy were often located in the suburbs of the Hellenic city, like the garden we associate with the philosopher Epicurus.

In medieval times, we have seen, too, that the monastery often settled outside the city's walls after the twelfth century, before the city, by its further growth, surrounded it. In every case, the suburban pattern was typically an open one: gardens and orchards and shaded walks, not just gaping space, accompanied the buildings. Great universities like Oxford and Cambridge, which grew up in country towns, sought and wrought for themselves the same kind of parklike environment: perhaps indeed their efforts to secure the luxury of space intensified the antagonism between town and gown.

The early appearance of the suburb points to another, even more important, fact: the life-maintaining agencies, gardening and farming, recreation and games, health sanatoria and retreats belong to the surrounding countryside, even when the functions they fostered spring from the town's needs or deficiencies. By the eighteenth century, it is true, the romantic movement had produced a new rationale for the suburban exodus, and the increasingly smoky and overcrowded town provided a new incentive. But it would be an error to regard suburbanism as a mere derivative of this ideology, for it had older, deeper roots. What needs to be accounted for is not the cult of nature that became popular in the eighteenth century, affecting everything from medicine to education, from architecture to cookery, but rather the obstinacy with which people had often clung for centuries to a crowded, depleted, denatured, and constricted environment, whose chief solace for misery was the company of equally miserable people.

By the time maps and airviews of late medieval cities were made, we find detailed evidence of little huts, cottages, and villas, with ample gardens, springing up outside the city's walls. By the sixteenth century the land so used served for more than summer residence and recreation. As early as the thirteenth century, indeed, Villani reported that the land for a circle of three miles around Florence was occupied by rich estates with costly mansions; and Venetian families were not behind in their villas on the Brenta. From the beginning, the privileges and delights of suburbanism were reserved largely for the upper class; so that the suburb might almost be described as the collective urban form of the country house—the house in a park—as the suburban way of life is so largely a derivative of the relaxed, playful, goods-consuming aristocratic life that developed out of the rough, bellicose, strenuous existence of the feudal stronghold.

A few centuries after Villani, Stow noted that outside the walls of London people were laying out little gardens and fantastic summer houses, "like midsummer pageants, with towers, turrets and chimneys," a full two hundred years before anyone began self-consciously to produce the fantastic villas and follies of the gothic revival. There is an allusion to the new type of suburb in 'The English Courtier.' "The manner of most gentlemen and noblemen also is to house themselves (if they possibly may) in the suburbs of the city, because most commonly, the air being there somewhat at large, the place is healthy, and through the distance from the body of the town, the noise is not much; and so consequently quiet. Also for commodity, we find many lodgings, both spacious and roomethy, with gardens and orchards delectable. So with good government, we have as little cause to fear infection there as in the country; our water is excellent and much better than you have any, on grounds and fields most pleasant."

Though the hygienic superiority of the suburb was one of its major attractions, persistently recommended by physicians, something more than this lured men from the city. And just as one finds the earliest evidence of the back-to-nature movement in Piero di Cosimo's paintings, so one finds an esthetic and psychological justification of suburban development in Alberti's treatise on building. Alberti observed that "there is a vast deal of satisfaction in a convenient retreat near the town, where a man is at liberty to do just what he pleases." That sounds the true suburban note: indeed, it even anticipates the present 'exurban' emphasis on informal clothing, for Alberti insists that "I, for my part, am not for having a [villa] in a place of such resort that I must never venture to appear at my door without being completely dressed."

As for the esthetic attributes of both house and site, Alberti's first perceptions might almost stand as the classic last word. "The great beauties of such a retreat are being near the city, upon an open airy road, and on a pleasant spot of ground. The greatest commendation of itself is its making a cheerful appearance to those that go a little way out of the town to take the air; as if it seemed to invite every beholder. . . . Nor should there be any want of pleasant landscapes, flowery mead, open champains, shady groves, or limpid brooks, or streams and lakes for swimming, with all other delights of the same sort. Lastly . . . I would have the front and whole body of the house perfectly well lighted, and that it be open to receive a great deal of light and sun, and a sufficient quantity of wholesome air." When he goes on to advocate both round and square rooms, and all rooms possible on one floor, one must ask how much he left for the early twentieth-century architect to invent. The whole suburban domestic program is there.

Though the retreat from the city held manifest advantages for health and family life, it was equally an attempt to achieve liberation from the sometimes dreary conventions and compulsions of an urban society: an effort, given the necessary financial means, to have life on one's own terms, even if it meant having it alone: the anarchism of the well filled purse, the heresy of the private individual's seeking to take over within the limits of a private family the functions of a whole community. This applied to both the suburban occupant and his house; and here again Alberti supplies the classic citation, on the difference between town and country house life—"which is, that in town you are obliged to moderate yourselves in several respects according to the privileges of your neighbor; whereas you have much more liberty in the country."

To be your own unique self; to build your unique house, mid a unique landscape: to live in this Domain of Arnheim a self-centered life, in which private fantasy and caprice would have license to express themselves openly, in short, to withdraw like a monk and live like a prince—this was the purpose of the original creators of the suburb. They proposed in effect to create an asylum, in which they could, as individuals, overcome the chronic defects of civilization while still commanding at will the privileges and benefits of urban society. This utopia proved to be, up to a point, a realizable one: so enchanting that those who contrived it failed to see the fatal penalty attached to it—the penalty of popularity, the fatal inundation of a mass movement whose very numbers would wipe out the goods each individual sought for his own domestic circle, and, worse, replace them with a life that was not even a cheap counterfeit, but rather the grim antithesis.

The ultimate outcome of the suburb's alienation from the city became visible only in the twentieth century, with the extension of the democratic ideal through the instrumentalities of manifolding and mass production. In the mass movement into suburban areas a new kind of community was produced, which caricatured both the historic city and the archetypal suburban refuge: a multitude of uniform, unidentifiable houses, lined up inflexibly, at uniform distances, on uniform roads, in a treeless communal waste, inhabited by people of the same class, the same income, the same age group, witnessing the same television performances, eating the same tasteless pre-fabricated foods, from the same freezers, conforming in every outward and inward respect to a common mold, manufactured in the central metropolis. Thus the ultimate effect of the suburban escape in our time is, ironically, a low-grade uniform environment from which escape is impossible. What has happened to the suburban exodus in the United States now threatens, through the same mechanical instrumentalities, to take place, at an equally accelerating rate, everywhere else—unless the most vigorous countermeasures are taken.

But before we confront this final caricature of the unfettered suburban life, lived according to nature, for the sake of health and child nurture, let us consider more closely the actual development of the suburban container. For we shall see that out of this breakup of the old urban forms, out of the chaotic freedom and spatial looseness of the suburban community, came the first substantial changes in urban structure, which matched, unconsciously, the changes that have been taking place in our whole conception of the cosmos. The open basketwork texture of the suburb bears little resemblance to the solid stone container of late neolithic culture. Though the suburb lacked many of the attributes of the ancient city, it has served as an experimental field for the development of a new type of open plan and a new distribution of urban functions.

Thus the suburb has prepared the way for a better order of planning, not yet fully expressed or achieved anywhere, in which both the static and dynamic functions, those of the container and the magnet, would find fresh expression. Though the suburb, as such, belongs to the past and has already been enveloped by the conurbation, some of the lessons that modern planners first mastered in the suburb must be incorporated into the new concept of the city.

2: PHASES OF SUBURBAN GROWTH

From the thirteenth century on, the dread of plague prompted a periodic exodus from the city; and in that sense, one may say that the modern suburb began as a sort of rural isolation ward. Even today, in a survey of the suburbanite's reasons for moving from Cleveland to the outskirts, the largest percentage of reasons in favor of this move, 61 per cent, was "to live in a cleaner, healthier neighborhood," while only 48 per cent of the answers favored better schools or the opportunity to own their homes, and only 28 per cent wished to have a yard or garden.

In every age, then, the fear of the city's infections and the attractions of the open countryside provided both negative and positive stimulus. Both operated, plainly, in the case of Boccaccio's ladies and gentlemen in 'The Decameron,' who fled from plague-ridden Florence, menaced equally by the corpses of the dead and the ordure of the living, to a country villa on the heights of Fiesole, whose very situation shows that the Etruscans had a better appreciation of a salubrious site than the Romans who founded Florence.

Pure air and water, freedom from raucous human noises, open fields for riding, hunting, archery, rural strolling—these are qualities that the aristocracy everywhere has always valued; and they are responsible per-haps for their bodily fitness and self-confidence, which contrasts with the occupational disabilities and deformations of the specialized urban drudge, too long confined to the workshop, the counting house, the library. By the time of Queen Elizabeth, the great houses of the aristocracy lined the Strand in London, and their gardens went down to the waterfront, while a stretch of farmland separated them from the Temple and the busy city to the east. The hotels of the gentry in Paris, on the Left Bank, were likewise suburban in their amplitude, even though their walled courtyards and mansions, forming a continuous street façade, concealed the generous gardens behind.

Let me emphasize the demand for space, which changed the whole scale of urban planning once the protective fortification ceased to be essential for security. Whatever else the suburb has stood for, it has demanded an enlargement of the areas of open green and garden, as proper appurtenances of the city. What only kings could demand once, was now the prerogative of every commoner who could get hold of the land itself. The more constricted the old quarters of the city, the more closely packed its streets and houses, the greater was the visual relief of the suburb's openness: indeed part of the esthetic value of the suburb, its special psychological virtue, springs from the daily shuttling to and from the city, with its alternation of openness and enclosure, freedom and constriction, easy movement and clogged traffic, spaciousness and overcrowding. All the inherent esthetic values of the suburb are sharpened by these contrasts.

As the crowding of the great metropolises and the spreading industrial towns became chronic in the eighteenth century, the demand to get away from the city therefore became more imperative and undeniable. If one did not quit the city for good on one's own initiative, the doctor's orders would prompt one to take temporary quarters in a health resort, a bath or a spa or a seaside retreat, or permanent quarters in a suburb beyond the grimy town. Soame Jenyns remarked in 1795 that tradesmen's wives who felt suffocated by the smoke of London must have their villas at Clapham; and Hampstead was an even more favored spot for those who could afford it, for its elevated site still gives it clear air when the rest of London is choking and sputtering in the smog. By the middle of the nineteenth century, the menace of poverty added a further incentive to the exodus. "Nothing," remarked a writer in the 'Quarterly Review' in 1850, "has so much contributed to drive away the opulent from the dwellings of the poor as the dread of their unwholesomeness and dirt."

This suburban movement developed more slowly in strictly industrial urban areas, where smoke-clogged vegetation grew with difficulty and potential parks and gardens were seized for refuse dumps and slagheaps, where in fact the massing of factory chimneys produced sufficient effluvia to defile a whole countryside. But the suburb flourished around towns with a more mixed population, with its infiltration of rural aristocracy and leisured people; and eventually, as at Edgbaston in Birmingham, it embraced the most hardened Bounderbys and Gradgrinds. At first, no doubt, the possibilities of suburban living were limited to those who, like John Ruskin's father, could sport a horse and carriage and coachman, or could at least afford the expensive daily journey by public coach; but by the end of the eighteenth century in London—later of course elsewhere —a new environment was taking shape on the outskirts: Barnes, St. John's Wood, Hampstead, later Bedford Park, Putney, and Hammersmith. The railroad and metropolitan mass transit only widened the economic basis of a movement that had begun among the upper classes long before their invention.

For a while, the street pattern of these new villa districts remained regular and hardly distinguishable from that of the central city. There was little in its formal arrangement to mark an early Victorian suburb, except the amplitude of garden space; and even this did not differ from the new quarters of an independent health resort and pensioners' retreat like Great Malvern. The houses were the usual spacious urban houses, with regular, often square, ground plans and high-ceilinged rooms: Palladian if not gothic villas or—in America—pseudo-Greek temples, aping marmoreal dignity mid a spreading lawn that never grew in Greece. But by the middle of the nineteenth century the romantic impulse in landscape planning began to affect architecture and urbanism, favoring the 'natural,' that is, the informal, the accidental, the capricious, and the wild. The principle of laissez-faire was applied by the new urban planners to both the environment and the buildings of man. Romantic order was a revolt against order: a relief from the implacable necessities of a monotonous and over-regimented daily routine. This exaggeration of playfulness and spontaneity, with its rejection of traditional guidances and workmanlike disciplines, finally made its way into the education of the young.

The romantic artist preferred rude originality to polite conformity, even if that rudeness was collectively tolerable only by complete spatial detachment from the rest of the community. Only in the landscape park could these principles of studied accident and willful wantonness be carried to their ideal limit; so the new form of the suburb became that of scattered buildings in a park. In every sense, the park preceded the new urban form and stamped it with certain characteristics that had never before been desired or contrived. This freedom paved the way for fresh inventions. In its system of circulation, Olmsted and Vaux's Central Park was superior to any conventional two-dimensional city plan; for, by using overpasses and underpasses wherever possible, it provided four independent traffic networks: footways for pedestrians, bridlepaths for horseback riders, carriage drives for wheeled vehicles, and crosstown transverses for city traffic. In its provisions for unhampered circulation and safe crossings, this scheme made a unique contribution to city planning.

Following romantic principles, the suburban house and plot and garden were deliberately de-formalized. The street avoided straight lines, even when no curves were given by nature: it might swerve to save a tree, or even to preserve the robust contours of a hillside. Toward the end of the nineteenth century, this impulse to respect nature led to treating minor variations in contour as definitive guiding lines, for the sake of the irregularity they produced: an exaggerated rebuke to the municipal engineer's costly practice of disregarding them completely.

Now it happens that simple natural forms are often less expensive than their mechanical substitutes: this was no small discovery in an age that preferred iron fences to privet hedges, paving to greensward, or paper and wax flowers made in sweatshops to flowers grown in the earth. This is still worth remembering in our present age, when architects lay out buildings without regard to orientation or view or micro-climate in order to justify a mechanically elaborate air-conditioning system, and seal their buildings in glass walls and Venetian blinds, which remove all the hygienic values derivable from open sunlight and naturally pure air.

By contrast with the present spurious 'romanticism of the machine' the architects and planners of the early romantic movement were demonstrably more scientific and rational. Because the suburban plan economized on mechanical conveniences, it had space and facilities for more vital functions. The suburban house was often consciously oriented for sunlight, for summer breezes, for a view; while plantations of trees and bushes served as windbreaks for both garden and home. Out of respect for a whole complex of biological and domestic interests, the suburban dwelling house achieved a new form, more congenial to family life in all its stages of development.

From the suburb, in fact, sprang a new domestic architecture, organically at one, both in function and image, with the life within and the landscape without: houses and gardens that brought to conscious perfection the traditional virtues of the farmhouse, with new utilities possible only in our own day. By economizing on paving, curbing, high masonry walls, unnecessarily wide roadways and avenues, the suburban planner saved money for trees, gardens, woods, playgrounds. By setting the houses in many-acred blocks, from two to five times as big as the standard city blocks, the new suburban residential density of from one to twelve houses to the acre was maintained in part by the plan itself. From H. H. Richardson to Frank Lloyd Wright the most graciously original expressions of modern form were achieved in the suburban house.

In these new suburbs the problem of creating an urban environment favorable to the health and nurture of children was solved by the middle classes as it had never been solved before, except in the almost equally open country town or village. The mere opening up of space was an essential part of the solution. Yet the change of scale and the scattering of dwellings raised an older rural problem, that of isolation; and, to achieve any degree of social advantage, it magnified the need for private vehicular transportation, since, again, the very dispersal of dwellings made any more public system of transportation for short hauls prohibitive.

In the end, once suburban growth became untrammeled, the open plan made rapid locomotion and an extravagant road system a necessity, at the expense of most of the other qualities that had made the suburb originally attractive. Thus in overcoming the difficulties of the over-crowded and over-extended city, the suburb proved to be both a temporary and a costly solution. As soon as the suburban pattern became universal, the virtues it at first boasted began to disappear.

As long as the suburb remained a convenient annex to the city, the part it played, if temporary, was often a salutary one. But even at an early stage, the popularity of the mode of escape undermined some of the results it aimed to achieve, above all privacy and solitude. What Francis Parkman had said of the westward march of the pioneer was equally true of the suburb: "The sons of civilization, drawn by the fascinations of a fresher and bolder life, thronged to the western wilds in multitudes which blighted the charm that had lured them." That form of suburban blight was visible at an early date. Land values went up in the newly invaded areas, once they were made accessible by railroad: the better the transit provisions, the higher the values and the wider the suburban ring. As the city crept nearer the suburbs, the rural note vanished: presently the sub-urbanite had the advantages of neither society nor solitude. Even in the nineteenth century, the social weaknesses of the suburb were apparent: one paid a heavy price for fresh air.

But there was a moment when the suburb's compensatory freedoms made it seem the answer to the growing city's growing problems: if one could not conquer the city one could at least escape it. If nothing more, the suburb was a protest against the inevitability of the inevitable. J. M. Richards, in his nostalgic wartime *jeu d'esprit*, 'Castles on the Ground,' did justice to both the mood and the product: the dreamful unexpectedness of suburban architecture, the sudden lift of a gable, the bulge of an oriel or a tower, the outburst of ungrammatical chatter in a foreign language, the eruption of an oasis of beflowered rocks in the middle of a velvety green-sward: cheap excursions into distant lands or into past moments of history. What were all these artful domestic exhibitions but Suburbia's service to 'Every Man in his Humor'? Dickens caricatured these private crotchets in 'Great Expectations,' in his picture of the Old 'Un, Mr. Wemmick's father, with his castellated house, his moat and his drawbridge and his sunset salute with a toy cannon. But something that had been lost in the city was here coming back in an innocent form—the power to live an imagined life, closer to one's inner grain than what the daily routine imposes.

Thus in its earliest form, the suburb acknowledged the varieties of human temperament and aspiration, the need for change, contrast, and adventure, and above all, for an environment visibly responsive to one's personal efforts, as even the smallest flower garden is responsive. Here nothing was too absurd to be attempted in architecture or gardening: hardly anything too private or too neurotic to be openly expressed. Domestic whimsy offset productive rigor and utilitarian monotony.

To sum up: the early romantic suburb was a middle-class effort to find a private solution for the depression and disorder of the befouled metropolis: an effusion of romantic taste but an evasion of civic responsibility and municipal foresight. The instincts that prompted this exodus were valid: caught in the new urban wreckage, the old cry, "Women and children first," was a sound one. Life was actually in danger in this new urban milieu of industrialism and commercialism, and the merest counsel of prudence was to flee—flee with all one's goods, as Lot and his household had fled from the sultry hell of Sodom and Gomorrah. But unfortunately this sound motto did not apply to the women and children of the working classes, despite many pious hopes vouchsafed in the middle of the nineteenth century that cheap fares and special workers' trains would at once solve the housing problem of the poor and permit everyone to spend part of his day in a rural environment. Even more unfortunately, to the extent that the lower middle classes did follow, they carried their depressed if respectable environment with them.

For the happy few, the suburb met the needs of child-bearing and child-rearing: with woman predominating in this community throughout the day, it was a sort of return to the archaic matriarchy, in a more playful and relaxed mood. Seemingly, for a while, the suburbanites held a hand uplifted over their fate: disease, disorder, prostitution, crime, violence, were all far away, in a festering metropolis. But only part of life went on here: all those mobilizing and quickening forces, all those dialectical tensions and struggles that had made actual life in the city stirring and significant were now relegated to the novel. What was needed was not a plan to widen the retreat from the city, but to return to the original core, with a new method of containing and distributing its great numbers, so that in the heart of the city the achievements of the suburb would be perpetuated in a more suitable and enduring form.

Taking the suburb at its best, it provided a parklike setting for the family dwelling house; and for all the domestic activities associated with it. In the kitchen, the garden, the workshop, activities that had once been necessities of country life could now be carried on as a relief from the grim, monotonous, imprisoned collective routine of the city. For a short while, indeed, old country habits had been carried over to the suburb, so that Ruskin, for example, would remember not merely the rural setting of his parents' home in Denmark Hill, but the generous vegetable gardens, the horse and the stable, and even the pigs and chickens that enriched the dinner table. This was in effect a colorable reproduction of the older Country House culture, with daily rather than seasonal excursions to town.

Beginning as a mechanism of escape, the suburb has turned into its very opposite. All that is left of the original impulse toward autonomy and initiative is the driving of the private motor car; but this itself is a compulsory and inescapable condition of suburban existence; and clever engineers already threaten to remove the individual control by a system of automation. The current cost of this form of 'freedom' in the United States—40,000 dead and more than a million people injured or maimed for life every year—must be partly debited from the favorable side of the suburban movement.

3: THE SUBURBAN WAY OF LIFE

At the beginning the suburb was the expression of a new way of life, less effortful, less regimented, less sterile, less formalized in every way than that of the production-minded urban centers; and as the emphasis has, with further gains in production, shifted to consumption, this new way of life has tended to become more universal and is no longer purely an expression of discontent with the disordered city; for even tiny historic towns, like Villeneuve-les-Avignon, now have their new suburban fringe.

By the very nature of the retreat, the suburb could be identified by a number of related social characteristics. And first, it was a segregated community, set apart from the city, not merely by space but by class stratification: a sort of green ghetto dedicated to the elite. That smug Victorian phrase, "We keep ourselves to ourselves," expresses the spirit of the suburb, in contrast to the city; for the city, by its nature, is a multi-form non-segregated environment. Little groups may indeed form social islands within a city, as the various tribes tended to do in the early cities of Islam, or again as people from a Greek or a Polish village might form temporary nests together in the same block in Chicago or New York. But the metropolis was a mixture of people who came from different places, practiced different occupations, encountered other personalities, meeting and mingling, co-operating and clashing, the rich with the poor, the proud with the humble.

Except where the suburb enclosed an original small town core, it tended to remain a one-class community, with just a sufficient fringe of tradesmen and servants to keep it going—the latter often condemned to use the central metropolis as their dormitory. Segregation, in practice, means compulsory association, or at least cohabitation; for if there are any choices, they lie outside the immediate community. Hence the great residual freedom of the suburbanite is that of locomotion. For esthetic and intellectual stimulus, the suburb remains dependent upon the big city: the theater, the opera, the orchestra, the art gallery, the university, the museum are no longer part of the daily environment. The problem of re-establishing connections, on a regional rather than a metropolitan basis, is one of the main problems of city planning in our time.

Not merely did the suburb keep the busier, dirtier, more productive enterprises at a distance, it likewise pushed away the creative activities of the city. Here life ceased to be a drama, full of unexpected challenges and tensions and dilemmas: it became a bland ritual of competitive spending. "Half your trouble," Rudyard Kipling wrote to William James in 1896, "is the curse of America—sheer, hopeless, well-ordered boredom; and that is going some day to be the curse of the world." Kipling put his finger, at that early date, upon the weakness of the suburban way of life.

Thus the genuine biological benefits of the suburb were undermined by its psychological and social defects: above all, the irreality of its retreat. In the town poor men demonstrated: beggars held out their hands in the street: disease spread quickly from poor quarters to the residences of the comfortable, via the delivery boy, the washerwoman, the seamstress, or other necessary menials: the eye, if not carefully averted, would, on a five-minute walk in any direction, behold a slum, or at least a slum child, ragged and grimy.

Even in the heyday of Coketown, sensitive and intelligent souls could not remain long in such an environment without banding together to do something about it: they would exhort and agitate, hold meetings and form parades, draw up petitions and besiege legislators, extract money from the rich and dispense aid to the poor, founding soup kitchens and model tenements, passing housing legislation and acquiring land for parks, establishing hospitals and health centers, libraries and universities, in which the whole community played a part and benefitted.

In the suburb one might live and die without marring the image of an innocent world, except when some shadow of its evil fell over a column in the newspaper. Thus the suburb served as an asylum for the preservation of illusion. Here domesticity could flourish, forgetful of the exploitation on which so much of it was based. Here individuality could prosper, oblivious of the pervasive regimentation beyond. This was not merely a child-centered environment: it was based on a childish view of the world, in which reality was sacrificed to the pleasure principle.

As an attempt to recover what was missing in the city, the suburban exodus could be amply justified, for it was concerned with primary human needs. But there was another side: the temptation to retreat from unpleasant realities, to shirk public duties, and to find the whole meaning of life in the most elemental social group, the family, or even in the still more isolated and self-centered individual. What was properly a beginning was treated as an end.

In many places, the change toward playful emptiness and civic irresponsibility can be dated. In private conversation Mr. Justice Brandeis once observed to me that he remembered the time, at the turn of the century, when the wealthy citizens of Boston told their sons, when they reached maturity: "Boston holds nothing for you except heavy taxes and political misrule. When you marry, pick out a suburb to build a house in, join the Country Club, and make your life center about your club, your home, and your children."

That advice was widely followed, not merely by the patricians of Boston and Philadelphia, but by their counterparts in many other big cities in the Western World. Though the result was a wide scattering of upper-class suburbs in the first and second wave of the metropolitan outflow, the exodus also quickened the inner corruption of the city and worked toward its destruction.

Only as a nursery for bringing up children did the suburb prove a more adequate environment, particularly in the early days of the railroad suburb, when each settlement was surrounded by a broad greenbelt of woods and fields. Here children could gambol safely, without supervision; and around the suburban schools was play-space so ample that it became the ideal requirement for all future schools: space for lawn tennis and croquet, for cricket or baseball, football or bowls. Emerson had noted these advantages clearly in his 'Journal,' in 1865: "There is no police so effective as a good hill and wide pasture in the neighborhood of a village, where the boys can run and play and dispose of their superfluous strength and spirits." The suburb established such play space as an essential part of the city: not to be crowded out by high land values. That was a permanent contribution.

But too soon, in breaking away from the city, the part became a substitute for the whole, even as a single phase of life, that of childhood, became the pattern for all the seven ages of man. As leisure generally increased, play became the serious business of life; and the golf course, the country club, the swimming pool, and the cocktail party became the frivolous counterfeits of a more varied and significant life. Thus in reacting against the disadvantages of the crowded city, the suburb itself became an over-specialized community, more and more committed to relaxation and play as ends in themselves. Compulsive play fast became the acceptable alternative to compulsive work: with small gain either in freedom or vital stimulus. Accordingly, the two modes of life blend into each other; for both in suburb and in metropolis, mass production, mass consumption, and mass recreation produce the same kind of standardized and denatured environment.

Even children suffered from this transformation of the whole community into a mere recreation area. For such a segregated community, composed of segregated economic strata, with little visible daily contact with the realities of the workaday world, placed an undue burden of education on the school and family. The smallest village where people still farm and fish and hunt, the drabbest industrial town whose population still engages in essential productive enterprises, has educational possibilities that the suburb lacks. In the end, the operative differences between the contemporary suburb and the big city become increasingly minimal: for in these seemingly different environments reality has been progressively reduced to what filters through the screen of the television set.

But both childhood and the suburb are transitional stages: so a well-planned urban community must have a place for other phases of life and other modes of living. A universal suburb is almost as much of a nightmare, humanly speaking, as a universal megalopolis: yet it is toward this proliferating nonentity that our present random or misdirected urban growth has been steadily tending. A large scale pattern of expressways and airfields and sprawling car parks and golf-courses envelops a small scale, increasingly shrunken mode of life.

Yet in its original effort, when the suburb approached nearest the romantic goal, it made a positive contribution to the emerging conception of the city as a mixed environment, interwoven in texture with the country; and many of these contributions need to be appraised and selectively adapted and improved, not discarded.

4: NOTHING GAINED BY

OVERCROWDING

In hybridizing maize a stunted, seemingly feeble species may often prove more productive in combination with one of more normal characteristics than two equally well-developed kinds. This odd source of hybrid vigor seems to hold equally for the suburb. What was essentially a stunted urban mode of life, favoring a single function, produced in combination with rural opportunities a whole series of improvements over the plan of the existing city.

In its free use of space, the suburb was the precise opposite of most historic cities in the West. In the latter we find a scattering of open spaces, behind and between buildings, sometimes considerable cultivated areas within the walls. In the suburb, on the other hand, there was a scattering of buildings in the midst of open spaces; the garden, the park, the arcade of trees, the approaching road, formed an esthetic continuum. Rows of buildings no longer served as continuous walls, bounding streets that formed a closed corridor: the building, divorced from its close association with the street, was embosomed in the landscape and deliberately absorbed by it. With this opening up of the close texture of the traditional city came a necessary change in the size of the residential block.

By the middle of the nineteenth century, the suburban superblock had come into existence, many times the size of the ordinary city block. Access to its interior was provided by cul-de-sac or narrow U and L shaped roadways, meant for limited local use. This innovation not merely provided for large gardens and freedom from disturbing through-traffic: it likewise economized on costly road building. In addition, the planner of suburbs, following the contours and narrowing the service roads, saved on both capital expenditure and upkeep, while preserving the parklike character of the whole environment. These innovations seem to have occurred spontaneously at more than one place, but so unconsciously with so little theoretic appreciation until a generation ago, that it is difficult to date them.

Yet none of the planning done within the nineteenth century, not even that done under Haussmann, compares in freshness of form and boldness of design with the best of the suburbs, from Olmsted's Riverside, near Chicago, to his Roland Park near Baltimore, from Llewellyn Park in New Jersey to Unwin and Parker's superb achievement at Hampstead Garden Suburb, in which the buildings were an integral part of the whole design.

So charming was the physical environment of the better suburbs that for long it drew attention away from their social deficiencies and oversights. By getting away from the standard gridiron plan and high ground rents, by accepting the co-operation of nature instead of stamping out every trace of environmental character, the new planners and builders evolved a new form for the city, or at least, the rough outlines of a new form. This achievement deserves an historic monograph that has still to be written, in which Clarence Stein's 'New Towns for America' would form a chapter. Here I will deal only with the general conclusions to be drawn from the best suburban practice.

The insight that seems intuitively to have guided the most effective suburban planners was first put rationally, perhaps, by Raymond Unwin, in a modest little pamphlet, 'Nothing Gained by Overcrowding.' Unwin began by examining the typical English bye-law street, the product of England's earliest municipal regulations. These regulations provided for a minimum amount of street width, backyard, daylight, and sanitary facilities for each house: but, as it turned out, with superfluous provisions for traffic—an unfortunate bias that has been carried over even into the neighborhood designs of the recent British New Towns. Unwin demonstrated that this seemingly parsimonious utilitarian plan provided for an extravagant number of streets, duly paved for heavy duty, at an excessive cost. For lack of any suitable other spaces, these traffic ways became playgrounds for children. Unwin further showed that by cutting down on the number of needless streets and devoting the areas so dedicated to internal gardens, he could provide almost the same number of houses, each with more usable garden land, and with more gracious surroundings, at the same price.

That in fact was what the suburban planner had often been doing. But the original cheapness of the land was usually credited with economies actually due to low development costs, through the elimination of curbing, over-wide streets, unnecessarily heavy paving, and—sometimes—the avoiding of municipal sewage systems, by using domestic cesspools, possible only in open communities of low density. Unwin proved that the dreariness of the congested quarters of London, Manchester, Philadelphia, Chicago, even when composed of only one-family houses, could be accounted for partly by bad planning, with wasteful expenditure of capital on utilities that a more imaginative plan, directed to serving human needs, would reduce.

This analysis also had a certain retrospective merit: not merely did it account for the success of innovations in planning like the superblock and the cul-de-sac, but it likewise showed the soundness of those monastic and collegiate plans, on the medieval pattern—The Temple and Gray's Inn in London, and the older colleges at Oxford and Cambridge—that had created self-enclosed quarters, withdrawn from wheeled traffic.

Unwin's perception that pleasant open spaces and parks and playgrounds were not an upper-class luxury, but could be incorporated without extra cost in the most modest housing scheme, simply by saving on needless utilities and streets, was a discovery of the first order. Here was a way to make the stony urban desert bloom, provided one did not, like the painter Mondrian, detest the sight of growing things in the city. But the new prescription was not self-administering. To preserve open land at low density, there must be effective public control over the exploitation of land, either by national or municipal ownership, or by the legal establishment of firm standards of residential density in areas zoned for residential use, as well as legal control to prevent private building that lacks adequate open areas.

In addition, major through traffic streams must be routed around residential areas, on roads that have no local function to perform. Thus the positive lessons of suburban planning needed, if they were to be effective, a kind of municipal statesmanship that has been slow in coming into existence. One of the surest evidences of that statesmanship is that its planning would be directed toward the elimination of the suburb as such, and the building of new communities of a higher and more complex order.

5 : THE SUBURB AS NEIGHBORHOOD UNIT

The fact that suburbs were originally small and self-contained communities had still another effect on their development: it helped to re-create a new consciousness of something that had been lost in the rapid growth of the city—the sense of the neighborhood. Traced back to its origins, this turns out to be the old village component, as essential to a balanced urban life as are its centers of higher culture and purposeful association.

In many suburban communities, the very absence of any structure of local government promoted neighborly organization; so that Robert Wood, in his curiously ambivalent and self-contradictory survey of Suburbia in the United States, pointed out correctly that the suburb restored, in some ways, the earlier ideas of democratic participation and local initiative. Though the New England town meeting had once been such an organ of conscious civic association, it had never been incorporated in the larger political structure; and with the growth of the city there had been, accordingly, a constant shift from the primary community of family and neighborhood, to more purposeful, selective, secondary associations that took care of the citizen's more specialized interests but were not related to his domestic life.

Plainly, in the great metropolises for the past century, family and neighborhood association have largely become residual facts. Excess of numbers, a constant influx of strangers, frequent shifting of domiciles, lack of identifiable boundaries or common centers for meeting, all lessened the stabilizing processes of neighborhood life. Yet in cities as unified as Paris, Chombart de Lauwe and his colleagues have shown, the whole life of a working class family centers in its 'quarter,' almost as rooted, almost as immune to outside influences, as if it were in a village a hundred miles away from the Place de la Concorde. Though the residents of a suburb might retreat from the formidable political challenges of a growing city, they often assumed active responsibilities in their local community, if only to assure themselves of a good water supply or well-managed schools.

On the scale of values that the psychologist, Edward L. Thorndike, erected, the suburbs of the United States ranked high above other communities in desirable qualities, with small towns coming next, and the industrial towns far down on the list. (The biggest cities, curiously, fell in between.) Doubtless Thorndyke's scale to some extent favored just those traits in which the suburb excelled. But on any scale that ignored the specific functions of the city, the suburb would probably rank high.

Some of the activities of the middle-class suburb were doubtless due to the superior education of its members and the relatively large amount of leisure that the women of the community enjoyed. The latter thus approximated, in modern terms, the conditions required for citizenship in the Greek polis: leisure, detachment from base occupations, concern for public goods.

"The suburban town emerges," as Robert Wood observes, "equipped with a limited constituency, a homogeneity, a type of civic attitude, and an amount of leisure which bid fair to put small town democracy into practice for more people and more governments than has been possible for a hundred years. The overwhelming majority of suburbs are relatively small in size and their population is manageable in number." Thus though the motive for the suburban exodus was largely an escapist one, spurred by the moral disorders and environmental foulness of the city, not the least of its gains was a political one. Politically the suburb might be described as an attempt to reduce the functional urban community to a size small enough for an individual family to cope with.

The suburb superficially restored the dream of Jeffersonian democracy, almost effaced by the oligarchic proclivities of capitalism, and provided the conditions essential for its success: the small face-to-face community of identifiable people, participating in the common life as equals. Gardening and politics were both 'do-it-yourself' activities in the suburb. And just as long as the community retained its natural limitation of area and numbers, it continued to foster this neighborly life. It was no accident, therefore, that Clarence Perry framed the concept of the neighborhood unit, after experiencing the benefits of a well-planned suburban environment as a resident of a model suburban development on Long Island, Forest Hills Gardens. What Perry did was to make more explicit, in a better defined structure, the life that he had there found rewarding.

Perry's original interest in the neighborhood principle had started at the political end. But it had been anticipated earlier by the Settlement House movement, which gave to the slums of cities like London, Chicago, and Pittsburgh something that even its best areas lacked: an organizing social nucleus, which provided the necessary facilities for working and co-operating in all manner of neighborly activities. He was a leader in the movement, which had started in the provincial industrial town of Rochester, New York, to restore through community centers some of the vitality of American political life. What the new Settlement Houses had seemed about to achieve in the first generation of their existence, he and his fellow-workers hoped to introduce into every American community.

The community center was a place for discussion and debate and co-operative action, on all public issues: its purpose was to restore initiative, self-consciousness, and self-direction to the local group: a challenge to partisan loyalties, one-sided decisions and remote control. Once established, the community center might launch out in many directions, as Toynbee Hall and Hull House had, fostering participation in amateur theatricals, the practice of the arts and crafts, forming a center for the spiritual and cultural life of the neighborhood, as the church had once done.

After 1920, the community center idea seemed to languish as a movement; and the hopes it quickened seemed to die out. Yet in part this was because of its very success; for in the following years it became standard practice, in the United States, to plan schools with facilities for serving as adult community centers, even in the day time. Perry, at all events, carried the whole conception further by conceiving a unified structure that would be more favorable to neighborhood activities and functions, and yet would take an active part as the suburb did not, in the larger urban program.

The principle of neighborhood organization was to bring within walking distance all the facilities needed daily by the home and the school, and to keep outside this pedestrian area the heavy traffic arteries carrying people or goods that had no business in the neighborhood. Once the walking distance was established, as the very criterion of a face-to-face community, it followed that no playground for school children should be more than a quarter of a mile from the houses it served; and the same principle applied with variations to the distance of the primary school and the local marketing area. Both the population and the peripheral spread of such a community was limited and might be physically defined by either a road system or a greenbelt, or both. Perry placed the population of such an urban neighborhood at about five thousand: large enough to supply a full variety of local services and appurtenances, always allowing for a generous flow across the borders; for it is only partisan opponents of the neighborhood unit idea who regard it as a sealed-in unit designed to prevent intercourse with the rest of the city. In his concept of the neighborhood Perry had identified the fundamental social cell of the city and established the principle of cellular growth.

Clarence Perry had in effect restored, with modern ideas and modern facilities, above all with self-conscious art, one of the oldest components of the city, the quarter, which we found in early Mesopotamia. But he had transposed the temple or church, as the attractive nucleus, into the school and the community center, and he had incorporated the playground and the park as an essential part of the whole design, thus bringing back into the city some of the rural elements it had too complaisantly forfeited. By restoring the pedestrian scale and lessening the amount of unnecessary transportation, the neighborhood plan proposed to free the traffic arteries for more efficient penetration into larger areas, without the endless cross-hauls and time-wasting that a random scattering of urban facilities entails.

In three different communities, one fitted into a gridiron street system, another on a rolling agricultural land, and the third on a hill site, Henry Wright and Clarence Stein demonstrated the value of the ideas Perry had formulated, and the universal application of the experience he had consciously projected into a new city pattern.

Out of these concrete applications two new planning features developed. One was the separation of through transportation avenues from local roads and streets, as advocated by Perry: this was carried to its logical conclusion in Radburn, where the pedestrian paths and the vehicular roads form two independent systems, as noted previously. The other was the neighborhood park, conceived either as a Greenbelt around the neighborhood, as in many English New Towns, or as a ribbon of internal green, uniting the superblocks as in Radburn. In the plan for Chandigarh, Le Corbusier wisely carried through, in his more systematic Cartesian manner, the Radburn plan originally laid down for that capital by Albert Mayer and Matthew Nowicki. So far, apart from the British New Towns, that is the largest application of the idea of cellular neighborhood development in an organized and unified city plan.

Thus one of the most striking innovations in modern city planning derives directly from both physical and social innovations made in the original planning of the romantic suburb. And the desire for this more genial environment for domestic activities, particularly those of a growing family with the personal responses possible only in a small community, helped to popularize the suburban movement. Unfortunately the suburb itself has lost the conditions that preserved the landscape around it and provided for spontaneous association and common enterprises. What the suburb retains today is largely its original weaknesses: snobbery, segregation, status seeking, political irresponsibility.

In a recent study in Boston, a survey showed that only one male resident out of three spends any time on community or civic activity in his dormitory suburb, and that he likewise fails to participate actively in his professional or business association. In effect, the suburbanite renounces the obligations of citizenship at both ends; and the farther he goes from the center the more dissociated he becomes. Neither neighborhood nor city give cohesion to the suburb of the 'motor age.' The suburban shopping centers, the suburban factories and business office and research institutions, provide a minimum of facilities for association while imposing through their random distribution a maximum exertion of effort—whether counted in time, mileage, or cost.

These fast moving particles are the fallout of the metropolitan explosion. They are no longer held together either by the urban magnet or the urban container: they are rather emblems of the 'disappearing city.' But this movement from the center carries no hope or promise of life at a higher level. Just as our expanding technological universe pushes our daily existence ever farther from its human center, so the expanding urban universe carries its separate fragments ever farther from the city, leaving the individual more dissociated, lonely, and helpless than he probably ever was before. Compulsory mobility provides fewer, not more opportunities for association than compulsory stability provided in the walled town.

What began as a flight from the city by families has become a more general retreat, which has produced, not so much individual suburbs as a spreading suburban belt. While the big organizations of the metropolis have become more highly organized, by large-scale bureaucratic supervision, mechanized accountancy, and centralized financial control, they have scattered their fragments—department stores, hotels, insurance offices, laboratories, banks—over the whole metropolitan landscape: sometimes, confessedly, to shorten the distance to work for the owners and managers. This in itself is an admission that the tedious metropolitan journey to work had become not merely intolerable but unnecessary. Unfortunately, the sum of all these dispersals does not produce a new urban constellation. Though potentially they provided the elements for a new kind of multi-centered city, operated on a regional scale, their effect has so far been to corrode and undermine the old centers, without forming a pattern coherent enough to carry on their essential cultural functions on anything like the old level. Within a generation, when they lose the momentum they now derive from the historic city, the resulting deterioration will be serious. Left to themselves, as Los Angeles already demonstrates, these forces will automatically destroy the city.

6: RAILROAD LINE, GREENBELT,
MOTOR SPRAWL

The suburbs built between 1850 and 1920 owed their existence primarily to the railroad, though those nearer the central city were, after 1895, likewise indebted to the electric trolley car (tramway) and the underground. Sometimes land speculators promoted rapid transit, but as often as not electric power and transit magnates—like the van Sweringens in Cleveland (Shaker Heights) and Insull in Chicago (Niles Center)—promoted the suburbs. The bold initiative of Frank Pick, as head of the London Underground, played no small part in London's twentieth-century suburban development.

The earlier type of suburb, which was most dependent on the railroad, had a special advantage that could be fully appreciated only after it had disappeared. These suburbs, strung along a railroad line, were discontinuous and properly spaced; and without the aid of legislation they were limited in population as well as area; for the biggest rarely held as many as ten thousand people, and under five thousand was more usual. In 1950, for example, Bronxville, New York, a typical upper-class suburb, had 6,778 people, while Riverside, Illinois, founded as early as 1869, had only 9,153.

The size and scale of the suburb, that of a neighborhood unit, was not entirely the result of its open planning, which favored low densities. Being served by a railroad line, with station stops from three to five miles apart, there was a natural limit to the spread of any particular community. Houses had to be sited "within easy walking distance of the railroad station," as the advertising prospectus would point out; and only those wealthy enough to afford a horse and carriage dared to penetrate farther into the open country.

Through its spaced station stops, the railroad suburb was at first kept from spreading or unduly increasing in numbers, for a natural greenbelt, often still under cultivation as market gardens, remained between the suburbs and increased the available recreation area. Occasionally, in a few happy areas like Westchester, between 1915 and 1935, a parkway, like the Bronx River Parkway, accompanied by a continuous strip of park for pedestrian use, not yet over-run by a constant stream of metropolitan traffic, added to the perfection of the whole suburban pattern. Whatever one might say of the social disadvantages, this was in many ways an idyllic physical environment. But it lasted less than a generation.

Probably it was the very existence of these natural greenbelts, insulating the small, self-contained, but closely linked suburban communities, that prompted the economist, Alfred Marshall, to suggest in 1899, a "national fresh air tax," in England, as a means of securing permanent green belts between towns. "We need," he observed, "to increase the playgrounds in the midst of our towns. We need also to prevent one town from growing into another, or into a neighboring village; we need to keep intermediate stretches of country in dairy farms, etc. as well as public pleasure grounds."

More timely and perspicuous advice could not have been offered to municipal governments: indeed more than half a century later, it is still timely and far more urgent. That it was not at once followed up by city planners and municipal officials, that it is still far from being appreciated

and acted upon in most growing urban centers, is a disgrace to these professions and a blot on our common civic intelligence. (The New Towns
movement in England and the far-sighted policies of a few notable cities,
such as Rotterdam, Amsterdam, and Stockholm, contrast with the dismal
failure of New York to protect Westchester and Long Island, or of San
Francisco to protect the Bay Region, and even more the vineyards and
orchards of Santa Clara Valley: to choose but two sorry examples out
of scores.)

Had Marshall's advice been promptly heeded, by introducing appropriate zoning and land-use legislation, and providing for the large-scale
acquisition of public land for settlement with every fresh highway development, a radical change in the urban pattern could have been introduced.
Not merely would it have been possible to prevent the consolidation and
extension of vast masses of suburban and sub-suburban housing, but we
could have taken positive steps to build up a more organic form, on a
regional scale, in keeping with our modern facilities for transportation
and communication.

Instead of creating the Regional City, the forces that automatically
pumped highways and motor cars and real estate developments into the
open country have produced the formless urban exudation. Those who
are using verbal magic to turn this conglomeration into an organic entity
are only fooling themselves. To call the resulting mass Megalopolis, or
to suggest that the change in spatial scale, with swift transportation, in
itself is sufficient to produce a new and better urban form, is to overlook
the complex nature of the city. The actual coalescence of urban tissue
that is now taken by many sociologists to be a final stage in city development, is not in fact a new sort of city, but an anti-city. As in the concept
of anti-matter, the anti-city annihilates the city whenever it collides with it.

What has happened to the suburb is now a matter of historic record.
As soon as the motor car became common, the pedestrian scale of the
suburb disappeared, and with it, most of its individuality and charm.
The suburb ceased to be a neighborhood unit: it became a diffused low-
density mass, enveloped by the conurbation and then further enveloping
it. The suburb needed its very smallness, as it needed its rural background,
to achieve its own kind of semi-rural perfection. Once that limit was overpassed, the suburb ceased to be a refuge from the city and became part of
the inescapable metropolis, 'la ville tentaculaire,' whose distant outlying
open spaces and public parks were themselves further manifestations of the
crowded city. This fact that will not cease to be true even if jet transportation brings an area twelve hundred miles away as near as one sixty miles
distant today. For when one conquers space one also increases the populations to whom that distant space is accessible. The prospective net gain is
considerably less than zero.

As long as the railroad stop and walking distances controlled suburban growth, the suburb had a form. The very concentration of shops and parking facilities around the railroad station in the better suburbs even promoted a new kind of market area, more concentrated than the linear market along an avenue. This was a spontaneous prototype of the suburban shopping center, whose easy facilities for parking gave it advantages over more central urban establishments, once the private motor car became the chief mode of transportation. But the motor car had done something more than remove the early limits and destroy the pedestrian scale. It either doubled the number of cars needed per family, or it turned the suburban housewife into a full time chauffeur.

These duties became even more imperative because the advent of the motor car was accompanied by the deliberate dismantling of the electric (rail) transportation system. In the more urbanized parts of America, electric transportation, often on its own private right of way, like the steam railroad, achieved far higher rates of speed than the present motor bus. Far from supplementing public rail transportation, the private motor car became largely a clumsy substitute for it. Instead of maintaining a complex transportation system, offering alternative choices of route and speed to fit the occasion, the new suburban sprawl has become abjectly dependent upon a single form, the private motor car, whose extension has devoured the one commodity the suburb could rightly boast: space. Instead of buildings set in a park, we now have buildings set in a parking lot.

Whilst the suburb served only a favored minority it neither spoiled the countryside nor threatened the city. But now that the drift to the outer ring has become a mass movement, it tends to destroy the value of both environments without producing anything but a dreary substitute, devoid of form and even more devoid of the original suburban values. We are faced by a curious paradox: the new suburban form has now produced an anti-urban pattern. With the destruction of walking distances has gone the destruction of walking as a normal means of human circulation: the motor car has made it unsafe and the extension of the suburb has made it impossible.

As a result, Unwin's salutary demonstration, 'Nothing Gained by Overcrowding,' must now be countered with a qualifying admonition: 'Something Lost by Overspacing.' This applies to every feature of the suburban conglomerate. The once modest highway whose Roman width of fifteen feet remained standard almost until the Parkway was invented, now demands thousands of acres, with rights of way broader than mainline railroads required in the height of their expansion.

To ensure the continuous flow of traffic, even in rural areas, immense clover leaves and jug-handles are designed, demolishing still more open space. And instead of freight yards and marshalling yards at the far terminals of a railroad system, the very dispersion of motor traffic demands similar facilities around every individual building where people congregate. Thus, each new factory or office, each new department store or shopping center, established in the midst of the open country, demands parking lots so ample that those who park on the rim have a far longer walk to the shop than they would have in a densely crowded city after leaving their bus or their subway train, though they still obstinately retain the illusionist image of the motor car's taking them from 'door to door.'

All this is a far cry from the aristocratic enjoyment of visual space that provided the late baroque city with open squares and circles and long vistas for carriage drives down tree-lined avenues. In the new suburban dispensation, wasteful spacing has become a substitute for intelligent civic design, far-seeing municipal organization, or rational economy. Each separate building sprawls in lazy, one-story plans over the maximum possible building area, insulated from its neighbors, if any, by an ever-enlarging parking lot, the latter again increasing steadily in size as mass transportation falls into completer disuse. Yet when the dispersed plant releases its workers at the end of the day, the time-wasting congestion at the exit may fully equal that in the big city.

Under the present suburban regime, every urban function follows the example of the motor road: it devours space and consumes time with increasing friction and frustration, while, under the plausible pretext of increasing the range of speed and communication, it actually obstructs it and denies the possibility of easy meetings and encounters by scattering the fragments of a city at random over a whole region.

At the bottom of this miscarriage of modern technics lies a fallacy that goes to the very heart of the whole underlying ideology: the notion that power and speed are desirable for their own sake, and that the latest type of fast-moving vehicle must replace every other form of transportation. The fact is that speed in locomotion should be a function of human purpose. If one wants to meet and chat with people on an urban promenade, three miles an hour will be too fast; if a surgeon is being rushed to a patient a thousand miles away, three hundred miles an hour may be too slow. But what our experts in transportation are kept by their own stultifying axioms from realizing is that an adequate transportation system cannot be created in terms of any single limited means of locomotion however fast its theoretic speed.

What an effective network requires is the largest number of alternative modes of transportation, at varying speeds and volumes, for different functions and purposes. The fastest way to move a hundred thousand people within a limited urban area, say a half mile radius, is on foot: the slowest way of moving them would be to put them all into motor cars. The entire daytime population of historic Boston could assemble by foot on Boston Common, probably in less than an hour if the streets were clear of motor traffic. If they were transported by motor car, they would take many hours, and unless they abandoned their unparkable vehicles would never reach their destination.

Our highway engineers and our municipal authorities, hypnotized by the popularity of the private motor car, feeling an obligation to help General Motors to flourish, even if General Chaos results, have been in an open conspiracy to dismantle all the varied forms of transportation necessary to a good system, and have reduced our facilities to the private motor car (for pleasure, convenience, or trucking) and the airplane. They have even duplicated railroad routes and repeated all the errors of the early railroad engineers, while piling up in the terminal cities a population the private motor car cannot handle unless the city itself is wrecked to permit movement and storage of automobiles.

If technical experts and administrators had known their business, they would have taken special measures to safeguard more efficient methods of mass transportation, in order to maintain both the city's existence and the least time-wasting use of other forms of transportation. To have a complete urban structure capable of functioning fully, it is necessary to find appropriate channels for every form of transportation: it is the deliberate articulation of the pedestrian, the mass transit system, the street, the avenue, the expressway, and the airfield that alone can care for the needs of a modern community. Nothing less will do.

By favoring the truck over the railroad for long-distance traffic, we have replaced a safe and efficient service by a more dangerous and inefficient one. If we want to improve our highway system, we should be zealous to keep as large a part of goods haulage as possible on the rails. Not the least reason for saving the passenger and freight railroad service and mass transportation is to ensure free movement by private vehicles on highways. Similarly, if the expressways that we have built around our cities are to function as such, mass transit must be improved and widened, not permitted to go out of existence.

The only effective cure for urban congestion is to so relate industrial and business zones to residential areas that a large part of their personnel can either walk or cycle to work, or use a public bus, or take a railroad train. By pushing all forms of traffic onto high speed motor ways, we burden them with a load guaranteed to slow down peak traffic to a crawl; and if we try to correct this by multiplying motor ways, we only add to the total urban wreckage by flinging the parts of the city ever farther away in a formless mass of thinly spread semi-urban tissue. The spatial dissociation of functions in suburbia results in an extreme specialization of the individual parts: segregated residence areas without local shops:

segregated shopping centers without industries: segregated industrial plants without eating facilities unless provided by the management. In escaping the complex co-operations of the city Suburbia recovers the original vices of overspecialization and rigid control.

Good urban planning must provide a place for the motor car: that goes without saying. But this does not in the least mean that the motor car must be permitted to penetrate every part of the city and stay there, even though it disrupts all other activities. Neither does it mean that the auto shall dictate the whole scheme of living; nor yet does it mean that its manufacturers should be permitted to flout the requirements of the city by designing ever broader and longer vehicles. Quite the contrary, the time has come to discriminate between two functions of the motor car— urban movement and countrywide movement. For the latter, a big car with plenty of room to house a family and hold their baggage is admirable. In the city, however, such cars should be encouraged to stay on the outskirts, and be heavily taxed for the privilege of parking within it; while special favors should be given to the design and distribution of small cars, electric powered, for ordinary intra-urban movement, to supplement rather than replace mass transportation. Moderate speed, quiet, ease and compactness of parking—these are the characteristics of a town car.

It is an absurdly impoverished technology that has only one answer to the problem of transportation; and it is a poor form of city planning that permits that answer to dominate its entire scheme of existence.

7: MASS SUBURBIA AS ANTI-CITY

Under the present dispensation we have sold our urban birthright for a sorry mess of motor cars. As poor a bargain as Esau's pottage. Future generations will perhaps wonder at our willingness, indeed our eagerness, to sacrifice the education of our children, the care of the ill and the aged, the development of the arts, to say nothing of ready access to nature, for the lopsided system of mono-transportation, going through low density areas at sixty miles an hour, but reduced in high density areas to a bare six. But our descendants will perhaps understand our curious willingness to expend billions of dollars to shoot a sacrificial victim into planetary orbit, if they realize that our cities are being destroyed for the same superstitious religious ritual: the worship of speed and empty space. Lacking sufficient municipal budgets to deal adequately with all of life's requirements that can be concentrated in the city, we have settled for a single function, transportation, or rather for a single part of an adequate transportation system, locomotion by private motor car.

By allowing mass transportation to deteriorate and by building expressways out of the city and parking garages within, in order to encourage the maximum use of the private car, our highway engineers and city planners have helped to destroy the living tissue of the city and to limit the possibilities of creating a larger urban organism on a regional scale. Mass transportation for short distances, under a mile, should rely mainly upon the pedestrian. By discouraging and eliminating the pedestrian, by failing to extend and to perfect mass transportation, our municipal officials and highway engineers have created a situation that calls for extremely low residential densities. Here again the monopoly of private space not merely reduces the social facilities of the city but sacrifices public open space to private.

The absurd belief that space and rapid locomotion are the chief ingredients of a good life has been fostered by the agents of mass suburbia. That habit of low density building is the residual bequest of the original romantic movement, and by now it is one of the chief obstacles to reassembling the parts of the city and uniting them in a new pattern that shall offer much richer resources for living than either the congested and disordered central metropolis or the outlying areas reached by its expressways. The *reductio ad absurdum* of this myth is, notoriously, Los Angeles. Here the suburban standards of open space, with free standing houses, often as few as five houses to the acre, has been maintained: likewise the private motor car, as the major means of transportation has supplanted what was only a generation or so ago an extremely efficient system of public transportation.

Los Angeles has now become an undifferentiated mass of houses, walled off into sectors by many-laned expressways, with ramps and viaducts that create special bottlenecks of their own. These expressways move but a small fraction of the traffic per hour once carried by public transportation, at a much lower rate of speed, in an environment befouled by smog, itself produced by the lethal exhausts of the technologically backward motor cars. More than a third of the Los Angeles area is consumed by these grotesque transportation facilities; *two-thirds* of central Los Angeles are occupied by streets, freeways, parking facilities, garages. This is space-eating with a vengeance. The last stage of the process already beckons truly progressive minds—to evict the remaining inhabitants and turn the entire area over to automatically propelled vehicles, completely emancipated from any rational human purpose.

Even in cities as spacious as Washington, it is only the original central area that has a residential density of ten or more families per acre: on the spreading outskirts, under ten is the rule, and a fast moving tide is putting an even larger tract under a density of settlement less than five per acre. This is ruinous both to urban living and to leisured recreation; for the attempt to service the distant areas with expressways will not merely sterilize more and more of the land, but will scatter social facilities that should be concentrated in new cities, organized so as to diffuse and amplify the central facilities.

The conclusion should be plain. Any attempt to create an adequate transportation system without creating in advance sufficient reserves of public land, without laying down a desirable density for balanced urban occupation *higher than the present suburban level,* without providing for a regional network largely independent of the bigger trunk line highways, will degrade the landscape without bringing any permanent benefits to its new inhabitants.

To keep the advantages first incorporated in the romantic suburb, we must acclimate them to the building of cities. To keep the advantages first discovered in the closed city, we must create a more porous pattern, richer in both social and esthetic variety. Residential densities of about one hundred people per net acre, exclusive of streets and sidewalks, will provide usable private gardens and encourage small public inner parks for meeting and relaxing. This can be achieved without erecting the sterile, space-mangling high-rise slabs that now grimly parade, in both Europe and America, as the ultimate contribution of 'modern' architecture. If we are concerned with human values, we can no longer afford either sprawling Suburbia or the congested Metropolis: still less can we afford a congested Suburbia, whose visual openness depends upon the cellular isolation and regimentation of its component families in mass structures.

8: FAMILIES IN SPACE

As it has worked out under the impact of the present religion and myth of the machine, mass Suburbia has done away with most of the freedoms and delights that the original disciples of Rousseau sought to find through their exodus from the city. Instead of centering attention on the child in the garden, we now have the image of 'Families in Space.' For the wider the scattering of the population, the greater the isolation of the individual household, and the more effort it takes to do privately, even with the aid of many machines and automatic devices, what used to be done in company often with conversation, song, and the enjoyment of the physical presence of others.

The town housewife, who half a century ago knew her butcher, her grocer, her dairyman, her various other local tradesmen, as individual persons, with histories and biographies that impinged on her own, in a daily interchange, now has the benefit of a single weekly expedition to an impersonal supermarket, where only by accident is she likely to encounter a neighbor. If she is well-to-do, she is surrounded with electric or electronic devices that take the place of flesh and blood companions: her real companions, her friends, her mentors, her lovers, her fillers-up of unlived life, are shadows on the television screen, or even less embodied voices. She may answer them, but she cannot make herself heard: as it has worked out, this is a one-way system. The greater the area of expansion, the greater the dependence upon a distant supply center and remote control.

On the fringe of mass Suburbia, even the advantages of the primary neighborhood group disappear. The cost of this detachment in space from other men is out of all proportion to its supposed benefits. The end product is an encapsulated life, spent more and more either in a motor car or within the cabin of darkness before a television set: soon, with a little more automation of traffic, mostly in a motor car, travelling even greater distances, under remote control, so that the one-time driver may occupy himself with a television set, having lost even the freedom of the steering wheel. Every part of this life, indeed, will come through official channels and be under supervision. Untouched by human hand at one end: untouched by human spirit at the other. Those who accept this existence might as well be encased in a rocket hurtling through space, so narrow are their choices, so limited and deficient their permitted responses. Here indeed we find 'The Lonely Crowd.'

The organizers of the ancient city had something to learn from the new rulers of our society. The former massed their subjects within a walled enclosure, under the surveillance of armed guardians within the smaller citadel, the better to keep them under control. That method is now obsolete. With the present means of long-distance mass communication, sprawling isolation has proved an even more effective method of keeping a population under control. With direct contact and face-to-face association inhibited as far as possible, all knowledge and direction can be monopolized by central agents and conveyed through guarded channels, too costly to be utilized by small groups or private individuals. To exercise free speech in such a scattered, dissociated community one must 'buy time' on the air or 'buy space' in the newspaper. Each member of Suburbia becomes imprisoned by the very separation that he has prized: he is fed through a narrow opening: a telephone line, a radio band, a television circuit. This is not, it goes without saying, the result of a conscious conspiracy by a cunning minority: it is an organic by-product of an economy that sacrifices human development to mechanical processing.

In a well-organized community, all these technological improvements might admirably widen the scope of social life: in the disorganized communities of today, they narrow the effective range of the person. Under such conditions, nothing can happen spontaneously or autonomously— not without a great deal of mechanical assistance. Does this not explain in some degree the passiveness and docility that has crept into our existence? In the recent Caracas revolution that deposed a brutal dictatorship in Venezuela, the starting signal, I have been told by an eye-witness, was the honking of motor car horns. That honking, growing louder, coming nearer, converging from every quarter of the city upon the palace, struck terror into the hearts of the rulers. That, too, was an urban phenomenon. Suburbia offers poor facilities for meeting, conversation, collective debate, and common action—it favors silent conformity, not rebellion or counter-attack. So Suburbia has become the favored home of a new kind of absolutism: invisible but all-powerful.

I might be uneasy about the validity of this analysis had not the prescient de Tocqueville anticipated it long ago, in 'Democracy in America.' He sought to "trace the novel features under which despotism may appear in the world." "The first thing that strikes observation," he says, "is an uncountable number of men, all equal and alike, incessantly endeavoring to produce the petty and paltry pleasures with which they glut their lives. Each of them living apart, is a stranger to the fate of all the rest—his children and his private friends constitute to him the whole of mankind; as for the rest of his fellow-citizens, he is close to them, but he sees them not; he touches them, but he feels them not; he exists but in himself and for himself alone; and if his kindred still remain to him, he may be said at any rate to have lost his country."

De Tocqueville was describing in anticipation the temper and habit of life in Suburbia, a habit that has worked back into the city and made even democratic nations submit, with hardly a murmur, to every manner of totalitarian compulsion and corruption. What this great political philosopher foresaw with his inner eye, less gifted observers can now see with their outer eye. This is the last stage in the breakup of the city. The expansion of our technology only quickens the pace of this change. What is left, if no counter-movement takes place, will not be worth saving. For when the container changes as rapidly as its contents nothing can in fact be saved.

9: PLANNING FOR URBAN GROWTH

Fortunately, the countermovement began over half a century ago; and it was directed both against the suburban exodus and against the metropolitan congestion that prompted it. The first forward-looking interpretation of the urban situation in general, in terms of new processes and potentialities already visible in civilization, was made by two remarkable observers toward the end of the nineteenth century. They dealt with the formative forces as a whole, and they treated the city's relationship to countryside and region as an integral part of its own life and as essential in any larger scheme of urban improvement.

The earlier contribution was made by the geographer, Peter Kropotkin, in the remarkable book called 'Fields, Factories, and Workshops.' Almost half a century in advance of contemporary economic and technical opinion, he had grasped the fact that the flexibility and adaptability of electric communication and electric power, along with the possibilities of intensive, biodynamic farming, had laid the foundations for a more decentralized urban development in small units, responsive to direct human contact, and enjoying both urban and rural advantages. Industry, he saw, was no longer tied to the coal mine, even when coal remained a source of power; nor was it tied to the railroad and the big city: neither efficiency nor economy was to be equated with big units of production. Kropotkin foresaw what many big corporations were to discover only during the Second World War; namely, that even when the total assemblage was a big one, the farming out of special industrial operations in 'bits and pieces' actually often made the reputed economies of concentrated large scale organization, the industrial tendency that justified other forms of metropolitan bigness, dubious. The finer the technology, the greater the need for the human initiative and skill conserved in the small workshop. Effective transportation and fine organization were often superior to the mere physical massing of plant under one roof.

Kropotkin realized that the new means of rapid transit and communication, coupled with the transmission of electric power in a network, rather than a one-dimensional line, made the small community on a par in essential technical facilities with the overcongested city. By the same token, rural occupations once isolated and below the economic and cultural level of the city could have the advantages of scientific intelligence, group organization, and animated activities, originally a big city monopoly; and with this the hard and fast division between urban and rural, between industrial worker and farm worker, would break down too. Kropotkin understood these implications before the invention of the motor car, the radio, the motion picture, the television system, and the worldwide telephone—though each of these inventions further confirmed his penetrating diagnosis by equalizing advantages between the central metropolis and the once peripheral and utterly dependent small communities. With the small unit as a basis, he saw the opportunity for a more responsible and responsive local life, with greater scope for the human agents who were neglected and frustrated by mass organizations.

Ebenezer Howard, who was influenced by Kropotkin, as he had been influenced by earlier utopian writers like Thomas Spence and James Silk Buckingham, carried these ideas a large stride further. Behind the new concept of the Garden City he saw "the splendid possibilities of a new civilization based on service to the community." He saw that the growth of the big city was self-defeating, for with every new increment of population, its traffic became more congested, its central institutions less accessible, and the larger part of its population was as little benefitted by its higher institutions of culture as if they were entirely outside its orbit. He believed that the time had come to establish a new pattern of city development: one that would use modern technical facilities to break down the widening gap between the countryside, with its depleted economic and social facilities, and the city, with its equally depleted biological and natural advantages: he proposed to overcome both the prevalent apoplexy at the urban center, and the paralysis at the extremities, by promoting a new pattern of city growth. Unlike the advocates of continued urban expansion, he rejected the suburb as a tolerable compromise; indeed, he hardly considered it. Howard saw that the relief of congestion was not a matter of widening the dormitory areas of the city, but of decentralizing all its functions. In rejecting the temporary, transitional form of the suburb he sought a stable marriage between city and country, not a weekend liaison.

In 'Garden Cities of Tomorrow,' Howard re-introduced into city planning the ancient Greek concept of a natural limit to the growth of any organism or organization, and restored the human measure to the new image of the city. To achieve this, he also introduced the Greek practice, which had been reformulated in fresh terms by Robert Owen and Edward Wakefield, of colonization by communities fully equipped from the start to carry out all the essential urban functions. Against the purposeless mass congestion of the big metropolis, with its slums, its industrial pollution, and its lengthening journeys to work, Howard opposed a more organic kind of city: a city limited from the beginning in numbers and in density of habitation, limited in area, organized to carry on all the essential functions of an urban community, business, industry, administration, education; equipped too with a sufficient number of public parks and private gardens to guard health and keep the whole environment sweet. To achieve and express this reunion of city and country, Howard surrounded his new city with a permanent agricultural greenbelt. This two-dimensional horizontal 'wall' would serve not merely to keep the rural environment near, but to keep other urban settlements from coalescing with it: not least, it would, like the ancient vertical wall, heighten the sense of internal unity. Apart from the concept as a whole, the principle of establishing permanent greenbelts around urban communities was a major contribution. Possibly the best name for such communities would be 'Greenbelt Towns.'

Certain aspects of this new form had already been prefigured in the self-contained early suburb, from Riverside, Illinois, on; but Howard's greatest contribution was less in recasting the physical form of the city than in developing the organic concepts that underlay this form; for though he was no biologist like Patrick Geddes, he nevertheless brought to the city the essential biological criteria of dynamic equilibrium and organic balance: balance as between city and country in a larger ecological pattern, and balance between the varied functions of the city: above all, balance through the positive control of growth in the limitation in area, number, and density of occupation, and the practice of reproduction (colonization) when the community was threatened by such an undue increase in size as would lead only to lapse of function. If the city was to maintain its life-maintaining functions for its inhabitants, it must in its own right exhibit the organic self control and self containment of any other organism.

Howard sought, in other words, to give to the new kind of city all the advantages that the big city possessed before its inordinate expansion put them beyond the means or beyond the reach of its inhabitants. He saw that, once it has achieved an optimum size, the need for the individual town is not to increase its own area and population, but to be part of a larger system that has the advantage of large numbers and extensive facilities. Unlike those who fled from the city, he, a born Londoner, did not underestimate these urban advantages, any more than, as an assiduous inventor of machines, he underrated the advances of the new technology. Rejecting the pattern of the suburb, he believed that industry should be an integral part of the city, and that the workshop and factory—he was not reckoning here with chemical industries, blast furnaces, coal pits—should usually be within a reasonably short distance of every home. He estimated that with a population of 32,000 people, of whom two thousand would be in the agricultural belt, the new city would provide a variety of enterprises, a mixed population with different vocations, and a thriving social life.

Howard proposed to test the possibility of creating a viable urban form by building an experimental model, so superior in both its social organization and its physical layout to the existing villages, country towns, suburbs, industrial conurbations, or congested metropolises that it would set a new pattern for future city building: instead of agglomeration, planned dispersal; instead of monopolistic concentration, decentralization; instead of disorganization, a higher type of unity. Once the feasibility of his conception was established, other advances would be possible: for with the land in corporate or municipal ownership, as would be necessary in founding a new community, the unearned increment of growth, which hitherto had gone to the individual landlord and had tended to promote profitable overgrowth, the bonus would go to the improvement of the community, either through reduced taxes or added services.

By changing constant urban expansion by piecemeal addition, to orderly de-centralization in 'self-contained' cities, Howard believed it would be possible to halt the continued congestion and expansion of London. So in time a sufficient proportion of the metropolitan population would be drawn off to lower land values and make possible the reconstruction of the historic center on more open lines, with greater respect for health, social convenience, and the amenities. The success of the new garden city would give back to the overpopulated center the fresh air, sunlight, and beauty that its own inordinate growth had largely robbed it of.

In Howard's mind, the Garden City was a sensible invention, like the railroad, based on welding into a workable whole a number of different factors, some practical, some ideal. The very simplicity of Howard's premises gave sharpness and clarity to his concrete proposals. He did not have to wait for a total canvass of the urban situation, such as Charles Booth had begun in his all too exhaustive survey of London, or for a national conversion to his point of view, as his contemporary Henry George had sought in his program for land reform before moving into action. Still less did he wait for the motor car to open a technical exit for escaping the city's congestion. Howard did what a capable engineer does today when he seeks to create a new type of structure whose complexity produces strains and stresses that are incalculable on the basis of past experience and traditional forms: he created a small model and tested it out; or rather he persuaded other people with sufficient capital and faith to join with him in this experiment, the building of the First Garden City of Letchworth, which was begun in 1904. Half a generation later, he started another garden city, Welwyn: and the fresh pattern of growth has laid the beginning of what is now a persistent movement toward urban integration.

Such an experiment was worth years of statistical research and carefully marshalled reports—judiciously inconclusive, nicely calculated to frustrate action. Indeed the building of the new town in the long run proved far cheaper, as well as far more effective, than the kind of exhaustive 'urban research' that is so popular today. For the new community within a reasonable time liquidated the cost of its own promotion and answered, more definitely than any purely hypothetic formulation could have done, the question of whether such a new urban unit could survive even though it ran contrary to the established canons of profit-making, land speculation, and metropolitan domination. When one considers the institutional and psychological obstacles opposing Howard's demonstration, it stands out as a consummate piece of statesmanship, on a par with the founding of the Mormon communities in Utah, or the Cooperative Wholesale Society in England.

In framing his new program, Howard had stuck to essentials, and had not tried to give the architectural and planning details the stamp of his own imagination. He had come forth, not with a new plan for the city— he carefully refrained from confusing the essential issues with any visual image whatever—but with a new program for the balanced organization and contained growth of cities, in a general process that could take care of an indefinite increase in the national population. Howard expressed his diagnosis and his program by means of a series of clarifying diagrams: but even the scheme that pictures the arrangement of the physical parts of the city was carefully labelled "A Diagram Only." His idea of the balanced community lent itself to a variety of urban forms, from that of his utopian predecessor, Charles Fourier, to that of Le Corbusier; and more than once, often in the guise of refuting Howard or demolishing the garden city idea, the principles of balance and functional completeness which Howard enunciated have been re-invented or re-stated without such assignment of credit to Howard as he himself always made to his precursors.

Many of the elements in Howard's proposal were already familiar; neither in his ideas nor in his practical initiatives did he seek to start from scratch: his ideal city was a combination of the possible and the practical, ideal enough to be desirable, close enough to contemporary practice to be realizable. His genius was to combine the existing organs of the city into a more orderly composition based on the principle of organic limitation and controlled growth. He began, not with the inertia of disintegration, but with an analysis of the life-maintaining human functions as related to the urban and rural environments. Though his analysis was not a profound one, it had the merit of doing justice to the variety and interrelationship of urban activities. What was significant about the garden city was not the mere presence of gardens and open spaces: what was radically new was a rational and orderly method for dealing with complexity, through an organization capable of establishing balance and autonomy, and of maintaining order despite differentiation, and coherence and unity despite the need for growth. This was the transformative idea.

The title that Howard chose for this new urban conception proved unfortunate: not only because it had been pre-empted much earlier by the dingy railroad metropolis of Chicago, but also because the existence of gardens, though integral to the new city, was not its distinctive feature; since it characterized even more copiously many a contemporary suburb. Howard in his book had suggested a density of 70 to 100 people per acre, if one derives this number from his suggested block and lot sizes. Now that is a truly urban density, approximately that of the New York Plan of 1811, when its new streets were lined with two and three story buildings. Such a density is higher than that of the usual suburb: five times as high as many contemporary parts of Los Angeles. Superficial students patently ignorant of Howard's work still unfortunately make the error of calling suburbs garden cities, or the suburban open plan a 'garden city type of plan': even worse, critics who should know better often refer to the classic garden cities, Letchworth and Welwyn, or to the British New Towns of later vintage, as if they were mere suburbs, because they were all laid out in an open—perhaps too open—framework.

But the garden city, in Howard's view, was first of all a city: a new kind of unit whose organic pattern would in the end spread from the individual model to a whole constellation of similar cities. It was in its urbanity, not in its horticulture, that the Garden City made a bold departure from the established method of building and planning.

Viewed in historic perspective, more than half a century after its inception, Howard's proposal has proved more realistic—and immensely more fruitful—than Soria y Mata's Linear City, or any of the later 'Roadtowns' that made transportation the sole determinant of the city plan. What Le Corbusier put forward as an improvement, the so-called Vertical Garden City, is in fact only a vertical suburb, whose very alternation of isolated high-rise buildings with uncultivated open areas makes the word city meretricious. In the English Garden City, gardens actually abound, rich in fruit trees, flowers, and vegetables; but Howard's new formulation gained distinction precisely because he refused to be tied down to a particular physical image of the city or a particular method of planning or a particular type of building. The specific forms of such a city would be a resultant of the landscape and the climate, the industries and the technological facilities available, and above all, the arts of the builders and the inhabitants: as for the ideal elements, he expressed them almost as mathematical abstractions.

Not that Howard was infallible. In his original picture of the coming decentralization of London, Howard—fortunately perhaps for his experiment—underestimated the gravitational pull of a big metropolitan center in a money-oriented economy, where salesmanship is the supreme art, where success demands the magnification of crowds, and where high rents and expensive congestion have a status value. Howard was doubtless correct in believing that many essential metropolitan goods and services were by-products of congestion itself and would, like the long journey to work, be greatly reduced or vanish in the new town. But his concrete proposal to create a self-contained community of thirty-two thousand people, as an alternative to the overburdened life of London, did not by itself do full justice to the social and technical complexities of present-day culture. He was nevertheless right in believing that 32,000 people formed a sufficiently big experimental unit to test the validity of this new method of city growth; and though his life was dominated by the necessity of taking this first step and following it through, his vision went beyond that practical limitation.

If anything were needed to establish the extraordinary range and penetration of Howard's thinking, his chapter on Social Cities should suffice. For Howard, the garden city did not imply either isolation or parochial self-containment, in the fashion of a sleepy country town in a remote inaccessible area. Howard was not disconcerted by the fact that a minority of the New Town's inhabitants would, for professional reasons, have to go either occasionally or even daily to London; for it was enough if there was a sufficient concentration of economic opportunities and social interests to keep most of the inhabitants fully occupied for most of the time, in an environment that possessed many positive urban values that London itself could no longer give even to the wealthy. As if to anticipate the temptation to regard the town of limited size as capable of completely containing and transmitting our modern culture, Howard sought to find an equivalent pattern, based not on congestion but on decentralized organization.

In his concept of Social Cities, even before the first garden city was founded, he carried this development to its next stage. If the garden city was not to depend for its higher functions upon the over-burdened metropolis, reducing its own status to that of mere satellite, then the smaller new towns, once they were sufficient in number, must deliberately group together in a new political and cultural organization, which he called a "Social City"—that which Clarence Stein and his colleagues were later to call the Regional City—to pool their resources and provide such facilities as large numbers alone make possible: a technical college or a university, a specialized hospital or a professional symphony orchestra. Howard pointed out that ten cities of thirty-thousand population each, connected by fast public transportation, politically federated and culturally associated, could enjoy all the advantages that a single unitary city of three hundred thousand could make possible; and it could have these advantages without the disabilities of the larger unit. What was once done by close building could now be done by close organization, thanks to rapid transportation and instantaneous communication.

By this federating device, a phase of his thought too long neglected,

Howard intuitively grasped the potential form of the etherialized city of the future, which would unite the urban and the rural components into a porous regional complex, multi-centered but capable of functioning as a whole. If the first step was to erect an experimental model of the new urban unit to demonstrate the feasibility of decentralization and self-contained growth, the next step was to create a new kind of large-scale urban community, in which the garden city would become a co-operating member.

Howard's thought was couched in the simple pieties of Victorian rationalism, colored by Christian benevolence; and though he was a persuasive preacher by word of mouth, disarming in his own personal simplicity, this fact served to make his most original insights seem more old-fashioned than they are. Actually, his vision was not merely in advance of current thinking about the nature and destiny of cities; it penetrated farther than some of his devout followers; and even today many people find it is easier to dismiss the full implications of his thought than to follow them through. Though the main value of the Garden City, from Howard's point of view, was to establish the possibility of a more organic method of city growth, which would reproduce, not unrelated fragments of urban order, but unified wholes, bringing together urban and rural values, it had still another office: it called general attention to the essential nature of the city itself, and promoted examination of the whole process of city development that had hitherto been lacking.

Above all, by his insight into the corporate and unified structure of a city, Howard called attention to the fact that the growth of a city must be in the hands of a representative public authority; and that the best results could be achieved only if this authority had power to assemble and hold the land, plan the city, time the order of building, and provide the necessary services. No longer were the most essential agents of city development to be left to the individual investor, whether speculator or owner, dealing with individual building lots, individual houses, individual business sites; for no individual exercise of either foresight or public spirit could produce the equivalent of a co-ordinated and meaningful whole. Nor was the city's responsibility to provide for the well-being of all its inhabitants to be recognized only after the maximum amount of disorder had been created by unregulated private effort.

Howard's emphasis on unity and balance and self-containment remains a salutary contribution to every kind of urban renewal; and it is no accident that the finest examples of civic design in the twentieth century have been in cities like Amsterdam, Frankfurt-am-Main, and Stockholm, where the medieval tradition of corporate responsibility had not been completely overthrown by the speculative scramble and ideological laissez-faire of the nineteenth century. It was perhaps only by proposing to build a new city that all the functions, activities, and purposes of a fully developed city could be recognized, since many of these had lapsed, while others had become grossly overemphasized, in the undirected growth of existing cities.

So antipathetic is Howard's organic approach to the life and growth of cities to the dominant ideology and practice of our time, that many people of considerable competence in the practice of city-planning still regard his program as a wholly chimerical one, doomed to failure by the very nature of our expanding technological economy. So large is this blind spot, that they dismiss as unreal every evidence of its success. But the fact is that in the first generation of its existence, Howard's 'impractical' proposals succeeded in bringing about the establishment of two Garden Cities, Letchworth and Welwyn; and both of these communities, starting as private enterprises, with limited prospects of gain, not merely survived indifference and opposition, but have affected the pattern of housing and city-building in many areas, from Scotland to India. It was the success of these cities that led Sir Anthony Montague Barlow's parliamentary committee to recommend the industrial decentralization in garden cities as a remedy for the increasing congestion of London; and this led in turn to the New Towns Act of 1946, which projected a ring of New Towns around London and in various other parts of England.

This is surely a singular kind of 'failure.' What other new conception of city improvement has resulted in the layout and building of fifteen New Towns, in Britain alone, to say nothing of similar foundations, either achieved or in process, in Sweden, in The Netherlands, in Italy, and in Soviet Russia? To belittle this achievement by saying that the congestion of London is still unabated, is to overlook the fact that in Britain half a million people, thanks to Howard's idea, are now living under physical and biological conditions immensely superior to those enjoyed by the majority of Londoners: conditions equal to, if not better than those prevailing in the richer suburbs of the past, since they hold more of the social ingredients of genuine urban life.

The fact that the New Towns program was abruptly terminated at the moment that searching criticism of its achievements and further experiments in the formal organization of new towns was needed, was a failure of the British political imagination, not a failure of the New Towns themselves, and still less a failure of the premises upon which they were built.

Both the premises and the program demanded revision in the light of further experience: the need for creating New Towns on a regional scale and inventing a new kind of administrative authority, with facilities both for construction and administration on the scale of the great Port Authorities and the London County Council has still to be recognized. But those who cry failure at the beginning of a movement, perhaps in the hope that their hue and cry will produce the end, actually show what a radical challenge to their complacencies and unexamined premises this new mode of city growth presents.

What Howard called the "town-cluster," set in a permanent green matrix to form a new ecological and political unit, was in fact the embryonic form of a new type of city that would transcend the spatial limitations of the historic city, even that of the metropolis, and yet overcome the boundless expansion and random diffusion of the conurbation. The next step in defining this new urban unit, in which the visible parts formed an invisible but tightly knit whole, was taken by Henry Wright and his associates in the New York State Commission for Housing and Regional Planning.

In analyzing the urban growth of New York State, Wright pointed out that the continuance of metropolitan growth at the terminal cities of New York and Buffalo would heap up their already massive disabilities; whereas it was now possible to plan for a new kind of urban diffusion. This would be different from the first period of decentralized community building, focussed in the village, and based upon the canal, the local railroad (not yet unified into a system), the use of water power, and the highroad for horse-drawn vehicles. The new urban pattern would be a more confined one, which would withdraw a permanent population from the Adirondack Mountains, turning them back into forests and recreation area, and would confine the new region of settlement to a broad band, running along the Hudson and the Mohawk Valleys, and upward into the favorable but poorly serviced area bordering Lake Erie. This constituted the new region of urban settlement, favorable to the renewal of older communities drained of their life blood by metropolitan centralization, and to the building up of new communities, limited in size, set in prosperous agricultural land, and interconnected in a new highway network based on the motor car.

Had there been sufficient political and economic initiative in New York State to follow this new pattern, both the big cities and the rest of the state would have profited by this development. Instead, all the planning since has been in terms of intensifying the pattern of metropolitan congestion. The through motorway from New York to Buffalo merely duplicates the railroad line and cuts into the essential public services of the railroad: whereas, under Wright's plan, the new townless highways outlined in 1929 by Benton MacKaye, instead of following the inner line of transportation, could have skirted the band of settlement and served as the backbone for a regional system of distribution. This would have provided both maximum access to the mountainous recreation areas beyond, and a serviceable system of transportation, private *and* public, using canal, river, railroad, highroad, and air. The concept of the balanced city must now be widened to the balanced region, deliberately remodeled as a work of art.

On this basis, four or five new regional entities might have been created, focussed in existing cities, but far more widely diffused, capable of directing further growth into balanced communities. This would have carried Howard's concept of Social Cities to its conclusion. Instead, the combined efforts of the Highway Commission and the Port of New York Authority have been to increase terminal congestion and extract profit from further disorder.

So far, then, Howard's proposals have failed to halt, or even retard, the automatic processes that are at work in our civilization. The underlying reason for this failure is that Western civilization is still carried along by the inertia of three centuries of expansion: land expansion, industry expansion, and population expansion; and these movements have taken place at a rate that would have made public organization and containment difficult, even if the need for a more stable life-economy had been recognized. From the beginning all three movements exhibited irrational and disruptive features, and so far from having diminished during the last two generations, they have been intensified. As both anxiety and disorder widen, the possibility of achieving planned distribution, a dynamic equilibrium, and normal growth decrease. The present planless suburban spread, with its accompanying metropolitan congestion and blight, is an ignoble substitute for civic order and regional design.

So much must be granted. But response to the present disintegrations may already be in process, concealed as Christianity was concealed for two full centuries under the panoply of the Roman Empire. Should the forces of integration reassert themselves, all communities will have to take account of Howard's theorem: that every city, every organ of the community, indeed every association and organization, has a limit of physical growth, and with it the corollary that every plan to overpass that limit must be transposed into an etherialized form.

This holds as true for the overcentralized hospital or research institution as it has already proved for the elephantine department store. In effectively planning the new dimensions and the new purposes of the city, we shall no doubt go beyond Howard's vision; but we shall still owe him a debt of gratitude for first outlining the basis of this wider order.

CHAPTER SEVENTEEN

The Myth of Megalopolis

1: ACCRETIONS OF POWER

The increase in the area of arable land, the improvement of agriculture, the spread of population, and the multiplication of cities have gone hand in hand throughout history: never more so than during the last century. Many countries are now entering an era when the urban population will not merely be greater than the rural population, but when the actual area occupied or pre-empted by urban growth will rival that devoted to cultivation. One of the signs of this change has been the increase in the number, area, and population of great cities. Megalopolis is fast becoming a universal form, and the dominant economy is a metropolitan economy, in which no effective enterprise is possible without a close tie to the big city.

Does this represent a final stage in urban development? Those who believe that there are no alternatives to the present proliferation of metropolitan tissue perhaps overlook too easily the historic outcome of such a concentration of urban power: they forget that this has repeatedly marked the last stage in the classic cycle of civilization, before its complete disruption and downfall. There is surely no evidence of stability in a civilization that has, within forty years, undergone two world wars and prematurely terminated the lives of some sixty million people, on the lowest careful estimate: a civilization that has resurrected the most barbarous forms of compulsion, torture, and wholesale extermination, and that now threatens, in future struggles to 'extend communism' or 'preserve freedom,' to annihilate the population of entire continents and perhaps make the whole planet permanently uninhabitable. This metropolitan civilization contains within itself the explosive forces that will wipe out all traces of its existence; and to make plans for the future without taking account of this fact is to betray one of the typical symptoms of that divorce from reality which has characterized the current exploitation of the scientific agents of mass extermination and mass destruction.

Before we can assess the more vital resources at the disposal of mankind, which may at last save it from its irrational misuse of science and technological invention, we must look more closely into the forces that have produced this metropolitan economy, and have battened on its proudly disastrous success. Perhaps a consciousness of the historic evolution of cities will provide an insight, hitherto lacking, that will enable new measures of control to be introduced into their otherwise automatic, because unconscious, processes. Even many present factors that now seem blind and spontaneous may prove, in fact, to be conscious and calculated efforts to stimulate growth that should be curbed, or to concentrate functions and powers that should be diffused.

Possibly one of the reasons for the oft-repeated urban cycle of growth, expansion, and disintegration, as I suggested earlier, lies in the very nature of civilization itself. We have seen that in many instances the city tends to encase the organic, many-sided life of the community in petrified and overspecialized forms that achieve continuity at the expense of adaptation and further growth. The very structure of the city itself, with the stone container dominating the magnet, may in the past have been in no small degree responsible for this resistance. In the end it has made physical disintegration—through war, fire, or economic corrosion and blight—the only way of opening the city up to the fresh demands of life.

If this is true, the prime need of the city today is for an intensification of collective self-knowledge, a deeper insight into the processes of history, as a first step toward discipline and control: such a knowledge as is achieved by a neurotic patient in facing a long-buried infantile trauma that has stood in the way of his normal growth and integration.

Cities like Rome, which historically came to the full end of their cycle before resuming growth again at a lower stage, afford an abundance of data for studying the rise and fall of Megalopolis. But unfortunately that data is too scattered and much of it is too illegible to provide a full insight into the facts. Though in our time Warsaw, Berlin, Tokyo, and many other cities were close to physical extinction, enough of the living tissue of the culture was preserved elsewhere to make possible their swift reconstruction, with many minor improvements, if with no decisive functional alteration. The persistence of these overgrown containers would indicate that they are concrete manifestations of the dominant forces in our present civilization; and the fact that the same signs of overgrowth and overconcentration exist in 'communist' Soviet Russia as in 'capitalist' United States shows that these forces are universal ones, operating almost without respect to the prevailing ideologies or ideal goals.

While one must recognize such facts, it would be premature to believe that these processes are final and irreversible: we have already surveyed a vast amount of data that demonstrates that, even in cultures far less committed to quantitative growth than our own, there comes a point when the tumorous organ will destroy the organism at whose expense it has reached such swollen dimensions. Meanwhile normal birth, growth, and renewal may elsewhere shift the balance.

Sociologists and economists who base their projects for future economic and urban expansion on the basis of the forces now at work, projecting only such changes as may result from speeding up such forces, tend to arrive at a universal megalopolis, mechanized, standardized, effectively dehumanized, as the final goal of urban evolution. Whether they extrapolate 1960 or anticipate 2060 their goal is actually '1984.' Under the guise of objective statistical description, these social scientists are in fact leaving out of their analysis the observable data of biology, anthropology or history that would destroy their premises or rectify their conclusions. While rejecting the scholastic doctrine of final causes, these observers have turned Megalopolis itself into a virtual final cause.

Much of the thought about the prospective development of cities today has been based upon the currently fashionable ideological assumptions about the nature and destiny of man. Beneath its superficial regard for life and health lies a deep contempt for organic processes that involve maintaining the complex partnership of all organic forms, in an environment favorable to life in all its manifestations. Instead of regarding man's relation to air, water, soil, and all his organic partners as the oldest and most fundamental of all his relations—not to be constricted or effaced, but rather to be deepened and extended in both thought and act—the popular technology of our time devotes itself to contriving means to displace autonomous organic forms with ingenious mechanical (controllable! profitable!) substitutes.

Instead of bringing life into the city, so that its poorest inhabitant will have not merely sun and air but some chance to touch and feel and cultivate the earth, these naïve apostles of progress had rather bring sterility to the countryside and ultimately death to the city. Their 'city of the future' is one levelled down to the lowest possibility of active, autonomous, fully sentient life: just so much life as will conform to the requirements of the machine. As we shall see, this would only carry the present forces at work in Megalopolis to their ultimate goal—total human annihilation. Such prophecies tend to be self-fulfilling. The more widely they are believed the better they work. But by the same token the more swiftly they work, the sooner they may come to a dire climax.

Today the end of our whole megalopolitan civilization is all-too-visibly in sight. Even a misinterpreted group of spots on a radar screen might trigger off a nuclear war that would blast our entire urban civilization out of existence and leave nothing behind to start over with—nothing but death by starvation, pandemic disease, or inexorable cancer from strontium 90 for the thrice-miserable refugees who might survive. To build any hopes for the future on such a structure could occur only to the highly trained but humanly under-dimensioned 'experts' who have contrived it. Even if this fate does not overtake us, many other forms of death, equally sinister, if more insidious and slow, are already at work.

But the cyclic process we are in the midst of is not necessarily a fixed and fatal one. On this fact all wise plans must be based. Our modern world culture, with its ever deepening historic sources and its ever widening contacts, is far richer in still unused potentialities, just because it is world-wide, than any other previous civilization.

Our problem in every department is to slow down or bring to a halt the forces that now threaten us: to break into the cycle of expansion and disintegration by establishing new premises, closer to the demands of life, which will enable us to change our direction and in many areas, to make a fresh start. The very existence of the New Towns of England and Sweden, though they have not yet altered the dominant metropolitan pattern, still bears witness to the possibility of a different mode of urban growth. That small sign may be the harbinger of a larger transformation.

In the present chapter, I purpose to look more closely at some of the formidable negative aspects of metropolitan civilization. This will serve as a prelude to a fresh analysis of the role of the city as magnet, container, and transformer, in modern culture.

2: "THE SLAVERY OF LARGE NUMBERS"

The basis for metropolitan agglomeration lay in the tremendous increase of population that took place during the nineteenth century: this probably surpassed, relatively as well as absolutely, that in neolithic times which made possible the original conquests of urbanism. The peoples of European stock multiplied from about two hundred million during the Napoleonic Wars to about six hundred million at the outbreak of the First World War. This stock, which accounted for only about one-sixth of the population of the earth in Malthus' day, rose to about a third of it in a little over a century, though meanwhile some of the other peoples who came under their influence, like the population of the Netherlands East Indies, likewise reproduced and survived as never before.

In 1800 not a city in the Western World had even a million people: London, the biggest, had only 959,310, while Paris had little more than half a million, far less than Amsterdam today. By 1850, London had over two million and Paris over a million inhabitants; and though other cities increased rapidly, too, they were still without serious rivals. But by 1900 eleven metropolises with more than a million inhabitants had come into existence, including Berlin, Chicago, New York, Philadelphia, Moscow, St. Petersburg, Vienna, Tokyo, and Calcutta.

Thirty years later, as the result of a feverish concentration of capital and financial direction, along with the profitable mechanical means for urban congestion and extension, there were twenty-seven cities with more than a million inhabitants, headed by New York and grading down to Birmingham, England, including metropolises on every continent, even Australia. By the middle of the twentieth century there were a host of new metropolitan areas, with bulging and sprawling suburban rings that brought many more within the general metropolitan picture.

The rise of cities with a population of over a hundred thousand was equally marked; and these smaller cities, too, had their suburban rings: even in such areas as North Carolina, where there was an almost providential opportunity to create a regional balance, in separated constellations of cities, no one of which might be more than 100,000 in number, these separate entities tended to coalesce into an undifferentiated, formless urban mass, or "conurbation." By 1930 nearly half of the population of the United States lived within a radius of twenty to fifty miles of cities with over a hundred thousand population; while by 1950 they were to be found in 168 urban areas with 50,000 or more people: in all 83,929,863. Similar tendencies prevailed everywhere: by 1950 13.1 per cent of the world population lived in cities of 100,000 or over, as against 1.7 in 1800.

This alteration in numbers, scale, and area under urbanization, resulted in qualitative changes in all these centers and in addition, extended the sphere of urban influence, bringing the goods, the habits, and the ideological values of the city to hitherto almost self-contained villages, still pursuing a round of life basically similar in content to that of the neolithic culture. Even the chief tools of primitive life in the jungle, the ax and the machete of the South American Indians, were no longer produced close at hand, but in Newark or Sheffield. These changes likewise affected the natural range of sizes in cities: for this apparently varies in numbers and distribution roughly with the size of the biggest city in the series. Above all, this building and multiplication of cities altered the whole balance between the urban and the agricultural population. Cities had once been islands dotting a wide agricultural sea. But now, in the more populated parts of the earth, the productive agricultural areas tended to be isolated green islands, slowly disappearing under a sea of asphalt, concrete, brick, and stone, either entirely covering up the the soil, or reducing its value for any purpose other than more paving, piping, and building.

To give an account of all the factors that brought about this change, would be to paint a much fuller picture of the development of our mechanical civilization during the last three centuries than I have attempted here: let my account in 'Technics and Civilization' supplement the previous chapters in this book. But in brief one may say that by a process of substitution and forced growth, mechanical processes had supplanted organic processes, in one department after another; and that the total result was to displace living forms and to encourage only those human needs and desires that could be profitably attached to the productive mechanism, whether for profit and power, as in early risk capitalism, for security and luxury, as under welfare capitalism, or for security and power together as under the monopolistic state capitalism of the so-called communist countries.

In any event the final result was much the same. Along with this change went a shift to more distant sources of supply, and from the producing towns to the financial centers, where the market was manipulated and the profits spent. 'Free competition' which was the slogan that broke the old feudal and municipal monopolies gave way to large-scale efforts to achieve monopoly or quasi-monopoly, now called 'oligopoly,' so that a minority of organizations could control the market and fix prices almost as successfully as if they were in fact one unit. The great metropolis was both an agent of this process and a symbol of its overwhelming success.

This general movement brought the various sectors of modern society within the same large urban container; and so it broke down in no little degree the separation between the various ruling groups and classes. Land, industry, finance, the armed forces, and officialdom formed a coalition in the leading Western countries, to effect the maximum amount of pecuniary exploitation and the maximum exercise of effective political control. Governmental agents of power began to direct 'national interests' toward the service of the industrialist and the financier, for, as Cecil Rhodes observed, "Expansion is everything."

Thus the specific forces naturally promoting the expansion of the metropolis were augmented by a general push in the same direction. The industrialist, abandoning his creed of laissez-faire and free enterprise, came to rely upon his imperialist allies to protect industry against the instabilities of the market: hence every form of 'protection,' from tariffs and subsidies to armies and navies that opened up closed markets or collected debts.

If the original form of the city was effected through the union of paleolithic and neolithic economies, that of the ultimate metropolis would seem the result of two forces that detached themselves in institutional forms very swiftly after the seventeenth century: a productive economy (industrial) utilizing energies on a scale never before available, and a consumption economy (commercial) heretofore confined to the court and the aristocracy, quickly multiplying the comforts and luxuries available to the few and gradually widening the entire circle of consumers.

Both economies became hyper-active under the pressure of continued invention: power, speed, quantity, and novelty became ends in themselves, and no effective attempt was made to control power and quantity with respect to other human needs than expanding production and consumption. Thus the great metropolises brought into one vast complex the industrial town, the commercial town, and the royal and aristocratic town, each stimulating and extending its influence over the other.

The standards of the factory and the market quickly spread to every other institution in the metropolis. To have the biggest museum, the biggest university, the biggest hospital, the biggest department store, the biggest bank, the biggest financial corporation was to fulfill the ultimate urban requirement: and to produce the maximum number of inventions, the maximum number of scientific papers, the maximum number of books became as much a mark of metropolitan success as the maximum number of tons of pig-iron in Pittsburgh or Essen. In short, every successful institution of the metropolis repeats in its own organization the aimless giantism of the whole. In reacting against the ancient conditions of dearth and scarcity, the metropolitan economy thus went to the other extreme and concentrated on quantity, without paying attention to the necessity for regulating the tempo, distributing quantity, or assimilating novelty. The organic, the qualitative, the autonomous were reduced to a secondary position, if not obliterated in every department.

Both the citadel and the wall had long been obsolescent in the great capitals; but at the very moment they disappeared, a network of organizational controls centering in the dominating capital city, ramifying by instant communication everywhere, came into existence and performed the same functions more effectively. Just to the extent that the new powers were shadowy, impossible to pin down or come to grips with, etherialized, they were all the more effective. One might breach a city wall or kill a king: but how could one assault an international cartel? Only when one national capital came into conflict with another capital did it become apparent that all the archaic and disruptive forces in the old citadels were still active—and indeed had become grossly magnified and increasingly irrational.

The growth and multiplication of great metropolises were both the proofs of this general tendency toward monopolistic concentration and the means by which it was effected. Even in the most self-complacent provincial town, the pattern of institutional life became increasingly that of the metropolis: the shibboleths of power politics, the orgiastic surges of nationalism, the general acceptance of both the commercial and the cultural trade-marks of the metropolis, to the shame-faced exclusion of local products, became well-nigh universal by the beginning of the twentieth century.

To the great consternation of Herbert Spencer and his followers, who innocently believed that industrialism made for peace, it became plain by the end of the nineteenth century that just the opposite had happened: it had widened the magnitude and destructive efficiency of war, by giving it the benefits of mass production and mechanization. Once more the soldier appeared in the center of the city and with him, the colors of life, ebbing from the insensate milieu of the industrial town, flowed back into the metropolis, in the gay uniforms of the Guards and the Cuirassiers. No part of life could escape this general regimentation. Under the peaceful surface and orderly routine of the metropolis, all the dimensions of violence had suddenly enlarged. As these forces developed, the metropolis became more and more a device for increasing the varieties of violent experience, and every citizen became a connoisseur in the arts of death.

This negative picture of metropolitan organization does not, let me emphasize, tell the whole story. One must judge what has happened during the past century, and what threatens us so banefully now, not only by the actual transformations that have taken place, but by many brave potentialities that may, in the long run, offset them and lift the whole level of life to a higher plane. Some of these potentialities have indeed, alas! already been wiped out. Thus the preservation and transmission of primitive cultures, for the contributions that they might have made in overcoming the sterilities now so painfully evident in our own, was not attempted till irreparable damage was done. So, too, many humane procedures and discoveries in medicine and education that have been perverted by metropolitan civilization, still await their full service in a culture directed to more human ends. But if the history of the nineteenth-century city is, as Lavedan has well said, the history of an illness, that of the twentieth-century city might be called the story of a strange kind of medical care and treatment which sought to allay the symptoms, while sedulously maintaining all the agonizing conditions that caused the disease—and actually produced side reactions that were as bad as the disease.

With a few outstanding exceptions, like Patrick Geddes, Peter Kropotkin, Ebenezer Howard, and Max Weber, one still looks in vain for fullness of understanding of the normal processes that the city furthers. Though there have been a multitude of studies of urban disorder and decay, the few that attempt to deal with urban health and to establish better norms for growth and development are still, for the most part, innocently utopian in their unqualified belief in the dubious imperatives of an expanding economy; likewise in their conceiving as all-important and all-sufficient the role science and technics would play in the city's future development.

Yes: the present metropolis, even in its most confused and corrupted form, reveals certain fresh achievements in diffusing human culture that hardly existed in earlier times, when all the higher forms were a monopoly of citadel and temple. The historic metropolitan core still has a function to perform, once its members understand that neither its original monopoly, nor its present disintegration can be indefinitely maintained. The great problem of today, if one may borrow a cliché from physics, is to transmute physical mass into psychic energy. We must invent new agencies for turning automatic congestion into purposeful mobilization: for etherializing the container, for repolarizing the magnet and widening the field. These possibilities will perhaps become more tangible, if we examine the miscarriages of effort that have taken place.

3: THE TENTACULAR BUREAUCRACY

The hypnotic attraction of the big city derives from its original position as an instrument of the national state, and a symbol of its sovereign power: one of the earliest of all urban functions. Except for Washington and Canberra, the cities that first set the pattern for inordinate and unrestricted growth were the national or imperial capitals: through their grandeur and wealth they drew both population and trade away from the smaller centers whose traditional ways of life were forced to yield to the immense prestige of king and court.

But political and military power must be sustained by economic organization. The means of continued urban agglomeration were the worldwide lanes of commerce that were opened from the sixteenth century on, tapping the hinterland by means of canals and rivers, then in the nineteenth century by continental railroad systems, and finally, in the middle of the twentieth century, by airlines whose very speed on non-stop flights caused smaller urban aggregations to be by-passed, and favored further concentration at a few terminals.

These varied means brought an endless flow of distant foods and raw materials into the metropolis, along with workers and intellectuals, traders and travellers, drawn from remote areas. "All roads lead to Rome," and railroads promoting regional diffusion were abandoned, or allowed to become obsolete and pushed into bankruptcy, in order to favor main-line travel and terminal congestion. Even the later motor expressways, potentially admirable agents of diffusion, have been planned, or rather adroitly misplanned, for this purpose.

The political condition that hastened the pace of this concentration and established it in sub-centers as well, was the increasing importance of the process of administration itself in every type of enterprise: industry, business, philanthropy, education. In its later phases, the growth of the big city is a by-product of the growth and widening influence of the bureaucracy, which pushed into every sphere the controls and regimentations we examined first in the baroque city.

Once the means of instantaneous communication were available, there was a fresh incentive to concentrate the organs of administration: production could now be directed, the shipment of goods routed, orders given and cancelled, sales made, credits extended and drafts cleared, at a single spot. Remote control, first embodied in the separation of staff and line in the army, spread to business operations. With the manufacture of the type-writer in the eighteen-seventies, and the coincident spread of high-speed stenography, more and more business could be conducted profitably on paper. Mechanical means of communication: mechanical means of making and manifolding the permanent record: mechanical systems of audit and control—all these devices aided the rise of a vast commercial bureaucracy, capable of selling in ever-remoter territories by establishing the fashionable patterns of the metropolis as identical with civilization itself, or with any-thing that could be called 'real life.'

The word bureaucracy had indeed become a discouraging by-word for tortuous inefficiency by the middle of the nineteenth century. Dickens needed no special powers of invention to create Sir Tite Barnacle and the Circumlocution Office. Everyone experienced, throughout the financial and the political world, the difficulty of getting things done by direct action. The simplest civil act required legal sanctions, documents, verifications. From the searching of a deed up to the establishment of civil rights in mar-riage, no one could move without the aid and slow consent of special func-tionaries. Lawyers who knew the prescribed forms and technicalities formed a large part of the growing professional population: their services were needed in the observance, and even more in the tactful breach, of the law.

In all this development the political bureaucracy served as a special target for chronic disparagement: it was supposed to have a monopoly of roundabout methods and a finicking, time-wasting attention to form. But the business man's self-righteous indignation about the monstrous growth of political bureaucracy was extremely humorless. Such an attitude overlooked the fact that the greatest development of bureaucracy during

THE TENTACULAR BUREAUCRACY 535

the last century took place within the realm of business itself: this put to shame the punier additions to the governmental bureaucracy. Plainly no great corporate enterprise with a worldwide network of agents, correspondents, market outlets, factories, and investors could exist without relying upon the services of an army of patient, clerkly routineers in the metropolis: stenographers, filing clerks, and book-keepers, office managers, sales managers, advertising directors, accountants, and their varied assistants, right up to the fifth vice-president whose name or O.K. sets the final seal of responsibility upon an action.

The housing of this bureaucracy in office buildings and tenements and residential suburbs constituted one of the major tasks of metropolitan expansion. Their transportation to and from work, within a limited timespan, raised one of the difficult technical problems that confronted the city planner and the engineer. And not merely did the bureaucracy itself require office space and domestic space: the by-products of its routine demanded an increasing share of the new quarters: files, vaults, places for live storage and dead storage, parade grounds and cemeteries of documents, where the records of business were alphabetically arrayed, with an eye to the possibility of future exploitation, future reference, future lawsuits, future contracts.

This age found its form, as early as the eighteen-eighties in America, in a new type of office building: symbolically a sort of vertical human filing case, with uniform windows, a uniform façade, uniform accommodations, rising floor by floor in competition for light and air and above all financial prestige with other skyscrapers. The abstractions of high finance produced their exact material embodiment in these buildings, and the tendency to multiply bureaucratic services and extend the far-reaching system of controls has not, even now, reached a terminus; for as members increase and transactions become more complicated, mechanical bureaucratic processes must replace direct human contact and personal intercourse. While in England and Wales, for example, between 1931 and 1951 total employment grew by eight per cent, office employment grew by sixty-three per cent; and in London the number of persons employed in offices is twice the national average.

With this development, a new trinity dominated the metropolitan scene: finance, insurance, advertising. By means of these agents, the metropolis extended its rule over subordinate regions, both within its own political territory and in outlying domains: directly or indirectly, they expedited the flow of tribute back into the big centers. Economic enterprise, political power, social authority, once divided over the length and breadth of the land, now concentrated in the new Romes. To obtain money, one must go to the metropolis: to exercise influence, one must achieve a prominent financial position in the metropolis. Here and there, a lone wolf, like the senior Henry Ford, would temporarily remain outside the system, or, like Walter Rathenau, would try to control it for higher human ends. But such isolation, such control, would be largely an illusion. Mark how Ford himself, who once manufactured a car adapted to popular needs and rural life, finally succumbed to the lure of metropolitan style.

Monopolistic organization: credit finance: pecuniary prestige—these are the three sides of the metropolitan pyramid. (Each has its equivalent in the planned, state-managed economies of 'communist' countries.) Whatever goes on in the big city ultimately traces back to one or another of these elements. The metropolis is the natural reservoir of capital under this economic phase; for its banks, its brokerage offices, its stock exchanges, serve as a collecting point for the savings of the surrounding country, and in the case of world capitals, for the surplus capital of foreign investors. Investors and manufacturers both gravitate to the metropolis. The more constant the need for credit capital, the more important for the borrower to be close to the big banks that can advance it.

The concentration of financial power in national or semi-national banks, like the august Bank of England, and in the hands of politically irresponsible private bankers, like the Houses of Rothschild and Morgan, was a characteristic early feature of this regime: but in turn even greater banking networks of national scope arose; so that sooner or later a large part of the population, as investors, depositors, borrowers, speculators, were drawn into the metropolitan scheme. As Balzac saw clearly at the very beginning of this concentration, the banker was supreme. Directly or indirectly the banker manipulated the puppets that appeared on the political stage: he contributed to the funds of the political parties and his sanction was as necessary to the success of a political policy or an industrial enterprise as his veto was fatal.

Now, mortgages on metropolitan real estate, whose values are 'secured' by the continued prosperity and growth of the metropolis, became a mainstay of savings banks and insurance companies. In order to protect their investments, these institutions must combat any attempt to lessen congestion; for this would also deflate the values that are based on congestion. Note how the program for slum replacement and suburban re-settlement mapped out by the Roosevelt administration after 1933 was undermined by the fact that the administration created at the same time another agency whose main purpose was to keep intact the existing structure of mortgages and interest rates. This policy made it impossible to scale down the burden of inflated urban land values and fixed urban debt to the general level of prices. Note, further, how the generous provisions for writing off part of high slum land values, in the interest of urban renewal, by the Federal government has resulted, not in lower densities and better housing for the poor people thus displaced, but often in even higher densities and larger profits through housing upper-income groups. (Characteristically, not the slum dwellers but the speculative financiers and builders have been the main beneficiaries.)

Though based on dynamic expansion, the whole system becomes cumulatively rigid and less capable of meeting new situations: it can neither maneuver nor retreat. Not the least rigid part of it, indeed, is the compulsion to carry through the processes of expansion. In the medieval order, the fatalities and insecurities of life were offset by the organization of guilds and friendly societies. In the metropolitan regime, these services are mainly performed by special financial corporations: insurance companies. Fire, flood, sickness, disability, accident, and death are all covered by one or another form of insurance. In the calculations made to ascertain the rates of insurance the first advances in statistical sociology took place; and in intensive work toward health maintenance and disease prevention, great organizations like the Metropolitan Life Insurance Company have demonstrated the cash value of improvement in these departments by education and medical aid.

Unfortunately, within the current metropolitan scheme, insurance is an attempt to achieve security by piling together at one point the maximum number of risks. In the short run the insurance company may be solvent: in the long run it becomes itself one of the elements contributing to the bankruptcy of the regime as a whole. As long as the productive mechanism is in working order, the flow of goods and services is continuous. But a drought, a dust-storm, an earthquake, a glut of commodities, to say nothing of a war, will shake the fabric; and the assertion of these implacable metropolitan claims then stands in the way of rational political adjustment. If this held before the invention of nuclear weapons, what shall we say of this form of security now? If the system had in fact a rational basis, all the surplus funds of insurance organizations would be addressed to the one risk that now makes all other risks microscopic: insurance for world peace, a prudent proposal that the philosopher, Josiah Royce, broached long ago.

To complete the process of metropolitan monopoly, its one-sided control must be pushed even further: by buying up and assembling local enterprises, forming chains of hotels or department stores that may be placed under centralized control and milked for monopoly profits. To seal this control one further step is necessary: the effective monopoly of advertising, news, publicity, periodical literature, and above all, of the new channels of mass communication, radio and television. These various departments have diverse points of origin and represent various initial interests; but historically they have been loosely tied together since the beginning and within the metropolitan framework they finally coalesce.

All these media work to a common end: to give the stamp of authenticity and value to the style of life that emanates from the metropolis. They establish the national brand: they control the national market: they make every departure from the metropolitan pattern seem deplorably provincial, uncouth, and what is even more heinous, out-of-date. The final goal of this process would be a unified, homogeneous, completely standardized population, cut to the metropolitan pattern and conditioned to consume only those goods that are offered by the controllers and the conditioners, in the interests of a continuously expanding economy. In countries like the United States where this development has been swiftest, that goal is already clearly in sight. Need one wonder that in this country, during the past decade, something like twice the sum was spent per family on advertising as was spent on primary and secondary public education? Control without kingship: conformity without choice: power without the intervention of personality.

Where the organs of finance and publicity are concentrated, the possessing classes, no matter where they originate, are likewise brought together; for the ritual of their life, as lived in public for the benefit of the illustrated newspapers and the television programs, is an essential part of the pecuniary lure. Montesquieu, observing this regime at an early stage, described the social consequences with his usual insight and precision. "Luxury," he noted, "is also in proportion to the populousness of towns, and especially of the capital; so that it is in proportion to the riches of the states, to the inequality of private fortunes, and to the number of people settled in particular places." The concentration of the rich is a typical metropolitan phenomenon. The princely ritual of conspicuous expenditure, no longer confined to the royal court, gives rise to the special luxury industries of the metropolis: dress, food, adornment, cosmetics. Because of the universal nature of metropolitan standards, the exotic fashions of the rich are presently copied and reproduced on a mass scale for the benefit of the entire populace: that indeed is a necessary pillar of an expanding economy.

Though greed, avarice, and pride are the main motivators of the metropolitan regime, in the second and third generations of money-making philanthropy itself becomes an auxiliary business of high repute. In countries where the supertax on income is high, charitable and educational foundations serve the new art of giving away money and yet retaining a firm control over its disposition, so as to protect the system that makes it possible. Just as a few hundred great corporations control about half the industrial capital in the United States, so do a relatively small group from the financial and managerial classes control the organs of culture. When new lines of activity are to be promoted in the arts and sciences, it is to the swollen purses of the metropolis that the promoters direct themselves: there, more often than not, the new foundation settles.

Thus a multitude of associations and organizations of national and international scope naturally have their headquarters in New York, London, or Paris. Here patrons and clients come together: here competitive patronage increases the opportunity for special interests to find support. Since a disproportionate share of power and influence and wealth has been drained away from the hinterland, it is necessary for the provincial who would recapture any of these things to leave his home and fight for a place in the metropolis.

Still a third condition abets the insensate agglomeration of population. Victor Branford suggested that the growth of imperial bureaucracies, coming as a result of political centralization in war, was one of the agents that either transformed the industrial town or caused it to yield in power and influence to the metropolis. War is the forcing house of political bureaucracy. During the nineteenth century, as population heaped further into a few great centers, they were forced to rely more fully on distant sources of supply: to widen the basis of supplies and to protect the 'life-line' that connects the source with the voracious mouth of the metropolis, became the functions of the army and navy.

In so far as the metropolis, by fair means or foul, is able to control distant sources of food and raw materials, the growth of the capital can proceed indefinitely. Even in a country like the United States, the outlying rural areas were for long treated as colonial possessions, and deprived by metropolitan bankers of the capital necessary to build their own steel works, even to further local consumption. It needed the Second World War to force the establishment of steel mills on the Pacific Coast.

Do not suppose that these efforts to promote agglomeration and congestion are wholly spontaneous. On the contrary, strenuous efforts were made—and continue to be made—to ensure it. Railroad systems were deliberately designed to compel passengers and goods to pass through the metropolis before going elsewhere. Each great metropolis still sits like a spider in the midst of a transportation web, though the railroads themselves have been sacrificed to the motor car and the jet plane. In the United States, in addition, as Warren Thompson long ago pointed out, the railroad rate structure is not based on the actual cost of service; the charges are arbitrarily equalized in such a fashion as to give a subsidy to the big cities at the expense of rival towns that are perhaps nearer the shipping point, even though the cost of handling freight in big cities has always, by reason of their very congestion, been disproportionately high— and is now almost prohibitive.

The public subsidy of air transportation works to the same end: that of achieving the maximum amount of congestion and nullifying the very improvements that the technological advances themselves have, potentially, brought about. Thus many of the boasted advantages of the metropolis, with its command of every resource of technology, turn out to be illusory: like Alice's Red Queen, by great exertion and utmost speed the metropolis barely manages to remain in the same position: in fact many of its services, for the last half century, have gone backward. Technological adroitness is no cure for political incompetence and social uninventiveness.

4: THE REMOVAL OF LIMITS

Let us now view the situation of the metropolis in more general terms: what some have called the urban explosion is in fact a symptom of a more general state—the removal of quantitative limits. This marks the change from an organic system to a mechanical system, from purposeful growth to purposeless expansion.

Until the nineteenth century the limitations of both local and regional transportation placed a natural restriction upon the growth of cities. Even the biggest centers, Rome, Babylon, Alexandria, Antioch, were forced to respect that limit. But by the middle of the nineteenth century the tendency toward metropolitan monopoly was supplemented with a new factor brought in by the effective utilization of coal and iron and the extension of the railroad: in terms of purely physical requirements the area of settlement coincided with the coal beds, the ore beds, the railroad network. Patrick Geddes, early in the present century, pointed out the significance of the new population maps, which graphically disclosed a general thickening and spreading of the urban mass: he showed that entire provinces and counties were becoming urbanized, and he proposed to differentiate such diffused formations by a name that would distinguish them from the historic city: the 'conurbation.'

Meanwhile the original forces that created the conurbation were supplemented by the electric power grid, the electric railway, and still later by the motor car and the motor road: so that a movement that was at first confined largely to the area accessible to the railroad now is taking place everywhere. Whereas the first extension of the factory system produced a multitude of new cities and greatly augmented the population of existing centers, the present diffusion of the area of settlement has largely halted this growth and has enormously increased the production of relatively undifferentiated urban tissue, without any relation either to an internally coherent nucleus or an external boundary of any sort.

The result threatens to be a universal conurbation. Those who ignored Geddes's original definition half a century ago have recently re-discovered the phenomenon itself, and treated it as if it were an entirely new develop-ment. Some have even misapplied to the conurbation the inappropriate term Megalopolis, though it represents, in fact, the precise opposite of the tendency that brought the original city of this name into existence. The overgrown historic city was still, residually, an entity: the conurbation is a nonentity, and becomes more patently so as it spreads.

What this removal of limits means can perhaps best be grasped by referring to the extension of historic centers. When Rome was surrounded by the Aurelian Wall in A.D. 274, it covered a little more than five square miles. The present area of London is 130 times as great as this; while it is roughly 650 times as big as the area of medieval London, which was 677 acres. The conurbation of New York is even more widespread: it covers something like 2,514 square miles. If no human purposes supervene to halt the blotting out of the countryside and to establish limits for the growth and colonization of cities, the whole coastal strip from Maine to Florida might coalesce into an almost undifferentiated conurbation. But to call this mass a 'regional city' or to hold that it represents the new scale of settlement to which modern man must adapt his institutions and his personal needs is to mask the realities of the human situation and allow seemingly automatic forces to become a substitute for human purposes.

These vast urban masses are comparable to a routed and disorganized army, which has lost its leaders, scattered its battalions and companies, torn off its insignia, and is fleeing in every direction. "Sauve qui peut." The first step toward handling this situation, besides establishment of an over-all command, is to re-group in units that can be effectively handled. Until we understand the function of the smaller units and can bring them under discipline we cannot command and deploy the army as a whole over a larger area. The scale of distances has changed, and the 'regional city' is a potential reality, indeed a vital necessity. But the condition for success in these endeavors lies in our abilities to recognize and to impose organic limitations. This means the replacement of the machine-oriented metropolitan economy by one directed toward the goods and goals of life.

Though the removal of limits is one of the chief feats of the metropolitan economy, this does not imply any abdication of power on the part of the chiefs in charge: for there is one countervailing condition to this removal, and that is the processing of all operations through the metropolis and its increasingly complicated mechanisms. The metropolis is in fact a proc-essing center, in which a vast variety of goods, material and spiritual, is mechanically sorted and reduced to a limited number of standardized articles, uniformly packaged, and distributed through controlled channels to their destination, bearing the approved metropolitan label.

'Processing' has now become the chief form of metropolitan control;

and the need for its constant application has brought into existence a whole range of inventions, mechanical and electronic, from cash registers to electronic computers, which handle every operation from book-keeping to university examinations. Interests and aptitudes that do not lend themselves to processing are automatically rejected. So complicated, so elaborate, so costly are the processing mechanisms that they cannot be employed except on a mass scale: hence they eliminate all activities of a fitful, inconsecutive, or humanly subtle nature—just as 'yes' or 'no' answers eliminate those more delicate and accurate discriminations that often lie at one point or another in between the spuriously 'correct' answer. That which is local, small, personal, autonomous, must be suppressed. Increasingly, he who controls the processing mechanism controls the lives and destinies of those who must consume its products, and who on metropolitan terms cannot seek any others. For processing and packaging do not end on the production line: they finally make over the human personality.

In short the monopoly of power and knowledge that was first established in the citadel has come back, in a highly magnified form, in the final stages of metropolitan culture. In the end every aspect of life must be brought under control: controlled weather, controlled movement, controlled association, controlled production, controlled prices, controlled fantasy, controlled ideas. But the only purpose of control, apart from the profit, power, and prestige of the controllers, is to accelerate the process of mechanical control itself.

The priests of this regime are easy to identify: the whole system, in its final stages, rests on the proliferation of secret, and thus controllable, knowledge; and the very division of labor that makes specialized scientific research possible also restricts the number of people capable of putting the fragments together. But where are the new gods? The nuclear reactor is the seat of their power: radio transmission and rocket flight their angelic means of communication and transportation: but beyond these minor agents of divinity the Control Room itself, with its Cybernetic Deity, giving His lightning-like decisions and His infallible answers: omniscience and omnipotence, triumphantly mated by science. Faced with this electronic monopoly of man's highest powers, the human can come back only at the most primitive level. Sigmund Freud detected the beginnings of creative art in the infant's pride over his bowel movements. We can now detect its ultimate manifestation in paintings and sculpture whose contents betray a similar pride and a similar degree of autonomy—and a similar product.

One of the ancient prerogatives of the gods was to create man out of their flesh, like Atum, or in their own image, like Yahweh. When the accredited scientific priesthood go a little farther with their present activities, the new life-size homunculus will be processed, too: one can already see anticipatory models in our art galleries. He will look remarkably like a man accoutered in a 'space-suit': outwardly a huge scaly insect. But the face inside will be incapable of expression, as incapable as that of a corpse. And who will know the difference?

5: SPRAWLING GIANTISM

Circle over London, Buenos Aires, Chicago, Sydney, in an airplane or view the cities schematically by means of an urban map and block plan. What is the shape of the city and how does it define itself? The original container has completely disappeared: the sharp division between city and country no longer exists. As the eye stretches toward the hazy periphery one can pick out no definite shapes except those formed by nature: one beholds rather a continuous shapeless mass, here bulging or ridged with buildings, there broken by a patch of green or an unwinding ribbon of concrete. The shapelessness of the whole is reflected in the individual part, and the nearer the center, the less as a rule can the smaller parts be distinguished.

Failing to divide its social chromosomes and split up into new cells, each bearing some portion of the original inheritance, the city continues to grow inorganically, indeed cancerously, by a continuous breaking down of old tissues, and an overgrowth of formless new tissue. Here the city has absorbed villages and little towns, reducing them to place names, like Manhattanville and Harlem in New York; there it has, more happily, left the organs of local government and the vestiges of an independent life, even assisted their revival, as in Chelsea and Kensington in London; but it has nevertheless enveloped those urban areas in its physical organization and built up the open land that once served to ensure their identity and integrity. Sometimes the expanding street system forms an orderly pattern, sometimes it produces only a crazy network that does not even serve traffic: but the difference between one type of order and another is merely a difference in the degree of sprawl, confusion, de-building.

As one moves away from the center, the urban growth becomes ever more aimless and discontinuous, more diffuse and unfocussed, except where some surviving town has left the original imprint of a more orderly life. Old neighborhoods and precincts, the social cells of the city, still maintaining some measure of the village pattern, become vestigial. No human eye can take in this metropolitan mass at a glance. No single gathering place except the totality of its streets can hold all its citizens. No human mind can comprehend more than a fragment of the complex and minutely specialized activities of its citizens. The loss of form, the loss of autonomy, the constant frustration and harassment of daily activities, to say nothing of gigantic breakdowns and stoppages—all these become normal attributes of the metropolitan regime. There is a special name for power when it is concentrated on such a scale: it is called impotence.

The giantism of the metropolis is not the result of technological progress alone. Contrary to popular belief, the growth of great cities preceded the decisive technical advances of the last two centuries. But the metropolitan phase became universal only when the technical means of congestion had become adequate—and their use profitable to those who manufactured or employed them. The modern metropolis is, rather, an outstanding example of a peculiar cultural lag within the realm of technics itself: namely, the continuation by highly advanced technical means of the obsolete forms and ends of a socially retarded civilization. The machines and utilities that would lend themselves to decentralization in a life-centered order, here become either a means to increase congestion or afford some slight temporary palliation—at a price.

The form of the metropolis, then, is its formlessness, even as its aim is its own aimless expansion. Those who work within the ideological limits of this regime have only a quantitative conception of improvement: they seek to make its buildings higher, its streets broader, its parking lots more ample: they would multiply bridges, highways, tunnels, making it ever easier to get in and out of the city, but constricting the amount of space available within the city for any other purpose than transportation itself. Frank Lloyd Wright's project for a skyscraper a mile high was the ultimate reduction to absurdity of this whole theory of city development. The ultimate form of such a city would be an acre of building to a square mile of expressways and parking lots. In many areas this is rapidly approaching fulfillment.

When both the evil and the remedy are indistinguishable, one may be sure that a deep-seated process is at work. An expanding economy, dedicated to profit, not to the satisfaction of life-needs, necessarily creates a new image of the city, that of a perpetual and ever-widening maw, consuming the output of expanding industrial and agricultural production, in response to the pressures of continued indoctrination and advertising. Two centuries ago the need for such an economy was indisputable, and in many poverty-stricken countries that need still remains, to lift the population above the margin of starvation and helpless depression. But in the countries of the West, particularly in the United States, the problem of scarcity has been solved, apart from distribution and relation to organic needs, only to create a new set of problems just as embarrassing: those of surfeit and satiety. Today, accordingly, expansion has become an end in itself: to make it possible the rulers of this society resort to every possible device of pyramid-building.

For unfortunately, once an economy is geared to expansion, the means rapidly turn into an end, and "the going becomes the goal." Even more unfortunately, the industries that are favored by such expansion must, to maintain their output, be devoted to goods that are readily consumable, either by their nature, or because they are so shoddily fabricated that they must soon be replaced. By fashion and built-in obsolescence the economies of machine production, instead of producing leisure and durable wealth, are duly cancelled out by mandatory consumption on an ever larger scale.

By the same token, the city itself becomes consumable, indeed expendable: the container must change as rapidly as its contents. This latter imperative undermines a main function of the city as an agent of human continuity. The living memory of the city, which once bound together generations and centuries, disappears: its inhabitants live in a self-annihilating moment-to-moment continuum. The poorest Stone Age savage never lived in such a destitute and demoralized community.

Now organic processes are purposeful, goal-seeking, self-limiting: indeed all organisms have built-in controls that serve to co-ordinate action and limit growth. The expanding economy, like the technological system on which it is so largely based, has no such limitations: its stabilization takes the form of multiplying the number of consumers and intensifying their wants. But to ensure continued productivity, it limits these wants to those that can be supplied at a profit by the machine. Thus this economy produces motor cars and refrigerators galore; but has no motive to supply durable works of art, handsome gardens, or untrammelled, nonconsuming leisure. Our economic establishment is better equipped to destroy the product outright than to give it away or to limit the output at source.

The image of modern industrialism that Charlie Chaplin carried over from the past into 'Modern Times' is just the opposite of megalopolitan reality. He pictured the worker as an old-fashioned drudge, chained to the machine, mechanically fed while he continued to operate it. That image belongs to Coketown. The new worker, in the metropolis, has been progressively released from the productive process: the grinding, impoverished toil that made the nineteenth-century factory so hideous has been lifted by social services and security, by mechanical aids and by complete automation. Work is no longer so brutal in the light industries: but automation has made it even more boring. The energy and application that once went into the productive process must now be addressed to consumption.

By a thousand cunning attachments and controls, visible and subliminal, the workers in an expanding economy are tied to a consumption mechanism: they are assured of a livelihood provided they devour without undue selectivity all that is offered by the machine—and demand nothing that is not produced by the machine. The whole organization of the metropolitan community is designed to kill spontaneity and self-direction. You stop on the red light and go on the green. You see what you are supposed to see, think what you are supposed to think: your personal contributions, like your income and security taxes, are deductible at source. To choose, to select, to discriminate, to exercise prudence or continence or forethought, to carry self-control to the point of abstinence, to have standards other than those of the market, and to set limits other than those of immediate consumption—these are impious heresies that would challenge the whole megalopolitan myth and deflate its economy. In such a 'free' society Henry Thoreau must rank as a greater public enemy than Karl Marx.

The metropolis, in its final stage of development, becomes a collective contrivance for making this irrational system work, and for giving those who are in reality its victims the illusion of power, wealth, and felicity, of standing at the very pinnacle of human achievement. But in actual fact their lives are constantly in peril, their wealth is tasteless and ephemeral, their leisure is sensationally monotonous, and their pathetic felicity is tainted by constant, well-justified anticipations of violence and sudden death. Increasingly they find themselves "strangers and afraid," in a world they never made: a world ever less responsive to direct human command, ever more empty of human meaning.

6: THE SHADOWS OF SUCCESS

To believe, therefore, that human culture has reached a marvellous final culmination in the modern metropolis one must avert one's eyes from the grim details of the daily routine. And that is precisely what the metropolitan denizen schools himself to do: he lives, not in the real world, but in a shadow world projected around him at every moment by means of paper and celluloid and adroitly manipulated lights: a world in which he is insulated by glass, cellophane, pliofilm from the mortifications of living. In short, a world of professional illusionists and their credulous victims.

The swish and crackle of paper is the underlying sound of the metropolis. What is visible and real in this world is only what has been transferred to paper or has been even further etherialized on a microfilm or a tape recorder. The essential daily gossip of the metropolis is no longer that of people meeting face to face at a cross-roads, at the dinner table, in the marketplace: a few dozen people writing in the newspapers, a dozen or so more broadcasting over radio and television, provide the daily interpretation of movements and happenings with slick professional adroitness. Thus even the most spontaneous human activities come under professional surveillance and centralized control. The spread of manifolding devices of every sort gives to the most ephemeral and mediocre products of the mind a temporary durability they do not deserve: whole books are printed to justify the loose evacuations of the tape recorder.

All the major activities of the metropolis are directly connected with paper and its plastic substitutes; and printing and packaging are among its principal industries. The activities pursued in the offices of the metropolis are directly connected with paper: the tabulating machines, the journals, the ledgers, the card-catalogs, the deeds, the contracts, the mortgages, the briefs, the trial records: so, too, the prospectuses, the advertisements, the magazines, the newspapers. As early as the eighteenth century Mercier had observed this metropolitan form of the White Plague. Modern methods of manifolding have not lessened the disease: they have only exchanged easygoing slipshod ways, which often sufficed, for a more exact record, whose elaboration and cost are out of all proportion to the value of what is recorded. What was a mere trickle in Mercier's day has now become a ravaging flood of paper.

As the day's routine proceeds the pile of paper mounts higher: the trashbaskets are filled and emptied and filled again. The ticker tape exudes its quotation of stocks and its report of news; the students in the schools and universities fill their notebooks, digest and disgorge the contents of books, as the silkworm feeds on mulberry leaves and manufactures its cocoon, unravelling themselves on examination day. In the theater, in literature, in music, in business, reputations are made—on paper. The scholar with his degrees and publications, the actress with her newspaper clippings, and the financier with his shares and his voting proxies, measure their power and importance by the amount of paper they can command. No wonder the anarchists once invented the grim phrase: "Incinerate the documents!" That would ruin this whole world quicker than universal flood or earthquake, if not as fatally as a shower of hydrogen bombs.

That life is an occasion for living, and not a pretext for supplying items to newspapers, interviews on television, or a spectacle for crowds of otherwise vacant bystanders—these notions do not occur in the metropolitan mind. For them the show is the reality, and "the show must go on!"

This metropolitan world, then, is a world where flesh and blood are less real than paper and ink and celluloid. It is a world where the great masses of people, unable to achieve a more full-bodied and satisfying means of living, take life vicariously, as readers, spectators, listeners, passive observers. Living thus, year in and year out, at second hand, remote from the nature that is outside them, and no less remote from the nature that is within, it is no wonder that they turn more and more of the functions of life, even thought itself, to the machines that their inventors have created. In this disordered environment only machines retain some of the attributes of life, while human beings are progressively reduced to a bundle of reflexes, without self-starting impulses or autonomous goals: 'behaviorist man.'

7: CONGESTION AND DE-CONGESTION

The facts of metropolitan congestion are undeniable; they are visible in every phase of the city's life. One encounters congestion in the constant stoppages of traffic, resulting from the massing of vehicles in centers that can be kept in free movement only by utilizing human legs. One encounters it in the crowded office elevator or in the even more tightly packed subway train, rank with the odor of human bodies. Lack of office room, lack of school room, lack of house room, even lack of space in the cemeteries for the dead. Such form as the metropolis achieves is crowd-form: the swarming bathing beach by the sea or the body of spectators in the boxing arena or the football stadium. With the increase of private motor cars, the streets and avenues become parking lots, and to move traffic at all, vast expressways gouge through the city and increase the demand for further parking lots and garages. In the act of making the core of the metropolis accessible, the planners of congestion have already almost made it uninhabitable.

The costs of congestion itself, in impeding the essential economic activities of the metropolitan area, are augmented by the costs of the purely mechanical methods overcoming this congestion. These costs, even if they were humanly tolerable, would long ago have been rejected because of their financial extravagance, if rational economic standards had played any part in forming the metropolitan myth.

The purely physical limits to metropolitan expansion are set mainly by three conditions: the amount of water that can be tapped by one population mass without encroaching on a competing neighbor: the amount of land available before one metropolis mingles and merges with the next: finally, the costs of transportation in both time and money, since with mere increase of distance from the center there comes a point at which the gravitational pull of the metropolis will weaken to a stage that will favor transportation to other more accessible centers, provided they offer comparable economic advantages. Let us observe how these limitations operate.

First, the demand for water. As the metropolis becomes more crowded, the local springs and wells are progressively abandoned for larger reservoirs of water, such as the rivers from whose befouled drinking water more than one great city, including Paris, London, and Rome, poisoned itself as late as the mid-nineteenth century. Even now, without the antiseptic administration of chlorine the drinking water of most big cities, particularly during winter months, would be dangerous to consume. In addition to the Croton system, opened in 1842, New York little more than half a century later reached back into the Catskills, a hundred miles away. Each additional mile of tunnel and pipe, each additional reservoir, adds to the unit cost; but a year of drought, such as New York experienced in 1951, can bring the city very close to the danger point. Meanwhile the spread of the metropolis itself not alone closes down local sources of supply, but, by filling in swamps and denuding hillsides of vegetation lowers the water table; while the industrial use of water, plus its widespread utilization in the United States for air-conditioning systems, brings famine still nearer even at existing population levels.

The only prospect of relieving this chronic shortage of water in metropolitan agglomerations would be the distillation of sea-water in wholesale quantities; but even if that were possible through utilizing cheap solar or nuclear energy it would probably be no more potable than that which is now manufactured aboard ship; and no matter how inexpensive the energy used to effect this conversion, the cost of the process would be one further addition to the mounting cost of water.

The cost of the internal transportation system in a big city is equally massive; yet some of the most important factors elude exact calculation. The initial capital cost for underground systems, for tunnels, bridges, and accessory highways, with their difficult excavation and boring, is necessarily high; but this is only a part of the total burden. Year by year one must add the cost of the coal and electricity consumed in the haulage of human bodies: above all, one must add on the human cost, in physiological wear and tear, the boredom and harassment and depression, brought about by this daily shuttling between dormitory and work-place: minutes and hours which at the peak of traffic cannot even be utilized in achieving the anesthesia of the daily newspaper. Add to this the fatigue of the journey, the exposure to infectious diseases in overcrowded cars, the disturbance to the gastro-intestinal functions caused by the strain and anxiety of having to reach the office or factory on time. Certainly any plan for improving the quality of life in metropolitan areas would, as a minimum requirement, demand a lessening of the time and distance needed for daily transportation.

Emerson said that life was a matter of having good days; but it is a matter of having good minutes, too. Who shall say what compensations are not necessary to the metropolitan worker to make up for the strain and depression of the twenty, forty, sixty, or more minutes he spends each night and morning passing through these metropolitan man-sewers—even if they are as efficient as those in London or Paris, as luxurious as that in Moscow? By contrast a walk to work, as much as a mile each day, is at most seasons a tonic, especially for the sedentary worker, who plays such a part in metropolitan offices and factories, at the typewriter, the linotype machine, the sewing machine, the filing cabinet.

By building up sub-centers, based on pedestrian circulation, within the metropolitan region, a good part of urban transportation difficulties could have been obviated. (In cities that are multi-centered and have been partly decentralized, such as London, by political regrouping into semi-autonomous boroughs, some forty per cent of the night population, according to Westergaard, had jobs within their own local authorities.) To make the necessary journeys about the metropolis swift and efficient the number of unnecessary journeys—and the amount of their unnecessary length—must be decreased. Only by bringing work and home closer together can this be achieved. Toward that end the Barbican scheme in London is a necessary complement to the New Towns policy—though unfortunately conceived at a density that may defeat its purpose.

What applies to the daily shuttling of people to and from the center of the metropolis applies equally to the transportation of goods; for congestion not merely slows down the passage of goods through the streets but also increases the time needed for unloading: and both raise the cost. The multiplication of motor vehicles capable of high speeds has in fact resulted in the progressive retarding of transportation and the piling up of costs. Horsedrawn vehicles in New York, according to a traffic study made in 1907, moved at an average speed of 11.5 miles an hour: today automobiles crawl at the average daytime rate of some six miles an hour; and as the density of building per acre increases in both business and residential areas, even this speed will slow down further. As for the costs of such congestion, during the nineteen-twenties a conservative estimate put it at $150,000,000 a year. By now goods shipped from one borough to another in New York must pay an extra cartage charge; and the total figures —augmented by the toll to the gangster-aided unions that dominate the trucking business and the waterfront—have reached astronomical dimensions.

But if the costs of metropolitan congestion are appalling the costs of de-congestion are equally formidable. In the United States, with the eager connivance of municipal authorities, an ever-larger part of the population is spreading over the countryside, seeking, as we have seen, the conditions for homelife, the space, the freedom of movement, that have become impossible within the central core, hoping too, but vainly, that the lower land values and taxes of the outlying areas will remain permanent even after the necessary civic improvements have been made. And all over the world the same sort of urban dispersal is now taking place, at an accelerating rate. In attempting to overcome congestion, the leaders of this dispersal have acted as if unlimited space were an effective substitute for a well-organized and well-designed community.

The chief factor that keeps this dispersal from being of an entirely random nature are the expressways and connecting roads that have made it possible: funnels that help to blow the urban dust farther from the center, once the top soil of a common life has been removed. "The thrust of technology," a recent observer of 'The Deserted City' notes, "seems persistently toward high speed facilities which will drive us ever further outward." This opinion is so widely shared that the writer does not bother to support it. So he does not explain why the thrust of technology should by itself determine human needs and be treated as a final end before which all other human purposes must bow. To attempt such an explanation would be to question the premises, indeed the sacred dogmas, upon which the economy of the metropolis has been built.

8 : THE BURSTING CONTAINER

By now it should be plain that congestion and expansion in the metropolis are in fact complementary movements, though they represent the beginning and end of the megalopolitan cycle. The dominant world metropolises represented huge concentrations of political, financial, and technological power, developing mainly in this very order: in time they were abetted by religious and educational concentrations of the same magnitude. So effective was this monopoly, so firm this mode of control, so rich its rewards, that they obscured for a time the human penalties of urban congestion: conditions that should have been a badge of shame became almost a mark of honor.

Strangely the greatest justification for metropolitan congestion has passed almost unnoticed. Through the operation of these forces the big city, in the nineteenth century, served by the very size and variety of its population to foster functions that had never been sustained on anything like the same scale before: corporate associations and societies of like-minded persons, pursuing special interests that covered every aspect of human life. Up to this time, the church, the university, the school, the guild, had been the main foci of associated activities, apart from the city itself. But from the early Renascence onward, these new associations began to flourish and took a thousand different forms: scientific societies, museums, sociable clubs, insurance associations, political parties, economic groups, historic societies, fellowships of all kinds.

Though the nineteenth-century metropolis boasted of its individualism, it was actually more significant because of the range and variety of its voluntary corporate associations. Consult the classified telephone directory of a big American city under its listing of clubs and associations: the immense number of purposeful associations you will find there are in part the by-product of metropolitan concentration, and they flourished as long as a large part of their members could conveniently come together for at least weekly or monthly meetings. With that solid core of participation, wider organizations of national and international range became possible.

Just as the concentration of political and economic power in the citadel produced urban institutions and social benefits not directly intended by the rulers, so did this proliferation of clubs and societies. However vast the metropolis, within it one could find at least a handful of like-minded people, to enhance and sustain any conceivable interest. This was a precious contribution to human development; and not a little of the credit for creativity and productivity that has gone to our technological inventions and our industrial organizations could be traced in the first place to these multitudinous organs of association.

In short, though the congestion of the metropolis has tended to suppress or destroy the organic tissue of neighborhoods and smaller communities, it has helped to create new organs of a more specialized and more selective nature, made possible by their accessibility to an unusually large population. This has an important bearing on the future reconstruction of cities and regions.

We are now faced with a condition for which, so far as I know, there is no precedent in history. Though the metropolitan container has burst, the institutional magnets still maintain to a large degree their original attractive power. In every metropolitan area the population is spilling over new suburban, exurban, and rural areas much faster than it is being accumulated in the reservoir at the center. But the reservoir itself, the metropolitan core, is not becoming empty. Now up to 1940 the prospect of a lowered rate of population growth, approaching stability by 1980 in more than one country, seemed definite: so steady and sure had been the decline in England, for example, that the best plans for post-war building took a lower urban population as a fundamental—and helpful—condition for rebuilding on a less congested pattern.

But both the general and the urban rates of growth have undergone a sudden reversal during the last twenty years, even in highly industrialized areas, accompanied by an even sharper upward movement in more primitive economies. This has been abetted, in technically more advanced countries, by the general shift in employment from agricultural and industrial occupations to the services and professions. In certain cases, like London, the increased employment offered by administrative activities has heightened the fashionable attractions of the center, with its opportunities for competitive spending and titillating forms of consumption. This has effectively counteracted the tendency of many industries to move out to the country: indeed, it has even served in England to draw industry away from the murkier industrial centers of Lancashire and West Riding, if only to pleasure the managerial and technical staffs—and their wives.

As a result, there has been no substantial decrease in the metropolitan population, apart from the temporary annihilation or evacuation of wartime: rather the contrary. But the fastest rate of growth has been in the outlying areas; and, to enlarge the whole scope of the urban problem, provincial towns and regional centers, which could often boast better housing, more ample park space, and more accessible recreation areas than the big city have themselves become the focus for still further metropolitan growth. These towns begin to display the same environmental deficiencies, the same unbalanced budget, the same expenditure on glib mechanical planning remedies instead of on positive human improvements, that their larger historic rivals boast. Thus the new megalopolitan form is fast becoming a universal one.

The important thing to recognize about this whole process is that although rapid transportation and instant communication have altered the scale of urban development they have not so far altered the pattern. This whole vast change has in fact been taking place within an obsolete urban framework. Rapid technological advances in pursuit of obsolete or humanly primitive goals—this is the very nature of the final stage of megalopolitan disintegration, as visible in its day-to-day city planning as in its ultimate plans for atomic, bacterial, and chemical genocide. Even the excessive birthrate may be a symptom of this deterioration: for, as W. M. Wheeler noted of insect societies, inordinate reproduction accompanies an arrest of other forms of biological development.

Yet the continued expansion of the metropolis into the formless megalopolitan conurbation, and the multiplication and extension of these conurbations reveal the depth of the plight every society now faces. Hence it is hopeless to think that this problem is one than can be solved by local authorities, even by one as colossal and competent as the London County Council. Nor is it a problem that can be successfully attacked by a mere extension of the scope of political action, through creating metropolitan governments. Philadelphia brought such an administrative unit into existence as early as the middle of the nineteenth century, turning a great county into a city long before most of its component towns were more than little villages. This metropolitan government area cannot now be distinguished from those that remained un-unified, except where the independence of the latter has happily preserved some greater measure of individuality and self-government. The internal problems of the metropolis and its subsidiary areas are reflections of a whole civilization geared to expansion by strictly rational and scientific means for purposes that have become progressively more empty and trivial, more infantile and primitive, more barbarous and massively irrational.

This is a matter that must be attacked at the source; whereas most of our present plans, including those that would impose some wholesale scheme of political administration upon even vaster urban areas, are the equivalent of turning the contents of Vesuvius back into the crater once it has erupted, or, no less unrealistically, of pretending that the lava-seared earth need only be united into larger fields to make profitable a new scheme of cultivation.

One cannot bring about the renewal of the city by replacing old structures with new buildings that only confirm the obsolete pattern of city growth and that rest solely on the equally obsolete ideological foundations of 'mechanical progress.' As long as the present forces remain in operation the area of urban disorganization will widen; and in the act of expanding indefinitely, in response to the 'thrust of technology' and the desire for immediate profit, one metropolis will merge physically with its neighbor. In that merging each metropolis will lose the neighboring landscape that served it for education and recreation, along with its residue of urban individuality.

Thus the very effort to escape from Megalopolis blocks all its roads. Nothing can happen in this new type of infra-urban society unless it can be done by a mass organization, working through a uniform apparatus controlled by central headquarters. Since it will no longer matter where this remote control center is, the last reason for the great city's existence will vanish at the very moment that it takes the form of a boundless conurbation. At that point the stage will be set for 'Post-historic Man.'

Those who think that there are no alternatives to this urban fate, and no human way out, may prove correct in their estimate of probabilities. But if this is so, it will be because our contemporaries have a limited insight into the forces of history, a poor understanding of the functions of the city, and a naïve tendency to overvalue the instruments of technology, considered apart from any relevance to human ends. At bottom they are the victims of a quasi-scientific metaphysics incapable of interpreting organic processes or furthering the development of human life.

The very defects of the prevailing ideology of our leaders will tend to bring about a fulfillment of their prophecies, and thus justify their dismal plans. The controllers themselves have, with exquisite irony, produced a collective mechanism that is not, in fact, under control, and once set in motion is not capable of being brought under control by the kind of mind that has devised it. They console themselves over their helplessness with the quaint notion that "you cannot put the hands of the clock back." But that ill-chosen metaphor reveals the basic error. Who would trust a clock to keep time accurately if its hands could not be put back: a clock subject to only one form of regulation—that for going faster?

The more automatic our organizations become, the more necessity there is for a system of regulation; and that system, like the clock's, must be adjusted in terms of an external standard, independent of the mechanism. In the case of a clock—the revolution of the earth: in the case of human institutions—the whole nature of man, not just that portion of it which has been fascinated by the machine and become submissive to *its* needs. So with cities: to correct the deficiencies of our over-mechanized civilization, we shall have to build up a multi-centered system of control, with a sufficient development or morality, intelligence, and self-respect to be able to arrest the automatic processes—mechanical, bureaucratic, organizational— at any point where human life is in danger or the human personality is threatened with loss of values and choices.

9: DESTINY OF MEGALOPOLIS

In following the growth of megalopolitan culture to its conclusion we reach a whole series of terminal processes, and it would be simple-minded to believe that they have any prospect of continuing in existence indefinitely. A life that lacks any meaning, value, or purpose, except that of keeping the mechanism of breathing and ingestion going, is little better than life in an iron lung, which is only supportable because the patient still has hope of recovery and escape.

The metropolitan regime now threatens to reach its climax in a meaningless war, one of total extermination, whose only purpose would be to relieve the anxieties and fears produced by the citadels' wholesale commitment to weapons of annihilation and extermination. Thus absolute power has become in fact absolute nihilism. Scientific and technological over-elaboration, unmodified by human values and aims, has committed countries like the United States and Russia to collective mechanisms of destruction so rigid that they cannot be modified or brought under control without being completely dismantled. Even instinctual animal intelligence remains inoperative in this system: the commitment to the machine over-throws all the safeguards to life, including the ancient law of self-preserva-tion. For the sake of rapid locomotion, we in the United States kill some 40,000 people outright every year and fatally maim hundreds of thousands of others. For the sake of wielding absolute nuclear power our leaders are brazenly prepared to sacrifice from fifty to seventy-five million of their own citizens on the first day of an all-out nuclear war, and mutilate, or even possibly in the end eliminate the human race. The illusionist phrase to cover these psychotic plans is 'national security,' or even, more absurdly, 'national survival.'

Now, in every organism, the anabolic and the catabolic processes, the creative and the destructive, are constantly at work. Life and growth depend, not on the absence of negative conditions, but on a sufficient degree of equilibrium, and a sufficient surplus of constructive energy to permit continued repair, to absorb novelties, to regulate quantities, and to establish give-and-take relations with all the other organisms and communi-ties needed to maintain balance. The negative factors in metropolitan existence might have provided the conditions for a higher development if the very terms of expansion had not given them the upper hand and tended to make their domination permanent, in ever more destructive processes.

When 'The Culture of Cities' was written in the mid-nineteen-thirties, the external forces that threatened metropolitan civilization were clearly visible: so much so that at this stage of the analysis I laid them out in the form of a 'Brief Outline of Hell.' I then sought to clarify the picture further by giving a résumé of Patrick Geddes's interpretation of the urban cycle of growth, from village (eopolis) to megalopolis and necropolis. That cycle has described the course of all the historic metropolises, including those that arose again out of their own ruins and graveyards. Even in 1938, when the book was published, this characterization seemed to more than one critic unduly pessimistic, indeed perversely exaggerated and morbidly unrealistic. Many were sure, then, that no dangers worse than chronic unemployment threatened the Western World; above all they were certain that war and the total destruction of cities were both highly improbable.

But today the one section of my original chapter on the metropolis that could not be re-published except as an historic curiosity is precisely this 'Brief Outline of Hell,' just because all its anticipations were abun-dantly verified. Though a prediction that is fulfilled naturally no longer concerns us, I recall this *fait accompli,* lest the reader dismiss with equal confidence in its unreality the present portrayal of our even more dire condition. I would remind him that, all too soon, the tensions increased and the war came, with the large-scale destruction of Warsaw in 1939 and that of the center of Rotterdam in 1940. In five years far vaster urban areas were totally destroyed, and large populations were exterminated from London to Tokyo, from Hamburg to Hiroshima. Besides the millions of people—six million Jews alone—killed by the Germans in their suburban extermination camps, by starvation and cremation, whole cities were turned into extermination camps by the demoralized strategists of democracy. Random killing and limitless death gave their final stamp to the realities of megalopolitan expansion.

Though the ruin was widespread, large patches of healthy tissue fortunately remained. By an immense gathering together of resources, helped in many countries by the generous initiatives of the Marshall Plan, the enormous task of rebuilding cities and transportation systems was successfully undertaken. Sometimes this constituted a sentimental task of imitative restoration, of "Bilder aus der Vergangenheit," as in so many towns in Germany: sometimes it produced a bold effort at old-fashioned rationalization, as in the reconstruction of Cherbourg: sometimes, as in Rotterdam or in Coventry, it became an energetic effort to achieve a fresh form for the urban core, which would do justice in wholly contemporary architectural terms to traditional values neglected in the nineteenth century. In two countries, Sweden and England, an even larger effort was made to conceive a new urban pattern that would break away from the automatic concentration and the equally automatic spread of the big city. In the case of England's New Towns, the feasibility of directing and controlling urban growth in relatively self-contained and balanced communities, with a sound industrial base, was amply demonstrated.

Remarkably, the wholesale rehabilitation of the cities of Europe at a higher level than they had achieved in the past, took place in less than a dozen years. That almost superhuman mobilization of energies demonstrated that urban reconstruction and renewal on a far greater scale might be accomplished, within a single generation, provided the economy was directly oriented to human needs, and that the major part of the national income was not diverted to the studious consumptive dissipations and planned destructions demanded by the expanding metropolitan economy: above all, by ceaseless preparations for collective genocide and suicide.

Unfortunately, as soon as the economy recovered and returned to the pursuit of its original ends, all its irrational features likewise came back: to keep going, an ever larger part of its energies must be dissipated in pyramid-building. Nowhere have the irrationalities of the current metropolitan myth been more fully exposed than in the development of so-called 'absolute' weapons for limitless nuclear, bacterial, and chemical genocide. The building up of these weapons among the 'Nuclear Powers' has given the 'death-wish' the status of a fixed national policy, and made a universal extermination camp the ideal terminus of this whole civilization.

Even if the nations take timely measures to eliminate the stock of such weapons, it will be long before the vicious moral effects of this policy are dissipated: adult delinquency, on the scale not merely contemplated but actually prepared for in detail, requires therapeutic counter-measures that may take a full century to show any positive effect. This is the last and worst bequest of the citadel (read 'Pentagon' and 'Kremlin') to the culture of cities.

In a few short years our civilization has reached the point that Henry Adams, with uncanny prescience, foresaw more than half a century ago. "At the present rate of progression, since 1600," he wrote, "it will not need another century or half a century to tip thought upside down. Law, in that case would disappear as theory or a priori principle and give place to force. Morality would become police. Explosives would reach cosmic violence. Disintegration would overcome integration." Every part of this prophecy has already been fulfilled; and it is useless to speculate about the future of cities until we have reckoned with the forces of annihilation and extermination that now, almost automatically, and at an ever-accelerating rate, are working to bring about a more general breakdown.

Metropolitan civilization thus embodies and carries to its conclusion the radical contradiction we found already embedded in the life course of the city from the moment of its foundation: a contradiction that comes out of the dual origin of the city, and the perpetual ambivalence of its goals. From the village, the city derives its nature as a mothering and life-promoting environment, stable and secure, rooted in man's reciprocal relations with other organisms and communities. From the village, too, it derives the ways and values of an ungraded democracy in which each member plays his appropriate role at each stage in the life cycle.

On the other hand, the city owed its existence, and even more its enlargement, to concentrated attempts at mastering other men and dominating, with collective force, the whole environment. Thus the city became a power-trapping utility, designed by royal agents gathering the dispersed energies of little communities into a mighty reservoir, collectively regulating their accumulation and flow, and directing them into new channels —now favoring the smaller units by beneficently re-molding the landscape, but eventually hurling its energies outward in destructive assaults against other cities. Release and enslavement, freedom and compulsion, have been present from the beginning in urban culture.

Out of this inner tension some of the creative expressions of urban life have come forth: yet only in scattered and occasional instances do we discover political power well distributed in small communities, as in seventeenth-century Holland or Switzerland, or the ideals of life constantly regulating the eccentric manifestations of power. Our present civilization is a gigantic motor car moving along a one-way road at an ever-accelerating speed. Unfortunately as now constructed the car lacks both steering wheel and brakes, and the only form of control the driver exercises consists in making the car go faster, though in his fascination with the machine itself and his commitment to achieving the highest speed possible, he has quite forgotten the purpose of the journey. This state of helpless submission to the economic and technological mechanisms modern man has created is curiously disguised as progress, freedom, and the mastery of man over nature. As a result, every permission has become a morbid compulsion. Modern man has mastered every creature above the level of the viruses and bacteria—except himself.

Never before has the 'citadel' exercised such atrocious power over the rest of the human race. Over the greater part of history, the village and the countryside remained a constant reservoir of fresh life, constrained indeed by the ancestral patterns of behavior that had helped make man human, but with a sense of both human limitations and human possibilities. No matter what the errors and aberrations of the rulers of the city, they were still correctible. Even if whole urban populations were destroyed, more than nine-tenths of the human race still remained outside the circle of destruction. Today this factor of safety has gone: the metropolitan explosion has carried both the ideological and the chemical poisons of the metropolis to every part of the earth; and the final damage may be irretrievable.

These terminal possibilities did not, I repeat, first become visible with the use of nuclear weapons: they were plain to alert and able minds, like Burckhardt in the eighteen-sixties, and like Henry Adams at the beginning of the present century.

Adams' contemporary, Henry James, put the human situation in an image that curiously holds today: that of the Happy Family and the Infernal Machine. "The machine so rooted as to defy removal, and the family still so indifferent, while it carries on the family business of buying and selling, of chattering and dancing, to the danger of being blown up." The machine James referred to was the political machine of Philadelphia, then the classic embodiment of corruption and criminality; but only a too-guileless observer can fail to see that it applies to other demoralized mechanisms in our expanding metropolitan civilization. Once-local manifestations of criminality and irrationality now threaten our whole planet, smugly disguised as sound business enterprise, technological progress, communist efficiency, or democratic statesmanship. No wonder the popular existentialists, mirroring our time, equate 'reality' with the 'absurd.' A large portion of the painting and sculpture of the past generation symbolically anticipates the catastrophic end products of this death-oriented culture: total dismemberment and dehumanization in a lifeless, featureless void. Some of the best of this art, like Henry Moore's archaic pinheaded figures, foretells a new beginning at a level so primitive that the mind has hardly yet begun to operate.

Now, if the total picture were as grim as that I have painted in the present chapter, there would be no excuse for writing this book; or rather, it would be just as irrational a contribution as the many other irrationalities and futilities I have touched on. If I have duly emphasized the disintegrations of the metropolitan stage, it has been for but one reason: only those who are aware of them will be capable of directing our collective energies into more constructive processes. It was not the die-hard Romans of the fifth century A.D., still boasting of Rome's achievements and looking forward to another thousand years of them, who understood what the situation required: on the contrary, it was those who rejected the Roman premises and set their lives on a new foundation who built up a new civilization that in the end surpassed Rome's best achievements, even in engineering and government.

And so today: those who work within the metropolitan myth, treating its cancerous tumors as normal manifestations of growth, will continue to apply poultices, salves, advertising incantations, public relations magic, and quack mechanical remedies until the patient dies before their own failing eyes. No small part of the urban reform and correction that has gone on these last hundred years, and not least this last generation—slum demolition, model housing, civic architectural embellishment, suburban extension, 'urban renewal'—has only continued in superficially new forms the same purposeless concentration and organic de-building that prompted the remedy.

Yet in the midst of all this disintegration fresh nodules of growth have appeared and, even more significantly, a new pattern of life has begun to emerge. This pattern necessarily is based on radically different premises from those of the ancient citadel builders or those of their modern counterparts, the rocket-constructors and nuclear exterminators. If we can distinguish the main outlines of this multi-dimensional, life-oriented economy we should also be able to describe the nature and the functions of the emerging city and the future pattern of human settlement. Above all, we should anticipate the next act in the human drama, provided mankind escapes the death-trap our blind commitment to a lopsided, power-oriented, anti-organic technology has set for it.

10: CULTURAL FUNCTION OF THE
WORLD CITY

Having faced the worst we are at last in position to understand the positive function of the historic metropolis, not as the focus of a national or imperial economy, but in its far more important potential role, as world center. Blindly moving to fulfill this essential but still-unrealized role, it has attempted to achieve by a mere massing together of forces and functions and institutions what can only be accomplished by a radical re-organization.

The conscious motives that concentrated so much power in a few great centers would not be sufficient to account for their immense powers of attraction or for the part they play in the culture of our time. And the fact is that metropolitan massiveness and congestion has actually a deeper justification, though it is not fully recognized: it is a focus of those activities that, for the first time, are bringing all the tribes and nations of mankind into a common sphere of co-operation and interplay. What Henry James said of London may be said equally of its great rivals: it "is the biggest aggregation of human life, the most complete compendium of the world. The human race is better represented there than anywhere else." Its new mission is to hand on to the smallest urban unit the cultural resources that make for world unity and co-operation.

Thus the very traits that have made the metropolis always seem at once alien and hostile to the folk in the hinterland are an essential part of the big city's function: it has brought together, within relatively narrow compass, the diversity and variety of special cultures: at least in token quantities all races and cultures can be found here, along with their languages, their customs, their costumes, their typical cuisines: here the representatives of mankind first met face to face on neutral ground. The complexity and the cultural inclusiveness of the metropolis embody the complexity and variety of the world as a whole. Unconsciously the great capitals have been preparing mankind for the wider associations and unifications which the modern conquest of time and space has made probable, if not inevitable.

Here we have, too, the essential reason for the most typical institution of the metropolis, as characteristic of its ideal life as the gymnasium was of the Hellenic city or the hospital of the medieval city—the Museum. This institution sprang out of the very necessities of its own excessive growth.

Inevitably the museum has taken on many of the negative characteristics of the metropolis: its random acquisitiveness, its tendency to over-expansion and disorganization, its habit of gauging its success by the number of people who pass through its gates. Too often physical size serves as a substitute for adequate organization, as in the labor market; and mechanical expansion is confused with significance. Yet in its rational form the museum serves not merely as a concrete equivalent of the library, but also as a method of getting access, through selected specimens and samples, to a world whose immensity and complexity would otherwise be far beyond human power to grasp. In this rational form, as an instrument of selection, the museum is an indispensable contribution to the culture of cities; and when we come to consider the organic reconstitution of cities we shall see that the museum, no less than the library, the hospital, the university, will have a new function in the regional economy. Already, in travelling exhibitions and extension departments, many museums have begun to transcend some of their original megalopolitan limitations.

But if the big city is largely responsible for the invention and public extension of the museum, there is a sense in which one of its own principal functions is to serve as a museum: in its own right, the historic city retains, by reason of its amplitude and its long past, a larger and more various collection of cultural specimens than can be found elsewhere. Every variety of human function, every experiment in human association, every technological process, every mode of architecture and planning, can be found somewhere within its crowded area.

That immensity, that retentiveness, is one of the greatest values of the big city. The breadth of human experience that the dynamic, still healthy metropolis offers is rivalled by its density and depth, its capacity for making available layer upon layer of human history and biography, not merely through its own records and monuments, but through distant areas that its great resources make it possible to draw upon. A civilization as complex and many sided as ours needs such a stable urban organization, capable of attracting and holding in close co-operation many millions of human beings, to carry on all its activities. But what is on one side the city's capacity for cultural inclusion makes it, through the very necessities of condensation and storage, an agent of digestion and selection. If all the materials of our culture were too widely scattered, if the relevant data and artifacts were not capable of being assembled in one place, assorted, made available for redistribution, they would exercise only a small fraction of their influence.

Though the great city is the best organ of memory man has yet created, it is also—until it becomes too cluttered and disorganized—the best agent for discrimination and comparative evaluation, not merely because it spreads out so many goods for choosing, but because it likewise creates minds of large range, capable of coping with them. Yes:

inclusiveness and large numbers are often necessary; but large numbers are not enough. Florence, with some four hundred thousand inhabitants, performs more of the functions of the metropolis than many other cities with ten times that number. One of the main problems of urban culture today is to increase the digestive capacity of the container without letting the physical structure become a colossal, clotted, self-defeating mass. Renewal of the inner metropolitan core is impossible without a far greater transformation on a regional and inter-regional scale.

11: THE INVISIBLE CITY

There is another side to this reorganization of the metropolitan complex that derives from the de-materialization, or etherialization, of existing institutions: that which has already partly created the Invisible City. This is itself an expression of the fact that the new world in which we have begun to live is not merely open on the surface, far beyond the visible horizon, but also open internally, penetrated by invisible rays and emanations, responding to stimuli and forces below the threshold of ordinary observation.

Many of the original functions of the city, once natural monopolies, demanding the physical presence of all participants, have now been transposed into forms capable of swift transportation, mechanical manifolding, electronic transmission, worldwide distribution. If a remote village can see the same motion picture or listen to the same radio program as the most swollen center, no one need live in that center or visit it in order to participate in that particular activity. Instead, we must seek a reciprocal relation between smaller and larger units, based upon each performing the sort of task for which it is uniquely fitted. The visible city then becomes the indispensable place of assemblage for those functions that work best when they are superimposed one on another or within close range: a place where meetings and encounters and challenges, as between personalities, supplements and reduces again to human dimensions the vast impersonal network that now spreads around it.

Let me approach the more abstract relations of the invisible city by drawing a parallel to the new relation on a more visible plane: a small but accurate sample. Scattered over France, often in remote villages and monasteries, are many superb examples of early fresco painting. Under the earlier metropolitan regime, many of these paintings would have been removed, often not without damage, from their original site and housed in a museum in Paris. This would have left a gaping hole in the place of origin, and would have deprived the inhabitants of a possession that had both communal and economic value, without providing in Paris any true sense of their original setting. Today a better program has been achieved. In the Museum of Murals in the Palais de Chaillot, a large number of admirable replicas of these paintings have been brought together. In a single afternoon one may see more paintings than one could take in comfortably in a fortnight of travelling. For those who wish a more intimate experience of the original on the site, the paintings have been identified and located: so that they have become more accessible, without their being wantonly dissociated from their original setting and purpose.

This is the first step toward a more general etherialization. With color slides now available, the process could be carried even further: any small-town library or museum might borrow, and show in a projection room, an even larger collection of murals. Gone is primitive local monopoly through isolation: gone is the metropolitan monopoly through seizure and exploitation. This example will hold for a score of other activities. The ideal mission of the city is to further this process of cultural circulation and diffusion; and this will restore to many now subordinate urban centers a variety of activities that were once drained away for the exclusive benefit of the great city.

This illustration serves all the better because the idea of the museum as a guide to regional resources, rather than as a substitute for them, was evolved spontaneously, almost surely without any thought for an ideal system of inter-urban co-operation. From industry and business there have been, during the last generation, many indications that similar processes are at work, extending and diffusing, to some degree decentralizing, functions that were hitherto highly concentrated in a few centers. Chains of banks, markets, department stores, hotels, factory units, have been organized on a continental scale; and though the purpose of this diffusion is, all too usually, to establish financial monopolies and ensure non-competitive profits—sometimes merely to give scope to voracious egos—the method of organization, particularly in metropolitan areas, indicates that the process runs with the grain of many other activities. The technical facilities that have been developed to achieve corporate control, would lend themselves equally to an economy that promoted a more autonomous action within the small unit, and a reciprocal, two-way system of communication and direction.

Not by accident, then, have the old functions of the urban container been supplemented by new functions, exercised through what I shall call the functional grid: the framework of the invisible city. Like the old container the new grid, in all its forms, industrial, cultural, urban, lends itself to both good and bad uses. But what is even more significant is the fact that the form has appeared in so many different places, as an organic response to present day needs. The new image of the city must be in part an expression of these new realities. On that score, both the old metropolis and the new conurbation lamentably fail for they have tended to efface instead of reintegrating the essential components of the city.

Technologically, two of the most perfect examples of this new network are in our power and communication systems: particularly clear in the electric power grid. A centralized power system has very definite limits of expansion. Beyond a given point, not merely are losses in transmission excessive, but a breakdown in the central station or a local disruption of the transmission wires can cause great hardship at every point. The electric power grid, in contrast, is rather a network of power plants, some big, some small, some worked by waterpower, some by coal, scattered over a large area, often thousands of square miles. Some of these plants by themselves could supply only their immediate community, others have greater range.

Each unit in this system has a certain degree of self-sufficiency and self-direction, equal to ordinary occasions. But by being linked together, the power stations form a whole system whose parts, though relatively independent, can upon demand work as a whole, and make good what is lacking in any particular area. The demand may be made at any point in the system, and the system as a whole may be drawn on to respond to it. Though the whole is at the disposal of the part, it is the local user who determines when it shall be used and how much shall be taken. No single central power station, however big, would have the efficiency, the flexibility or the security of the whole grid, nor would it be capable of further growth, except by following the pattern of the grid.

This pattern is not purely a technological one: it has a parallel in the realm of culture; in particular, in the working of the national library loan system in England. If the borrower at a branch library in a small town does not find the book he needs, he may put in a request that will be transmitted to the regional library center, situated in the principal town of the county. The regional library has a catalogue of all the co-operating libraries in the region, on which it can draw, if the book is not in the central regional library. If this fails, the request is passed on to the national center, which has command of the total resources of the co-operating libraries.

Thus, without having at hand a local library of large dimensions, any single unit in this system has a far larger collection of books at call than even the largest city can afford to offer to the local borrower. With our present resources for cataloguing, duplicating, and swift transportation, a country village could have facilities for study and research that few metropolises could boast—at least if nations were half as generous with library budgets as they now are with military installations.

Mark the departure in both examples. Large resources are no longer dependent upon topographic congestion or topheavy centralized control. With both the electric power grid and the library loan system, the largest facilities become available, not by heaping them together, but by articulating them into a system that enables the individual user, provided he uses an organized unit in the local area, to switch on this or that resource as needed. The last provision is important to note: no such facilities could be economically handled if the individual sought by his own initiative alone to satisfy his needs by dealing at long distance with the central agency: only by diffusion and articulation can the whole system function efficiently. The further advantage of such networks is that they permit units of different size, not merely to participate, but to offer their unique advantages to the whole: thus a little library holding a precious collection of manuscripts need not surrender them to the bigger institution in order to make sure of their adequate use: it can be an effective part of the whole, making demands, communicating desires, influencing decisions without being swallowed up by the bigger organization. This gives back to the region its proper autonomy without impeding—indeed rather encouraging—the universal processes.

Here is a pattern for the new urban constellation, capable of preserving the advantages of smaller units, and enjoying the scope of large scale metropolitan organization. In a well ordered world, there would be no limits, physical, cultural, or political, to such a system of co-operation: it would pass through geographic obstacles and national barriers as readily as X-rays pass through solid objects. Given even the present facilities for telephotography as well as fast transportation, such a system could in time embrace the whole planet. Once technics releases itself from the costly wholesale preparations for genocide that now engross the big national states and empires, or from the fulsome production of salable goods designed mainly for premature obsolescence and a profitable rapid turnover, there would be abundant facilities for perfecting such large scale intercultural associations; and the new regional city, visible and invisible, would be the chief instrument.

What this points to is a more organic method of creating and diffusing the goods of the city, than those practiced by the historic metropolis or in the present day conurbation. The original limitations of the city, once imposed by its monopoly of communication and political control, cannot be overpassed by a mere augmentation of numbers or a mere extension of roads and buildings. No organic improvement is possible without a reorganization of its processes, functions, and purposes, and a redistribution of its population, in units that favor two-way intercourse, I-and-Thou relationships, and local control over local needs. The electric grid, not the stone age container, provides the new image of the invisible city and the many processes it serves and furthers. It is not merely the pattern of the city itself, but every institution, organization, and association composing the city, that will be transformed by this development. In this radical innovation, the great universities and libraries and museums, if they were capable of self-regeneration, might lead the way, as their predecessors did in creating the ancient city.

The building materials for a new urban order, if I have interpreted the facts correctly, are at hand. But the possibility that they will continue to be misused and perverted by the existing political systems is high. The prospect of a massive extension of our present mechanical-electronic facilities, without any change in social purpose, or any attempt to translate the product into higher terms of human association, remains ominous. Countries like Soviet Russia, theoretically immune to the usual seductions and corruptions of contemporary capitalist enterprise, are plainly open to the same temptations—under equally virtuous disguises—to push bureaucratic command of power and centralized authority at the expense of free human association and autonomous development.

But the essential promise of this new order was expressed a century ago by Emerson: "Our civilization and these ideas," he observed, "are reducing the earth to a brain. See how by telegraph and steam the earth is anthropolized." The thought was independently elaborated in our own day by Teilhard de Chardin; but even he did not understand the ambiguous nature of this promise, or see the necessity of forfending these new dangers.

Our civilization is faced with the relentless extension and aggrandizement of a highly centralized, super-organic system, that lacks autonomous component centers capable of exercising selection, exerting control, above all, making autonomous decisions and answering back. The effective response to that problem, which lies at the very heart of our future urban culture, rests on the development of a more organic world picture, which shall do justice to all the dimensions of living organisms and human personalities. The thinkers who will do for this organic and human conception what Galileo, Bacon, and Descartes did for our now-insufficient and even dangerously outmoded concepts of science and technology have long been at work. But it may need another century or two before their contributions will have dethroned our Cybernetic Deities and restored to the center of our existence the images and forces and purposes of Life.

CHAPTER EIGHTEEN

Retrospect and Prospect

In taking form, the ancient city brought together many scattered organs of the common life, and within its walls promoted their interaction and fusion. The common functions that the city served were important; but the common purposes that emerged through quickened methods of communication and co-operation were even more significant. The city mediated between the cosmic order, revealed by the astronomer priests, and the unifying enterprises of kingship. The first took form within the temple and its sacred compound, the second within the citadel and the bounding city wall. By polarizing hitherto untapped human aspirations and drawing them together in a central political and religious nucleus, the city was able to cope with the immense generative abundance of neolithic culture.

By means of the order so established, large bodies of men were for the first time brought into effective co-operation. Organized in disciplined work groups, deployed by central command, the original urban populations in Mesopotamia, Egypt, and the Indus Valley controlled flood, repaired storm damage, stored water, remodelled the landscape, built up a great water network for communication and transportation, and filled the urban reservoirs with human energy available for other collective enterprises. In time, the rulers of the city created an internal fabric of order and justice that gave to the mixed populations of cities, by conscious effort, some of the moral stability and mutual aid of the village. Within the theater of the city new dramas of life were enacted.

But against these improvements we must set the darker contributions of urban civilization: war, slavery, vocational over-specialization, and in many places, a persistent orientation toward death. These institutions and activities, forming a 'negative symbiosis,' have accompanied the city through most of its history, and remain today in markedly brutal form, without their original religious sanctions, as the greatest threat to further human development. Both the positive and the negative aspects of the ancient city have been handed on, in some degree, to every later urban structure.

Through its concentration of physical and cultural power, the city heightened the tempo of human intercourse and translated its products into forms that could be stored and reproduced. Through its monuments, written records, and orderly habits of association, the city enlarged the scope of all human activities, extending them backwards and forwards in time. By means of its storage facilities (buildings, vaults, archives, monuments, tablets, books), the city became capable of transmitting a complex culture from generation to generation, for it marshalled together not only the physical means but the human agents needed to pass on and enlarge this heritage. That remains the greatest of the city's gifts. As compared with the complex human order of the city, our present ingenious electronic mechanisms for storing and transmitting information are crude and limited.

From the original urban integration of shrine, citadel, village, workshop, and market, all later forms of the city have, in some measure, taken their physical structure and their institutional patterns. Many parts of this fabric are still essential to effective human association, not least those that sprang originally from the shrine and the village. Without the active participation of the primary group, in family and neighborhood, it is doubtful if the elementary moral loyalties—respect for the neighbor and reverence for life—can be handed on, without savage lapses, from the old to the young.

At the other extreme, it is doubtful, too, whether those multifarious co-operations that do not lend themselves to abstraction and symbolization can continue to flourish without the city, for only a small part of the contents of life can be put on the record. Without the superposition of many different human activities, many levels of experience, within a limited urban area, where they are constantly on tap, too large a portion of life would be restricted to record-keeping. The wider the area of communication and the greater the number of participants, the more need there is for providing numerous accessible permanent centers for face-to-face intercourse and frequent meetings at every human level.

The recovery of the essential activities and values that first were incorporated in the ancient cities, above all those of Greece, is accordingly a primary condition for the further development of the city in our time. Our elaborate rituals of mechanization cannot take the place of the human dialogue, the drama, the living circle of mates and associates, the society of friends. These sustain the growth and reproduction of human culture, and without them the whole elaborate structure becomes mean-ingless—indeed actively hostile to the purposes of life.

Today the physical dimensions and the human scope of the city have changed; and most of the city's internal functions and structures must be recast to promote effectively the larger purposes that shall be served: the unification of man's inner and outer life, and the progressive unification of mankind itself. The city's active role in future is to bring to the highest pitch of development the variety and individuality of regions, cultures, personalities. These are complementary purposes: their alternative is the current mechanical grinding down of both the landscape and the human personality. Without the city modern man would have no effective de-fenses against those mechanical collectives that, even now, are ready to make all veritably human life superfluous, except to perform a few sub-servient functions that the machine has not yet mastered.

Ours is an age in which the increasingly automatic processes of pro-duction and urban expansion have displaced the human goals they are supposed to serve. Quantitative production has become, for our mass-minded contemporaries, the only imperative goal: they value quantifica-tion without qualification. In physical energy, in industrial productivity, in invention, in knowledge, in population the same vacuous expansions and explosions prevail. As these activities increase in volume and in tempo, they move further and further away from any humanly desirable objectives. As a result, mankind is threatened with far more formidable inundations than ancient man learned to cope with. To save himself he must turn his attention to the means of controlling, directing, organizing, and subordinating to his own biological functions and cultural purposes the insensate forces that would, by their very superabundance, undermine his life. He must curb them and even eliminate them completely when, as in the case of nuclear and bacterial weapons, they threaten his very existence.

Now it is not a river valley, but the whole planet, that must be brought under human control: not an unmanageable flood of water, but even more alarming and malign explosions of energy that might disrupt the entire ecological system on which man's own life and welfare depends. The prime need of our age is to contrive channels for excessive energies and impetuous vitalities that have departed from organic norms and limits: cultural flood control in every field calls for the erection of em-bankments, dams, reservoirs, to even out the flow and spread it into the final receptacles, the cities and regions, the groups, families, and per-sonalities, who will be able to utilize this energy for their own growth and development. If we were prepared to restore the habitability of the earth and cultivate the empty spaces in the human soul, we should not be so preoccupied with sterile escapist projects for exploring inter-plane-tary space, or with even more rigorously dehumanized policies based on the strategy of wholesale collective extermination. It is time to come back to earth and confront life in all its organic fecundity, diversity, and creativity, instead of taking refuge in the under-dimensioned world of Post-historic Man.

Modern man, unfortunately, has still to conquer the dangerous aberra-tions that took institutional form in the cities of the Bronze Age and gave a destructive destination to our highest achievements. Like the rulers of the Bronze Age, we still regard power as the chief manifestation of divinity, or if not that, the main agent of human development. But 'absolute power,' like 'absolute weapons,' belongs to the same magico-religious scheme as ritual human sacrifice. Such power destroys the sym-biotic co-operation of man with all other aspects of nature, and of men with other men. Living organisms can use only limited amounts of energy. 'Too much' or 'too little' is equally fatal to organic existence. Organisms, societies, human persons, not least, cities, are delicate devices for regulating energy and putting it to the service of life.

The chief function of the city is to convert power into form, energy into culture, dead matter into the living symbols of art, biological repro-duction into social creativity. The positive functions of the city cannot be performed without creating new institutional arrangements, capable of coping with the vast energies modern man now commands: arrangements just as bold as those that originally transformed the overgrown village and its stronghold into the nucleated, highly organized city.

These necessary changes could hardly be envisaged, were it not for the fact that the negative institutions that accompanied the rise of the city have for the last four centuries been falling into decay, and seemed until recently to be ready to drop into limbo. Kingship by divine right has all but disappeared, even as a moribund idea; and the political functions that were once exercised solely by the palace and the temple, with the coercive aid of the bureaucracy and the army, were during the nineteenth century assumed by a multitude of organizations, corporations, parties, associa-tions, and committees. So, too, the conditions laid down by Aristotle for the abolition of slave labor have now been largely met, through the har-nessing of inorganic sources of energy and the invention of automatic machines and utilities. Thus slavery, forced labor, legalized expropria-tion, class monopoly of knowledge, have been giving way to free labor, social security, universal literacy, free education, open access to knowl-edge, and the beginnings of universal leisure, such as is necessary for wide participation in political duties. If vast masses of people in Asia, Africa, and South America still live under primitive conditions and depressing poverty, even the ruthless colonialism of the nineteenth century brought to these peoples the ideas that would release them. 'The heart of darkness,' from Livingstone on to Schweitzer, was pierced by a shaft of light.

In short, the oppressive conditions that limited the development of cities throughout history have begun to disappear. Property, caste, even vocational specialization have—through the graded income tax and the 'managerial revolution'—lost most of their hereditary fixations. What Alexis de Tocqueville observed a century ago is now more true than ever: the history of the last eight hundred years is the history of the progressive equalization of classes. This change holds equally of capitalist and communist systems, in a fashion that might have shocked Karl Marx, but would not have surprised John Stuart Mill. For the latter foresaw the conditions of dynamic equilibrium under which the advances of the machine economy might at last be turned to positive human advantage. Until but yesterday, then, it seemed that the negative symbiosis that accompanied the rise of the city was doomed. The task of the emerging city was to give an ideal form to these radically superior conditions of life.

Unfortunately, the evil institutions that accompanied the rise of the ancient city have been resurrected and magnified in our own time: so the ultimate issue is in doubt. Totalitarian rulers have reappeared, sometimes elevated, like Hitler, into deities, or mummified in Pharaoh-fashion after death, for worship, like Lenin and Stalin. Their methods of coercion and terrorism surpass the vilest records of ancient rulers, and the hoary practice of exterminating whole urban populations has even been exercised by the elected leaders of democratic states, wielding powers of instantaneous destruction once reserved to the gods. Everywhere secret knowledge has put an end to effective criticism and democratic control; and the emancipation from manual labor has brought about a new kind of enslavement: abject dependence upon the machine. The monstrous gods of the ancient world have all reappeared, hugely magnified, demanding total human sacrifice. To appease their super-Moloch in the Nuclear Temples, whole nations stand ready, supinely, to throw their children into his fiery furnace.

If these demoralizing tendencies continue, the forces that are now at work will prove uncontrollable and deadly; for the powers man now commands must, unless they are detached from their ancient ties to the citadel, and devoted to human ends, lead from their present state of paranoid suspicion and hatred to a final frenzy of destruction. On the other hand, if the main negative institutions of civilization continue to crumble—that is, if the passing convulsions of totalitarianism mark in fact the death-throes of the old order—is it likely that war will escape the same fate? War was one of the 'lethal genes' transmitted by the city from century to century, always doing damage but never yet widely enough to bring civilization itself to an end. That period of tolerance is now over. If civilization does not eliminate war as an open possibility, our nuclear agents will destroy civilization—and possibly exterminate mankind. The vast village populations that were once reservoirs of life will eventually perish with those of the cities.

Should the forces of life, on the other hand, rally together, we shall stand on the verge of a new urban implosion. When cities were first founded, an old Egyptian scribe tells us, the mission of the founder was to "put the gods in their shrines." The task of the coming city is not essentially different: its mission is to put the highest concerns of man at the center of all his activities: to unite the scattered fragments of the human personality, turning artificially dismembered men—bureaucrats, specialists, 'experts,' depersonalized agents—into complete human beings, repairing the damage that has been done by vocational separation, by social segregation, by the over-cultivation of a favored function, by tribalisms and nationalisms, by the absence of organic partnerships and ideal purposes.

Before modern man can gain control over the forces that now threaten his very existence, he must resume possession of himself. This sets the chief mission for the city of the future: that of creating a visible regional and civic structure, designed to make man at home with his deeper self and his larger world, attached to images of human nurture and love.

We must now conceive the city, accordingly, not primarily as a place of business or government, but as an essential organ for expressing and actualizing the new human personality—that of 'One World Man.' The old separation of man and nature, of townsman and countryman, of Greek and barbarian, of citizen and foreigner, can no longer be maintained: for communication, the entire planet is becoming a village; and as a result, the smallest neighborhood or precinct must be planned as a working model of the larger world. Now it is not the will of a single deified ruler, but the individual and corporate will of its citizens, aiming at self-knowledge, self-government, and self-actualization, that must be embodied in the city. Not industry but education will be the center of their activities; and every process and function will be evaluated and approved just to the extent that it furthers human development, whilst the city itself provides a vivid theater for the spontaneous encounters and challenges and embraces of daily life.

Apparently, the inertia of current civilization still moves toward a worldwide nuclear catastrophe; and even if that fatal event is postponed, it may be a century or more before the possibility can be written off. But happily life has one predictable attribute: it is full of surprises. At the last moment—and our generation may in fact be close to the last moment—the purposes and projects that will redeem our present aimless dynamism may gain the upper hand. When that happens, obstacles that now seem insuperable will melt away; and the vast sums of money and energy, the massive efforts of science and technics, which now go into the building of nuclear bombs, space rockets, and a hundred other cunning devices directly or indirectly attached to dehumanized and de-moralized goals, will be released for the recultivation of the earth and the rebuilding of cities: above all, for the replenishment of the human personality. If once the sterile dreams and sadistic nightmares that obsess the ruling élite are banished, there will be such a release of human vitality as will make the Renascence seem almost a stillbirth.

It would be foolish to predict when or how such a change may come about; and yet it would be even more unrealistic to dismiss it as a possibility, perhaps even an imminent possibility, despite the grip that the myth of the machine still holds on the Western World. Fortunately, the preparations for the change from a power economy to a life economy have been long in the making; and once the reorientation of basic ideas and purposes takes place, the necessary political and physical transformations may swiftly follow. Many of the same forces that are now oriented toward death will then be polarized toward life.

In discussing the apparent stabilization of the birthrate, as manifested throughout Western civilization before 1940, the writer of 'The Culture of Cities' then observed: "One can easily imagine a new cult of family life, growing up in the face of some decimating catastrophe, which would necessitate a swift revision in plans for housing and city development: a generous urge toward procreation might clash in policy with the views of the prudent, bent on preserving a barely achieved equilibrium."

To many professional sociologists, captivated by the smooth curves of their population graphs, that seemed a far-fetched, indeed quite unimaginable possibility before the Second World War. But such a spontaneous reaction actually took place shortly after the war broke out, and has continued, despite various 'expert' predictions to the contrary, for the last twenty years. Many people who should be vigilantly concerned over the annihilation of mankind through nuclear explosions have concealed that dire possibility from themselves by excessive anxiety over the 'population explosion'—without the faintest suspicion, apparently, that the threat of de-population and that of over-population might in fact be connected.

As of today, this resurgence of reproductive activity might be partly explained as a deep instinctual answer to the premature death of scores of millions of people throughout the planet. But even more possibly, it may be the unconscious reaction to the likelihood of an annihilating outburst of nuclear genocide on a planetary scale. As such, every new baby is a blind desperate vote for survival: people who find themselves unable to register an effective political protest against extermination do so by a biological act. In countries where state aid is lacking, young parents often accept a severe privation of goods and an absence of leisure, rather than accept privation of life by forgoing children. The automatic response of every species threatened with extirpation takes the form of excessive reproduction. This is a fundamental observation of ecology.

No profit-oriented, pleasure-dominated economy can cope with such demands: no power-dominated economy can permanently suppress them. Should the same attitude spread toward the organs of education, art, and culture, man's super-biological means of reproduction, it would alter the entire human prospect: for public service would take precedence over private profit, and public funds would be available for the building and rebuilding of villages, neighborhoods, cities, and regions, on more generous lines than the aristocracies of the past were ever able to afford for themselves. Such a change would restore the discipline and the delight of the garden to every aspect of life; and it might do more to balance the birthrate, by its concern with the quality of life, than any other collective measure.

As we have seen, the city has undergone many changes during the last five thousand years; and further changes are doubtless in store. But the innovations that beckon urgently are not in the extension and perfection of physical equipment: still less in multiplying automatic electronic devices for dispersing into formless sub-urban dust the remaining organs of culture. Just the contrary: significant improvements will come only through applying art and thought to the city's central human concerns, with a fresh dedication to the cosmic and ecological processes that enfold all being. We must restore to the city the maternal, life-nurturing functions, the autonomous activities, the symbiotic associations that have long been neglected or suppressed. For the city should be an organ of love; and the best economy of cities is the care and culture of men.

The city first took form as the home of a god: a place where eternal values were represented and divine possibilities revealed. Though the symbols have changed the realities behind them remain. We know now, as never before, that the undisclosed potentialities of life reach far beyond the proud algebraics of contemporary science; and their promises for the further transformations of man are as enchanting as they are inexhaustible. Without the religious perspectives fostered by the city, it is doubtful if more than a small part of man's capacities for living and learning could have developed. Man grows in the image of his gods, and up to the measure they have set. The mixture of divinity, power, and personality that brought the ancient city into existence must be weighed out anew in terms of the ideology and the culture of our own time, and poured into fresh civic, regional, and planetary molds. In order to defeat the insensate forces that now threaten civilization from within, we must transcend the original frustrations and negations that have dogged the city throughout its history. Otherwise the sterile gods of power, unrestrained by organic limits or human goals, will remake man in their own faceless image and bring human history to an end.

The final mission of the city is to further man's conscious participation in the cosmic and the historic process. Through its own complex and enduring structure, the city vastly augments man's ability to interpret these processes and take an active, formative part in them, so that every phase of the drama it stages shall have, to the highest degree possible, the illumination of consciousness, the stamp of purpose, the color of love. That magnification of all the dimensions of life, through emotional communion, rational communication, technological mastery, and above all, dramatic representation, has been the supreme office of the city in history. And it remains the chief reason for the city's continued existence.

BIBLIOGRAPHY

ACKNOWLEDGMENTS

INDEX

BIBLIOGRAPHY

An asterisk (*) before the title indicates books particularly important for fur
ther understanding of the main theme, though many other books of equal im
portance are not so marked. Please note the following abbreviations:

AR: Architectural Review
JAIA: Journal of the American Institute of Architecture
JAIP: Journal of the American Institute of Planners
JRIBA: Journal of the Royal Institute of British Architects
JSAH: Journal of the Society of Architectural Historians
JTPI: Journal of the Town Planning Institute
TCP: Town and Country Planning
TPR: Town Planning Review

Abercrombie, Patrick. *Town and Country Planning.* New York: 1933.
Brief introductory sketch (Home University Series).

Ideal Cities: Victoria. In TPR: March 1921.
Summary of James Silk Buckingham's ideal city, which influenced Howard. One of
a series by Abercrombie on Ideal Cities.

Greater London Plan. 1944. London: 1945.
Immense advance on all previous plans for metropolitan areas. Based on conceptions of community planning, and of relation of town and country, clearly derived
from Howard's proposals, and ably expanded. Their influence is visible on the New
Towns actually built.

Abercrombie, Patrick, and J. H. Forshaw. *County of London Plan: Prepared
for the London County Council.* London: 1943.
Full of admirable detailed suggestions; but vitiated by an unexamined premise: the
necessity and the desirability of retaining the bulk of the existing population of the
County of London.

Abrams, Charles. *Revolution in Land.* New York: 1939.

Abrosimov, Pavel, et al. (editors). *Construction and Reconstruction of Towns:
1945–1957.* 3 vols. Moscow: 1958.
Prepared for the Fifth Congress of the International Union of Architects, the first
two volumes in English and Russian.

Ackerman, Phyllis. *The Symbolic Sources of Some Architectural Elements.* In
JSAH: Dec. 1953. (See also Lethaby.)

Adams, Charles C. *The Relation of General Ecology to Human Ecology.* In
Ecology: July 1935.

Adams, Thomas. *Outline of Town and City Planning: A Review of Past Efforts and Modern Aims.* New York: 1935.
Chiefly English examples and precedents.

579

Regional Plan of New York and Its Environs. Vol. II: *The Building of the City.* (See *Regional Survey of New York and Its Environs.*)

Addison, William. *English Spas.* London: 1951.

*Alberti, Leone Battista. *Ten Books on Architecture.* Florence: 1485. Translated into Italian by Cosimo Bartoli (1568) and into English by James Leoni (1726). London: 1955.
     The outstanding theoretical work prior to Camillo Sitte. With its continued emphasis on natural conditions and functional requirements, biological and economic, this treatise is rather an explicit formulation of medieval ideas, in renascence terms, than an expression of the new concepts of human and spatial regimentation.

*Albright, W. F. *The Archaeology of Palestine.* Harmondsworth: 1956. First ed.: 1949.

From the Stone Age to Christianity. New York: 1957.
     Magistral in every aspect, including the philosophy of history.

Alexandersson, Gunnar. *The Industrial Structure of American Cities: A Geographic Study of Urban Economy in the United States.* Lincoln, Neb.: 1956.

Alihan, Milla Aissa. *Social Ecology: A Critical Analysis.* New York: 1938.
     Though the approach is critical, the author dwells too heavily on the rather narrow area pre-empted by the Chicago School.

Allee, Warder Clyde. *Animal Aggregations: A Study in General Sociology.* Chicago: 1931.

Animal Life and Social Growth. Baltimore: 1932.

Allen, Edith Louise. *American Housing as Affected by Social and Economic Conditions.* Peoria: 1930.
     A sketch that needs to be filled out.

Allen, George Cyril. *The Industrial Development of Birmingham and the Black Country: 1860–1927.* Illustrated. London: 1929.
     Valuable paleotechnic data.

Andersen, Hendrik Christian. *Creation of a World Center of Communication.* 4 parts in 2 vols. Paris: 1913–1918.
     A first effort at visualizing the organs of a world culture.

Anderson, William (editor). *Local Government in Europe.* New York: 1939.

Andrae, W. *Das Wiederstehende Assur.* Leipzig: 1938.

The Story of Uruk. In Antiquity: June 1936.

Andreae, Johann Valentin. *Christianopolis.* Trans. by F. E. Held. New York: 1916.
     A late-medieval utopia, particularly interesting for its sidelights on cities.

*Aristotle. *Politics.* Athens: Fourth Century B.C.
     The *Politics* still repays close reading for its methodology as well as its civic insight.

Armillas, Pedro. *Meso-American Fortification.* In Antiquity: June 1951.

Aronovici, Carol. *Community Building: Science, Technique, Art.* New York: 1956.
     A comprehensive handbook, in terms of American practice.

Arts and Crafts Exhibition Society. *Art and Life, and the Building and Deco-ration of Cities: A Series of Lectures by Members.* London: 1897.
See especially the lecture by Lethaby.

Ashby, Thomas. *The Capitol, Rome: Its History and Development.* In TPR: June 1927.

Ashby, Thomas, and S. Rowland Pierce. *The Piazza del Popolo: Rome.* In TPR: Dec. 1924.

Astengo, Giovanni. *Town and Regional Planning in Italy.* In TPR: July 1952.

Atkinson, William. *The Orientation of Buildings: or Planning for Sunlight.* New York: 1912.
Pioneer modern study. (But see Rey, Augustin.)

Atlas portratif ou le théâtre de la guerre en Europe: contenants les cartes géo-graphiques avec le plan des villes et fortresses les plus exposés aux révo-lutions présentes. Amsterdam: 1702.

*Auzelle, Robert. *Encyclopédie de l'Urbanisme.* Paris: 1950–.
Superb collection of photographs and plans in a series of fascicules, usually featur-ing individual elements, but sometimes presenting whole plans and views. Particu-larly valuable because the drawings are all to the same scale and therefore com-parable. Selection is wide-ranging but unsystematic, with perhaps undue attention to relatively unimportant recent work.

*Avenel, Baron Georges d'. *Histoire économique de la propriété des salaires, des denrées et de tous les prix en général depuis l'an 1200 jusqu'en l'an 1800.* 7 vols. in 6. Paris: 1894–1926.
A work of exhaustive scholarship: indispensable. (See especially Vol. VI, Book V, Chapters 5 and 6.)

Histoire de la fortune française; la fortune privée à travers sept siècles. Paris: 1927.
(See Chapters 9 and 10 on Prix et Loyers des Maisons.)

Ayyar, C. P. Venkatarama. *Town Planning in Ancient Dekkan.* With an In-troduction by Professor Patrick Geddes. Madras: n.d.
The author draws on old Tamil texts for a description of the development of cities in southern India. Illustrates the universal nature of the pattern first discernible in Mesopotamia. An early essay in a field badly needing cultivation.

Badawy, Alexander. *Orthogonal and Axial Town Planning in Egypt.* In Zeit-schrift für Agyptische Sprache und Altertumes Kunde. Bd. 85. Erster Heft. Berlin: 1960.
Valuable. (But see also Fairman, H. W.)

Bailey, Francis A. *The Origin and Growth of Southport.* In TPR: Jan. 1951.

Balzac, Honoré de. *Le Père Goriot.* Paris: 1835.

Le Cousin Pons. Paris: 1847.
Two fine examples from *Scènes de la Vie Parisienne.* It was not for nothing, as Brunetière pointed out, that Balzac was a contemporary of Auguste Comte.

Bannister, Turpin C. *Early Town Planning in New York State.* In JSAH: Jan.–April 1943

Barbour, Violet. *Capitalism in Amsterdam in the Seventeenth Century.* The Johns Hopkins University Studies in Historical and Political Science. Series lxvii. No. 1.
Valuable. (See Burke, Gerald.)

*Bardet, Gaston. *Pierre sur Pierre. Construction du Nouvel Urbanisme.* Paris: 1946.
Sound, vivid, humane city-planning studies which contrast with Le Corbusier's expositions.

L'Urbanisme. Paris: 1947.

Mission de l'Urbanisme. Paris: 1947.

Qui est-ce-l'Urbanisme? Paris: 1947.

Naissance et Méconnaissance de l'Urbanisme. Paris: 1951.
Rich in both historic data and insight.

Barlow, Sir Anthony Montague (Chairman). *Report of Royal Commission on Distribution of Industrial Population.* H.M. Stationery Office, London: 1940.
A statesmanlike contribution which had decisive influence in laying the foundations for the New Towns policy.

Bartholomew, Harland, and Jack Wood. *Land Uses in American Cities.* Cambridge, Mass.: 1955.

Bates, Marston. *The Forest and the Sea: A Look at the Economy of Nature and the Ecology of Man.* New York: 1960.
Recommended to planners and administrators who alter man's ecology without looking at it or appraising the results of their intervention.

Bauer, Catherine. *Modern Housing.* Boston: 1934.
Too good to be laid aside merely because of limitations associated with its date.

Housing in the United States. In International Labor Review: July 1945.

Social Questions in Housing and Town Planning. London: 1952.

Economic Progress and Living Conditions. In TPR: Jan. 1954.

Baxter, Sylvester. *Greater Boston: A Study for a Federalized Metropolis Comprising the City of Boston and Surrounding Cities and Towns.* Boston: 1891.
Classic proposal for federal urban organization retaining and utilizing existing local authorities, following on organization of London County Council. Had Baxter's timely lead been followed, Boston might have carried to its conclusion the work well begun in metropolitan unification of transit, water supply, and parks. Note date.

Becatti, G., and G. Calza. *Ostia.* Rome: 1955.

Behrendt, Walter Curt. *Die einheitliche Blockfront als Raumelement im Stadtbau: Ein Beitrag zur Stadtbaukunst der Gegenwart.* Berlin: 1911.

Die Holländische Stadt. Berlin: 1928.
Rich in insight and illustrations.

Modern Building: Its Nature, Problems and Forms. New York: 1937.
Unrivalled in clarity, brevity, and depth.

Bellamy, Edward. *Looking Backward: 2000–1887.* First Edition. Boston: 1888. New edition. Boston: 1931.
Partial anticipations of neotechnic urban organization (mechanical).

Bellet, Daniel, and Will Darville. *Ce que doit être la cité moderne: son plan, ses aménagements, ses organes, son hygiene, ses monuments et sa vie.* Paris: 1914.
Cross section of accepted improvements before World War I.

Beloch, J. *Antike und Moderne Groszstädte.* In Zeitschrift für Sozialwissenschaften. Breslau: 1898.

Below, George Anton Hugo von. *Das ältere Deutsche Städtewesen und Bürgertum.* In Monographien zur Weltgeschichte, Vol. VI: Bielefeld: 1898.

Mittelalterliche Stadtwirtschaft und Gegenwärtige Kriegswirtschaft. In Kriegswirtschaftliche Zeitfragen, Vol. 10: Tübingen: 1917.

Die Enstehung des Modernen Kapitalismus und die Hauptstädte. In Schmollers Jahrbuch, Vol. 43, pt. 1: München: 1919.
Keen criticism of Sombart's position in his second edition.

Aus Sozial- und Wirtschaftsgeschichte; Gedächtnisschrift für Georg von Below. Stuttgart: 1928.
(See essays by Hapke and Schneider.)

Bennett, H. S. *Life on the English Manor: A Study of Peasant Conditions, 1150–1400.* Cambridge: 1948.
(See chapter on town as the "Road to Freedom.")

Bennett, John W., and Melvin M. Tumin. *Social Life: Structure and Function: An Introductory General Sociology.* New York: 1952.
Good chapter on city: but lacking in analysis of dynamic social processes—greeting, meeting, working, assembling, recording, storing, celebrating, etc.

Benoit, Fernand. *Avignon: au Double Visage.* Paris: 1940.

Benoit-Levy, Georges. *La Ville et son Image.* Paris: 1910.

Bérard, Jean. *L'Expansion et la colonisation Grècques jusq'aux guerres médiques.* Paris: 1960.
Excellent: part of a larger study left unfinished by the author's death.

Beresford, M. W., and J. K. S. St Joseph. *Medieval England: An Aerial Survey.* Cambridge: 1958.
Valuable.

Beresford, Maurice. *History on the Ground: Six Studies in Maps and Landscapes.* London: 1957.

Berlepsch-Valendàs. *Die Gartenstadtbewegung in England.* München: 1911.
Like Kampffmeyer's study, this testifies to the strong impression made by the garden-city movement in a single decade.

Bernoulli, Hans. *Die Stadt und Ihr Boden (Towns and the Land).* Erlenbach-Zurich: 1946.

Blanchard, Raoul. *Grenoble: Étude de Géographie Urbaine.* 3rd edition: 1935. (First ed.: 1911.)

Annecy: Étude de Géographie Urbaine. Annecy: 1917.
Both studies are exemplary products of the great French school of urban geography.

Blanckenhagen, Peter H. von. *The Imperial Fora*. In JSAH: Dec. 1954.

Blomfield, Reginald. *Sébastien le Prestre de Vauban: 1633–1707*. London: 1938.
Essential to an understanding of seventeenth-century planning.

Blumenfeld, Hans. *Form and Function of Urban Communities*. In JSAH: Jan.–April 1943.

Russian City Planning of the 18th and Early 19th Centuries. In JSAH: Jan. 1944.

Theory of City Form. In JSAH: July–Dec. 1949.

Scale in Civic Design. In TPR: Apr. 1953.
Blumenfeld's studies are outstanding in both theoretic and practical grasp.

Boekle, Erich, and Werner Lindner. *Die Stadt: Ihre Pflege und Gestaltung*. München: n.d.

Boëthius, Axel. *The Golden House of Nero*. New York: 1960.
Valuable data on ancient Rome and its influence on medieval buildings.

Bogue, Donald J. *Population Growth in Standard Metropolitan Areas: 1900–1950*. Washington: 1953.

Metropolitan Growth and the Conversion of Land to Non-Agricultural Uses. Chicago: 1956.

The Structure of the Metropolitan Community: A Study of Dominance and Sub-dominance. Ann Arbor: 1950.

Bolkestein, H. *Economic Life in Greece's Golden Age*. Dutch edition: 1923. Trans. Leiden: 1958.

Bonner, Robert J. *Aspects of Athenian Democracy*. Berkeley: 1933.

Booth, Charles. *Life and Labour in London:* 17 vols. Begun in 1889. London: 1902.
A monumental survey, exhaustive in details, but as difficult to grasp as a whole as the city it describes.

Booth, Charles, and others. *New Survey of London Life and Labour*. Vol. I–IV. London: 1930–1933.

Bossert, H. Th., and W. Zschietzschmann. *Hellas and Rome: The Civilisation of Classical Antiquity*. New York: 1936.
With 575 reproductions, some not found in similar works.

Botero, Giovanni. *A Treatise Concerning the Causes of the Magnificence and Greatness of Cities*. Trans. London: 1606.

Bowra, Sir Maurice, *et al. Golden Ages of the Great Cities*. New York: 1952.
Historic vignettes, some excellent, notably Runciman on Constantinople.

Bradford, John. *Ancient Landscapes: Studies in Field Archaeology*. London: 1957.
Much on ancient urban patterns as revealed by aerial photography.

Braidwood, Robert J. *The Near East and the Foundations of Civilization*. Condon Lectures. Eugene, Ore.: 1952.

Jericho and Its Setting in Near Eastern History. In Antiquity: XXXI, 1957.
Part of an 'agonizing reappraisal' which involves a more adequate differentiation of
the stages of urban growth.

Near Eastern Prehistory. In Science: June 20, 1958.
Careful study of transition from food collecting to village farm community. (See also
Sauer, Carl.)

Branford, Victor V. *Outlines of the Sociology of London: An Introduction
to the Study of Social Science.* London: 1908.
Pioneer London University Extension lectures by Geddes' redoubtable colleague.

Civics and Eugenics: An Introduction to the Science of Sociology. London:
1909.

The Drift to Revolution. London: 1919.
One of the 'Papers for the Present' that Branford edited. Brilliant.

Westminster: Spiritual and Temporal. London: 1920.
Still suggestive.

Sociological View of Westminster. In Sociological Review: July 1930.

Branford, Victor V., and Patrick Geddes. *The Coming Polity.* London: 1917.

Our Social Inheritance. London: 1919.
Branford's chapter on Westminster is full of insight. My own walks with Branford
around Westminster in 1920 left an imprint on all my later thinking.

*Braunfels, Wolfgang. *Mittelalterliche Stadtbaukunst in der Toskana.* Berlin:
1953.
In many respects the best monograph on the medieval city, based on original documents and covering many aspects besides the art of building cities: but lacking in
regard for the development of the plan as a whole. This neglect perhaps leads to an
overemphasis of the role of the master builder of the cathedral as general city architect.

Breasted, James Henry. *The Conquest of Civilization.* New York: 1926.
Still a good general introduction to ancient civilizations, though written as a textbook, and naturally needing revision in the light of the last generation's important
work. (See Frankfort and Childe.)

The Dawn of Conscience. New York: 1938.
Important analysis of the moralization of power in Egypt, leading to new concepts
of law, justice, and righteousness.

Bredius, Abraham, and others. *Amsterdam in de Zeventiende Eeuw.* 3 vols.
'sGravenhage: 1897–1904.

Breton, Nicholas. *The Court and the Country.* London: 1618.

Brett-James, N. G., and M. B. Honeybourne. *Precincts and Trade Quarters.*
In AR: Nov. 1946.

Bridenbaugh, Carl. *Cities in the Wilderness: The First Century of Urban Life
in America, 1625–1742.* New York: 1938.

Vol. II. *Cities in Revolt: Urban Life in America, 1743–1776.* New York:
1950.
Excellent study, if unfortunately weak on the physical and esthetic attributes. Has
important data on early flight from city.

Briggs, Martin S. *Town and Country Planning.* London: 1948.

Brinckmann, A. E. *Deutsche Stadtbaukunst in der Vergangenheit.* Second revised edition. Frankfurt-am-Main: 1921.

Brugmans, H., and C. H. Peters. *Oud-Nederlandsche Steden in Haar Onststaan, Groei en Ontwikkeling.* 3 vols. Leiden: 1909–1911.

*Brunhes, Jean. *Human Geography: An Attempt at a Positive Classification: Principles and Examples.* Translated. New York: 1920.
Classic.

Buber, Martin. *Paths in Utopia.* Translated. Boston: 1958.

Buchanan, C. D. *Mixed Blessing: The Motor Car in Britain.* London: 1958.
A sober appraisal. (For a more satiric exposition see John Keats' The Insolent Chariots.)

Bücher, Karl. *Die Bevölkerung von Frankfurt-am-Main in XIV Jahrhundert.* Tubingen: 1886.
Occupational statistics, as well as general ones. Important as an introduction to early municipal statistics in general.

Die Grosstadt: Vorträge und Aufsatze zur Stadteausstellung. Dresden: 1903.

Buckingham, James Silk. *National Evils and Practical Remedies.* London: 1849.
Contains plan for a model town which influenced Howard.

Buer, Mabel Craven. *Health, Wealth & Population in the Early Days of the Industrial Revolution.* London: 1926.
Warped picture of medieval sanitation and misleading in interpretation of later paleotechnic industry. But useful in its account of the mainly eotechnic inter-regnum.

Bunin, H. *The Reconstruction of Urban Centres.* In AR: May 1947.

Bunting, Bainbridge. *The Plan of the Back Bay Area in Boston.* In JSAH: May 1954.

Burckhardt, Jacob. *The Civilization of the Renaissance in Italy.* Translated from the Fifteenth Edition. New York: 1929.
Still pregnant, though no longer adequate. While the conceptual core was unsound, it was productive of fresh understanding.

Burgess, Ernest W., and others. *Environment and Education.* Supplementary Educational Monographs No. 54. Chicago: 1942.

The Urban Community. Chicago: 1927.

Burke, Gerald L. *The Making of Dutch Towns: A Study in Urban Development from the Tenth to the Seventeenth Centuries.* London: 1956.
Long needed and admirably done.

Burke, Thomas. *The English Townsman: As He Was and As He Is.* London: 1946.

Burnham, Daniel H., and Edward H. Bennett. (Charles Moore, editor.) *Plan of Chicago.* Chicago: 1909.
Magnificent in its outlines, narrow in its social purposes.

Bushnell, Horace. *Work and Play.* New York: 1864.
Address on City Plans for the Public Improvement Society of Hartford. See pp. 308–336: *note date.*

Bylinkin, N. *Reconstruction and Housing.* In AR: May 1947.
Interesting Russian contribution.

Cacheux, Emile. *État des Habitations Ouvrières à la Fin du XIXe Siècle.* Paris: 1891.
Highly useful documentation of evils and remedies.

Cadoux, G. *La Vie des Grandes Capitales: Études Comparatives sur Londres —Paris—Berlin—Vienne—Rome.* 2nd ed. Paris: 1913.
On water and transportation.

Caemmerer, H. P. *Washington: The National Capital.* Washington: 1932.

Calza, Raissa, and Ernest Nash. *Ostia.* 163 plates. Firenze: n.d. (1959?).

Campbell, Argyll, and Leonard Hill. *Health and Environment.* London: 1925. (IV, V.)
So far one of the best books on a subject still insufficiently explored.

Carcopino, Jerome. *Daily Life in Ancient Rome: The People and the City at the Height of the Empire.* Translated. New Haven: 1940.
Deals with the physiology of Rome, as Homo deals with its anatomy.

Carden, Robert Walter. *The City of Genoa.* London: 1908.

Carne, Elizabeth T. *Country Towns: And the Place They Fill in Modern Civilization.* London: 1868.

Carol, Hans, and Max Werner. *Staedte wie wir sie wuenschen: ein Vorschlag zur Gestaltung schweizerischer Grosstadt-Gebiete, dargestellt am Beispiel von Stadt und Kanton Zuerich.* Zurich: 1949.
Discriminating analysis of the growth of a metropolitan area, with constructive proposals for a more orderly and satisfactory development. Based on Zurich, but with wider reference.

Carrier, Robert, and Oliver Lawson Dick. *The Vanished City: A Study of London.* London: 1957.
Reproductions of old prints with commentary.

Carrington, R. C. *Pompeii.* Oxford: 1936.
Compact description, with plans, of this well-preserved ruin. (See Maiuri.)

Cerda, Ildefonso. *Teoría General de la Urbanizacíon.* Madrid: 1867.

Chadwick, Edwin. *Report on the Sanitary Condition of the Labouring Population of Great Britain.* London: 1842.
A classic summary of paleotechnic horrors. Sedulously overlooked or played down by zealous whitewashers of this period.

Chadwick, Edwin. (B. W. Richardson, editor.) *The Health of Nations.* 2 vols. London: 1887.
Summaries and extracts of Chadwick's numerous papers.

Champdor, Albert. *Babylon.* New York: 1958.
Excellent. Second volume in a useful new series, Ancient Cities and Temples.

Chancellor, Edwin Beresford. *The History of the Squares of London: Topographical and Historical.* London: 1907.

The Pleasure Haunts of London During Four Centuries. New York: 1925.
Full of valuable data.

Chapman, Brian and J. M. *The Life and Times of Baron Haussmann: Paris in the Second Empire.* London: 1957.
Useful.

Chapman, Edmund H. *City Planning under Industrialization: The Case of Cleveland.* In JSAH: May 1953.

*Childe, V. Gordon. *Man Makes Himself.* London: 1936.
Childe gave to the complex changes that took place around 3000 B.C. the name, The Urban Revolution. He distinguished himself among archaeologists by his attention to the city as a whole, in contrast to those who cannot see the city for the buildings and their artifacts, but he perhaps overestimated the technical and economic factors and failed to reckon sufficiently with the active role of religion.

Prehistoric Communities of the British Isles. London: 1940.

What Happened in History. Harmondsworth: 1942.
Compact survey of growth of ancient civilizations. (But see also Frankfort, Breasted, Mortimer Wheeler, Woolley, and others.)

Progress in Archaeology. London: 1944.

Cave Men's Buildings. In Antiquity: London: March 1950.
Report on Gorodtsov's discovery of *paleolithic* hamlet and buildings.

The Urban Revolution. In TPR: April 1950.
Condensed but richly concrete interpretation of the origin of the city, with emphasis on the settlement of the previously nomadic specialized craftsmen, but with only a passing reference to the role of the citadel. (Admirable: but see Frankfort.)

The Dawn of European Civilization. Sixth ed. revised. New York: 1958.

Chombart de Lauwe, Paul H., et al. *Paris et l'agglomération Parisienne.* 2 vols. Vol. I: *L'Espace social dans une grande cité.* Vol. II: *Methodes de recherches pour l'étude d'une grand cité.* Paris: 1952.
Admirable in both scope and method.

Chroniken der deutschen Städte von 14. bis ins 16. Jahrhundert. Lübeck. 5 vols. Transcription of Original Chronicles, edited by Historical Commission of Royal Academy of Science, München. Leipzig: 1884–1911.
There are equally voluminous chronicles for other cities.

Churchill, Henry S. *The City Is the People.* New York: 1945.

Clapham, John Harold. *An Economic History of Modern Britain.* 2 vols. Cambridge: 1930–1932.
A corrective to unfavorable one-sided accounts: but itself one-sided in its too studious optimism.

Clark, J. G. D. *Prehistoric Europe: The Economic Basis.* London: 1952.
(But see also: *A History of Technology,* edited by Charles Singer, et al.)

Clarke, Maude Violet. *The Medieval City State: An Essay on Tyranny and Federation in the Later Middle Ages.* London: 1926.

Clay, Rotha Mary. *The Medieval Hospitals of England.* London: 1909.

Collins, George R. *The Ciudad Lineal of Madrid.* In JSAH: May 1959.

Linear Planning Throughout the World. In JSAH: Oct. 1959.

Colvin, Brenda. *Land and Landscape.* London: 1948.
Useful introductory discussion.

Commelin, Caparus. *Beschrijvinge van Amsterdam*. 2 vols. Amsterdam: 1693–1694.

Constans, L. A. *Arles Antique*. In Bibliothèque des Ecoles Françaises d'Athènes et de Rome. No. 119. Paris: 1921.

Contenau, Georges. *Everyday Life in Babylon and Assyria*. New York: 1954.
Excellent, though meager in presentation of city through lack of (still unearthed) evidence.

Cooley, Charles Horton. *Social Organization: A Study of the Larger Mind*. New York: 1909.
Stresses role of primary group.

Human Nature and the Social Order. Revised ed. New York: 1922.
By one of the wisest of American sociologists.

Coolidge, John. *Mill and Mansion: A Study of Architecture and Society in Lowell, Massachusetts, 1820–1850*. New York: 1942.
Mainly esthetic orientation, but a useful contribution to the history and town planning of the factory period.

Coon, Carleton S. *The Story of Man: From the First Human to Primitive Culture and Beyond*. New York: 1954.
Secure when dealing with material remains; somewhat dogmatic on matters where equally competent interpreters may differ. With Teilhard de Chardin, he sees world unification as the next step in human development. The final chapter is full of wise words.

Coppolani, Jean. *Le réseau urbain de la France: sa structure et son aménagement*. Paris: 1959.

Coste-Messelière, Pierre de la. *Delphes*. Paris: 1957.
Georges de Mire's 246 photographs of Delphi are superb, revealing aspects the visitor rarely sees.

Coulborn, Rushton. *The Origin of Civilized Societies*. Princeton: 1959.
Important problem, inadequately formulated.

Coulton, George Gordon. *The Medieval Village*. Cambridge: 1925.
Does not deal with layout or physical character.

Medieval Panorama. Cambridge: 1939.
Good in general, not least for the picture of the English town in the Middle Ages—following, perhaps too closely, Maitland's trail.

Counaert, Emile. *Les Ghildes Médiévales: (V–XIV Siècles)*. In Revue Historique: Jan.–Mars et Avril–Juin: 1948.

Court, W. H. B. *The Rise of the Midland Industries: 1600–1838*. London: 1939.

*Creutzburg, Nikolaus. *Kultur im Spiegel der Landschaft: das Bild der Erde in seiner Gestaltung durch den Menschen: Ein Bilderatlas*. Leipzig: 1930.
Magnificent picture book which should be part of every planner's background. (But see late studies by Chombart de Lauwe and Gutkind.)

Crowe, Sylvia. *Tomorrow's Landscape*. London: 1956.
Excellent introductory sketch.

The Landscape of Power. London: 1958.
Deals with the formidable esthetic problem of generating stations, pylons, airports, etc.

Crozet, R. *Une Ville Neuve du XVIe Siècle: Vitry-le-François.* In La Vie Urbaine: Aug. and Oct. 1923.

Curie-Seimbres, M. A. *Essai sur les villes fondées dans le sud-ouest de la France aux XIII et XIV siècles sous le nom genérique de bastides.* Toulouse: 1880.
Pioneer study. (See Tout.)

Dahir, James. *The Neighborhood Unit Plan: Its Spread and Acceptance: A Selected Bibliography with Interpretive Comments.* New York: 1947.
Valuable.

   Region Building. New York: 1955.
   An illuminating interpretation of the Tennessee Valley and the TVA.

D'Ambrosio, Raffaele. *Alle Origini della Citta: Le Prime Esperienze Urbane.* Naples: 1956.
The first book after Fustel de Coulanges to deal extensively with the origins of the city and bring together the existing data.

Dasman, Raymond F. *Environmental Conservation.* New York: 1959.

Davidsohn, Robert. *Geschichte von Florenz.* 4 vols. in 8. Berlin: 1896–1927.
An exhaustive study.

Davis, William Stearns. *A Day in Old Rome.* New York: 1925.
A textbook; but it draws well on the sources.

Defoe, Daniel. *The Complete English Tradesman.* 4th ed. London: 1738. Also 2 vols. London: 1726–1732.
Invaluable.

DeForest, Robert Weeks, and Lawrence Veiller. *The Tenement House Problem.* 2 vols. New York: 1903.
A quaint landmark of housing reform.

Delcourt, Marie. *Les Grands Sanctuaires de la Grèce.* Paris: 1947.
Not as good as Dempsey, though wider in scope.

Demangeon, A. *Paris: La Ville et sa Banlieue.* Paris: 1933.

Dempsey, T. (Rev.). *The Delphic Oracle: Its Early History, Influence and Fall.* Oxford: 1918.
Good.

De Voe, Thomas F. *The Market Book.* New York: 1862.

Dewhirst, Robert K. *Saltaire.* In TPR: July 1960.

Dickens, Charles. *Sketches by•Boz.* London: 1836.
Here and in his later sketches Dickens left many valuable impressions of London. (See Mayhew.)

   Hard Times. London: 1854.
   Classic picture of Coketown itself, with archetypal characters of Gradgrind, Bounderby, and M'Choakumchild.

Dickinson, Robert E. *The West European City.* London: 1951.

Diedrichs, Eugen. *Deutsches Leben in der Vergangenheit in Bildern: Ein Atlas mit 1760 Nachbildungen.* 2 vols. Jena: 1908.
Graphic history of German social life: immensely rewarding to those who can read images as well as letters.

Dill, Samuel. *Roman Society: In the Last Century of the Western Empire.* Second Ed. revised. London: 1899.

Roman Society: From Nero to Marcus Aurelius. London: 1905.
Masterly.

Dobriner, William M. (editor). *The Suburban Community.* New York: 1958.
Representative collection of essays: but like most contemporary American sociology with a one-generation perspective, and with no perceptive understanding as yet of the physical aspects of community. (See Douglass, Harlan Paul.)

Dodd, George. *Days at the Factories: or, the Manufacturing Industry of Great Britain Described; Series I.* London: 1843.

Dohlmann, Robert von. *Aus Altertum und Gegenwart.* München: 1911.
(See Chapter V: Die Wohnungsnot des Antiken Grosstadte.)

Doob, Leonard W. *The Plans of Men.* New Haven: 1940.

Dopsch, Alfons. *The Economic and Social Foundations of European Civilization.* Wien: 1923–1924. Trans. New York: 1937.
Though S. W. Maitland began to correct the dismal traditional picture of the Dark Ages before the middle of the nineteenth century, Dopsch's re-examination of the evidence opened a new period. He emphasizes the pre-Carolingian continuities but tends to minimize the post-Carolingian hiatus.

Dorau, Herbert B., and A. G. Hinman. *Urban Land Economics.* New York: 1928.
Comprehensive but conventional. (See Hurd.)

Doty, Duane (Mrs.). *The Town of Pullman: Its Growth with Brief Accounts of Its Industries.* Pullman, Ill.: 1893.

Dougill, Wesley. Wythenshawe: *A Modern Satellite Town.* In TPR: June 1935.
Barry Parker's pioneer application of neighborhood planning in Wythenshawe has been insufficiently appreciated.

Douglass, Harlan Paul. *The Little Town: Especially in Its Rural Relationships.* New York: 1919.

The Suburban Trend. New York: 1925.
One of the earliest studies, and not the worst; useful for comparative appraisal of both the suburban situation and the differences in sociological method over a generation.

Doxiadis, K. A. *The Greek City Plan.* In Landscape: Autumn 1956.

The Science of Ekistics. In Architectoniki: Jan.–Feb. 1959.
(See also *Report of Proceedings of the Town and Country Planning Summer School.* Southampton: 1959.)

Raumordnung im Griechischen Städtebau. Berlin: 1938.
Perhaps the first attempt to do esthetic justice to the principles of spatial design in Hellenic planning.

Dubash, Peshoton S. G. *Hygiene of Town Planning and Vegetation.* London: 1919.

Du Camp, Maxime. *Paris: ses organes, ses fonctions et sa vie: dans la seconde moitié du 19e siècle.* Sixth ed. 6 vols. Paris: 1875.
One of the few comprehensive but not exhaustive works on civic institutions—ecclesiastical institutions for example are omitted—made all the more valuable by excellent historic introductions.

Duncan, Otis Daley, and Albert J. Reiss, Jr. *Social Characteristics of Urban and Rural Communities, 1950*. In the United States Census Monograph series. New York: 1956.
Of high immediate interest.

Dunham, H. Warner, and Robert E. Faris. *Mental Diseases in Urban Areas*. Chicago: 1939.

Dürer, Albrecht. *Unterricht zur Befestigung der Städte, Schlösser und Flecken*. First Ed.: 1527. Also Berlin: 1840, Paris: 1870.

Dyos, H. J. *The Growth of a Pre-Victorian Suburb: South London, 1580–1836*. In TPR: April 1954.
Valuable. Points to a lack of such studies covering period 1836–1936.

Eberstadt, Rudolph. *Handbuch des Wohnungswesen und der Wohnungsfrage*. 2 Ed. Jena: 1910. 4 Ed. Jena: 1920.
A comprehensive digest.

Die Spekulation im Neuzeitlichen Städtebau. Jena: 1907.
Reply to economists who justified the 'free market' in land.

Neue Studien über Städtebau und Wohnungswesen.

Vol. I. *Städtebau und Wohnungswesen in Belgien. Wiener Wohnverhältnisse*. Jena: 1912.

Vol. II. *Städtebau und Wohnungswesen in Holland*. Jena: 1914.

Vol. III. *Die Kleinwohnungen und das Städtebauliche System in Brüssel und Antwerpen*. Jena: 1919.
Important discussion of old and new housing types, with valuable plans of late medieval housing foundations for the indigent.

Ebert, Max (editor). *Reallexikon der Vorgeschichte*. Berlin: 1924–1932.
An encyclopedic sourcebook of ancient archaeology: the articles on Haus, Vol. II, and Siedlung, Vol. XII, are valuable, but that on the Stadt, Vol. XII, is almost worthless.

*Egli, Ernst. *Geschichte des Städtebaues. Erste Band: Die Alte Welt*. Zurich: 1959.
Comprehensive and detailed. Fills in certain areas sketchily treated in Lavedan, but is neither so exhaustive in its town-planning appraisals nor so richly illustrated.

Flugbild Europas. Zurich: 1958.
Superb air views of landscapes and cities.

Ehrenberg, Richard. *Capital and Finance in the Age of the Renaissance: A Study of the Fuggers and their Connections*. New York: n.d.
Does much to illuminate the part played by Antwerp, Lyons, and Amsterdam as commercial emporia in this age of transition; particularly, the influence of the free market, under the agency of the bourse. (See Barbour, Violet.)

Eliade, Mircea. *The Myth of the Eternal Return*. New York: 1954.

Patterns in Comparative Religion. Translation of the *Traité d'histoire des Religions*. New York: 1958.
The chapter on Sacred Places gives an essential key to understanding both the form and purpose of the ancient city.

The Sacred and the Profane. New York: 1959.

Eliot, Charles W. (Committee of the American Society of Landscape Architects). *Preservation of Open Spaces.* In Landscape Architecture: Jan. 1958.

Encyclopédie, ou dictionnaire raisonné des sciences, des arts et des métiers. Recueil de planches. 33 vols. Paris: 1751–1777.
The city as such is neglected: a significant omission. But the illustrations of urban life, particularly on the industrial side, are important.

Engels, Friedrich. *The Condition of the Working-Class in England in 1844.* Leipzig: 1845. Trans. London: 1887.
Terrible but incontrovertible picture. (For more favorable side, see Clapham.)

Engerand, Fernand. *Les Amusements des Villes d'Eaux à Travers les Ages.* Paris: 1936.
Useful description of spas, baths, and watering resorts.

English Courtier, The, and the Country Gentleman: Of Civil and Uncivil Life. London: 1586.

English Sanitary Institutions: Reviewed in Their Course of Development and in Some of Their Political and Social Relations. London: 1890.
Exhaustive and excellent.

*Ennen, Edith. *Frühgeschichte der Europäischen Stadt.* Bonn: 1953.
The best account of the romanesque transition to the fully formed medieval town.

Espinas, Georges. *La Vie Urbaine de Douai au Moyen Age.* 4 vols. Paris: 1913.
The last two volumes present the historic evidence and documents.

Les Origines du Capitalisme. Vol. III. *Deux fondations de villages dans l'Artois et la Flandre Française (X–XV siècles): Saint Omer.* Lannoy-du-Nord. Paris: 1946.
Admirable attempt to make the city plan a source of history.

Esteve, Gabriel Alomar. *Teoría de la Ciudad; Ideas Fundamentales Para un Urbanismo Humanistas.* Madrid: 1947.

Etienne, Charles, and John Liebault. *Maison Rustique, or the Countrey Farme.* London: 1616.

Evans, Arthur John. *The Palace of Minos.* London: 1921–1935.
Dealing with the discoveries that re-opened the history of Crete.

Evelyn, John. *Fumifugium: or The Inconvenience of the Aer and Smoake of London Dissipated.* London: 1661. Reprinted London: 1933.
Early zoning proposals; with a view to removing a nuisance that has persisted in London since the early Middle Ages.

London Revived: Consideration for its rebuilding in 1666. Edited by E. S. de Beer. Oxford: 1938.
Reprint of one version of *Londinum Redivivum,* Evelyn's proposals to restore London "to far greater Beauty, Commodiousness and Magnificence" after the Great Fire. Not merely are the three alternative plans interesting in their own right, with their provision for parish churches at regular intervals; but the details also throw light on the current urban scene, in its disorder and early industrial foulness.

Eyre, Edward (editor). *European Civilization: Its Origin and Development.* 7 vols. Oxford: 1935.

Fairman, H. W. *Town Planning in Pharaonic Egypt*. In TPR: April 1949.
Sketchy but useful. By the Brunner Professor of Egyptology at the University of Liverpool.

Fawcett, C. B. *A Residential Unit for Town and Country Planning*. London: 1944.

Feder, Gottfried. *Die Neue Stadt*. Berlin: 1939.

Federal Housing Administration. *The Structure and Growth of Residential Neighborhoods in American Cities*. Washington: 1939.
Realistic description of modes of American city growth.

Ferguson, William Scott. *Greek Imperialism*. Boston: 1913.
Comprehensive political study.

Fiennes, Celia. *The Journals of Celia Fiennes*. London: 1949.
Remarkable glimpses, indeed, detailed reports, on places and cities, from Land's End to Scarborough, including a near view of Bath, from 1685 to 1698.

Finegan, Jack. *Light from the Ancient Past*. Princeton: 1946.

Fish, T. *The Place of the Small State in the Political and Cultural History of Ancient Mesopotamia*. Bulletin of John Rylands Library: March 1944.

The Cult of King Dung, During the Third Dynasty of Ur. Manchester: 1927.
Evidence for worship of king as god at Lagash, Umma, Dreben, and Ur.

Fisher, F. J. *The Development of the London Food Market: 1540–1640*. In Economic History Review: April 1935.

Fletcher, Joseph S. *Memorials of a Yorkshire Parish*. London: 1917.

Florence, Philip Sargant. *Economic Advantages and Disadvantages of Metropolitan Concentration*. In *Columbia Conference on The Metropolis and Modern Life*. New York: 1954.

Follett, Mary Parker. *Creative Experience*. New York: 1924.
Pioneer study of the autonomous group.

Ford, James, and others. *Slums and Housing: with Special Reference to New York City: History; Conditions; Policy*. 2 vols. Cambridge, Mass.: 1936.

Fourastié, Jean. *Machinisme et Bien-Être*. Paris: 1951.
Has brief but acute analysis of contemporary city.

Fourier, François Marie Charles. *Le Nouveau Monde Industriel et Sociétaire*. 1 vol. Paris: 1829. 2 vols. Paris: 1840.
A book whose wide influence has hardly yet been adequately estimated or understood. Godin's Phalanstery at Guise directly stems from it, and it is still producing such queer progeny as Le Corbusier's Maisons de l'Unité d'Habitation.

Fournel, Victor. *Le Vieux Paris*. Tours: 1887.

*Fowler, W. Warde. *The City-State of the Greeks and Romans*. First ed.: 1893. 16th ed.: 1952.
Still valuable.

Frankfort, Henri. *The City of Akhenaten*. 3 vols. London: 1923.

Kingship and the Gods: A Study of Ancient Near East Religion as the Integration of Society and Nature. Chicago: 1948.
Brilliant study, rich in detailed knowledge, fruitful in hypotheses. (But see Hocart for a wider interpretation, which brings out similarities between cultures.)

*Town Planning in Ancient Mesopotamia. In TPR: July 1950.
This article with those of Childe and Fairman are so far the best presentation of the ancient city in the Near East.

*The Birth of Civilization in the Near East. Bloomington: 1954.
Outstanding both as presentation and interpretation.

The Art and Architecture of the Ancient Orient. Baltimore: 1955.

Franklin, Alfred Louis August. La vie privée autrefois; arts et métiers, modes, moeurs, usages des Parisiens du XIIe au XVIIIe siècle. 27 vols. Paris: 1887–1902.
Highly useful.

Freeman, Edward, and W. Hunt (editors). Historic Towns Series. 11 vols. London: 1889–1893.
One of the early stirrings of the cities movement, with parallel manifestations in Germany, Holland, and the United States.

Freeman, Kathleen. Greek City-States. London· 1950.
A case history of nine cities, from Thourioi to Byzantium.

Freeman, T. W. Geography and Planning. London: 1958.

*Friedländer, Ludwig. Town Life in Ancient Italy. Trans. of Staedetwesen im Italien im Ersten Jahrhundert: 1879, by W. E. Waters. Boston: 1902.

Roman Life and Manners Under the Early Empire. Trans. from 7th ed. of Sittengeschichte Roms. 4 vols. London: 1936.
Vols. I and II have more relevant data on the Roman city than any other general work.

Friedmann, Georges (editor). Villes et campagnes; civilisation urbaine et civilisation rurale en France. Paris: 1953.
Stimulating many-faceted report of a sociological conference dealing with the historical and contemporary problems of city and country, many as yet scarcely touched by scholarship.

Fritsch, Theodor. Die Stadt der Zukunft (Gartenstadt). Leipzig: 1912.

Fry, E. Maxwell. Chandigarh: The Capital of the Punjab. JRIBA: Jan. 1955.
Description of Le Corbusier's bold plan for a New Town, based on the Radburn principle: far more significant than Brasilia.

*Fustel de Coulanges, Numa Denis. The Ancient City: A Study on the Religion, Laws, and Institutions of Greece and Rome. Paris: 1864. New York: 1956.
The first work to give due emphasis to the religious foundations of the city: still a towering landmark in the whole literature. Full of pregnant observations worthy of further reflection and research.

Gadd, C. J. Ideas of Divine Role in the Ancient East. London: 1948.
History and Monuments of Ur. New York: n.d.
Based on the documents. (But see also Kramer and Woolley.)

Gaffney, M. Mason. Urban Expansion—Will It Ever Stop? In United States Yearbook of Agriculture. Washington: 1958.

Galpin, Charles Josiah. Social Anatomy of the Rural Community. In University of Wisconsin Bulletin No. 34.

Rural Relations of the Villages and the Small City. In University of Wisconsin Bulletin No. 411.

Ganshof, François Louis. *Étude sur le développement des villes entre Loire Rhin au moyen age.* Bruxelles: 1943.

Gantner, Joseph. *Die Schweizer Stadt.* München: 1925.

Grundformen der Europäischen Stadt. Wien: 1928.
Worthy but somewhat over-formalized attempt to establish the historic filiation of modern urban forms.

Gardner, Edmund G. *The Story of Siena and San Gimignano.* London: 1905.
One of the most interesting books in this rewarding Medieval Towns Series.

Garnier, Charles, and A. Amman. *L'Habitation Humaine.* Paris: 1892.
By an "historian who knew little architecture and an architect who knew little history" (Preface). Emphasis of course on isolated house; but a step beyond Violette-le-Duc's *The Habitations of Man in All Ages.*

Garnier, Tony. *Étude pour la Construction des Villes.* Paris: 1917.
Les Grands Travaux de la Ville de Lyon. Paris: 1924.
Une Cité Industrielle. Paris: 1932.
This project, worked out between 1901–1904 parallels both in time and in aim Howard's Garden City; and on the architectural side had the advantage of Garnier's vigorous rational use of modern forms. But it was published belatedly; and re-discovered by a younger generation who claimed for it a distinction as idea that belonged, in fact, to Howard. Garnier's work is, rather, to be compared with Le Corbusier's, to which it is decisively superior by reason of its social and human insight.

Garvan, Anthony. *Architecture and Town Planning in Colonial Connecticut.* New Haven: 1951.
Exemplary. Valuable for light thrown on colonial urbanization generally.

Gaskell, P. *Artisans and Machinery: The Moral and Physical Condition of the Manufacturing Population Considered with Reference to Mechanical Substitutes for Human Labour.* London: 1836.
Gaskell, writing with a belief in the established order, presents a damning view of early paleotechnic industry, whose defects revolted him.

Geddes, Patrick. *City Development: A Study of Parks, Gardens and Culture Institutes.* Edinburgh: 1904.
Report to the Carnegie Trustees on the development of Dunfermline. The beginning of Geddes' career as professional planner.

Civics as Applied Sociology. Parts I and II. In *Sociological Papers:* Vols. I and II: London: 1905–1906.

A Suggested Plan for a Civic Museum. In *Sociological Papers:* Vol. III: London: 1907.

Cities: Being an Introduction to the Study of Civics. University of London Extension Lectures Syllabus. London: 1907.

City Deterioration and the Need of City Survey. In Annals of the American Academy of Political and Social Science: July 1909.

The Civic Survey of Edinburgh. Edinburgh: 1911.
From the 'nineties onward Geddes was a tireless advocate of city surveys as preliminary to intelligent town-planning and city design; and this little pamphlet indicates how much one who knows his subject can put in small compass. (See also Poëte, Marcel.)

Cities in Evolution. London: 1915. New Edition: London: 1949.
Most popular and available of Geddes' writings on cities; made up chiefly of scattered papers, but with a unified point of view. The new edition omits some characteristic Geddesian contributions, but adds other unpublished materials.

Town Planning in Patiala State and City. Lucknow: 1922.

Town Planning Toward City Development: A Report to the Durbar of Indore. 2 vols. Indore: 1918.
Between 1914 and 1924 Geddes made or revised plans for some fifty cities in India and Palestine. The Report on Indore is the completest expression of his town-planning methods and his sociology and philosophy. Vol. II, which deals with the cultural foundations, is particularly recommended.

Geddes, Patrick, and Victor Branford. See Branford.

Geisler, Walter. *Die Deutsche Stadt: Ein Beitrag zur Morphologie der Kulturlandschaft*. Stuttgart: 1924.

George, M. Dorothy. *London Life in the XVIII Century*. New York: 1925.
Thoroughly documented "picture of the conditions of life and work of the poorer classes."

George, Pierre. *La Ville: Le Fait Urbain à Travers le Monde*. Paris: 1952.
A world survey of cities, with representative samples from every part of the world. Suggests, by both its success and its limitations, the need for a world encyclopedia of cities.

La Campagne: Le Fait Rural à Travers le Monde. Paris: 1956.

George, Pierre, and others. *Études sur la Banlieue de Paris*. Paris: 1950.

Gerard, P. (C.E.). *How to Build a City: Designed for the consideration of founders of towns, architects, civil engineers, sanitary organizations, municipal authorities, builders, and especially the managers of the various railroads to the Pacific*. Philadelphia: 1872.

*Gerkan, Armin von. *Griechische Städteanlagen*. Berlin: 1924.
Study of Greek city layouts, with particular reference to the more orderly Hellenistic plan attributed to Hippodamos. Von Gerkan contrasts Greek planning and architectural conceptions with the Roman-Italic order. The most acute and comprehensive study yet available; magistral, in fact. (But see also Wycherley and Roland Martin.)

Gerlach, Walther. *Die Entstehungszeit der Stadtbefestigungen in Deutschland: Ein Beitrag zur Mittelalterlichen Verfassungsgeschichte*. In Leipziger Historische Abhandlungen: Vol. XXXIV: Leipzig: 1913.
Analysis of various concepts of city and village in German Middle Ages.

*Gibberd, Frederick. *Town Design*. New York: 1953. Revised and enlarged: 1960.
An outstanding book by a distinguished practicing architect and planner. Does for our period what Sitte and Unwin did for theirs, using both historic and contemporary material. (See also Rasmussen.)

Giedion, Sigfried. *Space, Time and Architecture; the Growth of a New Tradition*. First ed. 1941. Third ed. 1954.
Brilliant: but often cavalier in presenting facts and judgments.

Gierke, Otto. *Political Theories of the Middle Age.* Trans. Cambridge: 1900. *Natural Law and the Theory of Society: 1500 to 1800.* 2 vols. Trans. Cambridge: 1934.
From *Das Deutsche Genossenschaftsrecht:* one of the best early statements of the modern sociological theory of groups. (See also Maitland, Follett, and Cooley.)

Gilbert, William. *The City: An Inquiry into the Corporation, its Livery Companies, and the Administration of their Charities and Endowments.* London: 1877.

Giovannoni, G., et al. *L'urbanistica dall'antichita ad oggi.* Firenze: 1943.

Giry, A. *Histoire de la Ville de Saint Omer.* Paris: 1877.
Important source of data on 'advanced liberties' of medieval town.

Giry, A., and A. Reville. *Emancipation of the Medieval Towns.* Trans. in *Historical Miscellany:* New York: 1907.
Translated from Chapter VII of Lavisse and Rambaud's *Histoire Générale.* Still one of the best descriptions of the emergence of the medieval town as a corporate entity, with a due discrimination of the difference between north and south, old Roman foundations and new towns, and all the varying local circumstances of habit, custom, law, and history.

Glass, David. *The Town.* London: 1935.

Glass, Ruth (Mrs.). *Social Aspects of Town Planning.* In TPR: March 1945.

Gleichen-Russwurm, Alexander von (editor). *Kultur- und Sittengeschichte aller Zeiten und Völker.* 24 vols. in 12. Hamburg: 1929.
Valuable for its many illustrations.

Glikson, Artur. *Regional Planning and Development.* Leiden: 1955.
Perhaps the best treatise in English on the philosophy of regional planning since Benton MacKaye's lonely classic, *The New Exploration;* particularly good in its ecological considerations and its detailed analysis of the planning problems of Israel and the Netherlands. (See also Thomas, William L., Jr.)

Notes on the Relation of Regional Planning to Conceptions of Technological Progress. The Hague: 1957.

Glotz, Gustave. *The Greek City; and Its Institutions.* Paris: 1928. Trans. New York: 1930.

Glueck, Nelson. *Rivers in the Desert: A History of the Negev.* New York: 1959.
Important for its study of water conservation by underground cisterns and reservoirs in a land otherwise unfit for urban occupation.

Godfrey, Hollis. *The Health of the City.* Boston: 1910.
A fair early treatment of air, waste, noise, and housing.

Goethe, Johann Wolfgang von. *Dichtung und Wahrheit.* Trans. London: 1848.
See the many admirable passages on medieval urban survivals.

Gomme, George Laurence. *The Village Community: With Special Reference to the Origin and Form of its Survivals in Britain.* New York: 1890.

Goodman, Percival and Paul. *Communitas; Means of Livelihood and Ways of Life.* Chicago: 1947.
Fresh utopian hypotheses and criticisms.

Gothein, Marie Luise. *A History of Garden Art*. 2 vols. London: 1928.
More than a half-century old, but still valuable, even though it cries for a successor.

Gottman, Jean. *Megalopolis, or the Urbanization of the North-Eastern Seaboard*. In Economic Geography: July 1957.

Revolution in Land Use. In Landscape: Winter 1958–1959.

Gouhier, Jean. *Le Mans: naissance d'une grande cité au milieu du XXe siècle*. Paris: 1953.

Gould, Elgin R. L. *The Housing of the Working People: A Special Report of U.S. Committee of Labor*. Washington: 1895.

Graham, Edward H. *Natural Principles of Land Use*. New York: 1944.

Graham, Michael. *Human Needs*. London: 1951.
A fresh assessment by a naturalist, equally at home on the sea, in pasture, on the slag heap, and in the dens of men.

Gras, Norman S. B. *An Introduction to Economic History*. New York: 1922.
Correlates economic and city development. Follows the general line of Bücher, but leaves the impression that metropolitanism is a final stage.

History of Agriculture in Europe and America. New York: 1925.
One of the few books available on a topic closely related to early city building, whose history has received even less attention than that of cities.

Gravier, Jean-François. *Paris et le Désert Français*. Paris: 1947.
Admirable study of the problem of achieving urban and regional equilibrium: the fruit of two generations of scholarship in an area where the French have been pre-eminent.

Gray, Richard. *The Future of the Backs: University Development in Cambridge*. In TPR: Jan. 1956.

Green, Alice Stopford. *Town Life in the Fifteenth Century*. 2 vols. London: 1894.
Classic.

Gregorovius, Ferdinand Adolf. *History of the City of Rome in the Middle Ages*. 8 vols. Stuttgart: 1859–1872. Trans. 13 vols. London: 1894–1902.

Grenier, Albert. Bologne: *Villa-novienne et Étrusque: VIII–IVe siècles avant notre ére*. In Bibliothèque Française d'Athène et de Rome. Paris: 1912.

Griffith, Ernest S. *The Modern Development of City Government*. 2 vols. Oxford: 1907.
(See Robson, William A.)

Grisebach, August. *Die alte deutsche Stadt in ihrer Stammeseigenart*. Berlin: 1930.
Richly illustrated; particularly with a varied lot of house-types.

Gropius, Walter. *Rebuilding Our Communities*. Chicago: 1945.

*Gross, Charles. *The Gild Merchant: a Contribution to British Municipal History*. 2 vols. Oxford: 1890.
A solid work in which the conclusions in Vol. I are backed by a second volume of citations from original sources.

Grosstadt, Die. *Vorträge und Aufsätze zur Städteausstellung*. Dresden: 1903.
Includes essays by Bücher and Ratzel and Simmel—the latter on The Big City and the Spiritual Life.

Grunsfeld, Ernest A., and Louis Wirth. *Plan for Metropolitan Chicago*. In TPR: April 1954.

Gut, Albert. *Der Wohnungsbau in Deutschland nach dem Weltkriege*. München: 1928.
Richly illustrated description of the earlier postwar housing in Germany, mainly on traditional lines.

Gutkind, E. A. *Creative Demobilisation*. Vol. I. *Principles of National Planning*. Vol. II. *Case Studies in National Planning*. London: 1943.
Wide ranging in scope and full of important material; but somewhat peremptory in its handling of the political and educational problems of large-scale planning.

Revolution of Environment. London: 1946.

Community and Environment: A Discourse on Social Ecology. London: 1953.

The Expanding Environment: The End of Cities; The Rise of Communities. London: 1953.
Close in spirit and outlook to Frank Lloyd Wright's The Disappearing City, but on a firmer basis of scholarship and planning experience.

Our World from the Air: An International Survey of Man and His Environment. Foreword by G. P. Gooch; Introduction by Lewis Mumford. New York: 1953.
Excellent survey of cities and landscapes, indispensable for those who would think clearly and sharply on these subjects.

Haarhoff, T. C. *The Stranger at the Gate: Aspects of exclusiveness and co-operation in Ancient Greece and Rome*. New York: 1938.
A significant study by a South African scholar, generalizing the problem of 'apartheid.'

Hackett, Brian. *Man, Society and Environment*. London: 1950.
A first effort to encompass a subject as yet still insufficiently explored by the preliminary sciences. An overall view, often shaky in details.

Hahn, Edouard. *Die Entstehung der Pflugkultur unseres Ackerbaus*. Heidelberg: 1909.
Important.

Hallenbeck, Wilbur. *American Urban Communities*. New York: 1951.

Haller, William, Jr. *The Puritan Frontier: Town Planning in New England Colonial Development 1630–1660*. New York: 1951.

Halpert, L., and Noel P. Gist. *Urban Society*. 2nd ed. New York: 1941.

Hammarstrand, Nils. *Pietro Cataneo. A Resurrected Writer on City Planning*. In JAIA: Dec. 1925.
Hammarstrand's pioneer studies in this Journal between 1923 and 1926 should long ago have been collected.

Hammond, John Lawrence and Barbara. *The Skilled Labourer (1760–1832)*. London: 1911.
Graphic, well-documented studies: indispensable for an understanding of the paleotechnic town.

Harrison, Jane. *Ancient Art and Ritual*. London: 1913.

*Haskins, Caryl P. *Of Societies and Men*. New York: 1951.
Recommended.

Hassert, Kurt. *Die Städte: Geographisch Betrachtet*. Leipzig: 1907.
Admirable pioneer study.

Haverfield, Francis J. *Ancient Townplanning*. Oxford: 1913.
Useful at certain points despite date.

Hawkes, Jacquetta. *Man on Earth*. New York: 1955.
Both thought and felt.

Hawley, Amos H. *The Changing Shape of Metropolitan America: Deconcentration since 1920*. Glencoe, Ill.: 1937.

Human Ecology: A Theory of Community Structure. New York: 1950.

Haworth, Lawrence L. *An Institutional Theory of the City and Planning*. In the JAIP: 1957.

Hayes, William C. *The Scepter of Egypt*. 2 vols. Cambridge, Mass.: 1959.
A thorough work, based on the collections of the Metropolitan Museum of New York.

*Hegemann, Werner. *Der Städtebau: nach den Ergebnissen der Allgemeinen Städtebau-Austellung*. 2 vols. Berlin: 1911.
The best single document on city planning and housing relating to the period before the First World War.

City Planning: Housing. 3 vols. New York: 1938.

Der neue Bebauungsplan für Chicago. Berlin: n.d.

Hegemann, Werner, and Elbert Peets. *The American Vitruvius*. New York: 1922.
Voluminous study of historic planning. Still valuable.

*Heichelheim, Fritz M. *An Ancient Economic History: From the Paleolithic Age to the Migrations of the Germanic, Slavic and Arabic Nations*. Vol. I. Leiden: 1958.
Rich in details, exhaustive in bibliography, but unhappily translated with a literalism that verges on illiteracy.

Heil, B. *Die Deutschen Städte und Bürger im Mittelalter*. Leipzig: 1912.

Heilig, Wilhelm. *Stadt- und Landbaukunde*. Berlin: 1935.

Heitland, William Emerton. *The Roman Fate*. Cambridge: 1922.

Last Words on the Roman Municipalities. Cambridge: 1928.
Extremely suggestive.

Herlihy, David. *Pisa in the Early Renaissance: A Study of Urban Growth*. New Haven: 1958.
Useful on political and economic history; but hardly touches on physical form.

*Herodotus. *History*. Literally translated by Henry Cary. London: 1891.
Herodotus has weathered the corrections of the archaeologist, and his work emerges once again as an indispensable introduction to the history and legend of the ancient world.

Herron, Ima Honaker. *The Small Town in American Literature*. Durham, N. C.: 1939.

Heyne, Moritz. *Das Deutsche Wohungswesen von den ältesten geschichtlichen Zeiten bis zum 16. Jahrhundert*. Vol. I in 'Fünf Bücher Deutscher Hausaltertümer.' Leipzig: 1899.
Valuable.

Hibbert, Arthur, and Ruthardt Oehme. *Old European Cities*. London: n.d.
Twenty-four sixteenth-century maps, with texts from the *Civitates Orbis Terrarum* of George Braun and Franz Hogenberg. (See Merian.)

Higbee, Edward. *The Squeeze: Cities Without Space*. New York: 1960.

Hilberseimer, Ludwig. *The New City: Principles of Planning*. Chicago: 1944.
Formalistic.

The Nature of Cities: Origin, Growth, and Decline; Pattern and Form; Planning Problems. Chicago: 1955.
An earnest and well-conceived attempt to pass beyond the limitations of the earlier work.

Hill, Ida Thallon. *The Ancient City of Athens: Its Topography and Monuments*. London: 1953.
A valuable guide to all that is now known.

*Hiorns, Frederick R. *Town-building in History: An outline review of conditions, influences, ideas, and methods affecting 'planned' towns through five thousand years*. London: 1956.
Wide in scope, conventional in both historic and esthetic judgment. But since there is no translation of Poëte and Lavedan in English, it has a genuine value, enhanced by its ample, wide-ranging illustrations. (But see also Egli.)

Hocart, A. M. *Kings and Councillors: An Essay in the Comparative Anatomy of Human Society*. Cairo: 1936.
Interprets the city as primarily a ritual center, with the oriented rectangular plan as an expression of ritual needs. Apart from Hocart's oversight of Roman planning, which would have served as confirmation of his views, his interpretation seems to deserve more serious consideration than many anthropologists and archaeologists have been willing to give.

Social Origins. London: 1954.
Full of shrewd observations, but with the main preoccupation the problem of kingship.

Hodgson, Francis. *Venice in the Thirteenth and Fourteenth Centuries (1204–1400)*. London: 1910.
(See Molmenti.)

Hoffbauer, Theodore J. H. *Paris à travers les ages: aspects successifs des monuments et quartiers historiques de Paris depuis le XIIIe siècle jusqu'à nos jour. Fidèlement restitués d'après les documents authentiques*. 2 vols. Paris: 1875–1882.
Illustrations excellent. Contributions by authorities like La Croix and Franklin. (See Poëte and Bardet.)

Hole, Christina. *English Home Life: 1500–1800*. London: 1947.
Juicy.

English Custom and Usage. Third Edition. London: 1950.

Holford, William. *Green Cities of the 20th Century*. In JTPI: May–June: 1947.

St. Paul's: Report on the Surroundings of St. Paul's Cathedral in the City of London. In TPR: July 1956.
A new approach to a difficult problem of keeping alive historic structures of great esthetic importance in an overdynamic economy: specially good because of Holford's rejection of the obvious cliché with which he himself first approached the situation.

The Tall Building in the Town. In JTPI: March 1959.
Able historic summary, though it leaves out one important consideration: the effect of such high-density concentrations in generating traffic already impeded at much lower densities.

Trading Estates. In JTPI: March 1939.
Holford's own Team Valley Estate set a new standard.

Holsti, Rudolph. *The Relation of War to the Origin of the State*. Helsingfors: 1913.
A neglected contribution that now needs re-statement and amplification.

Homo, Léon. *Rome Impériale et l'Urbanisme dans l'Antiquité*. Paris: 1951.
Exhaustive study dealing with every aspect of municipal life, roads, sanitation, police, etc., for which there are sufficient documents. Useful bibliography. (On the social aspect of this urbanism, see Friedländer.)

Honeybourne, M. B., and N. G. Brett-James. *Precincts and Trade Quarters*. In AR: Nov. 1946.

Hoover, Edgar M., and Raymond Vernon. *Anatomy of a Metropolis: The Changing Distribution of People and Jobs within the New York Metropolitan Region*. Cambridge, Mass.: 1959.
Part of a larger study.

Houston, J. M. *A Social Geography of Europe*. London: 1953.
Discusses the rural landscape and house types as well as the morphology of cities.

The Scottish Burgh. In TPR: July 1954.

*Howard, Ebenezer. *Garden Cities of Tomorrow*. London: 1902. First edition entitled: *Tomorrow: A Peaceful Path to Land Reform*. New edition, with Foreword by F. J. Osborn and Introduction by Lewis Mumford. London: 1946.
A close study of this classic is important for every serious student of urban development. Apart from the direct practical influence it has already exerted, it has had an indirect effect on planning in many other directions. But its most fundamental theorems, on constructive ways of both limiting and augmenting the size of urban units, have still to be adequately grasped. (See Osborn, F. J., Purdom, C. B., Stein, Clarence S., and Rodwin, Lloyd.)

Howe, Frederick. *The Modern City and Its Problems*. New York: 1915.
A pioneering work in a decade that started a fresh interest in city development in the United States. (See Yeomans, Alfred.)

Hoyt, Homer. *One Hundred Years of Land Values in Chicago: 1830–1933*. Chicago: 1933.
Study of the relation of city growth to land values seen in its historic perspective.

Forces of Urban Centralization and Decentralization. In American Journal of Sociology: May 1941.

Hrozny, Bedrich. *Ancient History of Western Asia, India and Crete.* Trans. New York: 1953.

Hughes, Thomas, and E. A. G. Lamborn. *Towns and Town Planning, Ancient and Modern.* Oxford: 1923.
Once useful, now outdated. (For English survey, see Hiorns, Frederick R.)

Hugo-Brunt, Michael. *George Dance, the Younger: as Town Planner (1768–1814).* In JSAH: Dec. 1955.

Huizinga, Johann. *The Waning of the Middle Ages.* Trans. New York: 1924.
Deals with complexities and contradictions of the disintegrating medieval idolum.

*Homo Ludens: A Study of the Play-Element in Culture. London: 1944.
Original and important.

Huntington, Ellsworth. *The Human Habitat.* New York: 1927.
Perhaps the soundest if not the most original of the author's numerous studies.

Hurd, Richard Melanchthon. *Principles of City Land Values.* First ed.: New York: 1903. Fourth ed.: New York: 1924.
Deservedly of high repute in a field where it long stood alone. Many illustrations of early stages of growth in American cities. By a businessman who really understood his business. Still available.

Hürlimann, Martin. *Berlin: Berichte und Bilder.* Berlin: 1934.

Hutchinson, R. W. *Prehistoric Town-Planning in Crete.* In TPR: Oct. 1950.

Prehistoric Town-Planning in and Around the Aegean. In TPR: Jan.–Apr. 1953.
By far the best accounts available of the predecessors of the Greek city. (See Wycherley for later Greek examples.)

Hutton, William. *The History of Birmingham.* Fourth Ed. London: 1819.

A Journey from Birmingham to London. Birmingham: 1785.

Hyde, Francis E. *The Growth of a Town: A study of the economic forces controlling the development of Stony Stratford in the Middle Ages.* In TPR: July 1949.

Ikle, Fred Charles. *The Effect of War Destruction upon the Ecology of Cities.* In Social Forces: May 1951.
Resumption of original pattern by returning inhabitants.

Jackson, J. B. (editor). *Landscape: Magazine of Human Geography.* 1951–current.
This quarterly rarely fails to present one or more articles of importance on city and landscape.

Jacobsen, Thorkild. *Mesopotamia: The Cosmos as a State.* In *The Intellectual Adventures of Ancient Man.* Chicago: 1946.
Gives Jacobsen's interpretation of primitive village democracy in Mesopotamia through analysis of later religious documents.

James, Edmund. *The Growth of Great Cities in Area and Population.* In Annals of American Academy of Political Science: Jan. 1899.
Still valuable.

James, Edwin Oliver. *The Ancient Gods: The History and Diffusion of Religion in the Ancient Near East and the Eastern Mediterranean.* London: 1960.
Useful general introduction.

*James, Henry. *The American Scene.* New York: 1907.
An urban commentary and interpretation, unrivalled in delicacy and depth.

Jastrow, Morris, Jr. *The Civilization of Babylonia and Assyria.* Philadelphia: 1915.
A landmark. (But see Kramer, Childe, Frankfort, Contenau.)

Jefferson, Mark. *Distribution of the World's City Folks.* In Geographical Review: July 1931.

Jeremiah, Keith. *A Full Life in the Country. The Sudbury and District Survey and Plan.* London: 1948.

Johnson-Marshall, Percy. *Comprehensive Redevelopment.* In JRIBA: April–Dec. 1959.

*Jones, A. H. M. *The Greek City: From Alexander to Justinian.* Oxford: 1940.

Athenian Democracy. Oxford: 1957.
Defense of realities of Athenian democracy against scurrilous attacks of its avowed enemies from Plato and the Old Oligarch on. Useful counterpoise if not the whole truth.

Jones, Thomas Jesse. *The Sociology of a New York City Block.* New York: 1904.
Pioneer study.

Jones, Victor. *Metropolitan Government.* Chicago: 1942.
Though dated by statistical changes since its writing, still valuable.

Jurgens, Oskar. *Spanische Städte: Ihre Baulich Entwicklung und Ausgestaltung.* Hamburg: 1926. In *University of Hamburg Abhandlungen: Bd. 23.*
First part systematic descriptions of twenty-seven Spanish cities; the second part deals with their planning and building. Useful bibliography but inadequate illustrations.

Justement, Louis. *New Cities for Old.* New York: 1946.

Juvenal. *Works.* Loeb's classics. New York.
Important as source, after one has made allowance for satirical bias. See especially *The City.*

Kampffmeyer, Hans. *Die Gartenstadt Bewegung.* Leipzig: 1909.
Excellent early study.

Karan, Pradyuma Prasad. *The Pattern of Indian Towns: A Study in Urban Morphology.* In JAIP: 1957.

Kellogg, Paul U. (editor). *The Pittsburgh Survey.* 6 vols. New York: 1909, 1914.
Monumental survey of a representative industrial city: an overhauling not unlike the later Middletown, but with more emphasis on the social workers' point of view and specific interests. Lacking on the civic and urban side, it is nevertheless one of the outstanding demonstrations of the survey method.

Kenyon, Kathleen M. *Digging Up Jericho.* London: 1957.
> Description of what seems, if the dating is correct, to be the earliest urban settlement in the Near East: a discovery that may revolutionize the archaeology and chronology of this area and urban development generally.

Kidder Smith, G. E. *Sweden Builds.* First Ed. New York: 1950. Second Ed. 1957.
> Rich in admirable photos and not least in plans, particularly good on the Swedish New Town of Vällingby.

Italy Builds: Its Modern Architecture and Native Inheritance. New York: 1955.
> Rare combination of good photography and architectural understanding, with a sense of the underlying human values as well.

Kirsten, Ernst, and Wilhelm Kraiker. *Griechenlandkunde: Ein Führer zu Klassischen Stätten.* Heidelberg: 1957.
> A modern Pausanias: invaluable. (But the 'Guide Bleu' to Greece is also excellent.)

Kite, Elizabeth S. *L'Enfant and Washington: 1791–1792.* Baltimore: 1929.

Kizer, Benjamin H. *Regional Planning in the Columbia River Area.* In TPR: July 1951.

Kligman, Miriam. *Human Ecology and the City Planning Movement.* In Social Forces: Oct. 1945.

Koenigsberger, Otto H. *New Towns in India.* In TPR: July 1949.

Kohl, Johann Georg. *Der Verkehr und die Ansiedlungen der Menschen in Ihrer Abhängigkeit von der Gestaltung der Erdoberfläche.* 1841. Second Ed. Leipzig: 1850.
> Sombart pokes fun at this work; but its emphasis on transportation as one of the critical factors in city development is not unsound.

Korn, Arthur. *History Builds the Town.* London: 1953.
> Rich in illustrations.

Kouenhoven, John A. *The Columbia Historical Portrait of New York.* New York: 1953.
> Rich in pictorial data.

Kraeling, Carl H., and Robert M. Adams (editors). *City Invincible: A Symposium on Urbanization and Cultural Development in the Ancient Near East. Held at The Oriental Institute of the University of Chicago, Dec. 4–7, 1958.* Chicago: 1960.
> A fascinating symposium that hardly does justice to its title, but at least leads up to it.

Kramer, Samuel Noah. *History Begins at Sumer.* New York: 1959.
> Many urban sidelights both in text and translation, by an outstanding scholar in this field. See his translations in Pritchard, J. B.

*Kropotkin, Piotr. *Fields, Factories, and Workshops: or Industry Combined with Agriculture, and Brainwork with Manual Work.* First Ed. Boston: 1899. Revised Ed. London: 1919.
> Sociological and economic intelligence of the first order, founded on Kropotkin's specialized competence as a geographer and his generous social passion as a leader in communist anarchism. Recommended especially to all concerned with planning for undeveloped areas.

Mutual Aid. London: 1904.
Pioneer work on symbiosis in sociology: one of the first attempts to redress the one-sided Darwinian emphasis upon the more predatory aspects of life. Note chapter on Mutual Aid in the Medieval City.

Kuhn, Emil. *Ueber die Enstehung der Staedte der Alten: Komenverfassung und Synoikismos.* Leipzig: 1878.
Almost as surprising for its subject matter and its high quality of thought as Fustel de Coulanges' work, especially considering its date.

Labò, Mario. *Strada Nuova.* In *Scritti di Storia dell'Arte in Onore di Lionello Venturi.* Rome: 1956.
Description of the new aristocratic quarter of Genoa designed by Galeazzo Alessi.

Lanciani, Rodolfo Amadeo. *Ancient Rome in the Light of Recent Discoveries.* 8th Ed. Boston: 1892.

New Tales of Old Rome. London: 1901.

Ancient and Modern Rome. London: n.d. (1927?).
Much in small compass, by a pioneer investigator.

Larrabee, Eric, and Rolf Meyersohn (editors). *Mass Leisure.* Glencoe, Ill.: 1959.
(See also *Mass Culture,* by the same editors.)

Larsen, J. A. O. *Representative Government in Greek and Roman History.* Berkeley: 1955.
Important fresh examination.

Larwood, Jacob (pseudonym for H. D. J. van Schevichaven). *The Story of the London Parks.* London: 1881.

Lavedan, Pierre. *Qu'est-ce-que l'urbanisme? Introduction à l'histoire de l'urbanisme.* Paris: 1926.
An introduction to the documents, plans, and other sources for a history of urbanism, rather than to the subject itself. More for the specialist than the general student.

*Histoire de l'Urbanisme. Vol. I. *Antiquité, Moyen Age.* Paris: 1926. Vol. II. *Renaissance et Temps Moderne.* Paris: 1941. Vol. III. *Époque Contemporaine.* Paris: 1952.
Classic work on the history of the town planner's art, rich in documentation, illustrations, and plans.

Géographie des Villes. Paris: 1936. Revised Ed.: 1959.

Représentation des Villes dans l'Art du Moyen Age. Paris: 1954.

Urbanisme et architecture: études écrites et publiées en honneur de Pierre Lavedan. Paris: 1954.

Layard, Austen Henry. *The Monuments of Nineveh: From drawings made on the spot.* In two series. London: 1853.
Still valuable.

Lebreton, Jean. *La Cité Naturelle: Recherche d'un urbanisme humain.* Paris: 1945.
Far sounder than the more widely publicized conceptions of Le Corbusier.

*Le Corbusier. *Urbanisme*. Paris: 1924. Trans. *The City of The Future*. New York: 1930.
> Suggestions for an elaborately mechanical metropolis, with widely spaced skyscrapers and multiple-decked traffic ways: closer to a genuine order than the gaudy projects of the New York skyscraper architects of the same period but just as bureaucratically oriented. But despite its arid conception of the city—or because of it—the most influential treatise of its generation.

Précisions. Paris: 1930.
> The gist of Le Corbusier's South American lectures, with even more extravagant schemes for skyscraper roadtown.

La Ville Radieuse: Collection de l'Equipement de la Civilisation Machiniste. Boulogne: 1934.
> Perhaps symptomatic of a transformation from purely mechanical ideology to the more biotechnic outlook.

Concerning Town Planning. Trans. by Clive Entwistle. New Haven: 1948.
> Brief recapitulation of Le Corbusier's views, not yet modified by his work in Chandigarh.

Le Corbusier, and François de Pierrefeu. *The Home of Man*. London: 1948.

Lee, Rose Hum. *The City*. Chicago: 1955.

Lestocquoy, J. *Les Villes de Flandre et d'Italie sous le gouvernement des patriciens (XI–XV siècles)*. Paris: 1952.
> Excellent analysis of the role of the rising merchant class in certain cities of Italy and the Low Countries. But by virtue of concentration, it neglects the role of the industrial workers and craftsmen.

Lethaby, W. R. *Architecture, Nature, and Magic*. New York: 1956.
> The recasting in 1928 of a study first published in 1892, analyzing the magical and religious sources of architecture.

Form in Civilization. London: 1922. Second Ed. New York: 1957.
> Precious for its down-to-earth human qualities, mostly lacking in the brittle criticism of our own period.

Of Beautiful Cities. In *Art and Life, and the Building and Decoration of Cities*. London: 1897.

Lettmayer, Ferdinand. *Wien um die Mitte des XX. Jahrhunderts: Ein Querschnitt*. Wien: 1958.
> Massive collaborative survey of this decapitated but still vital city.

Letts, Malcolm. *Bruges and Its Past*. Second Ed. Bruges: 1926.

Levy, Gertrude Rachel. *The Gate of Horn: A Study of the Religious Conceptions of the Stone Age, and their Influence upon European Thought*. London: 1948.
> Particularly good in its interpretation of paleolithic material, in cavern and labyrinth.

Levy, Hermann. *The Economic History of Sickness and Medical Benefit Before the Puritan Revolution*. In The Economic History Review, Vol. XIII, Nos. 1 and 2, 1943.

Lichtenberg, Freiherr Reinhold von. *Haus, Dorf, Stadt*. Leipzig: 1909.
> In its time an excellent study of the early developments of house, village, and city. Though much has been added to these data during the last half-century, especially in Mesopotamia, there is still a solid core of useful research in this volume.

Lichtwark, Alfred. *Deutsche Königstädte.* Berlin: 1912.

Liepmann, Kate K. *The Journey to Work: Its Significance for Industrial and Community Life.* London: 1944.
Uncritical in its assumptions, and lacking important data on frequency of change and potentialities of choice. Confuses accessibility and variety of industries with the necessity for their agglomeration.

Lille University. *Niveaux optima des villes. Essai de définition d'après l'analyse des structures urbaines du Nord et du Palais-de-Calais.* Lille: 1959.
Fresh study of size and diversification of town clusters.

Lindblom, C. E., and R. A. Dahl. *Politics, Economics and Welfare.* New York: 1953.

Lindner, Werner, and Erich Boekle. *Die Stadt: Ihre Pflege und Gestaltung.* München: n.d.

Little, Bryan. *The Building of Bath 1747–1947: An Architectural and Social Study.* London: 1947.

Lloyd, Nathaniel. *A History of the English House: From Primitive Times to the Victorian Period.* London: 1931.
Excellent.

Lock, Max. *Civic Diagnosis: An Outline Summary of Planning Research Undertaken by the Hull Regional Survey.* Hull: 1943.
Emphasis on social factors gives this brief study distinction.

Logie, Gordon. *The Urban Scene.* London: 1954.
Pictorial analysis of the city, in terms of enclosure of space, street furnishings, silhouette, etc. Supplements Rasmussen and Gibberd.

Loosley, Elizabeth W., John R. Seeley, and R. Alexander Sim. *Crestwood Heights: A Study of the Culture of Suburban Life.* New York: 1956.

Lopez, Robert S., and Irving W. Raymond. *Medieval Trade in the Mediterranean World: Illustrative Documents Translated with Introductions and Notes.* New York: 1955.
Rich in documents, admirable in scholarly critiques.

Lot, Ferdinand. *Recherches sur la superficie des cités remontant à la période Gallo-Romaine.* In Bibliotéque de l'École des Haute Études: Nos. 287, 296, 301: Paris: 1945.

L'Evolution des Communes Françaises. In Revue Historique: Jan.–March 1949.

Louis, Paul. *Ancient Rome at Work; an economic history of Rome from the origins to the Empire.* New York: 1927.

Lunt, Paul S., and W. Warner. *The Social Life of a Modern Community.* New Haven: 1941.

Lynch, Kevin. *The Form of Cities.* In the Scientific American: April 1954.
An original contribution.

The Image of the City. Cambridge, Mass.: 1960.

Lynch, Kevin, and Lloyd Rodwin. *A Theory of Urban Form.* In JAIP: No. 4, 1958.

Lynd, Robert S. and Helen M. *Middletown*. New York: 1929.
An able survey, though weak on the geographic side and lacking in comparative cultural reference. (See Kellogg, P. U.)

Macfadyen, Dugald. *Sir Ebenezer Howard and the Town Planning Movement*. Manchester: 1933.

Mackay, Ernest. *Early Indus Civilizations*. Second ed. revised and enlarged by Dorothy Mackay. London: 1948.

MacKaye, Benton. *The New Exploration: A Philosophy of Regional Planning*. New York: 1928.
Important not merely for point of view but for suggestions of method. MacKaye, originally a forester, and the founder of the Appalachian Trail, is a regionalist in the great tradition of Thoreau, Marsh, and Shaler.

Townless Highways for the Motorist. In Harper's Magazine: Aug. 1931.
Forecast the final form of the expressway in every feature except the extravagant but often unnecessary cloverleaf.

Regional Planning. In *Encyclopaedia Britannica*. 14 Edition.

Maclear, Anne Bush. *Early New England Towns*. In *Studies in History, Economics and Public Law*. New York: 1908.

Maitland, Frederic William. *Township and Borough: together with an appendix of notes relating . . . to Cambridge*. Cambridge: 1898.

Maiuri, Amedeo. *Pompeii*. Seventh Ed. Rome: 1954.
Detailed guide.

Pompeii. Novara: 1957.
Comprehensive and well-illustrated.

Herculaneum. Fifth Ed. Rome: 1958.

Mann, Peter H. *The Socially Balanced Neighborhood Unit*. In TPR: July 1958.

Marsh, George Perkins. *The Earth as Modified by Human Action*. Third Edition. New York: 1888.
A seminal work which demonstrated man's active part in changing the face of the earth and established his moral responsibility for his frequently destructive practices. (See Sauer, Carl, and Thomas, W. L.)

Marshall, John Hubert. *Mohenjo-Daro and the Indus Civilization*. 3 vols. London: 1927.

Martin, Alfred von. *Deutsches Badewesen in vergangenen Tagen*. Jena: 1906.

*Martin, Roland. *L'Urbanisme dans la Grèce Antique*. Paris: 1956.
Continues and carries further the work of von Gerkan and others, correcting earlier preconceptions about the work of Hippodamos, and stressing the functional nature of Greek town planning. Well-illustrated.

Maunier, René. *Essais sur les Groupements Sociaux*. Paris: 1929.

L'Origine et la fonction économique des villes: étude de morphologie sociale. Paris: 1910.
Important less for what it establishes than for what it attempts.

Mayhew, Henry. *London Labor and the London Poor.* 4 vols. London: 1861–1862.
Journalistic but full of interesting material.

Mayo, W. L. B., S. D. Adshead, Patrick Abercrombie, and W. H. Thompson. *The Thames Valley from Cricklade to Staines: A Survey of Its Existing State and Some Suggestions for Its Future Preservation.* London: 1929.

McAllister, Gilbert, and Elizabeth Glen. *Town and Country Planning: A Study of Physical Environment: The Prelude to Post-War Reconstruction.* London: 1941.

McClenahan, B. A. *Communality the Urban Substitute for the Traditional Community.* In Sociology and Social Research: March–April 1946.

McDonald, William A. *The Political Meeting Places of the Greeks.* In *The Johns Hopkins University Studies in Archaeology:* No. 34: Baltimore: 1943.
Excellent.

McKelvie, Blake. *Rochester: The Water-Power City.* 2 vols. New York: 1954.

Meakin, Budgett. *Model Factories and Villages.* London: 1905.

Meiggs, Russell. *Roman Ostia.* Oxford: 1960.

Meikelham, Robert. *On the History and Art of Warming and Ventilating Rooms and Buildings.* 2 vols. London: 1845.
Important: a rare book in a poorly explored field. Needs an even more exhaustive successor.

Mercier, Louis Sebastien. *The Picture of Paris: Before and After the Revolution. Paris: 1781–1788.* Trans. London: 1929.

Memoirs of the Year 2500. Trans. Liverpool: 1802.
Utopia interesting for historic sidelights.

Merian, Matthaeus. *Topographia Bohemiae, Moraviae et Silesiae.* Frankfurt-am-Main: 1650.

*Topographia Germaniae. Frankfurt-am-Main: 1642. Reprinted in small format. München: 1935.
Handsome woodcuts of cities, with curious and sometimes historically informative data. One of the great sources of knowledge as to the state of the late medieval town. Hill and church tower took the place of the airplane for the artist. (The works of W. J. Blaeu, Sebastian Munster, and John Speed are also worth consulting when available.)

Topographia Hassiae. Franckfurt am Mayn: 1655. Facsimile Reproduction. Basel: 1959.

Metz, Friedrich. *Die Hauptstaedte.* Berlin: 1930.

Meuriot, Paul. *Des agglomerations urbaines dans l'Europe contemporaine: essai sur les causes, les conditions, les conséquences de leur développement.* Paris: 1898.
Statistical study of urban concentration in the nineteenth century with special reference to France.

Du Concept de Ville Autrefois et Aujourd'nui. In *La Vie Urbaine:* Paris: 1919.

Meyerson. Martin, and Barbara Terret (editors). *Metropolis in Ferment.* In The Annals of the American Academy of Political and Social Science: Nov. 1957.
See particularly John Ely Burchard's essay on The Urban Esthetic. (Cf. Robert Mitchell below.)

Michell, H. *The Economics of Ancient Greece.* New York: 1940.
Thorough. (See Alfred E. Zimmern for a less detailed account in a wider social setting.)

Mirabilia Romae: Indulgentie et Reliquie ad Urbis Rome in Latino. Rome: c. 1495.
Reputedly the first 'modern' guidebook. (But see Pausanias!)

Mitchell, Robert B., and Chester Rapkin. *Urban Traffic: A Function of Land Use.* New York: 1954.

Mitchell, Robert B. (editor). *Building the Future City.* In The Annals of the American Academy of Political and Social Science: Nov. 1945.
Excellent conspectus as of this date, though with little attention to the esthetic and intellectual functions of the city.

Molmenti, Pompeo G. *Venice, Its Individual Growth from the Earliest Beginning to the Fall of the Republic.* 6 vols. Trans. Chicago: 1906–1908.
Admirable.

Mookerji, Radhakumud. *Local Government in Ancient India.* Oxford: 1919.

Moret, Alexandre. *The Nile and Egyptian Civilization.* New York: 1927.

Villes Neuves et Chartes d'Immunité dans l'ancien Empire. In Journal Asiatique. Juil.–aout 1912, mars–avril 1916, nov.–dec. 1917.
Important.

Morgan, Arthur E. *The Community of the Future.* Yellow Springs, Ohio: 1957.
Assessment of the qualities and functions of the small community, on village scale.

*Morley, Sylvanus Griswold. *The Ancient Maya.* Stanford: 1946.
Notable. Has an adequate chapter on Mayan cities, whose existence is sometimes disputed.

Mukerjee, Radhakamal. *Regional Sociology.* New York: 1926.
Good conspectus.

Man and His Habitation: A Study in Social Ecology. London: 1940.

Muller, Emile. *Habitations Ouvrières et Agricoles.* Paris: 1856.

Muller, Emile, and Emile Cacheux. *Les Habitations Ouvrières en Tous Pays.* First Ed. Paris: 1879. Second Ed. 1903.
Exhaustive survey of model housing schemes for the working classes; the second edition shows many plans exhibited at the Paris Exposition of 1900. (See Hole, Christina.)

Mumford, Lewis. *City Development: Studies in Disintegration and Renewal.* New York: 1945.

The Culture of Cities. New York: 1938.
See especially chapters on Regionalism.

The Transformations of Man. New York: 1957.
An essential introduction to the present volume. See, particularly, chapters on civilized and Post-historic Man.

The Fourth Migration. In Survey Graphic: May 1925.

A World Center for the United Nations. In JRIBA: Aug. 1946.

Planning for the Phases of Life. In TPR: April 1949.

The Modern City. In *Forms and Functions of 20th Century Architecture:* Vol. IV: New York: 1952.

The Neighborhood and Neighborhood Unit. In TPR: Jan. 1954.

A New Approach to Workers' Housing. In International Labour Review: Feb. 1957.
Critical analysis of shallow fashionable alternative between high-rise metropolitan dwellings and single family suburban quarters for low cost housing.

University City. In *City Invincible.* Edited by Kraeling, Carl, and Robert Adams. Chicago: 1960.

Munster, Sebastian. *Cosmographia.* Basel: 1552.
Valuable.

Munter, Georg. *Die Geschichte der Idealstadt.* Berlin: 1928.

Muntz, E. E. *Urban Sociology.* New York: 1938.

Mylonas, George E. *Ancient Mycenae: The Capital City of Agamemnon.* Princeton: 1957.

National Council of Social Service. *The Size and Social Structure of a Town.* London: 1943.
Useful study of a much neglected subject.

National Resources Committee. *Urban Planning and Land Policies.* 2 vols. Washington: 1939.
Vol. II contains descriptions of American and European new communities.

Neumann, Erich. *The Origins and History of Consciousness.* New York: 1954.
Though vulnerable to severe methodological criticisms, it is full of bold and often fruitful intuitions that might have been repressed by a more rigorous form of proof.

The Great Mother: An Analysis of the Archetype. New York: 1955.
The concept of the archetype as a dynamic agent remains elusive, almost defiant of systematic presentation, yet this opens some fresh trails into the study of human development.

New York State Housing and Regional Planning Commission: *Final Report.* Albany: 1926.
A bench mark of regionalism in American politics. With Clarence S. Stein as Chairman and Henry Wright as Planning Adviser, the Commission made a series of important investigations, culminating in the above report. (See also MacKaye, Wright, Stein.)

Nicholas, R. *City of Manchester Plan.* London: 1945.
Notable for incorporating the time-dimension, with the planning process proceeding by stages, instead of by wholesale demolition and replacement. One of the first reports to recognize time-sequences and organic processes in city development. Methodologically a notable contribution still not adequately assimilated.

Nolen, John. *New Towns for Old*. Boston: 1927.

Nougier, Louis-René. *Géographie Humaine Historique*. Paris: 1959.
Recommended.

Oberhummer, Eugen. *Der Stadtplan: Seine Entwicklung und geographische Bedeutung*. Berlin: 1907.
Examples largely from older cities.

Olmsted, Frederick Law. *Public Parks and the Enlargement of Towns*. Cambridge, Mass.: 1870.
One of the earliest and best expositions of comprehensive park planning.

Olmsted, Frederick Law, Jr., and Theodora Kimball. *Frederick Law Olmsted, Landscape Architect: 1822–1903*. 2 vols. New York: 1928.
Professional papers and significant biographic data, but too largely centered on Central Park. An exhaustive study of Olmsted's life and work is badly needed.

Osborn, F. J. *New Towns after the War*. London: 1918. Revised ed.: 1942.
Statesmanlike proposal, no less timely in 1942 than in 1918, to provide housing, not by nondescript and sporadic town extensions or internal reconstruction, but by building balanced communities or garden cities.

Transport, Town Development and Territorial Planning of Industry. No. 20, New Fabian Research Bureau. London: 1934.
Able criticism of centralizing tendencies, with suggestions for new policy which anticipated the main lines of the Barlow Report (*q.v.*).

The Planning of Greater London: with foreword by Sir Raymond Unwin. London: 1938.
Brief but effective criticism of the chaotic expansion of London, with definite proposals for rectifying it: proposals whose wisdom not only anticipated the situation caused by the Blitz but proposed a comprehensive way of attacking it.

The Future of Town and Countryside. In The Political Quarterly: Jan.–March 1943.

Green-belt Cities: The British Contribution. London: 1946.
After Howard's own book, the best brief introduction to the Garden City idea.

Progress of the New Towns. In TCP: London: Jan. 1950.
Interim report by the editors and others.

Osterweis, Rollin G. *Three Centuries of New Haven: 1638–1938*. New Haven: 1953.

Owen, Robert. *A New View of Society*. London: 1813.

Owen, Wilfred. *The Metropolitan Transportation Problem*. Washington: 1956.
Good. (But see also Mitchell and Rapkin.)

Cities in the Motor Age. New York: 1959.
Summary of the contributions to a symposium on highway planning and metropolitan development.

Page, J. W. *From Hunter to Husbandman*. London: 1939.

Palladio, Andrea. *The Architecture of Palladio in Four Books*. Venice: 1581. Trans. London: 1742.
Indispensable clues to the baroque plan.

Pallin, Professor H. N. *Anatema over Storstaden* (*Anathema on the Great Cities*). In Bulletin 19 of the Institutionen for Vagbyggnad och Kommunikationsteknik. Stockholm: 1943.
> To judge by the summary in English, an explanation of the expansion and destruction of great cities, in terms of the economic dynamism brought in by a pecuniary economy. Likewise a withering criticism of *The Culture of Cities.*

Park, Robert. *Human Communities: the City and Human Ecology.* Glencoe, Ill.: 1952.
> Valuable contributions by one of the leaders of the Chicago School in urban sociology.

Park, Robert E., E. W. Burgess, and R. D. McKenzie. *The City: with a Bibliography by Louis Wirth.* Chicago: 1925.
> Paper relating to the city as an ecological formation.

Parke, H. W., and D. E. W. Wormell. *The Delphic Oracle.* Volume I: *History.* Oxford: 1956.
> The best book available, though—true to its enigmatic subject—it naturally leaves open many teasing and probably insoluble problems. (But see Dempsey.)

Parkins, Maurice F. *City Planning in Soviet Russia.* Chicago: 1953.

Parrot, André. *Ziggurats et Tour de Babel.* Paris: 1949.

Passarge, S. *Stadtlandschaften der Erde.* Hamburg: 1930.

*Pausanias. *Description of Greece.* 6 vols. Translated with commentary by J. G. Frazer. London: 1898.
> The *Baedeker* of the second-century Roman world, enlivened for the Romans and often deadened for posterity by voluminous commentaries on local history, legend, and myth. But a mine for those who care to work it.

Pearson, S. Vere. *London's Overgrowth: And The Causes of Swollen Towns.* London: 1939.

Peel, J. *Topographia Galliae.* Amsterdam: 1660–1663.

Peets, Elbert. *Haussmann.* In TPR: June 1927.

Current Town Planning in Washington. In TPR: Dec. 1931.

Peets, Elbert, and Werner Hegemann. *The American Vitruvius.* New York: 1922.
> Rich compendium of historic urbanism.

Pepler, George L. *Open Spaces.* In TPR: Jan. 1923.

Perkins, J. B. Ward. *Early Roman Towns in Italy.* In TPR: Oct. 1955.
> Important.

Pernoud, Régine. *Les Villes Marchandes aux XIVe et XVe Siècles. Imperialisme et Capitalisme au Moyen Age.* Paris: 1948.
> Mainly political and economic.

Perret, Jacques. *Des Fortifications et Artifices.* Frankfurt-am-Main: 1602.
> Demonstrates how completely the town was sacrificed as an entity to artillery defense.

Perrot, Georges, and Charles Chipiez. *A History of Art in Ancient Egypt.* London: 1883.

A History of Art in Chaldea and Assyria. 2 vols. New York: 1884.

Perry, Clarence. *The Neighborhood Unit: A Scheme of Arrangement for the Family-Life Community*. In Vol. VII of the *Regional Survey of New York and Its Environs*. New York: 1929.
Classic summation by a pioneer in the community center movement. (See Dahir's Bibliography. Also Bardet's analysis of the 'echelons' of community.)

Housing for the Machine Age. New York: 1939.

Peterson, Arthur Everett, and George W. Edwards. *New York as an Eighteenth Century Municipality*. 2 vols. New York: 1917.
Medieval survivals in the New World.

Peterson, Eller Theodore, et al. *Cities Are Abnormal*. Norman, Oklahoma: 1946.
More than a little naïve.

Petit-Dutaillis, Ch. *Les Communes Française au XII Siècle*. In Revue du Droit Français et Étranger: 1945, 1946.

Petrie, William Flinders. *Deshasheh*. London: 1898.

The Revolutions of Civilization. London: 1911.

Some Sources of Human History. New York: 1919.
These two little books sum up the experience and knowledge of this redoubtable archaeologist, now neglected by the generation overshadowed by his gigantic figure. Not to be overlooked by the serious student.

Pevsner, Nicolaus. *Model Houses for the Laboring Classes*. In AR: May 1943.

Pichon, Armand. *Urbanisme et societé: suivi d'une note sur la ville et le sacré*. Paris: 1942.

Pierrefeu, François de, and Le Corbusier. *The Home of Man*. London: 1948.

Pinkney, David H. *Napoleon III and the Re-building of Paris*. Princeton: 1958.
One of a number of books devoted to the appreciation and rehabilitation, not only of Napoleon III but of the redoubtable Haussmann: an act of justice postponed by their ignominious exits.

Pirenne, Henri. *Medieval Cities: Their Origins and the Revival of Trade*. Princeton: 1925.
Despite its excellent basic scholarship, a misleading interpretation, which assigns to international commerce a role in urban production and population growth it could not and did not perform. Unfortunate because of its influence upon Carl Stephenson (*q.v.*) and others.

Les Villes et Les Institutions Urbaines. 2 vols. Bruxelles: 1939.
Collections of works on city, including: *Les Villes du Moyen Age:* 1927; *Histoire de la Constitution de la Ville de Dinant au Moyen Age:* 1889; *Les Anciennes Démocraties des Pays-Bas:* 1910; and various articles.

Pirenne, Jacques. *Les Villes dans l'ancienne Egypte*. In *La Ville*. Vol. VII. *Recueils de la Société Jean Bodin*. See Société Jean Bodin.
Valuable but limited to the economic and social aspects, chiefly during the feudal periods. (See Fairman.)

Poëte, Marcel. *Comment s'est formé Paris*. Paris: 1925.
A tiny book packed with a lifetime's knowledge. See below.

*Introduction a l'Urbanisme: l'Évolution des Villes: la Leçon de l'Antiquité. Paris: 1929.
Recommended. First third analyzes the social, economic, and geographic components of the city plan; the remainder is a specific study of the city in ancient civilization, Egyptian, Mesopotamian, and Greco-Roman. The approach is organic and historical.

*Une Vie de Cité Paris: de sa Naissance à nos Jours. 3 vols. text; 1 vol. illustrations. Paris: 1924–1931. Vol. II. Paris: 1927.
A monumental work of the first order.

Urban Development. In TPR: July 1950.
Brief but significant study of urban dynamics.

*Pöhlmann, Robert. Die Uebervölkerung der Antiken Grosstädte: in Zusammenhange mit der Gesammtentwicklung städtischer Civilisation. Leipzig: 1884.
Study of overgrowth of ancient metropolises seen in the perspective of nineteenth-century congestion.

Polanyi, Karl, C. A. Avenberg, and H. W. Pearson (editors). Trade and Market in the Early Empires. Glencoe, Ill.: 1957.
Admirable in its attempt to interpret early economic systems without superimposing latterday concepts of trading and price. But confusing in its effort to identify the market system with the formal marketplace, and open to challenge at other points.

Pope, Arthur Upham. Persepolis as a Ritual City. In Archaeology, Vol. 10, No. 2: Summer, 1957.
Important in its emphasis on the religious significance of the city, as late as the time of Darius.

Powell, Lyman P. (editor). Historic Towns of New England. New York: 1898.

Historic Towns of the Middle States. New York: 1899.

Historic Towns of Southern States. New York: 1900.

Pratt, Edward Ewing. Industrial Causes of Congestion of Population in New York City. New York: 1911.

Preuss, Hugo. Die Entwicklung des Deutschen Städtewesens. Vol. I: Leipzig: 1906.
Excellent.

Preusser, Conrad. Die Wohnhäuser in Assur. In Ausgrabungen der Deutschen Orient-Gesellschaft in Assur, No. VI: Berlin: 1954.

Princeton University Conference. Urban Development and Urban Transportation. Princeton: 1957.

Pritchard, James B. The Ancient Near East in Pictures. New York: 1954.

*Ancient Near Eastern Texts. Second Ed. Princeton: 1955.
Though selected for their relationship to the Old Testament, this is the best group of translations of ancient documents of all kinds in English: a mine of important material from which I have gratefully drawn. Beautifully complemented by the picture book.

Pritchett, C. Herman. *The Tennessee Valley Authority: A Study in Public Administration.* Chapel Hill, N. C.: 1943.

*Purdom, C. B. *The Garden City: A Study in the Development of a Modern Town.* London: 1913.
A pioneer study by one of Howard's ablest colleagues.

The Building of Satellite Towns: A Contribution to the Study of Town Development and Regional Planning.* London: 1925. Revised: 1949.
Acute and exhaustive, if at times capricious in documentation. (See Osborn.)

Britain's Cities To-morrow. London: 1942.

How Should We Rebuild London? London: 1945.

(Editor). *Town Theory and Practice.* London: 1921.
Symposium by various writers, including important chapters by Sir Raymond Unwin foreshadowing his Regional Plan for London.

Quaroni, Ludovico. *Una Città Eterna—quattro lezioni da 27 secoli.* In Urbanistica: June 1959.
Major interpretation of Rome's development.

Queen, Stuart Alfred, and Lewis Francis Thomas. *The City: A Study of Urbanism in the United States.* New York: 1939.

Radig, Werner. *Frühformen der Hausentwicklung in Deutschland.* Berlin: 1958.
Good critical summary of early work on primitive dwelling house, and well-illustrated presentation of later findings.

Raleigh, Walter. *Observations Concerning the Causes of the Magnificencie and Opulency of Cities.* In *Works.* Vol. II. London: 1751.
Still not devoid of interest.

Rannells, John. *The Core of the City.* New York: 1956.
A statistical attempt to discover a central focus of urban activities.

Rapkin, Chester, and William C. Grigsby. *Residential Renewal in the Urban Core.* Philadelphia: 1960.

Rappaport, Phillipp. *Sitten und Siedlungen im Spiegel der Zeiten.* Stuttgart: 1952.

Rasmussen, Steen Eiler. *London: The Unique City.* New York: 1937.
Sympathetic interpretation of the life and architectural forms of the most lovable of great capitals.

Towns and Buildings. Cambridge, Mass.: 1951.
Beautifully imagined, keenly perceived, charmingly illustrated, by an architect who is also, in the most intimate meaning of the word, a humanist.

The Dutch Contribution.* In TPR: Oct. 1953.

Neighborhood Planning. In TPR: Jan. 1957.

Raval, Marcel. *Histoire de Paris.* Paris: 1948.

Reclus, Elisée. *The Evolution of Cities.* In Contemporary Review: Feb. 1895.

Redfield, Robert. *The Primitive World and its Transformations.* Ithaca: 1953.
Outstanding.

Reed, Henry Hope, and Christopher Tunnard. *American Skyline.* New York: 1956.
The first consecutive account of American city development, particularly stimulating and colorful by reason of its drawing on hitherto unexploited literary sources. Anti-historic in its acceptance of imitative historic forms as an antidote for coarse, un-imaginative modern design. A book whose defects somewhat outweigh its excellences. (See Tunnard, Christopher.)

Regional Survey of New York and Its Environs. 8 vols. New York: 1927–1931.

Reichow, Hans Bernard. *Organische Stadtbaukunst.* Braunschweig: 1948.

Die Autogerechte Stadt: ein Weg aus dem Verkehrs-Chaos. Ravensburg: 1959.
A German elaboration of the Radburn idea.

Reid, James S. *The Municipalities of the Roman Empire.* Cambridge: 1913.
Still useful.

Reiss, Albert J., Jr., and Paul K. Hatt. *Cities and Society. The Revised Reader in Urban Sociology.* Glencoe, Ill.: 1957.

Renard, G. F., and G. Weulersse. *Life and Work in Modern Europe: Fif-teenth to Eighteenth Centuries.* London: 1926.
Valuable.

Reps, John W. *Planning in the Wilderness: Detroit, 1805–1830.* In TPR: Jan. 1955.

William Penn and the Planning of Philadelphia. In TPR: April 1956.

Town Planning in Colonial Georgia. In TPR: Jan. 1960.

The Green Belt Concept. In TCP: July 1960.

Revesz-Alexander, Dr. Magda. *Die Alten Lagerhäuser Amsterdams: eine Kunstgeschichtliche Studie.* First Ed. Amsterdam: 1928. Second Ed.: The Hague: 1954.

Rey, Augustin. *The Healthy City of the Future.* In TPR: July 1915.
Mainly on orientation for sunlight, by one of the pioneers in this belated rediscovery of principles known to Xenophon and his contemporaries.

Rey, Augustin, Justin Pidoux, and Charles Barde. *La Science des Plans des Villes.* Paris: 1928.
Comprehensive; but in need of restatement.

Richards, J. W. *A Theoretical Basis for Physical Planning.* In AR: Feb.–March 1942.

Castles on the Ground. London: 1946.

Richardson, Benjamin War. *Hygeia: A City of Health.* London: 1876.
Though in his program of hospitalization Richardson is still in advance of contempo-rary communities, some of his most 'advanced' prescriptions are now significantly be-low standard.

Rider, Bertha Carr. *The Greek House: its history and development from the Neolithic period to the Hellenistic Age.* Cambridge: 1916.
Fuller than the publication date might suggest.

Riehl, Wilhelm Heinrich. *Culturstudien aus drei Jahrhunderten.* Stuttgart: 1859.
See essays on Das Landschaftliche Auge and the Augsburgen Studien.

Die Naturgeschichte des Volkes als Grundlage einer deutschen Social-Politik. Vol. I: *Land und Leute;* Vol. II: *Die bürgerliche Gesellschaft;* Vol. III: *Die Familie;* Vol. IV: *Wanderbuch (als zweiter Theil zu Land und Leute).* Sixth Ed. Stuttgart: 1866–1882.
Important work by a great cultural historian of the same rank as De Sanctis in Italy. See especially chapters on the city in Vols. I and IV, and on the house in Vol. III.

Riemer, Svend. *The Modern City.* New York: 1952.

Riesman, David. *The Suburban Dislocation.* In The Annals of the American Academy of Political and Social Science: Nov.: 1957.

The Lonely Crowd. New York: New Haven: 1950.

Rivet, Paul. *Maya Cities.* New York: 1954.

Roberts, Lewes. *The Treasure of Trafficke.* London: 1641.

Robinson, Charles Mulford. *The Improvement of Towns and Cities.* New York: 1901.

Modern Civic Art, or The City Made Beautiful. New York: 1903.
An excellent book in its time and still worth consulting.

The Width and Arrangement of Streets: A Study in Town Planning. New York: 1911.
Pioneer studies following Olmsted.

Robson, William A. *The Government and Misgovernment of London.* London: 1939.
Penetrating.

Robson, William A. (editor). *Great Cities of the World: Their Government, Politics and Planning.* New York: 1955.

Rochette, M. Raoul. *Histoire critique de l'établissements des colonies Grècques.* 4 vols. Paris: 1815.
So good in its time it apparently has discouraged further investigation.

Rodgers, Cleveland, and Rebecca Rankin. *New York: The World's Capital City.* New York: 1948.

Rodwin, Lloyd. *The British New Towns Policy: Problems and Implications.* Cambridge, Mass.: 1956.
Scholarly appraisal, appreciative of the British New Towns policy, yet not altogether free from misleading preconceptions as to Howard's original intentions and premature conclusions about the final outcome of the policy. (See F. J. Osborn's counterattack in *Land Economics:* Aug. 1956.)

Rogers, E. N., J. Tyrwhitt, and J. L. Sert (editors). *The Heart of the City.* New York: 1952.

Romanelli, Pietro. *The Palatinate.* Rome: 1956.

The Roman Forum. Rome: 1959.

Roper, Marion Wesley. *The City and the Primary Group.* Chicago: 1935.

Rosenau, Helen. *The Ideal City*. London: 1959.
Excellent in intention, disappointing in execution.

Rosenstock, Eugen. *Werkstatt aus Siedlung: Untersuchungen Uber den Leben-straum des Industrie Arbeiters*. Berlin: 1922.

Rostovtzeff, Michael I. *Out of the Past of Greece and Rome*. New Haven: 1932.
See chapters on A City Arisen and Caravan Cities.

The Social and Economic History of the Hellenistic World. 3 vols. Oxford: 1941.
Meager references to the city.

Rostovtzeff, Michael I., and others. *Urban Land Economics*. Ann Arbor: 1922.
Note especially Rostovtzeff on Cities in the Ancient World, and Dr. Mary Shine's Urban Land in the Middle Ages.

Roupnel, Gaston. *La Ville et la Campagne au XVIIe Siècle*. Paris: 1922.

Rouse, Clive. *Old Towns of England*. London: 1936.

Roussel, Pierre. *Delos: Colonie Athénienne*. In Bibliothèque Française d'-Athène et de Rome. Paris: 1916.

Rowntree, B. Seebohm. *Poverty: A Study of Town Life*. New York: 1901.

Poverty and Progress. London: 1942.
Two studies of York, a generation apart. Significant.

Royal Institute of British Architects. *Transactions: the Town Planning Conference, London 10–15 October 1910*. London: 1911.
An epoch-marking conference, whose papers rival those of later meetings in Antwerp and Berlin. See Hegemann.

Ruskin, John. *The Stones of Venice*. 2 vols. London: 1851.
Social interpretation of architecture and architectural interpretation of societies both have their essential beginnings here, but the neglect of the civic whole shows the characteristic limitations of this period.

Russell, Josiah Cox. *Late Ancient and Medieval Population*. Philadelphia: 1958.

Ryerman, D. (editor). *Country Towns in a Future England*. London: 1944.
Beginning of a collective assertion by British country towns of their claims vis-à-vis the greater cities.

*Saarinen, Eliel. *The City: Its Growth, its Decay, its Future*. New York: 1943.
Perspicuous plea for decentralized reorganization of great centers, by a distinguished architect and planner.

Samonà, Giuseppe. *L'Urbanistica e l'Avvenire della Città*. Bari: 1959.

Sanders, S. E., and A. J. Rabuck. *New City Patterns: The Analysis of and a Technique for Urban Reintegration*. New York: 1946.

*Sauer, Carl O. *Agricultural Origins and Dispersals*. Bowman Memorial Lectures: Series Two. New York: 1952.
Wide observation and acute reasoning that reinterprets the whole process of domestication and human settlement. An outstanding contribution by the dean of American geographers, with a command of broader prospects that links him closely to George Perkins Marsh.

Savage, Wm. *The Making of Our Towns.* London: 1952.

Savoia, Umberto. *Turin, the "Regular" Town.* In TPR: June 1927.

Schaal, Hans. *Ostia: Der Welthafen Roms.* Bremen: 1957.
Good.

Schedel, Hartmann. *Das Buch der Chroniker.* (*The Nuremberg Chronicle.*) Nürnberg: 1493.
Richly illustrated by woodcuts of cities done by Michael Wohlgemuth. The technique is rough and the factual accuracy dubious: one stock cut, for example, is used over and over again to represent various cities.

Schevill, Ferdinand. *History of Florence: From the Founding of the City through the Renaissance.* New York: 1936.

Schlesinger, Arthur Meier. *The Rise of the City: 1878–1898.* New York: 1933.
Sound interpretation of American history with a view to various urban manifestations; but without grasp of the city as an entity. (See Bridenbaugh.)

Schmokel, Hartmut. *Ur, Assur und Babylon: Drei Jahrtausende im Zwei-stromland.* Stuttgart: 1955.
Historical study with occasional glimpses of the city. (See Contenau.)

Schmoller, G. *Deutsches Städtewesen in Alterer Zeit.* In Bonner Staatswissenschaftliche Untersuchungen. Heft 5. Bonn: 1922.

Schneider, Arthur. *Stadtumfange in Altertum.* In Geog. Zeitschrift: 1, 1895.

Schultz, Alwin. *Das hausliche Leben der Europäischen Kulturvolker vom Mittelalter bis zur zweiten Hälfte des XVIII Jahrhunderts.* München: 1903.

*Schultze-Naumburg, Paul. *Kulturarbeiten.* Vol. 1: *Hausbau;* Vol. 2: *Garten;* Vol. 3: *Dorfer und Kolonien;* Vol. 4: *Städtebau;* Vol. 5: *Kleinburger-hauser.*

Die Gestaltung der Landschaft durch den Menschen: Vol. 7. Part 1: *Wege und Strassen.* Part 2: *Die Pflanzenwelt und ihre Bedeutung im Land-schaftsbilde.* Vol. 8. Part 3: *Der Geologische Aufbau der Landschaft und die Nutzbarmachung der Mineralien.* Part 4: *Die Wasserwirtschaft.* Vol. 9. Part 5: *Industrie.* Part 6: *Siedelungen.* München: 1916.
A work of fundamental importance upon the artful and orderly transformation of the environment by man. One of the original monuments of its generation.

Schumacher, Fritz. *Darstellungen des Soziologischen Zustandes im Hamburg-isch-Preussischen Landesplanungsgebiet.* Hamburg: 1931.

Wesen und Organisation der Landesplanung im Hamburgisch-Preussischen Planungsgebiet. Hamburg: 1932.
Two of a series of reports on land planning in the Hamburg area, by the outstanding architect-planner of his generation in Germany.

Das Werden einer Wohnstadt: Bilder vom neuen Hamburg. Hamburg: 1932.

Schwann, Bruno. *Town Planning and Housing Throughout the World.* Berlin: 1935.
An International Symposium. (See Hegemann for an earlier and better one.)

Scott, Mel. *The San Francisco Bay Area: A Metropolis in Perspective.* Berkeley: 1959.
Well-rounded study, worthy of wide imitation in other urban areas.

Scott Report. *Report of Committee on Land Utilization in Rural Areas.* H. M. Stationery Office. London: 1942.
Chiefly concerned with safeguards for agriculture and countryside interests in applying Barlow Report policy of industrial dispersal.

Scotto, Francesco. *Itinerario d'Italia: ove si Decrivono Tutte le Principali Città d'Italia.* Rome: 1747.

Seidensticker, Wilhelm. *Umbau der Städte.* Essen: 1959.

Self, Peter. *Cities in Flood: The Problems of Urban Growth.* London: 1957.
Intelligent and well-rounded presentation of this complex subject.

Sert, José Luis. *Can Our Cities Survive? An A B C of Urban Problems.* Cambridge, Mass.: 1942.
Development of a collaborative study made by the Congrès International des Architectes Modernes (C.I.A.M.), handicapped by the original limitations of the program, which restricted the functions of the city to housing, transportation, recreation, and business.

The Human Scale in City Planning. In *The New Architecture and City Planning* (Paul Zucker, editor): New York: 1944.

Sestieri, Pellegrino Claudio. *Paestum.* Rome: 1958.

Shambaugh, Bertha. *Amana that was and Amana that is.* Iowa City: 1927.
Description of the most successful of utopian communities, notable for both civic and regional plan. A fuller study while the evidence is still accessible is urgently needed. The bypassing of this extraordinary experiment is a reproach to scholarship.

Sharon, Arieh. *Planning in Israel.* In TPR: April 1952.

Collective Settlements in Israel. In TPR: Jan. 1955.

Sharp, Thomas. *Town and Countryside: Some Aspects of Urban and Rural Development.* New York: 1933.
Vigorous argumentative book on the principles of urban and rural planning by an able planner, somewhat marred by a perverse animus against the garden city, which he equates with bad open suburban planning.

Town Planning. Harmondsworth: 1940.

Cathedral City: A Plan for Durham. London: 1945.

Exeter Phoenix: A Plan for Rebuilding. London: 1946.
Both these studies are admirable in form as well as content: while they stress the physical and esthetic sides of planning, they do not overlook the social and political elements.

Shillabar, Caroline. *Edward I: Builder of Towns.* In Speculum, No. 3: 1947.

Siedler, Ed. Jobst. *Markischer Städtebau im Mittelalter: Beitrage zur Geschichte der Entstehung, Planung und baulichen Entwicklung der markischen Stadte.* Berlin: 1914.
Thorough work on German colonization towns.

Sieffert, P. Archangelus. *Altdorf: Geschichte von Abtei und Dorf.* Strasbourg: 1950.
Though this monastic community never developed into a city, its history illustrates a process carried further in other places. The scholar who follows this up will perform a service to urban history.

Sigerist, Henry E. *Landmarks in the History of Hygiene.* New York: 1956.

Simmel, Georg. *The Great City and Cultural Life.* In *Die Grosstadt:* Dresden: 1903.

Simon, Ernest (Lord Simon of Wythenshawe). *The Re-Building of Manchester.* New York: 1935.
By the wise industrialist who played a leading part in Manchester's resurgence.

Simon, John. *Reports relating to the Sanitary Condition of the City of London.* London: 1854.
Important documentation.

Sinclair, Robert. *Metropolitan Man: The Future of the English.* London: 1937.

Singer, Charles, E. J. Holmyard, and A. R. Hall (editors). *A History of Technology.* Vol. I: *From Early Times to Fall of Ancient Empires.* Vol. III. *The Mediterranean Civilizations and the Middle Ages.* Oxford: 1954.
Much useful material in these volumes, if not in the remaining three.

Sisi, Enrico. *L'urbanistica negli studi di Leonardo da Vinci.* Firenze: 1953.
Gathering together of Leonardo's sundry notes, until now available only in scattered references in the Notebooks.

Sismondi, Jean C. L. *History of the Italian Republics in the Middle Ages.* Recast and supplemented by William Boulting. London: 1895. First published in 16 vols. in 1815.

*Sitte, Camillo. *Der Städtebau nach seinen kunstlerischen Grundsatzen.* Wien: 1899. Fifth Ed. 1922. Trans. but abridged. New York: 1935.
Analysis of city forms from the esthetic and social point of view: the first real appreciation of the method of layout in the medieval city, particularly in the squares with their frequently asymmetrical arrangement.

Sjobert, Gideon. *The Preindustrial City: Past and Present.* Glencoe, Illinois: 1960.

Sly, John Fairfield. *Town Government in Massachusetts, 1620–1930.* Cambridge: 1930.

Smailes, A. E. *The Geography of Towns.* London: 1953.
Admirable introduction. (See also Griffith, Taylor, Dickinson, and Hassert.)

Smith, Adam. *An Inquiry into the Nature and Causes of the Wealth of Nations.* 2 vols. London: 1776.
Chapters I and III in Book III show that Smith had a fundamental understanding of the political economy in its fullest sense, including the economy of cities and public works. The dropping out of this view from the later economists was symptomatic. But Marshall, and still more, Bücher, Sombart, and N. S. B. Gras have helped restore the city.

Smith, E. Baldwin. *Architectural Symbolism of Imperial Rome and the Middle Ages.* Princeton: 1956.

Smith, Robert. *Colonial Towns of Spanish and Portuguese America*. In JSAH: Dec. 1955.

Smith, Wilfred. *Industry and the Countryside*. In TPR: Oct. 1954.

Snow, W. Brewster (editor). *The Highway and the Landscape*. New Brunswick, N. J.: 1959.

Société Jean Bodin, La. *La Ville*. Première partie. *Institutions administratives et judiciaires*. Bruxelles: 1954. Deuxieme partie. *Institutions économiques et sociales*. Bruxelles: 1955.
These papers by divers scholars cover a wide historic and geographic range.

Sombart, Werner. *Der Moderne Kapitalismus*. 4 vols. München: 1902–1927.
See Vol. II, Second Part, on Ursprung und Wesen der Modernen Stadt, for his theory of the city: also Chapter 25, Vol. III (first half) for relation of population movements and city building. Sombart, like Bücher, Schmoller, and Max Weber, has much to say about the city; and his notion of the city as primarily a group of consumers, is logically and historically correct—as opposed to the usual emphasis upon the market and the function of exchange as primary.

Der Begriff der Stadt und das Wesen der Stadtebildung. In Brauns Archiv: Vol. 4: 1907.

Krieg und Kapitalismus. München: 1913.

Luxus und Kapitalismus. München: 1913.
Both these books throw much light on the baroque city.

Soria y Mata, Arturo. *La Ciudad Lineal*. Madrid: 1931.
Suggested as early as 1882. (For full account see Collins, George.)

*Sorre, Max. *Les Fondements de la Géographie Humaine*. Vol. I: *Les Fondements Biologiques*. Vol. II: *Les Fondements Techniques*. Vol. III: *L'-Habitat*. Paris: 1950–1952.
Admirable in every aspect of human geography.

Speed, John. *England, Wales, Scotland and Ireland*. London: 1627.

Speiser, Ephraim Avigdor. *The Beginning of Civilization in Mesopotamia*. In *The Beginning of Civilization in the Orient*. American Oriental Society Symposium. Baltimore: 1939.
(See also his translations in Pritchard.)

Spengler, Oswald. *The Decline of the West*. München: 1920. Trans. 2 Vols. New York: 1928.
Important because of emphasis upon the role of the city as a formative factor in culture.

Spielvogel, Samuel. *A Selected Bibliography in City and Regional Planning*. Washington: 1951.
Still useful, particularly in areas omitted or poorly represented in present notes.

Staley, Eugene. *World Economy in Transition*. New York: 1938.

Stamp, L. Dudley. *Man and the Land*. London: 1955.

Stanislavski, D. *The Origin and Spread of the Grid Pattern Towns*. In Geographical Review: 1946.

Early Spanish Town Planning in the New World. In Geographical Review: 1947.

Starkey, Thomas. *England in the Reign of Henry VIII: A Dialogue between Cardinal Pole and Thomas Lupset.* Written between 1536–38. London: 1878.

*Stein, Clarence S. *New Towns for America.* New York: 1951.
A critical and self-critical study of the series of housing and planning experiments in which Stein played a leading part, from Sunnyside Gardens to Radburn, from Greenbelt to Baldwin Hills Village. Indispensable for the serious student. (See Wright, Henry.)

Stockholm Builds a New Town. In Planning: 1952.

Stephenson, Carl. *Borough and Town: A Study of Urban Origins in England.* Cambridge, Mass.: 1933.
A thorough study, with due reference to the growth of the medieval town on the continent; but unhappily over-influenced by Pirenne.

Stephenson, Flora and Gordon. *Community Centres.* London: 1946.

Stephenson, Gordon. *Town Planning, Contemporary Problem of Civic Design.* In TPR: July 1949.

Design in Its Relation to Economic Factors. In TPR: Jan. 1953.

The Wrexham Experiment. In TPR: Jan. 1954.

Stephenson, Gordon, and others. *The Planning of Residential Areas.* In JRIBA: Feb. 1946.

Stewart, Cecil. *Naarden—Stellar City.* In JTPI: April 1953.
Study of one of the most perfect of the surviving baroque fortification layouts, a veritable lily-pad town. See Plate 49.

Stöckli, Arnold. *Die Stadt: Ihr Wesen und Ihre Problematik; eine Soziologische und Stadtebauliche Betrachtung.* Köln: 1954.

Stokes, I. N. P. *Iconography of Manhattan.* 6 vols. New York: 1915–1928.
Invaluable source book, unfortunately produced only in limited edition.

*Stow, John. *A Survey of London: Conteyning the Originall, Antiquity, Increase, Modern Estate, and Description of That City, etc.* First Ed. London: 1528. Second Ed. 1603. (Reprinted in Everyman Series.) Sixth Ed., revised and edited by John Strype. 2 vols. London: 1754–1755.
One of the classics in urban historiography.

Sullenger, T. Earl. *Sociology of Urbanization: A Study in Urban Society.* Ann Arbor: 1956.

Tait, James. *Mediaeval Manchester and the Beginnings of Lancashire.* Manchester: 1904.

The Medieval English Borough: Studies on Its Origins and Constitutional History. Manchester: 1936.

Tanzer, Helen H. *The Common People of Pompeii: A Study of the Graffiti.* In The Johns Hopkins University Studies in Archaeology. No. 29. Baltimore: 1939.
From the signs, notices, and random scrawls left abundantly on the walls of the destroyed city, the author pieces together a picture of the daily life of this provincial town, which partly makes up for the lack of other kinds of literary references to Roman provincial life.

Tappan, Henry P. *The Growth of Cities.* New York: 1855.

Tarn, W. W. *Hellenistic Civilisation.* London: 1927. Third Ed. revised, with
G. T. Griffith: 1952.
Has a whole chapter on the Greek cities of this period, plus a good discussion of
Monarchy, City, and League. Admirable. (But for special light on role of kings, see
Jones, A. H. M.)

Taylor, E. A. *The Relation of Open Country Population to Villages and
Cities.* Ithaca: 1934.

Taylor, Graham Romeyn. *Satellite Cities: A Study of Industrial Suburbs.* New
York: 1915.
An early study of the internal decentralization of the metropolis through the building of an industrial rim for the heavy industries. Proves that tendencies now so
palpable have in fact been long at work.

Taylor, Griffith. *Environment, Village and City: A Genetic Approach to Urban Geography; with Some Reference to Possibilism.* In the Annals of
the Association of American Geographers: March 1942.

*Urban Geography: A Study of Site, Evolution, Pattern and Classification
in Villages, Towns and Cities.* London: 1949.

Taylor, William Cooke. *Notes on a Tour in the Manufacturing Districts of
Lancashire in a Series of Letters to His Grace the Archbishop of Dublin.*
London: 1842.

*Factories and Factory System: from Parliamentary Documents and Personal
Examination.* London: 1844.

Terpenning, Walter A. *Village and Open Country Neighborhoods.* New York:
1931.
A pioneer study that still needs to be followed up and enlarged.

Thackrah, Charles Turner. *The Effects of the Principal Arts, Trades, and Professions, and of Civic States and Habits of Living, on Health and Lon-
gevity with a Particular Reference to the Trades and Manufactures of
Leeds.* London: 1831.
Valuable for sidelights on the Industrial Town.

Thomas, James Henry. *Town Government in the Sixteenth Century.* London:
1933.

*Thomas, William L., Jr. (editor). *Man's Role in Changing the Face of the
Earth.* Chicago: 1956.
This book is the exhaustive record of a memorable symposium, dedicated in spirit to
George Perkins Marsh and presided over by his distinguished successor, Carl Sauer.
See especially the following articles:
Brown, Harrison. *Technological Denudation.*
Glikson, Artur. *Recreational Land Use.*
Harris, Chauncey D. *The Pressure of Residential-Industrial Land Use.*
Klim, Lester E. *Man's Ports and Channels.*
Landsberg, H. E. *The Climate of Towns.*
Mumford, Lewis. *Natural History of Urbanization.*
Sauer, Carl O. *The Agency of Man on Earth.*
Thompson, Warren A. *The Spiral of Population.*

Thompson, Homer A. *Stoa of Attalos.* In Archaeology: Autumn 1949.
Detailed examination of Pergamon's contribution to Hellenistic Athens.

The Agora at Athens and the Greek Market Place. In JSAH: Dec. 1954.

Thompson, J. Eric S. *The Rise and Fall of Maya Civilization.* Norman, Okla.: 1954.
Supplements Morley; but not as full in its treatment of the city. (See Rivet.)

Thomson, Robert Ellis. *The History of the Dwelling House and Its Future.* Philadelphia: 1914.
An early attempt based on insufficient data: the subject still waits its master.

Thornbury, Walter. *Old and New London: A Narrative of its History, its People, and its Places.* 6 vols. London and New York: n.d.
By internal evidence the last chapter was written in 1878. Its closeness to some of the material makes up at times for its lack of scholarly care.

Thorndike, Edward L. *Your City.* New York: 1939.
A suggestive attempt to apply a value-scale to the comparative achievements of American cities.

Thorndike, Lynn. *Sanitation, Baths, and Street-cleaning in the Middle Ages and Renaissance.* Reprinted from *Speculum.* Cambridge, Mass.: 1928.
Important critical judgment that should wipe away ignorance and misinterpretation in a field where popular American scholarship, even now, remains deficient.

Tomkinson, Donald. *The Marseilles Experiment.* In TPR: Oct. 1953.

The Landscape City. In JTPI: May 1959.

Tout, Thomas Frederick. *The Collected Papers of Thomas F. Tout: with a Memoir and Bibliography.* Manchester: 1934.
See especially the chapters on Medieval Town Planning and on the origin of the English bureaucracy. While Tout's survey of the new towns and bastides opened new ground, his contribution is weakened by the fact that he held a restricted notion as to what constitutes plan.

Toutain, J. *Les cités Romaine de la Tunisie: Essai sur l'histoire de la colonisation romaine dans L'Afrique du Nord.* Paris: 1896.
Admirable.

Town and Country Planning Association (then Garden City Association). *Evidence to Barlow Royal Commission.* London: 1938.
Relates Garden City thesis to national planning policy. Influenced findings of Commission.

Town Planning Institute. *Report on Planning in the London Region.* London: 1956.
Brief but comprehensive.

Town Planning Review, The. Liverpool: 1911–current.
Invaluable.

Toy, Sidney. *A History of Fortification: from 3000 BC to AD 1700.* London: 1955.
Suggestive but incomplete; witness the omission of Vauban, the man who consummated and undermined the art.

Toynbee, Arnold Joseph. *A Study of History.* 10 vols. London: 1934.
Good in its analysis of the general environment; but so far inadequate because of failure to recognize the critical importance of the city and the cloister in the development of both institutional forms and personality. (See Spengler.)

Tucker, T. G. *Life in Ancient Athens.* New York: 1906.
Elementary but still useful.

Tunnard, Christopher. *The City of Man.* New York: 1953.
Much fresh material on the city and its planning during the last few centuries, often brilliantly presented. Properly critical of the anti-esthetic bias of much of what passes for town planning and modern architecture today: yet with a tendency to indulge too charitably the infirmities of a nostalgic eclecticism that evades the unevadable challenges of our time for continuity and rational order. While the caprices of judgment make this book stimulating, it is perhaps not safe to put in the hands of the untutored. Still, its excellences sufficiently outweigh its defects. (See Reed, H. H.)

Tyrwhitt, Jacqueline (editor). *Patrick Geddes in India.* London: 1947.
An admirable selection.

Size and Spacing of Urban Communities. In JAIP: Summer 1949.

*Unger, Eckhard. *Das Stadtbild von Assur.* In Der Alte Orient, Vol. 27, No. 3.
Description of the layout and contents of the city of Assur based on both excavations and the text of a description of the city from the seventh century B.C. This combination of evidence is both rare and important. (See Herodotus.)

United States Public Health Service. *Air Pollution in Donora, Pa.* Public Health Bulletin 306. Washington: 1949.

United States Resettlement Administration. *Greenbelt Towns: A Demonstration in Suburban Planning.* Washington: 1936.

Unwin, Raymond. *High Building in Relation to Town Planning.* In JAIA: March 1924.
A classic paper.

Nothing Gained by Overcrowding. London: n.d. c. 1903.
Another classic, which laid the foundation for the open plans of British housing estates after 1920. Even more significantly, it demonstrated the reckless sacrifice of recreation space to streets and roads in most current planning, and thus paved the way for Stein and Wright's superblock.

The Housing Problem: How Planned Distribution May Prevent Crowding. In Journal of the Royal Sanitary Institute. No. 10, 1936.

Town Planning in Practice: An Introduction to the Art of Designing Cities and Suburbs. First Ed. London: 1909. Republished: 1932.
Coming after Olmsted, Unwin was (with his partner, Barry Parker) the outstanding town planner of his generation. This book is a compendium of his background and his experience; but Unwin's most effective contributions were in terms of open planning. A generous appraisal of his life and work is badly needed.

Urban Redevelopment: The Pattern and the Background. Paper read before the Town Planning Institute, 12 July 1935.

Urbanisme et Habitation. Special number: July–Dec. 1953.
On Haussmann and his planning.

Urbanistica: Rivista Trimestrale dell'Istituto Nazionale di Urbanistica. Turin: 1930–current.
Over the years this review has published a series of important monographs, with handsome illustrations, maps, and plans, dealing with the development of cities, mainly but not exclusively Italian. Recommended.

Uthwatt Report. *Report of Expert Committee on Compensation and Betterment.* H.M. Stationery Office. London: 1942.
    Masterly analysis of problem of increases and reductions of land values involved in dispersal planning and shifts of population.

Vance, Rupert B., and Nicholas J. Demerath (editors). *The Urban South.* Chapel Hill, N. C.: 1954.

Van der Bent, T. J. *The Problem of Hygiene in Man's Dwellings.* New York: 1920.

Vandier, J. *D'Archéologie Egyptienne.* Paris: 1955.

Van Traa, Ir. C. (editor). *Rotterdam: de geschiednenis van tien jaren weder opbouw.* Rotterdam: 1955.
    The rebuilding of Rotterdam.

Vernon, Raymond. *Metropolis: 1985.* New York: 1960.
    Summary volume of a series of detailed studies of metropolitan New York. See for comparison the Regional Survey of New York by Thomas Adams and his associates.

Vidal de la Blache, Paul Marie Joseph. *Principles of Human Geography.* Trans. New York: 1926.

Vie Urbaine, La. Periodical. 1919–.
    Originally published by l'Institut d'Histoire, de Géographie, et d'Économie Urbaine de la Ville de Paris. After 1923 by l'Institut d'Urbanisme de Université de Paris.

Vigman, Fred K. *The Crisis of Cities.* Washington: 1955.

Villes d'art Célèbres, Les. 76 vols. Paris: 1906–1936.
    Mainly useful for pictorial documentation. (See also Hürlimann.)

Violich, Francis. *Cities of Latin America: Housing and Planning to the South.* New York: 1944.
    Pioneer reconnaissance.

Visser, Elizabeth. *Polis en Stad.* Amsterdam: 1947.

Voelcker, H. (editor). *Die Stadt Goethes: Frankfurt am Main im XVIII Jahrhundert.* Frankfurt am Main: 1932.

Voigt, A. H., and P. Goldner. *Kleinhaus und Mietskaserne.* Berlin: 1905.
    Defense of speculation in land and speculative building. Eberstadt called it a "catechism for speculatordom."

Volckers, Otto. *Dorf und Stadt: Eine deutsche Fibel.* Leipzig: 1944.
    Demonstrates the close relation of village and city in pattern and design in Central Europe.

Wade, Richard C. *The Urban Frontier: The Rise of Western Cities 1790–1830.* Cambridge, Mass.: 1960.

Wagner, Martin. *Wirtschaftlicher Staedtebau.* Stuttgart: 1911.
    Wagner, one time city planner of Berlin, had both technical competence and theoretic grasp.

Wagner, Otto. *Die Grosstadt: eine Studie.* Wien: 1911.

Wales, H. G. Quaritch. *The Mountain of God: A Study in Early Religion and Kingship.* London: 1953.

Walker, Robert A. *The Planning Function in Urban Government.* Chicago: 1941.

Warner, W. L., and Paul S. Lunt. *The Social Life of a Modern Community*. New Haven: 1941.

Wattjes, J. H., and P. A. Warners. *Amsterdam: vier eeurwen bouwkunst*. Amsterdam: 1956.
Synopsis in English. Survey of four centuries of architecture that unfortunately stops short with the nineteenth century.

Webb, Sidney and Beatrice. *The Manor and the Borough*. Parts 1 and 2. New York: 1908.

English Local Government from the Revolution to the Municipal Corporation Act. The Story of the King's Highway. New York: 1913.

*Webber, Adna Ferrin. *The Growth of Cities in the Nineteenth Century: A Study in Statistics*. New York: 1899.
Classic pioneer work: but the whole subject needs careful re-study.

Weber, Adolf. *Die Grosstadt: und ihre Sozialen Probleme*. Leipzig: 1908.

Weber, Alfred. *Theory of the Location of Industries*. Chicago: 1929.
Attempt to work out theoretical distribution in terms of costs of transportation and labor, working regionally, and agglomerative factors within industry. (But see later work by Florence, P. Sargant.)

Weber, Max. *Wirtschaft und Gesellschaft*. 2 vols. 2nd Ed. Tubingen: 1925.
Second Part of Vol. I has chapter on the city.

The City. Translated. Glencoe, Ill.: 1958.
Excellent for its day (1921) but no longer adequate as a general theory of the city. See Sjobert, Gideon.

Weeden, William B. *Economic and Social History of New England, 1620–1789*. 2 vols. Boston: 1890.
Extraordinarily good, even now.

Wehrwein, George S., and Richard T. Ely. *Land Economics*. New York: 1940.

*Wells, Herbert George. *Anticipations of the Reaction of Mechanical and Scientific Progress upon Human Life and Thought*. London: 1902.
The chapters on locomotion and the probable diffusion of great cities are landmarks in social prophecy.

A Modern Utopia. London: 1905.

Tono-Bungay. London: 1909.

New Machiavelli. London: 1911.
Noteworthy descriptions of London here and in *Tono-Bungay*.

West Midland Group. *Conurbation: A Planning Survey of Birmingham and the Black Country*. London: 1948.

Westergaard, John. *Journeys to Work in the London Region*. In TPR: April 1957.
Important because it brings out many factors overlooked in Kate Liepman's study.

Wetzel, Friedrich. *Die Stadtmauern von Babylon*. Leipzig: 1930.
See article herein by Eckhard Unger: *Zur Topographie Babylon nach der Keilinschriftlichen Ueberlieferung*.

*Wheeler, Mortimer. *The Indus Civilization*. In the *Cambridge History of India*. Cambridge: 1953.
Excellent summary of present knowledge by the able sometime director-general of archaeology in India.

Wheeler, William Morton. *The Social Insects and Their Origin and Evolution*. New York: 1928.

Emergent Evolution and the Development of Societies. New York: 1928.
Brief but important discussion of the doctrine of emergence, as applied to societies.

Whitaker, Charles Harris. *From Rameses to Rockefeller*. New York: 1934.
A social interpretation of architecture by a challenging critic whose work as editor of the *Journal of the American Institute of Architects* put the housing and community-planning movement in the United States on new foundations.

White, Richard W. *A Study of the Relationship between Mental Health and Residential Environment*. Cambridge, Mass.: 1957.

White, William H., Jr. *The Exploding Metropolis*. New York: 1958.
Argues the case for the city as meeting place against Suburbia and high rise regimentation.

Wibberley, G. P. *Agriculture and Urban Growth: A Study of the Competition for Rural Land*. London: 1959.

Wiener, Norbert. *The Human Use of Human Beings*. First ed. New York: 1950. Revised: 1954.
Important in regard to the city as communications center.

Wiese, Leopold von. *Ländliche Siedlungen*. In *Handworterbuch der Soziologie*. Stuttgart: 1931.

Willey, Gordon R. (editor). *Prehistoric Settlement Patterns in the New World*. Viking Fund Publications in Anthropology. No. 23. New York: 1956.
Studies by many authorities, not least the editor, in a field heretofore neglected by anthropologists.

Williams, James M. *An American Town*. New York: 1906.
A pioneer study. (See Lynd, Robert.)

Williams-Ellis, Clough. *England and the Octopus*. London: 1928.
Virile attack on the destroyers of landscape.

Wilson, John A. *The Burden of Egypt: An Interpretation of Ancient Egyptian Culture*. Chicago: 1951.
Emphasis on mobility and adaptation corrects once popular view of an entirely rigid and arrested culture.

Wirth, Louis. *Community Life and Social Policy: Selected Papers*. Chicago: 1956.
Includes his notable discussions of Localism, Regionalism, and Centralization, The Metropolitan Region as a Planning Unit, and Urbanism as a Way of Life. One of the best products of the Chicago school of sociology, but with an open bias in favor of the big city.

Wittfogel, Karl A. *Oriental Despotism: A Comparative Study of Total Power*. New Haven: 1957.
The early chapters on the relation of hydraulic civilization to the growth of concentrated state power have relevance for the interpretation of the rise of the city.

Wolf, Gustav. *Die Schöne Deutsche Stadt.* Vol. I: *Mitteldeutsch.* München: 1911. Vol. II: *Suddeutsch.* München: 1912. Vol. III: *Norddeutsch.* München: 1913.

Wood, Edith Elmer. *The Housing of the Unskilled Wage Earner.* New York: 1919.

Slums and Blighted Areas in the United States. Washington: 1936.

Introduction to Housing: Facts and Principles. Washington: 1940.
Succinct summary by a zealous worker for better housing. (See Bauer, Catherine.)

Wood, Robert C. *Suburbia: Its People and Their Politics.* Boston: 1959.
Fresh study of suburbia as the modern embodiment of the small community; but ambivalent in its values and curiously self-contradictory in its conclusions.

Woolley, Leonard (Sir). *Excavations at Ur: A Record of Twelve Years' Work.* London: 1954.
An amplification and revision of the findings first published in *Ur of the Chaldees.* (See also the more generalized interpretations by Childe and Frankfort.)

Alalakh: An Account of the Excavations at Tell Atchana in the Hatay, 1937–1949. Oxford: 1955.

Woolston, Howard. *The Urban Habit of Mind.* In American Journal of Sociology: March 1912.

Metropolis: A Study of Urban Communities. New York: 1938.

Wright, Frank Lloyd. *The Disappearing City.* New York: 1932.
Brief exposition of a possible type of urban organization in which agriculture would be the fundamental occupation and an acre the minimum area occupied by a family. Clear anticipation (romantically rationalized) of the contemporary exurban sprawl.

Frank Lloyd Wright on Architecture: Selected Writings 1894–1940. Edited with an introduction by Frederick Gutheim. New York: 1941.

The Living City. New York: 1958.

*Wright, Henry. *Report of the Commission of Housing and Regional Planning for the State of New York.* Albany: 1926.
The pioneer American study in the regional background of urban development. (But see also Abercrombie's classic reports on Doncaster and The Deeside.)

Re-Housing Urban America. New York: 1934.
Early study by one of the ablest planners of his generation. (See Stein, *New Towns for America.*)

Wright, Henry Myles. *The Motor Vehicle and Civic Design.* In JRIBA: Jan. 1957.

Wright, Lawrence. *Clean and Decent: The Fascinating History of the Bathroom and the Water Closet.* London: 1960.
Contents more scholarly than the title: an effective first flushing.

*Wycherley, R. E. *How the Greeks Built Cities.* London: 1949.
The best work in English to date. Its emphasis on the components of the Greek city, fortifications, walls, gymnasia, stoa, etc., make it an indispensable complement to Lavedan, who neglects some of these elements. (But see Martin, Roland.)

Hellenic Cities. TPR: July 1951.
Summary of findings expressed at greater length in *How the Greeks Built Cities.*

Hellenistic Cities. In TPR: Oct. 1951.
Valuable. (But see Martin, Roland, and Tarn, W. W.)

Wymer, Norman. *English Town Crafts: A Survey of Their Development from Early Times to the Present Day.* London: 1949.

Yadin, Yigael. *The Earliest Record of Egypt's Military Penetration into Asia. Some aspects of the Narmer Palette.* In Israel Exploration Journal: Jerusalem: 1955.

Yeomans, Alfred. *City Residential Land Development.* Chicago: 1916.
Results of significant competition held by Chicago City Club to encourage plans for the development of a neighborhood unit for a quarter-section. The intervention of the war possibly kept this competition from having the influence it might have had on later neighborhood design.

Ylvisaker, Paul N. *Innovation and Evolution: Bridge to the Future Metropolis.* In the Annals of the American Academy of Political and Social Science: Nov. 1957.

Young, George Malcolm (editor). *Early Victorian England: 1830–1865.* 2 vols. New York and London: 1934.
Excellent.

Country and Town: A Summary of the Scott and Uthwatt Reports. Harmondsworth: 1943.

Zeiller, Martin. *Topographia Franconiae.* Frankfurt-am-Main: 1648.

Topographia Helvetiae, Rhaetiae et Valesaiae. Frankfort-am-Main: 1654.
Illustrated travel books, invaluable for their woodcuts of medieval survivals. (See Merian.)

Zevi, Bruno. *Architecture as Space.* New York: 1957.
Admirable constructive analysis that applies to cities as well as buildings.

Zimmerman, Carle C. *The Changing Community.* New York: 1936.
A study of the local community, valuable for its short surveys of actual communities, but embarrassed by a terminology even more ambiguous than Pareto's.

*Zimmern, Alfred E. *The Greek Commonwealth.* Oxford: 1911. Fifth Ed. revised. Oxford: 1931.
Magnificent survey of the Greek polis, still unrivalled.

Solon and Croesus; and other Greek Essays. Oxford: 1928.
Contains some material left out of *The Greek Commonwealth;* including a careful inquiry into the status of slave labor.

Zimmern, Helen. *The Hansa Towns.* New York: 1889.

Zucker, Paul. *Entwicklung des Stadtbildes: die Stadt als Form.* Wien: 1929.
Good bibliography of older literature and pictorial documentation.

New Architecture and City Planning. New York: 1944.

Town and Square: From the Agora to the Village Green. New York: 1959.
Comprehensive work on an important subject, richly illustrated, with an excellent bibliography.

ACKNOWLEDGMENTS

Since I am a generalist, not a specialist in any single field, the study of cities has occupied only a portion of my thinking life. But this interest has spanned the better part of a lifetime; and I cannot list all my personal and intellectual debts without courting an Homeric tediousness. During the last quarter-century, since the publication of 'The Culture of Cities,' these obligations have multiplied; and I now hesitate more than ever to draw up a roster of all the scholars, planners, architects, municipal officials, and corporate bodies that have helped me in my work. Let them not suppose that my silence implies any failure of humility or gratitude. I must content myself with lighting a candle at 'The Altar of the Dead': Victor Branford, Patrick Geddes, Henry Wright, Charles Harris Whitaker, Raymond Unwin, Walter Curt Behrendt, Barry Parker, Patrick Abercrombie, Matthew Nowicki, and Alexander Farquharson. But my immediate debts are easier to fix and acknowledge: the freedom for travel, research, and reflection that enabled me to devote the last four years to this book I owe to a John Simon Guggenheim Memorial Fellowship (1956), a Visiting Bemis Professorship at the Massachusetts Institute of Technology (1957–1960), and a Ford Research Professorship in the Institute for Urban Studies at the University of Pennsylvania (1959–1961). To those responsible for these appointments I give my warmest thanks.

—L. M.

INDEX

Brackets around numerals denote plate numbers in the Graphic Sections.

637